Unpriced Values

Unpriced Values

Decisions without Market Prices

JOHN A. SINDEN

The University of New England
Armidale, New South Wales
Australia

ALBERT C. WORRELL

Yale University
New Haven, Connecticut

A WILEY-INTERSCIENCE PUBLICATION

JOHN WILEY & SONS

New York • Chichester
Brisbane • Toronto

Library of Congress Cataloging in Publication Data:

Sinden, J A
Unpriced values.

"A Wiley-Interscience publication."
Includes index.
1. Value. 2. Valuation. 3. Externalities (Economics) 4. Environmental policy—Decision-making. I. Worrell, Albert Cadwallader, 1913- joint author. II. Title.

HB201.S599 338.5'21 78-24183
ISBN 0-471-02742-1

Printed in the United States of America

10 9 8 7 6 5 4 3 2

To Mallee and Helen

Preface

Human existence has become increasingly complex as populations have increased and standards of living have risen. The resulting pressures on environmental resources and on people have reached levels where more thorough planning and more effective policies are urgently needed.

Many problems are complicated by the presence of things that have not been bought and sold in markets and are therefore unpriced. People cannot decide whether such things are worth having by comparing selling price to money cost. Nor can they choose between them on the basis of comparative prices. But these decisions are still basically economic, because they arise from competing demands for scarce resources.

People can be observed making decisions about such things every day, and it is obvious that their lack of monetary prices does not prevent them from being treated as economic goods. But rational planning and policy development about unpriced goods and actions require reliable evidence as to their comparative values. So we hear planners and policy makers asking questions about the values of scenic views, California condors, improvements in health, and savings in commuting time.

Many people feel it is impossible to place values on such things. Others feel that they can only be compared by assigning monetary prices to them. We do not agree with either of these views. We believe that it is possible to determine comparative values for unpriced things and that valid comparisons can be made without always resorting to monetary prices.

People in various disciplines have tried to resolve this problem in their own areas. We have seen the published results of many of these efforts and of most of the methods that have been developed. From our perusal of them and our own experience and study we have arrived at the approach followed in this book. We are concerned with the general problem of unpriced values in policy decisions. The book attempts to assist such decisions by clarifying the nature of value, by discussing the measurement of unpriced values, and by indicating more effective ways of analyzing decisions.

We believe that economic theory can provide an appropriate basis for environmental policy. But its application to practical problems is severely restricted by its underlying assumptions, such as perfect competition. We try to overcome this weakness as follows: (a) Rather than try to rationalize theory with complex assumptions, we rely on the basic notions of utility, disutility, and value. We feel that careful interpretation of these fundamental concepts can lead to a wider and more helpful application of economic principles. (b) Rather than search for optimal decisions, we search for improved decisions. A close scrutiny of available methodology appears more fruitful at this time than attempts to develop new methodology. So we try to clarify the roles and potentials of existing methods, to set them in context, and to generalize them between disciplines. (c) Rather than always search for the money values of objects, we concentrate on the nature and characteristics of problems. Policy requires the making of decisions and not the calculation of values as such. An understanding of the real nature of problems often permits a wider and simpler use of economic principles and methods.

We try to put this all together in a form that will be useful to managers, planners, policy analysts, and policy makers. This is in no sense a "cookbook." But it is addressed to people who are actually working with problems, and it shows how to formulate, use, and apply the methods to such problems.

The book can be used in various ways, but all readers should go through all the chapters at least once. Part I considers the nature of values, the kind of value information needed for decisions, the usefulness of comparative values, and the nature and application of basic economic concepts. Part II gives the reader an appreciation of the large number and wide range of methods that have been developed to measure unpriced values and of how each fills a special niche. Part III considers why decisions involving unpriced values are perceived as difficult and shows how appropriate analyses can overcome this.

Having obtained a general appreciation of the arguments by reading through the entire book, administrators and policy makers should concentrate on Parts I and III, to review what is possible and to understand the concepts that underly it. Analysts and planners, by contrast, should concentrate on Parts II and III to further understand the methods and how to apply them to actual situations.

We have used this as a text with students while developing the ideas and material. It has been found useful by students of diverse backgrounds in a variety of environmental areas. The flexibility of the subject matter is indicated by its use with undergraduate and graduate students in courses in valuation of unpriced benefits and costs, advanced natural-resource economics, values for environmental planning, and recreation economics.

The student with no field experience often takes time to assimilate the concepts of Part I, even though we have tried to explain them in simple terms. A useful approach for such students is to read Chapters 1 through 7 in sequence and then briefly review Chapters 18 through 20 before reading Chapters 7 through 20 in detail.

We have been interested in the general problem of unpriced values for many years. Our active collaboration began in 1973, when Sinden was a visiting lecturer at Yale University and we conducted a graduate seminar together. The success of the seminar encouraged us to carry our ideas into book form. Progress was slow and frustrating until early 1975, when Worrell spent three months at the University of New England. Sinden's department freed him of teaching responsibilities for that period, and we were able to devote full time to the interchange of ideas. Sinden was again a visiting lecturer at Yale in the fall of 1977, when we could test the manuscript with a graduate seminar and put it in final shape. Our collaboration has been so close that we no longer are able to identify with any certainty what our individual contributions have been.

We wish to thank G. M. Brown, Jr., R. O. Brush, J. R. Gray, T. R. Gupta, J. Hammack, I. W. Hardie, D. R. Helliwell, P. W. O'Hanlon, J. E. Opie, B. R. Payne, G. A. Shumaker, R. W. Vickerman, and B. R. Vile, each of whom reviewed at least one chapter in detail. Our students at Yale and the University of New England helped us develop material and reviewed the work in progress. P. Crawford, M. T. Hitchens, P. W. Liesch, J. Promkutkeo, D. G. Read, I. K. Reynolds, and D. J. Thampapillai collected data and tested methods as part of their graduate studies. K. M. Pollack checked every reference and read the final manuscript, making many helpful suggestions. J. B. Wyckoff of Oregon State University provided Sinden an opportunity to develop methodology and review the field of valuation during a study leave in 1972.

Many secretaries have had a part in the work involved and have been more helpful than might normally be expected. We particularly thank Sue Lucas of Armidale, who has persisted with us over the entire project. Yale University and the University of New England have provided study leaves and support in many other forms, without which we could not have completed the book. And finally, we thank both our families, who have lived with and encouraged this book for so long.

Armidale, New South Wales
New Haven, Connecticut
January 1979

John A. Sinden
Albert C. Worrell

Contents

PART I CONCEPTS OF VALUATION

1 Policy, Planning, and Values 3

The Significance of Values, 3
The Concept of Value, 4
What Kind of Value Estimate Does a Planner Need? 9
Values Without Prices, 10
The Process of Value Determination, 12

2 An Economic Basis for Valuation 17

Exchange as an Economic Phenomenon, 17
A Basic Model of Exchange, 18
Utility and Demand, 34
Disutility, Cost, and Supply, 41
How Useful Are Actual Market Prices? 43
Use of the Market Model for Valuation, 52

3 Individual Valuations 53

The Basic Role of Individuals in Determining Values, 53
Determinants of Individual Utility, 53
From Individual Utility to Individual Value, 57
Determinants of Individual Value, 58
An Individual's Process of Comparative Valuation, 61
Individuals in Social Groups, 62

4 Social Valuations 63

What Is Social Value? 63
Determinants of Social Utility, 64
From Social Utility to Social Value, 72
Value to a Social Group, 73

Social Valuation Processes, 78
Social Values and Social Decisions, 80

5 Valuation and Decision Making **82**

Decision Situations, 82
When Is a Monetary Value Necessary? 86
Administrative Hierarchy of Decision Making, 88
Implications of Some Questionable Decision Criteria, 91
Value Information for Complex Decisions, 95
Decision Procedures Which Can Ease Valuation Problems, 101
Summary, 104

6 Valuation as a Process **105**

Steps in the Valuation Process, 105
Adapting the Traditional Theory of Choice, 112
Conclusion, 116

PART II METHODS OF VALUATION AND ANALYSIS

7 Selection of a Valuation Method **119**

The Process of Valuation, 119
Selection of a Group of Methods, 121
Different Approaches to Valuation, 123
Validation of Values, 126
Nature and Scope of the Methods Chapters, 128

8 Analyses Involving Multiple Objectives **130**

An Environmental Policy Example: A Gorgelands National Park, 130
With No Extra Data, 134
With an Ordering of Outcomes, 135
With Orderings of Objectives and Outcomes, 137
With Constraints on Objectives, 139
Direct Approaches with Weights, 142
Less-Direct Approaches with Weights, 148
With Combinations of Data, 154

With Sequential Interaction with Decision Makers, 158
Discussion, 159

9 **Analyses Involving Characteristics of the Environment** **162**

The General Approach, 162
An Environmental Policy Example: Improving the Quality of Life in Australian Country Towns, 165
Standardized Difference Methods, 171
Standardized Proportion Methods, 176
Standardization by Utility Ratings, 180
Standardization by Ranked Classes, 183
Discussion of the Methods: Quantitative Concepts of "Good" and "Bad", 184
Conclusions: The Role of the Methods, 186

10 **Estimation of Total Utility—The Expedient Methods** **188**

An Environmental Policy Example: A Choice Between Landscapes, 188
Describing the Alternatives, 191
Ranking the Alternatives, 195
Rating the Alternatives, 200
Discussion and Conclusions, 209

11 **Estimation of Total Utility—The Rigorous Methods** **213**

An Environmental Policy Example: Selecting a Level of Pollution Control, 215
Rank Order and Equality Judgments, 219
Rating Judgments, 226
Proportional Judgments, 232
Probability Judgments, 235
Estimating Comparative Total Utilities, 243
Discussion and Conclusions, 245

12 **Estimation of Monetary Values—Opportunity-Cost Methods** **250**

An Environmental Policy Example: Allocating Resources Among Competing Land Uses, 250
Observation and Interpretation of Costs, 254
Structured Comparisons of Costs, 261

Cost as a Loss in Money Income, 266
Do Increases in Expenditure Increase Utility? 271
Discussion, 273

13 Estimation of Monetary Values—Interpretation of Market and Land Prices **276**

An Environmental Policy Example: Pest Control, 277
Conventional Market-Price Method, 279
Production-Function Method, 283
Residual Method, 287
The Land-Price Method, 290
Market-Comparison Method, 299
Discussion, 301

14 Estimation of Monetary Values—Direct Questioning **303**

Applying the Basic Model of Exchange, 304
An Environmental Policy Example: Air-Pollution Abatement, 306
The Single Direct Question, 307
Developments of the Single Direct Question, 312
The Single Trade-Off Game, 315
Developments of the Single Trade-Off Game, 319
The Costless Choice Method, 322
The Priority-Evaluator Technique, 324
The Indifference-Mapping Method, 329
Discussion, 331

15 Estimation of Net Social Benefit—Direct Methods **335**

Net Social Benefit as an Ideal for Valuation, 335
An Environmental Policy Example: Maintenance of Wildlife Habitat, 337
Direct Methods for Calculating Net Social Benefit, 347
Application to Various Kinds of Decisions, 357
Summary, 363

16 Estimation of Net Social Benefit—Structured Methods **364**

The Travel-Cost Method, 364
The Structured Sensitivity Analysis, 374

The Opportunity-Cost Procedure, 377
Adjustments to the Estimate of Value, 378
Discussion and Conclusions, 379

17 Estimation of Social Values **383**

The Formation and Analysis of Social Values, 383
Adapting Standard Economic Principles, 386
Forming a Consensus, 390
Analyses of Past Decisions, 392
Analyses of Past Behavior, 400
Weighting the Components of Social Value, 402
Decisions in which Individual Values Are not Fully Recognized, 409
Discussion and Conclusions, 410

PART III RATIONAL DECISIONS WITHOUT MARKET PRICES

18 Why Decisions Involving Unpriced Values Are Considered Difficult **415**

Difficulty in Distinguishing What Is Actually Exchanged, 415
Lack of Understanding of Alternative Valuation Methods, 422
Lack of Appreciation of Why Some Things Are Not Priced, 433
Incomplete Consideration of the Decision Situation, 436
Conclusion, 443

19 Reputedly Difficult Valuations—Analyses of Examples **444**

What is the Value of a Reduction in Noise? 444
What is the Value of a Person's Time? 447
What is the Value of Open Space? 451
What is the Value of an Endangered Species? 454
What is the Value of Gradual Change? 457
What is the Value of Human Life? 459
Conclusions, 463

20 Complex Decisions Involving Unpriced Values—Analysis of an Example **465**

Problem Formulation: A Gorgelands National Park, 466
Identifying the Significant Outcomes, 469

A Monetary Approach, 470
A Utility Approach, 479
A Mixed Approach, 484
A Comparison of the Approaches, 488
An Overview, 490

INDEX 509

PART I

CONCEPTS OF VALUATION

"Tiny rivulets turned into sparkling diamonds, as the sun crept over the canyon rim. . . . and nevermore, will the beauty of this section of rugged and freely running river, be available to you and yours. . . . These ten miles are not only easy on the eyes, but. . . . (have) a tremendous potential as a white water challenge. . . . tomorrow there may not be a ruggedly beautiful scenic river where you can slip your boat through the white foam, let your children frolic in crystal clear pools, or just dangle your toes in the cool currents. . . ." —*Hoff (1972)*

CHAPTER 1

Policy, Planning and Values

A flood-control dam was being planned for the South Santiam River near Cascadia, Oregon to protect the Willamette Valley. The Army Corps of Engineers had made a careful benefit-cost analysis of the monetary benefits of flood protection and the monetary costs of construction. Net benefits were estimated to be in the millions of dollars. But opponents argued that the Corps had not included all the costs. They spoke of scenery and white-water canoeing and frolicking children, and insisted that these, too, were important components of a construction decision.

How should the Corps have compared scenery and frolicking with flood protection and construction costs? Emotional appeals like this show that people consider them important, but emotions are not very helpful in analyzing problems. Better means are available, and it is the purpose of this book to show that useful comparative valuations of such things can be made for planning and policy formation.

1. THE SIGNIFICANCE OF VALUES

The mere acts of living and using natural environments require people to make endless decisions. Since they cannot do or have everything, they must choose among alternatives. Their decisions fall in two broad classes: (a) is it worthwhile to obtain a thing or carry out an action and (b) is it better to choose one thing instead of its possible alternatives?

Both questions involve a concept of value. Anything that is worthwhile having or doing is said to be of value to the persons involved. When a number of things would all be of value, those that would be more advantageous are said to have the greater value. Value is used as a measure or indicator of relative importance, and the comparative values of alternative things or actions provide guides for choices and decisions.

Individual people can estimate the relative values of things to themselves reasonably well, even though they sometimes make mistakes. But many decisions explicitly involve other people. We often make choices intentionally for their effects on others, such as the decisions parents make about the lives of their children. And all social groups make decisions that affect part or all of their individual members.

In such situations a complete evaluation of the consequences requires information about values to people other than the decision makers. This leads to attempts to "plan" decisions on the basis of values to all involved. Because of this, we often use the terms "planner" or "analyst" when referring to those who are analyzing situations and developing information to guide decisions. We do not necessarily mean formally trained professional planners.

2. THE CONCEPT OF VALUE

Value is a property of things, but a different kind of property from color or weight. A flower is blue regardless of whether this makes any difference to anyone, but things only have value when their existence does make a difference to someone. The value of a thing derives basically from some need or desire which it has the capacity to satisfy. The greater this capacity, the greater its value will usually be. We can summarize this as follows:

$$\text{Value} = f\,(\text{capacity to satisfy}) \tag{1.1}$$

2.1. Variation In Values

Value—as a property of a thing—can only be measured in terms of some desideratum, that is, some characteristic which people want in the thing. Using this desideratum as their criterion, people can rank things in an order of relative values. Those that have a high capacity for providing the desideratum are assigned a high value and those with a low capacity, a low value.

Foodstuffs are usually compared in terms of their capacity to provide nutrition. Oatmeal, for example, is said to have a high nutritive value. However, people do not always look at foods in terms of nutrition. A gourmet will be seeking more than that in a meal, and if he is otherwise well-fed, he may not be interested in nutritive value at all. He may compare foods in terms of taste and rank oatmeal rather low. Oatmeal could thus have a low gustatory value even though it has a high nutritive value.

This suggests that the value of a thing depends partly on the circumstances under which it is evaluated. Value is not a fixed, inherent property. Rather, it is a variable property whose magnitude depends not only on the nature of the thing itself but also on who evaluates it and the environment in which it is assessed. A thing i may have different values for different purposes, at different times, to different people, under different conditions (the physical environment in which the evaluator finds himself), and in different circumstances (the personal, physical, emotional, psychological, social, and political situation of the evaluator at the time he makes the valuation). We may emphasize this idea as follows:

$$\text{value}_i = f(\text{desideratum used as criterion, capacity to satisfy that desideratum, environmental conditions, circumstances of evaluator at time of valuation}) \tag{1.2}$$

If value is such a variable property, how can it be useful as a guide for decisions? The answer lies in the nature of choice and decision: people do not make general or universal decisions. They never choose, for example, to take wheat bread in preference to rye everywhere and under every conceivable circumstance. Instead, they make limited choices that appear the best solutions to the problems facing them. Human problems tend to be specific, and the decisions made about them are also specific.

2.2. Determination Of Values

Values are always determined for some purpose. A planner needs to know the comparative values of certain alternatives to choose among them. These values must be measured in terms of desiderata, but which particular ones are relevant depends on the purpose of the decision.

2.2.1. Only One Desideratum Involved. Comparative valuation is straightforward when only one desideratum, such as nutrition, is involved. Some things like stones have none of the properties necessary for nutrition. Others are nutritious for some organisms but not for humans and would be ruled out if the purpose is to nourish people. The purpose of the valuation determines which things have potential value and which do not.

Things that have the essential characteristics vary in their potential. But since only one clearly specified desideratum is involved, a scientific appraisal can be made of the capacities of the alternative things to provide that desideratum. On the basis of this appraisal, the alternatives can be ranked in the order of their relative values. If there is sufficient factual information on the capacities of the alternatives to provide the specific desideratum, it may be possible to quantify their relative values. For example, it might be possible to say that foodstuff X has twice the nutritional value of foodstuff Y.

It is not always necessary to obtain an absolute measure of the capacities of two things to compare their values. An indicator of comparable magnitudes may be all that is needed. Suppose, for example, a choice has to be made between two scenic outlooks because only one can be preserved. Let us assume that the purpose of preservation is to provide aesthetic satisfaction. This is difficult to define, let alone measure. But if one outlook provides a view of a lake and distant snow-covered mountains and the other overlooks an automobile junkyard, the relative aesthetic values may be easy to determine.

2.2.2. A Choice between Desiderata. Many choices involve alternatives that meet different desiderata. How does one determine the comparative values of a foodstuff and an item of clothing, for example? Because people make such choices, it must be possible to compare the values of diverse things, but what is the basis of valuation?

Again we must know its purpose. Suppose, for example, a decision maker must choose between a ton of bread and a ton of wool sweaters. An emergency situation has arisen, and he has the responsibility for sending help. He must decide whether it should be food or clothing. Bread has a high nutritive value, and wool sweaters have a high warming value. But the question facing the decision maker is which will have the greatest value to victims of the catastrophe. The relevant desideratum is what these victims need.

The real choice facing the decision maker is not between bread and sweaters but between two desiderata: nutrition and protection against cold. Their values to the victims must derive from some more basic desideratum, which in this case is maintenance of viability or health. The extent to which bread or sweaters can contribute to health depends on how valuable they are, respectively, for nutrition or warmth. But no matter how valuable they may be in terms of these desiderata, it is their potential contribution to the health of the victims that determines their value. Like the values of individual things, values of desiderata vary with the circumstances of the people involved. If the catastrophe in our example were a blizzard, protection from cold might be of more immediate value than nutrition. If it were a crop failure, the reverse might well be true.

2.2.3. An Ultimate Desideratum. The preceding discussion used a more basic desideratum as a measure of the comparative values of other desiderata. But situations also arise in which people have to choose between such more basic desiderata. Let us take as an example a group of people who have a limited amount of time and energy available for the production of more goods like food and clothing or for organized singing and dancing. Let us assume that they must choose one or the other. Their appraisal problem is: which use of their available time and energy will produce the greatest value? The question seems to be: which is more valuable—physical comfort (obtainable through food and clothing) or aesthetic satisfaction (obtainable through singing and dancing)?

These value objects can only be appraised in terms of some other desideratum, but it will have to be a very basic one. What common desire leads people to want and value both physical comfort and aesthetic experiences? Baier suggests that this ultimate desideratum is a worthwhile life and that people value things which have a capacity to make favorable differences to their lives (Baier, 1969). He therefore proposes a favorable difference to someone's life as the ultimate criterion for appraising value. Anything that has no capacity to make a favorable difference to someone's life is without value. By contrast, things that have a capacity to make large favorable differences are very valuable.

Economists use the term *utility*, which they define as the satisfaction of a human want or desire. This is virtually synonymous with a capacity to make a favorable difference to someone's life. We use utility as a shorthand for Baier's longer and more precise terminology. We can now rewrite Equation 1.2 as

$$\text{value}_i = f(\text{utility, environmental conditions, circumstances of evaluator at time of valuation}) \qquad (1.3)$$

2.3. Persons Relevant to Valuation

Baier's definition of value as a capacity to make a favorable difference to someone's life appears to imply that anything is valuable which has a capacity to make a favorable difference to any person's life. This definition seems too general to be useful; if valuation is to be a guide in actual decision situations, it must be specific.

This consideration adds another dimension to valuation: what person or persons must be included in the appraisal? Unless this is specified, the resulting value statement will be vague and perhaps even meaningless. There are at least three specifications for which useful appraisals might be made: (1) the personal value to an individual evaluator, (2) the value to an individual evaluator and other people for whom he has a personal concern, and (3) the value to other specific groups of people.

To specify the persons relevant to an appraisal, it is necessary to know why the valuation is being undertaken. The immediate and obvious reason for most valuations is to form a basis for a rational decision. But there is always some more basic reason why this decision must be made. It is in terms of this basic reason that the decision will be rational or not.

2.3.1. Evaluator and Personal Acquaintances. Suppose a person has to choose between two housing units that are for sale at the same price. The rational thing to do is to choose the unit with the highest value. But the buyer cannot appraise their comparative values unless he keeps in mind why he has to choose a housing unit in the first place.

It will make considerable difference, for example, whether he is a single, free-lance artist who works at home or a married man with two young children. The artist needs a place where he can both live and work, and from experience he knows what kind of housing is most congenial to his life-style. He is probably the only one who has to be considered in the valuation.

The father, by contrast, has to find satisfactory housing for four individuals who live together as a close-knit unit. He has a reasonably good understanding of the needs and attitudes of individual members of his family and the problems they have in sharing a dwelling. He has the further advantage of knowing that because of their close relationship, something that benefits one will probably make a favorable difference to the lives of the others. But father, mother, and children are all relevant to the valuation. It would not be surprising if the father and the artist differed about the relative values of the two housing units.

2.3.2. Other Groups of People. Many decisions are more complex than the preceding question. For example, imagine a housing authority which must choose between two kinds of dwelling units that could be erected at the same cost in a planned housing development. The authority has to make this choice to fulfill its responsibility for providing the best possible housing—within budgetary limitations—for low-income people. It must determine which kind of unit is most valuable for this purpose. But what people should it consider in the appraisal?

Because members of the housing authority will not live in the development themselves, the choice will not affect their own lives. Furthermore, those who will live in the development are not likely to be relatives, friends, or others with whom the housing authority members identify closely. The problem is to determine the comparative values of the two kinds of dwelling units to another group of people—those who will occupy them when they are completed. It will make a great deal of difference in the appraisal whether they are elderly people, young families with children, members of some ethnic group, or a mixture of different kinds of people. We discuss this problem in detail in Chapter 4, on Social Valuations.

2.4. A Favorable Difference To Someone's Life

The ultimate criterion of value proposed by Baier appears both logical and useful, but it presents difficulties in practical application. Two questions arise: exactly what is a favorable difference and how can such differences be measured?

Making a favorable difference to someone's life implies that if a person receives the thing being valued, his life will not only be different but also in some sense "better" than it would have been otherwise. But what does it mean to say that life is "better"? What is the criterion of "goodness"? For that matter, against what standard can a life be compared to determine whether it is good or bad? It is generally agreed that there is no such external standard that can be used. The criterion has to be an empirical one based on what people actually find to be worthwhile. We analyze this factor more closely for individuals in Chapter 3 and for social groups in Chapter 4.

The ultimate evidence for a value appraisal has to come from the people whose lives are affected. Even if a person has complete information on the differences to his life that would result from the alternatives being compared, it is still necessary for him to decide which of them would be most favorable in view of the kind of life he finds worthwhile. Part II of this book is devoted to ways of obtaining this information from the people relevant to valuations.

3. WHAT KIND OF VALUE ESTIMATE DOES A PLANNER NEED?

The role of a planner or analyst is to assemble and analyze information on relative values of possible alternatives. It is not his role to make a decision but to assist those who have that responsibility to carry it out as wisely as possible.

In the majority of cases a planner will be appraising values to people other than himself. The preceding section argued that the ultimate evidence for a value appraisal must come from the people whose lives are affected. A planner's basic problem is to predict the comparative valuations the affected people would make themselves if they had an opportunity to do so. If we can assume that people would choose the alternatives which are most beneficial to them, the planner's role is to indicate the alternatives that would have the most favorable effects on these people.

It seems reasonable to assume that people are rational in most of their decisions and that they try to obtain the greatest net value, in whatever sense they define it. In a free choice they will take the alternative that has the highest value to them. The value information that would enable them to make rational decisions—and therefore the information a planner should seek—must satisfy certain requirements. Depending on the problem, the estimates must:

(**a**) express benefits in terms comparable with costs,

(**b**) express values of all alternatives in comparable units,

(**c**) express values for all individuals in comparable units.

The conventional unit for valuation has been a monetary one, because it will usually satisfy the above requirements. However, any index that meets these requirements may be satisfactory for a planner or analyst. For some problems units of time may be as effective as units of money. For others an index of relative value may be all that is needed.

Because problems and planning are specific, universal values are not necessary. What are needed are the values of the benefits and costs to the particular people affected by the specific choice or decision.

4. VALUES WITHOUT PRICES

The problem that led to the South Santiam Dam controversy with which we introduced this chapter was a lack of comparable values for all benefits and costs. The Corps of Engineers was able to estimate values for flood protection and construction costs, but because there were no ready indicators of value for scenery and whitewater canoeing, the Corps omitted them from its appraisal. Why do these kinds of benefits present such problems for planners and policy makers? What characteristics do they have that apparently make it difficult to appraise their values? An analysis of the terms people use to refer to them will help us see where the problem lies.

4.1. Apparently Special Characteristics

Intangible. The term *intangible* is often used to describe this kind of benefit or cost. Literally, it means "incapable of being touched or perceived by touch" and some of them, like scenic views, certainly cannot be touched in the same sense as an apple. But many things that apparently are readily valued also have strong and important intangible qualities. Houses and automobiles are examples.

Another interpretation of intangible is discussed by Schmid (1967). We may be vaguely aware of some want but not sure how particular goods or services might satisfy it, as in the case of people who feel that mental health could be improved by regular exposure to pleasant scenic views. Schmid suggests that people call things intangible when they lack a knowledge of how a good (scenic view) satisfies a want (mental health). We might carry this interpretation further and hypothesize that the reason people use the label *intangible* is that they have not thought enough about the utility or satisfaction they get from the good. Perhaps they cannot fully articulate in monetary terms what they would be willing to give up in order to get the good.

Incommensurable. Hitch and McKean (1960) used this term in their study of the economics of defense. The characteristic of "lacking a common basis of comparison" fits such goods and services well. Management problems certainly arise from the fact that the benefits of a view or a preserved species cannot readily be measured in the same units as are management costs.

Environmental Goods. This term has been used by Pendse and Wyckoff (1972), among others. It is often convenient, because many of these benefits and costs do occur in the environmental area. However, it is not universally applicable. Benefits from national security, a relaxed life-style, and improved health are all "intangible" but would not normally be regarded as "environmental goods."

Indirect Benefits and Costs. This is a term that is frequently used in benefit-cost studies. Many of these benefits and costs do occur as by-products or spillovers from other activities. But many of them—like recreation and improved health—are deliberately produced by people as a main objective.

The concepts of intangibility, incommensurability, environmental origin, and indirectness are not very helpful, because they lack analytical content. They describe some characteristics of some of these goods but do not come to grips with the basic problem that concerns us.

4.2. Conventional Characteristics

Nonmarket Goods. This term is nearer the mark as an analytical description and concept. These things are not exchanged in organized markets with regular market prices, and in this sense they certainly are nonmarket goods.

Extra-Market Goods. This is a more appropriate term because although these goods are not exchanged in regular markets with monetary prices, they are exchanged. Societies do choose between alternative ways of preserving the environment, for example, and even between preserving the environment and providing employment. Because the groups that make these decisions always have limited resources, they treat these as economic goods in the usual sense of the term economizing. Scarce resources are allocated between competing ends and, in effect, exchanged for these particular goods. But the exchange does not take place in an ordinary market with monetary prices. In this sense, they are extra-market goods.

4.3. Unpriced Goods and Services

In his book, *Economics of American Forestry,* Worrell (1959) used the term *unpriced* for a certain kind of good or service. This term makes the central point that the price system does not measure people's relative desire to consume and willingness to produce certain goods and services, which therefore have no monetary prices. It conveys a meaning similar to extra-market but does not have the connotation that no market exists. Because some sort of market—in the sense of an arrangement for exchange—usually does exist, and because the universal and important feature of these things is their lack of a monetary price, we use the term *unpriced* throughout this book.

5. THE PROCESS OF VALUE DETERMINATION

We have now looked at various aspects of values and their use. Based on these, it is our opinion that the most reliable evidence of people's relative valuations is their willingness to pay, that is, what they are actually willing to give up in order to have things. The rest of Part I is concerned with the process of value determination—how people determine what they are willing to pay. In this section we lay some groundwork for that more detailed consideration.

5.1. Schematic Models of Value Determination

The values people ascribe to various things are affected by many factors. Whether they recognize it explicitly or not, people take them into account in their valuations. The flowcharts of Figures 1.1 and 1.2 try to show in a general way how these inputs come together in the valuation process. Although presented in the form of a decision path, we are not necessarily suggesting that people always follow such a path in making evaluations. The models are intended to be explanatory rather than analytical or predictive.

We present two models because individual and social valuations are not identical. They are clearly interrelated, as the models show, but social values frequently differ from individual values.

These models try to picture the process that takes place in response to a problem. Values are being appraised to aid some decision which must be made at that time. Because of this, time is not explicitly included in the models, and the feedback loops that would involve points at different times are omitted. The inevitable feedback of society on environment through time is also omitted. One outcome of any decision is more information for the next decision. If our models were to be generalized, they would also have to include a feedback loop from the final valuation to the evaluator's stock of knowledge. As a result of such feedback, individuals and societies change their perceptions, stocks of knowledge, and institutions over time. The valuation response to an event may therefore also change over time.

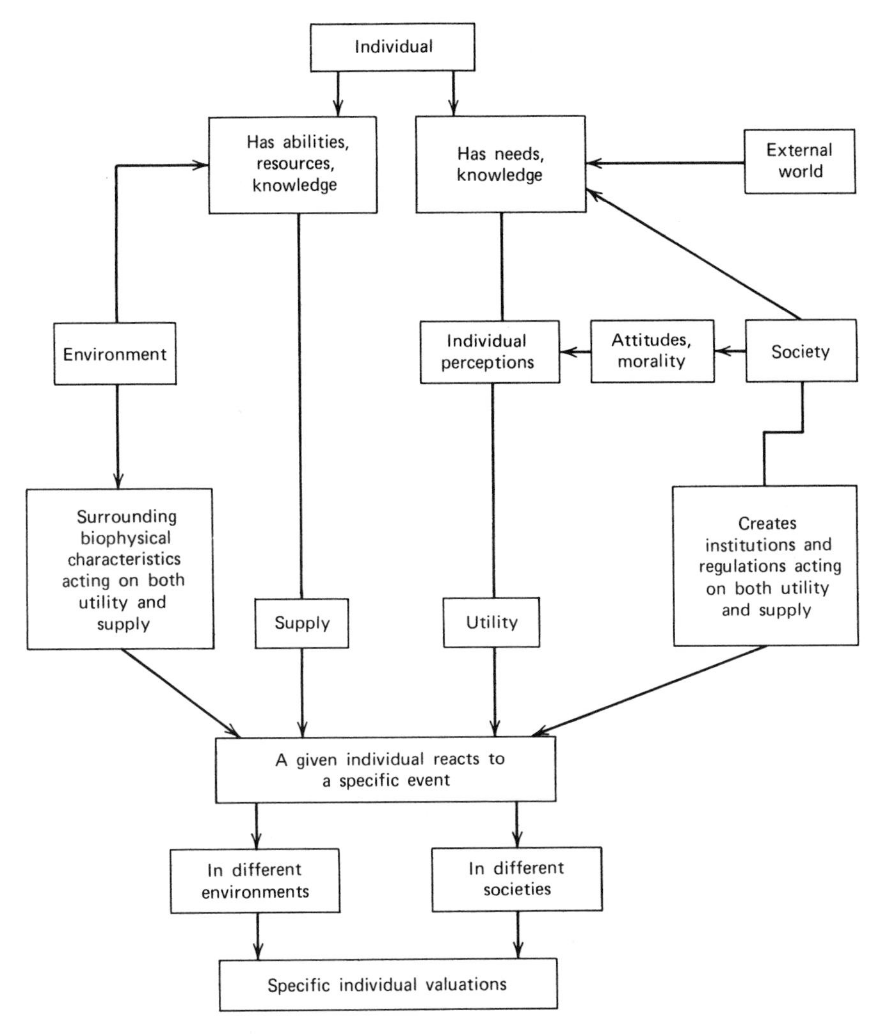

Figure 1.1. An individual's valuation path at a particular time.

However, at the time when a specific valuation is being made, any previous feedback is already contained in the factors forming the background for that decision. At the moment of decision, the situation closely approximates that shown in the models.

There are four main sources of input to the valuation process: (1) individual people, (2) the social group of which these people are a part, (3) the immediate biophysical environment of these people, and (4) the external

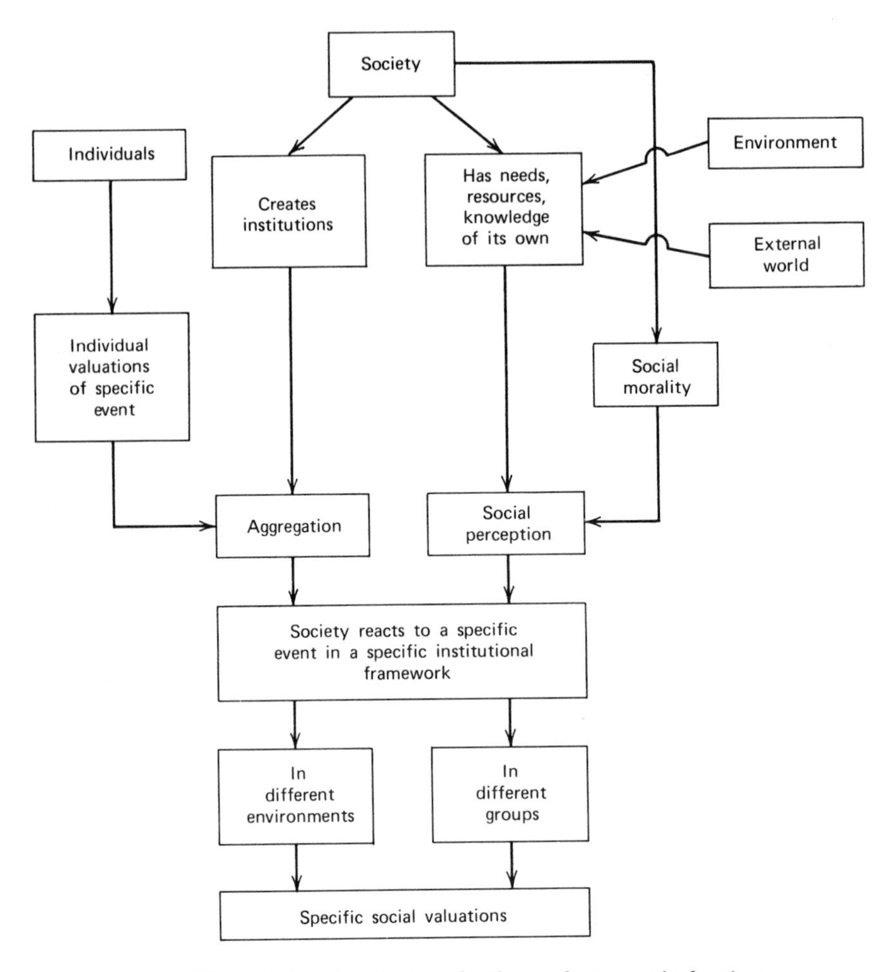

Figure 1.2. A society's valuation path at a particular time.

world outside the relevant environment. The same four inputs affect both individual and social valuations, though in somewhat different ways.

We present these models for the purpose of setting in focus the independent parts or inputs of the valuation process and for highlighting the interrelationships between them. This will make it possible to consider one input or relationship in detail without losing sight of where it fits into the overall process. Useful estimates of comparative values can sometimes be derived from analyses of the key inputs or relationships in a specific decision situation. But in order to do this, a planner must understand the flow of inputs in the situation he is trying to analyze.

5.2. A Model of Individual Value Determination

Figure 1.1 shows how various factors fit together in determining the value an individual places on a thing in a specific situation. He finds himself at this time with certain needs and desires and some knowledge of how to satisfy them. He also has certain abilities, skills, and resources and some knowledge of how to use them. These determine what he can do to satisfy his needs himself or through exchanging with other people.

Some of his needs are inherent in his physiological makeup, but most are determined by the environment in which he lives and the social group to which he belongs. The external world also exerts some influence on them. However, it is not just the needs that determine his valuation but also his perception of the thing being evaluated in relation to them. And his perceptions are strongly influenced by the attitudes of his social group, particularly with respect to morality.

The social group may also have created institutions or imposed regulations that affect what this person can have. Because of different institutions, for example, he could have exclusive property rights to land in the United States but not in the Soviet Union. Finally, the environment not only partially determines his needs but may also influence the potential of various things for filling them. For example, he may need recreation, but whether skiing is a valuable way to fill this need depends on the environment in which he lives. As a result of all these influences, individuals have rather definite feelings about the utilities of alternative things at the times when they must choose between them.

In a similar way the abilities, resources, and knowledge a person has are largely determined by his environment and social group, and these may also influence how he uses them. Because he has available only a limited amount of what he would need to obtain the things he is evaluating, any choice he makes will have an opportunity cost in the form of other things foregone.

When an individual has to make a decision, he evaluates each alternative in terms of both its utility to him and the opportunity cost of getting it. He thus arrives at comparative values of the alternatives. But since both utility and supply are affected by his environment and social group, he might arrive at different valuations if he were living in a different environment or were a member of a different social group.

5.3. A Model of Social Value Determination

Figure 1.2 shows how various factors fit together in determining the value a society places on a thing in a specific situation. The society finds itself with certain needs, resources, and knowledge of its own. In some sense these are in addition to or independent of the needs, resources, and knowledge of its individual members. Some of a society's needs and resources are inherent in its own makeup, but most are determined by its immediate environment and by the external world around it.

Every society has certain moral feelings and attitudes that affect its perception of the values of various things to it. Most societies also create various institutions with the aim of facilitating or stabilizing the coexistence of their individual members. A major source of information for a society in evaluating an event is appraisals by its members of the value of that event to them personally. Because these valuations differ from person to person, society has a problem of aggregating them, and society utilizes some of its institutions in this process.

A society, then, combines the aggregated individual valuations with its perception of the value of the event to the group as a whole and arrives at a social valuation. Because individual valuations and social perceptions of group value are both affected by the environment in which the group exists and the makeup of the group itself, social value may be different in different environments and for different groups.

CHAPTER 2

An Economic Basis for Valuation

Chapter 1 presents the ideas that value derives from the capacity of things to make favorable differences to people's lives, that values are indicators of relative importance, and that values are used as guides in making choices between alternatives. Economics is the study of how people make choices in using scarce resources and in distributing goods and services among relatively unlimited wants. Some of the theories and models that have been developed for explaining economic activities may therefore be useful in analyzing valuation problems.

1. EXCHANGE AS AN ECONOMIC PHENOMENON

The two basic economic activities of production and consumption come together in the equally basic activity of exchange. People obtain many of the goods and services they want by exchanging something they have for something someone else has. They also make many exchanges that do not involve other people, as when they use some of their time and wealth to produce something for their own consumption. All these exchanges involve choices and rest on comparative valuations of the things exchanged.

1.1. The Concept of a Market

A market is basically an arrangement by which buyers and sellers come together and exchange things. Some markets—like the New York Stock Exchange—are actual places where large numbers of buyers and sellers regularly make many exchanges. But the markets for many things—like dwelling houses—consist of nothing more than arrangements for bringing potential buyers and sellers together.

When a market system involves many exchanges over a long time, there is a tendency for recognizable prices to develop. People notice what is happening in other exchanges and adjust their asking or offering prices accordingly. Since rational people would not sell a thing for less than it is worth to them nor buy it for more than it is worth, market prices are indicators of values to those involved in exchanges.

1.2. Relevance of Economic Theories for Valuation

Economists have developed theories to explain the behaviors of both parties to market exchanges. Demand theory explains how buyers or consumers respond to the prices at which things are offered for sale and how their responses would differ if the prices were higher or lower. Supply theory explains how sellers or producers respond to the prices people offer to pay for things and how their responses would differ if the prices were higher or lower. Price theory explains how market prices develop in response to the demand for and supply of goods and services and how prices serve as regulators to bring demand and supply into balance.

Demand and supply theories explain behavior in response to effective prices, regardless of how those prices have been formed. They are as useful with nonmonetary prices (such as travel time) as with monetary prices. Price theories, by contrast, rest on assumptions about the form and competitiveness of the market; the number, size, and knowledge of participants; and their mobility. These assumptions may not fit actual exchange situations. We can therefore use demand and supply models with more confidence than we can models of price formation. This chapter concentrates on the key concepts of demand and supply and how the basic exchange models can help in valuation.

2. A BASIC MODEL OF EXCHANGE

Exchanges only take place when both buyers and sellers agree on an acceptable market price. The buyers must feel the value to them of the thing being exchanged is greater than the price, and the sellers must feel the opposite or they would not willingly exchange it. Because money is commonly used as a medium of exchange, the models usually show price in monetary units. However, they can also be used effectively to explain market behavior with price expressed in nonmonetary units.

Although both buyers and sellers respond to market prices in terms of comparative values, the bases of their value judgments differ, and different models are needed to explain their behaviors.

2.1. Demand Schedules as Models of Buyer Behavior

The economic concept of demand rests on the theory that at a given time and under given circumstances, the amount of a thing people buy is determined by the price they have to pay for it. The theory does not say that people will always buy different amounts at different prices; rather, it states that there is a general tendency for the amount purchased to vary with the market price when everything else is equal. Demand is thus visualized as a schedule of the amounts that would be purchased at different prices by the same people, in the same market, at the same time, and under the same circumstances.

Let us take as an example an Englishman who likes to visit historic castles and abbeys, and let us assume there is a privately owned abbey near his home that charges an entrance fee. How many visits might he make to this abbey during a three-month summer period? Because his money and time are limited, he might not visit the abbey more than five times, even if there were no entrance fee. He might also consider an entrance fee of £3 to be excessive and not visit the abbey at all. Between these extremes, his visits might vary as follows:

Price per visit (pounds)	3.0	1.5	1.0	0.5	0.25	0.0
Number of visits	0	1	2	3	4	5

This schedule shows his demand for visits to the abbey in a summer.

For analytical purposes, demand schedules are often presented in graphic form, with price on the vertical axis and quantity on the horizontal axis, as in Figure 2.1. Demand theory states that the relationship between price and quantity purchased is ordinarily an inverse one, so demand curves usually slope downward to the right. This agrees with the common observation that people usually buy more of a thing when the price is low than when it is high. The nature and scale of our simple example are patterned on results reported by Snaith (1975) in a study of National Trust properties in Britain.

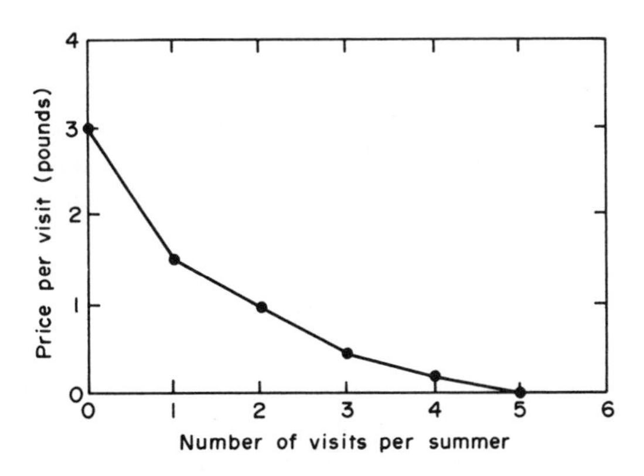

Figure 2.1. A hypothetical demand schedule for visits to an abbey.

The Trust administers historic houses, castles, and abbeys, as well as larger areas of landscape interest. In the nine groups of houses investigated by Snaith, the number of visits did vary inversely with the size of the admission fee.

The factors that determine demand are analyzed in detail in Section 3. But first we should look at the supply side of the market and the general way in which demand and supply come together in exchanges.

2.2. Supply Schedules as Models of Seller Behavior

The economic concept of supply rests on the theory that at a given time and under given circumstances, the amount of a thing people sell is determined by the price they can receive for it. The theory does not say that people will always sell different amounts at different prices; rather, it states that there is a tendency for the amount sold to vary with the market price when everything else is equal. Supply is thus visualized as a schedule of the amounts that would be sold at different prices by the same people, in the same market, at the same time, and under the same circumstances.

To continue our earlier example, let us assume that the abbey in question is owned by a duke who is considering allowing people to visit it. However, he is not willing to do this for free, so at a zero price he would not supply any visits. If people are willing to pay a minimum admission fee, he will allow some of them to visit the abbey. If they are willing to pay a higher fee, he will admit more. His behavior conforms to supply theory which says that the relationship between price and the quantity sold is ordinarily a direct one.

For analytical purposes, supply schedules are often presented in graphic form, with price on the vertical axis and quantity on the horizontal axis. The resulting supply curve is usually upward sloping, as illustrated in Figure 2.2.

2.2.1. Supply Situations.

Two different situations may be found on the supply side. A stock situation is one in which only some limited amount of the thing exists, as in the case of land. The physical supply of such things is restricted to this stock. A production situation is one in which it is possible to produce more of the things, as in the case of manufactured goods. The physical supply of such things is variable.

Stock Situations. In stock situations supply is determined by reservation demand on the part of those who possess the goods. The quantity they are willing to sell at any price depends on how valuable they feel the thing is for their own consumption, some other use, or possible future sale. The abbey

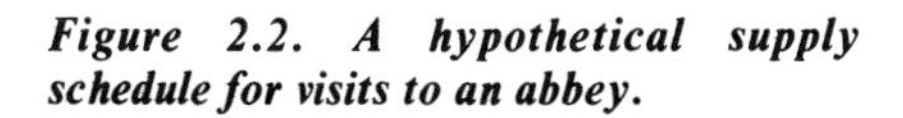
Figure 2.2. A hypothetical supply schedule for visits to an abbey.

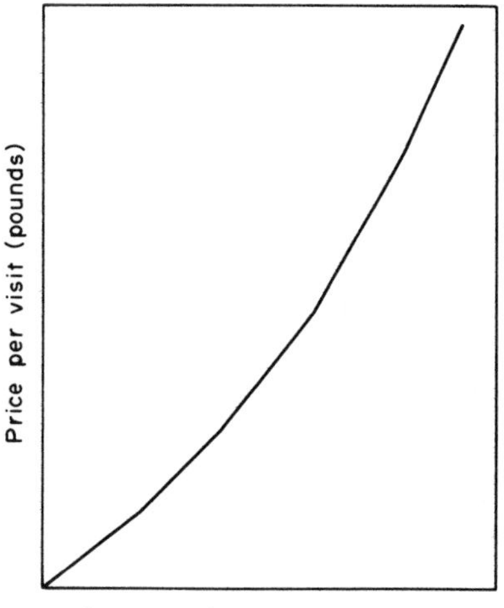

in our example presents a stock situation. People want to visit it because of its interest, but additional historical abbeys cannot be produced. The duke may value the abbey exclusively for his own enjoyment. Admitting visitors would impose a cost on him in the form of loss of exclusive use. But he might be willing to accept this opportunity cost in exchange for some amount of money and would therefore admit visitors if the price were right. Presumably a few visitors would not be as much of a nuisance as many, so the number of visits the duke will permit is only likely to increase with higher admission fees.

Production Situations. In production situations supply is determined by cost of production. A supplier will not ordinarily produce something unless he feels the price he can obtain for it will be greater than the cost of producing it.

Our duke and his abbey do not represent a purely stock situation. He may find it possible to accommodate additional visitors by paving a parking lot or providing guides. He may also increase the attraction of the abbey by developing a museum, landscaping the grounds, or even adding a zoo. All these actions would require monetary outlays, and the extent to which he pursues them will depend on the size of the admission fee people are willing to pay.

2.2.2. Long-Run and Short-Run Supply. Production situations may have two time dimensions—long run or short run. In the long run everything involved in production can be changed: land can be shifted to other uses, capital can be converted to other forms, labor can engage in other activities. In the short run some of these factors may be fixed. A producer's problem then is to obtain the maximum benefit from these limited resources. We will analyze short-run behavior in the following sections, but first must look more closely at the long run.

Long-Run Supply. In the long run all productive factors can shift or be shifted to other uses. Long-run supply is therefore determined by long-run opportunity costs and may be greater or less than short-run supply. For example, wages may be low in a region with limited employment opportunities. If economic development takes place and workers start to shift to new activities, an existing enterprise may have to raise its wage rate in order to keep going. The resulting higher costs will cause the long-run supply to be less than current short-run supply. The outcome could be the opposite if a scarcity of skilled workers were eliminated over time by a technician training program.

A supplier who is considering starting a new enterprise will take a long-run viewpoint. He will try to foresee all production costs and will not be willing to supply a good unless he feels the price will cover its total long-run cost. The duke will not begin to admit visitors to his abbey unless he is convinced the enterprise will be profitable in the long run.

Short-Run Supply. Once a supplier has decided to go ahead, however, he usually must take actions that cannot readily be reversed and that consequently create fixed costs. If the duke has paved a parking lot and landscaped the abbey grounds, he cannot recover the money thus invested by deciding not to admit visitors. From then on he must operate in a short-run situation. If his original decision was a mistake, he may not be able to obtain enough income from admission fees to cover his total costs, and in the long run he may have to give up the enterprise. In the short run, however, he will produce if he can cover his variable costs.

2.2.3. The Production Function. In the short run some productive factors are fixed but others are variable. The amount a supplier produces therefore depends on how much of the variable factors, such as labor, he uses in combination with fixed factors, such as land. The crop yield from a hectare of land will generally increase as more labor is applied.

In our example, certain of the factors necessary to provide visits are fixed at the start of a tourist season, such as the abbey itself, the landscaping, and parking facilities. The number of people employed to maintain them and serve the visitors can be varied, however. An increase in the number of employees will increase the number of visitors who can be accommodated during the season, as illustrated in Table 2.1 and in Figure 2.3*a*.

A production function is not ordinarily a straight-line relationship. At lower levels of input there may not be enough of the variable factor to use the fixed factors efficiently. An increase in input may, therefore, yield more than a proportionate increase in output. This is illustrated in Table 2.1, where ten employees can take care of more than twice as many visitors as five employees. The important statistic is that in column 3—the change in total output resulting from a given increase of input (five employees in this case). We use the term *marginal physical product* for a slightly more

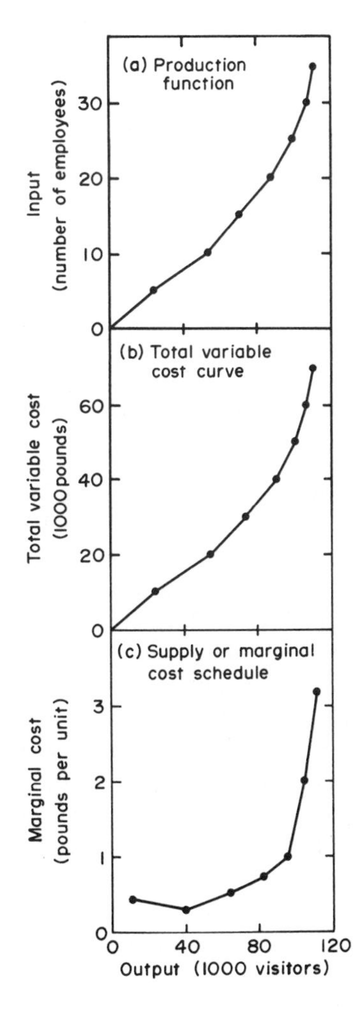

Figure 2.3. Derivation of a supply schedule for visits to a hypothetical abbey from underlying production and cost relationships.

Table 2.1. Production Function and Marginal Cost Schedule for Visits to a Hypothetical Abbey

Input	Output	Change in			
Number of People Employed	Number of Visitors (1000)	Output[a] Number of Visitors (1000)	Total Variable Cost[b] (£1000)	Change in Cost (£1000)	Marginal Cost Per Unit of Output[c]
1	2	3	4	5	6
0	0		0		
		25		10	0.4
5	25		10		
		30		10	0.3
10	55		20		
		20		10	0.5
15	75		30		
		15		10	0.7
20	90		40		
		10		10	1.0
25	100		50		
		5		10	2.0
30	105		60		
		3		10	3.3
35	108		70		

[a] The marginal physical product can be obtained by dividing each figure in this column by the change in input.
[b] Wages at £2000 per year.
[c] Column 6 = column 5/column 3.

specific statistic—the change in output for a one-unit change in the relevant input with all other inputs held constant.

In any production function a point is always reached beyond which the marginal physical product declines. In Table 2.1 this occurs at an input of ten employees. Beyond this point further intensification of production will yield diminishing returns. The production functions for many economic activities do not show an area of increasing returns because marginal productivity declines from the start. Diminishing marginal productivity occurs because it becomes progressively harder to combine more variable inputs effectively with a constant amount of fixed input. A small abbey staff would be so busy with maintenance that they could handle only a few visitors. Five more employees to provide guide and other services would make it possible to admit many more visitors, and their marginal productivity would be high. But if the duke already had thirty employees, it would be difficult to find productive work for five more. As parking lot attendants and messengers they might make it possible to accommodate a few more visitors, but their marginal productivity would be low. Beyond some level, additional inputs would not increase output at all.

2.2.4. Derivation of the Supply Schedule. A production function shows the various outputs that can be produced by combining different amounts of a variable input with some given fixed input. If this function is plotted on a graph, as in Figure 2.3*a*, one can read from the curve the physical cost (in units of variable input) of producing various outputs. But a supplier needs a production cost in monetary units that he can compare with the price people are willing to pay for his product. If he can buy or hire all the variable factor he needs at the same per-unit price, the physical production function can be converted to a cost function by multiplying the physical input units by the price per unit. This is illustrated in column 4 of Table 2.1 and in Figure 2.3*b*, using a wage cost of £2000 per employee year.

However, what the supplier needs to know is whether he should produce additional units in response to the price consumers are willing to pay. For this he needs the marginal cost of each additional unit. He can determine this by calculating the total cost of the additional variable inputs required and dividing by the number of additional units of output produced. This gives the marginal variable cost per unit of additional output, as illustrated in column 6 of Table 2.1.

For example, suppose our duke has already decided to employ ten people to take care of the 55,000 visitors he expects will pay to see the abbey this year. If he were to employ five more people, he could handle an additional 20,000 visitors with the existing facilities. The cost of providing these additional visits would be £10,000 at the going wage of £2000 or a marginal cost of £0.5 per visitor. If tourists are willing to pay an admission fee of £0.6, the duke could profitably provide for 75,000 visits. He would not supply more, however, because if he were to add five more employees and increase the total to 90,000 visitors, the additional 15,000 visits would cost £0.7 each or more than the admission price of £0.6.

The marginal cost of expanding output is therefore what determines a supplier's response to market prices. The marginal variable cost schedule illustrated in column 6 of Table 2.1 and Figure 2.3*c* is the short-run supply schedule. Because marginal costs normally increase because of diminishing marginal physical productivity, the result is an upward-sloping supply curve. Economic theory says that producers tend to expand output in the short run to a point where the marginal cost of additional output is equal to market price. The price at which a supplier willingly sells his product indicates the social value of that product in terms of marginal costs.

2.3. Interaction of Supply and Demand

The preceding sections have discussed supply and demand as individual phenomena. Isolated exchanges do take place between individual sellers and buyers, but most markets involve a number of people. In this section we look at the economic theory of behavior in such broader markets.

2.3.1. Market Supply and Demand Schedules. Market supply is the total of all individual supplies in a market. If all sellers were identical and had supply schedules like that pictured in Figure 2.3*c*, total market supply would be this individual schedule multiplied by the number of sellers. If each seller had a different supply schedule, market supply would be the sum of the individual amounts offered for sale at each price.

For example, suppose there are three abbeys in close proximity and the public perceives a visit to one as providing the same utility as a visit to any other. Let us assume that the supply schedule for our original abbey is pictured by curve 1 in Figure 2.4. The supply provided by the second abbey (curve 2) is less at every price than that of the original abbey, and that pro-

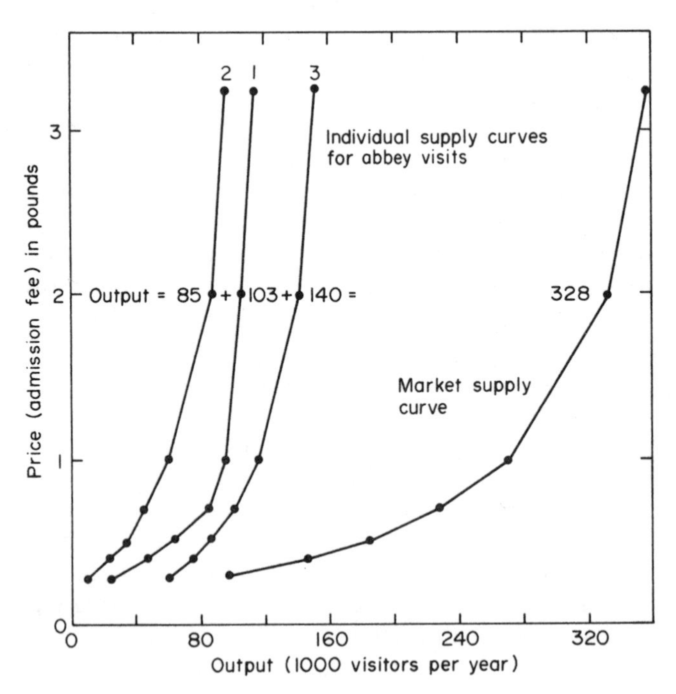

Figure 2.4. Market supply schedule for visits to hypothetical abbeys as an aggregate of individual supply schedules.

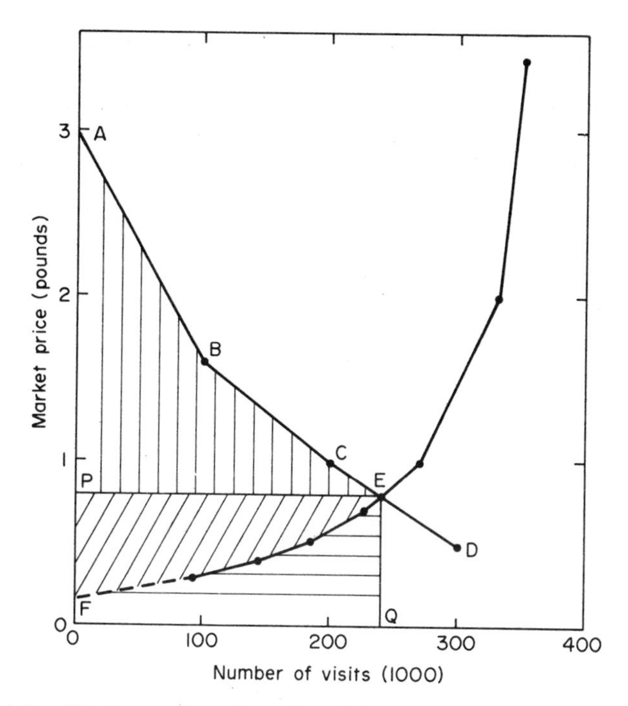

Figure 2.5. The interaction of supply and demand in a hypothetical market for visits to abbeys.

vided by the third abbey (curve 3) is greater. The total market supply schedule (right-hand curve) is equal to the sum of the three individual supplies. At a price of £2, 85,000 will visit abbey 2; 103,000, abbey 1; and 140,000, abbey 3. If people are willing to pay £2 for admission to an abbey, they can make a total of 328,000 visits in this area.

Market demand is also the total of all individual demands in a market. If every abbey visitor had an individual demand schedule like that in Figure 2.1, the total market demand schedule would be this individual schedule multiplied by the number of buyers. If each buyer had a different demand schedule, market demand would be the sum of all individual demands at each price.

2.3.2. Interaction in a Market. Buyers and sellers come together in markets to exchange goods and services. The expected behavior of buyers is shown by the market demand schedule for a good and that of sellers by its market supply schedule. Market demand and supply interact as illustrated in Figure 2.5. This shows how many abbey visits people would make and how many visits owners would provide at various admission fees from £0 to £4.

Figure 2.4 showed that at an admission price of £2, the three abbeys would offer a total of 328,000 visits. This is shown again by the market supply schedule in Figure 2.5. The pooled market demand of the potential visitors shown in Figure 2.5 indicates, however, that they would make only 74,000 visits if the admission fee were £2. Some would choose not to visit an abbey at all, and others would make only one or two visits. The abbey owners would find themselves prepared to handle more than four times the number of visitors who actually appeared.

By contrast, if the admission price were only £0.5, people would want to make 300,000 visits to the abbey (point *D* in Figure 2.5). However, if the abbey owners could only charge £0.5 for admission, they would provide for only 180,000 visitors. People could only make about half as many visits as they would like. In such a situation we would expect abbey owners to raise admission fees and try to hire more employees. The higher fees would discourage some potential visitors but not all.

In the case in which abbey owners are prepared to serve more visitors than are willing to pay for admission, we would expect them to reduce the price and lay off some employees. Market price is thus a variable that can move up or down in response to the efforts of buyers and sellers to make exchanges.

Economists have developed a theoretical model of a perfectly competitive market. It assumes there are large numbers of buyers and sellers, none of whom exchanges enough individually to affect the market. It also assumes that the product being exchanged is homogeneous and that both buyers and sellers have perfect knowledge and can enter or leave the market at will. Finally, it assumes that all participants compete actively with an objective of furthering their own economic interests.

If perfect competition existed in the market pictured in Figure 2.5, the price of an abbey visit would rise and fall in response to bids and offers until it eventually stabilized at £0.8 (point *P* in Figure 2.5). At this price people would want to make 240,000 visits (point *Q* in Figure 2.5), and abbey owners would provide for this number. Everyone willing to pay an admission fee of £0.8 could visit an abbey, and each abbey owner would find a customer waiting for every visit he was willing to provide for £0.8.

Under perfect competition there would be an efficient allocation of resources to the provision of abbey visits. Market price would cover the costs of all productive factors (abbeys, capital, labor, etc.), so abbey visits would be as valuable as anything these factors could produce in any other use. At the same time, because visitors are free to buy other goods and services, their paying for an abbey visit would indicate that it is worth more to them than the other things they could have bought. Market price thus indicates the value of the marginal unit exchanged to both buyers and sellers.

The model of perfect competition approximates actual market situations well enough to be useful in value analyses. However, real markets deviate enough from the assumptions underlying the model that actual market prices must be used with caution as indicators of social value. We discuss this in detail in Section 5.

2.4. Quantitative Expression of Supply and Demand

Demand and supply schedules provide simple quantitative expressions of buyer and seller responses. Although graphic models are helpful in analyzing these responses, they can be generalized and extended for valuation purposes better in mathematical form.

2.4.1. The Demand Function. ***Background.*** Economic theory assumes that individual consumers strive to maximize the utility (U) they derive from consuming goods and services, and therefore

$$U = U(Q_1, \cdots, Q_n) \tag{2.1}$$

where Q_i represents the quantity of the ith good consumed. Because consumers have limited resources, this is subject to the income constraint

$$Inc = P_1Q_1 + \cdots + P_nQ_n \tag{2.2}$$

where P_i is the price of the ith good and Inc represents income. Choices that maximize utility and meet the income constraint can be explained or predicted by the general function

$$Q_1 = f(P_1 \cdots P_i \cdots P_n, Inc) \tag{2.3}$$

This model theorizes that the consumption of a good depends on or is influenced by the price of the good itself, the prices of other goods, and the consumer's income. In environmental work it is common to add variables for other explanatory factors, giving a demand function of the form

$$Q_i = f(P_i, P_n, Inc, X_n) \tag{2.4}$$

where P_n now stands for the prices of all other goods and X_n represents all other factors.

The simplest demand function would be

$$Q_i = f(P_i) \tag{2.5}$$

or in arithmetic terms

$$Q_i = a - bP_i \tag{2.6}$$

The term a is a constant, and b is the coefficient that relates the amount of Q_i to that of P_i. This simple model says that quantity consumed is influenced solely by price and that an increase in price is associated with a decrease in consumption; hence the coefficient has a negative sign.

An Example. The demand relationship between number of visits to an abbey and admission price presented in Figure 2.1 can be expressed by the function

$$Q = 4.2 - 1.6P \tag{2.7}$$

which fits a linear relationship to the points in Figure 2.1. The coefficient of determination, which measures how closely the function fits the points, is .84. This indicates that differences in price account for 84 percent of the variation in visits to the abbey. Other factors that are responsible for the remaining 16 percent cause the actual demand function to have a curved form, rather than the linear one fitted by Equation 2.7.

The example shown in Figure 2.1 was an individual demand curve for one abbey visitor. Let us now consider a simple market demand example as shown in Table 2.2. There are seven consumers who have similar tastes but live at various distances from an abbey. All pay the same entrance fee, but because they incur different travel costs the effective price to them varies as shown in column 3. The number of visits they buy is shown in column 2. The following demand function can be fitted to these price and quantity

Table 2.2. Hypothetical Demand Information for Seven Visitors to an Abbey

Visitor	Quantity (visits per summer)	Effective Price per Visit[a] (£)	Income (£1000)
1	2	3	4
A	4	0.50	12
B	3	0.25	14
C	2	0.50	8
D	1	1.00	8
E	1	2.00	12
F	0.5	3.00	13
G	0	4.00	17
Average	1.64	1.61	

[a] The sum of entrance fee and travel costs.

figures

$$Q = 3.0 - 0.8P \tag{2.8}$$

The coefficient of determination of .62 shows there is a pattern to the relationship between price and quantity. The price variable alone accounts for 62 percent of the variation in visits among individuals.

We can now illustrate the effect of a nonprice factor—incomes of the individual consumers, which are shown in column 4. When income is added to the equation, we obtain the demand function

$$Q = 0.6 - 1.2P + 0.2Inc \tag{2.9}$$

The coefficient of determination is now .77, which shows that this function accounts for 15 percent more of the variation in consumption than does Equation 2.8. The number of visits to the abbey varies inversely with price but directly with personal income.

2.4.2. The Supply Function. A supply function is a mathematical expression of a supply schedule. It assumes people try to maximize net revenue within resource or input constraints. Since the underlying logic is the same, we do not analyze supply functions in the detail used with demand functions.

A supply function can be expressed as

$$Q_i = f(P_i, Inc, X_n) \tag{2.10}$$

The quantity offered for sale varies with market price, income, and other variables. A simple supply function is

$$Q_i = a + bP_i \tag{2.11}$$

2.4.3. Elasticity of Demand and Supply. Economic theory says that if everything else is equal, people will buy less at high prices and more at low prices, and do the opposite when selling. The extent to which they adjust their behavior in response to a difference in price is called elasticity. When the amounts bought or sold change greatly with price, the demand or supply is said to be elastic. When the quantity changes little with price, they are said to be inelastic.

Definition. Elasticity is defined as the proportionate change in quantity that would result from a proportionate change in price

$$\text{elasticity} = \frac{\text{change in quantity}}{\text{original quantity}} \div \frac{\text{change in price}}{\text{original price}} \tag{2.12}$$

It is most frequently expressed as the percentage change in quantity that would result in a 1 percent change in price. A demand or supply function with an elasticity greater than 1 is called elastic, and one with an elasticity less than 1 is called inelastic.

Equation 2.12 can be modified to permit the calculation of elasticity at any point on a demand schedule from the data in the demand function. The denominator of Equation 2.12 will be 0.01 because elasticity is based on a 1 percent change in price. From Equation 2.6 we know that

$$Q_i = a - bP_i \tag{2.13}$$

so a change in price will bring about a change in Q_i equal to the change in P_i multiplied by b, and the numerator of Equation 2.12 can be written as

$$\frac{b\,(0.01\ P_i)}{Q_i} \tag{2.14}$$

If both numerator and denominator of Equation 2.12 are now multipled by 100 to eliminate the decimals, we have

$$e = \frac{(bP_i/Q_i)}{1} \tag{2.15}$$

which can be simplified to

$$e = b\left(\frac{P_1}{Q_1}\right) \tag{2.16}$$

where e is elasticity, b is the coefficient of price in the demand function, and P_1 and Q_1 are the price and quantity at point 1.

We can illustrate this with the demand function (2.9) derived from the data in Table 2.2. The elasticity of demand at the point where quantity and price have mean values is

$$\text{elasticity} = -1.2\left(\frac{1.61}{1.64}\right) = -1.18 \tag{2.17}$$

At this point on the schedule, demand for visits to the abbey is somewhat elastic. A 1 percent increase in admission fee would result in a 1.18 percent decrease in the number of visits by this group of visitors.

Price elasticity of supply can be calculated in a similar manner from a supply function. It is important to note that elasticity is not usually the same over the whole range of a schedule. Demand or supply could be elastic at low prices but inelastic at high prices.

2.5. Usefulness of the Exchange Model in Valuation

Before elaborating on these theories in Sections 3 and 4, we should briefly see how they relate to valuation problems.

2.5.1. A Market Model Concept of Value. Individual demand schedules show buyers' willingness to pay for various quantities of goods or services. The schedule presented in Figure 2.1, for example, shows a particular Englishman is willing to pay £1.5 to visit an abbey once. He apparently feels a visit to an abbey has a value to him at least as great as £1.5. As he would not make two visits unless the admission fee were lower, he apparently feels a second visit to the same abbey would have a value of only £1. If the admission fee were £1 he presumably would still feel that his first visit has a value of £1.5, even though he only pays £1 for it. If he buys a £1.5 value for only £1 he will obtain what is called a consumer's surplus, which in this case will amount to £0.5.

Let us now look at the market demand situation in Figure 2.5. This shows aggregate willingness to pay of all consumers for visits to abbeys. At a market price of £0.8 they will make a total of 240,000 visits; thus each visit must have a value to them of at least £0.8. If the price were £1.0, these same people would make 200,000 visits (point *C* in Figure 2.5), and if it were £1.6, they would still make 100,000 visits (point *B* in Figure 2.5), which indicates they feel many of the visits they can obtain for the market price of £0.8 are actually worth more. At the market price, these people obtain an aggregate consumers' surplus indicated by the area *PAE*.

The consumers pay £0.8 apiece for 240,000 visits, as shown by the area *OPEQ* in Figure 2.5. But since they would have willingly paid the consumers' surplus also, if necessary, their actual total willingness to pay is indicated by the area *OAEQ*. In any market situation, therefore,

$$\begin{matrix}\text{total consumers'} \\ \text{willingness to pay}\end{matrix} = \begin{matrix}\text{consumers'} \\ \text{expenditures}\end{matrix} + \begin{matrix}\text{consumers'} \\ \text{surplus}\end{matrix}$$

In a given market the total revenue received by sellers must equal the total consumer expenditure. The actual cost to the sellers is the aggregate of the marginal variable costs indicated by the supply curve, or the area *OFEQ*. Because the producers would have been willing to sell their products at these marginal costs if necessary, the total revenue they obtain includes a producers' surplus of *FPE*.

Because consumers' total willingness to pay indicates the total benefit and producers' total costs indicate the cost of producing these benefits, the total net benefit is shown by the area *FAE*. In any market situation

$$\begin{matrix}\text{net social} \\ \text{benefit}\end{matrix} = \begin{matrix}\text{consumers'} \\ \text{surplus}\end{matrix} + \begin{matrix}\text{producers'} \\ \text{surplus}\end{matrix}$$

This is a useful economic concept of value.

2.5.2. An Overall Assessment. People's choices are based on their reactions to the differences they think the alternatives would make to their lives. Valuation does not necessarily have to consider how such differences would be created, but it must consider how people react to them. This behavior is a response to the satisfaction expected and the costs of obtaining it. Demand and supply schedules attempt to capture behavioral responses to satisfaction and cost. Together they provide a means of assessing the differences things make to people's lives.

The model of price formation described in Section 2.3.2 and Figure 2.5 is only accurate under conditions of perfect competition. But the models of demand and supply are useful in understanding behavior regardless of how prices are formed and whether they are expressed in monetary terms or not. The next two sections relate the demand and supply models to the motivations that underlie behavior.

3. UTILITY AND DEMAND

Demand is an outward expression of the utility a person can obtain from possession or use of a thing. The concept of demand therefore provides a transition between actual behavior, which can be observed, and the underlying satisfaction or "warm glow" which constitutes utility. It is a useful tool with which to express and then estimate relative utilities of alternative choices.

3.1. The Notion of Utility: Preference for a Single Good

The demand model is based on a belief that individuals behave in ways that satisfy their wants and desires. Anything they deliberately obtain can therefore be assumed to provide utility. Common behavior indicates that having more of most things increases the utility received. But it also suggests that the utility obtained does not increase in direct proportion to the quantity consumed. There is good reason to believe that for most things the relation between total utility and quantity consumed resembles that shown in Figure 2.6.

3.1.1. Diminishing Marginal Utility. In Figure 2.6 total utility is increasing up to four units, but each additional unit has added less than the preceding one. The marginal utility is diminishing.

This phenomenon can be explained on two grounds: (1) No human wants are insatiable, so that no matter how much is available, people will not consume infinite quantities of anything. At some point they become completely satiated, and an additional unit will have zero marginal utility, as illustrated by the fifth unit in Figure 2.6. Consuming more might even have negative utility, as in the case of overeating. (2) People almost always use or consume things in combinations. (A common meal consists of meat,

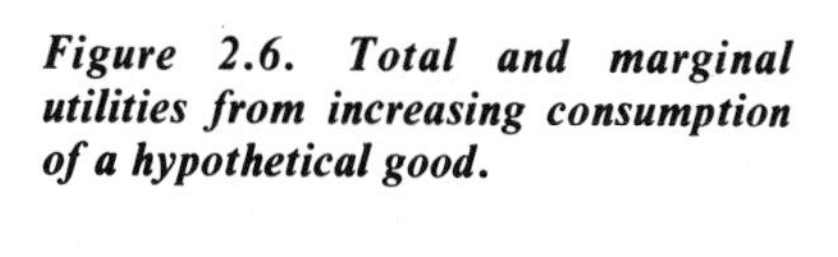

Figure 2.6. Total and marginal utilities from increasing consumption of a hypothetical good.

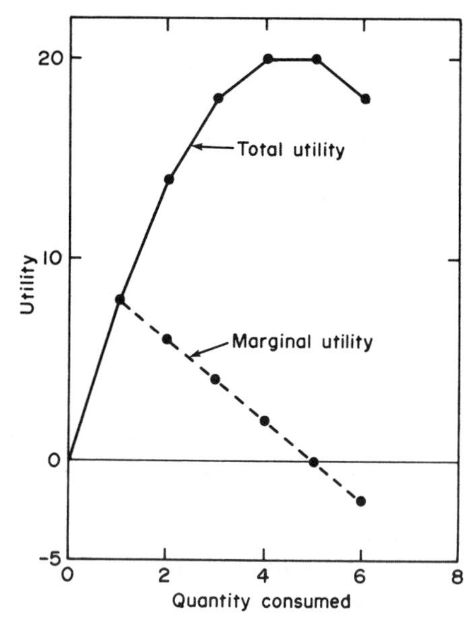

potatoes, and vegetables, for example.) Because the components of combinations are seldom perfect substitutes, more of any one component will not usually increase utility as much as its original amount did. (A second helping of vegetables might not add much utility to an already satisfactory meal.)

3.1.2. From Diminishing Marginal Utility to Demand. A buyer makes the transition from utility to demand by determining how much he is willing to pay for a good or service. Viner (1925) suggests the following causal sequence in determining willingness to pay for a thing:

(1) A recognition of its diminishing marginal utility.

(2) A more or less accurate visualization of its schedule of marginal utilities.

(3) An estimate of the expected utilities of the other things that would have to be sacrificed to obtain it.

(4) An estimate of the monetary sacrifice the buyer is willing to make to obtain a given quantity of the thing.

(5) An estimate of the monetary sacrifices he would be willing to make to obtain a range of other quantities.

Step 5 provides the data for a demand schedule.

In step 3 a buyer recognizes that he must give up other utilities to obtain the thing he wants. Because money serves as a proxy for all other things, he can determine the monetary value of the things he must sacrifice. This establishes the minimum price he is willing to pay; if the thing is not worth this much, he would be worse off buying it. If he feels its utility is greater than this cost, he will decide how much additional money he is willing to sacrifice to obtain it. This is step 4. Finally, in step 5 he applies this same procedure to other quantities. In each case it is the utility of the marginal unit that determines how much he is willing to pay per unit for the total quantity.

In a market economy money has utility because it can be exchanged for other things that have utility. If a person uses his first money to buy things of greatest utility and succeeding units to buy things of successively less utility, the marginal utility of money will diminish as he obtains more of it. A rational person shifting money from present uses to a new use would give up that use which has the lowest marginal utility. Because marginal utility diminishes, the utility that a dollar represents depends on how much money a buyer has. The marginal utility of one more dollar may be high to a poor person but low to a rich one. A wealthy person may therefore be willing to pay more for the same thing than a poor person.

An individual buyer presumably adjusts his purchases so that the marginal utility of a unit of his money is the same in all uses, and he cannot make himself better off by shifting money from one use to another. The behavior of buyers in a market is determined both by the marginal utilities of the things exchanged and the marginal utility of their money. A market demand schedule is heavily influenced by the incomes of buyers.

3.2. The Indifference Curve Approach: Preference between Two Goods

The utility theory of buyer behavior, which we discussed in the previous section, is based on preferences for single goods. We now consider an alternative approach which is based on relative preferences between goods. This approach makes the reasonable assumption that people can choose between combinations or "bundles" of goods as well as between single goods.

3.2.1. Indifference Curves. If people can compare bundles of goods, it seems reasonable that there must be some combinations which appear equally desirable to them. When faced with a choice, they would be indifferent as to which combination they received.

Suppose the Englishman of our example in Section 2.1 is not limited to visiting abbeys (A) during the summer but has an alternative of going to the beach (B). To simplify the illustration, let us assume that these are the only alternatives available to him. For the moment we will ignore any limitations imposed by the size of his income.

Let us start with a reference bundle of three visits to an abbey and four to the beach, which provides a total of U units of utility. This is presented as combination II in Table 2.3. Let us now assume that he would be equally satisfied if he could make five visits to an abbey and two to the beach (combination I) or two visits to an abbey and eight to the beach (combination III). He would obtain U units of utility from any of these combinations and would be indifferent as to which he had.

These three combinations are plotted on the indifference curve U in Figure 2.7. If this person could make fractional visits to abbeys and the beach, there would undoubtedly be other combinations on this curve to which he would be indifferent. The important feature of Figure 2.7 is that any combination of activities on curve U would provide the same total amount of utility.

Table 2.3 shows that if this person were starting with combination II, he would be willing to give up two visits to the beach for two more abbey visits (a move to I) or to give up one abbey visit for four more visits to the beach (a move to III). Another person might not be willing to make these same trade-offs, nor might this man at another time or under other circumstances.

3.2.2. The Indifference Map. Other indifference curves may be plotted on Figure 2.7 by finding other combinations of abbey and beach visits, all of which provide the same amount of total utility. For example, everything else being equal, people could be expected to prefer combination V ($5A + 5B$) to combination II ($3A + 4B$) because it contains more of both components. Other combinations can be found which provide the same total utility U', such as combinations IV and VI. When these are plotted in Figure 2.7, they give a new indifference curve U'. Any combination on this curve provides the same total utility, which is greater than that provided by

Table 2.3. Combinations of Visits to an Abbey and the Beach which Provide Different Levels of Total Utility

	Total Utility U			Total Utility U'	
	Number of Visits to			Number of Visits to	
Combination	A	B	Combination	A	B
I	5	2	IV	8	3
II	3	4	V	5	5
III	2	8	VI	3	10

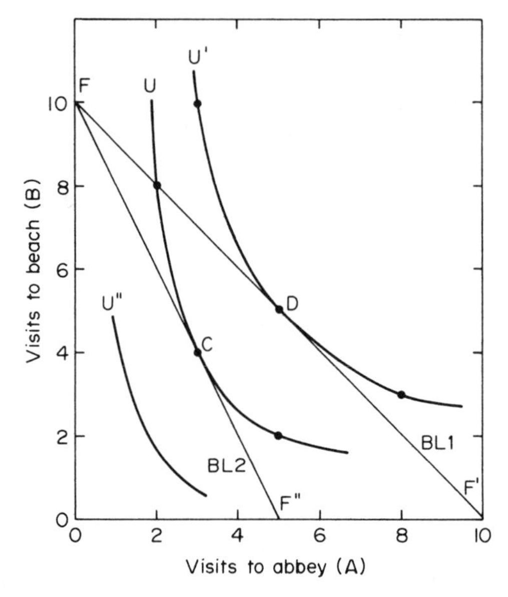

Figure 2.7. A hypothetical indifference map for visits to abbeys and the beach.

any combination on curve U. Other combinations providing a lower amount of total utility could also be found and plotted as curve U''. By continuing this procedure, Figure 2.7 could be filled with a family of indifference curves, whose utilities increased from the lower left to the upper right. The result is called an indifference map.

An indifference map indicates that the total utility obtained by an individual is a function of the quantities of the two goods consumed

$$U_i = f(Q_A, Q_B) \tag{2.18}$$

No attempt is made to define the absolute meaning of, say, U units of utility, but the relative magnitudes of utilities can be defined. Techniques for obtaining numerical measures of intervals between indifference curves have been developed by Ramsey (1931) and von Neumann and Morgenstern (1947) and are presented in Chapter 11. With these techniques, indifference maps can describe preferences in sufficient quantitative detail to permit the calculation of standard demand curves, as we show in Section 3.2.4.

3.2.3. The Budget Line. An indifference map is a useful characterization of a person's preferences about two things. If there were no limits on what he might choose, the indifference map could guide his choices, because he would always obtain the greatest possible amount of additional utility by making that choice which would put him on the highest indifference curve.

However, a decision maker must also consider prices and budget limitations as follows

$$Inc = (Q_A \times P_A) + (Q_B \times P_B) + \cdots + (Q_n \times P_n) \qquad (2.19)$$

where Q and P are the quantities and prices of various goods and Inc is the buyer's total income. Within the budget constraint imposed by his income, the quantity of any thing this person can buy is determined by the price of that thing and the quantities and prices of the other things he buys.

In our example in Figure 2.7, the budget this buyer has available for visits to abbeys and beaches can be used as follows

$$Inc = (Q_A \times P_A) + (Q_B \times P_B) \qquad (2.20)$$

If his budget were £10 and the price of a visit to either an abbey or the beach were £1, he could make ten visits to either one, or various combinations such as six to abbeys and four to the beach. These combinations all fall on the straight line F to F', which is called a budget line and labeled $BL1$ in Figure 2.7. If his budget were £5 instead of £10, he could make five visits to an abbey or five to the beach, and the budget line connecting these points would show other possible combinations.

If we now look at the indifference curves, we can see how a buyer will decide which combination of visits to select from all those possible with a budget of £10. If he chooses two abbey and eight beach visits, he will get the amount of utility indicated by indifference curve U. However, if he chooses five visits to each (point D in Figure 2.7), he will get the higher utility indicated by curve U'. Any other combination on his budget line would fall below curve U' and give him less utility. His best choice is indicated by point D where his budget line is tangent to the highest possible indifference curve U'.

If the budget remains the same but the price of one good changes, a new budget line becomes effective. If, for example, the charge for abbey visits were to increase to £2, a budget of £10 would permit only five abbey visits or any of the combinations indicated by the new budget line $BL2$. The best possible combination would now be three abbey and four beach visits (point C in Figure 2.7), because this would provide a utility of U. Any other combination would fall below this indifference curve. An increase in the relative price of one good not only forces the buyer to reduce his total purchases, but also causes him to substitute some of the cheaper good for the more expensive one.

3.2.4. Derivation of a Demand Schedule. We can now expand the idea of an indifference map to illustrate a person's attitude toward combinations of all the goods and services he might buy. Let the horizontal axis of Figure

2.7 remain in units of abbey visits, but imagine that the vertical axis now shows units of all other goods and services except abbey visits. The indifference curves indicate that the buyer feels some combinations of abbey visits and all other things would provide equal utility but that others would provide more or less utility.

Let us now imagine that this person has a budget of £10 and that the average market price of all other goods and services is £1 per unit. If the price of abbey visits is also £1, he could buy ten visits or ten units of other things or any of the combinations on the budget line *BL*1. His indifference curves indicate that the best combination would be at point *D*. At a price of £1, he could be expected to buy five visits. If the price of abbey visits were £2 but the prices of all other things remained the same, his purchase opportunities would be shown by budget line *BL*2. His best combination would now be at point *C*, so that at a price of £2 he could be expected to buy three visits. To emphasize the behavioral nature of these results, let us summarize the effect of price on quantity taken:

Price in £	Best combination	Quantity taken
1	D	5
2	C	3

If we use a fixed budget and assume that the prices of all other things remain constant, a range of other prices for abbey visits can be tested and the resulting quantities determined. In this way a complete demand schedule for abbey visits can be derived. The actual utility a purchaser obtains from an abbey visit does not have to be measured. All that is needed is information on the trade-offs he is willing to make between abbey visits and all other goods and services.

3.3. Comparative Utilities for Valuation

Economic theory does not attempt to relate utility to an ultimate or absolute degree of satisfaction. This is not necessary for valuation. As Alchian (1953) has noted, ". . . whether or not utility is some kind of glow or warmth, or happiness, is here irrelevant; all that counts is that we can assign numbers to entities or conditions which a person can strive to realize. . . ." What is needed is a scale to measure comparative utilities and predict choices, and this can be based on relative levels of utility rather than absolute measurements. Part II of this book is devoted to various ways of deriving such scales and estimating relative utilities.

4. DISUTILITY, COST, AND SUPPLY

Supply is an outward expression of the disutility a person suffers when he provides a thing to someone else. The concept of supply forms a transition between observed behavior and the disutility underlying it. The transition is made by way of the cost of the resources that must be used or given up to provide the supply. In a perfectly competitive market price indicates value to both buyers and sellers. The money cost of resources indicates the benefits that might be obtained by using this money for other purposes. The real costs of resources are the utilities from other opportunities a supplier must sacrifice. The disutility of providing the thing results from the necessity of sacrificing these utilities. Supply, therefore, also rests on estimates of comparative utilities.

4.1. Costs Sometimes Ignored

For supply to be a useful indicator of social value, a seller must take into account all the costs of providing a good or service. This may not be done when some of the costs are implicit or external.

Most supply costs are explicit, consisting of out-of-pocket monetary payments for wages, rent, interest, and materials. The seller is aware that he is incurring these costs and is sensitive to them. However, there may also be implicit costs for which no overt payment is made. The duke, for example, owns the abbey and facilities and provides managerial services. If he does not pay himself a salary, rent for the abbey, and interest on his invested capital, it appears that these do not cost anything. But all of them could be put to other uses, and the utilities they would produce in the best other uses are the opportunity costs of using them in the abbey enterprise. If the duke ignores these implicit costs, he may provide abbey visits at a price that does not cover the total disutility.

Most supply costs are internal to a production operation; that is, they are clearly part of the operation, and the producer is sensitive to them. Some costs, however, are external and occur as spillovers. They may fall on other people or even on the producer himself, but he may be unaware of them or ignore them. For example, a large number of visitors to an abbey will create noise, road congestion, and pollution. The noise and pollution may affect the duke and his family; the congestion will affect primarily other travelers. These externalities are part of the cost of providing abbey visits. If the duke ignores them, he may again provide abbey visits at a price that does not cover the total disutility.

4.2. Time as a Cost

Many decisions involve costs and benefits that will materialize in the future. A question then arises of how to add or compare utilities that will exist at future times with those that exist today. This is a subject on which there is considerable theoretical disagreement. All we can do here is present some approaches that are generally used and that are reasonably satisfactory for valuation purposes.

4.2.1. A Model of Response to Time. People generally consider things that are immediately available to have different utilities than those that will only become available in the future. They prefer to receive things now and consider having to wait as a cost that will reduce the value of a future receipt. However, people sometimes prefer to receive some things in the future rather than at the present.

If people prefer to receive a dollar now rather than later, future dollars must be weighted downward when comparing them with present dollars. By contrast, if they prefer a dollar later, future dollars must be weighted upward in value comparisons. The present worth (PW) of a future benefit is

$$PW = B_t \times WT_t \tag{2.21}$$

where B is the future benefit at time t and WT is the weighting factor.

Equation 2.21 is quite general, for it makes no assumptions about the direction or magnitude of preference for present versus future. WT will be less than 1 if people prefer the present, and more than 1 if they prefer the future. If they should be indifferent between present and future, WT would be exactly 1, and the present worth of B would be identical with its future utility.

In most cases people prefer to have things now and assign a weight of less than 1 to future utilities. Because they usually discount future values, the weight is commonly called a *discount factor.* It is important to remember, however, that people do not always discount future utilities.

It is a common observation that the farther things are in the future, the more heavily people tend to discount them. They deduct a waiting cost for the time that must pass before they can receive them. Economic analysis usually assumes that the size of the deduction is not directly proportional to the length of time. Rather, the size of the discount is assumed to increase with time at a compound rate in the same way that money allowed to remain in a savings account increases over time.

A major problem with the discounting model lies in deciding what rate of interest to use. Ultimately it is an arbitrary decision and is discussed in great detail in books on economic and benefit-cost analysis. Although the assumption that people discount future values at a compound rate can be questioned and present worth is very sensitive to the rate used, it is the best model of response to time which economic theorists have developed.

4.2.2. Arithmetic of Time Analysis. This section just briefly defines the terms and sets out the arithmetic to be used in later chapters.

Present worth is the worth of future benefits or costs discounted to the present. For future benefits this is

$$PW = B_1 + B_2WT_2 + \cdots + B_tWT_t \tag{2.22}$$

where WT_t is the discount factor for the specific year t.

Present net worth is the difference between discounted future benefits and discounted future costs

$$PNW = B_tWT_t - C_tWT_t \tag{2.23}$$

where C_t is cost at year t.

An *annuity* is an infinite stream of equal annual benefits or costs that are equivalent to a given present worth. The present worth of this stream is the sum of the discounted annual amounts

$$PW = \frac{a}{d} \tag{2.24}$$

where a is the annual amount and d is the discount rate. Rearranging this gives the value of an annual annuity as

$$a = PW \times d \tag{2.25}$$

Internal rate of return is the discount rate that would make the discounted benefits of a project equal the discounted costs.

5. HOW USEFUL ARE ACTUAL MARKET PRICES?

In a market economy people indicate their comparative valuations of goods and services by the amount of money they are willing to spend. If the market is large, prices indicate the combined valuations of many individuals. If it is freely competitive, they indicate the marginal willingness to pay of a whole group of people. Therefore, a large, competitive, organized market allows people to express and pool their comparative valuations of many goods and services.

But most actual markets are not large and competitive, and observed market prices and quantities must be used with care in estimating values.

This does not affect the usefulness of the model as an analytical device, but it does affect the usefulness of real world data as inputs to the model. Haveman and Weisbrod (1975) refer to the divergence of observed price and competitive price as "the measurement problem" and note that it is often severe.

An understanding of how real prices develop and how real markets differ from the model is important. We now consider this development and these differences in the context of three criteria from the basic model of exchange. Real prices are proper measures for social valuations if (1) market prices measure the willingness of those involved to pay for the marginal unit, (2) market prices are equal to marginal costs, and (3) marginal costs reflect true social costs. If any one criterion is not met, some adjustment of market prices is necessary.

5.1. Market Prices

We start this section with a description of market prices and their functions and then explore reasons why they may not indicate social values and what might be done to offset this deficiency.

5.1.1. What is Price? Price is the amount of other things people agree to exchange for a thing. If there is a monetary system, it is usually expressed in money. If there were no monetary system, exchanges would still take place, and there would still be prices, but they would be expressed in units of other goods and services.

Money is a medium of exchange, and people are not usually interested in it for its own sake but for the things they can buy with it. A sum of money is thus a surrogate for each of the other things it might purchase. A price of $1 does not mean a thing's value is equal to that of a $1 bill but rather to that of any other thing which could be purchased for one dollar.

5.1.2. How Do Market Prices Develop and Change? A market price develops in the interaction between buyers and sellers who wish to exchange some good or service. The buyer tries to obtain it as cheaply as possible, and the seller tries to obtain as much as possible for it. By bargaining, they arrive at a mutually acceptable price and an exchange takes place, or if they cannot agree, no exchange takes place and there is no market price.

When a number of people exchange a thing in a free market, there is a tendency for a single uniform price to develop. Everyone who is willing to pay this price can obtain what he wants, and everyone who is willing to sell at this price can sell what he desires. People who are not willing to pay or accept this amount are priced out of the market.

5.1.3. What Do Market Prices Indicate about Values? When an exchange takes place, the sellers must feel that the utility of the thing to them is less than the price, and buyers must feel it is higher than the price. Price is thus a compromise between the valuations of sellers and buyers. Because of diminishing marginal utility, the buyer may feel that once he has acquired this much of the good, additional amounts would have less utility to him. And the seller may feel that production of additional units will cost more than those he has just sold. As a result, the same buyer and seller may not be willing to exchange more units at the price they agreed on in the first transaction.

If demand is described by a typical downward-sloping curve, market price shows only the willingness to pay of the marginal buyer. All other buyers would be willing to pay more than market price, but because they can buy all they want at this price, they do not need to reveal their true willingness to pay. Market price underestimates the total value to the consumers who buy a good by the amount of the consumers' surplus.

Market prices are often used as indicators of the value of other units besides those exchanged or the value to other people than those involved in the exchanges. Neither of these extrapolations may be valid. The only sure value information conveyed by a market price is for the specific transaction in which it was involved. Even then it may only represent value to one party under peculiar circumstances. This is why the usual legal definition of fair market value specifies that the price must be agreed on by a willing buyer and a willing seller, neither of whom is under any unusual pressure to trade.

5.1.4. Market Prices as Indicators of Social Value. What market price indicates about value to society is best considered in two parts: (1) What does market price tell about the social value of the units actually being exchanged at this price, and (2) what does it tell about the social value of additional units that would be made available as a result of a decision?

Social Value of Things Currently Exchanged. The values of things people are exchanging must be at least as high as their market prices. Some people could mistakenly be paying more than a thing is worth, and others could have strategic or speculative reasons for paying more, but if all buyers are aggregated, market prices should be good indicators of minimum social values.

However, many buyers may be obtaining a consumer's surplus. The total consumers' surplus realized by all buyers depends on the elasticity of demand for the product. If the demand is relatively elastic, the consumers' surplus will be small, as shown by area *PAC* in Figure 2.8. In this case

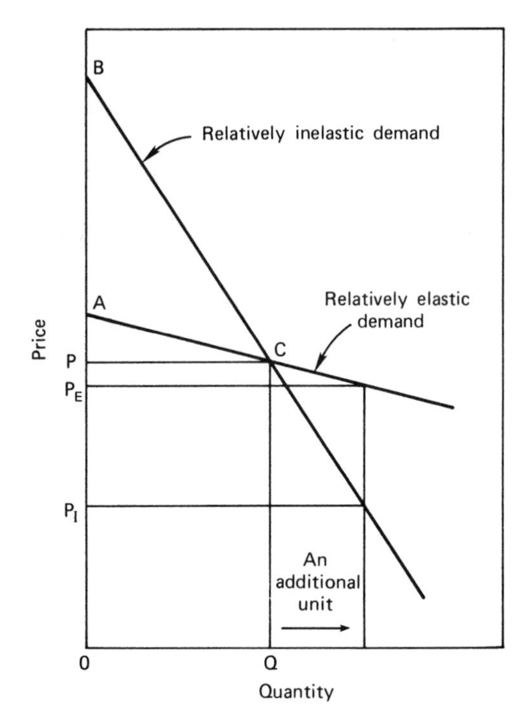

Figure 2.8. ***Effect of elasticity of demand on consumers' surplus and the price of an additional unit exchanged.***

market price will give a good estimate of social value when multiplied by quantity exchanged as in area *OPCQ*.

The less elastic demand is, the more people there are who would willingly pay more than the going price and the greater the consumers' surplus, as shown by area *PBC* in Figure 2.8. In this case market price will give a poor estimate of social value of the total quantity exchanged as shown by area *OPCQ* compared to the correct area *OBCQ*. Market prices must be supplemented with information about demand for and supply of the thing being appraised before they can be safely used as indicators of social value.

Social Value of Additional Units. If demand for a good is fairly portrayed by a typical downward-sloping demand curve, we would not expect people to buy more than the quantity now exchanged unless the price is lowered. The utility of an additional unit to the buyer will be less than the current market price. How much less depends on how elastic demand is. If it is relatively elastic, people would buy more at a slightly lower price (P_E)

and the utility of an additional unit is well indicated by current market price, as shown in Figure 2.8. However, if demand is relatively inelastic, people will buy more only if price is much lower (P_I), and current market price provides a poor estimate of the utility of an additional unit.

The situation on the sellers' side is similar. If supply is portrayed by a typical upward-sloping curve, we would not expect people to sell more unless the price is raised. Total cost to the seller of an additional unit would be greater than the current market price. How much greater depends on how elastic supply is. If it is relatively elastic, some people would sell more at a slightly higher price, and the value of an additional unit is only a little more than the current market price. However, if supply is relatively inelastic, people will sell more only if the price is raised substantially and the value of an additional unit is much greater than the current market price.

Where does this leave planners trying to analyze decisions that would add additional benefits to the amount people already enjoy? If the decision would add only a few more units, the current market price may be a reasonable indicator of value, especially if the demand is relatively elastic. If the decision would add a large amount to that already consumed, the value of the additional units is certain to be less than the current market price. How much less depends on the elasticity of demand. On the supply side, a large addition is almost certainly unobtainable at the current market price. If supply is inelastic, a much higher price will be required to bring forth a large addition.

In summary, market prices are always questionable as indicators of the social values of additional things. A benefit-cost analysis based on current market prices may be misleading if large quantities are involved. Furthermore, because of variations in the elasticities of demand and supply, it cannot safely be assumed that all prices diverge from real values to the same extent. Market prices must be supplemented with supply and demand information before they can be used as value indicators for additional units.

5.2. Market Failure

If society had the single goal of maximizing utility and recognized the amount of available resources as its only constraint on choices, a competitive market would theoretically lead to an optimal allocation of resources and production of goods and services. However, even then a market system might produce undesirable goods or unsatisfactory amounts of desirable goods, and market prices could give a distorted picture of social values. In the absence of such ideal conditions, a market system is even more likely to fail. Let us look at the main causes of market failure.

5.2.1. Through External Effects. Many economic activities produce effects that are not intended or perhaps even considered by the participants. Economists call them *externalities* and speak of external economies and diseconomies. They are also commonly called *indirect effects, spillovers,* or *side effects.*

In the process of manufacturing paper, for example, a plant may discharge waste products into a stream. As a result, downstream fish catches may be reduced, and people may be unable to swim safely. These downstream effects are part of the cost of making paper, but the company does not have to pay them and does not include them when determining the selling price of its product. The market price of paper is therefore likely to be lower than it would be if it took the full social cost of production into account. Because these external costs are ignored, the market price of paper is not a good indicator of social value. External effects can also exist on the demand side, and on both sides they can be detrimental or beneficial.

5.2.2. Through Different Recognition of the Future. Many market choices involve future goods and services. People's appraisals of their values are influenced by two main factors: uncertainty and time preference.

Uncertainty. Any estimate of a future outcome must be based on assumptions and predictions and will always be uncertain. In a decision about preserving open space, for example, one can assume that open space will have value for occupants of the area in the future. But will there still be people living here, and if so, how many will there be? Will they feel that open space is valuable, or will their values differ from ours? Because there is no reliable way of answering such questions, appraisals of future values always include a large element of uncertainty.

Time preference is at least partly a result of uncertainty. As we noted in Section 4.2, people generally prefer to have things now rather than in the future. They recognize this in valuations by determining a present worth for future benefits. Present worth is clearly a measure of value, but it may be distorted by different recognition of the future.

Anything very far in the future is discounted heavily by individuals and could even be considered to have no present worth. But society has a much longer time horizon and might feel that such things had present worth. The lifetimes of many groups are longer than those of individuals, who are likely to be unconcerned about future happenings no present member will live to see. Benefits to future members are more important to a group than to present members, and the group's valuation of their present worth is almost certain to exceed individual valuations. Although groups also exhibit time preference, they are not likely to discount future values as heavily as individual members would. A decision made in the market system may therefore not always be optimal for both society and the individual.

5.2.3. Through Lack of Appropriability. A market system can only function with things that can be appropriated from people who want them. Unless someone has exclusive control over a thing, he cannot force anyone else to pay for it. There is no opportunity then for people to express their relative valuations by exchanging the thing in a market. Suppose, for example, that because an adjacent hill overlooks the abbey, people cannot be excluded from observing animals in the zoo. Unless the duke can obtain control of the hill, he cannot appropriate "looking at the animals," and no market will develop for this benefit.

This sort of situation usually arises because the cost of appropriation is too high. It might involve excessive departures from tradition through fencing off land that has been used in common for centuries. Or there may be so many entry points that the cost of collecting payment from visitors would be higher than the potential revenue. The reasons may be traditional, legal, technical, or financial. The important point is that exclusive control cannot be established over inputs or outputs.

The goods in this example have one characteristic of the more general public goods situation. In addition to the nonexclusive characteristic, true public goods exhibit nonrivalry in consumption. That is, consumption by one person does not reduce the quantity available for others. Viewing a landscape and listening to radio programs are public goods that exhibit both characteristics of nonexclusion and nonrivalry.

5.2.4. Through Secondary Effects and the Multiplier. Because most choices and decisions affect more than one person, social values are aggregations of individual and group values. Large and complex decisions may also affect other people beyond those who directly benefit or bear costs.

Secondary benefits or costs are outcomes that occur as a consequence of direct outcomes. For example, the direct benefits of a decision to build an irrigation project may be increases in the production of sugar beets and the incomes of local farmers. But the additional supply of beets may make it possible for an entrepreneur to build a local sugar mill. The opportunity for unemployed people to find jobs in the new mill is a real secondary benefit of the irrigation project. Because all economic activity is interrelated, such linkages or chains of effect are common. The farther one attempts to trace them, the more questionable they become. The entrepreneur might have built the sugar mill and employed the people anyway, importing beets from some other source. In many cases, however, secondary effects are a real and important component of social value and should be measured and incorporated.

One particular kind of secondary effect is the multiplier effect, a financial phenomenon that occurs because people who receive money ordinarily spend it. The farmers in our example will have greater cash incomes from sale of the additional beets produced with the irrigation water. They will spend this on clothes, automobiles, farm equipment, and many other things. If they spend it locally, the haberdasher, automobile dealer, and other providers of goods and services will also experience an increase in income. They in turn will spend much of their new receipts for a variety of things they would not have purchased otherwise. The effect of the additional income to the farmers will thus be multiplied throughout the local economy.

5.3. Government Intervention

Many factors influence the responses of consumers and producers, the most influential probably being government intervention in the market. Such intervention influences or determines the situation in which households appraise their willingness to pay and firms their willingness to produce. The effects enter the basic model of exchange in three different but related ways. They may (1) change the slope of the demand and supply curves, (2) shift the position of one or both curves, or (3) limit or expand the quantities of outputs and inputs that can be exchanged.

If reasonable competition exists, market prices can often be used to estimate values. But government influences may depress or raise market prices away from a competitive level. Social costs, which indicate the real cost of using resources, will then diverge from private costs, and social benefits will be changed and diverge from private benefits. We now outline the direction of some of these effects.

Taxes and subsidies are basically transfers from one part of an economy to other parts. Taxes take purchasing power from private consumers, and the receipts are used to provide public services and to subsidize private consumers and producers. From society's point of view, taxes and subsidies are not social costs or social benefits but reallocations of social resources.

From an individual point of view, however, taxes are costs and subsidies are benefits. Depending on their incidence, they are therefore likely to affect individual willingness to pay and willingness to produce and through these may influence market demand and/or supply. Market price may still be determined by competition, but the marginal utility to the buyers and marginal cost to the sellers may be different than they would have been without the taxes and/or subsidies.

Quantity and quality controls are imposed by governments dissatisfied with the results produced by the market system. They may attempt to prevent prices from becoming too high or too low. Or they may try to assure a minimum quality of product or to ensure minimum standards of protection for people and the environment. In effect, governments are trying to get market prices to reflect what they feel the social values are. In their attempts to overcome market failure, however, they may prevent the competitive market system from functioning as it theoretically should. If prices are being deliberately manipulated for other social ends, they may be uncertain indicators of comparative values.

Socialization of some resources and production is tried by many countries as a means of achieving more equitable and efficient allocation and distribution than is provided by private enterprise. However, large government producers and consumers do not behave in the market like the small price takers assumed by the competitive market model. They may have other objectives than maximizing net revenues, may ignore many costs that are vital to private producers, and may affect prices directly by the size of their operations. Extensive government participation in the market for any product may divert price from the level indicated by private marginal costs and utilities. As in all government intervention, it is difficult to predict whether the resulting prices will be nearer to or farther from true social values.

5.4. Imperfect Competition

The validity for social valuation of the prices developed by the competitive market model depends heavily on all buyers and sellers being too small to affect the market and individually competing on the basis of price. In the real world both assumptions are often violated. Many markets consist of only a few buyers or sellers who either do not compete or do so only through advertising, product differentiation, or political influence. Some buyers and sellers are so large that they can act as price leaders, and other participants have no choice but to follow them. Prices are often set administratively and varied only through discounts, rebates, and similar techniques. Distress sales and desperation purchases are not uncommon. Even in free private markets, prices often do not bear a close relationship to marginal cost or marginal utility.

5.5. Summary

Market prices are not useless or even poor sources of value information. Where they exist, they are usually the best indicators available. But that is exactly what they are—indicators. They do not measure values; they indicate how people feel about the relative values of things they exchange with other people.

An individual buyer or seller indicates his comparative valuations by willingness to pay or willingness to be paid for various things. In a market situation this is translated into prices, which are commonly expressed in money. An organized market can provide useful social value information because it aggregates many individual valuations into one value indicator. However, analysts must question the degree to which available market prices reflect and can be used to measure social values. Although a lack of market prices complicates valuation, the mere existence of prices does not guarantee valid social values.

6. USE OF THE MARKET MODEL FOR VALUATION

The basic model of exchange consists of demand and supply schedules. Their combination provides a model of how exchange would take place if buyers and sellers were willing competitors who could participate without hindrance, and if quantities and prices were free to move in response to supply and demand. Under such ideal conditions, market exchanges would lead to equilibrium and an efficient allocation of resources. But even if these conditions are not met, demand and supply schedules can be used for valuation, because they model behavior. Demand schedules express buyers' willingness to pay as a function of utility, and supply schedules express suppliers' willingness to produce as a function of opportunity cost.

The demand and supply models can therefore help improve information for decisions by providing a useful foundation for analytical techniques to estimate comparative values. The challenge for the analyst is to find ways of applying them. Part II of this book sets out a range of possible ways of meeting this challenge.

CHAPTER 3

Individual Valuations

People almost always live and share their lives with others. The groups they form have permanence, structures, and patterns of action that extend beyond the lives of their members. But all groups are composites of individuals. This chapter analyzes the process by which individuals appraise values and the factors that apparently affect that process. Chapter 4 extends this to social valuation by groups.

1. THE BASIC ROLE OF INDIVIDUALS IN DETERMINING VALUES

Values of things and actions derive ultimately from their effects on individual lives. We have recognized this by deriving a definition of value from the concept of potential utility or capacity to make a favorable difference to someone's life. But what might be a favorable difference to one person could well be an unfavorable difference to someone else. The value of a thing to any person is always the utility he could derive from it minus the disutility to him of obtaining it.

Most comparative valuations are made by individuals for their own purposes. All of us appraise the values of many things every day, often without being overtly aware we are doing so. We also make frequent appraisals of the values of things to other people. Sometimes these other people do not agree with our appraisals. This usually happens because we have not appraised the values of the things as the others see them. Instead, we have appraised them on the basis of what they would be worth to us or what we feel they should be worth to other people. If such mistakes are to be minimized, we need to understand the process through which individuals arrive at their own value appraisals.

2. DETERMINANTS OF INDIVIDUAL UTILITY

People only consider a thing to have value if its possession or use would make a favorable difference to their lives. The thing must have a capacity to meet some need or fulfill some desire. But things that do cater to wants and needs vary in their capacity to meet them and consequently in their utility.

People's wants also vary; thus the utility of a thing depends on who is evaluating it. It might have utility for one person but not for another.

Utility is not an inherent and stable property of things but varies with people's wants and needs. As a first step toward a general value equation we have

$$U_i = f(PU_i, W_j) \tag{3.1}$$

where U_i is the utility that can be derived from a thing i, PU_i is the potential utility or capacity of the thing to satisfy, and W_j is the wants and needs of a person j. This says that utility is basically a function of both the potential of a thing and the wants and needs of the person receiving it.

2.1. Wants and Needs

The utility of many things derives from their capacity to meet basic physiological needs. To survive, grow, and carry on activities people need food, water, protection against the elements, rest, and other essentials. They have little interest in other things until these physiological requirements are satisfied.

Human needs are not limitless, however, A certain number of food calories a day is all that is needed for energy. The marginal utility of food diminishes as a person has more to eat. The same is true of other physiological needs, and once minimum requirements are met, people assign higher comparative utilities to things other than to those catering to physiological needs. People also have psychological, social, and spiritual needs which play important roles in determining utility after the physiological needs have been met. Beyond these needs a range of wants and desires determine utility for things that are not essential.

People's needs and wants vary with the circumstances in which they find themselves. The same thing can have great utility for people under one set of circumstances and little or none under another. We must therefore add the individual's circumstances as a second step toward a general value equation

$$U_i = f(PU_i, W_j, IC_j) \tag{3.2}$$

where IC_j is the individual circumstances of person j at the time he would obtain i.

Utility is always a marginal concept; as a person's needs or wants become satisfied, marginal utility diminishes. No matter how high a thing's potential utility may be, if the wants of an individual are completely satisfied, that thing will have no utility for him. The marginal utility of an additional unit depends on how much of the thing a person already has.

2.2. Environmental Situation

Equation 3.2 recognizes that the utility of a thing to a person depends on his individual circumstances. But this variable is too comprehensive to be useful for analysis, and we must divide "circumstances" into its major parts. One of these is the physical environment in which the individual lives or would use the thing being evaluated. So we can extend the value equation as

$$U_i = f(PU_i, W_j, IC_j, E_j) \tag{3.3}$$

where E_j is the environmental situation of individual j and IC_j is now all of his other circumstances.

Some physiological needs are strongly influenced by the environment. Protection from cold is more essential in an arctic environment, so warm clothing has higher utility. The problem of meeting a need can also vary with the environment. People have difficulty obtaining adequate nourishment in very dry climates, so food plants that require little moisture have high utility in dry regions. The activities in which people engage are largely controlled by their environment. Even activities that go on everywhere are modified by environment. Travel is a universal activity, but the comparative utility of different vehicles depends on where they are used.

What people find satisfying, are comfortable with, and find interesting often depend on how they feel about things rather than on needs for them. Many of these feelings have their origin in personal experience with a particular kind of environment. People who have grown up in rural areas may derive greater utility from open fields and forests than city people who have not experienced them. People's life-styles and the things they learn to do depend on the environment in which they live. This is especially important in recreation. The proportion of rural American men who hunt is much higher than that of urban men because the latter seldom have a chance to learn.

To summarize, an individual's appraisal of the utility of things is influenced by the environment in which he has spent his life and that in which he now lives or expects to be living at the time he uses the things. Human beings are adaptable, learn new skills and develop new attitudes, and are able to modify their environment to some extent, so an individual's value judgments are not absolutely conditioned by environment. But it is not possible to appraise the utility of something to an individual without considering his environment.

2.3. Social Situation

Our attitude toward life is always conditioned to some extent by the opinions and attitudes of other people. From the time we are babies, other people are exerting influences and pressures on us. We have all been taught many things by parents, teachers, religious leaders, and other associates. Much of what we "know" is what someone has told us. Only as we grow older do we have a chance to test this knowledge against personal experience.

Another part of an individual's circumstances, therefore, is the social situation in which he finds himself, and we can write

$$U_i = f(PU_i, W_j, IC_j, E_j, S_j) \tag{3.4}$$

where S_j is the social situation of individual j and IC_j is now all of his other circumstances except for his environment.

The quality of a person's life always depends to some extent on his relationships with other people in the groups of which he is a part. A secure position in the group is important, and individuals hesitate to take actions that meet with the disapproval of their peers. There is a tendency for individual attitudes to conform to those of the group. Status is important, and this places a premium on doing things other members approve of or of "keeping up with the Jones." Individual utility may depend heavily on the groups to which a person belongs. Unless social determinants are taken into account, it may often be difficult to understand an individual's attitude toward life and consequently to appraise correctly the utility of things to him.

An important part of individual attitudes toward things stems from feelings about right and wrong. Individual assessments of utility are at least colored by people's moral outlook and that is to a large extent determined by the social groups in which they live.

Social morality is the attitude of a group about what is right and wrong. This is concerned with relationships between individuals as members of organized groups and with relationships between groups. At issue is the effect of individual actions on other members of the group and on group existence itself. Every organized group prescribes norms of behavior for its members and usually provides sanctions for enforcing them. Concepts of social morality differ between groups, but any given group's concepts of social morality strongly influence the utility of many things and actions to its members.

Individual ethics are the beliefs of individuals about what is right or wrong. Some ethical attitudes are obviously just a reflection of the moral norms of society, but some originate within the individual. There are people who would not cheat even though they knew that cheating was tolerated by their group. Both social morality and personal ethics may strongly influence individual attitudes toward the utility of things and actions. Personal ethics are conditioned by the social groups in which a person grew up and lives and may vary greatly between societies and even between groups within a society. Unless these influences are understood and taken into account, it may be difficult to predict how individuals will evaluate the utility of a potential benefit.

3. FROM INDIVIDUAL UTILITY TO INDIVIDUAL VALUE

We have now seen that the utility of a thing to an individual is the result of a complex set of needs and desires that have their origin in or are conditioned by the individual's physiological makeup, his past and present environment, and his past and present social relationships. His perceptions may also be colored by personal characteristics, such as whether he is optimistic or pessimistic and skeptical or credulous. Taking all these into account (probably implicitly and not explicitly) and allowing for expected future events, an individual arrives at a perception of the utility he could derive from a thing.

If he goes through this same process with another thing, he obtains a similar appraisal of the utility of the second thing. Providing the two appraisals are complete and consistent, he has an indication of the comparative utilities of the two things. If he could have either one without cost, the comparative utilities would indicate comparative values. Other things being equal, if he had to choose between them, his rational course would be to choose the one with the highest utility.

But it is only in rare or trivial cases that individuals can obtain things free. Usually they must take some action or give up something else to obtain a thing they desire. An individual's rational criterion, therefore, is not the total utility of the thing he desires but rather the net utility that would result from the exchange. If he has to make a large sacrifice or suffer a large disutility to get the thing, it may have no value for him, even though its utility is very high. He may actually be worse off after he gets it than he would be without it.

Value is only incompletely indicated by utility. The disutility that will necessarily occur in the course of obtaining a thing and deriving utility from it must be recognized. The basic definition of value is

$$V_i = U_i - DU_i \qquad (3.5)$$

where V_i is the value of thing i and DU_i is the disutility involved in obtaining it.

Value is thus a function of both utility and disutility. From Equation 3.4 we know that utility is a function of various factors. Because the disutility of getting or using something consists of other utilities foregone, disutility is also a function of these factors. As the next step toward a general value equation, we can therefore replace U_i in Equation 3.5 with the factors in Equation 3.4 and

$$V_i = f(PU_i, W_j, IC_j, E_j, S_j, DU_i) \tag{3.6}$$

All these factors affect individual perceptions of comparative values. Most people probably take many of them into account only implicitly. But expressions like "not worth having" and "not worth the effort" indicate that people perceive values in terms of their total situations.

4. DETERMINANTS OF INDIVIDUAL VALUE

To benefit from potential utility, people must get possession or use of things and in many cases go through some process of deriving the utility from them. These actions represent costs to the users. Anything that adds to the utility of a thing increases its value, but, equally important, anything that contributes to the cost of realizing the utility decreases its value.

A given thing could have different values to the same individual in different situations, not because the utility would be different but because the cost of deriving the utility would be different. For example, suppose water of equal quality occurs in two acquifers at depths of 50 and 1000 feet. To a farmer the water will have the same utility whether it comes from one acquifer or the other. But to realize this utility he must drill a well and pump the water to the surface. The shallow acquifer is clearly more valuable than the deeper one. Value to individuals is almost always partly determined by more factors than utility alone. The following sections discuss the most important of these.

4.1. Disutility as a Determinant

Choices and decisions have to be made because people cannot have everything they need and desire. To make a gain in one place they have to make a sacrifice somewhere else. The real costs of realizing the utility of a thing are always opportunity costs. The cost to an individual of getting a thing is the utility he might have realized from the alternative opportunities he must forego.

The value equation could therefore be expressed as: The value of a thing i is equal to the utilities to be derived from having i minus the utilities that could have been derived from the other things that must be given up in order to obtain i. Disutilities are lost utilities. The disutility "work" is the foregone utility "leisure," and the disutility "air pollution" is the foregone utility "pure air."

Disutilities are determined by the same factors we discussed in Section 2—wants and needs and the environmental and social situations. The cost of obtaining something may represent a large disutility to one person but only a small one to another. Even though these people agreed on the utility of the benefit to be received, that benefit would have less value to the first person than to the second. For example, two people might agree that the view from a mountaintop, that could be reached by a 1-mile climb, would have great utility to them. But if one is young and healthy and the other is older and suffering from a heart condition, the differences in disutility of climbing the mountain might cause the view to have a high value for the young person but none at all for the older one.

4.2. Economic Determinants

A person's well-being is affected not only by what he presently has but also by what he is able to produce or obtain. What he can produce depends on what resources he has available. These resources include (1) land or natural resources, (2) technology, (3) personal knowledge, skills, and ability, (4) time, and (5) capital. The opportunity costs of most decisions will be closely related to the amounts of these resources available to him, as the following example illustrates.

Suppose a landowner is considering building a dam and developing a pond for fishing. He is an ardent fisherman and feels such a pond would have high utility. Whether the value of a pond will justify going ahead with the project will depend largely on the opportunity costs involved. (1) Is he a vegetable farmer with a 20-acre farm in an area where he cannot obtain more land or a rancher with several thousand acres of rangeland? (2 and 3) Does he have the technological knowledge to build a dam himself or would he have to hire an engineer? (4) Does he have slack time that he could devote to dam building, or is he already working seven days a week? (5) Does he have a bulldozer and other heavy equipment, or would he have to hire them? The disutilities (opportunity costs) might be very high or very low, depending on his resources.

But resources can often be substituted for each other. The vegetable farmer might use more capital for irrigation equipment, improve his disease-control technology, or work longer hours to produce the same amount of crops on less land. The actual opportunity costs depend on how a person combines the resources available to him.

An individual's assessment of value thus depends on his available resources. The values of things to him can be expected to change if resource availability changes. And people with different resource endowments will almost inevitably assign different values to the same things. We must therefore add an economic resource variable to the value equation

$$V_i = f(PU_i, W_j, IC_j, E_j, S_j, R_j, DU_i) \tag{3.7}$$

where R_j stands for the economic resources available to individual j and IC_j is the remaining unidentified circumstances.

4.3. Institutional Determinants

The valuation process is affected by certain social institutions that formalize arrangements through which members of a group deal with each other. We consider such institutions further in Chapter 4 and 5, but we briefly discuss them here as they affect individual evaluations.

4.3.1. Exchange at a Given Time through the Market System. Elaborate market institutions make it possible for people to exchange a variety of goods and services with other people. One alternative usually open to them is to exchange a thing for something else. So in making choices, individuals consider not only the direct value of a thing to themselves, but also the value of what they might acquire by exchanging it with someone else. Because farmers raise more wheat than they can consume themselves, the marginal utility of most of it to them as consumers is zero. But because they can exchange it for other things that do have utility to them, the value of the wheat as a guide to production decisions derives from the values of the other things wheat can buy in exchange.

4.3.2. Exchange over Time through the Credit System. Many benefits are not received at once but occur as flows over future periods. The same is often true of disutilities, which may arise gradually as streams of future opportunity costs. Valuation of a house, for example, is based on the utility of a stream of future benefits (shelter, privacy, amenities) minus the disutility of a stream of future costs (maintenance, repairs, property taxes).

Banking and credit institutions have developed to facilitate exchanges in situations like this. A seller can receive at once the full present worth of the future utilities to be provided by his house, and a buyer can spread the disutilities of paying for a house over many years. This may affect valuations by both seller and buyer. A seller may be willing to accept less for a house in one lump sum than he would if he had to receive payment in annual installments as the utilities materialize. And a buyer may be willing to pay more for a house if he can meet the opportunity costs in annual installments as he receives the utilities. The value of a thing to an individual will therefore be determined to some extent by how much access he has to a credit system and how much it costs to use it. In general, a readily available line of credit and low interest rates are likely to raise a person's valuations.

We can now take the final step in developing a general value equation by adding the institutional framework as a variable, and have

$$V_i = f(PU_i, W_j, E_j, S_j, R_j, IF_j, DU_i) \tag{3.8}$$

where IF_j is the institutional framework within which individual j makes his valuations. In our model the addition of IF_j completely describes the individual circumstances of j, and IC_j can be deleted.

4.4. A General Value Function

We have expressed individual value as a function of seven major variables, each of which is subject to various determinants. This provides a basis for analyzing valuation situations, since the variables must all be accounted for in one way or another. Part II of this book surveys the approaches that have been used to formulate value functions for unpriced goods and services.

5. AN INDIVIDUAL'S PROCESS OF COMPARATIVE VALUATION

The process used by individuals in making decisions is a comparative valuation of the alternatives, and this allows for some simplification of the value model.

Choices Are Marginal, not Global. People encounter problems piecemeal and do not have to make global choices or decisions about their whole lives at one time. Life is a succession of incremental choices and decisions, which individually are seldom of critical importance. Uncertainty about the future is so great that most decisions have to be made in the limited context of what is known about the immediate situation.

Some Factors Are Fixed. Although the number of factors affecting decisions is very large, most have already played their role in establishing the circumstances within which a specific decision must be made. These factors are fixed at the decision time, and the individual need only focus on the other factors that might cause values to vary in his situation.

An individual's comparative valuations start with the person himself. Because of his inherent makeup and the conditioning he has received from environment and society, he possesses a personal set of values and an attitude toward life that basically determine the kinds of things that can make favorable differences to him. Other individuals start from their own personal bases and may differ in their valuations.

One Factor May Dominate Choice. People do not evaluate everything in a logical manner. Built-in value attitudes are probably taken for granted and not consciously questioned. In some cases a basic attitude may dominate other considerations and, in effect, determine comparative value. In other cases the opportunity costs may be so large as to dominate the decision. And there are cases in which the utility of a thing to an individual is so great that he forgets both his personal attitudes and the opportunity costs involved.

An individual appraising comparative value to himself in one situation has to consider only the factors relevant to his evaluation. If these factors can be identified and understood, it may be possible to predict with considerably accuracy what that individual's valuation will be.

6. INDIVIDUALS IN SOCIAL GROUPS

In this chapter we have shown that social groups affect individual valuations. The social nature of people also creates two kinds of valuation problems.

Many decisions affect not only the person making them but also other people. Parents, teachers, administrators, and politicians make frequent choices for other people that have little or no effect on their own lives. The values of things to these other individuals are determined by the factors described in this chapter. But in this case they are being assessed by someone other than the affected individual himself.

The problem becomes more complicated with something that has value to a whole group of people. The often-mentioned conflict between individual and social values suggests that sometimes the value to a group is different from the sum of the values to its individual members. This, in turn, suggests that social values may be determined by factors other than those we have discussed as affecting individual values, or that these same factors operate differently in determining social values. These and other aspects of social valuations are discussed next in Chapter 4.

CHAPTER 4

Social Valuations

At the end of Chapter 3 we noted that the groups to which people belong not only influence their individual valuations but also make valuations of their own. Since planning almost always involves more than one person, the information needed for decision making is usually the social value or, where relevant, the group value rather than the individual value. This chapter discusses the factors that influence social appraisals and how individual values combine to determine group or social value.

1. WHAT IS SOCIAL VALUE?

People spend most of their lives in close association with other people. Some associations are casual, as in the case of people who pass on the street and never see each other again, but many are more permanent and some endure over a lifetime.

People form groups with others who have something in common, and these range from fellow passengers on planes to citizens of the same country. The members of groups identify with other members, share many things, conform more or less to group norms, and have a feeling of "belonging" and security that separates them from the rest of the world.

Groups have a structure and existence that to some extent is independent of the lives of their members. There clearly are close relationships between individuals and the groups to which they belong. A group conditions the attitudes and actions of its members, and the members influence and to some extent form the attitudes and policies of the group. But a group is more than a collection of individuals; it continues to exist and to act as a group despite what may happen to any of its members.

A social group is an entity that bases its decisions on their effects on the group. Any thing or action that could make a favorable difference to the life of the group has value to it. This social value may or may not agree with individual members' values. A case of general agreement is the Salk polio vaccination program. The nature and level of benefits was different for individuals than for society, but the program had a positive value for both. A case of partial disagreement is a successful defensive war. This has positive value to the nation and many of its citizens but a negative value to those who are disabled or killed.

There are many different social groups, and most people probably belong to more than one. Each group exists for some reason and has its own objectives, aspirations, and concept of what is beneficial. Because of such differences, various groups cannot be expected to agree on the values of things. The American Association of Retired People and the Boy Scouts of America have different desiderata in mind when appraising values. An efficient, low-cost prescription drug service is considered of great value by the AARP but would probably not appear very valuable to the Scouts.

What, then, is social value? It cannot be the value to humanity as a whole, but must refer to a particular group that is well enough organized to function as a social entity, define desiderata, and make decisions regarding them. The value of something to this group is a social value, in contrast to its personal values to individual members.

2. DETERMINANTS OF SOCIAL UTILITY

Things that have a capacity to satisfy a group need vary in that capacity and consequently in their potential utility. Group wants and needs also vary, so that the same thing can have utility for one group and not for another. As a first step toward developing a general social value equation we have

$$U_{ig} = f(PU_{ig}, W_g) \tag{4.1}$$

where U_{ig} is the utility of i to group g, PU_{ig} is the potential utility of i to group g, and W_g is the wants and needs of group g. This says that social utility is a function of both the potential utility of a thing and the wants and needs of the group.

2.1. Wants and Needs

In much the same way that certain things are essential to the functioning of individual organisms, some things are essential to the functioning and survival of groups. The most obvious of these is the health and survival of a minimum number of members. Unless a critical membership is maintained, a group will not be able to function and will eventually disintegrate. Anything that will help maintain a viable membership has utility to a group.

Things like adequate food and shelter provide group utility as well as individual utility. Medical care has group utility not only because it reduces suffering and makes life better for individual members, but also because it keeps them in shape to carry on their functions in the group. Some members play more critical roles than others, and things essential to their health have greater utility to the group than those necessary for the health of ordinary members. Care is usually lavished on the health and survival of group leaders, and higher utility is attached to the nourishment and protection of children than to that of adults.

A social group may be more flexible than an individual in its "physiological" needs. A critical mass of members may be maintained through recruitment as well as through protection of present members. A high birthrate has great utility to a society with low life expectancies, as does a compulsory draft system to an army suffering combat losses.

Another essential need of all groups is cohesiveness. The members must hold together and act in a coordinated fashion. If each goes his own way, the group will disintegrate. There must be some structure that ties individuals together and enables them to function as a group. Things that promote identification with the group and close working relationships among its members have utility to the group.

The wants and needs of groups vary with the circumstances in which the groups find themselves. Maintaining membership is always necessary but may not ordinarily be a problem. However, sometimes the loss of members may be serious, and anything that helps maintain membership has great utility. The circumstances of the group are a second variable in the social value function

$$U_{ig} = f(PU_{ig}, W_g, GC_g) \tag{4.2}$$

where GC_g is the circumstances of group g at the time it obtains i.

2.2. Environmental Determinants

The utility of many things depends on the environment in which a group exists. In large part this stems from environmental effects on what has utility for individual members. Many specific-purpose groups, such as ski clubs, exist because their members want to use a particular environment. In some cases the environment also affects the group as a whole. Protection forests have utility for mountain communities in areas subject to avalanches and torrents. We must therefore add the effects of environment to the social value function

$$U_{ig} = f(PU_{ig}, W_g, GC_g, E_g) \tag{4.3}$$

where E_g is the environment surrounding group g and GC_g is now the other circumstances of the group.

Social groups also adapt to their environments. They develop cultures that to some extent are a response to the environment. The aboriginal inhabitants of Australia lived successfully for thousands of years with only the simplest technology in an environment that was often hostile. The culture they developed enabled them to exist in balance with their ecosystem and, perhaps most important, provided means of limiting their numbers to what the environment could sustain.

Large social groups, such as a religious sect or state, occupy many environments simultaneously, and some things have utility to them in certain parts of their territories but not in others. This complicates the appraisal of comparative values to the group as a whole.

2.3. External World Determinants

Every social group exists in a larger world inhabited by other people, and to some extent this external world determines what does or can have utility to the group. Because of the speed of modern travel and communication, groups are constantly subject to outside influences.

Any group will find part of the outside world acting as an antagonist or competitor and limiting the things from which the group can derive utility. For example, oil reserves in one country may have no utility to the people of another if the first country refuses to give the second access to the oil through direct exploitation or the market. And military force may not have utility to the second nation as a means of obtaining the oil if the external world will not permit its use. In an extremely antagonistic world, things or actions that contribute to a group's defense have high utility, and military budgets are justified on the grounds of the utility of defensive works and weapons.

Part of the outside world is also likely to be cooperative, and things may have utility a group could not take advantage of alone. Existing mineral deposits may be of little utility to a developing country, but if other countries are willing to provide technical knowledge and capital, the same deposits may assume great utility.

In general, groups function as representatives of their members in dealing with the outside world. Because of this, the outside world primarily affects group utility, and affects individual utility only secondarily and through the group. This is in contrast to many physiological and environmental determinants, which work primarily through their effects on individual utilities to affect group utility.

We can now add the external world as one more variable in the social value equation

$$U_{ig} = f(PU_{ig}, W_g, GC_g, E_g, EW_g) \tag{4.4}$$

where EW_g is the external world situation of group g and GC_g is now the remaining circumstances of the group.

2.4. Individual Member Determinants

The people who make up social groups do not lose their individual characters as group members. They may conform to the group, subordinate themselves to it, or even be dominated and controlled by it, but what has utility for the individual members will to some extent determine what has utility for the group. We must therefore add utility to individual members as a variable in the social value equation

$$U_{ig} = f(PU_{ig}, W_g, GC_g, E_g, EW_g, U_{ij}) \tag{4.5}$$

where U_{ij} is the utility of i to individual members j.

Utility to individuals is determined by many of the same factors that determine utility to a group. The important point is that social utility is composed of both the utility to the group as such and the individual utilities to its members. Except for U_{ij}, the variables identified in Equation 4.5 are intended to show their role in determining utility to the group and not to its individual members.

2.5. Group Characteristics

Not only are there many social groups, but they are of many different kinds. The utility of things to a group is determined not only by the factors discussed in the preceding sections but also by the characteristics of the group itself. We will identify the most important of these characteristics, but first let us add them to the social value equation

$$U_{ig} = f(PU_{ig}, W_g, GC_g, E_g, EW_g, K_g, U_{ij}) \tag{4.6}$$

where K_g is the characteristics of group g. The following discussion recognizes six kinds of characteristics that seem to be most important in determining group utility. The order in which they are presented does not necessarily indicate their relative significance.

Lifetime. Groups do not usually consider their lifetimes to be limited by the life expectancies of individual members. Their time horizons are often longer, and they tend to be concerned about their future members. The effect on valuation depends on the specific lifetime of the group, as the following diagram indicates:

Example	Ship's passengers		Family
Spectrum	Temporary	⟵⟶	Permanent
Effect on Valuation	Short-run choices and interests		Long-run choices and interests

The arrow indicates that individual groups may fall anywhere between the extremes shown.

Territorial Hierarchy. The territory occupied by group members and affected by member actions varies considerably among groups. (This is a geographic phenomenon, in contrast to the numbers phenomenon to be discussed next.) Many are actually subgroups of larger groups that share most other characteristics. The effects on valuation depend on the territorial scope of the group, as in the following example:

Example	Church congregation	Religious sect
Spectrum	Local ←——→	International
Effect on Valuation	Operates within rules and adapts these to local conditions	Makes rules; entire concern is with group values

Number of Members. Groups vary considerably in the size of their membership. This is often related to the territorial phenomenon just discussed, but some large social groups occupy small geographic areas, and some relatively small groups spread over large areas. The effects on valuation vary with the size of the groups.

Example	Family	Nation
Spectrum	Small ←——→	Large
Effect on Valuation	Certain actions prescribed; greater recognition of group attitudes	Few actions prescribed

Reason for Formation. Some groups form for specific purposes, and others form just as a result of living together. Most of the latter are old groups that formed in the past and have survived to the present. Most of their members have been born into an existing group; they are not there as the result of a conscious choice. By contrast, people voluntarily join groups of the first class because of the specific purposes for which they were formed. The effects on valuation are illustrated by the following example:

Example	Labor union	Ethnic group
Spectrum	Specific purpose ←→	General purposes
Effect on Valuation	Group goals close to individual goals	Group strongly influences individual members

Age of Group. Groups that form for specific purposes can be separated into old existing groups and newly formed ones. Regardless of their purposes, the significant characteristic of the old groups is that they became established and survived. Many of the attitudes developed during their histories have become institutionalized. The longer one remains a member, the more likely he is to conform to these group attitudes, and the "old guard" are often considered conservative because they do not want to see the group change. By contrast, a recently formed group's attitudes are new and in many cases still being formed. They are dominated by the attitudes of the individuals who formed the group. Eventually there will be disagreements among members, and some will have to conform or resign. If the group survives, it will gradually become like the old existing ones.

Example	Environmental group	Professional group
Spectrum	New ←——→	Old
Effect on Valuation	Group likely to recognize individual attitudes	Members likely to conform to group

Reason Members Joined. The membership of some groups is entirely voluntary. People join to accomplish certain objectives, and if the group does not help achieve them they withdraw, and the group may disband. Utility to such groups is almost completely determined by what has utility to their members. At the opposite extreme are groups whose objectives are specific but whose membership is compulsory. Because people are coerced into being members, their individual preferences have little influence on group decisions.

Example	Social club	Military organization
Spectrum	Voluntary ←——→	Compulsory
Effect on Valuation	Individual goals dominant	Group goals dominant

As indicated by the arrows in the diagrams, most groups fall somewhere between the extremes of most characteristics. Many have been in existence for a long time, have diversified memberships, and have general or varied objectives. They are concerned for the welfare of their members, but they recognize that individual aspirations often conflict and what would benefit some might well harm others. Utility to the group must be a compromise among the utilities and disutilities to individual members. How these are aggregated in group valuations is discussed in Section 4.

2.6. Group Attitudes

Social groups—like individuals—have attitudes toward life in general and toward specific aspects of it that have a fundamental influence on their valuations. These attitudes are often related to the reasons for a group's existence, particularly in those groups that formed for specific purposes. The attitudes of the broader ethnic, religious, and political groups have evolved as responses to various influences. We briefly consider some of these in the following sections, but first we should add attitudes as another variable in the social value equation

$$U_{ig} = f(PU_{ig}, W_g, GC_g, E_g, EW_g, K_g, A_g, U_{ij}) \tag{4.7}$$

where A_g is the attitudes of group g.

Historical Determinants. The present attitudes of any group result to a large extent from what it has done and what has happened to it in the past. Attitudes evolve and accumulate with the passage of time. They tend to adapt and adjust to changing situations but sometimes persist long after their usefulness has ended.

This historical process is nicely illustrated by the changes over time in the social attitudes of national groups toward the environment. The United States Department of the Interior (1967) has identified four stages in American attitudes: (1) exploitation in the earliest years, (2) preservation as a reaction to exploitation, (3) government regulation, and finally (4) a more balanced ecological approach.

In the exploitation phase the natural environment is a barrier to expansion. The objective of individual and social action is to push frontiers outward, to populate the land, and to use natural resources primarily to assist these short-term objectives.

The exploitation stage was coming to an end when Marsh's book *Man and Nature* was published in 1864. His major contribution was showing that just as man changes the environment when he exploits it, so the environment exerts an inevitable influence on man. Partly because of Marsh, the American attitude gradually changed from one that all forests should be cleared for farming to one of preserving the remaining forests for future needs and environmental protection.

As the preservationists "matured," regulated management prevailed. The objective was to provide benefits for society now and in the future through constraints, such as timber cutting limits, soil conservation practices, and the reservation of natural areas. This phase was partly a reaction against the use of private resources for exclusive individual interests.

The fourth phase was heralded by increasing environmental problems. The public began to see that man was only one component of the natural environment. The current ecological phase is based on an attitude that understanding environmental interactions is of first importance. The objective is still satisfaction of people's wants, but a definite constraint is recognized in the need to maintain a balance in nature.

The Effect of Wealth. Part of the historical change in American attitudes toward the environment was a result of increasing affluence. Well-fed and well-clothed people have the time and inclination to demand high standards of air and water quality and low levels of noise and congestion. The effects on valuation are indicated by the following diagram:

Example	Developed nation	Developing nation
Spectrum	Rich ⟵⟶	Poor
Effect on Valuation	More concern for luxuries or qualities than for quantities	More concern for essentials and quantities than for qualities

Moral Determinants. It is clear that some group attitudes have a moral basis rather than a utilitarian one. Most groups believe that some actions are good and others bad, that some are socially acceptable and others are not. The resulting attitudes may lead to behavior that appears irrational to others, but which is the only kind that is morally acceptable to the group and of value to it.

External World Determinants. Every social group exists in a larger world inhabited by other groups, and most of its members also belong to some of them. This poses problems for a group in terms of maintaining its identity and objectives and holding the interest and allegiance of its members. A group's attitude toward many things depends on how important it feels they are to its relations with the rest of the world. Status, pride, security, a sense of inferiority or superiority, and many other factors affect a group's attitudes.

The external world also conditions many group attitudes. Smaller groups often have to be "licensed" by some broader authority before they can form, and certain attitudes may be discouraged or even outlawed by this authority. Many built-in group attitudes, which are now accepted parts of their culture, were probably originally responses to external world influences.

3. FROM SOCIAL UTILITY TO SOCIAL VALUE

Anything has value to a social group that can make a favorable difference to the group's life. The components of a favorable difference are the same as those described in Chapter 3 for individuals. The attitudes of a group are very important in determining value. If dancing is considered sinful, for example, it cannot be a valuable form of recreation, but if the attitude toward dancing is favorable, valuation becomes a question of utility. If dancing would provide needed relaxation for busy people, contribute to health through exercise, and keep young people out of mischief, it would have utility to the group.

But value also depends on what the group has to give up in exchange for the benefits of dancing. If it is harvest time and everyone is needed to salvage a crop that is the only source of food, the opportunity cost of dancing would be very high. Dancing may have high utility, but engaging in it now would make an unfavorable difference to the group's life. Harvesting the crop has greater current utility than does dancing, so at this time harvesting has value and dancing does not.

Valuation is essentially a problem in comparison. Value derives from utility but depends also on the disutilities involved in realizing it. We can express this in the same form as we did for individuals

$$V_{ig} = U_{ig} - DU_{ig} \tag{4.8}$$

where V_{ig} is the value of i to group g and DU_{ig} is the disutility to group g of obtaining i.

As the next step in developing a general social value equation we can substitute the definition of group utility from Equation 4.7 in Equation 4.8. Because this is now in terms of value, we must also change the factor "utility to individual members" in Equation 4.7 to value to individual members. This gives

$$V_{ig} = f(PU_{ig}, W_g, GC_g, E_g, EW_g, K_g, A_g, V_{ij}, DU_{ig}) \tag{4.9}$$

where V_{ij} is the value of i to the individual members of the group.

Finally, it is necessary for us to recognize the importance to valuation of economic resources, as we did with individuals. What a group can produce depends heavily on the economic resources available to it. Because of diminishing marginal productivity, the more resources a group has, the less important are the marginal units of those resources. The marginal opportunity costs (disutilities) of diverting resources from other production vary with the amount of resources available and are an important determinant of the disutility of obtaining additional goods or services. Economic resources is the final component of the group circumstances we recognized in Equation 4.2. We can now remove the variable for group circumstances and add a variable for economic resources to give

$$V_{ig} = f(PU_{ig}, W_g, R_g, E_g, EW_g, K_g, A_g, V_{ij}, DU_{ig}) \tag{4.10}$$

where R_g is the economic resources available to group g. This is the final form of a general equation for social value.

4. VALUE TO A SOCIAL GROUP

The determination of social value by comparing group utilities and disutilities is similar to the determination of individual value by comparing individual utilities and disutilities, but the comparisons are somewhat more difficult. In the rest of this chapter we analyze the difficulties, set them in perspective, and suggest how they can often be simplified by focusing on the nature of the decision.

4.1. Comparisons Involving Only Utility

The simplest valuation situations are those in which there are no costs. The criterion is simply whether the thing or action has utility for the group. If it does, it has value to the group, no matter who benefits from it. Anything that makes at least one person better off without making anyone else worse off is valuable to a group.

Real examples of this simple situation are not common. One might be a case in which a philanthropist has offered to donate a rare old book to a university. If accepting the gift would involve no costs, the value of the book depends on whether it would have utility to the university. If just one professor or student would be better off as a result of this book being in the library, the welfare of the university as a whole will be increased by its acceptance, for no one would be worse off as a consequence. By contrast, suppose the philanthropist has offered to donate a portrait of himself that has no artistic value and in which no member of the university community is interested. The university could reject the offer as being of no value because it lacks utility, even though it would not cost anything to accept it.

The problem becomes more complex if it involves not just an either/or decision but a choice between alternatives. Suppose the philanthropist has offered to buy for the university either a rare old book or a valuable painting, but not both. If there are no costs to accepting the gift, either would appear to have value, and the university should logically accept one. But which should it choose? The comparison of utilities is complicated by the fact that both gifts would not benefit the same people. How can the university compare the utility of a painting to art students and faculty, scholars, and visitors to the art gallery with the utility of a book to literature students and faculty, scholars, and others who use the library?

What must be compared is the marginal differences these gifts could make, and that depends to a large extent on the university's present situation. For example, a choice between book and painting would not be difficult if (1) the university had no art gallery or courses in art but did have an excellent library and program in literature or (2) another philanthropist had just given the university a collection of the works of a famous artist, the only gap in which is the painting the first philanthropist has offered to buy.

Valuations that involve no costs are rare, but decisions are common in which the costs are fixed. Suppose, to stay with the same example, a donor has given a university a sum of money to be spent on either books or paintings. The university does not have to decide whether the utility of this purchase will exceed the opportunity cost, for the donor has already made that decision. All the university has to decide is whether books or paintings would have greater utility. Valuations are often simplified by proceeding in these two stages: (1) deciding that expenditure of a certain budget for a general purpose would have social value and (2) allocating this fixed budget between alternative ways of accomplishing the general purpose. The fixed-budget comparisons in the second stage can be approached as if there were no costs involved.

4.2. Comparisons Involving Only Opportunity Costs

Many social valuations involve choices in which the utilities of the alternatives are identical. A choice between alternative ways of producing some given benefit is an example. In such cases, the comparative values are determined solely by the opportunity costs of the alternatives.

Decisions that only involve opportunity costs can often be formulated in a straightforward manner. Suppose, for example, a local community has decided to build a new school. There is general agreement that it will have value, and the taxpayers have approved a bonding program to borrow the necessary money. But where should it be built? If the municipality already owns two suitable tracts of land and it would be very expensive to acquire more land elsewhere, the decision must be based on the comparative opportunity costs of locating the school on each of the two tracts. It will have value regardless of where it is located, but the value will be greatest where the opportunity cost is least.

The comparative opportunity costs may be obvious if, for example, one possibility is a former landfill disposal area and the other contains the last remaining example of a unique natural ecosystem. Even less extreme situations may be rather easy to compare, as in the case where one site is a highly developed and heavily used park and the other an undeveloped park that is less popular with the public.

Some comparisons may be more difficult. For example, both alternatives may be parks that have identical facilities and heavy use, but one may be located in a newer, affluent residential area and the other in an older, poorer neighborhood. The comparison reduces to identical physical sacrifices by a group of wealthy people and a group of poor people. Which would cause the greatest disutility to the whole community? Attitudes about distribution of wealth would probably carry more weight in such a choice than would any attempt to calculate comparative opportunity costs.

Comparative assessments of social utilities and opportunity costs may not be easy but they are possible. When real-life decisions are analyzed, many prove susceptible to rather simple comparative appraisals. Throughout the book we attempt to identify situations where relatively simple appraisals are adequate to guide decisions.

4.3. Comparisons of Social Values

As shown in Equation 4.8, many valuations require an appraisal of both utility and disutility. Value is the net difference an object's possession or use could make to the life of a group. Comparison of the social values of two objects requires a determination of this net difference for each. This involves the aggregation of various utilities and disutilities.

4.3.1. Aggregating Individual Values. This is basically the same process that individuals go through in making comparative valuations, except that social value is a composite of values of individual members and any additional value to the group as a whole. The component values may be positive or negative. The key problem of social valuation lies in aggregating the component values into a social value.

There appear to be two ways of approaching this aggregation. One is to appraise the positive or negative utility to each individual affected by the decision, calculate a net value for each individual, and then add these to give a total value to the group as a whole. The other is to appraise and total the utilities to all who will receive them, including the group as a whole; appraise and total the opportunity costs to all who will bear them, including the group; and then determine the net difference between the totals of the utilities and opportunity costs.

The first approach requires separate appraisals of the net differences that the object will make to each individual life and to life of the group. These net differences must then be combined into a total net difference to the lives of all involved.

The second approach does not require an evaluation of the net effects on individual lives. It is based on overall assessments of effects on the group. It requires a list of all who will receive utility with an estimate of how much each will receive and a list of all who will bear opportunity costs with an estimate of how much each will bear. The total utilities are then compared with the total opportunity costs. It is not always necessary that all utilities and opportunity costs be expressed in the same units. A subjective assessment of total utility and total opportunity costs may be all that is needed for a decision.

The first approach to aggregating values appears most feasible when there are no externalities; that is, when the same individuals receive the utilities and bear the costs. It may then be possible to obtain their individual appraisals of value. If they are similar people, it may be reasonable to add their individual valuations without differential weightings and to take only a small sample and extrapolate it to the total. The smaller the number of individuals involved, the more feasible this approach would seem to be.

The second approach to aggregating utilities and disutilities seems to have advantages where the benefits and costs are so unevenly distributed that there would be extreme differences in individual valuations, including many negative ones. Large numbers of individuals may also be handled more easily by this approach.

4.3.2. Weighting Individual Effects. Because of the complex nature of social valuations, questions are likely to arise about how much weight to give to effects on individual people. Three characteristics of social valuation affect this differential weighting.

Group Effects Dominate Individual Effects. Practically all social valuations include appraisals of effects on both the group and its individual members. If there is a conflict between these, the effects on the group are likely to be considered more important than those on the individual members. Since individual utility is a strong determinant of group utility, there is not much likelihood that something that has a positive value for a group might have negative individual values for all its members. But there are many situations in which the costs of obtaining group utility are borne by only some of the members. The judgment then may be that the benefits to the group outweigh the costs to these few individuals. Where something important to the maintenance or survival of the group is involved, the effects on individual members are likely to receive little weight. An example is a defensive war in which individual lives are sacrificed to protect the group.

All Affected Persons Are Included. Social valuations tend to include all those affected by choices or decisions. When an individual appraises the value of an action, he may ignore some benefits or costs that affect other people but do not affect him. A group does not ordinarily ignore any effects on its members. It often gives different weights to different people on the basis of their relative importance to the group, but it usually considers all individuals who are affected.

Groups may ignore effects on people outside their own membership or on other groups, but most are very much aware of their relationships with the outside world. They are likely to include some consideration of the effects on their external political situation. When the feedback of external effects is considered, a choice that apparently benefits outside people more than the group's own members may make the greatest favorable difference in the long run.

Groups Are More Concerned about the Future. Because of their relatively long lifetimes, groups give more weight to future utilities and opportunity costs than individuals do. Individuals worry about the future too, but their limited range of life expectancy places a fairly short time horizon on their valuations. People have some concern for those who will survive them, particularly for relatives and close friends, but few give much weight to future people they will never see. The uncertainties of life are such that most people also discount rather heavily things that may happen to them personally in the future. In general, the farther something is in the future, the less weight individuals give it in their personal valuations, and beyond some point the tendency is to give it no weight at all.

Social groups are more concerned about the future, and many of their actions are aimed at their continued viability and activity (and perhaps growth). Future utilities and future opportunity costs may be very important to them, and their scope of consideration must extend to future membership as well as present.

Nevertheless, few social groups evaluate future utilities or opportunity costs as equivalent to present ones. They try to forecast what their future situations will be when the utilities or costs accrue to them. Depending on how situations change, a given thing could be more or less important to them in the future than it is now. Progress in all human areas has been so great during the past century that practically all social groups believe things will be better in the future than they now are, and this exerts a strong bias toward the present in social valuations.

4.4. Useful Estimates of Social Value

We have seen that the values of things to a social group are determined by many potentially conflicting factors, as shown in the value function of Equation 4.10. At any particular time many of these factors are built-in to the group's attitudes or the situation that gives things utility. For most valuations there is no need to know why the group's attitude or situation is what it is. The valuation question is simply how much favorable difference the thing could make to the life of the group under these given conditions.

In any situation certain variables may dominate the other factors and alone determine the value. It may not be necessary even to analyze the other components. In a natural disaster such as a flood, for example, the social utility of rescuing the victims is so obvious that no one questions the cost or asks which individuals should be rescued. When there are numerous benefits or opportunity costs, it may not be necessary to appraise all with the same accuracy. If the most significant ones can be measured with confidence, rough estimates or even mere listings of the others may suffice to indicate the magnitudes of the total utilities or costs. It is never possible to establish a true or exact social value, but it is possible to obtain estimates that are sufficiently reliable to serve as guides for policy and planning decisions.

5. SOCIAL VALUATION PROCESSES

Our discussion of social values has focused on their nature, composition, and determination and has said little about how groups actually make valuations. Because of their complexity, social values can only be estimated; they cannot be measured precisely. However, the method a group uses in appraising values is bound to have an effect on the results it gets. The rest of this section presents three processes groups use in estimating comparative social values. Each provides a means of doing the two things necessary in social valuations: estimating the utilities and opportunity costs involved in the decision and aggregating the effects on individual members and the group. Because none of them alone does this perfectly, they are often used in combinations.

5.1. The Market Process

Whenever people willingly exchange things, they are expressing comparative valuations. Each party indicates that he thinks what he is receiving has more utility to him than what he is giving for it. How much more utility it may have is not evident from the exchange, but the fact he has willingly given up something for it indicates he feels its possession has value to him. Willingness to pay in the form of market price is an indicator of the minimum utility of an item to its buyer.

In organized markets many buyers and sellers interact with each other, as described in Chapter 2, and market prices indicate their pooled judgment about the values of the things exchanged. These prices multiplied by the number of units exchanged aggregate individual valuations into indicators of social value. However, as we pointed out in Chapter 2, market price has its weaknesses. Even in perfectly competitive markets, price only shows the willingness to pay of the marginal consumers. And price may only show the marginal utility to the rich if the poor are unable to express their valuations by competing in the market.

All objects of social valuation are not traded in organized markets because only those that can be appropriated are susceptible to exchange. Many large objects of social valuation—such as schools, dams, and highways—are seldom, if ever, bought and sold in markets.

5.2. The Political Process

All social groups of any size have elite subgroups or leaders who make decisions and take actions for them. These leaders obtain and retain their powers through the political process and in turn are controlled, or at least influenced, by the rest of the group through the same process. This process is quite complex, but two general explanations that have been advanced for it help see how it functions to estimate individual utilities and opportunity costs and to aggregate these into social values.

One explanation is that people transmit their individual appraisals upward to their elected representatives, who aggregate them and convert the aggregates into policies and laws. These in turn are passed on to government agencies for implementation. This explanation assumes that people are aware of needed decisions and willing to participate in the political process to contribute their assessments. It also assumes that the representatives receive complete and accurate information, and that the formation of a consensus is appropriate to the problems dealt with, or is at least acceptable to the people.

A second explanation is that the political process is pluralistic and that government decisions are made at many points in the organizational structure. This explanation assumes that only a few people are directly involved in, concerned about, or affected by any one decision and that they play an active role in that decision while the rest of the public remains passive. The active groups bring pressure to bear on government agencies or through their elected representatives. The utilities and opportunity costs to the affected people are appraised by them, partly aggregated by their pressure groups, and further aggregated by politicians and government officials.

Both explanations conform to observation, and the political process in most cases is probably a combination of the two. Social valuations that are unsuited to the market process or poorly handled by it are often made through this political process.

5.3. The Judicial Process

All social groups develop ways of resolving or settling disputes between individual members and between members and the group. In larger social groups these are formalized in a judicial system. Because many disputes involve or have their origins in conflicting valuations, part of the judicial process is a search for comparative social values.

The judicial process consists of three steps. The first is an attempt to determine what past decisions or judgments by the social group have a bearing on the case at hand. A court seeks such information in the constitution, statutory laws the legislative bodies have enacted, and regulations and other administrative laws developed by administrative agencies. In the English system the court also scans the common law, which enbodies the findings of centuries of judicial decisions about group values. In this first step, a court is trying to find out how the group has expressed its attitude toward similar value problems in the past.

The second step is an advocacy proceeding in which representatives of various alternatives present evidence to support their views. An important part of the advocacy proceeding is an attempt to offset or discredit evidence presented by opposing advocates. At the end of this step a court presumably has the best information obtainable about the comparative values involved.

The final step is a judgment or finding about the comparative values. There is always a subjective element in this, and various devices such as juries, panels of judges, and hearing boards are used as means of avoiding individual biases. As a further safeguard, the judicial process provides for appeals to higher courts or authorities if the judgment of the first court is questioned.

The judicial system is not designed specifically to appraise social values, and courts avoid accepting this as a direct responsibility. But in the course of discharging their accepted duties they must make many social valuations. Because these include a thorough consideration of the utilities and opportunity costs involved and an attempt to consider all affected individuals, they play an important role in social decisions.

6. SOCIAL VALUES AND SOCIAL DECISIONS

We have tried in this chapter to identify the nature of social values, the process of value formation, and the role of values in social decisions. The nature and formation of social values are similar to those of individual values, but groups often recognize different variables and interpret similar variables in different ways.

Groups often recognize externalities when their individual members do not. They are concerned with some variables and objectives that are explicitly of a group nature, such as maintenance of group size and cohesiveness. Groups also differ from individuals in their perceptions of the same things. They tend to have longer time horizons than individuals and to weight benefits and costs to some members more heavily than those to others. In any given situation, therefore, a group's values may differ from the sum of its members' individual values.

All groups aggregate individual and group values in their assessments of social value. For an analyst attempting to estimate social value, this aggregation process is the most difficult part to duplicate. In this chapter we have identified three points that can be of help. (1) The characteristics of a group, as discussed in Section 2.5, strongly determine how it weights and aggregates individual values. (2) Social values can be compared in various ways, as described in Section 4, and those which require estimating and aggregating individual values are the most difficult and expensive. (3) Groups are constantly assessing values and making decisions, and by studying these an analyst can often discover useful patterns on which to base future estimates.

The nature of the decision is critical in determining the kind of comparative valuation that is useful or necessary. In the next two chapters we show how an analysis of decisions can assist in the valuation of unpriced benefits and costs.

CHAPTER 5

Valuation and Decision Making

Meaningful values are only determined in the context of a decision. People do not ordinarily prepare in advance lists of values to which they refer when they must make a decision. Instead, they appraise the values of things or actions in particular situations, often not until the time when a decision must be made. This is true even of things on which there is general and consistent agreement about values. For example, most people would agree that gold is more valuable than steel. But a knife manufacturer would choose steel as a raw material because for his decision it is the more valuable of the two.

Because values are appraised in the course of making decisions, they are affected by the decision process itself. How good values are as decision guides depends partly on how the decisions are made. This chapter discusses the most important relationships between decision making and the valuation process.

1. DECISION SITUATIONS

Decisions that require valuations can be divided into three broad types: either/or situations, compensation situations, and alternative choice situations. The kind of value information necessary for a decision depends on the type of situation in which it is being made. We discuss each type separately and illustrate them with the indifference map shown in Figure 5.1. This shows how a hypothetical decision maker might feel about the utility he could obtain from one thing X compared to the utility he could obtain from all other things he might consume Y. The indifference curves in Figure 5.1 show various combinations of X and Y that this decision maker feels would give him the same total utility. We have only shown two of the great number of curves that make up his total indifference map.

1.1. Either/Or Situations

In an either/or situation a decision maker has to choose between doing something or not doing it. As a guide to this choice, he needs to determine whether doing it would make a favorable difference to his life. If it would have value to him, he should decide to do it; if not, he should choose not to act. All he needs to know is whether it would have value; the amount is not important because any additional value will make him better off.

Figure 5.1 shows that this may not be as simple as it sounds. To obtain the additional utility offered by the choice, he must also suffer some disutilities. Suppose, for example, he does not now have any of the good X and is at point A on his indifference map where he has Y_a of other things. The decision he faces would provide him with X_b of the new thing at an opportunity cost of reducing his consumption of other goods and services from Y_a to Y_b. He would move from point A to point B on the indifference map. The indifference curve shows that the total utility he would receive after the choice would be the same as it is now, and he would be no better off. Although the amount of X he would receive would have utility, this would be completely offset by the disutility of giving up some Y so that X_b would have no value to him. If he could obtain X_b at a sacrifice of less then $Y_a - Y_b$, it would have value, and he should choose to get it. If it would require a sacrifice of more than $Y_a - Y_b$, getting it would make him worse off, and he should not choose it. An either/or decision requires a comparison of the total value after the choice with that of before.

1.2. Compensation Situations

The problem in compensation situations is to make an injured person as well off as he was before he suffered a loss. We seek a compensation value that will exactly offset the loss he has suffered. For example, suppose the person in Figure 5.1 has lost some of the X that he had. His original situation was at point C where he had X_c of this and Y_c of all other things. The combination gave him a total amount of utility pictured by indifference curve U_{20}. After the loss he has only X_b of X and is at point D. He still has Y_c of all other things, but his total utility has been reduced to that shown by the lower indifference curve U_{10}. The decision problem is how to compensate him for the loss of value $U_{20} - U_{10}$.

If it is not possible to compensate him in kind by giving him enough X to bring his holdings back to X_c, it is necessary to find a compensation value that will bring his total utility back up to U_{20}. In Figure 5.1 we see that this could be accomplished by giving him enough other things to bring his total holding up to Y_b, which will put him on indifference curve U_{20} at point B. A combination of Y_b and X_b has the same total utility for him as his original combination of Y_c and X_c. The required compensation value is therefore $Y_b - Y_c$.

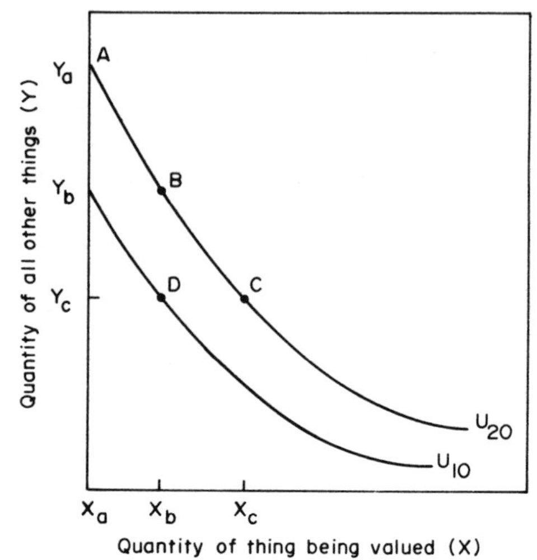

Figure 5.1. ***Indifference map showing total utility received from various combinations of one thing X and all other things Y.***

Figure 5.1 shows that the amount of compensating utility required depends on how a person feels about various combinations of the thing he has lost and all other goods and services. Compensation situations require the identification of other things whose value to the damaged person will offset the value he has lost. This compensation value is often, but not necessarily, expressed in money.

1.3. Alternative Choice Situations

In alternative choice situations a decision maker must choose one of various available alternatives. We illustrate this using two alternatives, but the same analysis applies if there are more. The decision must be made in two steps. First, one must determine whether the alternatives would have value to the affected person in an either/or situation like that discussed in Section 1.1. If he is now at point *A*, any alternative that would not move him to a higher indifference curve can be eliminated. In some cases this may be the only step needed. If one alternative would not have value, it is rational to choose the other one. The amount of value is unimportant because people would clearly be better off to get some additional value rather than none.

If both alternatives would have value, a second step is necessary: their comparative values must be determined. If the person involved does not have any of either alternative thing, his situation would be like that shown for thing *X* at point *A* in Figure 5.1. His indifference maps would probably not be the same for both things, but in both cases he would be starting with a supply of other goods and services and none of the thing in question. In each case he will have to bear some opportunity cost to obtain the thing. The preferred choice is that one that will give him the greatest total amount of utility. (In graphic terms, this choice would raise him to the highest indifference curve.)

If the person already has some of both goods, the choice will add a marginal amount to his stock of the one he chooses. We can picture his situation on the indifference map of Figure 5.2, which shows the total utility received from various combinations of alternative goods X and Z. The effect on total utility of a marginal increment in one good will depend on the combination of these goods the person already has. For simplicity, let us assume that the choice is between a marginal increment of five units in either X or Z. If he already has 15 units each of both goods and is obtaining a total utility of U_{10}, as shown at point A, an increase of five units in either good would increase his total utility to U_{20}, as shown by points A_2 and A_3, which are both on the same indifference curve. In this case the values of both alternatives are identical.

However, if he has 40 units of Z and only five units of X and is obtaining a total utility of U_{10}, as shown at point B, an increase of five units of X

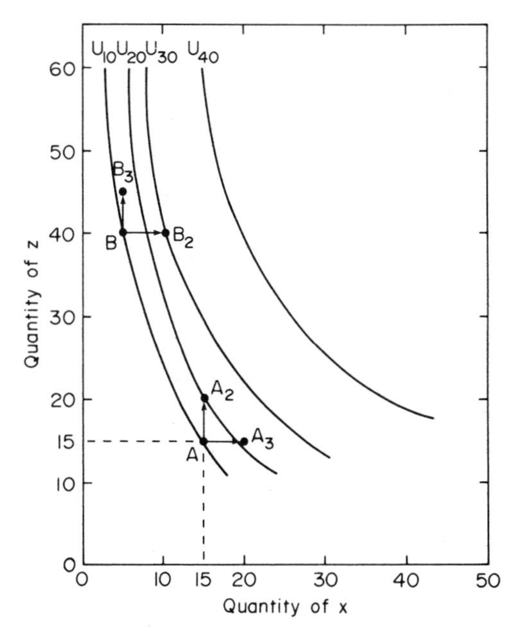

Figure 5.2. Indifference map showing total utility received from various combinations of two different things.

would raise his total utility to U_{30}, as shown by point B_2, but an increase of five units of Z would only raise it slightly, as shown by B_3. Diminishing marginal utility has progressed much further with good Z because of the large amount already possessed. In this case a marginal amount of X would have a much higher value than one of Z, and X should be chosen.

1.4. Implications for Decision Making

We can see from this section that the nature of the decision has a major influence on the kind of valuation needed as a guide. An either/or decision needs only to determine whether the thing or action would have value. An alternative-choice decision needs only to determine which of the possible alternatives would have the greater value. In neither case is it necessary to know value with any exactitude. Many compensation decisions are similar. If the only concern is to make an injured person at least as well off as he was before, it is only necessary to know that the compensation value is greater than the loss. It is only when an injured party must be compensated exactly for his loss that a precise value determination is necessary.

2. WHEN IS A MONETARY VALUE NECESSARY?

The preceding discussion indicates that values have to be measured if decision makers are to say they are greater than other values, equivalent to values lost, or even just greater than zero. Because of the prevalence of market exchanges and prices, it is common to measure values in monetary terms. This section shows that this is not always necessary for rational decisions.

Figure 5.3 classifies decisions to show what kinds of values are needed for particular situations. The starting point is the importance of monetary costs to the decision. In some cases they are relatively unimportant as, for example, in deciding on the route for a Sunday afternoon drive. Time and distance are likely to be more critical than the cost of gasoline. Once a decision has been made to go somewhere, the aesthetic benefits to be obtained from various routes will be weighed against their length and the time required to traverse them. Monetary values will not be needed in decisions of type *D*1.

When monetary costs are important, they may be fixed or variable. If his budget is fixed, a decision maker can only manipulate outputs, and his criterion must be to maximize benefits. If only one kind of benefit, such as recreation days, can be produced, the rational choice is the one that will provide the greatest number of days. A monetary measure of the benefits is not needed in decisions of type *D*2; they can be based on comparisons of the quantities produced by the alternatives.

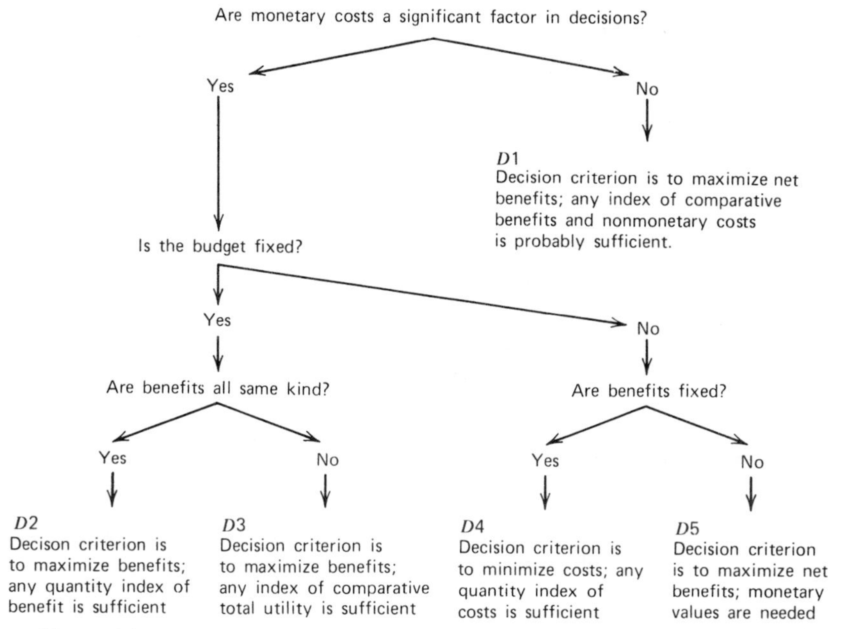

Figure 5.3. A classification of decisions to show when monetary values are needed.

If the budget is fixed but alternative outputs are of different kinds—such as overnight camping and daytime picnicking—the benefits must be compared by some index of total utility. Chapters 10 and 11 present methods for obtaining such indexes. Decisions of type *D*3 do not require monetary measures.

If the budget or monetary costs are not fixed, the kind of valuation hinges on whether the benefits are fixed or not. If the benefits to be produced are specified, the decision maker can only manipulate costs, and the relevant criterion is to minimize them. Monetary costs can be compared directly, and other costs may be compared in quantitative terms, such as hours of travel time. No measure of benefits—either monetary or nonmonetary—is needed for decisions of type *D*4.

The analysis of alternative management strategies for national fish hatcheries by Brown and Hussen (1974) provides examples of both benefit maximization (*D*2) and cost minimization (*D*4) decisions. Rearing and feeding strategies were first examined with an objective of maximizing the pounds of fish released. Costs in each of several management activities were fixed, and different combinations of activities were compared in terms of fish weight produced (decision type *D*2). The problem was then restructured as a cost-minimization decision. An implicit assumption was made that benefits of sport fishing depend on the weight of fish caught, and management strategies were compared on the basis of cost for a given weight of catch. If the benefit level (weight of catch) stays the same while overall costs are lowered, net benefits or value must increase. Using these two kinds of decisions permitted an analysis of hatchery problems without a specific value for the benefits of fishing.

The only clear case in which a monetary value is necessary is when both benefits and costs can vary and the decision criterion must be to maximize net benefits (type *D*5). Because different kinds of benefits and costs cannot be added or compared directly, it is necessary to measure all in a common unit. The most useful one is a monetary unit, and the methods presented in Chapters 12 to 16 provide various ways of estimating values in these terms.

3. ADMINISTRATIVE HIERARCHY OF DECISION MAKING

Any large group must delegate the making of social decisions to certain members. These people formulate social policies and administer the programs that implement them. They become organized in hierarchies, in which the extent of individual authority and responsibility varies with the level in the organizational structure. The pattern is similar for governments and private groups. The general nature of this decision hierarchy is illustrated in Figure 5.4. We now expand on the kinds of decisions made at different levels and their implications for valuation.

3.1. Decisions at Different Administrative Levels

Different levels in the hierarchy tend to be concerned with different kinds of decisions. The hierarchic structure presented in Figure 5.4 shows only four levels of decision making. More than four levels can be distinguished in many hierarchies, but because those shown illustrate the major differences, we limit ourselves to them in the following discussion.

3.1.1. At the Executive Level. At the highest level we find policy-making bodies, such as legislatures or boards of directors, and administrators, such as presidents and chief executive officers. The relationships among them vary from organization to organization, but it is clear that top administrative officers often play a major role in policy formulation. We therefore treat this as a single level rather than try to break it down.

At this level, two kinds of major decisions are made: (1) how large the organization should be and (2) how resources should be allocated among departments, programs, or products. The standard technique of benefit-cost

	Level in the Hierarchy	Type of Decision
High		
	Government (Executive or legislative level)	How is the social budget to be allocated between major sectors, such as the environment, education, transportation, etc.?
	Department (Secretarial or vice presidential level)	How is the departmental budget to be allocated to divisions of the department or to major programs?
	Operational district (Managerial level)	How are fixed budgets to be used to achieve given goals?
	Totally delegated job (Single employee level)	Choices between alternatives, all of which are acceptable.
Low		

Figure 5.4. An illustrative hierarchy of decisions.

analysis has proven least useful at this level. Part of the difficulty lies in determining the total benefits and opportunity costs of transferring resources from one sector to another. The long time periods involved in such major decisions increase the difficulty.

Neither benefits nor costs are likely to be fixed at this top level, and most decisions are of the nature of *D*5 in Figure 5.3. They also involve multiple benefits and costs that often cannot be measured in common physical units. Monetary measures of value are therefore desirable.

3.1.2. At the Departmental Level. At this second level, immediate decisions concern the allocation of departmental resources among competing but similar projects. Long-term decisions concern the size of the departmental budget because this can be varied over the years. It is important to recognize that policy decisions are not all made at the top and merely carried out by the lower levels. The budget-formation process, for example, progressively aggregates the budgets of the various levels to arrive at a total budget. Each level makes valuations in the context for which it is responsible.

The nature of decisions at this level is different than at the higher level, and it is often unnecessary to value both benefits and costs in monetary terms. An example is presented by Buchanan (1970) from the 1957 budget of the Bureau of Land Management. Approximately 70,000 acres of rangeland were treated for weed control at a cost of some $712,000. The decision variables were area, level of weed removal per acre, and budget. Three possible criteria could be identified by holding two of the variables constant:

(**a**) Fixed budget and area—maximize quantity of weeds removed per acre,

(**b**) Fixed budget and level of weed removal—maximize number of acres treated,

(**c**) Fixed level of weed removal and area—minimize cost of treatment.

In all these cases the objective to be optimized could be specified quantitatively, but a value for weed control did not have to be determined.

At this level, benefits can often be measured in terms of a performance standard, such as area sprayed. Although this does not in any way measure the utility derived from spraying, it does make rational decisions possible.

3.1.3. At the Managerial Level. At this level, a manager or operator—such as a field forester or park ranger—has a budget to spend and a forward budget to estimate. Once a budget has been allocated to his district, the decision criterion is likely to be cost effectiveness. The aim is to maximize the benefits from a fixed budget (decision types *D*2 or *D*3) or to minimize the cost of achieving a given goal (type *D*4). In neither case is it necessary to compare benefits with costs directly, and monetary values are not essential.

3.1.4. At the Totally Delegated Level. At this lowest level in the administrative hierarchy, decisions are made by foremen and crew bosses. They are assigned specific jobs to do as a result of someone higher having weighed benefits and costs. Their only choices are between alternative ways of completing a task, and even these alternatives may be carefully prescribed. Comparative valuations at this level can be very simple in nature.

3.2. Implications for Valuation

A Risk of Suboptimization. Programs that appear desirable at a departmental or managerial level sometimes prove undesirable at a broader level. For example, an agency charged with flood protection may consider constructing a large dam and reservoir to be an efficient means of achieving its ends. However, consideration of the project at an interagency level may call attention to the role of floods in maintaining marshes for wildlife and enriching river bottom fields through silt deposit. When these opportunity costs are included in the social valuation, a program that appears optimal at the agency level may be clearly suboptimal at a departmental or governmental level.

Decisions near the top of an administrative hierarchy must try to consider all benefits and costs to all affected people. At lower levels some benefits and costs are ignored, not because they should be but because part of the decision has already been made at a higher level. At the lowest levels, where budgets are fixed and objectives clearly specified, rational decision making may merely do things efficiently without any question of their desirability.

The Need For Valuation. Valuation is most necessary at higher administrative levels. The need to value all benefits and costs decreases progressively at lower levels. However, because of the danger of suboptimization, complex and difficult valuations are probably best referred to higher administrative levels, where subjective judgments are more broadly informed.

Criteria are most easily defined at lower administrative levels and have most immediate potential there for valuation. But the criteria used at each level must be rational in terms of the broader social values recognized at higher levels if they are not to produce merely individual or local valuations.

The potential use for efficiency criteria and their implications for valuation always depend on the particular decision involved. We saw in Chapter 2 that efficient resource allocation can theoretically be achieved by expanding use to the point where marginal cost is equal to marginal benefit. This can often be done at lower administrative levels by comparing market values and monetary costs. However, at higher levels unpriced values become important on both the cost and benefit sides, and market prices alone may provide unsatisfactory guides.

4. IMPLICATIONS OF SOME QUESTIONABLE DECISION CRITERIA

In Figure 5.3 we saw that decisions can be separated into five different classes according to the nature of the costs and benefits involved, and that a rational decision criterion can be identified for each of these. To facilitate administration, decision makers tend to convert relevant criteria into specific decision rules. These are working versions of the criteria, and decisions are often based on them in a routine manner. For example, a public forest may be managed with a fixed budget set by the legislature. The appropriate decision criterion apparently is to maximize benefits. The agency may interpret this to establish a decision rule that timber is always to be sold to the highest bidders in public auctions.

The criteria and decision rules accepted and used by decision makers largely determine their comparative valuations. The public forest manager above is saying, in effect, that the social value of merchantable timber is represented by the highest price that can be obtained in an open auction. However, preservationists and others have questioned whether such market-determined values accurately reflect social value, and we must consider the implications for valuation of such commonly used decision criteria.

4.1. Budget First, Allocate Afterward

In this approach a total budget is set on the basis of what can be afforded rather than on the benefits to be produced. The size of the budget may be visualized as an absolute maximum: "We cannot afford to spend more than X million dollars or we will bankrupt the nation." Or it may be based on gross comparisons: "Why are we spending only X million dollars on this program when we are spending Y million on liquor and tobacco?" In neither case is any real assessment made of the marginal benefits of the proposal and its marginal costs.

4.2. Requirements for Essential Needs

The requirements approach is based on some concept of "needs." This may be what people would like if they could have it or what someone thinks they should have. The expressed attitude is that these needs are so clear that they must be fulfilled regardless of cost. But as Eckstein (1967) points out, there would always be some cost that could not be justified by any amount of utility from such requirements. Because economic resources are scarce, obtaining any utility always involves opportunity costs in terms of other utilities foregone. If value represents a favorable difference to someone's life, it is clear that a requirements approach does not measure value, because it is not a net concept and considers only the utility gained and not that lost.

4.3. Standards as Policy Guidelines

The designation and enforcement of standards is a common technique in environmental policy. For example, upper limits are set on allowable concentrations of toxic wastes in streams and on the number of animals that can be grazed on public rangelands. Standards are relatively easy to enforce, but they are often applied indiscriminately to all similar rivers and lands because of the great cost of determining optimal qualities for individual units.

All standards contain implicit valuations. The discussions which precede their establishment may compare benefits and costs in some manner. But as Thomas (1972) says, "The setting of a standard is in effect an imputation of a certain finite level of utility or benefit accruing to life, to health, or to well-being." And the use of a standard implies that its total benefit is at least equal to its cost.

Standards also contain implications about benefits above and below the specified levels. Take, for example, the standard set by the Clean Air Act that 1977 model cars could not emit more than 15 grams per mile of carbon monoxide. The benefit from eliminating emissions above 15 grams was apparently considered greater than any cost involved. But elimination of emissions below 15 grams was apparently considered to have no value. Standards seem to be an all-or-nothing approach to valuation.

4.4. Technical Criteria

Decisions about environmental policies require information on changes in the environment and on the effects of these changes. This information is often presented as technical facts which provide clear and unambiguous indicators of environmental change and have found a valid niche in this role. For example, Lipscomb (1972) developed a damage-risk criterion as an indicator of danger from noise exposure. His index combines the noise threshold in decibels with measures of duration and frequency.

Technical indices are appropriate measures of technical efficiency but poor guides to decisions. Candler and Sargent (1962) have called this the "technologist's dilemma." If diminishing marginal utility has progressed far enough or if people are satiated with a good or service, a decision could raise a technical index while adding little to total utility. Because of this, a change that ranks low on a technical index could actually increase utility more than some alternative with a high index. Because many decisions will cause increases in some things and decreases in others, an increase in total value may be accompanied by decreases in some technical indexes.

Technical criteria may be useful in fixed-budget decisions, as we discuss later. However, it is generally better to try to estimate directly the utilities and disutilities involved in the acquisition and consumption of the things in question.

4.5. Ratios of Financial Performance

Financial ratios are used as decision criteria under a variety of names, such as interfirm comparisons, farm standards, and performance ratios. Information is collected from firms in an industry on such items as sales volume and revenue, profit, and quantities and costs of inputs. Various ratios are then calculated, such as profit per unit of total revenue and output per unit of labor or land input. Individual firms can then compare their own performance with the average of the industry and isolate key areas needing improvement.

These ratios can sometimes be accurate guides to profit-increasing decisions but may be distorted for two reasons. The first is that no one ratio may give a true picture of a firm's performance. For example, if only one product of a multiproduct firm is analyzed a proposed change may decrease total cost per unit of output and therefore appear desirable. If the entire firm operation is analyzed, however, it may be found that the proposed change would increase per unit costs of other products enough to more than offset the improved ratio obtained for the first product. All ratios must therefore be viewed together.

A second distortion can result from the practice of comparing individual firm performance with the average of, say, the top 10 firms. Any one firm's performance ratio may result largely from a particularly favorable cost or price situation or even a lucky production choice which happened to coincide with unforeseen high prices. If many firms are in the top 10 because of such accidental factors, their average performance ratio may be a poor basis for comparison. The effort required to assure that ratios are not distorted might better be devoted to a more complete measure of values.

4.6. Some Decision Rules

Decision making always involves costs. Although the quality of decisions can be improved, it is clear that the benefits obtained do not always justify the additional costs. Deciding how much to spend on decision making can be expensive in itself. Many decision makers therefore adopt rules or guidelines which they follow regularly for specific kinds of decisions. Such guidelines avoid the assessment of actual values for individual cases and thus reduce the costs of making decisions. But they imply assumptions about relative values and may not be an improvement over ad hoc procedures.

In an undated paper, Harry, Hendee, and Stein have suggested that for outdoor recreation decisions "priority in use be given to those users motivated by the more specific motives." Their logic is that more generally motivated recreationists have more alternative sites available and if excluded would presumably suffer less than those whose specific motives can be realized only in the particular area. But even if there are equal numbers of both kinds of users, this decision rule implies that the utility obtained by a specifically motivated user who is admitted is greater than the disutility suffered by a generally motivated user who is excluded. With no evidence of comparative values, this seems to be a shaky assumption.

In discussing land-management decisions, Downes (1972) proposed certain axioms to guide allocation to different uses. He suggested that the choice should go to (a) the use with the highest or most urgent priority, (b) the most flexible form of use in terms of ready conversion to other uses, (c) multiple uses as compared to single uses, and (d) uses that maintain stability and ensure the continued usefulness of the area. Although these all seem desirable as general guidelines, they imply comparative values that may not hold in specific cases. Open space has a high priority near centers of population, but it might be less valuable socially than sites for hospitals or schools would be. Flexibility would exclude the use of land for valuable purposes such as buildings and highways. A multiple-use guideline would eliminate wilderness areas, and a maintenance guideline would prevent mining and quarrying. Only by assessing the comparative social values of the alternative uses can it be determined whether such guidelines would lead to rational decisions in specific cases.

5. VALUE INFORMATION FOR COMPLEX DECISIONS

All decisions ultimately come down to comparisons of utilities and disutilities. A variety of systems have been developed for tabulating, presenting, or assessing the information needed for such comparisons. These systems are often presented as good substitutes for each other. But because of differences in geographic scope and purpose, decisions vary in their complexity and therefore in their information requirements. This in turn affects the amount of judgment required in selecting and presenting data. Because the various systems are not perfect substitutes, it is important to understand the implications of using them as decisions guides.

5.1. Causes of Complexity in Decisions

Purpose, Time Frame, and Geographic Scale. Decisions involving specific and limited purposes, very short time periods, and small geographic areas are usually simple and modest in their information requirements, as shown in Table 5.1. By contrast, those involving general purposes, long time periods, or broad geographic areas tend to be complex. The complexity of a decision—and its consequent data needs—depends on the combination of purpose, time frame, and scale with which it is concerned.

Table 5.1. Relationship between the Complexity of Decisions, Relevant Policy Questions, and Data Requirements

Kind of Decision	Kinds of Policy Questions that Must be Answered	Nature of Data Requirements	Examples of Display and Assessment Procedures
Least complex	What changes would occur in outputs, inputs, and the environment?	Technical data on changes in the environment, outputs, inputs, and costs. (Few money values, no comparative assessments.)	Environmental-impact statements.
More complex	As above, plus which alternative provides greatest output per unit cost or least cost per unit benefit?	As above, plus comparison of money costs with output levels.	Opportunity cost and cost-minimization techniques.
Most complex	As above, plus which alternative has greatest value?	As above, plus present money values for all costs and benefits. (All economic parameters can vary.)	Benefit-cost analysis.

Number of Fixed and Variable Parameters. All decisions can be expressed in terms of choices involving a few production parameters. These are the input, the output, and the production technique. In any decision some of these parameters, or parts of them, are fixed, and others are variable. Only a minimum amount of information is needed about the fixed parameters. They sometimes do not need to be valued at all (Table 5.1). The complexity of the decision depends almost entirely on how many of the parameters are variable.

At the most-complex level decisions concern optimum policies, plans, or whole groups of entire programs. None of the parameters are fixed—output, input, and technology can all be varied. Furthermore, the benefits and costs of the alternatives may differ in their timing and distribution among members of the society. Such complex decisions require large amounts of information, the expression of all utilities and disutilities in comparable value terms, and an aggregation of the values accruing to various individuals and to society as a whole.

The complexity of most decisions lies somewhere between the extremes of Table 5.1. The amount and kind of information needed to guide such decisions and the systems most suitable for presenting this information depend on how complex the decisions are.

The Policy Questions that Must be Answered. The information needed for a decision depends on the questions that must be answered to make that decision. The more numerous or involved these questions are, the more complex is the decision, and the greater is the amount of information needed to make it.

This is illustrated for three levels of complexity in Table 5.1. The least-complex decisions are those which can be based on information about the changes in inputs, outputs, or the environment that would result from the decision. An example is a choice between two locations for a power-generating plant. The critical question is: What changes in the environment would result from building the plant on each of the alternative sites? Such decisions may not require any value data at all.

The most-complex decisions are those which must be based on information about alternative values. An example is a decision on whether to build a major dam and which of several locations would be most suitable if it is built. The critical question is: What would be the social value of each proposed dam? Would the utilities produced by each dam exceed the disutilities involved in building it and, if so, by how much? Such decisions require aggregating a variety of value data in comparable form.

The kind of system that will be most appropriate for tabulating and presenting information depends on the questions that must be answered on the basis of the information. More-complex decisions require more judgment on the part of the analyst and the decision maker. The information presentation system must facilitate this judgment process.

5.2. Display Systems to Aid Decisions

Information for decisions is often set out in tabular form for convenience and ease of understanding. Two examples of such tabular statements are Hill's (1968) goals achievement matrix and Lichfield's (1970) planning balance sheet. These systems are often promoted as planning methods or decision-making procedures that could substitute for benefit-cost analysis. They are, in fact, none of these but are convenient ways of tabulating and displaying data.

The planning balance sheet is explicitly concerned with who benefits from and who pays for a given project. The major groups of gainers and losers are identified and classed as producers or consumers as in the example of Table 5.2. The cause of each benefit or cost is identified in column 2 and its monetary amount listed in columns 3 and 4. All relevant benefits and costs are listed, even though some cannot be valued. No

Table 5.2. The Planning Balance Sheet System for Presentation of Data for an Urban Redevelopment in Central London

Groups of Individuals (gainers or losers)	Utility or Disutility	Costs[a] (£ million)	Benefits[a] (£ million)
1	2	3	4
A. Producers			
1. Local government authorities	Construction costs	15	na
	Savings on services	na	*
2. Central government	Construction costs	7	na
3. Developers	Construction costs	50	na
4. Local business	Loss of trade, costs of disruption	38	na
5. Other business	Economies of scale and benefits from new shops	na	103
	Loss of trade	*	na
Totals		110	103
B. Consumers			
6. Existing residents			
Residents displaced	Cost of disruption	1	na
Residents not displaced	Loss of friends	*	na
7. Future residents	Benefits of new environment	na	6
8. Travellers	Time costs	11	na
	Loss of comfort	1	na
	Cost of accidents	*	na
9. City population at large	Loss of local character and gain in some amenities	*	*
10. Users of new facilities	Loss of local character and gain in some amenities	*	*
Totals		13	6

Source. After Alexander (1974).
[a] * = no data available, na = not applicable.

attempt is made to produce a single index of net value, such as a benefit-cost ratio or present net worth.

What do such display systems achieve, since a diligent analyst would always try to identify all benefits and costs and record their incidence? Their role is simply to provide a convenient way to present the data. The more difficult questions concern the implications of such systems for different data, policy questions, and decisions.

5.3. Assessment Systems

A variety of environmental assessment systems have been devised. They can report, describe, record, and interpret data for decisions. Some simply describe the characteristics of alternatives and leave the choices to decision makers. Others embody selection of alternatives and thus imply that valuations and decisions have already been made.

In a review of procedures for recording landscape quality, Steinitz (1970) identifies five types of display or assessment systems. Table 5.3 summarizes these. The five classes are quite general and can be applied to any environmental problem, not only to landscapes. They are distinguished mainly by the degree to which they actually make comparative assessments and valuations rather than merely describe resources. At one end of the scale are methods of inventory or description (type 1 in Table 5.3). These are concerned solely with listing measurements and records of environmental characteristics. The methods are entirely supply-oriented, with no attempt to introduce estimates of use or predictions of demand. Litton's (1968) work on the description of forest landscapes is an example of this type.

Table 5.3. A Range of Assessment Systems

Type	Description	Policy Information Available	Examples
1. Resource descriptions (resource inventories)	Quantitative description of physical, chemical, or other characteristics	No policy choices directly possible; entirely supply oriented	Litton (1968) on landscapes; environmental impact statements
2. Resource-centered analysis (resource-capability surveys)	As in 1, plus list of suitable uses	Range of choices that could be suitable, but only from an inventory viewpoint	Leopold and Marchand (1968) ranking of landscapes by uniqueness
3. Resource analysis with demand	As in 2, plus estimates of future use	Socioeconomic and demand estimates to compare and rate environments for future uses	McHarg (1968) overlay approach
4. Single product or use assessment systems	As in 3, plus predictions of consequences of different policies in specific environments	Physical characteristics of things like flood plains and predictions of consequences like flood damage	
5. Assessment and choice between many uses (decision methods proper)	As in 4, plus attempts to predict changes in use for many uses, with changes in environmental or population characteristics (the "if-then" study)	Answers to "What happens if *X* changes?" policy questions; happenings often defined in quantitative terms; choices between uses possible	Michigan recreation planning studies

Source. After Steinitz (1970).

At the other end of the scale are systems that combine inventory and estimates of future levels of consumption in selected uses. The analyst must attempt to predict and include outcomes for a number of interacting uses. Because the very act of selecting uses involves an evaluation of comparative benefits and costs, these planning methods incorporate valuations. The series of reports on outdoor recreation planning in Michigan (Michigan Department of Conservation, 1967) are often cited as examples of such planning techniques.

We have shown three classes between these extremes in Table 5.3, but in practice the five classes grade into one another. There are many examples within each class. Leopold and Marchand's (1968) system for tabulating and assessing data to rank landscapes is described in Chapter 9. One of the McHarg (1968) systems in class 3 is described in the next section. The different systems can aid different decisions, and conversely, different decisions require different data and different ways of assessment.

5.4. Implications of the Systems

Although the intent of the assessment and display systems is to present reliable information on which decision makers can base judgments about comparative values, the systems themselves often have built-in implications for valuation. The McHarg overlay approach is a good example of the way in which these systems can make important and often implicit judgments about valuation.

In one application the overlay approach was used to identify the "least social cost corridor" for the Richmond Parkway on Staten Island (McHarg, 1968). The approach combined physical characteristics such as slope, geology and drainage with another set of characteristics concerning danger to life and property on sites susceptible to floods and hurricanes. Each characteristic was mapped on a transparent overlay and divided into three categories represented by three degrees of shading, least cost being transparent and highest cost being shaded in the darkest tone. The same system of shading was applied to social as well as natural processes. When various overlays are combined, it is concluded that the least-shaded area represents the location with the least social cost.

The notion of value is central to McHarg's method, because he attempted to place a hierarchy of values on environmental characteristics or institutions that have no prices. His approach can be criticized because the overlay method equates values of equal shading. When wildlife quality and forest quality are both shaded with the same tone, the method is, in effect, equating forest quality with wildlife quality. This is in direct contradiction to McHarg's statement that there is no possibility of ranking between characteristics. Built into the technique is an explicit valuation of widely different things like historic buildings and steep slopes. Such valuations are not inappropriate, but they must be explicit and not hidden, consistent with the stated aims and procedure of the method, and always obvious to the decision maker.

6. DECISION PROCEDURES WHICH CAN EASE VALUATION PROBLEMS

Section 4 pointed out that some of the criteria used to guide decisions are questionable and that decision rules may have implications for valuation that are not appreciated by their users. Section 5 noted a need for methods of assessing and displaying value information but cautioned that the systems proposed may also contain unsuspected value implications. Rather than closing the chapter on such a discouraging note, we would like to describe briefly some ways of structuring decisions that can make the valuation process easier.

6.1. The Notion of a Threshold Comparison

Valuation difficulties can sometimes be reduced if there are two mutually exclusive alternatives and it is possible to value all the benefits and costs of one alternative in money. For example, Krutilla and Cicchetti (1972) compared preservation and hydroelectric power development as two mutually exclusive uses of Hells Canyon. They were able to calculate the net monetary benefits from power development and to convert these to an annual equivalent of $80,000. This provided a threshold value or bench mark showing the annual return that could be obtained from power development. If annual preservation benefits could be shown to exceed $80,000, preservation would be a more valuable alternative than power development.

The threshold-value method is particularly useful in cases involving recreation and preservation because estimates of monetary value are hard to make for them. In a situation similar to Hells Canyon, for example, it might be possible to assess a minimum value for the recreation that could continue if the area were preserved but not if it were developed. Recreation is only one of the potential benefits from preservation, but if its value alone proved to be greater than the threshold value from development, preservation would be the most valuable alternative, and a decision could be reached even though the other preservation benefits could not be valued in money.

6.2. Constraints instead of Values

Framing decisions as constrained optimization problems is another way to overcome valuation difficulties. For example, a land-management decision may have a number of objectives, such as timber production, land preservation, employment, and water quality. Only one of these might be nominated as the objective function to be optimized. In this case it might be income from timber, because this can be readily measured and quantified. The other objectives could then be formulated as constraints. The expression of such constraints in physical quantity units avoids the valuation problem. In this example, the constraints might be:

(a) Employment must not be less than X jobs per year.

(b) At least Y acres of land must be devoted to preservation.

(c) Water quality must be better than Z milligrams of dissolved oxygen per liter.

A conventional method for handling such problems is linear programming.

This procedure has been widely advocated (O'Brien and Roy, 1971; Gray and Anderson, 1964a). But it has some important implications for valuation that are closely related to the notion of setting standards, which we discussed in Section 4.3. A minimum constraint of 500 jobs, for example, implies that the benefits from every job up to 500 are larger than the resulting losses in timber production, no matter how great those losses might be. Similarly the benefits from every acre preserved up to the constraint are assumed to be worth more than the opportunity costs. This technique can be helpful, but the implications of constraints must be carefully recognized.

6.3. The Simple-Betterness Method

The principle of simple betterness can sometimes be used to narrow the range of alternative choices. Rickard, Hughes, and Newport (1967) provide an example of the method in the context of managing a Douglas-fir forest for timber and landscape benefits. Figure 5.5 is a hypothetical display of the monetary net benefits from timber and the nonmonetary benefits from landscape for five alternative ways of managing a tract of land. Timber benefits are scaled in dollars of net present worth. The landscape scale is undefined (unmeasurable units) and indeterminate (has unknown limits); it is simply an approximate ranking of landscape benefits. The display indicates that alternatives 2 and 4 provide similar landscape benefits and that both provide greater landscape benefits than alternatives 1, 3, or 5.

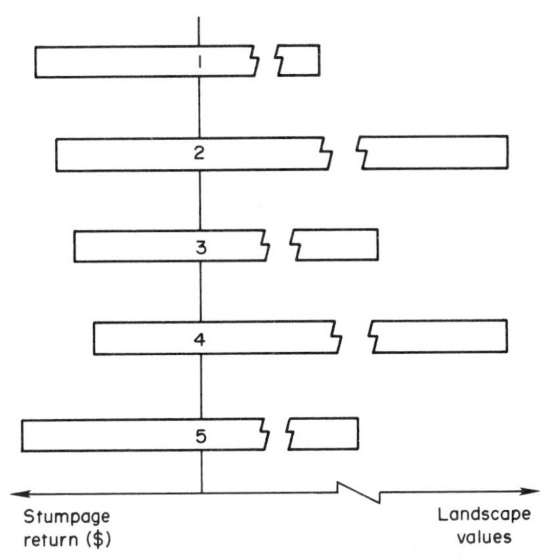

Figure 5.5. Simultaneous display of dollar and nondollar consequences of five alternative forms of forest managment. (After Rickard et al., 1967.)

The simple-betterness method searches for alternatives that are dominated by others in both monetary and nonmonetary aspects. For example, because alternative 2 produces both larger timber benefits and larger landscape benefits than alternative 3, alternative 3 can be ignored. Alternative 2 is also superior to alternative 4; although it produces about the same landscape benefits, its timber benefits are greater. Alternative 4 can therefore also be ignored. Finally, because alternative 5 is superior to alternative 1 in both timber and landscape benefits, alternative 1 can be ignored. The decision can thus be reduced to a choice between alternatives 2 and 5.

6.4. Performance Budgets

Complex decisions must be structured in such a way that the right alternatives are considered and attempts are made to value and compare the right benefits and costs. McKean (1958) suggests that one way of doing this is through performance budgets. These entail complete, or nearly complete, breakdowns of costs by activities and outputs. Against each cost is then set an indicator or target of expected performance. For example, a forest-service budget might recognize activities of fire control, road development, and timber management. Against the fire-control costs might be set indicators of the control organization (men, equipment, etc.) that could be put in the field and the expected savings in timber and other forest values. To this could be added estimates of the changes in these indicators that would result if the budget were increased or reduced by, say, 1 percent. A decision about a specific aspect of fire control could then be approached in terms of its effect on the general fire-control situation of the forest service.

This procedure is similar to the financial performance ratios that we criticized in Section 4.5. However, the directions of the two approaches are different. Performance budgets place little reliance on single ratios based on actual past costs. Instead, they examine the whole program and the marginal changes that could result from the decisions under consideration.

7. SUMMARY

We have tried to show in this chapter the close relationship between decisions and valuation. Because of their importance for the rest of the book, we recapitulate the points made. We assume that the reason for making valuations is to guide choices and other decisions. Because decisions differ in their nature, the data sources and precision that are appropriate also differ. Whether monetary estimates of value are needed depends on how many of the economic parameters are fixed in the decision. The scope of decisions varies with the administrative level at which they are made, and the need for monetary estimates varies accordingly. Certain decision criteria are in common use and sometimes provide good indicators of value, but they must be used with care, because they are not perfect substitutes for explicit valuation. Finally, the policy questions that underlie decisions determine the kind of information needed and how it can best be assessed and displayed for the decision makers. The various systems that have been developed for tabulating and presenting information do not reduce the need for technical data and quantitative value estimates.

CHAPTER 6

Valuation as a Process

In the preceding five chapters we have stressed the point that value is always specific to people and their situations. We have shown that appraisals are made to guide decisions and that the kind of valuation needed varies with the kind of decision. But we do not want to leave the impression that every appraisal is a unique event. Valuation is a process, and there is a general pattern to the application of economic reasoning that can make this process efficient and effective.

1. STEPS IN THE VALUATION PROCESS

For clearer exposition we present the valuation process as a sequence of steps. In actual practice these steps are often telescoped, and they are not necessarily always carried out in this order.

1.1. Define the Problems and the Alternatives

Some choices involve simpler valuations than others, and different decisions may require different concepts of value. The logical starting place is a clear definition of the problem and each alternative. The following questions are important.

Persons Involved. Who are the gainers and who are the losers? Does the decision concern a single person, a group of people, or society as a whole? Answers to these questions will guide the definition of benefits and costs and provide information on who should be interviewed.

Objectives. Does the decision involve many objectives, or does it rest on one alone? If there are multiple objectives, what are the priorities among them?

Value Object. Does the decision involve consuming more or less of a given thing, or does it involve a new thing? Does it represent an either/or, alternative choice, or compensation situation? The answers will indicate the nature of the data that must be collected and what kinds may already be available.

Kind of Action. Does the decision involve a whole program or just a single, marginal project? Does the project include only one activity or good, or a number of them? The answers will alert the analyst to the level of difficulty to be expected.

Nature of the Alternatives. Are similar alternatives to be compared, or does the decision involve choices between quite different things? Choices between similar things can sometimes be analyzed without monetary values.

Resources and Constraints. What scarce resources and what constraints are involved? More specifically, what is the nature of the budget, and is it or the output level fixed?

Answers to these questions will guide the specification of benefits and costs, the selection of valuation methods, and the nature of the final comparative assessment. If adequate answers can be found, the subsequent analysis will be much simplified.

1.2. Identify the Participants

The next step is to identify the people involved, because it is the value to these people that must be measured. When markets and prices exist, the producers and consumers can usually be identified, but this is more difficult with unpriced goods. For example, people may benefit from knowledge that an environment is being preserved, but these consumers are spread throughout society and are hard to identify, because no goods are actually being exchanged.

Market prices are formed in exchanges between producers and consumers who are different people. But an analogous exchange takes place when one person is both producer and consumer. In many forms of recreation, individuals select locations and produce activities whose benefits they personally consume. They exchange resources such as time and money for benefits like scenery and solitude. There is no market or market price, but value is indicated by the willingness to pay of the individual. The analyst's challenge is to identify the participants and what is being exchanged so the basic economic principles of valuation can be applied.

1.3. Define the Utilities and Disutilities

The third step is to define the nature of the things being valued. The importance of the step and the problems involved can best be shown by examples.

Many attempts have been made to evaluate the benefits of hunting and fishing. Participants clearly obtain utility in the form of satisfaction from these sports, but this satisfaction is hard to define. Potter, Hendee, and Clark (1973) hypothesized that hunting satisfaction consists of the following major elements: being outdoors and close to nature, changing routine, having companionship, shooting, challenging skills, living vicariously, displaying trophies, taking game, owning equipment, and having verbal and visual experiences. But if satisfaction derives from so many dimensions, how can an analyst ever conceptualize the valuation problem? Potter offers a clue in his observation that hunters who seek the same prey may generally obtain the same kinds of satisfaction. The type of prey that particular hunters seek—waterfowl or elk, for example—may define the dimensions of satisfaction that make the sport valuable to them. Valuation should therefore start from information about the thing involved—in this case the type of prey being sought.

Another example is the valuation of the improved water quality resulting from pollution control. Pickle, Rucks, and Sisson (1973) identified the major benefits of water pollution control in Alabama as: (a) increased recreational opportunities, (b) increased value of land adjacent to the river, (c) reduced loss of fish and wildlife, and (d) reduced cost of water treatment by industries downstream. These benefits were indicated by changes in the following measurable items: number of recreation days, amount of land traded, quantity of fish caught, and quantity of water intake by industry. Because these changes can be related to changes in certain characteristics of the river, the total utility resulting from pollution control can be expressed as:

$$\begin{aligned}\text{total utility} &= f(\text{quantity of benefits}) \\ &= f(\text{characteristics of river}) \qquad (6.1)\end{aligned}$$

Valuation should start from information on the basic changes in the thing being appraised.

1.4. Define the Things Exchanged

The next step is to define the things actually exchanged or produced. Goods and services with regular monetary prices pose few problems at this stage—a particular type of meat or automobile can be defined in detail. But unpriced goods and services seem harder to define. The main reason is the apparent difficulty in distinguishing between the physical resource, the products traded, the activities involved, and the ultimate utilities. For example, questions like the following are often raised about landscape benefits: Are we trying to value the warm inner glow derived from a view or the landscape that provides it? Are we trying to value the whole view or just that part which provides satisfaction? Are we trying to value the intangible thing called beauty or some manifestation of it?

This distinction between a resource (the landscape) and an ultimate utility (beauty) is important. In the case of scenic views it would be very difficult to define and measure the utility called "beauty." But there is a difference between a person's perception of a utility and his reaction to it. The psychological process of appreciating beauty may defy measurement, but the physical reaction to beauty can often be measured in terms of number of visits to a particular view, for example.

The reasoning is not limited to landscapes. Foods differ in flavor, which is just as hard to define as beauty. It is not obvious how one can measure the difference in flavor, between beef and lamb, for example. But people's reactions to various foods can readily be observed, and these are good indicators of the foods' comparative utilities.

A single resource, such as a landscape, might provoke different reactions in different individuals. Presumably, they receive different utilities from it. The focus of valuation should therefore not be on the landscape resource itself but on the activity of viewing it, which is what the viewers derive utility from. This activity is the object of exchange, and the willingness to pay for it can be observed as an indicator of its value.

However, some decisions, such as which of several open-space areas should be preserved, do involve choices between resources. The physical things being exchanged here are resources, but because their comparative values derive from the benefits they can produce, the choice is really between the potential benefits from the alternative areas. The potential benefits will vary with certain critical characteristics of the areas. If these characteristics can be accurately defined, the comparative values of alternative areas can be estimated directly from them.

Workers in the landscape field in particular have been ready to identify characteristics that are important in determining comparative values. Linton (1968), for example, started out by hypothesizing that only two basic elements—land form and land use—were important in determining the value of scenic resources and did not analyze any others. Leopold and Marchand (1968) identified 32 characteristics of riverscapes, but then did not weight them in any way and thus implied that they were all of equal importance. Litton (1972) argues that choices in landscape management can best be made with a systematic method of landscape description. He identified six recognition factors and six composition types, but he implicitly assumed that utility is derived equally from all of these attributes by all people. Unfortunately, little evidence has usually been offered to support such identifications.

Another example of a different type may help make the point. Considerable effort is being devoted to improving the quality of urban environments. What is being exchanged as a result of these urban improvement decisions? The ultimate utility involved is a favorable change in the quality of people's lives, which is hard to define and even more difficult to measure. But the benefits people actually receive as the results of decisions are specific things like better health, less damage to trees and gardens, or higher real estate values. Valuations must start with a determination of the effects on such products of a proposed improvement, illustrating the general need to concentrate valuation on the things actually exchanged.

1.5. Identify the Causal Chain from Characteristics to Utility

Utility is derived from the characteristics of things rather than from the things themselves. The preceding section discussed several studies whose authors felt characteristics were the basis of utility. If such hypotheses can be tested and verified, it becomes possible to estimate utility from measurements of the significant characteristics. It is important for an analyst to identify as well as he can the causal chain along which utility is derived from characteristics of the thing being valued.

Lave and Seskin (1970) report several studies that quantify and establish relationships between health and air quality. One study used data from 117 standard metropolitan statistical areas in the United States. The dependent health variable was measured as the total mortality rate, and the independent variables included the amount of suspended particulates and the concentration of sulfates. The equations for the relationships explained 80 and 81 percent, respectively, of the variation in mortality rates between areas. This suggests that the effects of an air pollution control program on social utility can be traced through the program's effects on suspended particulates and airborne sulfates.

Causation can rarely be proved conclusively, but any analysis will be on firmer ground if reasonable justification can be developed from relating utility to certain characteristics of the things being valued. If models have been analyzed and compared validly and if there are good basic hypotheses on relationships, strong evidence of correlation may justify an inference of causation.

1.6. Select Scales for Measuring Benefits and Costs

Once the thing to be exchanged has been identified and defined, it must be scaled in some kind of numerical units. Products like meat can be scaled in kilograms, but how are products such as views to be scaled? Money is a handy yardstick for utility, but other scalars are often adequate.

Workers in the landscape area have made numerous attempts to scale the comparative utility of different views. We discuss many of these techniques in detail in Part II, and only mention them briefly here as examples of this step in the valuation process.

In preparing guidelines to improve the scenic beauty of highways, Burke, Lewis, and Orr (1968) developed a simple scale whose midpoint was the common landscape "that occurs most of the time—the average condition." Views were scaled +1 if superior and −1 if inferior to the common landscape, which was scaled 0. Fines (1968) proposed a more elaborate scale for landscapes which ranged from 0 to 32. The most complex scale for landscape values is probably Leopold's (1969) uniqueness ratio. Assuming that utility is somehow related to uniqueness, he rated various characteristics of riverscapes on a scale of 0 to 1.0, where 0 indicated not at all unique—very common and 1.0 indicated absolutely unique—no other like it. The scales for a number of individual characteristics were then aggregated into a uniqueness ratio for each landscape.

1.7. Measure Quantities Exchanged and Used

The selection of a useful scale to measure quantities is an important step in any comparative valuation. The kind of scale selected has a major influence on the cost and difficulty of the appraisal, so it is important to remember what must be measured and what can be accomplished with the various scales. Let us look briefly at the major kinds of scales and what is required for their use.

Objective, Continuous, Numerical Scales. Characteristics of resources can often be measured in objective units, as can the width and depth of a river. These are observed facts, uncolored by the observer's subjective feeling. The scales are continuous, and each observation fits on a scale of known intervals and unbroken sequence.

Subjective, Continuous, Class Scales. Characteristics of resources can often be classified according to subjective scales. An example is Linton's (1968) scale of landforms: lowlands, low uplands, plateau uplands, hill country, bold hills, mountains. This is a continuous scale from lowlands to mountains, and any landscape can be classified as being at some point on this scale. Although such scales do not actually measure resources, they can facilitate comparative valuations.

Present/Absent Discrete Scales. These scales are objective in the sense that there is no room for the observer's feelings to affect the classification. For example, certain species of plants or animals either are present in an area or they are not. But such scales represent only the two end points of the continuum that must actually exist. They are only useful if utility depends entirely on the presence or absence of a characteristic.

Qualitative, Noncontinuous Scales. These scales attempt to indicate an ordering in terms of some characteristic felt to be important in determining utility. An example of such a characteristic might be vegetative cover, and the classes in the scale might be bare, grassy, woodland, and forest. A subject must be classified in one "slot" because these scales are not continuous, but the classification can be quite objective. If the ordering reflects a meaningful gradation of the benefit involved, such scales may serve as useful indicators of comparative value.

1.8. Estimate Value Information

The analyst has now defined the problem and alternatives in the decision for which he is preparing information. He has identified the participants and the utilities and disutilities involved, has defined the things that will be exchanged, and has identified the causal chain between characteristics of these things and utility. With all this in mind, he has selected suitable scales and determined how to use them in measuring the quantities of the things exchanged. He is now prepared to obtain comparative value information on these things.

We saw in Chapters 3 and 4 that the value of a thing is determined by the utility it can provide to the people whose lives are affected and the disutility they must bear in order to have it. In Chapter 2 we saw that disutility can be expressed as opportunity cost—the alternative utilities people must sacrifice to obtain a particular utility. The basic value equation can be written

$$V_i = U_i - OC_i \tag{6.2}$$

where V_i is the value of thing i to the participants in the decision, U_i is the utility thing i could provide these participants, and OC_i is the opportunity cost they must bear in order to have i.

Because opportunity costs are utilities foregone, the analyst is seeking information as to which alternative would provide the greatest net utility. As we noted in Chapter 5, the utility is specified for some decisions, and only opportunity costs can vary; for other decisions the opportunity costs are specified, and only utility can vary. In such cases indices based on characteristics may suffice to indicate comparative values. If these are not adequate, an assessment of relative utilities in comparative numbers may suffice, the type of assessment needed being determined by the particular situation.

In more complex decisions, when both utilities and opportunity costs are variable, everything must be measured in comparable units, and monetary estimates are usually most satisfactory. The best indicator of people's assessment of utility is their willingness to pay, that is, what they are actually willing to exchange for the thing in question. A useful form of the basic value question is

$$V_i = WTP_i - OC_i \tag{6.3}$$

where WTP_i is the willingness of the participants to pay for thing i and all variables are expressed in a common monetary unit (which is not necessarily market price).

Chapter 7 extends this discussion to the choice of a method from those presented in Part II. We merely wish to emphasize here that the choice of a method always depends on the particular decision involved and is influenced by the availability of data, analytical skills, and resources of time and money.

1.9. Present a Final Comparative Assessment

The goal of the valuation process is to provide information on the comparative values of decision alternatives. The analyst's role is to present these comparative assessments in a form that is useful to decision makers. The data that are presented vary from problem to problem.

At one extreme, it may be possible to derive monetary values for all benefits and costs and to present a single monetary figure for the value of each alternative. This could be presented as follows:

$$V_1 = \$100 \qquad V_2 = \$250 \qquad V_3 = \$200$$

A similar presentation can be made whenever values can be assessed in a common unit, even though it is not a monetary one. As we will see in Part II, this situation occurs rather frequently.

At the other extreme, it may be impossible to derive monetary values for any of the unpriced things. The most the analyst can do is list all benefits and costs and describe them as best he can. A useful example is shown in the planning balance sheet of Table 5.2.

There are various intermediate ways of presenting comparative assessments which we will illustrate as the book proceeds. Each chapter in Part II has as its theme a different environmental example involving different kinds of assessment.

2. ADAPTING THE TRADITIONAL THEORY OF CHOICE

Traditional economic theory assumes that individuals try to maximize utility, and—as shown in Equation 2.3 of Chapter 2—that the quantity of any good consumed is a function of its price, the prices of other goods, and consumer income. The theory further assumes that goods are consumed as goods, that they are considered as whole units, and that the process of consuming them does not affect the amount consumed. This has two important deificiencies, for it ignores the characteristics of goods and it ignores the process by which goods produce utility. The following sections show how the traditional theory has been adapted to overcome these deficiencies and to make it more useful for the assessment of values.

2.1. Assessing Utility from Characteristics

Lancaster (1966) has proposed an approach to consumer choice that departs from the traditional theory in two respects: the characteristics of goods, rather than the goods themselves, are assumed to provide utility, and the process of consumption is assumed to be as important as the goods in providing utility.

Lancaster's second assumption recognizes that the time spent in preparation, acquisition, consumption, and recollection has an important effect on utility. Along with Becker (1965), he suggests that households combine time and goods into basic activities, that decisions are made about these basic activities, and that the utility function a household seeks to maximize is

$$U = U(\text{activity}_i \cdots \text{activity}_n) \tag{6.4}$$

where activity_i is the activity of consuming good i subject to both time and income constraints. This reformulation with activities in place of goods is intuitively appealing, because many unpriced benefits—such as extensive recreation—involve a high input of time and a negligible input of goods or money.

Lancaster's first assumption, that utility derives from the characteristics of things rather than from the things themselves, makes it possible to express a household's utility function (Equation 6.4) in terms of characteristics. Three further assumptions are now necessary: (1) that each consumption activity involves a fixed set of characteristics, (2) that the quantity of goods consumed for a given level of a particular activity is constant, and (3) that consumption of a given level of a particular activity will, *ceteris paribus*, provide a fixed level of utility. The utility maximization function can then be rewritten as

$$U = \mathrm{U}\,(K_{11} \cdots K_{nn}) \tag{6.5}$$

where K_{ij} is the quantity of the ith characteristic of the jth activity.

A household now chooses activities in terms of the utility derived from their characteristics, within the time and budget constraints. This model is particularly attractive in the environmental area, because it provides a systematic framework for accomodating some of the conceptual problems we recognized earlier. For example, the utility derived from fishing can be related to such characteristics of the activity as climate, number of fish caught, and scenic surroundings. The utility of water consumed by industrial plants can be related to such characteristics of the water intake as temperature, dissolved oxygen, and sulfide content.

2.2. Assessing Utility from Part of a Resource

When a resource is the object of valuation, do we value the whole resource or just part of it? All resources are composed of many characteristics. Landscapes, for example, comprise such things as vegetation, water, topography, access, composition, and land use. The difficulty with valuing an entire resource is that all of its characteristics are viewed equally and simultaneously. In an analytical context, characteristics that are unimportant may obscure the important ones we wish to study. In a philosophical context, Baier (1969) argues that the values of things relate only to characteristics that are wanted. For example, it is not the whole landscape that provides utility but only those characteristics that people wish to see.

Presumably, an individual's response to a resource is an aggregate reaction to its characteristics. An analyst must try to determine which of the characteristics are important to the kinds of utility he is trying to value. In some cases he may have to consider the whole resource. In others he may consider all characteristics, but give them different weights in the final analysis. In still other cases he may be able to isolate certain significant characteristics, measure only the response to these, and ignore all others. In no case does it make sense to analyze characteristics that have little or no influence on the utility realized by the relevant people.

2.3. Assessing Utility from Intermediate Products

Many decisions about actions on resources affect utility only through a long causal chain. Take, for example, a decision about constructing an effluent disposal system. What social value would the system have? Clearly, people will receive little, if any, utility directly from the facilities themselves. Their value will derive from the effects they have on water quality. But water quality is a result of various river characteristics, such as odor, temperature, and bacteria content. The effects of treatment will show up as changes in such characteristics, and the value of the facility will depend on the utility of these changes. But changes in odor, temperature, or bacteria content will not in themselves create utility. People will only benefit from the effects these changes might have on health, quality of fishing, or the amenities of living along the river.

The generation of utility can be visualized as a sequence. Utility is a function of benefits received (such as improved fishing). Benefits received are a function of changes in some characteristics of a resource (such as a reduction in water temperature). And changes in characteristics are a function of the resource itself (such as a river) and the input of other factors (such as construction and operation of a treatment facility).

$$U = f(B) = f(K) = f(ER, I_1 \cdots I_n) \tag{6.6}$$

where U is utility, B is benefits received, K is characteristics of a resource, ER is the environmental resource itself, and I is the inputs that would be made as a result of the decision.

Land-classification schemes often attempt to relate characteristics of land directly to utility, although terms like "suitability" and "capability" are sometimes used instead of utility. Young (1973) reviews such schemes and discusses one promoted by the U.S. Department of Agriculture. This scheme (Klingebiel and Montgomery, 1961) classified land mainly on the basis of limitations or hazards resulting from such characteristics as slope, soil depth, and drainage. The system consisted of eight suitability classes based on the degree of overall hazard, and land with similar levels of the characteristics was assigned to the same class. Appropriate uses were then recommended for each class of land.

It is impossible to make recommendations about overall suitabilities without implicitly making certain assumptions about the relationships between land characteristics and land uses. Such recommendations assume that the effects of nonland inputs are constant and less significant than those of the land input, that the prices of all outputs are constant, and that the production of utilities from other uses is constant. Such schemes may predict the uses that would have maximum utility in restricted situations and under constant conditions, but they cannot be expected to choose the uses of highest utility under all conditions.

A popular approach seems to be to relate utility directly to characteristics or even to the inputs made as a result of the decision. In general, any attempt to represent intermediate products like quality characteristics as final payoffs should be viewed with suspicion. Ignoring the full causal chain from basic resource to ultimate utility may lead to ending the analysis at the wrong point (such as characteristics) or beginning at the wrong starting point (again characteristics). Valuation should concentrate on the utility derived from the things ultimately exchanged.

3. CONCLUSION

We have seen in this chapter that when valuation is viewed as a process it is possible to recognize certain necessary and logical steps. Part I of this book has focused on the first four steps of defining the problems and alternatives, identifying the participants, defining the utilities and disutilities involved, and defining the things exchanged. Part II covers the remaining five steps. Its task is to review and describe the kinds of methods that appear useful for collecting data on unpriced values and making comparative value assessments.

PART II

METHODS OF VALUATION AND ANALYSIS

CHAPTER 7

Selection of a Valuation Method

Part I discussed the concept of value and the nature of valuation. Part II now reviews various valuation methods and shows how they can be used with unpriced benefits and costs. In this chapter we discuss the problem of selecting an appropriate group of methods. Each group is then the subject of a separate chapter, and the selection of specific methods within each group is considered in its chapter.

1. THE PROCESS OF VALUATION

In Part I we argued that value derives from the favorable difference a thing can make to someone's life and can be expressed by the general definition

$$\text{value of something} = \text{utility from its use} - \text{disutility of obtaining and using it} \tag{7.1}$$

In the symbols of Equation 3.5 of Chapter 3 we have

$$V_i = U_i - DU_i \tag{7.2}$$

Valuation is the process of implementing this equation.

Values are indicators of relative importance and can be used to guide choices among alternatives. Economics is concerned with choices and many of its principles apply to valuation. The conceptual definition of value in Equation 7.2 can be given operational content by employing two economic principles: willingness to pay (*WTP*), which can measure utility and recognize income constraints, and opportunity cost (*OC*), which measures disutility. Equation 7.2 can be re-expressed as

$$V_i = WTP_i - OC_i \tag{7.3}$$

The analyst's problem is to find ways to measure *WTP* and *OC*.

1.1. Values Are for Decisions

Different problems and different decisions may need different interpretations of the basic value concept. The relevant points from Part I can be summarized as follows:

(a) Values are neither intrinsic nor general; they are always specific to given desiderata, times, places, individuals, and decisions. The marginal nature of decisions means that people rarely try to determine optimal bundles of things or to consider all possible choices at one time. Usually they analyze smaller groups of choices to move a step toward higher utility.

(b) The specificity of decisions assists and often simplifies valuation. Certain parameters like attitudes and relevant persons are fixed for specific choices.

(c) The three major kinds of decisions require different degrees of detail and accuracy and pose different levels of difficulty for analysts. Compensation decisions require precise estimates of value. Either/or decisions require comparisons between single new things and existing situations. Choices between alternatives require estimates of relative value.

(d) Decision objectives and budget constraints influence the kinds of value information needed. The maximization of benefits from a given budget and the minimization of cost for a specified benefit do not necessarily require monetary estimates of benefit. Where money costs are insignificant, benefits can often be measured by a proxy for money.

(e) The nature of a decision varies with the level at which it is made in the decision-making hierarchy. The decision criterion, the nature of the required value estimate, and the appropriate valuation method all vary with this level.

(f) Decisions are often based on criteria other than value, such as the distribution of benefits and costs. The analyst's task is to identify and define these other criteria and the role that value data have.

Overall, valuation difficulties may be simplified by focusing on the decision.

1.2. Values for Individuals, Groups, and Society

Chapters 3 and 4 discussed the nature of individual, group, and social values. The main points may be summarized as follows:

(a) Different viewpoints lead to different definitions of value, so any given policy problem may be viewed differently by various people. For example, an individual businessman may equate value with net monetary income, but society will normally equate value with all the benefits and costs to everyone involved and not with monetary benefits and costs alone.

(b) Social value may be a composite of the values to individual members, or it may include additional values that accrue to the group as a whole, such as group cohesiveness and longevity.

2. SELECTION OF A GROUP OF METHODS

The appropriate method depends on the nature of the decision and the value information required. Important aspects of the decision are the existence of multiple or single objectives; the need for individual, group, or social values; and the existence of fixed costs or benefits.

The choice is also influenced by the availability of research resources and data. A shortage of research time and skill or a lack of available data will limit consideration to expedient or less-demanding methods, whereas greater resources of time, skill, and data will permit more rigorous analytic methods.

By carefully considering some questions relating to these factors an analyst can focus on a group of methods and then select the particular method that suits his problem. Figure 7.1 lays out some of these questions and shows how they can lead to specific groups of methods. The logical starting question is whether more than one factor must be considered and therefore whether utilities can be measured on a single scale. The search for a method can then proceed as follows:

(1) If more than one factor is involved, these may be multiple objectives or multiple characteristics. (If only one factor is involved, proceed to step 4.)

(2) If they are multiple objectives, they may be things society wants, such as net benefits, distribution of income, or environmental protection. Each objective involves a different scale and the objectives must be aggregated. The methods in Chapter 8 are suitable for such cases.

(3) If they are multiple characteristics, there must be a different scale for each. For example, an air-quality decision may require measurement and aggregation of several characteristics of the air. Chapter 9 covers methods for converting such measurements to an index of value.

(4) If there is only one factor involved, the cost may be fixed or variable. (If the costs are variable, proceed to step 8).

(5) If the costs are fixed, insignificant, or can otherwise be ignored, comparative value must be indicated by total benefits, and methods that estimate total utility will be appropriate. The question then is whether the decision justifies much or little research.

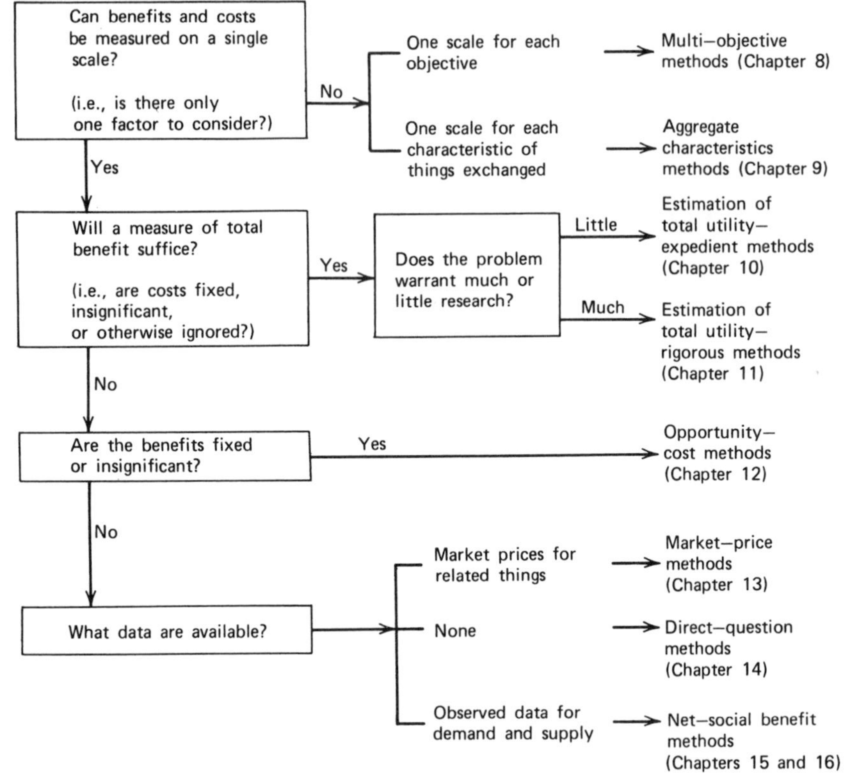

Figure 7.1 A schematic diagram of the selection of a group of methods.

(6) If the decision does not justify high costs, one of the expedient methods of Chapter 10 can be used. Some of the expedient methods are suspect, because they aggregate data on different scales and involve untenable assumptions. But the methods are rapid, and data can be collected for a large sample. Analysts often justify using such methods when they need an answer quickly or when research resources are limited.

(7) If the decision is important enough to justify the cost of obtaining very reliable information, the rigorous methods of estimating total utility described in Chapter 11 should be used.

(8) If the costs are not fixed, the benefits may or may not be fixed. (If the benefits are not fixed, proceed to Step 10.)

(9) If the benefits are fixed or insignificant, comparative value must be measured by the opportunity-cost methods of Chapter 12.

(10) If the benefits are not fixed or insignificant, comparative values must be based on estimates of net monetary benefits. The choice of a method then depends on what data are available for the analysis. The three following situations are possible.

(11) If market prices are available for related things, the methods of Chapter 13 can be used to estimate or derive monetary values for the things in question.

(12) If no data are available, information must be obtained by one of the direct-questioning methods of Chapter 14.

(13) If data for demand and supply exist or can be obtained, net social benefit can be estimated by the methods of Chapters 15 and 16.

(14) Finally, if the decision requires information on group or social values, the methods of Chapter 17 are appropriate to aggregate estimates obtained by other methods.

Specific decisions or problems require specific kinds of methods. No method will satisfy all problems, no matter how well it analyzes some of them. The choice of a method should rest on how well it suits the decision and not on its intrinsic merits. As we illustrate in Chapter 12, some methods that give no value information in the form of net utility can in certain situations provide related information that is helpful for decisions. Some of the methods in that same group can only provide values in very specific situations. The choice should depend on whether such situations exist rather than on the inherent merits of the method.

3. DIFFERENT APPROACHES TO VALUATION

The various groups of methods provide different kinds of valuations for the decision situations just discussed. Some important aspects of these differences are now considered in more detail.

3.1. Different Ways to Implement the Value Model

The different groups of methods implement the value model of Equation 7.2 in different ways. The full model, with its estimation of social utility and disutility, is implemented only by the net-social-benefit methods of Chapter 15. The other groups of methods implement the model less completely or with certain restrictive assumptions, as shown in Figure 7.2. For example, if costs can be ignored, the total-utility methods of Chapters 10 and 11 provide estimates of value. With an assumption of constant net benefits per unit, the quantity exchanged can measure value. With an assumption that a given net benefit accompanies a given level of some characteristic, the characteristic methods of Chapter 9 provide accurate indices of value.

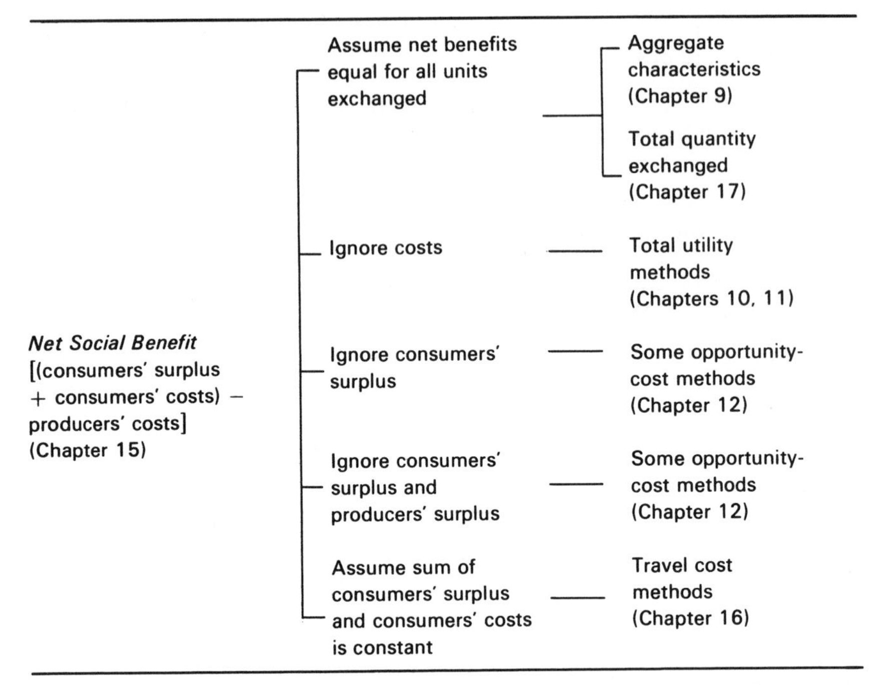

Figure 7.2. ***Relationship of some groups of methods to net social benefit.***

3.2. Different Value Units

Some methods can be applied with either monetary or nonmonetary value units. The appropriate unit depends on the specific problem, because it is the problem that dictates the criteria the unit must meet. The five possible criteria are as follows:

If interpersonal comparisons are needed, or if individual values are to be aggregated to group or social values, the method should have (1) a common scale for all individuals, (2) a common base point, and (3) units on the scale which are known and equal. Criterion 2 would exclude simple rank orders even though such a scale could satisfy criteria 1 and 2.

If comparisons involve different products or different times, the method needs (4) identical units for each product or time period.

If benefits are to be compared to costs, the method needs (5) benefits and costs in the same units.

The most obvious measure that meets all five criteria is a monetary unit, which means a method from Chapters 12 through 17. But there are other situations in which all five criteria do not apply and other units are suitable. For example, hours of time or miles of travel will satisfy criteria 1 through

4. There also are several methods and decision procedures that can satisfy all criteria without using money as the yardstick.

There is a spectrum of "numericalness" in the units of value and in the way they meet the criteria. At the nonnumerical extreme are methods with verbal assessments such as good or bad, satisfied or dissatisfied. Such methods meet only criterion 1. At the other end of the spectrum are methods that provide quantitative data on comparable additive scales and meet all five criteria.

The value scale may be ordinal, without specific intervals between each unit. Alternative values can then only be ranked. Because the distances between individual ranks may vary greatly, these "measurements" cannot be manipulated in any rigorous way. Or the value scale may be cardinal or numerical. The distances on these scales may be natural simple units such as the dollar or arbitrary simple units such as the utile, which economists invented for this purpose. In other cases they may be complex distances such as the ratios or percentages of the value indices of Chapter 9.

3.3. Different Methods for Different Data

There are various possible sources of data for valuations, and each may promote the use of different methods. Data sources for air pollution, for example, may be: physical and biological data on pollution effects, technical data on production and consumption, expenditure information, opinion surveys of air-pollution sufferers, data from court decisions, and political expressions of social choice.

Data sources are rarely substitutes for each other. For example, data on physical and biological effects may be suitable for the comparative value indices of Chapter 9. Expenditure information can provide data for the opportunity-cost (Chapter 12) and market-price (Chapter 13) methods. Opinion surveys suit the methods of Chapters 10 and 11 for estimation of total utilities or the direct-questioning methods of Chapter 14. However, an analyst may not need an opinion survey if data are already available on expenditures and market behavior. And conversely, if there are no observable market data, direct-questioning and utility methods may have to be used. An analysis of political decisions or court cases is only appropriate for group or social values.

Some methods are based on facts uncolored by opinions, such as data on actual behavior. Some of the opportunity-cost methods of Chapter 12 and net-social-benefit methods of Chapter 15 use data on actual consumption. At the other end of this spectrum are data based entirely on people's opinions. Such subjective data on what individuals think are completely personal and may be inconsistent or biased in unknown ways. However, some of the utility methods of Chapter 11 attempt to capture and formalize subjective thoughts in an objective way.

4. VALIDATION OF VALUES

In addition to selecting and applying appropriate methods, an analyst must also justify his results. Validation is the process of checking results to make sure that they measure what they are supposed to measure. There are various possible procedures, which vary in their concepts and rigor. We now discuss them in a descending order of rigor.

4.1. Prediction Tests

The strongest procedure is to test values for their predictive ability. Future behavior is predicted from the estimated values, actual future behavior is observed, and the predictions are then compared to the observations. Values that prove to be adequate predictors are suitable for further decisions. The rationale for this test is that planning should make the same choices as the people involved would have made themselves.

The most rigorous tests provide the strongest support. For example, there is considerable debate as to the objective that individual firms maximize. Officer and Halter (1968) and Lin, Dean, and Moore (1974) argued that farm firms try to maximize utility rather than monetary profit. They derived utility functions, predicted behavior from them, waited to observe this behavior, and compared predicted to actual behavior. In this strong prediction test, utility data provided acceptable and superior predictions. An implication for valuation is that money values may be less useful than utility values.

4.2. Concurrent Prediction Tests

A concurrent validation test differs from the preceding test in that the predicted behavior is compared to current actions. An acceptable relationship between predicted and current behavior validates the results. One variant is the back-projection test, in which predicted actions are compared to behavior in the immediate past.

The test may be performed in several ways, including regression, correlation, or visual observation, but in each case the analyst must decide on acceptable levels of comparability. LaPage (1968) measured the benefit from campground use in New Hampshire on the scale shown below. He collected data on current behavior (average length of stay) and expected behavior (plans to return), which gave the following averages:

Scale of Benefit	Average Length of Visit (days)	Percentage who Plan to Return
Highly satisfied	4.25	84
Well satisfied	3.25	60
Satisfied	3.25	56
Dissatisfied	1.50	23

Expected behavior and, to a lesser extent, current behavior closely follow the benefit scale. The visual test tends to validate the scale and the results of the study.

4.3. Internal-Consistency Test

The rationale of the internal-consistency test rests on the simple proposition that differences in values should be related to differences in characteristics of the people involved or of the things exchanged. This belief can be tested through statistical techniques, two of which are illustrated in Chapter 14. If value differences parallel other differences, the values are consistent with internal characteristics and are accepted.

The internal-consistency test is weaker than the prediction tests. But behavior may often be hard to observe, whereas data on socioeconomic or environmental characteristics are easier to collect. It can be a simple test and seems stronger than the following procedures.

4.4. Comparison of Results

Several validation tests involve justifying the results after they are obtained. One procedure is to demonstrate their similarity to other results. For example, Brookshire, Ives, and Schulze (1976) valued aesthetic benefits through a direct-question method. The results were justified by comparison with the numerical values obtained with the same method in a similar study and similar area by Randall, Ives, and Eastman (1974).

Another procedure can be used when the results being compared were all derived in the same study. The different results can be tested against each other to see if they follow expected patterns. Bohm (1971), for example, used several variations of a direct-question method to value benefits. The variations involve different systems of payment. He hypothesized that similar values for all payment systems would indicate valid results. A statistical test showed no significant differences between the values, so the results were accepted.

This sort of validation is usually easy to apply, but its logic is sometimes questionable. Similarity is only a reliable test if the other results have been justified.

4.5. Content Tests

The least-rigorous test concerns the nature of the valuation method. The analyst must be able to make one or more of the following arguments: (a) the method measures what it is supposed to measure, (b) the assumptions and content of the method follow theory and are applicable, (c) the data were collected carefully, or (d) the questions were structured carefully with built-in checks. Shaw and Wright (1967) term this the "content validity" test, because it rests on judgments about the content of the method itself. However, because the analyst in all cases should have checked the method, its assumptions, and the data collected, this test provides no real verification of the results.

Structuring questions with built-in checks does provide an interesting way to perform this test. Values obtained with the direct-question methods of Chapter 14 are often most in need of validation. Bohm (1971) and Tideman (1972) illustrate two kinds of built-in checks for them. Bohm argues that subjects should be left uncertain about how their responses might affect their liability to pay. A rational individual will then not perceive any advantage in understating or overstating his values. Tideman pursued the same idea for structuring methods to reduce bias. If the possibility of extra payment is just balanced by the possibility of lower payments, a rational individual will have no incentive to bias his responses.

5. NATURE AND SCOPE OF THE METHODS CHAPTERS

Part II reviews a large number of methods for interpreting or implementing the value model of Equation 7.3. These methods fall into 10 relatively homogeneous groups in terms of the value information they provide. Each group is the topic of a separate chapter.

Our attempt to review the whole range of methods in one book has meant that some associated topics have had to be omitted. There is not space to discuss risk, the cost of information, sampling methods, or forecasting. We regret this, because problems in valuation sometimes derive more from these causes than from a lack of concepts and methods.

Some of the methods involve such supporting procedures and knowledge as linear programming and questionnaire design. We have minimized discussion of these procedures in order to concentrate on the value questions and methods. The presentation employs a graphic, tabular, and written treatment. Mathematical interpretation has been avoided except where essential for application and summary purposes.

Our approach to valuation involves the collection, analysis, and interpretation of data. Comparative values indicate preferences. Empirical efforts to estimate values must therefore be based on certain beliefs or assumptions about these preferences. These assumptions are detailed more fully in texts such as Halter and Dean (1971), but can be summarized as follows:

(**a**) The preferences allow alternative things (*A*, *B*, *C*) to be ordered. The ordering may be a preference or an indifference among the alternatives.

(**b**) The ordering is transitive. If *A* is preferred to or equal to *B*, and *B* is preferred to or equal to *C*, then *A* is preferred to or equal to *C*.

(**c**) Preferences vary on continuous rather than discrete scales.

(**d**) The addition of a new and independent alternative does not change the preference ordering of the existing alternatives.

CHAPTER 8

Analyses Involving Multiple Objectives

Valuations appear particularly difficult when the problem involves several objectives, so our study of measurement begins with the methods usable for multiple objective decision making. These methods offer ways to combine monetary and nonmonetary values and procedures to account for unpriced things. They present several approaches to valuation for the multiple-objective decision.

All of the methods require a clear statement of each objective and data on the effects of each alternative on each objective. But apart from the simplest and least informative methods, they all require extra data, as shown in Figure 8.1. These data may be orderings of outcomes or objectives, constraints, weights between objectives, or combinations of these. One important basis for choosing a method is the availability of the necessary extra data. We present the methods in the order of their data requirements. After the methods themselves, we discuss in Section 9 a procedure for collecting data and implementing methods through a sequence of structured interactions with the decision maker.

Another important basis for choice is the information obtainable from each method and the criterion that each involves. The methods implement several criteria and are not perfect substitutes for each other. We note this sort of information about them as we proceed, summarize it in Table 8.4, and review it at the end of the chapter.

Most of the methods are explained sufficiently for direct applications. But several, like linear programming and goal programming, involve mathematical procedures that we do not detail. For comparison, the methods are explained in the context of a single environmental problem to which we now turn.

1. AN ENVIRONMENTAL POLICY EXAMPLE: A GORGELANDS NATIONAL PARK

There is currently a proposal to make a national park of some 424,000 acres at the headwaters of the Macleay River in New South Wales, Aus-

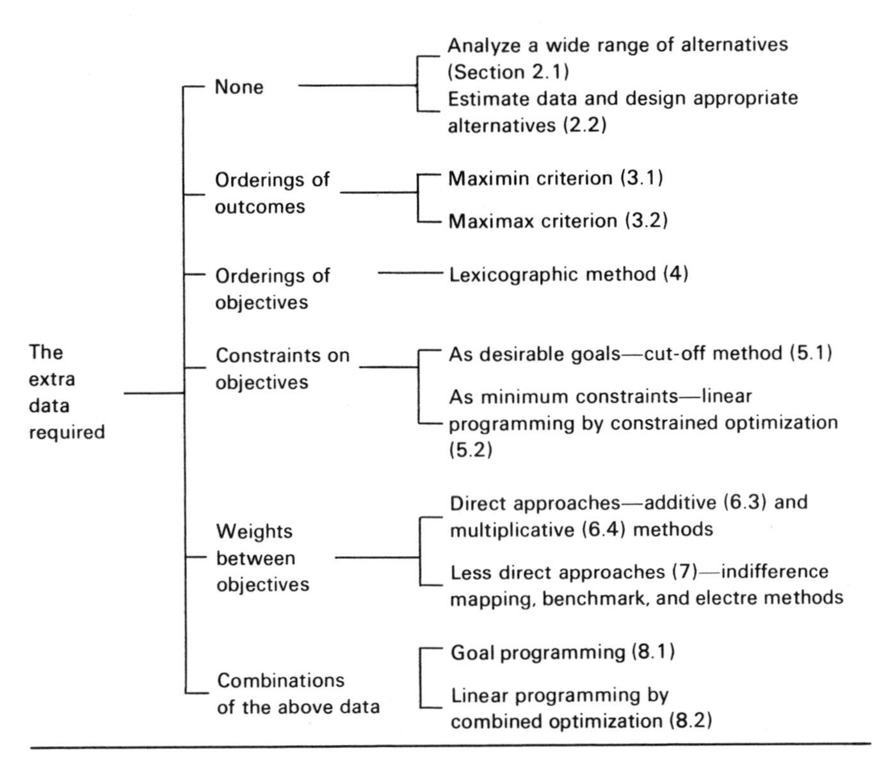

Figure 8.1. Multiple-objective methods classified by the nature of the extra data necessary.

tralia. The proposal is based on the spectacular gorgeland scenery, the relatively untouched natural state of some of the land, and the endangered habitats of a kangaroo species and a eucalypt species.

The area is presently public land that is leased by private parties from the crown. To establish a park, the government would have to buy out the leases and displace farm families and mining. We discuss the conflicting objectives next and then consider the alternative park possibilities and their outcomes. The relevant data on the alternatives are collected in Table 8.1.

1.1. The Multiple Objectives

The decision whether to establish a park will be made by the state government, which would administer the park, and the federal government, which

Table 8.1. Outcomes of Four Alternative Land Use Plans for a Gorgelands Park

Outcomes	Alternative			
	Existing	*A*	*B*	*C*
1	2	3	4	5
Present Uses Retained	**Cattle, Mining**	**Less Cattle, Mining**	**No Cattle, Mining**	**No Cattle, No mining**
Area of Park (1000 acres)	**0**	**292**	**424**	**424**
OBJECTIVES				
1. *Net monetary benefits*[a]				
(a) From cattle	51	12	0	0
(b) From mining	455	455	455	0
(c) Acquisition cost	0	−74	−90	−545
(d) Operating cost	0	−100	−100	−100
Total	506	293	265	−645
2. *Acquisition Cost*[a]	0	74	90	545
3. *Distribution of income*				
Number of farm families supported by area	32	25	24	24
4. *Number of recreation visits*	58,200	62,700	64,300	64,300
5. *Preservation of*				
(a) Major scientific projects (number)	1	1	1	1
(b) Habitat of endangered kangaroo	No	No	Yes	Yes
(c) Habitat of rare eucalypt	No	No	No	Yes
(d) Natural landscape vistas	No	Yes	Yes	Yes
Quantitative Index[b]	1	2	3	4
Qualitative Index	Little	Improved	More improved	Most improved

[a] Thousands of dollars present worth expressed as annuities at 10%.
[b] Number of the preceding (a) to (d) preserved.

would provide the money. The analysis must therefore be social in scope and will rest on various objectives, which are shown in Table 8.1.

Because both governments consider changes in aggregate net money benefits, objective 1 in Table 8.1 is net monetary benefit, which should be maximized. Acquisition costs may be a separate additional objective. The distribution of income is an important social consideration, which we define as the number of farm families wholly or partly supported by the area.

The environmental benefits arise from visits to the park and preservation of it. Dedication of the land as a national park will preserve habitats and natural vegetation and promote scientific research through its permanence as an experimental area. Objective 5 is clearly the preservation of the natural environment, but its definition and measurement are less clear. For the purposes of this chapter we define it qualitatively as shown on the last line in Table 8.1, and quantitatively as the number of dimensions with some positive contribution to preservation. We use both forms of measurement in the chapter to examine whether a method can accommodate a qualitative description or requires a quantitative index.

1.2. The Alternatives

The alternative land-use plans range from a continuation of the existing use to a complete park without cattle grazing or mining (alternative *C*). These alternatives and their outcomes for each objective are now considered in more detail.

The land within the proposed boundary is currently leased by 32 farmers and a mining company. Each year 1010 cattle are sold for a net farm income of $51,000. Gold and antimony are mined on some 5 acres in the most accessible area. For convenience, we ignore this small amount of land in the total area figures of Table 8.1. The net income to the mining company over the 20-year life of the mine can be expressed as an annuity of $455,000 at 10 percent. These net monetary benefits will be lost if a full park is established.

The grazing and mining leases can be purchased for some $900,000 and $4,550,000, respectively. Eight farmers live entirely from their leases, so under alternative *C* only those 24 who could support themselves with land outside the park would remain (objective 3). The mine would close, but the miners are largely itinerant and could readily find work elsewhere. Alternatives *A* and *B* (Table 8.1) are two partial parks in which the majority of the land would be preserved (*A*) or all would be preserved (*B*) but the mining would continue.

1.3. Role of the Example in this Chapter

We have specified the gorgelands problem sufficiently to illustrate this group of methods. But we have simplified it with constant operating costs for all size parks. Also, we have not detailed our calculation of net monetary benefits, although we did apply standard economic procedures to the actual data.

The gorgelands example also provides a theme for Chapter 20. In that chapter we apply the methods of Chapters 9 through 17 to convert some of the nonmonetary data of Table 8.1 to monetary values and to convert the net monetary benefits to net social benefits.

The kind of data in Table 8.1 is the kind of information that is normally available at the start of an analysis. Other data needed for multiple-objective decisions, such as weights, are introduced during this chapter. The application of the present methods to the data of Table 8.1 illustrates what the multiple-objective methods alone can achieve, even though we will not always apply them to selecting a single best alternative.

2. WITH NO EXTRA DATA

Two methods are appropriate when no extra data can be obtained and when the decision maker is inaccessible. The first is simply a display of information for a wide range of alternatives. In the second, the analyst estimates the missing data and then designs several appropriate alternatives or plans.

2.1. Analyze a Wide Range of Alternatives

Increasing attainment of one objective usually requires decreasing that of another. Because these trade-offs are the essence of multiple-objective decisions, the estimation and display of information about alternatives should improve such decisions. If nothing else, these displays allow the decision maker to pick the project or plan that provides the most appropriate set of benefits and costs.

Miller and Byers (1973) used the method for watershed planning. The two objectives of particular relevance were net monetary benefits to the nation and environmental quality, which was initially defined as the weight of sediment phosphorus. The mix of net benefit and quality depended on the combination of cropping practices, recreation and wildlife activities, and channel improvements. The combination that maximized net benefits subject to a given quality constraint was identified through mathematical programming. The constraint was systematically varied to identify a series of optimal combinations. This series provided the complete range of outcome mixes from maximum net money benefits at lowest environmental quality to minimum money benefit at highest quality. The decision maker could then select the combination that was socially appropriate. Various procedures were used to incorporate several environmental characteristics into the quality objective to extend the application.

This method concentrates on analyzing a wide range of projects or plans. In doing this it separates out and ignores the estimation of weights or constraints. However, information on the range of alternatives and the trade-offs between them is helpful in making decisions, because it makes clear the inevitable interaction between objectives. The U.S. Water Resources Council (1971) recommends as a general principle that the benefits and costs of each objective be made explicit. A wide enough range of alternatives should include the socially optimal project.

2.2. Estimate Data and Design Alternatives

The analyst can always try to estimate the missing information about orderings, constraints, weights, or goals. Then he can design several projects or prepare several plans that use these data in different ways. As Howe (1971) argues, the method is necessarily vague, because the estimated data are imprecise. A given objective might be optimized for several different constraints, or perhaps the constraints or weights may be too vague for any optimization procedure. Despite these problems, plans and projects can be presented together with information on their benefits and costs. This presentation may be adequate for a choice or may encourage the decision maker to provide more data.

2.3. Discussion

Some of the features of these methods are summarized in Table 8.4. Table 8.1, which presents information on four alternatives for the gorgelands example, resembles the method of Section 2.1 because it includes the two extreme alternatives (existing use and C). As the chapter proceeds we will follow the method of Section 2.2, estimate the missing data, and apply them directly to the choice between the park alternatives.

3. WITH AN ORDERING OF OUTCOMES

Decision makers who can order the outcomes for each separate objective and between different objectives can use the following two methods. Each method rests on a particular decision criterion and attitude toward uncertainty.

3.1. The Maximin Criterion

A pessimistic decision maker will determine the worst possible outcome for each alternative and choose that alternative whose worst outcome is better than those of the others. The "best of the worst" criterion requires decision makers to order the outcomes of different objectives. This ordering is difficult when objectives differ considerably, but should be easier when they are similar.

Let us apply the method to the gorgelands example.

(a) First the outcomes in terms of each objective are observed for any one of the alternatives. For existing use the outcomes are $506,000 net monetary benefits, $0 acquisition costs, 32 families retained, 58,200 visits, and little preservation (Table 8.1).

(b) The decision maker must select the worst of these outcomes. Let us assume he selects little preservation as the worst outcome of this alternative.

(c) Steps a and b are repeated for each of the alternatives. Assume that the complete list of worst outcomes is as follows:

Existing uses—little preservation

Alternative A—improved preservation

Alternative B—24 retained families

Alternative C—$545,000 acquisition cost

(d) The decision maker must now consider this list, select the best of these outcomes and thus identify the best alternative.

When the objectives are similar—as are different types of recreation—selection of the best and worst outcomes seems straightforward. But in our example the nature of the objectives is quite different. However, alternative *A* is better than existing use in terms of preservation, and an acquisition cost of $545,000 (alternative *C*) may be worse than displacing eight families (*B*). The maximin criterion would therefore reduce the problem to a choice between alternatives *A* and *B*.

The maximin criterion can assist choices without explicit data on weights or constraints. MacCrimmon (1973) claims that ordering outcomes is similar to—and possibly easier than—weighting objectives. But the method is only applicable when the value of an alternative is determined by a single outcome, as in cases in which objectives are achieved in sequence or where decision-makers are pessimistic.

3.2. The Maximax Criterion

This "best of the best" criterion complements and mirrors the previous method. An optimistic decision maker, who chooses the best single outcome for each alternative, would follow this procedure.

(**a**) The outcomes in terms of each objective are observed for any one of the alternatives. The outcome of highest utility is noted.

(**b**) All alternatives are observed, and the best outcome for each is chosen. In our example these might be as follows:

Existing uses—$506,000 net monetary benefits

Alternative A—62,700 visits

Alternative B—64,300 visits

Alternative C—Most improved preservation

(**c**) The decision maker now selects the best of these outcomes and thus identifies the best alternative.

Selection of the best (or worst) outcome is a direct comparison of the utilities of the outcomes. Suppose that most preservation were chosen as the best outcome. The decision maker would be informally, but no less definitely, saying that the utility from most preservation is higher than the utility from net benefits of $506,000 or from 64,300 visits.

Like the previous method, the maximax criterion is appropriate when the decision can rest on the outcome of any one objective. It also requires that the decision maker be optimistic.

3.3. Discussion

Neither of these methods requires extra data, but they both require access to a decision maker who can order all the outcomes. We believe the decision makers in New South Wales are more balanced than these optimitistic or pessimistic extremes, and we have not applied these methods to our gorgelands example.

4. WITH ORDERINGS OF OBJECTIVES AND OUTCOMES

A decision maker may be able to order all the objectives in terms of their importance for his particular problem and also order the outcomes for each objective. The ranking of outcomes for a given objective requires no extra information or ability beyond that needed for the preceding methods. But information on both orderings permits the use of the lexicographic method, which is named after the systematic ordering of things in a dictionary.

4.1 The Lexicographic Method

The method proceeds as follows:

(**a**) The decision maker orders the objectives in terms of their importance. Let us assume that the order for the gorgelands example is (1) preservation, (2) distribution of income, (3) net money benefits, (4) acquisition costs, and (5) visits.

(**b**) The most important objective (preservation) is selected and its outcomes are in turn ordered. This gives (1) most improved (alternative *C*), (2) more improved (alternative *B*), (3) improved (alternative *A*), and (4) little (existing use).

(**c**) If the first outcome is clearly preferred, the procedure stops and the alternative is chosen. If several alternatives have the same or similar outcomes the procedure continues.

(**d**) The outcomes for the second ranked objective are now ordered. This is distribution of income in our example. The problem is to choose between alternatives *C* and *B* because these had the preferred outcomes for the first ranked objective. Both of these alternatives have the same outcome (24 families) for the second objective. If these outcomes for the second objective were distinctly different and the order were clear, the procedure would stop. When this is not true, as in our example, the third objective (net money benefits) must be noted and the process repeated. Alternative *B* is clearly preferable to *C* for this third objective.

(**e**) The procedure continues until one alternative emerges as superior or all objectives have been examined.

If the "most improved" preservation from Alternative *C* is clearly preferable to the "more improved" from *B*, the procedure would stop at step c, and alternative *C* would be chosen. If not, the procedure would continue to step d, and alternative *B* would be chosen.

A different ordering of objectives can lead to a different choice of alternative. Suppose that distribution of income were ranked first and preservation second. The choice would now go to the existing use alternative (32 families) which failed steps b and c with the original ordering of objectives.

4.2. The Potential of the Lexicographic Method

This method requires close contact with the decision maker throughout the analysis. But as Boland (1974) notes, ordering objectives and outcomes may be simpler than providing weights and goals. The method is most appropriate when the decision maker cannot visualize or express the trade-offs between objectives. The potential for valuation seems promising because the method accommodates descriptive qualitative outcomes, like preservation, and ranked values through the orderings.

5. WITH CONSTRAINTS ON OBJECTIVES

The biophysical or technical standard is a common tool of environmental policy. It may be a maximum constraint on an undesirable thing like noise or a minimum on a desirable thing like habitat preservation. Several methods are available when objectives can be specified in terms of meeting standards. The cut-off method is appropriate when all objectives can be specified as constraints. Linear programming is appropriate when one dominant objective must be optimized but the rest can be specified as constraints. When weights as well as constraints are available, other methods that we discuss later in the chapter can be used.

The specification of constraints for the gorgelands example confronted some usual problems. A constraint on net money benefits was hard to specify, so although it would not be the single dominant objective, we left it to be optimized. We defined constraints for the other objectives as follows:

acquisition cost ≤ $1 million total (or $100,000 per year as an annuity at 10 percent)
distribution of income ≥ 24 retained families
number of recreation visits ≥ 58,200
environmental preservation ≥ substantial improvement

The preservation constraint is qualitative, but it is sufficient for the cut-off method. "Substantial" is defined as an improvement in two of the four preservation categories. Only alternative *B* (more improved) and alternative *C* (most improved) meet this definition. The constraint for recreation visits was set at the lowest of the outcomes in Table 8.1. We had no clear idea of what constraint the decision maker would place on distribution of income or acquisiton cost. So we set the former at the worst actual outcome and the latter at the apparently prohibitive figure of $1 million. The following two methods are based on these constraints.

5.1. The Cut-Off Method

In the cut-off method alternatives are eliminated if they fail to meet the constraints—hence its other name of "elimination by aspects." The method is best explained by example.

5.1.1. Application to the Gorgelands Example. The decision maker nominates a constraint for each objective, and the method then proceeds as follows:

(**a**) The objectives and their constraints are considered in any order. For example, consider acquisition cost first with its constraint of not more than $100,000 per year. All alternatives that fail to meet this standard are excluded, which eliminates alternative *C*.

(**b**) Consider the remaining alternatives against any other constraint, say, a substantial improvement in preservation. Once more exclude all alternatives that fail to meet this constraint. Existing use and alternative *A* are cut off to leave only alternative *B*.

(**c**) The process in step b is repeated for all the objectives. Any remaining alternatives must meet all the constraints. If only one remains, it is chosen—as is alternative *B* in our example. If more than one remains, an extra criterion must be used to choose among them. If none remain, no alternative is suitable, and the decision maker may wish to revise his constraints.

5.1.2. The Role of the Cut-off Method. This method resembles lexicographic ordering in the way objectives and alternatives are systematically considered. But there are important differences between the two methods. The cut-off method accepts all projects that meet the constraint for an objective, whereas the lexicographic method accepts only the best alternative for each objective. The cut-off method also considers all objectives and not just enough of them to isolate a single alternative. Unlike the lexicographic method, a different choice will not follow a different ordering of objectives. If constraints can be defined, the cut-off method is superior. In Chapter 9 we apply it to problems based on the characteristics of alternatives rather than objectives of the decision.

5.2. Linear Programming—Constrained Optimization

Haimes and Hall (1974) note that a classical approach to decisions about unpriced things has been to optimize a dominant priced objective while constraining choices for the unpriced objectives. Linear programming is the major mathematical technique that applies this approach.

5.2.1. The Nature of the Method. Linear programs consider a large group of alternatives and select those that optimize a given function subject to given constraints. A convenient dominant objective is minimization of costs. The constraints can then be given levels of unpriced benefits (in any quantitative measure), environmental standards, and other relevant data.

Linear programming designs the optimal plan (or alternative) by combining the available alternatives (or subalternatives) into an optimal group. Thus, as MacCrimmon (1973) says, the method solves a design problem rather than a choice problem. Nevertheless, the method generates much useful information for choices and is a step toward valuation.

Constrained optimization, in which all but one of the objectives are specified as constraints, is the simplest version of linear programming. Alternatively, several objectives can be combined in the function that is optimized. This approach, known as combined optimization, requires weights between objectives, and we consider it later in Section 8.2.

5.2.2. An Illustration. The gorgelands example is a choice between mutually exclusive alternatives rather than a grouping of alternatives in a plan. Linear programming cannot therefore be fully illustrated with this example, but the basic ideas can be shown. Suppose the objective is to maximize net monetary benefits subject to the constraints listed at the beginning of Section 5. Inspection of Table 8.1 shows that the constraint on acquisition costs excludes alternative *C* (as it did in the cut-off method). The constraint on preservation excludes existing use and alternative *A*. The distribution and visit constraints permit all alternatives. The choice is therefore limited to alternative *B*, as in the cut-off method. Suppose now that the preservation constraint were relaxed to "an improvement" rather than "a substantial improvement." The choice would then be between alternatives *A* and *B*. Because alternative *A* maximizes net money benefits, it would be chosen.

5.2.3. The Role of the Method. The potential of linear programming is affected by its optimization procedure and need for quantitative data. The requirement to optimize something may focus the analysis on an objective of little substance in the decision. Constraints are a convenient way to accommodate unpriced things, but they must be expressed numerically. A satisfactory numerical constraint is hard to specify for preservation in the gorgelands example. But quantitative data suit computer routines and allow large-scale sensitivity analyses. As we see in Chapter 12, the method provides much useful information on the opportunity costs of trading-off between objectives and resources and of changing resource levels.

5.3. Choice Between the Methods

The ease or difficulty of specifying constraints is the same for both methods. The cut-off method reaches a decision without optimizing anything, whereas linear programming must have a function to optimize.

The arithmetic simplicity of the cut-off method is partly offset by its inability to provide opportunity-cost information. However, the cut-off method accommodates unpriced outcomes rather easily. Linear programs require all constraints to be specified numerically, whereas the cut-off method can accept descriptive qualitative specifications.

6. DIRECT APPROACHES WITH WEIGHTS

The weighting approaches of Sections 6 and 7 recognize that the value of an alternative is proportional to the outcomes for all objectives. The direct methods of this section require explicit weights and apply them directly. The methods in Section 7 do this less directly. The two direct methods use additive or multiplicative functions to weight outcomes into an index of comparative value. Because they both follow the same general procedure and use the same weights, we consider these before discussing the methods themselves.

6.1. The General Procedure

(a) The nature of the value function is first stated in a formal way. For the gorgelands example we have

$$V_i = f\text{(net money benefits, acquisition cost, distribution of income, visits, and environmental preservation)} \tag{8.1}$$

where V_i is the value of alternative i.

(b) This relationship is specified more precisely by replacing the general objectives with their specific outcomes (X). With the five objectives of our example we can say

$$V_i = f(X_{i1}, X_{i2}, X_{i3}, X_{i4}, X_{i5}) \tag{8.2}$$

Because the outcomes must be specified quantitatively, we use the quantitative index of Table 8.1 (1 to 4) for preservation. All other outcomes in Table 8.1 are already in satisfactory numerical units.

(c) The outcomes may need to be standardized on a common scale, as we will discuss more fully in Chapter 9. For present purposes we follow McGaughey and Thorbecke (1972) and express all outcomes for a given objective as proportions of the mean of the objective. The standardized outcomes for the four gorgelands alternatives are shown in Table 8.2. This step is omitted in the multiplicative method, so we will continue to refer to outcomes for both approaches as X. This step is also omitted in the additive method when the decision maker can provide weights for the raw outcomes in their different units and levels. But the step is necessary for the additive method where the objectives are weighted as general concepts rather than as specific outcomes. These weights implicitly assess the utility of a given proportional change in one objective against the same change in another.

(**d**) The weights are now built into the model

$$V_i = f[(X_{i1}, WT_1), \cdots, (X_{i5}, WT_5)] \tag{8.3}$$

(**e**) The generalized model of Equation 8.3 is now given explicit mathematical structure. One possibility is the linear or additive form

$$V_i = (X_{i1} \times WT_1) + \cdots + (X_{i5} \times WT_5) \tag{8.4}$$

Another is the multiplicative form

$$V_i = X_{i1}^{WT_1} \times \cdots \times X_{i5}^{WT_5} \tag{8.5}$$

where the weights are entered as exponents. Psychological research often suggests that perception of differences between outcomes depends on the logarithm of the difference rather than the arithmetic difference (Huber et al., 1969). The same notion is also common in economics. The utility of money and time is often, if not usually, proportional to a curvilinear func-

Table 8.2. Application of the Additive Weighting Method

	Objectives[a]									
	1		2		3		4		5	
Alternatives	Net Monetary Benefits[b]		Acquisition Cost[b]		Distribution of Income		Recreation Visits (thousands)		Preservation	
1	2		3		4		5		6	
Existing Use	506	4.83	0	0	32	1.22	58.2	0.93	1	0.40
A	293	2.80	74	0.42	25	0.95	62.7	1.00	2	0.80
B	265	2.53	90	0.51	24	0.91	64.3	1.03	3	1.20
C	−645	−6.15	545	3.07	24	0.91	64.3	1.03	4	1.60
Total	419		709		105		249.5		10	
Mean	104.8		177.3		26.3		62.4		2.5	

[a] The left hand column for each objective lists the actual outcomes from Table 8.1, and the right-hand column lists the standardized outcomes. The standardized outcomes equal the actual divided by the mean. For example, 4.83 = 506/104.8 for objective 1 for existing use.
[b] The actual level is in present worth in thousands of dollars expressed as annuities at 10%.

tion of the quantity of the resource. These situations indicate some nonlinear form such as Equation 8.5.

(f) The final step is to obtain the weights and estimate the values from the model.

The methods are simple to use when the appropriate weights are available, and especially when the same weight applies to all outcomes of a given objective, as we assume for the gorgelands example.

6.2. The Derivation of Weights

All the direct approaches to multiple-objective decisions require explicit weights. If the relevant decision makers or population are accessible, the survey methods of Chapters 10 and 11 can provide these weights. For example, Gum, Roefs, and Kimball (1976) used the allocation of percentage ratings method, which we present in Chapter 11, to obtain weights for the social objectives of environmental projects. They inserted the following question for three of their many objectives in a mail survey of residents of Arizona and New Mexico:

> The aesthetics of water include clarity, odor, and floating objects. Allocate 100 points to indicate your desire for an improvement in each of these aspects of water aesthetics:
>
> | | |
> |---|---|
> | Clarity | _____ |
> | Odor | _____ |
> | Floating Objects | _____ |
> | Sum | 100 |

The observation and analysis of behavior can sometimes yield implicit weights, as we discuss in Chapter 17. In a similar way, weights can be derived from survey responses on simulated behavior, as Sinden and Smith (1975) and Shafer and Mietz (1970) have shown for landscape valuation.

6.2.1. Application to the Gorgelands Example. Weights for the five objectives of Table 8.1 were obtained from interviews with 30 randomly selected households with the paired comparison method of Chapter 11. (Promkutkeo et al., 1977). The objectives were expressed descriptively and generally as, for example, "increase in total recreational benefit from increase in number of recreational visits now and over time" for objective 4 and "increase in chances of scientific discovery" for part of objective 5. The weight for scientific discovery was pegged at 1.0 and the following weights were obtained:

1.	Net monetary benefits	0.7
2.	Acquisition cost	0.7
3.	Distribution of income	0.9
4.	Recreational visits	0.3
5.	Preservation—by classes	
	(a) Scientific discovery (peg)	1.0
	(b, c) Habitat preservation	1.5
	(d) Landscape vistas	1.3 (range 1.6 to 1.1)
Average (a) to (d)		1.3

For convenience, acquisition costs were assigned the same numerical weight as net money benefits, because both were dollar sums, although acquisition costs must be weighted negatively. A single average weight was used for preservation.

6.2.2. Discussion. The selection of weights raises some important issues. Should weights for objectives be elicited as descriptive qualitative concepts, as in Gum, Roefs, and Kimball (1976) and Promkutkeo, Mook, and O'Hanlon (1977), or should they be related directly to quantitative outcomes? And should different weights be elicited for different outcomes for the same objective? Clearly, different weights should be used at different levels of an objective if the utility of a given standardized change in the outcome varies with the level. Haimes and Hall (1974) developed their "surrogate worth trade-off" method as a version of weighting for this situation. But weights can be elicited for descriptive rather than quantitative outcomes if this is useful to the decision maker.

Arthur, Daniel, and Boster (1977) suggest that the direct weighting methods are inappropriate when no explicit weights can be obtained. In contrast, Coomber and Biswas (1973) argue that no weights should be used in this situation, thereby implying equal weights for all objectives. We take an intermediate position, following McGaughey and Thorbecke (1972). The sensitivity of the choice of alternative can be tested against a range of weights. The methods can still be used if the choice is not sensitive, but they must be rejected if the choice is sensitive to different weights.

6.3. The Additive Weighting Method

This method consists simply of inserting the weights and standardized outcomes into Equation 8.4 to calculate the value. The weights for the gorgelands problem were listed in Section 6.2.1 and the standardized outcomes in Table 8.2. With these data, the value for the existing use (V_{ex}) is calculated as follows:

$$V_{ex} = 4.83(0.7) - 0.0(0.7) + 1.22(0.9) + 0.93(0.3) + 0.40(1.3) = 5.28 \quad (8.6)$$

The comparative values for the other alternatives are 3.87 for A, 4.10 for B, and -3.25 for C. The existing use is the optimal choice based on these data.

Crawford (1973) used the method for a choice of highway routes and extended it by introducing probabilities. The objectives included safety, travel time, travel cost, scenic quality, and driving convenience. The outcomes for each objective were recorded directly on a standardized scale of $+3$ (strong positive impact) to -3 (strong negative impact), as in the Likert method of Chapter 10. The probability that an outcome would actually occur was estimated and inserted as an additional multiplier on the appropriate X in Equation 8.4.

This method is a logical approach to valuation, because it aggregates utilities in the manner of Equation 3.5. We illustrate it again as an application of the methods of utility estimation in Chapter 11. MacCrimmon (1973) concluded that the method had had widespread use and cited interesting applications to value heroes and choose soldiers to demobilize. He also discussed two variations of the additive method. A hierarchical procedure decomposes an objective into several subobjectives, each of which is measured and weighted separately, as in the methods of Chapter 9 (Figure 9.1). A quasi-additive procedure recognizes that aggregate utility may not be a simple sum as shown in this section, nor a multiplicative sum as shown in the next section. Other forms require other formulations of the basic model of Equation 8.3.

6.4. The Multiplicative Weighting Method

This method simply inserts the weights and unstandardized outcomes into the multiplicative formula (Equation 8.5) to estimate comparative values. Before applying the method to our example and discussing other examples, we consider the relevance of the method itself.

6.4.1. The Role of the Method. The multiplicative model is applicable when total utility is a multiplicative function of the outcomes. But it can also be used when outcomes cannot be standardized. Consider, for example, the addition of the raw outcomes for alternatives A and B:

$$\text{sum for } A = 293{,}000 - 74{,}000 + 25 + 62{,}700 + 2 = 281{,}727 \qquad (8.7)$$

$$\text{sum for } B = 265{,}000 - 90{,}000 + 24 + 64{,}300 + 3 = 239{,}327 \qquad (8.8)$$

The problem is that a linear transformation of one of these outcomes can change the ordering. Alternative A would be preferred with the two sums shown. But suppose the money outcomes were transformed from dollar units to thousand-dollar units. These items for alternative A would now be 293 and 74 instead of 293,000 and 74,000. The sums would now be 62,946 for A and 64,502 for B, and the preferred alternative is reversed. The possibility of such effects from a simple change in units rules out the addition of unstandardized outcomes as a useful comparative procedure. This problem is avoided if the numbers are multiplied instead of added, because a change in the units of one variable will change all the values by an identical amount. Division of the numbers will avoid the same problem for subtractions.

6.4.2. Application to the Gorgelands Example. We multiply the positive outcomes (benefits) together and divide by the negative outcomes (costs), with the weights as exponents, as indicated in Equation 8.5. For example, the value of alternative A (V_A) is calculated using the outcomes of Table 8.1 and the weights of Section 6.2.1 as follows:

$$V_A = \frac{293{,}000^{0.7} \times 25^{0.9} \times 62{,}700^{0.3} \times 2^{1.3}}{74{,}000^{0.7}} = 3278 \qquad (8.9)$$

In the same way, the comparative value of alternative B is 4266 and that of C is 0.000024. The value for C is low because C's net monetary benefit is negative (−$645,000) and must enter the denominator along with acquisition cost. The comparative value for existing use is undefined because the acquisition costs in the denominator are zero. The method provides comparative values, and we will consider their meaning after some more examples.

6.4.3. Further Examples from Aircraft Design and Pollution. The multiplicative model occurs in various guises. In economics, the benefit-cost ratio measures comparative value as benefits divided by costs. Epstein (1957) proposed a general "value function" for engineering and applied it to the choice of aircraft designs. The comparative value of design i might be indicated as

$$V_i = \frac{\text{rate of climb} \times \text{speed} \times \text{payload}}{\text{cost} \times \text{maintenance time} \times \text{fuel consumption}} \qquad (8.10)$$

The same notion was presented in simpler form by Seiler (1966) as a "cost-effective comparison." This comparative value, or "figure of merit," for aircraft involved only costs. In essence,

$$V_i = \frac{1}{\text{required runway length} \times \text{cost} \times \text{delivery time}} \qquad (8.11)$$

Reiquam (1972) proposed an index of environmental stress to measure the disutilities associated with pollution. This index of comparative value was measured as the simple product of persistence of the pollutant, transportability, and complexity. Hill and Alterman (1974) considered air pollution from power plants and reported an index proposed by Weston to compare sites. The essence of the index was the multiplicative model as the product of geographical coverage, pollution effects on land use, and national economic value of land uses.

6.4.4. Discussion. The arithmetic of the multiplicative weighting method can lead to peculiar numerical values, such as the 0.000024 for alternative *C*. There will be few of these arithmetic aberrations when there are continuous numerical scales and alternatives that involve only marginal changes, such as *A* and *B* in our example. The units of value also pose a problem in that the meaning of a unit made up of (money × number of visits × number of families × preservation ÷ money) is unclear. However, these apparent peculiarities do not preclude the use of the method for ranking. In fact, it is sometimes called the "dimensionless ranking method."

6.5. Discussion

Both of these methods aggregate utilities logically in the manner of Equation 3.5. The choice between them rests on the appropriate model to aggregate outcomes. Similar issues affect the choice between additive and nonadditive utility functions, which we discuss in Chapter 11.

The choice between these and other methods depends in part on the information they provide. These methods give no monetary cost information, although Keeney and Wood (1977) show how other tradeoff information can be derived through sensitivity analysis.

The methods order alternatives on a numerical scale and focus on the relationship or weights between objectives. Although the general procedure requires numerical data for the outcomes, these methods can accommodate descriptive or qualitative outcomes. Comparative utilities can replace numerical outcomes, as Crawford (1973) showed, and these utilities can easily relate to descriptive outcomes. This also avoids the need for monetary values for outcomes and can prove useful for valuing unpriced things.

7. LESS-DIRECT APPROACHES WITH WEIGHTS

A variety of methods can implement the general procedure of Section 6.1 without explicit weights. These less-direct approaches avoid weights through devices such as indifference maps, intensive series of indifference judgments, and the special weights of the electre method. We consider these in turn.

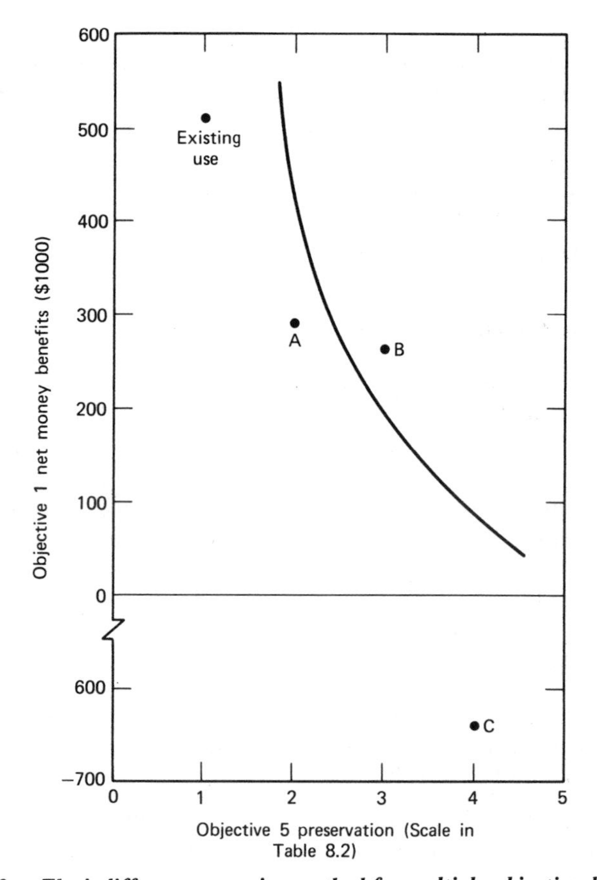

Figure 8.2. The indifference mapping method for multiple-objective decisions.

7.1. The Indifference-Mapping Method

The axes of an indifference map can readily depict two objectives, and each alternative can be represented by a single point, as in Figure 8.2. The decision maker's preferences can then be elicited as indifference curves (or an indifference surface, if there are more than two objectives). Alternatives on the same curve are equally preferred, and the one on the highest curve is most preferred. With the two objectives of the gorgelands example shown in Figure 8.2, alternative *B* would be most preferred.

An indifference curve depicts the rate at which a decision-maker is willing to substitute, say, net monetary benefits for preservation. The method therefore embodies explicit information on weights, but uses it indirectly to reach the decision. The potential of the method depends on an ability to obtain indifference functions and to handle problems with many objectives. The method seems useful for two objectives but appears difficult for problems with many objectives. Sinden and Wyckoff (1976) review procedures for obtaining indifference curves in two-good situations. The method that is described next is also based on indifference curves and appears more suitable for problems with many objectives.

7.2. The Benchmark Method

The benchmark method converts a multiple-objective decision to a single-objective decision through a series of systematic tradeoffs. The outcome for one objective of a base alternative is selected as a benchmark. The trade-offs are indifference judgments that convert other alternatives to hypothetical alternatives of equal utility. The outcomes of the hypothetical alternatives are identical with those of the base, except for the benchmark objective. The outcomes for the benchmark objective in the various alternatives are the indicators of comparative value.

7.2.1. The Nature of the Method.

(a) One alternative is selected as the base for comparison and its outcomes for each objective are noted. The outcomes for Alternative A are displayed in column 2 of Table 8.3.

(b) An objective with a numerical scale is chosen as the index for comparative valuation. Net monetary benefits is convenient in our example. The

Table 8.3. The Systematic Trade-Offs for the Benchmark Method

	Alternatives					
Objective	*A*	*B*	B_1	B_2	B_3	B_4
1	2	3	4	5	6	7
1. Net monetary benefits ($1000)	293	265	249	251	241	441
2. Acquisition cost ($1000)	74	90	74	74	74	74
3. Distribution (number of families retained)	25	24	24	24	25	25
4. Visits (1000)	62.7	64.3	64.3	62.7	62.7	62.7
5. Preservation	Improved	More improved	More improved	More improved	More improved	Improved

[a] Alternatives *A* and *B* are actual alternatives. B_1 to B_4 are hypothetical alternatives, all of which are of equal utility to *B*.

outcome for this objective for the base alternative ($293,000) is the benchmark.

(**c**) Another alternative is selected and its outcomes noted. We use alternative *B* in column 3. The outcomes for all of the nonbenchmark objectives (2, 3, 4, and 5) are different for alternatives *B* and *A*, so the outcomes for *B* must be converted to those of *A*.

(**d**) Select any one of the nonbenchmark objectives for conversion. Let us take acquisition cost. Its outcome must be converted to $74,000, which is the outcome in the base alternative *A*.

(**e**) The analyst then poses the following sort of question to the decision-maker: "A reduction in acquisition cost from $90,000 to $74,000 in Alternative B_1 would be an advantage. To be indifferent between alternatives *B* and B_1, you might accept a different net money benefit in B_1 in exchange for this lower acquisition cost. At what level of net monetary benefits (NMB^*) are you indifferent between the pair of outcomes [$265,000 NMB, $90,000 acquisition cost] for B and [NMB*, $74,000 cost] for B_1?" The figure nominated by the decision maker for NMB^* is inserted as an outcome in the hypothetical alternative B_1. Let us assume a figure of $249,000, because $1 of acquisition cost has the same utility as $1 of net money benefit.

(**f**) The outcome for the converted acquisition cost of $74,000 (now the same outcome as for alternative *A*) is entered in B_1. The outcomes for objectives 3, 4, and 5 are entered unchanged from *B*.

(**g**) Another objective is selected for a trade-off and the question to the decision maker of step e is suitably rephrased. Number of visits is reasonably straightforward in this example. If alternative B_1 is converted to match alternative *A*, 1600 visits will be lost (64,300 to 62,700). This second conversion requires a second hypothetical alternative (B_2). Because the loss of visits would be a disadvantage, the net monetary benefits of B_2 must be larger than those of B_1 if the decision maker is to be indifferent between them when all other outcomes remain the same. Let NMB^* for B_2 be $251,000 because the benefit of a visit was valued at about $1. Let us assume that the decision maker feels that $2000 more in net monetary benefits would offset the loss of 1600 visits and therefore nominates $251,000 as the NMB^* for B_2.

(**h**) The trade-offs continue in this systematic fashion. In the next indifference judgment between alternatives B_2 and B_3, the number of retained families is increased to the 25 of alternative *A*. This advantage is balanced by a loss of $10,000, making NMB^* $241,000 for B_3. A final judgment converts the last outcome (preservation) to match that of alternative *A*. B_4 is now the same as *A* except for the benchmark objective.

(**i**) The decision maker is now indifferent to alternatives *B*, B_1, B_2, B_3, and

B_4. The choice between A and B can therefore be made by choosing between A and B_4. The outcomes for these alternatives differ only in the objective net monetary benefits. Because an NMB of \$441,000 is preferable to one of \$293,000, B_4 and hence alternative B is selected as the most valuable.

7.2.2. The Potential of the Method. The method reduces a multiple-objective decision to the equivalent of a single-objective decision by using a simple index of comparative value for the final choice. The decision maker must make an intensive and perhaps lengthy series of indifference judgments. However, all multiple-objective methods require extra information, and these trade-offs focus on exactly the judgments that the decision maker should make. In an extensive formal treatment of the method, Raiffa (1968) suggests that sensitivity analyses and observations of behavior can assist with these trade-offs.

7.3. The Electre Method

Electre stands for "Elimination and (et) Choice Translating Reality." The method elicits weights directly, although these weights differ from those in the direct approach of Section 6. The electre method does not isolate a single best alternative or provide an index of comparative value. Instead, it narrows the number of relevant alternatives by dividing them into those that can be accepted, can be eliminated, or require more information, and then partially ordering the accepted alternatives (Roy, 1973). The decision maker must make explicit judgments about the preferences or different outcomes on the same objective, the forms of the weights to be given different objectives, and the thresholds for differences between alternatives.

7.3.1. The Nature of the Method. The method derives an index of concord, based on the proportion of the objectives on which an alternative ranks first, and an index of discord, based on the intensity of preference among the alternatives. Following David and Duckstein (1976), the steps in the preparation and use of these two indices are:

(a) Any pair of alternatives is selected. Let us select alternatives A and B with their outcomes in Table 8.1.
(b) The concord index rests on the frequency with which one alternative (A) is preferred to the other (B) for the various objectives. The pair of outcomes on each objective is observed. They are scored 2 if A is preferred to B, 1 if approximately equal, and 0 if B is preferred to A. The outcomes in Table 8.1 lead to the following scores:

Objective	1	2	3	4	5
Preference	$A > B$	$A > B$	$A > B$	$B > A$	$B > A$
Score	2	2	2	0	0

Weights can be incorporated here by using scores that differ for more- and less-important objectives. For example, preference on a less-important objective could be scored 1 rather than 2.

(**c**) The concord index is calculated by summing the scores from step b and standardizing them on the maximum possible score in the comparison. With a score of 2 per performance, the maximum possible is 10. The concord index for alternative *A* over *B* is 6/10 or 0.6.

(**d**) A concord index is calculated for each pair of alternatives.

(**e**) The first step toward the discord index is to identify the objectives in which the other alternative (*B* in this case) is preferred. These are objectives 4 (visits) and 5 (preservation) in step b.

(**f**) A utility scale is set up for each objective. The maximum point on the scale is determined by the relative importance of the objective and thus incorporates weights. Let the scale for our most-important objective (preservation) be from 1 to 20. The number of visits is a much-less important objective, so it is scaled from 1 to 8.

(**g**) Intervals are now assigned to the scales. The preservation objective is divided into the four classes of little, improved, more improved, and most improved (Table 8.1). If each class represented an equal interval, 5 utility units on this 20-point scale would be assigned to each class.

(**h**) The intensity of preference for *B* over *A* is measured by observing the number of intervals between the alternatives. Alternative *B* is one interval higher than *A* and so scores 5 points more.

(**i**) The intensity score from step h is standardized by dividing by the maximum point of the scale. This discord coefficient is therefore 5/20 or 0.25.

(**j**) Discord coefficients are calculated for all objectives where *B* is preferred to *A*. Objective 4 (visits) would have a coefficient of 0.13 (1/8) if 62,700 and 64,300 visits are one interval apart on an 8-point scale.

(**k**) The discord index for the alternative is the highest discord coefficient, 0.25 in this example. It is calculated for all pairs of alternatives.

(**l**) The decision maker now defines threshold levels for the concord and discord indices. The concord threshold is the minimum dominance that will be tolerated. For example, a threshold of 0.70 would indicate that *A* must dominate (or be preferred to) *B* on 70 percent of the objectives. Or, what is the same thing, alternative *A* must have a score of 2 on 70 percent of the objectives and 0 on the remainder. Alternative *A* has a concord index of 0.60 and would fail this test. The discord threshold is the maximum adverse preference that will be tolerated on any one objective. A threshold of 0.25 would indicate a maximum tolerance between outcomes on any objective of one interval on a four-class, 20-point scale (or its equivalent). The discord index between *B* and *A* just meets this test.

(**m**) Finally, the concord and discord indexes for each pair of alternatives are compared to the thresholds. Alternatives that do not meet the minimum degree of concord (or dominance) or the maximum degree of discord (or inferiority) are rejected.

7.3.2. The Potential of the Method. The electre method elicits the decision maker's preferences as yes/no/indifferent judgments for the concord index, as weights between maximum points on utility scales for the discord index and as absolute cut-offs for the thresholds. The first of these data are simple to obtain. The last two are harder to obtain, although no more difficult than data for most of the other multiple-objective methods.

Unlike Cohon and Marks (1975), we do not dismiss the electre method. The technique fails to provide opportunity cost information, fails to measure alternatives by comparative value, and is restricted to comparisons of discrete alternatives rather than designing alternatives. But it does concentrate on questions about weights and will reduce the number of relevant alternatives to be considered. The electre method will therefore assist in choices between large numbers of alternatives, although it may not indicate a single best choice.

7.4. The Role of the Methods

All of these methods are relatively new. Except for electre, they all require a considerable time input by the decision maker. But electre may not indicate a best choice. They all can handle descriptive rather than numerical outcomes, and all recognize that weights can change over the levels of an objective.

8. WITH COMBINATIONS OF DATA

We now consider two methods that use combinations of data. Both weight the objectives, although the nature of the weights differs in each.

8.1. Goal Programming

Goal programming requires goals for each objective, weights for deviations from each goal, an ordering between objectives, and constraints for resource levels. It optimizes a specific criterion and is appropriate when that criterion fits the problem and the necessary data are available.

8.1.1. The Nature of the Method. Goal programming selects the alternatives, and the quantities of each, that will optimize a specific function. The mathematical procedure solves a design problem, as does linear programming. But goal programming incorporates unpriced things in a different and sometimes more useful manner.

Goals are set for each objective. These might be a number of recreation days, a volume of water, a number of animal-months of grazing, or an area of habitat preserved. The alternatives under consideration would contribute variously to each of these goals.

The weights differ from those of other multiple-objective methods. They measure the disutility of deviations from one goal relative to deviations from another. The weights are equal if all one-unit deviations have equal disutility. They can allow positive deviations to be treated differently from negative deviations. A basic step in the method is to estimate

$$\sum_{j=1}^{n} (\text{derivation from goal } j \times \text{weight } j) \qquad (8.12)$$

for all alternatives, where n is the total number of objectives.

Decision makers may not be able to weight deviations in their different units. For example, one recreation visit is not comparable to one acre-foot or one animal-month. In such a case deviations can sometimes be standardized as percentages, as suggested by Field (1973). Then the decision maker need only weigh, for example, a 5 percent deviation from one goal against a 5 percent deviation from another.

Priority factors score or weight objectives in order of their importance. If preservation is considered twice as important as distribution of income, and it in turn is considered twice as important as recreation visits, the priority scores would be 4, 2, and 1, respectively. The factors can also reflect an ordinal ranking. However they are specified, their effect is preemptive—the goal of highest priority is met first. Field discusses approaches in which neither weights nor priorities can be precisely specified.

The criterion of goal programming is to minimize the sum of the weighted deviations from the goals. The mathematical procedure combines quantities of the alternatives in plans. The optimal plan minimizes

$$\sum_{j=1}^{n} [\text{priority } j \, (\text{deviation from goal } j \times \text{weight } j)] \qquad (8.13)$$

for all alternatives and subject to the usual resource constraints. The priority factors are denoted here by "priority j."

8.1.2. An Example: Multiple-Use Forest Management. Schuler, Webster, and Meadows (1977) report applications of goal programming to labor management, production schedules, and market strategies, but they indicate few applications to environmental problems. They applied the method to the management of a forest in Missouri.

The forest had to meet a range of different uses, including recreation (visitor-days), hunting (visitor-days), production of timber (volume), and grazing (animal-months). Priority scores between these objectives and the resource constraints were specified, together with the details of each management alternative.

Through goal programming, alternatives were selected to meet the constraints and minimize deviations from the specified goals. Then goals and constraints were systematically varied to investigate the sensitivity of the plans, or selected alternatives, to certain key variables. Because most of the goals cannot be met with the existing budget, trade-offs may be necessary. For example, the goals for hunting and timber production cannot both be met, but those for hunting and recreation or timber and recreation can. Three percent more hunting could be provided in exchange for a loss of 10 percent of other recreation. And a 55 percent increase in timber yield can be obtained for a loss of 17 percent of the recreation.

8.1.3. The Role in Valuation. Goal programming minimizes deviations and is methodologically identical to maximizing values. But deviations can be expressed in different units, whereas values have always been expressed in the same unit, usually in money. The deviations can be in numbers of visits, volumes of water, number of animal-months, or any convenient unit. The freedom from common units and monetary estimates of value is an advantage of goal programming.

Goals are important for both general policy and day-to-day management. The method recognizes this and provides information about which goals can be attained with existing resources and what trade-offs are necessary to provide more of one objective. This is important information for all decisions, although Cohon and Marks (1975) argue that the method is more suitable for private-sector decisions. Private enterprise usually has clearer goals and more-specific priorities and faces more-specific problems than does a government enterprise.

The method simultaneously considers all the objectives. However, this advantage is gained through a specific criterion of optimality that may not suit all problems. Furthermore, the method can generate neither monetary opportunity costs from increased quantities of unpriced things nor changes in income from changes in units of input.

8.2. Linear Programming—Combined Optimization

This version of linear programming weights several objectives in a single function, which is then optimized, subject to the usual resource constraints. The method is appropriate when decision makers wish to optimize several objectives and can specify the necessary weights, and when any other objectives can be treated as resource constraints.

8.2.1. The Nature of the Method. The method is identical to the constrained optimization version (Section 5.2) except for the objective function which is respecified. The procedure is to find the alternatives and associated quantities that maximize

$$\sum_{j=1}^{n} (\text{outcome from alternative } i \text{ for objective } j \times \text{weight } j) \qquad (8.14)$$

for all alternatives, where n is the total number of objectives.

8.2.2. Examples: Air Pollution and Land Use. Using objectives of cash income, quantity of capital assets, and air pollution, Candler (1973) applied the method to a firm. The outcomes of each alternative on the three objectives were scored on a standardized 1-to-100 scale. The weights were the trade-offs, such as those between cash income and decreases in pollution. They were obtained with the methods outlined in Section 6.2.

Thampapillai (1976) applied the method to estimate production possibilities for the two competing objectives of net social benefits (measured in money, as in Chapter 15) and environmental quality. The environmental objective was measured as the money value of recreation (through the travel-cost method of Chapter 16) and the monetary value of preservation (through the land-price method of Chapter 13). The weights on the two kinds of output were varied between 1.0 and 0.0 in a complementary manner. For example, one set of weights was 1.0 for net social benefits and 0.0 for environmental quality. Another was 0.4 for *NSB* and 0.6 for environmental quality. Each program used a different set of weights and provided a different land-use plan (different combinations of activities and quantities). The weights were varied over their entire range to provide a variety of land-use plans for which the decision maker could make his choice.

8.3. Discussion

These two programming methods rest on specific criteria and require more kinds of data than do previous methods. These disadvantages can be offset for goal programming by the way unpriced things are accommodated.

Linear programming with combined optimization embodies a weighted-objective function like the weighted approaches of Section 6 and can incorporate objectives as constraints. The implied criterion may therefore be closer to reality than in the constrained optimization version, and the extra data may be worth collecting.

9. WITH SEQUENTIAL INTERACTION WITH DECISION MAKERS

Various applications of the preceding methods rest on a progressive collection of data from the decision maker. The procedure, as shown in Figure 8.3, recognizes that weights, orderings, and constraints cannot always be elicited at the start, even though they are implicit in the problem. The analyst must make preliminary estimates of the missing data and then revise them through progressive interactions with the decision maker. The decision maker only has to say whether the results are satisfactory or choose a result from a small number presented at each interaction. He does not have to nominate specific weights, goals, orderings, or constraints.

Zionts and Wallenius (1976) apply the additive weighting method of Section 6 interactively. Arbitrary weights provide initial results. These are presented to the decision maker, together with the implied trade-offs between objectives. The decision maker says whether the results and trade-offs are satisfactory and thus indicates the need for and direction of revisions.

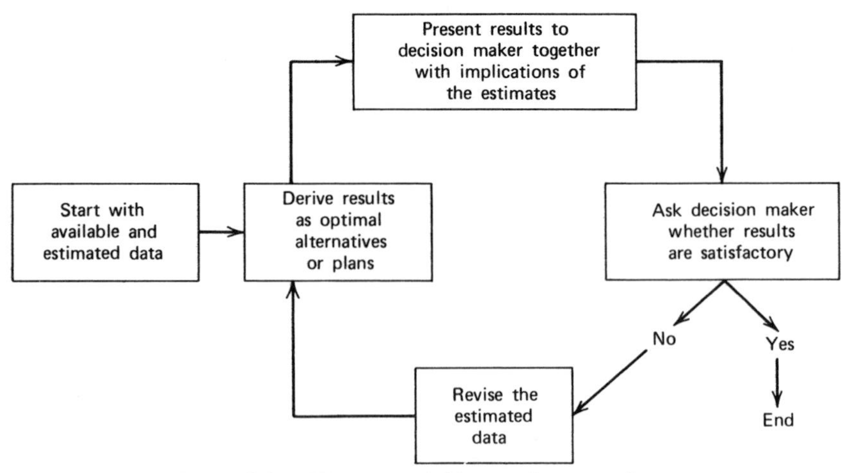

Figure 8.3. The sequential interaction procedure.

Monarchi, Kisiel, and Duckstein (1973) simulated a water use/pollution/production system with multiple objectives. At each interaction the decision maker was asked to name the single, most-important goal, which was then entered in the simulation. This procedure avoided an initial need for a complete ordering of objectives as in goal programming or lexicographic ordering.

Sequential interaction requires that the decision maker respond to concrete situations rather than to the abstract questions of some data-collection method. This should simplify the estimation of data, even though it requires continual access to the decision maker.

10. DISCUSSION

In concluding, we consider the choice of a method and the way the various methods accommodate unpriced things. Information about each method has been summarized in Table 8.4, which forms the basis for this discussion.

10.1. The Choice of a Method

As Cohon and Marks (1975) point out, the selection of a method is itself a multiple-objective decision. Several relevant objectives are included in Table 8.4, and others are now introduced.

An important initial question concerns the existence of any unusual decision criteria. The criteria for the maximin, maximax, and goal-programming methods are unusual in that they do not relate directly to the fundamental notion of value as an aggregate of utilities. All of the other methods rest on this fundamental notion, although they do so in different ways. A decision maker who specified an unusual criterion would use a method suited to it.

Opportunity-cost information is often important to a decision. Few of the methods can provide monetary data on income losses resulting from changes in output or input levels. More of them provide the information in the form of quantitative, nonmonetary trade-offs, as shown in Table 8.4.

Selection of a method also depends on the number of objectives involved. A large number will complicate use of the weighting methods, except perhaps for the electre technique. But a large number does not significantly increase the complexity or workload of the lexicographic, cut-off, or programming methods. As our application to the gorgelands problem shows, at least two of the weighting methods are practical with as many as five objectives.

The decision maker may need to identify an optimal group of projects rather than a single best alternative. All the methods can identify an

Table 8.4. Characteristics of the Multiple-Objective Methods

Method	Has an Unusual Decision Criterion	Provides a Quantitative Index of Comparative Value	Provides Opportunity Costs: In Money	Provides Opportunity Costs: In Other Units	Orders All Alternatives	Requires Quantitative Data for Outcomes	Requires Common, Quantitative Units for Benefits	Can Select an Optimal Package
1	2	3	4	5	6	7	8	9
Analyze a range (2.1)	X	X	√	√	X	√	?	?
Estimate data (2.2)	X	X	√	√	X	√	?	?
Maximin (3.1)	√	X	X	X	X	X	X	X
Maximax (3.2)	√	X	X	X	X	X	X	X
Lexicographic (4)	X	X	X	X	X	X	?	X
Cut-off (5.1)	X	X	X	X	X	X	?	X
Linear programming, constrained optimization (5.2)	X	√	√	√	X	√	√	√
Additive weighting (6.3)	X	√	X	√	√	√	X	X
Multiplicative weighting (6.4)	X	√	X	√	√	√	X	X
Indifference mapping (7.1)	X	X	X	?	√	X	X	X
Benchmark (7.2)	X	√	X	√	√	X	X	X
Electre (7.3)	?	X	X	X	?	X	X	X
Goal programming (8.1)	√	√	?	√	X	√	√	√
Linear programming, combined optimization (8.2)	X	√	√	√	X	√	√	√

Key: √ = Yes, X = no, ? = perhaps, depending on the application and the problem.

optimal alternative, but only some of them can combine alternatives into an optimal package or plan.

MacCrimmon (1973) suggests that methods be combined in the decision process. For example, the cut-off and electre methods can be used to filter out some alternatives. Then the preferred method can be applied, perhaps in a sequential, interactive way, to revise key data items.

10.2 Accommodation of Unpriced Things

The methods differ in their requirements for quantitative or descriptive outcomes and for monetary or nonmonetary benefits. Some, like the programming methods, must convert objectives into goals or constraints, so quantitative measurement is essential (columns 7 and 8, Table 8.4). Others can rest on simple orderings of outcomes by the decision maker, and qualitative descriptions will suffice. The cut-off and lexicographic methods are examples. The weighting methods can also use qualitatively described outcomes, if weights can be elicited for them. Linear programming by constrained optimization, however, seems to be more successful when more outcomes can be specified in money.

CHAPTER 9

Analyses Involving Characteristics of the Environment

A variety of methods have been developed to derive indices of value from measurements of the characteristics of environments. When applied to social problems, these methods have been called "social indicators"; when applied to resource conservation, they are called "scarcity indices" or "uniqueness ratios." The methods have been used to set acquisition priorities on landscapes, wildlife habitats, and river valleys, and to analyze and seek patterns in social disorders.

1. THE GENERAL APPROACH

These methods recognize that utility is a function of the characteristics of a good, activity, or environment. Lancaster (1966) sets out in a formal manner the functional relationships and assumptions underlying this approach. We discussed them in Section 2.1 of Chapter 6. In this chapter we review and illustrate a number of methods that implement this concept of utility and disutility arising from characteristics. These methods apply when the result of a decision will be a change in characteristics. They can be used whenever the characteristics are separable and measurable.

These methods all follow a similar pattern, as shown in Figure 9.1, although they vary in terminology. Cuttance (1974), in a study of poverty, used the terms "dimension" and "domain" where we use "concept" and "characteristic." Dee, Baker, Drobny, Duke, Whitman, and Fahringer (1973) used "category" and "parameter" for our same terms. These differences in terminology are minor. The important differences between the methods are in their procedures for standardizing measurements of and incorporating different weights for each characteristic. These differences are discussed as the chapter proceeds. In this section we summarize the general approach.

1.1. Nominating the Abstraction

The first step is to nominate a grand ideal or abstraction as the goal of policy. Leopold and Marchand (1968), for example, set out to describe the

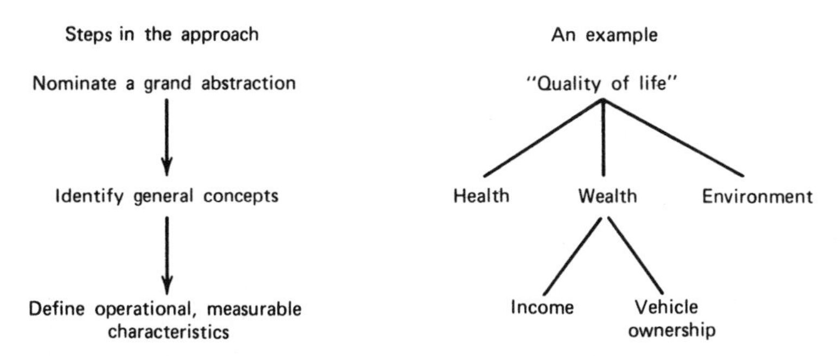

Figure 9.1. The general approach followed by methods involving characteristics of the environment.

factors comprising *social and aesthetic value.* Helliwell (1969) sought a system for comparing the *total benefit* of one wildlife resource with another. Perloff (1969) tried to provide a broad framework for valuing *quality of the urban environment.* The notion of social indicators hinges on the abstract grand ideal of *welfare and better-offness,* as seen in the U.S. Department of Health, Education and Welfare (1969) definition of a social indicator:

> A statistic of direct normative interest which facilitates concise, comprehensive and balanced judgment about the condition of major aspects of a society. It is in all cases a direct measure of welfare and is subject to the interpretation that, if it changes in the "right" direction, while other things remain equal, things have gotten better, or people are "better off."

1.2. Concepts to Capture the Abstraction

The abstraction or grand ideal must next be given a specific measurable identity. Those concepts that appear to capture the abstraction best are listed. For example, in an attempt to capture the abstraction "quality of the urban environment," Perloff (1969) first listed six major concepts: natural environment, spatial environment, transportation-utilities environment, community-neighborhood environment, household shelter, and workplaces. For each of these he listed a number of specific and measurable subconcepts. In the case of natural environment, some of these were the airshed, the watershed, quiet and noise zones, and sunlight exposure.

1.3. Characteristics to Measure the Concepts

The relation between the physical characteristics to be observed and the concepts to be measured must now be carefully identified. For example, in

Perloff's case we may readily acknowledge the airshed as a significant parameter for measuring quality of an urban environment. But air quality is open to a range of interpretations. Should it be operationalized as physical particles, noxious ordors, poisonous gases, reduced visibility, or all of these?

1.4. Numerical Scales to Measure the Characteristics

Developing these scales can be the most objective step so far. The examples in the rest of the chapter will show how various characteristics have been scaled. The scales can range from completely objective measurements, such as height of a waterfall in meters, to subjective rankings, such as "unattractive" versus "beautiful."

1.5. Aggregation of the Characteristics into an Index

This final step involves determining the weights for each characteristic and standardizing the measurements into a single index of value. The analyst's judgment is obviously needed in the selection of weights, but it also enters the method in his selection of a standardization procedure. Figure 9.2 presents a classification and outline of a range of procedures. As we discuss these different procedures in the rest of the chapter we try to indicate the relative effects on the final value index of the different ways in which an analyst's judgment might be incorporated.

The simplest way to aggregate a set of numerical measurements of characteristics would appear to be just to add them up. The impossibility of adding things measured in different units rules this out as a feasible method. But the following example demonstrates two further problems in such addition:

Characteristics	Park A	Park B
Size in acres	1280	2560
Number of lakes	3	1
Number of picnic sites	50	20
Totals	1333	2581

The total scores are clearly not valid evidence that park *B* is more valuable than park *A*. But it is also evident from this example that any characteristics that are measured in large absolute numbers dominate the comparison. Size of park overwhelms the numbers of lakes and picnic sites. If lakes and picnic sites are more important characteristics in determining park value than is size, they could be weighted more heavily in the aggrega-

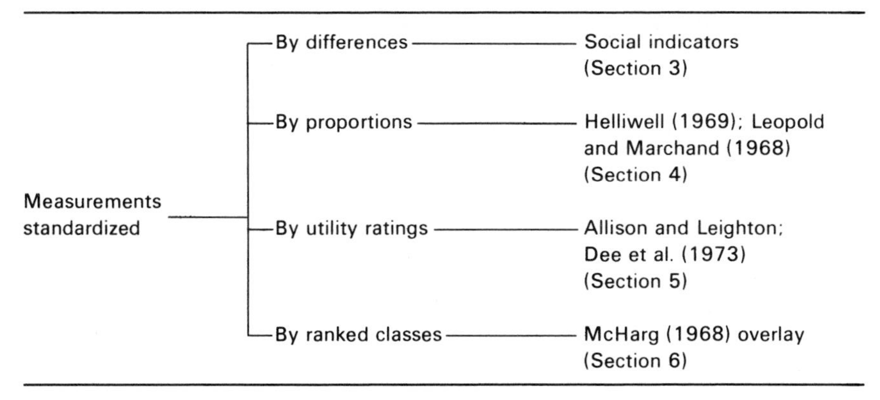

Figure 9.2. The range of methods for deriving a value index from characteristics of the environment.

tion. But even if they were given 10 times as much weight as size, the number of acres is relatively so large that park *B* would still have the larger total.

The second problem is that the rank order of the results obtained by addition may change with a linear transformation of only one variable. For example, if the size of the parks were transformed from acres to square miles, the figures for size would change to 2 for park *A* and 4 for park *B*. The totals would then become 55 for park *A* and 25 for park *B*. A mere change in the units in which one characteristic is measured reverses the apparent comparative values of the two parks.

The methods we present in Sections 3 to 6 are designed to prevent one characteristic from dominating the comparison and to produce rank orders that cannot be changed by simple linear rescaling or transformations.

To provide a base for considering and comparing the methods, we now introduce an actual environmental policy problem and use it in the rest of the chapter. This example provides a realistic theme for illustrating the methods, even though some data in our illustration might be revised in actual application.

2. AN ENVIRONMENTAL POLICY EXAMPLE: IMPROVING THE QUALITY OF LIFE IN AUSTRALIAN COUNTRY TOWNS

The drift of population into large metropolitan centers creates problems for both the expanding metropolis and the declining country towns. Policies for dealing with these problems require some criterion against which various alternatives can be judged. There is a need to measure the effects of broad policies on different areas and the changes such policies would cause over time at individual locations. The yardstick must measure what we call "quality of life." This abstraction consists of many dimensions, which must be judged in some objective, measurable way.

In this chapter we examine the characteristics of 25 country towns in New South Wales. The methods illustrated would apply equally well to cities and, in fact, to any problem where characteristics can be observed and aggregated by an analyst.

2.1. A Sample of Country Towns

The state of New South Wales contains three cities with over 100,000 population, which form a continuous urban strip along the coast and are not included in our study. This leaves 25 country towns which had populations over 8000 in 1971. All of them are included in the analysis. They range in size from Muswellbrook with 8100 people to Cessnock with 35,000. Because data were available for only one time period, comparisons were made between towns at one time rather than for one town at different times.

2.2. Nominating the Grand Abstraction

Our study concerns the quality of life in specific country towns. One difficulty with this abstraction is the data base. Towns are not, in themselves, ideal units for this sort of analysis, because the statistics ignore conditions in surrounding rural areas and in centers of less than 8000 population. However, the towns are the focus of schemes for locating new industries and tertiary institutions. In any event, data are not available for regional variations.

Another difficulty with this abstraction and the intertown analysis concerns aggregation. Quality of life is a personal concept and can be expected to vary widely between individuals. But an analysis of variations among towns requires the aggregation of data into town-size social groups. We would like to determine the aggregate utility obtained by each town from all priced and unpriced goods and services consumed in a given time period. Data for all individuals in all 25 towns are expensive to collect and pose problems of sampling and aggregation. However, these is consensus on the specific qualities of towns that should be observed, reviewed, and improved, so we focus on these qualities.

2.3. Capturing the Abstraction in Concepts

Quality of life has many facets, and a wide range of concepts must be recognized. Because people require a reasonable standard of living, an income or wealth concept is necessary. Adequate housing should be available. Families should be stable, with few broken homes, and there should be high levels of public safety, law, and order. These facets of social order are both important and hard to measure. There should be adequate employment opportunities and access to a pleasant natural environment. The whole population should have access to health and education services and recreational, cultural, and leisure opportunities. In summary, the general concepts needed to capture the abstraction "quality of life" appear to be:

Growth

Income and wealth

Housing

Social order and condition

Employment

Natural environment

Health and education services

Recreational, cultural, and leisure opportunities.

The difficulties in defining and agreeing on the nature of these concepts are obvious, but they do provide a basis for making the abstraction "quality of life" operational. In the next section they are converted as far as possible into measurable characteristics.

2.4. Making the Concepts Measurable through Characteristics

The definition of the concepts is difficult enough, but the analyst's problem is compounded by the need to convert them into measurable characteristics. These difficulties face any planner for any policy problem. This discussion of the 25 Australian towns can give some idea of how they can be faced and possibly solved, or at least circumvented.

Australian data on incomes are completely lacking below the state level. However, three reasonable surrogates are available on a town basis: value of retail sales, wages and salaries in manufacturing, and motor-vehicle ownership. These are shown in Table 9.1, along with two characteristics to measure growth.

Table 9.1. **Operational Characteristics for Quality-of-Life Concepts**

Key	Concepts and Characteristics	Direction of Contribution	Source of Data
Growth			
K_1	Annual rate of population growth, percent per year, 1966–1971	+	2
K_2	Total value of all new buildings in 1971–1972, $ million	+	2
Income and wealth			
K_3	Value of reatil sales, $ per capita in 1968–1969	+	2
K_4	Wages and salaries in manufacturing, $ per employee in 1969–1970	+	2
K_5	Percentage of private dwellings with motor vehicles	+	1
Housing			
K_6	Average rent per furnished private house, $ per week, 1971	–	1
K_7	Percentage of all dwellings on a sewer line, 1971	+	1
K_8	Property tax per private dwelling, $ per house 1971	–	2
Social organization			
K_9	Percentage of population born in Australia, 1971	+	1
K_{10}	Percentage of 1971 population residing in the town in 1966	+	1
K_{11}	Percentage of population who classify themselves as Church of England, 1971	+	1
Employment			
K_{12}	Percentage of labor force unemployed, 1971	–	1
K_{13}	Percentage of labor force in mining, 1971	–	1
K_{14}	Percentage of labor force in manufacturing, 1971	+	1
Natural environment			
K_{15}	Distance of town from nearest beach, miles	–	
K_{16}	Ranking of variety of natural resources, 1 worst to 5 best	+	
K_{17}	Number of rainy days 1968, deviation from Armidale with direction of deviation ignored	–	3
K_{18}	Maximum temperature (F°), deviation from Armidale, sign ignored	–	3, 4
K_{19}	Minimum temperature (F°), deviation from Armidale, sign ignored	–	3, 4

Sources. 1. Commonwealth Bureau of Census and Statistics, 1973. Census of Population and Housing, 30 June 1971. Bulletin 7. Characteristics of the population and dwellings, local government areas. Part 1. New South Wales.

2. Handbook of local statistics. Commonwealth Bureau of Census and Statics, 1973. New South Wales.

3. Commonwealth Bureau of Statistics, 1970. New South Wales, Statistical Register, Rural Industries and Settlement and Meteorology 1967–1968, and 1968–1969. Data from p. 182.

4. Extreme of all years recorded up to 1968.

Numerous data are available for the housing and employment concepts, but the analyst must exercise judgment in selecting the relevant characteristics. We restricted employment data to three characteristics: level of unemployment, percentage of labor force in mining, and percentage of labor force in manufacturing.

Characteristics may contribute in a negative or positive way to quality of life, as shown by the housing characteristics. Rents and property taxes have been assigned a negative weight, because increases in them have unfavorable effects on residents. The percentage of houses on sewer lines indicates something about the quality of living conditions.

Australian data on social order and health are lacking on a town basis. There are no published figures on legal convictions, disease outbreaks, and mental or physical health. This lack of data is a difficulty, but general observation suggests that variation in these factors is low among these 25 towns. The big variation in these characteristics is between metropolis and country towns rather than among individual towns (Stillwell, 1974). Three characteristics of the population that appear to be good indicators of social order and condition are included in Table 9.1.

Reliable statistics on recreational, cultural, and leisure opportunities are also unavailable. These presumably vary among towns and perhaps are correlated with some of the other characteristics shown in Table 9.1. One item—distance from nearest beach—is included with characteristics of the natural environment. Other than that, it appears best not to try to make this concept operational here.

Quality of life is strongly affected by the natural environment. Cleanliness of the air, diversity of available surroundings, and climate all affect an individual's sense of well-being. Five characteristics were selected to allow for these factors. Distance from the beach was given a negative weight to accommodate the Australian penchant for beach recreation. We also included a diversity index (1 to 5) based on our own judgment of the local natural environment.

For the climatic data, number of rainy days was used instead of amount of rainfall because it reflects humidity and inconvenience as well as amount of rain. At the bottom of the scale—few rainy days per year—more rain would be desirable, but at the top—many rainy days—less would be better. In terms of effect on quality of life, an arithmetic scale of rainy days is not acceptable, because the sign would have to be reversed about halfway up the scale. For our purpose, we arbitrarily adopted a "perfect climate" and recorded deviations from this for number of rainy days, maximum temperature, and minimum temperature. The town selected was Armidale with 116 rainy days per year. Any deviation above or below this level was considered undesirable, and the rainy-days characteristic was therefore negatively weighted. To avoid division by zero in the subsequent methods, Armidale's deviation from the optimum is recorded as 1.

2.5. Deriving a Set of Weights

The three items of information needed for these methods are raw data on characteristics, a set of weights, and a method for standardization and aggregation. The weights are derived in this section. Then the methods are described in Sections 3 to 6, whereas Section 7 discusses them.

The problem is to assign each of the 19 characteristics a weight to reflect its relative importance. In an actual decision situation, information for these weights must be obtained from the decision makers or from the people affected by the decision. Purely for illustrative purposes, we have arbitrarily

Table 9.2. Relative Weights for the Characteristics of Country Towns

Characteristic	Total Weight per Group	Weight per Characteristic[a]
Growth	15	
K_1		+10
K_2		+ 5
Income and wealth	20	
K_3		+ 6
K_4		+ 6
K_5		+ 8
Housing	25	
K_6		− 7
K_7		+11
K_8		− 7
Social organization	5	
K_9		+ 1
K_{10}		+ 3
K_{11}		+ 1
Employment	20	
K_{12}		−15
K_{13}		− 4
K_{14}		+ 1
Natural environment	15	
K_{15}		− 2
K_{16}		+ 4
K_{17}		− 5
K_{18}		− 2
K_{19}		− 2
Totals	100	100[b]

[a] With direction from Table 9.1.
[b] Ignoring sign.

assigned weights that we think are reasonable approximations of those that might be allocated by a state planner.

Using the allocation of percentage ratings method, which is described in Chapter 11, we divided 100 points among all the characteristics. Because 19 variables are too many to handle mentally in one allocation, we proceeded in two steps. First, the 100 points were distributed among the six groups of characteristics, as shown in column 2 of Table 9.2. This requires only a judgment about the relative importance of the major kinds of characteristics. Second, the total points for each group were divided among the characteristics within that group.

2.6. Some Observations Thus Far

Two things seem clear from this first stage of problem formulation and data collection.

Data omissions can be especially important with these methods. The true nature of the abstraction may depend as much on the characteristics that are omitted as on those that are measured. The data in this example seem reasonable for the physical and financial needs of people in the towns, but they ignore various psychological characteristics that must affect the quality of life, however it is defined.

The direction of the contribution of each characteristic will vary with the particular decision problems. The desirability of any given characteristic will also vary with the decision makers. For example, a person planning to construct and rent housing will normally regard high rents as desirable, but a family seeking a place to live will hold the opposite view.

3. STANDARDIZED DIFFERENCE METHODS

Rankings by the simple addition of characteristics are sensitive to variation in the units of any one characteristic, as we saw in Section 1.5. This difficulty can be overcome by converting the basic data into standardized scores. One such method is based on differences and standard deviations. Each characteristic is considered in turn. The difference between the observed measurement of that characteristic for each individual town and the mean for all towns is calculated. This difference is divided by the standard deviation of the towns from their mean. In application to problems of the urban environment, the resulting number has been called a "Z-score":

$$Z_{ij} = \frac{K_{ij} - \bar{K}_j}{SD_j} \tag{9.1}$$

where Z_{ij} is the Z-score of town i for characteristic j, K_{ij} is the observed

Table 9.3. Measurement of Characteristics for the Town of Albury with Means and Standard Deviations for All 25 Towns[a]

Characteristics		Albury	All 25 Towns: Mean	All 25 Towns: Standard Deviation
K_1	% population growth	2.5	2.2	1.9
K_3	Value retail sales ($/capita)	1421.0	1180.2	270.6
K_6	Average rent ($/week)	17.1	16.2	2.7
K_{12}	% unemployed	2.1	1.9	0.6
K_{16}	Variety of natural resources (rank)	3.0	3.6	1.1
K_{19}	Minimum temperature (deviation)	6.0	6.2	4.4

[a] Only part of the 19 characteristics are shown.

measurement of town i for characteristic j, $\bar{K}_j$ is the mean of characteristic j for all towns, and SD_j is the standard deviation from the mean of characteristic j for all towns.

This procedure overcomes the basic difficulty by eliminating the units of the scale. Z-scores of various characteristics can be added because they are all expressed in terms of standard deviations from their means. A decision rule of the following sort could be based on the results: Select or emulate that town which has the highest positive Z-score (number of standard deviations above the mean of all towns).

This kind of method is known as a "social indicator" in the urban literature. These indicators have been widely used to compare social well-being, or the quality of life, in different areas. They are well suited to analysis of the kind of policy problem we are using as our example.

3.1. The Unweighted Additive Social-Indicator Method

The simplest of these methods is the unweighted additive model. The procedure is as follows, using the town of Albury as an example (some of the 19 characteristics are shown in Table 9.3):

(a) Observe the numerical level of a given characteristic K_j for a given town. For K_1 (population growth) for Albury we have 2.5.

(b) Observe the mean ($\bar{K}_j$) and standard deviation (SD_j) for the characteristic for all towns. For K_1 we have a mean of 2.2 and a standard deviation of 1.9.

(c) Calculate the Z-score for each characteristic. For K_1 and Albury this is

$$Z_{ij} = \frac{K_{ij} - \bar{K}_j}{SD_j} = \frac{2.5 - 2.2}{1.9} = 0.158$$

The Z-scores of Albury for part of the 19 characteristics are shown in Table 9.4. They are separated into positive and negative characteristics in conformance with Table 9.1. The signs in Table 9.4 indicate the direction of the deviation from the mean.

(**d**) Aggregate the Z-scores of all the characteristics for each town. Because no weights are used in this method, the Z scores are just added. This is the quality-of-life score for our country towns example:

$$\text{quality-of-life rating for town } i = \sum_{j=1}^{n} Z_{ij} \qquad (9.2)$$

The calculation of the score for Albury, as shown in Table 9.4, is $(+1.650 - 4.071) = -2.421$.

Of the 25 towns in the example, the one with the highest quality-of-life score by the unweighted additive, social-indicator method is Taree, with a score of 5.8, and the one with the lowest score is Broken Hill, with a score of −18.8. The five towns with the highest scores and the five with the lowest are shown in Table 9.5. The scores of these 10 towns in their respective order in Table 9.5 are: 5.8, 5.3, 5.0, 4.9, 4.6; −4.0, −4.3, −4.5, −8.3, −18.8.

3.2. The Weighted Additive, Social-Indicator Method

In the preceding method, each characteristic was weighted equally. Another version of this method is to assign different weights to each characteristic, as follows:

$$\text{quality-of-life rating for town } i = \sum_{j=1}^{n} (WT_j \times Z_{ij}) \qquad (9.3)$$

where WT_j is the weight assigned to characteristic j.

Table 9.4. Calculation of Quality-of-Life Scores for Albury by the Standardized Difference Methods[a]

Positive Characteristics				Negative Characteristics			
K_j	Z_i	WT_j	$Z_j \times WT_j$	K_j	Z_j	WT_j	$Z_j \times WT_j$
K_1	0.158	10	1.580	K_6	0.333	7	2.331
K_3	0.890	6	5.340	K_{12}	0.333	15	4.995
K_9	−0.232	1	−0.232	K_{19}	−0.045	2	−0.090
K_{16}	−0.545	4	−2.180				
Totals	+1.650[b]		+13.948[c]		+4.071[b]		+22.050[c]

[a] Only part of the 19 characteristics are shown. Totals refer to all 19 characteristics.
[b] The total unweighted score is derived as follows: 1.650 − 4.071 = −2.421.
[c] The total weighted score is derived as follows: 13.948 − 22.050 = −8.102.

Table 9.5. A Summary of the Rankings of the Top and Bottom Five Towns by Six Methods of Analysis

	Social Indicators					
Rank	Simple	Weighted	Helliwell Unweighted	Helliwell Weighted	Leopold Weighted	McHarg Overlay
1	Taree	Queanbeyan	Orange	Queanbeyan	Queanbeyan	Taree
2	Orange	Muswellbrook	Queanbeyan	Armidale	Muswellbrook	Orange
3	Maitland	Taree	Armidale	Muswellbrook	Maitland	Maitland
4	Queanbeyan	Maitland	Goulburn	Orange	Goulburn	Queanbeyan
5	Grafton	Armidale	Maitland	Goulburn	Armidale Lismore	Grafton Goulburn
21	Dubbo	Dubbo	Cessnock	Dubbo	Inverell	[a]
22	Cessnock	Cessnock	Parkes	Shellharbour	Cessnock	Moree
23	Shellharbour	Shellharbour	Dubbo	Cessnock	Kempsey	Albury
24	Moree	Moree	Moree	Moree	Broken Hill	Cessnock
25	Broken Hill	Broken Hill	Broken Hill	Broken Hill	Moree	Broken Hill

[a] The 21st position has been left blank because the 19th position is occupied by three towns—Lithgow, Parkes, and Wagga.

Table 9.6. The Top and Bottom Towns as Ranked in Concept Groups by the Weighted Social-Indicator Method[a]

	Growth	Wealth	Housing	Social Condition	Employment	Natural Environment
Rank	K_1 and K_2	K_3 to K_5	K_6 to K_8	K_9 to K_{11}	K_{12} to K_{14}	K_{15} to K_{19}
1	Shellharbour	Queanbeyan	Casino	Lithgow	Lithgow	Armidale
2	Port Macquarie	Tamworth	Grafton	Maitland	Muswellbrook	Lismore
3	Queanbeyan	Inverell	Lithgow	Broken Hill	Maitland	Kempsey
4	Albury	Taree	Taree	Grafton	Goulburn	Taree
5	Armidale	Gunnedah	Maitland	Kempsey	Queanbeyan	Goulburn
21	Kempsey	Casino	Moree	Wagga	Cessnock	Parkes
22	Cessnock	Dubbo	Albury	Shellharbour	Inverell	Cessnock
23	Grafton	Lithgow	Port Macquarie	Port Macquarie	Broken Hill	Dubbo
24	Broken Hill	Shellharbour	Dubbo	Armidale	Kempsey	Moree
25	Lithgow	Cessnock	Shellharbour	Queanbeyan	Moree	Broken Hill

[a] The ranking is based on the sums of the weighted Z-scores for the characteristics included in each concept group.

The procedure is much the same as for the previous method, but after the Z-scores have been calculated, they are multiplied by their weights (from Table 9.2) and then aggregated. These three steps are shown for some of the characteristics for Albury in Table 9.4.

Albury receives a score of −8.10 by the weighted method, compared with −2.42 by the unweighted method. The important question, however, is how Albury compares with the other towns. The town with the highest quality-of-life rating by the weighted method was Queanbeyan, with a score of 60.4, and the one with the lowest rating was again Broken Hill, with a score of −76.2. The five towns with the highest scores and the five with the lowest are shown in Table 9.5. Those with the lowest ratings scored in the same order by both methods. At the upper end of the scale, however, not only did the order change but also the towns.

3.3. Should There be a Value Index for the Grand Abstraction or For Each Concept?

The rankings of Table 9.5 are based on aggregates of all 19 characteristics. These broad aggregates provide acceptable rankings when all characteristics are traded-off or considered together, but they can disguise important variations. In a similar sort of analysis, Cuttance (1974) reported social indicators by concepts such as wealth, housing, and the environment. Table 9.6 shows the top and bottom five towns as they rank according to the major concepts. Queanbeyan is at the top of the weighted-aggregate quality list in Table 9.5 but at the bottom in terms of the social-condition concept. Armidale also is in the top five in aggregate score but in the bottom five on social condition.

An analyst needs the overall grand abstraction score for policy purposes. But listing scores by concept may provide much extra information.

4. STANDARDIZED PROPORTION METHODS

Raw data must be standardized to overcome the problems involved in adding absolute numbers. The methods in this section do this through some form of proportional transformation. Numerical measurements are compared to a standard and then expressed as proportions of that standard.

4.1. Proportion of a Best Observed Level

The basic idea of this method is to use as a standard the best level of each characteristic that is observed among the alternatives being considered. The levels of this characteristic for the other alternatives are then converted to proportions of this best level, and the resulting figures for all characteristics are aggregated to give a total score for the alternative.

4.1.1. Helliwell's Conservation Value. Conservationists tend to place higher values on rare species of plants and animals than on common ones. Helliwell (1974a) translated this axiom into a quantitative criterion for wildlife preservation decisions by proposing that the following index be used to compare alternative sites:

$$\text{conservation value} = \frac{(\text{no. of individuals of a species at site})^{\text{const}}}{(\text{no. of ind. of species in whole country})^{\text{const}}} \tag{9.4}$$

where const is a constant 0.36.

A site that contains all known individuals of a species will have a conservation value of 1.0. One that contains 1000 individuals out of a total population of 10,000 will have a conservation value of

$$\frac{(1000)^{0.36}}{(10{,}000)^{0.36}} = \frac{12}{27.5} = 0.436$$

Following the logic of the criterion, the first site has a higher value and should be preserved in preference to the second.

In comparisons of the occurrence of plant species at different locations in Britain, Helliwell (1974a, b) used the occurrence of a species (yes/no) within 10-kilometer quadrats to derive an estimate of the total number of the species, thus avoiding the need to actually count individuals. Helliwell's value index provides a good example of a proportion method where the weighting procedure is based on the analyst's judgment. It was used to assess priorities for preservation between various areas in Britain.

4.1.2. Application to the Country-Towns Example. The notion of a conservation value, and its associated criterion, has obvious general relevance for preservation problems. But how might one adapt this index of scarcity to fit a situation of abundance or one of quality? The ratio really measures the proportion of some total number of things that a particular alternative provides. We can restructure this notion by rewriting the basic ratio for any alternative i as follows

$$\begin{array}{l}\text{quality score of}\\ \text{characteristic } j\end{array} = \frac{\text{observed level of } j \text{ in alternative } i}{\text{maximum level of } j \text{ in any of the alternatives}} \tag{9.5}$$

For example, the maximum level of characteristic K_2, total value of all new building construction, occurred in Albury (\$10.3 million). This is the maximum level that can be expected to occur. The level of K_2 for Armidale was $5.5 million, or 53.4 percent of the maximum level. The quality rating of Armidale on this characteristic is 0.534 compared to a rating of 1.000 for Albury.

The general idea in application is to calculate the percentage of desirability for each characteristic and to aggregate these percentages. We are thus comparing actual levels of occurrence against the maximum attainable in the sample.

The unweighted procedure for the proportion of best level method is as follows:

(**a**) Take the observed level of the first characteristic (K_1 percent population growth). For Albury this was 2.5.

(**b**) Take the maximum level that this characteristic reaches in any of the towns. This was 7.2 in Shellharbour.

(**c**) Calculate the proportion that Albury is of the maximum: 0.347.

(**d**) Add up the proportions for all characteristics for the particular town, remembering that the contribution of some is positive and that of others negative (Table 9.1). The total for Albury was +3.189.

(**e**) Divide the aggregate (+3.189) by the number of characteristics (19). This gives a score of 0.168 for Albury.

The town with the highest quality-of-life score by this method was Orange with 0.265 and the one with the lowest score was Broken Hill with −0.059. The towns with the five highest and five lowest ratings by this unweighted procedure are shown in Table 9.5.

The weighted procedure is the same as the unweighted one for the first three steps. Then the proportion determined in step c is multiplied by the weight assigned to the particular characteristic (Table 9.2). Because characteristic K_1 was assigned a weight of +10, this gives a weighted figure of 3.47 for Albury. The figures for all characteristics are then aggregated as in step d, giving a total of +12.964 for Albury, and again divided by 19. The final weighted score for Albury was 0.68.

The town with the highest quality-of-life score by the weighted method was Queanbeyan with 1.32 and the one with the lowest score was Broken Hill with −0.28. The towns with the five highest and five lowest ratings by this method are shown in Table 9.5.

4.2. Proportion of a Target Level

This method uses a target level as the standard for each characteristic. The observed levels of the characteristics are converted to proportions of these target levels, and the resulting figures for all characteristics are aggregated to give a total score for each alternative.

4.2.1. The ORAQI Index of Air Quality. The Oak Ridge air quality index (ORAQI) is an example of this method (Babcock and Nagda, 1972). The concentrations of five air pollutants are measured and compared to federal standards, or targets, as follows:

$$\text{ORAQI} = \left(5.7 \sum_{j=1}^{5} \frac{K_j}{TK_j}\right)^{1.37} \qquad (9.6)$$

where K_j is the concentration of pollutant j, TK_j is the target for pollutant j, and the scaling factors 5.7 and 1.37 set the index at 10 for unpolluted and 100 for completely polluted on all five characteristics.

The general suitability of this method for comparative valuations of environmental situations lies in the use of nominated targets and the standardization and aggregation of field observations.

4.2.2. Leopold's Index of Resource Scarcity. Leopold and Marchand (1968) present a methodology to "record the presence or absence of chosen factors that contribute to aesthetic worth." Their general procedure is identical with that for the other methods in this chapter. Their abstraction of aesthetic worth is broken down into three concepts: physical and chemical character, biological character, and human use and interest. These concepts are in turn broken down into a total of 32 characteristics.

The basic data are measurements of each characteristic for each site being considered. A set of weights could readily be used, but Leopold and Marchand do not, thereby implying equal weight for all characteristics.

The Uniqueness Ratio as a Scarcity Index. The authors set up a target for each characteristic. They then ask: How close is the level of each characteristic on each site to the target? Leopold and Marchand postulate that to be truly worth preserving, a characteristic should be unique. Their criterion of value is frequency of occurrence, with a target of uniqueness (a frequency of 1). The data on characteristics show the number of times each characteristic occurs in all the sites being considered. If this number is 1, the uniqueness ratio is $1 \div 1 = 1$; if it is 2, the ratio for this characteristic is 0.5. The decision criterion proposed is to select those sites that have the most nearly unique characteristics.

4.2.3. Application to the Country-Towns Example. The general relevance of this method lies in the use of a target level for each characteristic. Leopold and Marchand were interested in testing sites against a criterion of uniqueness and therefore set the target levels for each characteristic at one occurrence over all sites. But other target levels can also be used, including different targets for each characteristic, as we saw in the ORAQI index. The general principle can therefore be readily applied to problems like our country-towns example.

A target level was selected for each of the country-town characteristics. To save space, we do not list all these targets, but some examples are: 2 percent population growth for K_1, 95 percent of all dwellings on sewer lines for K_7, and 0.5 percent of labor force unemployed for K_{12}. The actual level of each characteristic in each town was then divided by the target level. For characteristic K_1, Albury had a population growth rate of 2.5 percent for a ratio of 1.25. The ratio of each characteristic was multiplied by its weight from Table 9.2, making Albury's ratio 12.5. The weighted ratios of all characteristics were then aggregated and divided by 19, giving a final score of -1.98 for Albury.

The town with the highest score by this method was Queanbeyan (0.5) and that with the lowest was Moree (-5.0). The five highest-ranking and five lowest-ranking towns are shown in Table 9.5. Because the towns tended to exceed the targets for the negative characteristics more than those for the positive characteristics, all the final scores had a negative sign except that for Queanbeyan, the top-ranked town. This is an artifact of the levels at which the targets were set and does not affect comparisons among the towns.

5. STANDARDIZATION BY UTILITY RATINGS

The methods presented in Section 4 use objective procedures to convert observed levels of characteristics to standardized proportions. In this section we consider two methods that use a more subjective procedure. They both convert measurements of the characteristics to utility ratings on a given scale. The first method has a continuous scale of 0 to 1.0, similar to the scale of 0 to 100 used by the scoring method, which we describe in Chapter 10. The second method has a scale consisting of four points—poor, fair, good, and excellent. The points can be given numerical ratings of, say, 5, 10, 15, and 20. These two methods are more subjective than those of Section 4 because the analyst is responsible for rating the measurements as well as selecting the characteristics to be measured.

5.1. An Environmental Impact Index

Dee, Baker, Drobny, Duke, Whitman, and Fahringer (1973) set out a methodology for evaluating the environmental impacts of water-resource development. Their work is representative of a number of methods of environmental impact analysis that rely on observation of physical characteristics and on weighting and aggregation procedures of varying complexity.

The grand abstraction is environmental impact. This is broken down into 18 concepts, which range from water pollution and noise pollution to a historical package. Each of the concepts is in turn subdivided into characteristics. The noise-pollution concept has only one characteristic, noise, but the water-pollution concept has 14, including temperature and dissolved oxygen content. These characteristics are all directly measurable.

The procedure is as follows:

(**a**) Each of the characteristics at a given site i is measured in physical terms.

(**b**) The analyst postulates a relationship between each characteristic and a utility scale. Figure 9.3 illustrates a relationship for dissolved oxygen.

(**c**) The measurement of each characteristic j is converted to a utility rating. On Figure 9.3 the measurement for dissolved oxygen at site i (K_{ij}) is read from the curve as 0.3.

(**d**) A set of weights is obtained similar to that in Table 9.2.

(**e**) The utility ratings for all characteristics are multiplied by their respective weights and aggregated to give an environmental impact score for the water resource being evaluated.

Dee, Baker, Drobny, Duke, Whitman, and Fahringer acknowledge that the scores or comparative values by themselves are rather meaningless. For

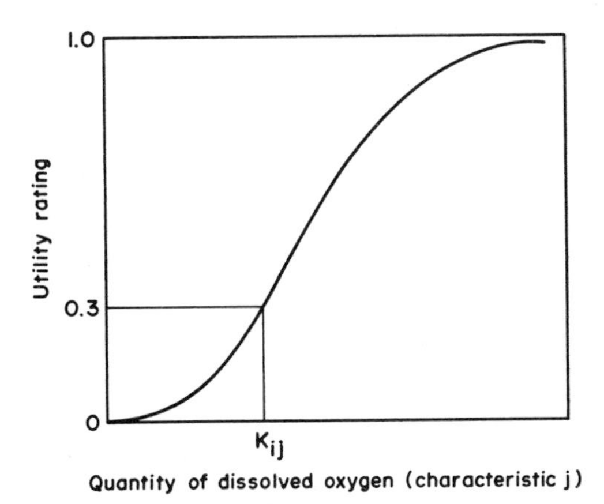

Figure 9.3. Conversion of measurements of dissolved oxygen to utility ratings. (After Dee et al., 1973.)

policy purposes, the scores must be put into some problem comparison. Dee et al. therefore suggest that the environmental impact of an expected change or proposed project be measured as the difference between the environmental impact scores (*EIS*) before and after the decision:

$$\text{environmental impact} = EIS \text{ after} - EIS \text{ before} \qquad (9.7)$$

If the environmental impact score, or comparative value, would increase as a result of the decision, the decision would be desirable.

5.2. The New Hampshire Resource-Success Index

Despite the natural beauty of New Hampshire, some forest campgrounds have been little used. Allison and Leighton (undated) suggest that improper selection of the site or natural-resource base is a key reason. They propose a numerical system based on environmental characteristics to value prospective sites for campground use.

The basis of their grading system is shown in Table 9.7. They observe and measure 42 physical and socioeconomic characteristics, such as available facilities, ease of access, and distance from urban centers. The procedure for a given site is to consider each site characteristic, such as size of water resource (K_1 in Table 9.7), observe its level at the site in question, and note from Table 9.7 the utility rating for this level. If the site has a lake of 200 acres, it represents an excellent level and receives a score of 20

Table 9.7. The New Hampshire System for Rating Campground Quality

	Characteristics	Excellent		Poor	
K_1	Size of water resource	Lake, over 200 acres	20	Small pond or stream	5
⋮			⋮		⋮
K_4	Water-depth fluctuation	Under 1 foot	20	Over 4 feet	5
⋮			⋮		⋮
K_{22}	Air drainage	No severe thunderstorm	20	Many severe thunderstorms	5
⋮			⋮		⋮
K_{42}	Fireplace wood	Free or service charge	15	None available	5

Source. Condensed from Allison and Leighton (undated). The original table shows 42 characteristics and also has columns for "good" and "fair" ratings.

points. The scores of all 42 characteristics are aggregated and compared with the overall rating standards provided. For example, if a site has a total score of 285 it is deemed a poor site. A total score of 600 or over is deemed excellent overall. The site with the highest score is the most desirable.

The method standardizes measurements for characteristics through utility ratings and compares existing conditions between sites or with the ideal conditions. It implicitly calculates the ratio of actual level to ideal level and is a kind of index of proportional achievement, like Helliwell's conservation value. This ratio is combined with the planner's judgment about what is excellent, good, fair, and poor and is expressed as the numerical scores of Table 9.7. For example, an excellent size of water resource scores 20 points, whereas a poor size scores only 5 points. Weighting is incorporated within characteristics by converting physical measurements to index scores and is also applied in the more usual way between characteristics. For example, in the case of K_{42}, an excellent availability of firewood scores only 15, not 20. The weights are incorporated through the planner's judgment and expressed in the utility rating per characteristic per site and not as a measurement per characteristic.

Because the principle is identical with that of Helliwell's method, the two methods can be expected to produce the same rank order if the same weights are used. The New Hampshire method, however, converts a measurement of each characteristic to a utility rating and aggregates these ratings rather than the standardized measurements. This is an advantage in that it readily allows for subjective qualitative measurements. For example, characteristic K_{21} concerns the abundance of wildlife, which can be very difficult to record. In the New Hampshire system this is measured only as abundant, fairly abundant, seldom seen, or rarely seen, and numerical scores are applied directly to these qualitative records.

6. STANDARDIZATION BY RANKED CLASSES

Standardization converts measurements on different scales to equivalent measurements on a common standard scale. The methods that use differences (Section 3) and proportions (Section 4) completely standardize onto a continuous scale. The method to be described in this section allocates a measurement to one of a number of ranked classes. Because this common scale consists of discrete points, the standardization is only partial. Nevertheless, the method may have wide potential, and we develop it from one of its popular forms—the McHarg overlay approach. Measurements are allocated to classes on the scale with explicit judgments about their utility relative to the common scale. This development with explicit judgments and a common scale overcomes the objections we raised in Section 5.4 of Chapter 5 to McHarg's original approach.

In McHarg's (1968) method each characteristic is divided into three classes: good, medium, or poor. For a geographical policy problem such as the location of an expressway, a map overlay is prepared for each characteristic. The overlay is left transparent for good, lightly shaded for medium, and heavily shaded for poor levels of the characteristic. Then the characteristics are aggregated by placing the overlays on top of each other. The regions that have the lightest overall shading are "best," and those that have the heaviest shading are "worst". The method thus provides ways to aggregate characteristics by combining overlays and to standardize data by grouping it into three classes.

We now apply this method in a modified form to the country-towns example.

Each of the 19 characteristics of Table 9.1 was considered and the measurements were divided into three classes: good, medium, and poor. The class limits were based on standard deviations, as in the social-indicator method of Section 3. Any measurements of more than one standard deviation above the mean were classed "good," and any of more than one standard deviation below the mean were classed "poor." Any measurements within one standard of the mean were classed "medium." The classes were scored 1 for good, 2 for medium, and 3 for poor.

The measurements for each characteristic for each town were scored 1, 2, or 3, and the scores were aggregated for each town. The lowest aggregate score indicates the best town. The equivalent of McHarg's transparent overlay (i.e., a town with a good score for every characteristic) is indicated by a score of 19. A score of 38 indicates a town of medium quality. The lowest score was 32 for Taree. The top six and bottom four towns are shown in Table 9.5.

The outstanding feature of this example is the extremely close results obtained by this method and the unweighted social-indicator method (Table 9.5). Neither method incorporates weights (or more precisely, both methods imply a unit weight for all characteristics). Both use the same standardization procedure with standard deviations, so the similarity is logical. The McHarg method apparently offers little new as far as decisions are concerned, but it does offer a convenient way to display data.

7. DISCUSSION OF THE METHODS: QUANTITATIVE CONCEPTS OF "GOOD" AND "BAD"

All the methods of this chapter incorporate quantitative judgments of goodness in the standardization as well as in the weights. The influence of the weights is readily recognized and acknowledged, but the influence of the standardization procedure is less obvious. In view of the differences in the ranking of towns by the different methods, even when the weights and other data are identical (Table 9.5), these judgments are important and should be acknowledged. In this section we consider the judgments involved in the choice of a method and a standardization procedure.

When should a town be considered of substandard quality? Cuttance (1974) argues, in the context of urban poverty, that a city needs treatment if it falls below one standard deviation less than the mean. The subjectivity involved in setting such limits is usually readily acknowledged. It is minimized in the social-indicator approach by first defining each characteristic in quantitatively measurable terms.

Cuttance attempted to measure family living standards in New Zealand and Australia. He selected the three concepts of clothing, social health, and accommodation to capture the grand abstraction "quality of urban life." Characteristics were chosen to represent each concept, and these were measured for each family. The measurements were standardized by the method of ranked classes (Section 6). The classes were scored from 1 to 5, and the scores for each characteristic were aggregated for each family up to the concept level, as in Table 9.6.

The means and standard deviations of the aggregate scores for each concept were then determined for each family in the sample. These provide the data to implement a definition of poverty. Families are judged to be impoverished if they have a significantly lower score on any one of the three concepts than the population as a whole. "Significant" is defined as more than one standard deviation below the mean. Cuttance makes no special case for the use of one standard deviation. This is not a direct indication of poverty as such, but it provides a statistically stable tool to measure differences in the social characteristics.

This indicator of quality is internally determined from the data in the method, and no objective external standards are used. It is not suitable for environmental studies that try to isolate unique or special areas from a whole population. But it is sensitive to the range of characteristics within the population. A wide variation in accommodations or health will show up as a high standard deviation, and the method will thus allow for the existing range of living standards and inequalities.

The standardized proportion methods introduce specific notions of goodness. Helliwell (1969) takes as his standard for preservation the best possible occurrence of a species. The ORAQI index and Leopold and Marchand's (1968) uniqueness ratio set targets against which things can be compared. The environmental impact assessment procedure (Dee et al., 1973) introduces a utility scale of 0 to 1 against which each characteristic is measured. These different approaches to standardization lead to different rankings, as we see in Table 9.5.

The standardized-proportion method, with a target, is based on an external concept of goodness; the social indicators on an internal concept. If a problem clearly involves external comparisons, external targets should be used. Many urban and social problems are measured by comparison with the whole population, and internal targets are therefore valid.

8. CONCLUSIONS: THE ROLE OF THE METHODS

The role of these methods depends on how well they provide answers and fit decision situations. Table 9.5 shows that the various methods can give different answers to the same policy question. The rankings are similar, but they can diverge substantially in some cases. All of the methods were applied to the same country-towns example and used identical characteristics, weights, and data throughout. The differences in outcomes must therefore be traceable to the type of method and the standardization procedure it uses. Let us see how this may affect use.

8.1. The Answers They Provide

When we look at Table 9.5, several questions arise. Why do some towns, like Armidale, rate in the top five with only some methods, whereas other towns, like Queanbeyan, are in the top five with almost every method? Why do some towns, like Broken Hill and Moree, fall in the bottom five with every method? The answers must lie in the measurement and combination of the following items:

(1) The characteristics that are chosen.

(2) The weights that are assigned.

(3) The method of standardization that is used.

(4) The level of each town on each characteristic.

The fourth is an objectively measured item and can perhaps be ignored. Proponents argue that the reliance on measurements of each characteristic lends an objectivity to the methods. Undoubtedly, the use of scales, like height in meters or milligrams of dissolved oxygen per liter, do produce objective measurements. Analysts can agree on 110 meters or 7.1 milligrams, but might not agree on subjective measurements like "very high" or "high." But the first three items are selected by the analyst himself. An analyst is therefore able to directly influence the results through his selection of characteristics, weights, and method.

We can make the following observations from the sample analyzed in this chapter:

(a) It appears that characteristics and weights can be selected satisfactorily. An analyst can consult his employers or his electorate to collect data or confirm his choices for these items. If this is so, the method of standardization is the item needing attention.

(b) The characteristics of some towns are pronounced enough to cause them to always fall in the top or bottom five. This is perhaps fortuitous and may be an artifact of these data and these towns. But it may result from two causes. First, as with Cessnock, a town may rate "bad" on all or most characteristics and therefore will rank at the bottom by any method. Second, a town may score so poorly on one undesirable characteristic that it inevitably comes out at the bottom of the aggregated scores. Broken Hill, with its high percentage of labor in mining, is an example. This suggests that an analyst should try several methods to check for differences in ranking.

8.2. The Problems They Pose and the Assumptions They Include

The assumptions of the methods must be very carefully stated and always kept in mind. They are principally the following:

(a) The *ceteris paribus* assumption that all other things are constant. Although this is perhaps intuitively obvious, it should be explicitly stated to avoid confusion. Consider average weekly rent (K_6), for example. We would normally expect the quality of houses to rise as rent rises. But we weighted this characteristic negatively, because we believe that high rents lower the quality of life when the variety and quality of the housing available remain constant.

(b) An implicit assumption that all people derive the same utility from the same things. If this assumption does not hold, the environmental-impact system proposed by Dee, Baker, Drobny, Duke, Whitman, and Fahringer (1973) is not applicable for evaluations involving more than one kind of person. However, this group of methods is useful when this assumption can be accepted.

CHAPTER 10

Estimation of Total Utility—The Expedient Methods

The basic model of value

$$\text{value}_i = \text{utility}_i - \text{disuitility}_i$$

indicates that comparative value equals comparative utility when disutility is the same for all alternatives. The great variety of methods for estimating total utility differ in the reliability of their utility estimates, their simplicity, and their speed of use. The methods presented in this chapter are simple but lack rigor. Chapter 11 reviews the more reliable but more complicated methods.

The range of simple methods is shown in Figure 10.1. Their data vary from written or verbal descriptions to numerical ratings on a standard scale. The analyses for comparative values range from simple observations of the distribution of responses, through calculations of frequencies, percentages, aggregates, and averages, to more complex manipulations of the same basic data. We refer to these more complex analyses in passing, but consider the simpler analyses in detail.

Data for these methods can be collected simply and analyzed rapidly, but this expedience is obtained at the cost of less-reliable indicators of utility. These utility measurements usually lack scales that permit reliable aggregation. We consider this problem as we proceed.

1. AN ENVIRONMENTAL POLICY EXAMPLE: A CHOICE BETWEEN LANDSCAPES

Appeals to the emotions, claims of intrinsic worth, and undue emphasis on the subjectivity of the benefits often cloud discussions on landscape policy. These arguments arise mainly from the unpriced nature of landscape enjoyment. Together with the paucity of cost data, they have promoted the use of nonmonetary methods—particularly the less-rigorous utility-estimation methods—in landscape assessment. Landscape choice therefore provides a good example to illustrate and contrast the methods discussed in this chapter.

1.1. The Landscape Alternatives

Landscape management requires selection of areas for preservation, enhancement, or other treatment, and any resource development inevitably involves benefits from different landscapes. The Cascadia Dam proposal, with which we introduced Chapter 1, involved damming a natural, free-flowing river for a reservoir. The new reservoir would be only 5 miles from an existing one and would add little to the diversity or number of recreation opportunities. But it would drastically change the local landscape. As part of a larger analysis of the proposal, Sinden (1973) assessed preferences for five landscapes.

These can be briefly described as follows:

Landscape	Water Resource	Existing Forest Resource	Artificial Features
A	Reservoir	Cutover	Dam with all facilities
B	Natural lake	Natural	Boating facilities only
C	Natural, free flowing river	Natural	None
D	Headwaters	Natural wilderness	None
E	Flat river through farmland	Cutover, partially removed	Small farms with rural roads

The problem for the Cascadia Dam decision was to compare the benefits of the new landscape (*A*) with those of the landscape that would be changed (*C*). The present adaptation compares the value of landscapes *A*, *C*, and three others in the same area (*B*, *D*, and *E*).

1.2. Problem Formulation

Drawings of each landscape were shown to 10 subjects. These subjects were familiar with these kinds of environments and each was given the same verbal description to supplement the drawings.

The environmental problem was presented to each subject as follows:

> Imagine that you live near Cascadia and that the river may be dammed for a reservoir. Consider all of the landscape benefits that your family would obtain from a picnic type visit to each of the five locations pictured. Which of the five areas would you prefer to have provided or retained?

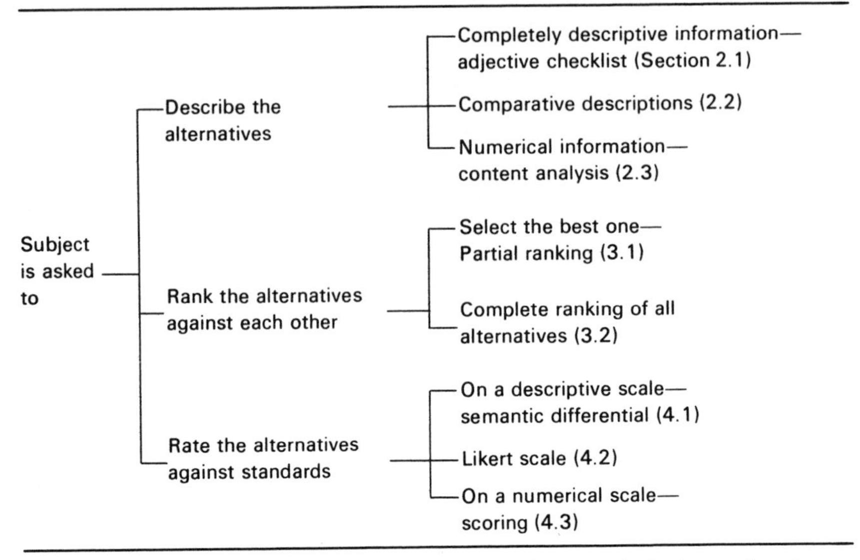

Figure 10.1. A classification of the expedient methods for estimating comparative utility by their data inputs.

This question on preferences will be expanded for each different method, as we come to them.

The subjects were simply asked to express their preferences in terms of one kind of activity—picnic visits. The results record total utility to each subject from this specific kind of visit. Although 10 subjects would be insufficient for a real survey, they are adequate to illustrate the methods.

1.3. Role of the Example in This Chapter

We are presenting this example to illustrate the methods and not as a pattern for a field survey. We therefore ignore some important issues of landscape analysis, such as whether actual landscapes or photographs or drawings are best and whether experts or users should be used as subjects. These are adequately covered in Cerny's (1974) review and in Daniel and Boster (1976).

The example poses a realistic set of alternatives in a relevant policy context. The methods are now considered and the comparative values they produce are summarized in Table 10.1 as we proceed. We return to the relevance of these results for policy at the end of the chapter.

Table 10.1. Comparative Utilities for Five Landscapes as Estimated by Various Expedient Methods

Landscape	Comparative description[a]	Partial Ranking		Complete Ranking	Likert Method	Scoring
	Number of High or Very High	Number in Best		Average Ranking	Total Rating[b]	Average Rating[b]
		One Choice	Three Choices			
1	2	3	4	5	6	7
		Results: Comparative Utilities				
A	2	2	6	3.3	38	52
B	7	4	9	2.0	42	67
C	6	1	6	2.7	38	63
D	4	3	4	3.4	34	51
E	1	0	5	3.6	34	45
		10	30			
		Ranking from Comparative Utilities[c]				
A	4	3	2	3	2	3
B	1	1	1	1	1	1
C	2	4	2	2	2	2
D	3	2	5	4	4	4
E	5	5	4	5	4	5

[a] Summarized from Table 10.2.
[b] For all 10 subjects.
[c] Where 1 = 1st or best; 5 = 5th or worst.

2. DESCRIBING THE ALTERNATIVES

A simple way to collect data is to record verbal impressions. These descriptive data suit several kinds of methods, ranging from the adjective checklist, through the selection of comparative descriptions, to detailed analysis of the content of impressions.

2.1. The Adjective Checklist

Adjectives such as "eroded" or "forested" describe alternatives, and others such as "pleasant" or "unpleasant" indicate relative values. Formal procedures have been developed by Craik (1972) and Sonnenfeld (1969) to use such adjectives to compare and understand outdoor environments.

2.1.1. Nature of the Method. The steps in the method can be generalized as follows: First, a group of adjectives is selected for the particular environments and subjects. Selection may involve the subjects themselves and the use of statistical criteria to isolate the most commonly used words. Then the selected adjectives and the environments in question are presented to the subjects. Finally, the frequencies with which the subjects use each adjective for a given environment are calculated. Presumably, a higher frequency indicates a more agreed upon description.

Descriptive phrases can readily replace adjectives, as Berry (1975) showed in his analysis of aesthetic benefits of open space land. Twelve phrases, including "a place for children to play," "a place to enjoy nature," and "a place to relax," were presented to 220 subjects in Philadelphia. The comparative criterion was the percentage of the respondents who selected each phrase to indicate their most-important uses or benefits. The results indicated the more-important utilities ascribed to the open space land.

2.1.2. Role of the Method. The relative importance of adjectives shows how an individual reacts to, or visualizes something. The method has been developed primarily to investigate perceptions and meanings, and thus it has a role in identifying and understanding utilities. Although sometimes vague and individualistic, this understanding is a start toward valuation (Brush, 1976). Further, the use of adjectives that are closely related to value, utility, and disutility emphasizes valuation.

Limitations arise from the descriptive nature of the method. An adjective may mean different things to different people. The next method extends the checklist idea and provides comparative values. The semantic differential and Likert methods, which we discuss subsequently, also extend the method for numerical values.

2.2. Comparative Descriptions

This method simply records directly on a descriptive scale how the subject feels about a thing's relative value.

2.2.1. Nature of the Method. A set of descriptions is presented to the subject, who is asked to allocate each alternative to its most appropriate category. The most frequently selected description, or sometimes an average description, indicates the comparative value.

The nature of the descriptions varies from study to study. A simple set is grade 1—extremely attractive, grade 2—attractive, grade 3—average, and grade 4—poor. Further qualifying descriptions can readily be added to standardize judgments. For example, average landscapes might be further described as "pleasant areas with no striking features."

The Hampshire Model (Penning-Rowsell and Hardy, 1973) attempts to improve the systematic nature and objectivity of the method. Features that contribute to or detract from attractive landscapes are described and then listed for each land unit in the survey. A balanced assessment of total landscape quality of each unit is derived by subjective averaging of these features.

Harrison (1962) recommended that large landscapes be broken into foreground and background. Then each of these zones should be assessed in one of the following three descriptive classes: ordinary quality—locally common and undramatic, medium quality—pleasing to most viewers, and high quality—tends to produce a strong feeling of appreciation by most viewers. As Hamill (1971) notes, Harrison provides no numerical ratings for these classes.

2.2.2. Application to the Landscape Example. The four Hampshire descriptions were supplemented by a lower "very poor" quality and applied to our example. To test the simplest version of the method, no further descriptions were provided. The 10 subjects were asked to allocate each landscape (*A* to *E*) to the category of landscape utility that they thought appropriate. Their allocations are shown in Table 10.2 and summarized in column 2 of Table 10.1. The subjects found no difficulty with the method. The results seem clear, with landscapes *B* and *C* most preferred.

2.2.3. Role of the Method. This method meets none of the criteria for interpersonal comparisons which we noted in Section 3.2 of Chapter 7. For example, the descriptive classes and the apparent base point of "medium quality" may mean different things to different people. However, a single evaluator could provide a consistent assessment. Alternatively, a small group of evaluators could be trained to produce similar assessments. In this context, Penning-Rowsell and Hardy (1973) note that this method has been extensively used by government agencies in Britain to select landscapes for

Table 10.2. Allocation of Landscapes to Descriptive Classes by Ten Subjects

	Landscapes				
Landscape Description[a]	*A*	*B*	*C*	*D*	*E*
Very high landscape value	2	2	1	2	0
High landscape value	0	5	5	2	1
Medium landscape value	4	2	0	0	5
Low landscape value	3	1	4	3	2
Very poor landscape value	1	0	0	3	2
Total	10	10	10	10	10

[a] The first four descriptions follow the Hampshire Model (Penning-Rowsell and Hardy, 1973).

preservation and enhancement. The simplicity and speed of the method promote its use for large-scale surveys.

2.3. Content Analysis

This method attempts to identify the meanings of texts such as letters or newspaper articles in a quantitative, objective manner. We review the nature of the method and then consider procedures for assessing meanings for valuation.

2.3.1. Nature of the Method. The first step is to decide whether relevant comparative values for the particular problem can be inferred from written material. For example, do comparative impressions about the problem lend themselves to written description, and can such descriptions relate directly to valuation? The second step is to define the appropriate data. These data may be words, sentences, complete letters, newspaper articles, radio broadcasts, or books and may be specially elicited. The third step is to select a system to classify the material for quantitative analysis. The final step is to define and perform the quantitative assessment.

2.3.2. Assessment of Content. A very simple system of assessment was used by Stankey (1972a) to analyze opinions on five alternative ways to manage a forest wilderness area. Five hundred letters were received in response to a request for comments on potential management plans. The favored alternative in each letter was noted, irrespective of the strength of opinion, and the results were expressed as percentage of the respondents in favor of each alternative. Kasperson (1969) investigated the perceived ownership of ponds in Massachusetts. His data were the possessive adjectives in newspaper articles about the ponds. He simply reported the total numbers of occurrences of the adjectives "our," "town's," "region's," and "state's."

A more-thorough system of assessment is provided by Mayntz, Holm, and Hoebner (1976) in their detailed discussion of the method. We now consider their system in the general context of our landscape-choice example. Each sentence is divided into its subject, predicate, and complement, as in the three simple examples of Table 10.3. Both predicate and complement are scored for the direction (utility +; disutility −) and intensity (high—3 to low—1) of the valuation. "Will increase" is of stronger intensity than "may increase" and of opposite direction from "will decrease." The scores assigned to the complements suggest that local business utilities are of lower intensity than those of recreation opportunities. The total score, which in this case is negative (−3), indicates the total value of the reservoir.

Table 10.3. A Content Analysis of Three Sentences for Reservoir Value

Subject	Predicate	Score	Complement	Score	Total[a] Score
1	2	3	4	5	6
The reservoir	may increase	+1	road congestion	−1	−1
The reservoir	will decrease	−2	recreation opportunities	+2	−4
The reservoir	will increase	+2	local business	+1	+2
Total					−3

[a] Column 6 = column 3 × column 5.

2.3.3. Role of the Method. The potential of the method for valuation rests on the ability to classify and assess the material. As Mayntz, Holm, and Hoebner note, there are no formal rules for the scoring system, so objectivity, generality, and reliability depend on the analyst. The method is only suitable when the only source of information is the written description.

2.4. Discussion

All these methods can successfully implement the basic notion of valuation, namely, the search for what people feel is worthwhile. But they do not implement the model of group value (Equation 4.8) so successfully. Written descriptions will inevitably mean different things to different people, which invalidates the apparently common scales and base points of comparative descriptions and content analysis.

3. RANKING THE ALTERNATIVES

People can usually order alternatives according to their preferences. Such rankings have no quantitative scale of utility, but they do provide simple comparative valuations. Preference usually represents total utility, but the methods seem equally applicable to ranking by net utility or value. We now consider the two general methods, partial and complete ranking, and several ways to interpret the information obtained.

3.1. Partial Ranking

Possibly the simplest valuation method of all is to ask a subject which alternative he prefers. We apply this method to our example and then consider some variations.

3.1.1. Application to the Landscape Example. The subjects were asked to consider the five landscapes and to name the one they most preferred. Then, in a modest extension of the method, they were asked to name their three most-preferred alternatives. At no stage in the method did we ask a subject to rank all the alternatives.

The only way to aggregate and record the results is to determine the frequency with which each alternative is selected. Landscape *B* was preferred by most subjects in both applications (Table 10.1, columns 3 and 4). But the second choice changed from *D* to *A* and *C* when the number of "best" preferences was increased from one to three.

3.1.2. Another Example: Preferences for Use of Forest Trails. The simplicity of the method promotes its use in large-scale surveys. McCay (1976), for example, investigated the preferences of different kinds of trail users in Ohio for trails with one or more uses. Each subject was asked how he preferred to travel on the forest trails. When more than one mode of travel was given, McCay assumed equal preference for all modes. Sixty-nine percent of hikers and 54 percent of horseback riders ranked single-use trails first, whereas 42 percent of motorcyclists ranked three-use trails first. Such percentages, and the distributions and rank orders of Table 10.1, are three quantitative ways of expressing comparative values.

3.1.3. Two Simple Variations. These variations both involve preferences between pairs of things. Neither provides quantitative values directly, but they follow some of the assessment and display systems discussed in Chapters 5 and 8 and can both present useful information for decisions.

Present or Absent? Listing the presence or absence of a benefit (or cost) is essentially a ranking in terms of that benefit. When everything else is constant, an alternative that has the benefit ranks more highly than one that does not. The method displays information for each alternative and may promote improved decisions. Conceivably, it could be applied to groups of subjects, but it is more suitable for factual descriptions by a single analyst, as shown by the following simple application to the landscape example, where *X* indicates "present."

	Landscape				
Benefit or Cost	*A*	*B*	*C*	*D*	*E*
Retain existing vegetation		X	X	X	X
Retain natural vegetation		X	X	X	
Extend road system	X				
Provide man-made things	X				X

When this display procedure is applied to environmental impact assessments, it is sometimes extended by more-complex but more-informative designations than just presence or absence (Warden and Dagodag, 1976).

Presence or absence information is methodologically identical to yes-or-no answers to survey questions. The standard Guttman and Scalogram procedures from sociology convert such answers into a numerical scale of relative attitudes. If the questions were value oriented, the scale would measure comparative value rather than comparative social attitude.

Better or Worse? A similar binary variation was used by Donnermeyer, Korsching, and Burdge (1974) to identify benefits and costs from relocation due to water resource development. Their object was to specify the factors that contributed to changes in the families' financial situation. Families were asked if their new situation was better or worse for factors such as rent, condition of house, cost of travel to work, and business volume. This list could readily be extended to include unpriced things.

3.1.4. An Extension: A Series of Partial Rankings. A complete ranking of all alternatives can be obtained by ranking a series of pairs of alternatives. If the alternatives are well-defined and the scale of preference is clear and unidirectional, there should be few inconsistencies. The method of paired comparisons which is presented in Chapter 11 involves comparisons of all possible pairs of alternatives. This maximum number of comparisons, with its built-in checks, lends more rigor to the partial-ranking method and more credence to the results.

3.1.5. Discussion. Partial rankings can provide much initial general information for valuation, but they provide little reliable data on comparative values. They may be most useful for prevaluation surveys to structure questionnaires, define problems, and display information.

3.2. Complete Ranking

In a complete ranking subjects are asked to order all the alternatives. The method itself needs little elaboration, but the interpretation of results is of some interest.

3.2.1. Application to the Landscape Example. Our 10 subjects were asked to rank all five landscapes in order of preference. The results are shown in Table 10.4 and summarized in Column 5 of Table 10.1.

Rankings have been aggregated and interpreted in several ways. The rank order numbers can be aggregated and averaged as in Table 10.4. On this basis, landscape *B* is most preferred (average 2.0) and *E* is least pre-

Table 10.4. Complete Rankings of Five Landscapes by Ten Subjects[a]

Landscape	Subject 1	2	3	4	5	6	7	8	9	10	Total	Average
A	5	1	5	3	3	1	5	3	4	3	33	3.3
B	3	2	4	1	1	2	3	2	1	1	20	2.0
C	2	4	2	4	2	4	2	1	2	4	27	2.7
D	1	5	1	2	4	5	1	5	5	5	34	3.4
E	4	3	3	5	5	3	4	4	3	2	36	3.6

[a] where 1 = most preferred and 5 = least preferred.

ferred (3.6), although *A*, *D*, and *E* are very close. Alternatively, the distribution of high and low rankings can be determined. The number of subjects ranking each landscape in the single best and three best preferences was identical to the results for partial ranking (columns 3 and 4 in Table 10.1). Both the average ranking and the distribution of high and low rankings assessed landscape *B* as most preferred. But the results for the other four landscapes differed. The average ranking interpretation placed *C* in second place, but the best single choice approach placed *C* in fourth place. Although this procedure for data collection provides a single consistent set of numbers, the different interpretations can lead to different comparative values.

3.2.2. Other Examples: Transmission Lines and Lakeshore Features. These two examples illustrate interpretation through both the total and the distribution of rank orders. Gray (1975) investigated planning procedures to locate transmission lines in Ontario. The aesthetic quality of several different landscapes was ranked by 62 subjects and the rankings were added. These totals, like those of Table 10.4, provided an ordering from which the landscapes were placed in nine quality classes. Subjects were then asked in which landscapes they preferred transmission lines to be located. Seventy-four percent of the landscapes preferred for the lines were in the lower four quality classes.

Day and Gilpin (1974) investigated the decision of 180 households to live near reservoirs. A major part of their results was a complete ranking of the importance of 14 factors in the decision. They used the term "order of merit technique" for complete ranking. They proceeded by having subjects repetitively select factors they considered highest and lowest in importance until all were ranked or declared unrankable. Forty-seven percent ranked proximity to valley parkland and 80 percent ranked proximity to a reservoir in their four least-important factors. Only 12 percent listed parkland proximity and 2 percent reservoir proximity among their top four factors. These two factors were clearly unimportant in the decision.

3.2.3. Discussion. The complete-ranking method should not be used for interpersonal comparisons, as we discuss more generally in Sections 3.3 and 5. Nevertheless, the method can be applied to group valuations in a restricted way. Day and Gilpin (1974) and others have demonstrated its suitability for surveys of many subjects. Some of the differences in comparative values they obtained were large and sufficiently clear for their purposes.

Another useful role is as simple scales of relative importance, as in the Fischer and Davies (1973) approach to environmental impact assessment. The impact of each activity, such as pest control, on each environmental resource or characteristic is ranked from 1 (low) to 5 (high) and qualified by + (benefits) or − (costs). The suffix *S* or *L* is added to denote short- or long-term effects. The resulting numbers are not aggregated but are displayed to aid the decision and to identify problems for further analysis.

Another approach to group valuation is to make assumptions about the statistical distribution and additivity of responses. The methods of equal intervals and successive intervals adopt this approach in converting rankings to a numerical scale of social attitudes. Gauger and Wyckoff (1973) applied the assumptions of the former method under the name "Q-sort" to rank water-based landscapes, although they did not continue to a numerical scale of comparative values.

3.3. Discussion of the Ranking Methods

Ranking provides an adequate measure of comparative value for a single person. But like the descriptive methods of Section 2, rankings lack a standard scale with a common origin and known interval. Comparisons of rankings for groups of subjects are therefore meaningless. For example, subjects 1 and 2 may gain the same total utility from landscape *B*, although they rank it slightly differently.

If interpersonal comparisons are meaningless, why have so many analysts used rankings in this way? Shafer and Mietz (1970), for example, asked 50 subjects to rank seven landscapes. The rankings were aggregated to give a total preference score between 50 and 350 for each landscape. These scores were used in further comparative assessments.

Part of the answer is the similarity of orderings between ranking and other methods that we discuss in Section 5. Part results from the speed of ranking. Hamill (1974) compared Leopold's uniqueness ratio (Chapter 9) and a ranking method to assess the aesthetic worth of river sites in Idaho.

Each of the 12 sites was ranked on many characteristics. The rankings by characteristic were aggregated into an overall evaluation number and the sites were then ordered by these numbers. Hamill concluded that ranking had much lower time requirements and much fewer opportunities for error than Leopold's approach.

4. RATING THE ALTERNATIVES

In these methods subjects are asked to rate total utility on a given scale. The scales are arbitrary, but provide common standards against which the subjects assess each thing. We discuss three methods which grade into each other. The semantic differential method has a descriptive scale, the scoring method has a numerical scale, and the Likert method has characteristics between the two.

4.1. The Semantic Differential

The semantic differential develops the adjective checklist further by pairing adjectives at each end of a scale and grading the intervening continuum. The method was devised by Osgood (1952) to investigate the meanings people attach to concepts and things. The method's primary role has been in this sort of perception problem, and we consider it in this context.

4.1.1. Nature of the Method. The concepts and problems are first defined. For example, Moeller, Machlaclan, and Morrison (1974) investigated people's perceptions of six "concepts" of the natural environment (national forest, wilderness, state park, lake, mountain, and wildlife) and four kinds of users (auto campers, wilderness hikers, picnickers, and park rangers). Next, adjective pairs are selected for the meanings and perceptions of interest. Moeller, Machlaclan, and Morrison were considering the perception of value for these concepts. They selected adjective pairs like valuable/worthless and pleasant/unpleasant.

A seven-point scale is prepared for each pair, like the following example:

	Very	Quite	Slightly	Neutral	Slightly	Quite	Very	
Pleasant	____	____	____	____	____	____	____	Unpleasant

The subjects indicate which point on each scale best fits each thing or concept.

The results are a set of checkmarks for each subject. They can be interpreted for valuation by rating the points from +3 for the favorable extreme to -3 for the unfavorable extreme. This procedure is similar to the Likert scale, which we discuss next. Average ratings can then be calculated for each thing or for each group of subjects.

The semantic differential must be applied comparatively. The perceptions provided by given subjects for one concept, like wilderness, can be compared to those for another concept, like natural forest. Alternatively, the perceptions different groups of subjects have of the same thing can be compared. For example, Shafer and Richards (1974) compared perceptions of photographs to those of real scenes. Their subjects used similar adjectives to describe the same landscape whenever the photograph contained most of the scenic variation.

4.1.2. Role of the Method. The difficulties with the semantic differential method arise from its reliance on single adjectives. A given adjective may convey different meanings to different people. Consensus on a rating for a given adjective might therefore result from different perceptions rather than from real agreement. Furthermore, some adjectives are hard to pair. For example, Shafer and Richards pair "satisfying" with "frustrating," which connotes making ones best efforts vain or ineffectual. Satisfying/unsatisfying would be a better pair of opposites.

The contribution to valuation must rest on effective comparisons of things and on information more closely related to values, choices, and behavior. The method can help to discover relevant utilities and to identify important characteristics of the environment. Berry (1975) argues that knowledge of the relevant utilities from unpriced things is necessary for a planner to make recommendations and to defend his choices. He used the semantic differential to derive information on how different resources, benefits, and costs were perceived. Adjective pairs, such as appealing/unappealing, pleasant/ unpleasant, valuable/worthless, or satisfying/unsatisfying, are direct measures of total utility. Peterson and Neumann (1969), for example, were close to valuation with their five-point scale for preference, only the end positions of which were defined:

Appealing ____ ____ ____ ____ ____ Unappealing

Kelly and Stephenson (1967) investigated the effect of store design and management on patronage. Their questionnaire included the following three scales to measure attitudes to prices: prices are (high to low) compared to other stores, values are (high to low) for money spent, and a (large to small) number of items are specially priced. The end result was an average rating for each store on each scale. This kind of information relates closely to valuation and choices.

4.2. The Likert Method

Likert pioneered the measurement of social attitudes through rating scales. His formal philosophy and its extension to the method of summated ratings are discussed elsewhere (Likert, 1932; Edwards, 1957). We consider here his basic ideas and some of their many practical variations and applications to valuation.

4.2.1. Nature of the Method. The fundamentals of the method are a series of statements that present a standard scale and a simple system of numerical rating. We illustrate two kinds of presentation for landscape assessment.

The first kind of statement and presentation was used by Murray (1974). He made statements like: "Views of undeveloped mountain ranges (or rural valleys, etc.) are of high visual quality." The subject was then asked to rate his response on a five-point scale such as:

Strongly Agree	Agree	Undecided	Disagree	Strongly Disagree

There are several ways to aggregate and interpret such ratings. The responses can be aggregated directly into frequencies or percentages. For example, Murray reported that 94 percent of his subjects agreed or strongly agreed with the statement about mountain ranges. Eighty-two percent favored or strongly favored views of rural valleys, whereas 64 percent disliked or strongly disliked views of industrial valleys. These well-defined measures of comparative utilities are directly useful for decisions. If viewing places are equally expensive to provide, views of mountain ranges and rural valleys should have precedence over views of industrial valleys. Views of undeveloped mountain ranges might be given some precedence over those of rural valleys.

Another aggregation procedure is to allocate numbers to each point on the scale and then add and average these ratings. In his original paper, Likert (1932) allocated 5 to one end of the scale (strongly agree) and 1 to the other end (strongly disagree). The method of summated ratings offers a third, but more complex, aggregation procedure (Edwards, 1957).

The second kind of presentation has one complete statement for each point on the scale, rather than the one or two words per point of the first presentation. Boster and Daniel (1972) used a simple version as the basis of their comparison of landscape benefits from six ways of logging a forest. Four of their ten points were presented and rated as follows:

9 I am absolutely certain that I LIKE the area represented by the sample

5 Just guessing—like

4 Just guessing—DISLIKE

0 I am absolutely certain that I dislike the area represented by the sample

These points really define a probability that a given level of utility or disutility will be obtained. But for practical purposes, the results were treated as if they were actual utility ratings.

4.2.2. Application to the Landscape Example. Our 10 subjects were asked to compare each landscape on a five-point scale. Their responses were distributed as shown in Table 10.5. These particular frequencies are difficult to interpret by simple observation. Landscape *B* appears to be the most preferred, because eight out of ten rated it as pleasant or better. Similarly, *C*, *D*, or *E* may be the least preferred. To interpret the responses differently, numerical ratings were assigned to each point. The utility ratings for each landscape were aggregated as the total of (rating × number of subjects) for all points. The results are listed in column 6 of Table 10.1. They confirm *B* as first choice, but indicate that *C* is not near the bottom.

4.2.3. Other Examples: Wilderness Encounters and Scenic Rivers. The technique of descriptive standards and numerical ratings has been applied in several ways. The following examples illustrate some of them.

Several scales in the same questionnaire can relate to different quantities or levels of the same thing. Then simple frequency data can be interpreted for results similar to a demand curve. For example, in a series of questions Stankey (1972b) asked visitors to a wilderness area how they felt about encounters with different numbers of other parties. Their response for each

Table 10.5. Responses of 10 People to a Statement about Five Landscapes (the Likert Method)

Landscape	Very Pleasant	Pleasant	Undecided	Unpleasant	Very Unpleasant	Totals
A	3	4	2	0	1	10
B	5	3	1	1	0	10
C	5	1	1	3	0	10
D	3	3	0	3	1	10
E	0	6	2	2	0	10
Rating	5	4	3	2	1	

number was recorded on a very pleasant/very unpleasant scale as in the preceding section. The percentage of subjects recording pleasant or better fell as the numbers of encounters increased. This relationship does not measure the level of aggregate utility. But Stankey argued that it does indicate the number of encounters at which the experience ceases to be pleasant (or utility ceases to be positive).

The number of points on the scale can readily be varied. For this method, three is the minimum, such as the high, medium, and low grades used by Zube for landscape assessment (Cerny 1974). Michalson (1972) used a four-point scale to assess the impact of trips down wild and scenic rivers in Idaho. Consider the following hypothetical results from 225 subjects for rivers *F* and *G*:

		Number of Responses		Rating × Number	
Scale	Rating	F	G	F	G
Excellent	+2	185	25	370	50
Satisfactory	+1	15	50	15	50
No opinion	0	0	0	0	0
Unsatisfactory	−1	25	150	−25	−150
		225	225	360	−50

The responses weighted by the ratings give total utility numbers of 360 and −50. The absolute meaning of these numbers is unknown. But they indicate that if the costs of obtaining the benefits are similar, *F* has greater value than *G*. In this example the numbers of responses at each point on the scale provide sufficient information for comparison and choice.

4.2.4. Extension to Multicharacteristic Situations. The speed and simplicity of the Likert method promotes its widespread use and permits detailed investigation of each thing involved in a decision. An interesting example of this detail is the investigation of multicharacteristic problems.

Moeller and Engelken (1972) applied the approach to investigate environmental characteristics important to a fishing experience. The characteristics they recognized were water quality, natural beauty, privacy, weather, access, facilities, size of fish, and number of fish caught. Each of these was rated 3 if very important, 2 if important, and 1 if unimportant. The authors noted that such artificial ratings do not provide precise interval measurements for each person. But they are useful for describing overall patterns among characteristics. Average ratings were calculated for each characteristic, and by age and other attributes of the 100 fishermen. Water quality and natural beauty were consistently rated as the most important characteristic contributing to a good fishing experience. Size and number of fish were less important.

4.2.5. Discussion. The Likert method derives numerical ratings from orderings on a scale. It is therefore a bridge between ranking and the scoring method that we discuss next. The numerical utility numbers should be interpreted as orderings and not as measures of "excellent" or "very pleasant" utilities. The following example illustrates this point.

Consider two rating schemes for the following responses for a different river H:

		Scheme 1		Scheme 2	
Scale	Number of Responses	Rating	Rating × Number	Rating	Rating × Number
Excellent	70	+2	140	+1000	70,000
Satisfactory	95	+1	95	+100	9,500
No opinion	20	0	0	+10	200
Unsatisfactory	40	−1	−40	+1	40
	225		195		79,740
Average per subject			0.87		354

Scheme 1 leads to an average rating per subject of 0.87—between no opinion (0) and satisfactory (+1). But scheme 2 leads to an absolute reading between satisfactory (+100) and excellent (+1000). As Payne (1976) points out, both schemes are valid, and the different absolute readings arise from converting ordinal data to numerical scales. This happened even though we have assumed that excellent means the same thing to all subjects. But each scheme rates river *H* higher than river *G* and lower than *F* was rated in Section 4.2.3, confirming visual observation of the distribution of responses. The Likert method should provide comparative values to guide choices, even though we cannot say by how much one thing is preferred to another.

As with the other methods in this chapter, we do not discuss the more-complex ways of converting the same basic data into continuous numerical scales of value. Edwards (1957) describes the method of summated ratings that converts a distribution of results by points on a scale. Boster and Daniel (1972) use a mathematical procedure they call the "theory of signal detection" to convert the same kind of data into numbers expressing the comparative values.

4.3. The Scoring Method

In this version of rating, subjects score total utility directly on a standard numerical scale. They choose the score that best represents their total utility. The scale may be short, with just five points like the Likert scale, or long, with a 1-to-100 scale. The scales are commonly arithmetic, but may be exponential, as is the one Fines (1968) developed for landscape assessment.

4.3.1. Application to the Landscape Example. The 10 subjects were asked to rate the total utility from each landscape on a 1-to-100 scale. The scale was anchored or standardized by defining 100 as the best landscape environment they could imagine and one they would visit for certain. A rating of 50 indicated an average landscape that they would be indifferent about visiting. The lowest rating of 1 was described as the worst imaginable landscape and one they would definitely never visit. The average ratings are shown in column 7 of Table 10.1.

4.3.2. Application by a Single Analyst. Another way to apply the method is for the analyst to place things on a continuum and score them himself. Linton (1968) applied the method to assess landscapes in Scotland, and Moore and Baker (1969) used it to investigate research-and-development projects.

Linton attempted to evaluate scenic resources in an objective and quantitative fashion. He claimed that landform and land use were the two basic elements of a scenic resource. They were assessed in the following manner. Landscapes were ordered on a landform continuum with a rating assigned to each form. The landforms and ratings were lowland (0), low uplands (2), plateau uplands (3), hill country (5), bold hils (6), and mountains (8). A land-use continuum from urbanized (−5) to wild landscapes (+6) was also specified. The scores obtained with the two scales were added for a composite assessment.

The scoring method is useful for assessing descriptive things like landscapes. But Moore and Baker (1969) also used it to rate research-and-development projects according to quantitative estimates of their probability of success, timing, and level of total benefits and total costs. The timing of the benefit stream was estimated and recorded as the percentage of total benefits received in each of several years. Each project was scored 3, 2, or 1 on the desirability of the timing, which is a different approach to discounting. Scores for probability of success, total benefits, and total cost were assessed on a 9-to-1 scale. An aggregate rating for the project was derived by adding the separate scores.

4.4. Some General Issues

The selection of standard scales for these three methods raises some questions about survey and methodology. We consider three questions raised by all these methods and, in the process, illustrate other applications and variations of the methods.

4.4.1. The Implied Weights. An apparent advantage of rating is the information obtained about the amount by which one thing is preferred to another. Consider, for example, the ratings on the equal interval, 1-to-100 scale (column 7, Table 10.1). The average subject seems to prefer *A* to *E* by some 15 percent and *B* to *E* by 50 percent. But this is only correct if the subjects have understood the scale and can "fit in" with its standards and equal increments.

Fines' (1968) 32-point exponential scale has an increasing numerical interval for its six descriptive categories. Unsightly is rated 0 to 1, undistinguished 1 to 2, pleasant 2 to 4, distinguished 4 to 8, superb 8 to 16, and spectacular 16 to 32. This weighting permits more-detailed assessments in the better categories. But it implicitly gives proportionately more weight to these better landscapes in the calculation of total ratings for a geographical unit from the ratings for each landscape in the unit.

Consider, for example, two units that are each composed of five landscapes. The first has one landscape rated at the top of the distinguished class (8) and four rated at the top of the undistinguished class (2). This gives it a total rating of 16. The second unit has five landscapes that are all rated at the middle of the pleasant class (3), giving it a total rating of 15. Since the total scores are almost the same, this scale implies that one better (distinguished) landscape can balance four poorer (undistinguished) landscapes in a comparative assessment.

The standard ratings or utility weights are quite arbitrary, but prior decisions must validate the implied utility comparisons. For example, if one distinguished landscape can balance one undistinguished one, these ratings must be at equal intervals above and below a mean. In the case of the scale used in Section 4.2.5, numbers must be selected for the intervals from "no opinion" to "satisfactory" and from "satisfactory" to "excellent." Should they be equal, as in scheme 1, or scaled up by 10, as in scheme 2? Finally, the analyst must decide whether "pleasant" or any other point on the scale means the same thing to different people. Answers to these questions will indicate the appropriate relative intervals. Then numbers and an arbitrary base point can be selected that will provide a scale that indicates the ordering among the things being assessed.

4.4.2. Anchoring the Scales. The rating scales must be defined, or anchored, to common standards. Quantitative things, such as numbers of animals or days of recreation, can be specified numerically. But more subjective things like landscapes must be defined in some other way. Common and useful procedures are the written or illustrated description and the known landscape. Fines (1968) anchored specific points on well-known or easily illustrated landscapes. Linton (1968) completed the entire assessment himself, so his ratings should be consistent. Nevertheless, he anchored each point on his landform and land-use scales to lengthy descriptions and specific qualifications. For example, mountains in the landform characteristic must have a relative relief exceeding 2000 feet and separateness.

There are three general ways to anchor scales: the known landscape, written and illustrated descriptions, and estimates of behavior (as illustrated in Section 4.3.1). Many analysts use a combination of them.

4.4.3. The Number of Points. The number of points on the scale can vary from a continuum (which in practice must be something like a 1-to-100 scale) to a minimum of three (as in the superior, typical, and inferior scale proposed by Burke et al., 1968). Too many points will exceed the subjects' ability to discriminate. But too few will ignore much of their natural ability to discriminate. Since there is no generally correct number of points on a rating scale, the analyst must try to fit the number to the problem. Matell and Jacoby (1971) concluded that the predictive ability of the results is independent of the number of points. But estimates of differences in utilities may need more careful selections, because, as Finn (1972) and Moore and Baker (1969) show, the number of points affects the mean ratings and variances. Moore and Baker further reported that nine and seven interval scales always performed well but three interval scales did not.

4.5. Discussion

The rating methods incorporate standards against which utility is judged, and they provide numerical results. They should therefore provide more information than does ranking and should suit more problems. The most important extra information they obtain is the amount by which the utility of one thing differs from that of another. Reliable quantitative information on these differences is, in fact, hard to obtain. The method and scales must be very carefully specified for this purpose.

Rating scales often include a "neutral" or "undecided" position. This neutral position should always convey the same meaning, so that the number of responses above or below this common point can be useful indicators of comparative value.

5. DISCUSSION AND CONCLUSIONS

All these methods are simple to apply and require relatively little time and skill to collect and analyze the data. Thus they are well suited to surveys of large numbers of subjects, to rapid surveys, and to analyses that warrant only small inputs of time and skill. But these advantages are obtained at a cost, which we consider in discussing the role of and choice between the methods. Table 10.6 summarizes the information that the methods provide.

5.1. Difficulties for and Approaches to Group Valuations

All the descriptive and ranking methods lack a standard scale with known intervals and a common origin. They should, therefore, not be used for comparisons among subjects. But they are useful for the single planner who makes all the assessments himself. Most applications of rating methods have also failed to meet these criteria.

A planner has a choice of several approaches when he has to use one of these expedient methods for group valuations. He could use one of the methods and subsequently try to validate his results in some way. We prefer one of the following approaches:

(a) A rating scale can be defined with a given, common origin (neutral point) and known appropriate intervals, as we attempted to do in our simple example in Section 4.3.1.

(b) Rating can be applied with an objective common unit such as time, travel distance, or money. With this change, rating grades into the direct-questioning methods for willingness to pay, which we discuss in Chapter 14.

Table 10.6. The Information Provided by the Expedient Total Utility Methods[a]

Method	Identify Basic Utilities	Identify Best Alternative	Order All Alternatives	Determine by How Much Things are Preferred	Numerical Comparisons
1	2	3	4	5	6
Adjective checklist	√	X	X	X	X
Comparative description	√	√	√	X	√
Content analysis	√	√	√	X	√
Partial ranking	X	√	X	X	√
Complete ranking	X	√	√	X	√
Semantic differential	√	X	X	X	X
Likert method	?	√	√	?	√
Scoring	X	√	√	?	√

[a] √ = yes, X = no, and ? = maybe.

(**c**) The proportion of the responses above and below some common origin can be calculated. Six of the methods provide numerical data (Table 10.6) from which proportions can be calculated. This approach meets the criteria for group comparisons.

(**d**) The basic data can be converted from comparative descriptions, rankings, and ratings into numerical scales through the sociological scaling techniques. We have indicated techniques for each kind of data but have not enlarged on them because they are well described elsewhere. The techniques all rest on special assumptions about the additivity of responses and the statistical forms the responses should fit. If these assumptions can be accepted, the data can be transformed into a scale.

5.2. Choice Between the Methods

These methods were developed to overcome some information gaps and to fulfill specific purposes. Their role in valuation depends on whether the way they do this is compatible with value assessment. We now consider how the characteristics of these methods suits them for various kinds of valuations.

5.2.1. On the Characteristics of the Methods. Comparisons between the methods must be based on the key criteria of consistency between subjects, validity of the results, and relevance of the orderings for the decision. In the landscape field Penning-Rowsell and Hardy (1973) contrasted two versions of comparative descriptions and ratings with Fines' (1968) scale. The orderings by all the methods were very close, but the results from the rating were more consistent because the rating scale was anchored to specific landscapes and descriptions.

Green and Swets (1966) compared rankings, ratings with scales from 4 to 34 points, and paired comparisons, which we discuss in Chapter 11. They reported that all these methods gave comparable numerical indexes, which indicates a similar ordering. Daniel and Boster (1976) asked 26 groups of subjects to compare six landscapes with scoring on a 1-to-10 scale. Only 16 of the 156 possible orderings differed. This general evidence that all the methods order things in the same way is supported by the results of our landscape example in Table 10.1. All the methods rank *B* first, all but one place *E* last, and all but one place *C* second.

The validity of the methods depends on their ability to provide comparative values that can predict behavior. Sinden (1973) tested ranking (1 to 5) and scoring (1 to 100) against a willingness to pay indicator of value. Data on willingness to travel to different sites (in extra travel time) proved a statistical predictor of behavior and provided a standard. The scoring data were much more highly correlated with willingness to pay and the better predictors of behavior. Scoring, therefore, appears to be the more valid method.

5.2.2. For Different Kinds of Decisions. An initial step in valuation is to identify the things exchanged and their associated utilities and disutilities. Four of the eight methods can readily assist in identifying basic utilities (Table 10.6).

All the methods are suitable for the either/or decision, which needs only a comparison between two things. Six of the methods are capable of identifying the single best alternative. The two doubtful ones (adjective checklist and semantic differential) also seem able to do this, if they are applied carefully.

The choice of a method for comparison of one thing with a number of others is more difficult, unless the thing happens to rank consistently best or worst. Although five methods provide complete orderings (Table 10.6), the order in the middle varies much more than that at the extremes. Landscape *A*, for example, is fourth by comparative description, third by scoring, and second by the Likert method. If a method is selected with the criteria of consistency, validity, and applicability to the problem, obtaining estimates of comparative utility is straightforward.

Only five of the eight methods are suitable when all things must be ordered, and the appropriate method requires careful selection. Complete utility orderings have numerous policy applications, as Penning-Rowsell and Hardy (1973) and Daniel and Boster (1976) have shown. Both studies used simple orderings of current landscapes to indicate areas for immediate preservation. This information can be easily mapped as aesthetic contours for a scenic beauty map.

Changes in utility numbers can identify areas for special treatment and can record changes. Penning-Rowsell and Hardy estimated changes in utilities from such treatments as tree planting and removal of eyesores like mine tailings. Fines estimated percentage changes from before and after comparisons of utility of views (Cerny, 1974). Similarly, Daniel and Boster (1976) discussed how "aesthetic recovery" changes over time can be monitored with these methods.

The choice of a method is also influenced by the nature of the area and the decision situation. For example, the appropriate words for the adjective checklist and semantic differential methods vary with the environment.

Some fixed-budget decisions require the selection of a group of projects. Unless all projects have the same cost, makeup of the group must be adjusted to meet the budget constraint and to maximize utility. For this decision one must know by how much the utility of one project exceeds that of another. Only the Likert and scoring methods can provide these cardinal utility numbers, and they can only do this with very careful specifications of the scale.

5.3. Conclusions

Comparative values are most useful in numerical form. All the methods of this chapter are simple and fast to use, but the rating methods seem to provide the most generally valid and consistent numbers. Furthermore, well-standardized ratings indicate quantitative differences in utility that can predict behavior. The rating methods, and numerical scoring in particular, seem to be the most generally applicable of the expedient methods.

CHAPTER 11

Estimation of Total Utility—The Rigorous Methods

Chapter 10 presented simple expedient methods of estimating total utility or disutility based mainly on single direct questions. The more rigorous methods of this chapter also estimate total utility, but provide for careful elicitation of information. They involve more-structured questions and more-detailed field procedures, and therefore are more expensive in terms of the time and skill needed for each interview.

The rigorous methods encourage careful responses in various ways, as shown in Figure 11.1. The simplest ones rank outcomes as does the ranking method of Chapter 10, but compare them to all other outcomes. The scoring method has also been made more rigorous, as we describe in Section 3. A third group requires subjects to judge when utilities from various alternatives stand in certain proportions to each other. A fourth requires subjects to decide when they are indifferent between alternatives that involve risky outcomes.

Methods for utility estimation have been developed in a wide range of disciplines, including economics, political science, psychology, and sociology. Despite some differences in approach, those developed in the different disciplines tend to blend with each other. A given method may be used, for example, to derive an attitude scale for a psychologist or a utility scale for an economist. The various disciplines often use different terms for the same things, which creates some confusion in transferring methods to other fields. Economists seem to have made the most use of these methods as value indicators for policy decisions, and in this book we use the economics terminology almost entirely.

Utility estimation has been approached in a variety of ways. Torgerson (1958) distinguished three major kinds of methods: (a) those that require only ordinal or ranking judgments, (b) those that require quantitative or numerical judgments, and (c) those, sometimes called the response methods, that explicitly "underdefine" the thing whose utility is to be estimated. The third class cannot be structured specifically enough for the kind of decisions with which we are concerned. Although theoretical models have been

Subject is asked to		
Estimate the order of, or identify equality among, outcomes	Rank order and equality judgments (Section 2)	Paired or ranked comparisons (2.1)
		Half-value sum method (2.2)
Rate outcomes relative to some given standard	Rating Judgments (Section 3)	Allocation of a single outcome to a point on a given scale-scoring method (Chap. 10)
		Allocation of percentage ratings (3.1)
		Estimation of numerical ratios (3.2)
		Checking for consistency (3.3)
Estimate when utilities from outcomes stand in a given proportion	Proportional judgments (Section 4)	Direct-midpoint method (4.1)
		Double-judgment method (4.2)
Estimate equality among outcomes involving probabilities	Probability judgments (Section 5)	von Neumann–Morgenstern method (5.1)
		Ramsey method (5.2)

***Figure 11.1.* A classification of the rigorous methods of estimating total utility.**

presented, little field work has been reported with them. We therefore omit this third class and concentrate on the first two kinds of methods.

Many decisions involve choosing among alternative packages of benefits and costs. For example, one possible vacation may consist of 6 days of hiking, 5 of fishing, and 3 of travel. An alternative may consist of 10 days of fishing, 3 of sightseeing, and 1 of travel. To determine the comparative utilities of the two alternatives, it is necessary to know the utility or disutility provided by each component and the weight that should be given each component when aggregating them into an estimate of total utility. Some of the methods in this chapter are suited to finding both utility and weights, but others can only be used for one or the other.

The next section presents a pollution-control example in which the alternatives involve a number of objectives. Then we show how the methods in Figure 11.1 can be used to estimate utility rankings or weights. Finally, Section 6 shows how the methods can be used to guide an overall decision as to which alternative will have the greatest social value.

1. AN ENVIRONMENTAL-POLICY EXAMPLE: SELECTING A LEVEL OF POLLUTION CONTROL

Pollution takes a variety of forms, but decisions about efforts to control it have a number of problems in common. (a) The damage is usually difficult to value, because it involves things that are hard to see as immediate effects, such as death, disease, and ecological damage. (b) To estimate the comparative social values of alternative actions, it is necessary to combine the benefits from control with their associated costs. (c) Decisions usually involve a choice between various levels of control, including those currently in effect. (d) The alternative actions inevitably involve different groups of people and different institutions. The methods of this chapter are suitable for dealing with the first three of these problems, and we now present an example involving them. The problem of aggregating effects on different people and institutions is postponed for consideration in Chapter 17.

1.1. A Case of Water Pollution Control

The example presented here is hypothetical, but is based on information from real situations. A city with a population of 250,000 lies at the mouth of a large river. Forty-two percent of the inhabitants are in the work force, and 25,000 of them are employed in manufacturing. The factories in the city are primarily zinc and iron ore refineries, and the waters of the estuary are critically contaminated with mercury, cadmium, lead, and zinc from these plants.

The high level of pollution and the importance of the industry to the city have stimulated controversy over what to do. The city already has a primary sewage treatment plant, but the industries and government have agreed to consider jointly financing a new pollution control facility. A decision must be made whether to build a new control facility and, if so, the level of control it should be designed to achieve.

There are various alternatives, including retention of the existing facility, as we show in Table 11.1. The five new alternatives would achieve various reductions in the level of mercury in the river, as shown in column 4. But these would require correspondingly higher costs, which are shown in column 6 as lump-sum capital outlays.

1.2. Basic Data on the Alternatives

The comparative values of the alternative facilities depend on the utilities and disutilities that would result from them. The six major ones are identified in Table 11.2 under the heading "objectives." The first four are utilities and the last two disutilities.

A causal chain between mercury intake and premature death and disease is well established. The intake is commonly through the consumption of poisoned fish. Some of the current 2000 deaths per year are known to result

Table 11.1. Characteristics of Six Alternative Pollution Control Facilities

Alternative	Type of Treatment Plant	Location of Disposal	Expected Level of Mercury in River	Regulations on Consumption of Fish	Additional Capital Outlays ($ million)
1	2	3	4	5	6
A_1[a]	Primary—old (existing)	River	Critical	Very strict	0
A_2	Primary—renewed	River	Serious but tolerable	Strict	80
A_3	New primary plus low-efficiency secondary	River	↓	Some	200
A_4	New primary plus high-efficiency secondary	River	↓	None	450
A_5	New primary plus high-efficiency secondary plus tertiary	River	↓	None	800
A_6	As for A_5	Sea	Negligible	None	1500

[a] A_1 is the existing facility.

Table 11.2. Outcomes of Pollution Control by Six Alternative Facilities in Terms of Major Objectives

Objectives	Alternative Control Facilities[a]					
	A_1	A_2	A_3	A_4	A_5	A_6
1. *Reduction in annual death rate*						
Number of deaths per year	2000	1995	1993	1992	1991	1990
Change from present	0	5	7	8	9	10
2. *Reduction in annual disease rate*						
Number of cases per year	22,500	22,490	22,485	22,482	22,480	22,480
Change from present	0	10	15	18	20	20
3. *Increase in number of fish species preserved*						
Number preserved	3	7	10	12	13	14
Change from present	0	4	7	9	10	11
4. *Increase in property value*						
Total value ($ million)	500	560	600	620	630	630
Increase from present (annuity equivalent)[b]	0	6	10	12	13	13
5. *Additional capital costs*						
Total outlay ($ million)	0	80	200	450	800	1500
(annuity equivalent)[b]	0	8	20	45	80	150
6. *Decrease in employment*						
Number employed	25,000	23,900	23,800	23,500	23,200	22,500
Relative decrease (%)	0	4.4	4.8	6.0	7.2	10.0

[a] As described in Table 11.1.
[b] Annuities calculated at 10 percent.

from mercury poisoning despite the strict regulations on consumption of fish from the estuary. The alternative new pollution-control facilities would reduce the level of mercury in the water as shown in Table 11.1, and consequently would reduce deaths by the numbers shown for objective 1 in Table 11.2.

Some of the 22,500 disease cases reported in the city each year are known to result from ingestion of mercury. The five alternative pollution-control facilities would reduce the number of cases by the amounts shown for objective 2. Although the numbers involved are not large, reductions in death and disease are usually considered to have high utility.

Only three species of fish now found in the river are edible, and fishing is actually banned in the estuary. The pollution reduction resulting from the more effective control facilities would be followed by restocking with additional species of edible fish, as shown for objective 3. Alternative A_6 would actually permit oyster harvesting, which has been stopped specifically because of mercury pollution.

The total value of houses and other real estate along the estuary is now estimated at $500 million. A decrease in water pollution would cause a rise in these values, as shown for objective 4. Since such changes in property value would only occur once, the annual increase is shown by an annuity calculated at 10 percent interest.

Finally, the new facilities would require employers to divert to pollution control resources that otherwise would be used to renew their capital equipment and maintain output. This will reduce total employment and must be included as a social cost. Line 6 shows the effect on total manufacturing employment of the various alternatives. These changes in employment are expressed as percentage decreases from the current level of 25,000 employees.

1.3. Determining the Comparative Values

The decision problem in the pollution control example is to select one of the six possible alternatives. The social value of each alternative can be described in terms of the outcomes that would result for each objective shown in Table 11.2. Each objective will contribute utility or disutility to the total value of the alternative. The comparison of the alternatives must therefore be based on a matrix of utilities, as shown in Table 11.3. For each alternative i there will be a set of utilities for the six objectives j.

A decision maker will usually not give equal weight to all the objectives involved in an alternative. The analyst must therefore determine the relative weights (WT) to be assigned to each of the objectives j. Once he has the utilities for the matrix in Table 11.3 and the weights for each objective, the value of any alternative can be calculated as follows

$$V_i = \sum_{j=1}^{6} (U_{ij} \times WT_j) \tag{11.1}$$

This equation simply says that the value of an alternative is the total of its weighted utilities for each objective.

Table 11.3. The Matrix of Utilities for the Six Alternatives and Objectives of the Pollution Control Example

Objectives	Alternatives (i)				
(j)	A_1	.	.	.	.	A_6
O_1	U_{11}	.	.	.	.	U_{61}
.	.					.
.	.					.
.	.					.
.	.					.
O_6	U_{16}	.	.	.	.	U_{66}

A rational decision about the level of pollution control can be made by selecting that alternative that has the highest comparative value. The value number itself has no absolute meaning, but it does indicate the relative desirability of the alternatives.

The problem for the analyst is to obtain reliable estimates for the utilities of Table 11.3 and for the weights to be assigned the objectives. The following sections show how the various rigorous methods for estimating total utility can be used for these two purposes.

2. RANK ORDER AND EQUALITY JUDGMENTS

The easiest tasks for a subject may be to rank two alternative outcomes in terms of utility and to state when two alternatives appear to be of equal utility. We therefore discuss these kinds of judgments first, and include both simple rank order and equality judgments. The methods in this group ask if the utility of one outcome is greater, equal to, or less than that of another.

2.1. Paired or Ranked Comparisons

Two closely related procedures are referred to as the paired comparison methods. Both rest on a series of rankings of pairs of outcomes, but they differ in their implementation and subsequent analysis. In the complete-paired comparisons method, outcome *A* is first compared to outcome ***B*** in the order *A*–***B*** and then in turn to each of the other alternative outcomes. Then all of the paired comparisons are repeated in the reverse order *B*–*A*. The partial paired comparisons method involves only one set of comparisons in the order *A*–***B***. The reversed set in the order *B*–*A* is not made. We will illustrate only the partial paired comparisons method here.

Two different procedures have also been developed for analyzing the judgments. Edwards (1957) derived his relative values by the conversion of the judgment data to simple proportions and then through probabilities to standard normal deviates. Eckenrode (1965), by contrast, derived his scale of values from simple proportions alone. We illustrate only Eckenrode's shorter analysis.

This method is merely a development of the simple rank orders we discussed in Chapter 10. We include it here because a systematic comparison of each alternative with all others can be expected to improve the validity of the results.

2.1.1. Procedure. The essence of this method is the comparison of each outcome with every alternative outcome. A convenient tabular means of recording the judgments made about each comparison is presented in Table 11.4. The procedure for applying this method to determine the

Table 11.4. Ranking of Pairs of Objectives by One Subject for the Partial Paired Comparison Method

	Objectives				
Objectives 1	Reduction in Disease Rate 2	Increase in Fish Species Preserved 3	Increase in Property Value 4	Additional Capital Costs 5	Decrease in Employment 6
1 Reduction in death rate	1	1	1	1	1
2 Reduction in disease rate		3	2	5	6
3 Increase in fish species preserved			3	5	3
4 Increase in property value				5	6
5 Additional capital costs					5

weights to be given the six objectives of the pollution control example is as follows:

(1) For the first paired comparison, the subject is asked: Do you consider Objective 1 more important than Objective 2? No equality judgments are allowed. The subject's ranking is recorded as 1 or 2. In Table 11.4, the subject has ranked reducing death rate higher than reducing disease rate, as indicated by the 1.

(2) The same question is asked for every other pair, and the number of the higher-ranked objective is recorded. A separate table, similar to Table 11.4, is obtained for each subject.

(3) The frequencies of the ranking judgments by all subjects are summarized for all comparisons. Table 11.5 is an example of a summary of individual tables like 11.4 for six subjects. It is read and interpreted in a column-to-row manner as follows: the 4 in column 1 and row 2 indicates that objective 1 is ranked higher than objective 2 by four subjects.

(4) The number of times that each objective was ranked higher than any other is found by adding the columns. In Table 11.5, for example, objective 1 was ranked higher than other objectives 25 times by the six subjects.

(5) The frequency data are then expressed as proportions of the possible maximum. The sums of the individual columns in Table 11.5 divided by 90 give the following proportional weights for the objectives:

Objective	Frequency	Weight (percent)
1	25	27.8
2	15	16.6
3	12	13.3
4	8	8.9
5	16	17.8
6	14	15.6
	90	100.0

These weights are recorded in Table 11.6 for comparison with those that will be derived later by other methods.

2.1.2. Discussion. The paired comparison method cannot be used to scale the utilities of alternative outcomes that are different levels of the same objective. In such cases, if more of the objective is always preferred to less, any scaling will always have equal intervals. The result will be constant marginal utility rather than the diminishing marginal utility that it is realistic to expect. For this reason, we cannot use this method to scale the utilities of the six alternative pollution-control facilities and have used it only to determine the weights to be given the various objectives.

We have illustrated only the method of partial paired comparisons. The complete paired comparisons method requires twice as many judgments from each subject in Step 2, but these judgments are still recorded as in Table 11.4 and are totaled for all subjects as in Table 11.5. The analysis proceeds exactly as in Steps 3 to 5.

Table 11.5. Frequencies of Ranking of Pairs of Objectives by Six Subjects for the Partial Paired Comparisons Method

	Objectives					
Objectives	**1**	**2**	**3**	**4**	**5**	**6**
1	—	2	0	0	2	1
2	4	—	3	2	2	4
3	6	3	—	3	3	3
4	6	4	3	—	5	4
5	4	4	3	1	—	2
6	5	2	3	2	4	—
Sums	25	15	12	8	16	14

Table 11.6. Weights for the Objectives of the Pollution-Control Example as Determined by Different Methods

Objectives	Paired Comparison Method	Allocation of Percentage Ratings	Estimation of Ratios
1. Reduction in death rate	27.8	50.0	51.0
2. Reduction in disease rate	16.6	15.0	17.0
3. Increase in fish species preserved	13.3	10.0	12.8
4. Increase in property value	8.9	5.0	6.4
5. Additonal capital costs	17.8	12.0	8.5
6. Decrease in employment	15.6	8.0	4.3

A choice between the two ways of analyzing the results must rest on the planner's beliefs about the distribution of the judgments. Eckenrode's procedure is appropriate when all judgments are of equal importance and are to be weighted equally in the analysis. Edwards' procedure assumes some particular probability distribution of the judgments and embodies this in the results.

2.2. The Half-Value Sum Method

This method is based on an assumption that people can tell when two simple groups of outcomes have equal utility. The analyst presents the two groups to a subject and varies the levels of the outcomes in one group until the subject feels that both groups are of equal utility. Then he calculates a set of utility numbers that satisfies these judgments.

This method is most appropriate when there are a large number of outcomes, when the outcomes provide a wide range of utilities, and when the outcomes vary continuously along a scale. It is not suited to the calculation of weights for objectives, since one objective cannot be continuously adjusted to another. It would be directly applicable to our pollution-control example if there were more than six outcomes. To use this same example, let us assume that for objective 3 (increase in the number of fish species preserved) there are 39 possible outcomes ranging from 2 to 40 species. We label them $2F$ to $40F$.

2.2.1. Procedure. The method is applied in the following steps:

(1) The subject is asked to rank the outcomes in order of preference. If he always prefers a higher level of preservation to any lower level, the order would be $2F, 3F, 4F, \ldots 40F$.

(2) Any two outcomes are selected that are separated by at least one other outcome. Because it is convenient to start at the bottom of the list, we select $2F$ and $4F$.

(3) The subject is then asked to select an outcome (nF) that will satisfy the equation

$$U(2F) + U(4F) = U(nF) \tag{11.2}$$

where U is utility. Let us assume the subject selects $6F$. He is telling the analyst that he would derive as much utility from an estuary with six fish species preserved as he would from two other estuaries in one of which two species were preserved and in the other four species. Equation 11.2 is a half-value sum identity.

(4) Two more outcomes are selected, and the subject is again asked to identify a single outcome that would satisfy the half-value sum identity. But this time the two outcomes are selected to straddle the outcome obtained in step 3. Because $5F$ and $7F$ straddle $6F$, the subject is asked to select a new nF that will satisfy the equation

$$U(5F) + U(7F) = U(nF) \tag{11.3}$$

Let us assume he selects $13F$.

(5) Step 4 is repeated to give a series of equality judgments. For illustrative purposes let us assume that the next one is

$$U(12F) + U(14F) = U(40F) \tag{11.4}$$

This must be the last one, because it exhausts the possible outcomes.

(6) An arbitrary origin is selected for the utility scale, such as

$$U(2F) = 1$$

(7) An assumption is now made that the utilities of the two outcomes on the left side of the equations in steps 4 and 5 are so close that they can be considered identical. The utility of the intermediate outcome must therefore also be identical, and we have from Equation 11.2

$$U(2F) = U(3F) = U(4F) = 1 \tag{11.5}$$

The utility of outcome $6F$ can now be calculated by inserting the utilities of outcomes $2F$ and $4F$ in Equation 11.2 to give

$$U(6F) = 1 + 1 = 2 \tag{11.6}$$

(**8**) Step 7 is repeated for each of the other half-value sum equations, giving

$$U(13F) = 2 + 2 = 4 \qquad (11.7)$$

$$U(40F) = 4 + 4 = 8 \qquad (11.8)$$

(**9**) The utilities calculated in steps 7 and 8 are now plotted over their respective outcomes and a curve fitted, as in Figure 11.2.

(**10**) The utilities for the outcomes of the alternatives being compared (the six pollution-control facilities, in our example) are read from the curve and standardized. In our example the standardization consists of setting the utility of the lowest outcome (three species) equal to zero and the interval between the two lowest outcomes (three and seven) equal to 10. The utilities of the other outcomes are then standardized by subtracting 1.0 and dividing the remainder by 0.12.

The results are

Outcome (No. of species)	Initial Utilities	Standardized Utilities
3	1.0	0.0
7	2.2	10.0
10	3.0	16.7
12	3.5	20.8
13	4.0	25.0
14	4.1	25.8

These standardized utilities are recorded in Table 11.7 for comparison with those that are derived by other methods.

2.2.2. Discussion. The half-value sum method is applicable to any decision that involves many outcomes and in which three adjacent outcomes each provide roughly the same utility. The basic judgments seem relatively easy for subjects to make, but they may have to include hypothetical alternatives. For example, in our pollution-control example it was necessary to visualize two estuaries and to aggregate their expected utilities when only one estuary actually existed. A similar need to abstract from reality occurs in some of the other utility-estimation methods.

2.3. Choosing Between the Methods

If a subject can report on a rank order, it seems reasonable that he could also report on an equality. The choice between these methods cannot be

Table 11.7. Utility Scalings for Various Fish Species Preservation Outcomes as Determined by Different Methods

Outcome (species preserved)	Half-Value Sum	Churchman-Ackoff	Direct Midpoint	Double Judgment	von Neumann-Morgenstern	Ramsey
14	25.8	24.3	20.0	22.5	16.7	21.8
13	25.0	22.9	18.8	20.8	15.8	20.6
12	20.8	20.0	17.6	19.0	15.0	18.8
10	16.7	12.9	15.0	15.5	13.3	15.3
7	10.0	10.0	10.0	10.0	10.0	10.0
3	0.0	0.0	0.0	0.0	0.0	0.0

based on the nature of the judgment required. It can, however, be based on the nature of the problem. The half-value sum method can only be used with outcomes whose levels can vary along a continuum. Scaling utilities meets this requirement, but determination of weights does not. In our pollution-control example, it proved easy to simulate enough additional fish-preservation outcomes to provide a continuum that permitted using the half-value sum method to scale their utilities. The methods of paired comparisons, by contrast, do not lend themselves to utility scaling and are best suited to determining weights for the various objectives.

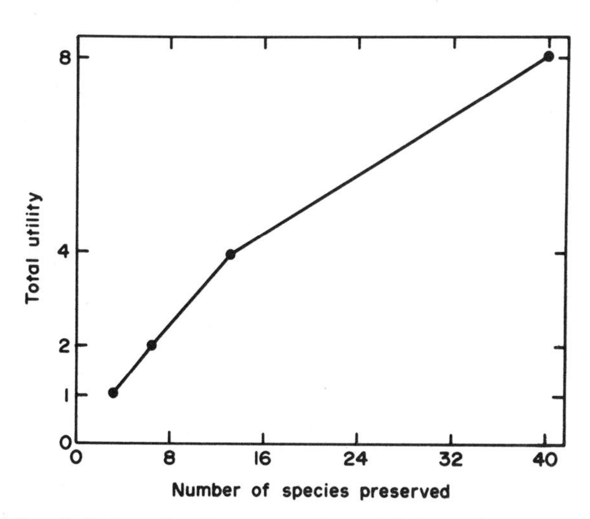

Figure 11.2. Relation of utility to number of fish species preserved, as estimated by the half-value sum method.

3. RATING JUDGMENTS

The methods in this group ask how the utilities of outcomes rate in relation to some given standard. The basic notions about rating and appoaches to it were discussed in Chapter 10. We consider here some more rigorous methods that encourage introspection and provide checks on the consistency of results.

The rating judgment methods divide into four broad classes, as shown in Figure 11.1. The first class has been covered in Chapter 10 and is not discussed here. It consists of allocating outcomes, one by one, to points on a given scale. The second class is a more rigorous version of scoring, which allocates all outcomes simultaneously rather than one by one (Section 3.1). The third class encourages subjects to think carefully about the relative utilities of pairs of outcomes. They are asked to compare pairs and to estimate the ratios between their relative utilities. These are discussed in Section 3.2. The final class, which we discuss in Section 3.3, consists of efforts to improve the validity of ratings with consistency checks. The latter three approaches can be expected to improve the validity of ratings over those obtained with the expedient methods of Chapter 10.

3.1. Allocation of Percentage Ratings

A relatively straightforward extension of the scoring method of Chapter 10 is to consider all outcomes simultaneously. Turban and Metersky (1971) used this as part of a procedure to derive weights and utility scalings for alternative systems of air defense. The method is based on an assignment of ratings to given outcomes. Because the ratings themselves are adjusted rather than the levels of the outcomes, the method can be applied to both discrete and continuous objectives. It can therefore be used to derive weights for different objectives as well as utility scalings for different levels of given objectives. We show only how it is used to derive weights.

3.1.1. Procedure. Turban and Metersky discuss the method in terms of generalized objectives rather than specific outcomes. They have been careful to express each defense objective in a measurable form, such as the expected probability of detection of a submarine by a single buoy. We can define and express the six objectives of the pollution control example in the same way. The method proceeds as follows:

(1) The subject is asked to rank the objectives in order of preference. Let us assume the ranking is

First—reduction in death rate

Second—reduction in disease rate

Third—additional capital costs

Fourth—increase in fish species preserved

Fifth—decrease in employment

Sixth—increase in property value

(2) The subject is then asked to allocate 100 points among the various objectives. He is expressly instructed to consider all factors simultaneously. Let us assume his allocation is

First—	50
Second—	15
Third—	12
Fourth—	10
Fifth—	8
Sixth—	5
	100

This is the desired weighting of objectives. These figures are entered in Table 11.6 for comparison with those derived by other methods.

3.1.2. Discussion. Turban and Metersky checked their results for consistency and also for reasonable agreement among subjects. On the basis of their experience, they claimed that simultaneous allocation of percentage ratings was superior to a series of single allocations. However, the subject in our pollution-control example found it difficult to allocate points among the six objectives simultaneously so that they added to exactly 100. In fact, he informally introduced several intermediate or back-up questions to help with the allocation. For example, he first estimated a single rating for the most preferred objective and then rated the other objectives in relation to it as well as to the scale itself. With numerous objectives, some other procedure or some formal intermediate questions may be appropriate.

The alternatives for this method are defined as generalized objectives rather than as specific outcomes. This can lead to differences from the weights obtained with other methods. For example, subjects may be especially sensitive to some objective, such as reducing the death rate, and may weight this heavily if it is expressed as a generalized outcome. However, if it is expressed as a specific quantitative outcome, such as a saving of 10 lives, they may view it in relation to total deaths from all causes and give it a different weight.

It is also possible that the ordering may change if the objectives are expressed as specific outcomes. For example, not making a high capital outlay may be considered more important than preserving a small number of fish species. The percentage ratings elicited would then imply that capital is weighted more heavily than fish species. However, if the subjects considered preserving a large number of fish species more important than making a small capital outlay, the apparent ordering of the objectives would be reversed.

3.2. Estimation of Ratios

Edwards (1972), in a study of the decision-making process of the National Aeronautics and Space Administration, advocated a method that rests on comparisons between pairs of objectives. The subjects estimate specific ratios to express the relative utilities of each pair in a sequence of pairs. This method can be used to derive weights for generalized objectives or for specific outcomes of objectives. We illustrate its use with specific outcomes. A slight variation of Edwards' procedure has been used by Stimson (1969), and we present both variants.

3.2.1. Procedure Starting with the Least-Preferred Outcome. Once the initial identification of outcomes for objectives has been completed, the method is applied as follows:

(1) The subject is asked to rank the specific outcomes for each objective in order of importance. (An example of such a ranking is shown in step 5).

(2) A rating of 10 is arbitrarily allocated to the least important outcome.

(3) The next least-important outcome is then rated in terms of an "importance preserving ratio." Suppose the least important outcome is a 4.4% decrease in employment and the next least important is an increase of $6,000,000 in property values, as shown in the example in step 5 below. The subject would be asked to consider how much more important the increase in property values is than the decrease in employment and to assign it a number that reflects this comparison. If he felt that it was twice as important, he would assign it a number of 20, because the decrease in employment has already been given a rating of 10. Let us assume he gives it a weight of 15, as shown below in Step 5.

(4) The other outcomes are then rated as in step 3, using the least important outcome rating of 10 as the base.

(5) The ratings are standardized to add to 100. For our example, this gives

Outcomes of Objectives	Initial Weights	Standardized Weights
Reduction in death rate (5 fewer deaths)	120	51.0
Reduction in disease rate (10 fewer cases)	40	17.0
Increase in fish preservation (4 extra species)	30	12.8
Additional capital costs ($8,000,000)	20	8.5
Increase in property value ($6,000,000)	15	6.4
Decrease in employment (4.4% decrease)	10	4.3
	235	100.0

These standardized weights are entered in Table 11.6 for comparison with those derived by other methods.

3.2.2. Procedure Starting with Most-Preferred Outcome. Instead of taking the least-preferred outcome as the base, this method can start with the most-preferred outcome. Stimson (1969) used this approach in analyzing the allocation of funds in a large public health program. He recognized seven objectives, such as services to the chronically ill and support of research, and proceeded as follows:

(1) Subjects were asked to rank the seven objectives in order of preference.

(2) An arbitrary rating of 100 was given to the most-preferred objective.

(3) A vertical scale was marked into 100 units and an arrow labeled "1" was placed opposite the 100 mark.

(4) Each subject was then asked to place six other arrows on the scale to indicate the relative weights he would give each of the other objectives compared to the rating of 100 for the most preferred one.

3.2.3. Discussion. The estimation of ratios method is usable with generalized objectives, such as minimize costs, or with specific outcomes, such as a cost of $8 million. Subjects appear to have little difficulty assigning ratios to alternative outcomes, but a mechanical aid like that used by Stimson may be helpful to them. The method works equally well when it starts from the least-preferred or most-preferred end of the scale. We have applied it to weight the specific outcomes of alternative A_2.

3.3. Checking for Consistency

Churchman and Ackoff (1954) provide a simple method for checking the utility numbers that individuals associate with each outcome in a set. The outcomes are ranked in order of preference, and ratings are allocated to them one by one as in the scoring method of Chapter 10. Comparisons are then made between the ratings of groups of outcomes. If these are not consistent, the individual ratings are adjusted enough to satisfy the comparisons. This method can be used to estimate total utilities of different levels of a single objective or to derive and check relative weights for various objectives. We illustrate it only for estimating utility.

3.3.1. Procedure. We illustrate the procedure with the third objective of the pollution control example—increase in fish species preserved. The lowest level of this objective is 3 species and the highest is 14. The method proceeds as follows:

(1) The subject is asked to rank the outcomes in order of preference. In our example, this might be:

$$14F > 13F > 12F > 10F > 7F > 3F.$$

(2) A rating of 100 is provisionally assigned to the most-preferred outcome.

(3) The subject is then asked to assign ratings to the other outcomes to reflect their relative utilities. These might be:

3 species—10	12 species— 85
7 species—45	13 species— 95
10 species—70	14 species—100

(4) The subject is then asked to compare the rating of the most-preferred outcome to the sum of the ratings of the next three outcomes as a group. This might turn out to be:

$$14F < (13F + 12F + 10F)$$

which says that this subject would prefer to see pollution controlled in three estuaries to the levels of the above outcomes rather than in only one estuary to the higher level that would produce $14F$. In other cases a subject might consider the most-preferred outcome to rate higher than or equal to the next three outcomes as a group.

(5) Step 4 is now repeated for the other possible comparisons. Suppose the results are:

$$13F < (12F + 10F + 7F)$$
$$12F < (10F + 7F + 3F)$$
$$10F < (7F + 3F)$$

(**6**) The individual ratings obtained in step 3 are now checked to see whether they are consistent with the comparisons obtained in steps 4 and 5. In our case they are consistent with all but the last comparison, $70 < (45 + 10)$, which is obviously not true.

(**7**) If some of the comparisons are not consistent, individual ratings must be adjusted to make them so. In our example the rating for $10F$ might be adjusted to 60, and those for $7F$ and $3F$ might be adjusted to 50 and 15, respectively. With these adjustments, all the above comparisons would be consistent.

(**8**) For comparative purposes, it is convenient to standardize the utility numbers. This can be done by setting an arbitrary base level of $U(3F) = 0$ and an arbitrary interval of $U(7F) - U(3F) = 10$. Subtracting 15 from each of the utility ratings, and dividing the results by 3.5 gives the following:

Outcome (no. of species)	Initial Utilities	Standardized Utilities
3	15	0.0
7	50	10.0
10	60	12.9
12	85	20.0
13	95	22.9
14	100	24.3

These standardized utilities are entered in Table 11.7 for comparison with those derived by other methods.

3.3.2. Discussion. This method is based on and essentially a check for the scoring method. Its strength lies in the check it provides on the consistency of the initial ratings in step 3 with the comparisons in steps 4 and 5.

3.4. Choice between the Rating Judgments Methods

The allocation of percentage ratings and the estimation of ratios methods are more straightforward than the Churchman–Ackoff method. There seems to be little choice between the first two methods, although the estimation of ratios may be more suitable for face-to-face surveys. The Churchman–Ackoff method is most useful as a check for consistency, the purpose for which it was originally proposed.

4. PROPORTIONAL JUDGMENTS

The methods in this group ask whether the utilities of the outcomes are proportional to each other. We illustrate this approach for just two of the possible proportions: the direct-midpoint method, in which the subject is asked to report when an outcome stands halfway between two other outcomes, and the double-judgment method, in which the subject is asked to adjust the level of an outcome until it provides double the utility of another fixed outcome. Geiger and Firestone (1933), in a study of the disutility of noise, asked their subjects to consider all of the following proportions: 1/100, 1/10, 1/4, 1/2 (the half judgment), 1, 2 (the double judgment), 4, 10, and 100. We believe the two we present here adequately illustrate the method.

This approach can be applied best when the level of an outcome can be varied continuously. These methods are therefore more suited to scaling utilities than to calculating weights for different objectives. We show how they can be used to estimate utilities.

4.1. The Direct-Midpoint or Half-Judgment Method

This method rests on utility judgments about the level of an objective that will lie halfway between two other levels of the same objective. If utility numbers are available for the two extremes, the utility of the level in question will lie halfway between them. Fishburn (1967) calls this the *direct-midpoint* method because of the directness and nature of the judgment. Torgerson (1958) calls it a *bisection* method.

4.1.1. Procedure. We illustrate this method with the same six outcomes for fish species preservation we used in Section 3.3.1. The method proceeds as follows:

(1) The subject is asked to rank the outcomes and to select the least-preferred and most-preferred ones. Let us assume that these are $3F$ and $14F$.

(2) He is then asked to consider the utilities of the two extreme outcomes and to specify an outcome whose utility lies halfway between them. A useful approach is to start with the midpoint in physical size of the outcomes, which in our example would be 8.5 species. The subject can then be asked whether he considers an increase from 3 to 8.5 species to have the same utility as an increase from 8.5 to 14. If diminishing marginal utility is present, he can be expected to rate the utility of the former increase higher than that of the latter. He can then be asked to adjust the midpoint until these two increases have equal utility. Let us suppose he selects a midpoint of 7.5 species because he feels an increase from 3 to 7.5 species would have as much utility as a further increase from 7.5 to 14.

(**3**) The subject is then asked to select another midpoint between the lower limit and the one just selected in step 2. Let us suppose he decides that an outcome of 5 species would have a utility exactly halfway between the utilities of 3 and 7.5 species.

(**4**) He is then asked to select another midpoint between the upper limit and the one selected in step 2. Let us assume he selects 10 species.

(**5**) An arbitrary base point and an arbitrary utility scale are now selected. Let us use $U(3F) = 0$ and $U(14F) = 100$.

(**6**) Because the range between 0 and 100 has been divided into four equal parts by the three midpoints, the utilities of those midpoints must be

$$5.0 \text{ species} = 25$$
$$7.5 \text{ species} = 50$$
$$10.0 \text{ species} = 75$$

Utility is now plotted over number of species for the two extremes and these three midpoints, and a smooth curve is fitted to the five points.

(**7**) From the curve developed in step 6, the utility numbers are read for each of the six possible outcomes and listed below to the nearest whole number. These initial utilities are then standardized as before, using an arbitrary base point of $U(3F) = 0$ and an arbitrary interval of $U(7F) - U(3F) = 10$. The results are

Outcome (no. of species)	Initial Utilities	Standardized Utilities
3	0	0.0
7	50	10.0
10	75	15.0
12	88	17.6
13	94	18.8
14	100	20.0

These standardized utilities are entered in Table 11.7.

4.1.2. Discussion. The extremes of the actual range of alternative outcomes provide good end points for a utility scale. Subjects are likely to be familiar with possibilities between these natural limits and to be able to visualize midpoints. However, when the range of outcomes is small, it may be necessary to make artificial subdivisions of natural units in order to establish midpoints. The subjects may then have some difficulty visualizing things like the 7.5 fish species in our example.

4.2. The Double-Judgment Method

The double-judgment approach is similar to the midpoint method just discussed. Galanter (1962) used it to derive a utility curve for money, and Fishburn (1967) to estimate the disutility of delays at highway toll booths. We use it to estimate the relative utilities obtained from different levels of fish species preservation.

4.2.1. Procedure. The method starts at the lower limit of the range of outcomes and proceeds as follows:

(1) The subject is asked to estimate an outcome whose utility is double that of the least-preferred one. In our example he is asked: If you are obtaining satisfaction from knowing that the estuary is still habitable by three species of fish, how many species would it have to support before you felt your satisfaction was twice as great? Let us suppose the reply is seven.

(2) Using the outcome from step 1, the subject is asked to estimate a new outcome that has twice as much utility. Suppose the reply is 18.

(3) Further questions are then asked, proceeding up the range of outcomes. In our example the second response was above the upper limit of the range (14 species), so questioning would stop with Step 2.

(4) Based on the subject's replies, the analyst now sets up a series of preference equations. In our example these are:

$$U(7F) = 2[U(3F)] \tag{11.9}$$

$$U(18F) = 2[U(7F)] \tag{11.10}$$

(5) An arbitrary origin is set and utility numbers are calculated with the preference equations. In our example the base can be set at $U(3F) = 10$. Substituting this in Equation 11.9 gives $U(7F) = 20$, and substituting this in Equation 11.10 gives $U(18F) = 40$.

(6) The utility numbers obtained in step 5 are plotted over their respective outcomes, and a smooth curve is fitted. Utility numbers are read from this curve for the actual outcomes and standardized in the usual way. The results are:

Outcome (no. of species)	Initial Utilities	Standardized Utilities
3	10.0	0.0
7	20.0	10.0
10	25.5	15.5
12	29.0	19.0
13	30.8	20.8
14	32.5	22.5

These standardized utilities are entered in Table 11.7.

4.2.2. Discussion. The double-judgment method presents several arithmetical problems. The arbitrary origin for the utility scale cannot be set at zero, as was done in the other methods. Because each successive estimate is double the first, all will be zero if the first is zero. This problem can be handled by the standardization procedure we used. More serious is the problem that the series of elicited numbers quickly runs off the scale of actual outcomes because of successive doubling. This may make it difficult for subjects to give true responses. It also means that the analyst will have very few points with which to plot the utility curve.

4.3. Choice between the Proportional Judgment Methods

The double-judgment method is a simple extension of ratio estimation, with the ratio set at 2 and the outcomes varied to fit this ratio. It seems most appropriate when the total utility curve is approximately linear and when there is a wide range of outcome sizes. When these characteristics do not exist, the direct midpoint method is preferable.

5. PROBABILITY JUDGMENTS

The methods in this group ask when the expected utility of prospect I is equal to the expected utility of prospect II. They are based on the expected utility theorem, which Dillon (1971) states as follows: Assume a decision maker whose preferences follow the axioms of ordering, transitivity, continuity, and independence, noted in Section 5 of Chapter 7. There will be a utility function that will assign a single number to any risky prospect faced by this decision maker. Among the useful properties of this utility function is the concept that the utility of any prospect is, in fact, its expected utility. If prospect I is a risky prospect with a set of outcomes distributed according to a probability distribution, the utility of prospect I will be equal to its statistically expected utility (EU)

$$U(I) = EU(I) \tag{11.11}$$

The mathematical expression for the expected utility of a prospect that has two possible outcomes a and b, whose probabilities of occurring are pr and $(1 - pr)$, respectively, can be expressed as

$$EU(I) = pr\,[U\,(a)] + (1 - pr)\,[U(b)] \tag{11.12}$$

Substituting this expression for $EU(I)$ in Equation 11.11 gives

$$U(I) = pr[U(a)] + (1 - pr)\,[U(b)] \tag{11.13}$$

The relatively simple concept expressed in Equation 11.13 is the basis of a number of methods for estimating the utility of outcomes. They all involve two prospects and seek to find the point of indifference between prospects by adjusting either the probability or the level of an outcome. Once this point has been found, a set of equations like 11.13 is obtained, from which utility numbers can be derived.

The idea underlying these methods has been applied to the analysis of decisions by Fishburn (1964) and Raiffa (1968). Of particular interest are the attempts to place numerical measurements on subjective utilities. Early efforts centered on estimating the utility of monetary outcomes, but recently they have been extended to forest-fire control, mineral exploration, and meteorology (Halter and Dean, 1971).

The methods differ in the number of outcomes and in whether adjustments are made to the outcomes and probabilities. The von Neumann–Morgenstern method presented in Section 5.1 has three outcomes that are fixed and two probabilities that are varied. The Ramsey method described in Section 5.2 has fixed probabilities and four outcomes, one of which is varied. When the outcomes are defined as different levels of a single thing, the methods can be used to estimate utilities. When they are defined as different objectives for one alternative, the methods can be used to derive weights for the objectives. We illustrate their use only for estimating utilities.

5.1. The von Neumann–Morgenstern Method

This method, developed by von Neumann and Morgenstern (1947), rests on choices between two prospects, the basic model for which is shown in Table 11.8. Prospect I is a two-element probability combination, the actual outcome from which depends on the probabilities. Prospect II consists of one outcome that would be obtained with certainty. The subject is presented

Table 11.8. The Basic Model for the von Neumann-Morgenstern Method

Prospect I			Prospect II		
Probability	**Outcome**	**Example**	**Probability**	**Outcome**	**Example**
pr	*a*	14	1.0	*c*	5
1 - pr	*b*	3			

with these two prospects, and then the probabilities of the two outcomes in prospect I are adjusted until he is indifferent as to which prospect he receives.

This method is sometimes called the *reference-contract* method because prospect I serves as a constant reference point for all choices. Outcome *a* in prospect I is usually the most-favorable possible outcome, and outcome *b* the least-favorable one. Prospect II is known as the *certainty equivalent,* because the probability of receiving the outcome is 1.0, or certainty. The method is also known as the *standard-gamble method* (Fishburn, 1967) in recognition of the gamble involved in prospect I and the basic position of the method in the field of decision analysis.

5.1.1. Procedure. We illustrate this method with different outcome levels of fish species preservation in the pollution-control example. The method proceeds as follows:

(**1**) The game is structured to suit the specific problem. In our example the most favorable possible outcome (a) is 14 species preserved, and the least favorable one (b) is 3 species, as shown in Table 11.8. Other outcomes between these extremes can be inserted as outcome *c*.

(**2**) The subject is now interviewed to determine the level of probability (*pr*) in prospect I at which he considers the two prospects to be of equal utility. This is done for enough different levels of outcome *c* to establish the relationship shown in Figure 11.3.

(**3**) Let us assume that the size of outcome *c* is set at 5 for the first run, as in Table 11.8. It is often convenient to begin by setting *pr* at one extreme or the other, that is, at 0 or 1.0. The questioning might start like this:

Question: If *pr* were 0, would you prefer prospect I or II?

Answer: If *pr* were 0, I would be certain to get outcome *b* or 3 species with prospect I. I prefer prospect II with its certain outcome of 5 species.

The size of *pr* would then be increased until an exhange like this was reached:

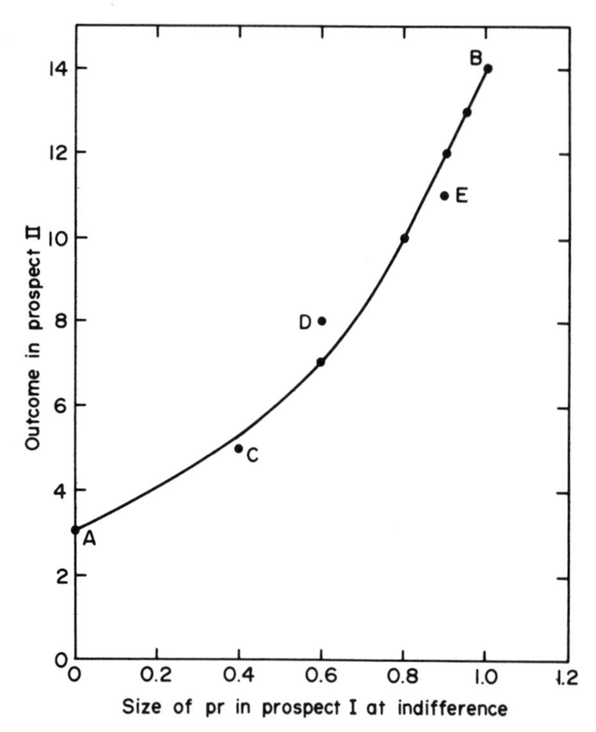

***Figure 11.3.** Relation between probability of obtaining the most favorable outcome in prospect I and the size of the certain outcome in prospect II at indifference between prospects in the von Neumann-Morgenstern method.*

Question: If *pr* were .4, would you prefer prospect I or II?

Answer: Prospect I would now give me a 40 percent chance of getting 14 species and a 60 percent chance of getting only 3 species, compared to a certainty of getting 5 with prospect II. I am not able to choose between these prospects. (The subject is indifferent as to which prospect he gets.)

(4) The *pr* of .4 at indifference is plotted against the respective outcome of 5 species as point *C* on Figure 11.3.

(5) Step 4 is now repeated using other convenient figures for outcome *c*. For illustration, let us assume that two more outcomes (c) of 8 and 11 species are tested and give probabilities (*pr*) of .6 and .9, respectively. These are plotted as points *D* and *E* on Figure 11.3.

(6) It is not necessary to follow step 3 for the most- and least-favorable outcomes. If in prospect II the certain outcome were 14 species, the subject would only be indifferent between the prospects if the probability (*pr*) of obtaining outcome *a* were 1. If the probability is less than 1, he is clearly better off to take the certain outcome of prospect II. The same would be true if outcome c were 3 species. He would prefer prospect I if there were any probability greater than zero of getting output a. He will only be indifferent between prospects I and II when $pr = 0$. The extreme points A and B in Figure 11.3 can therefore be anchored in advance. The interviews are needed to establish the points between these extremes.

(**7**) A curve is now fitted to the plotted points, and pr values are read from it for the outcomes that are actually possible. There are six of these in the pollution control example.

(**8**) The utility figure for the most-favorable outcome is arbitrarily set at 100 and that for the least-favorable one at 0. Based on the expected utility theorem and the knowledge that at indifference the expected utility of prospect II equals that of prospect I, we can write

$$1.0\,[U(c)] = pr[U(a)] + (1 - pr)\,[U(b)] \tag{11.14}$$

Substituting the arbitrary utility figures gives

$$1.0\,[U(c)] = pr(100) + (1 - pr)\,(0) \tag{11.15}$$

This can now be solved for the utilities of the various outcomes by entering the pr figures obtained in step 7. For an outcome of 7 species and its probability of .6 from Figure 11.3 this is

$$U(7) = 0.6(100) + 0.4(0) = 60$$

The resulting utilities are standardized in the usual way and give

Outcome (no. of species)	Original Utilities	Standardized Utilities
3	0	0.0
7	60	10.0
10	80	13.3
12	90	15.0
13	95	15.8
14	100	16.7

These standardized utilities are entered in Table 11.7.

5.1.2. Discussion. The success of the von Neumann–Morgenstern method depends on how well the subjects can handle the game displayed in Table 11.8, and particularly on how well they can handle choices involving probabilities. Much depends on how the interviewers introduce the subjects to the notion of probabilities. Once a subject has grasped the method, the necessary judgments are simple. He is only required to say that he prefers one prospect to another or is indifferent between them.

5.2. The Ramsey Method

The method developed by Ramsey (1931) is based on choices between two prospects, as was the von Neumann–Morgenstern Method, but presents four possible outcomes instead of two, as shown in Table 11.9. The probabilities are also different, in that all are fixed at .5 so that there is an equal chance of obtaining each outcome in each prospect. Officer and Halter (1968) claim that this equality is an advantage, because subjects may gain utility from the way an outcome is derived (i.e., gambling) as well as from the outcome itself. The presence of identical probabilities means that the gamble is the same in each prospect. The item adjusted to elicit the point of indifference is also different. In the Ramsey method the level of one outcome is adjusted rather than one probability.

5.2.1. Procedure. We illustrate this method with the fish preservation outcome levels. The method proceeds as follows:

(1) The conceptual model of Table 11.9 must first be structured to fit the particular problem. Positions a and c are occupied by different levels of the outcome being studied. It is convenient to start with outcome a being the lowest possible level—in our case, three fish species. Outcome c is the variable level that will be adjusted to achieve indifference. It is therefore shown as n in Table 11.9. The model works best when outcome position b is occupied by a good alternative to the thing whose levels occupy positions a and c and when position d is occupied by a neutral thing. Outcome b must be preferred to outcome d. The levels of b and d are held constant throughout the set of games. For our example, a reduction in the number of disease cases is a real alternative to fish species preservation. Outcome b will therefore be defined as a reduction of 10 disease cases and labeled "10 *DC*" in Table 11.9. A reasonably neutral thing would be provision of a new city park, so outcome d is defined as a two-acre park and labeled "2 *AP*".

(2) The subject is now interviewed to determine the figure for n that would make him indifferent between prospects I and II. Since outcome b is prefer-

Table 11.9. The Basic Model for the Ramsey Method

Prospect I			Prospect II		
Probability	Outcome	Example	Probability	Outcome	Example
0.5	a	3 species	0.5	c	n species
0.5	b	10 *DC*	0.5	d	2 *AP*

red to outcome d by definition, n must be greater than the figure for a, or three species in our example. The interview starts with this minimum level:

Question: If n were three, would you prefer prospect I or II, or be indifferent between them?

Answer: Since outcomes a and c are identical and I prefer 10 DC to 2 AP, I would choose prospect I.

The interviewer then selects a higher level for n.

Question: What would be your response if n were seven?

Answer: Now I would prefer prospect II.

The interviewer now knows that n at indifference must be between three and seven and tries other levels until the subject is indifferent. Let us suppose this occurs at five species.

(3) The game is now repeated as in step 2, but the figure obtained there (five species) is now used for outcome a. A series of questions are again asked to elicit a new indifference figure for n. Let us suppose this is 8.

(4) Step 2 is repeated several more times, using for a the figure obtained for n at indifference in the preceding game. Let us suppose these additional figures for n are 11, 15, and 20.

(5) An arbitrary origin and interval are selected for the utility scale. It is often convenient to set the origin at the lowest possible outcome, so we will use U (three species) = 0. The interval may be anything convenient, particularly if the final utility numbers are standardized. Let us use $U(10DC) - U(2\,AP) = 5$.

(6) Estimates of total utility are now derived. In step 2 the subject indicated that he would derive the same utility from both prospects when n was 5. At indifference, the expected utility of prospect I equals that of prospect II. Based on the expected utility theorem, which defines expected utility in terms of probabilities of each outcome as in Equation 11.12, we can write

$$.5[U(3F)] + .5[U(10\,DC)] = .5\,[U(5F)] + .5[U(2\,AP)] \qquad (11.16)$$

where F stands for fish species preserved. Multiplying through by 2 and transposing gives

$$U(10\,DC) - U\,(2\,AP) = U(5F) - U(3F) \qquad (11.17)$$

Substituting the arbitrary interval and origin from step 5 gives

$$5 = U(5F) - 0 = U(5F)$$

So we know that the utility of three species = 0 and of five species = 5.

(7) Step 6 is now repeated for the second n figure of 8 obtained in step 3.

Following Equation 11.16, we have

$$0.5\,[U(5F)] + 0.5\,[U(10\,DC)] = 0.5\,[U(8F)] + 0.5\,[U(2\,AP)] \quad (11.18)$$

and substituting the arbitrary interval and the utility of $5F$ from step 6 gives

$$5 = U\,(8F) - U(5F) = U(8F) - 5$$

and so the utility of eight species = 10.

(**8**) Step 6 is then repeated for the other n figures from step 4. The utilities for all outcomes are

3 species = 0	11 species = 15
5 species = 5	15 species = 20
8 species = 10	20 species = 25

The regular interval between the utilities of these outcomes results from the constant arbitrary interval of 5 assigned to $[U\,(10DC) - U(2\,AP)]$.

(**9**) The utilities obtained in step 8 are plotted over their respective n figures, and a smooth curve is fitted.

(**10**) Utility scalings for the actual outcomes are read from this curve and standardized, if necessary. The results are

Outcome (no. of species)	Initial Utilities	Standardized Utilities
3	0.0	0.0
7	8.5	10.0
10	13.0	15.3
12	16.0	18.8
13	17.5	20.6
14	18.5	21.8

These standardized utilities are entered in Table 11.7.

5.2.2. Discussion. The sequential manner in which outcome c is moved to become outcome a in each succeeding game distinguishes this method from the von Neumann–Morgenstern method. The Ramsey method has an advantage over the von Neumann–Morgenstern method in that some of the outcomes can be discrete rather than continuous. We have used this method to derive monetary values for recreation activities in Oregon (Sinden, 1974), for rural and recreational problems in Australia (Liesch and Sinden, 1976), and for the rural way of life in Chapter 14. In each application the model was extended by running several sets of games, with a new level of outcome *b* in each set. Outcomes *a* and *c* must be continuous, but outcome *b* can be discrete.

5.3. Discussion of the Probability Judgment Methods

5.3.1. Other Uses of the Methods. An interesting application of this kind of method is Keeney's (1973) comparison of sites for a new airport at Mexico City. He derived weights for various objectives by the probabilistic rating method, which is essentially the von Neumann–Morgenstern method with several outcomes in positions *a, b,* and *c*. Utilities for the outcomes of each objective were estimated by the probabilistic midpoint method, which is also based on von Neumann–Morgenstern, but has the probabilities fixed at .5 for *a* and *b* and at 1 for *c*. Outcome *c* was varied to achieve indifference. He then combined utilities and weights as in Equation 11.1 to estimate comparative values.

The aggregation procedure of Equation 11.1 can combine utilities and disutilities to express comparative values in net utility. We use this procedure in Section 6 to estimate comparative values for the pollution control alternatives.

5.3.2. Choice Between the Probability Judgment Methods. A choice between the methods in this group should be based on the reactions of subjects to the method and the relevance of different models for the particular valuation. The following observations can be made:

(**a**) If subjects obtain positive utility from gambling itself, as well as from the expected outcomes, the Ramsey method must be used. This is the only model in which all probabilities are the same.

(**b**) Some subjects have more difficulty responding to changes in probabilities than to changes in levels of outcomes. If this problem arises, a method with fixed probabilities is more suitable.

(**c**) Some models handle discrete factors more readily than others. If discrete factors are involved, a model with fixed outcomes is more appropriate than one in which the outcomes are adjusted.

6. ESTIMATING COMPARATIVE TOTAL UTILITIES

The previous sections have shown how the various rigorous methods can be used for estimating relative utilities and for estimating relative weights. This information must now be combined into estimates of comparative total utilities. We illustrate this process with the pollution control example. The problem is to choose one of the six alternative pollution control facilities. Using the estimates of relative utilities and weights from the preceding sections, we determine the total utility that each objective would provide in each alternative. By proper weighting, we then combine these into estimates of comparative values for the alternatives.

6.1. The Basic Model

The basic model for estimating comparative values was set out in Equation 11.1

$$V_i = \sum_{j=1}^{n} (U_{ij} \times WT_j) \tag{11.19}$$

This model says that the value of any alternative i can be calculated by multiplying the utility for each objective (U_{ij}) by the weight given that objective (WT_j) and adding the n products. This is one way of implementing the general value Equation 3.5.

A range of weights for the six objectives of the pollution control example is summarized in Table 11.6, and a range of utilities for one objective in Table 11.7. The procedure now is to (a) select an appropriate set of weights, (b) derive utility scalings for the other five objectives, (c) multiply the utility scalings by the weights, and (d) add the products.

6.2. Choosing the Utilities and Weights

Utilities. Table 11.7 shows that the utility numbers for different outcome levels of a given objective can vary with the methods used for estimating them. There may be several causes of this variation. In our case, the subject was questioned over a period of days, so some of the variations may reflect inconsistencies. Some may also be due to random causes. And different methods will inevitably elicit different numbers.

We selected the direct midpoint method because it encourages introspection and should motivate the subject. Its questions are also within the actual range of outcomes and so may record utilities more realistically. The direct midpoint method was applied to estimate utility numbers for the other five objectives. The resulting standardized utilities are shown in Table 11.10.

Weights. Table 11.6 shows that the weights assigned to different objectives can also vary with the methods used for determining them. Because the two rating judgment methods give reasonably close results, we have used the estimation of ratios method's weights, which are shown in Table 11.6.

Table 11.10. Standardized Utilities for the Six Objectives of the Alternative Pollution Control Facilities

Objectives	Alternatives					
	A_1	A_2	A_3	A_4	A_5	A_6
1. Reduction in death rate	0	10.0	14.0	16.0	18.0	20.0
2. Reduction in diease rate	0	10.0	13.3	14.9	15.9	15.9
3. Increase in fish species preserved	0	10.0	15.0	17.6	18.8	20.0
4. Increase in property values	0	10.0	14.7	16.6	17.2	17.2
5. Additional capital costs	0	10.0	30.0	90.0	185.0	500.0
6. Decrease in employment	0	10.0	40.0	180.0	390.0	1000.0

6.3. Calculating the Values

The standardized utilities from Table 11.10 were weighted and added in accordance with Equation 11.19. They were then divided by 100 and gave the following comparative values

	Alternative	Value
A_1	Primary—old (existing facility)	0.0
A_2	Primary—renewed	+7.4
A_3	New primary + low-efficiency secondary	+8.0
A_4	New primary + high-efficiency secondary	−1.4
A_5	New primary + high-efficiency secondary + tertiary	−17.1
A_6	Same as A_5, but disposal at sea	−68.9

6.4. Choosing an Alternative

Alternative pollution control facilities A_2 and A_3 show positive values. Because these values measure the net utility of a change from the present pollution control system (A_1), either of them would be desirable. The estimated values are so close that a choice is difficult. For alternatives A_4 to A_6, the extra disutilities (increases in costs) exceed the extra utilities (increases in benefits), and their comparative values are negative.

7. DISCUSSION AND CONCLUSIONS

7.1. Three Persistent Problems

The methods described in this chapter are fairly straightforward but present three persistent problems. One is the need to collect large amounts of data and to ask many questions of each subject. A second lies in distinguishing between additive and nonadditive utilities. A third is the need for realism to promote true responses from the subjects. Let us consider these problems in more detail.

7.1.1. Handling Large Amounts of Data. The difficulty of estimating utilities or weights increases rapidly with the number of outcomes. In our example with six objectives, the method of paired comparisons required 15 questions for each subject. Ten objectives would have required 45. The following procedures can help overcome this problem.

(**a**) Work with a subset of the outcomes and ignore the rest. In a study involving 40 different objectives, Turban and Metersky (1971) found that four to seven objectives provided 90 percent of the total utility. The rest contributed less than 10 percent and could be ignored.

(**b**) Start with a few objectives and add others gradually to see whether they affect the results. Fishburn (1964) suggested that a small number (6 to 10) of the more important objectives be selected first and that their weights and utilities be calculated and the comparative values determined. A second group of 6 to 10 objectives can then be added and the process repeated. If the second results agree with the first, the analyst can ignore any other objectives.

(**c**) Study a small number of objectives intensively, and insert these as pegs in the total list of objectives. Additional objectives need only be compared with these standard pegs and not with every other objective.

A decision to use one of these procedures instead of one of the others must depend on the skills and beliefs of the analyst and on some prior information about the preferences of the decision maker.

7.1.2. Additive and Nonadditive Utilities. The rigorous methods assume that utilities from different objectives can be added together. This asumption rests on a belief that all objectives contribute independently to overall utility. Additive models dominate the literature on riskless choice, partly because they are simple and relatively easy to use and partly because they permit analysis of some interesting problems. Because the methods of this chapter are strictly applicable only when the additivity assumption holds, we must consider how this affects their use.

Utilities can only be added if the outcomes are "utility independent." This situation exists when the nature of the alternatives is such that the level of one objective can be varied independently of those of other objectives and when the subjects' preferences for one objective are independent of the amounts of the other objectives they receive. When these requirements are met, the utilities from different objectives can be added.

The probability judgment methods are based on the expected utility theorem and explicitly overcome the additivity problem by introducing probabilities and combining them into expected outcomes. These outcomes are mutually exclusive, and because the subject knows he cannot have both, it is reasonable to assume that he will perceive the utilities as independent.

The assumptions necessary for an additive function will often be violated, but the methods described in this chapter may still be useful for decisions. Yntema and Torgerson (1967) have shown that in a majority of multiobjective cases, the additive effects tend to swamp the nonadditive ones. An additive method that does not accurately measure a particular utility may still serve adequately to discriminate among the total utilities of different alternatives. And it is sometimes possible to apply tests for additivity, as Keeney (1973) and Keeney and Wood (1977) have shown.

7.1.3. The Need for Realism. The examples in this chapter have elicited and recorded utilities in terms of numbers on a scale. Other recording procedures are sometimes used in the belief that realism will lead to truer responses. Many decisions about transportation and recreation facilities involve some travel. In such cases, subjects may be able to allocate travel time better than rating points.

The probability judgment methods often need some means of getting subjects to think in terms of probabilities. Some investigators have had their subjects move markers on diagrams to simulate the fall in pr for outcome a and rise in $(1 - pr)$ for outcome b. Others have drawn marbles from a bag. In agricultural applications it has been found helpful to express a probability of .25 in terms of something familiar to the subject, such as one crop in four years.

7.2. Choosing among the Total Utility Methods

Some subjects find it easy to express preferences in the numerical form of utility data, but others find it difficult. We have almost always been able to elicit data on utilities and weights when the subject is not overtly hostile. The key is to select a method that is adequately precise but also simple to apply.

7.2.1. Do Different Methods Give Similar Results? The rigorous methods can be expected to give similar results under certain circumstances. Harlow, Miller, and Newcomb (1962) found, when judging essays, that different methods agreed when the choice was among similar alternatives in the same general problem area. Because the estimation of utilities involves comparing similar things, we can expect the methods to agree more closely on utility scalings than on weights. Tables 11.6 and 11.7 support this.

Eckenrode (1965) compared the results of six methods—ranking, rating, three paired comparison methods, and the Churchman–Ackoff method—and reported that all produced "essentially the same" ordering of weights. Similar methods with similar kinds of judgment can be expected to give similar results.

If a group of methods would all give similar results, an objective choice among them must be based on other criteria. The following are useful:

(a) What kinds of problems does the method suit?

(b) How easily is the method understood by the subjects?

(c) What are the costs involved in using the method?

(d) What special features does the method have?

We expand on the first two criteria in the following sections.

7.2.2. What Kinds of Problem Do the Methods Suit? It is important to distinguish between objectives that are continuous and those that are discrete or binary. Outcomes for continuous objectives can occur at any level and can be tested as small increments. Discrete objectives, by contrast, can only occur at certain specific levels. The most extreme example—a binary objective—can occur at two levels. Table 11.11 summarizes some

Table 11.11. Important Characteristics of the Rigorous Total Utility Methods

Method	Kind of Objective That Can Be Analyzed[a]		Ease of Comprehension by Subject	Length of Interview Required
	Discrete	Continuous		
Paired comparisons	√	X	simple	short
Half-value sum	X	√	simple	short
Allocation of percentage ratings	√	√	simple	shortest
Estimation of ratios	√	√	simple	shortest
Churchman–Ackoff	√	√	satisfactory	short
Direct midpoint	X	√	satisfactory	rather short
Double judgment	X	√	satisfactory	rather short
von Neumann–Morgenstern	X	√	less satisfactory	long
Ramsey	√	√	less satisfactory	long

[a] √ = yes; X = no.

characteristics of the methods, including their need for continuous objectives. Almost all of them are suitable for continuous objectives, but only some can be used with discrete ones.

7.2.3. How Easily Are the Methods Understood? The ease with which subjects can understand a method and the cost of using it are closely related. The low-cost methods tend to be those that are easily understood. Furthermore, the low-cost methods require no special skills on the part of the interviewer, and the interviews can usually be relatively short. We have presented the methods in this chapter in the order of the difficulty of the judgments required from subjects. Some writers reject the simple methods, which ask subjects to make single, bold, direct judgments, presumably because they feel the lack of introspection will lead to a lack of precision. Our position, like that of Stevens (1959), is to test them experimentally rather than reject them *a priori.*

The literature suggests that the following general statements can be made about ease of understanding:

(a) Methods that require probability judgments involve gambles and are more difficult for subjects to grasp than are the ranking, rating, and proportional judgment methods. However, the probability judgments may encourage greater introspection and truer responses.

(b) Some methods need much explanation and explicit back-up questions and can be expected to require long interviews.

(c) The rating methods work directly with specific outcomes and are easier for an analyst to apply and interpret. This may also make them easier for subjects to grasp.

CHAPTER 12

Estimation of Monetary Values—Opportunity-Cost Methods

Because consumers will make purchases as long as the benefits exceed their costs, the value of a benefit is reflected in its cost. This simple principle underlies the valuation methods based on monetary cost, or opportunity cost as we have defined it. All the methods provide monetary estimates, but they sometimes estimate total benefit rather than value or net benefit.

Costs are often readily available or easy to measure, and a variety of opportunity-cost methods have been developed, as shown in Figure 12.1. A first approach uses production (or replacement) costs, consumers' expenditure, and the related concepts of gross national product and value added. A second approach makes structured comparisons. A third approach considers opportunity cost in its fundamental role as the benefits lost in the opportunities foregone.

All the methods rest on the principle that benefits are reflected in the costs of an exchange. They are further supported by the universal recognition of monetary costs as a measure of disutility.

Many opportunity-cost methods are widely, and often justly, criticized because they do not estimate value as such. We agree with much of this criticism, and we review it as the chapter proceeds. But our assessment is based on the methods' role in providing information for decisions, as well as in providing estimates of value. Therefore, we have a rather different perspective and reach different, more-favorable conclusions about the usefulness of the methods.

1. AN ENVIRONMENTAL POLICY EXAMPLE: ALLOCATING RESOURCES AMONG COMPETING LAND USES

Allocating uses to various land types is a general problem that must be faced by all forms of land management. Our example was selected because much data has been published by the Agricultural Experiment Station of

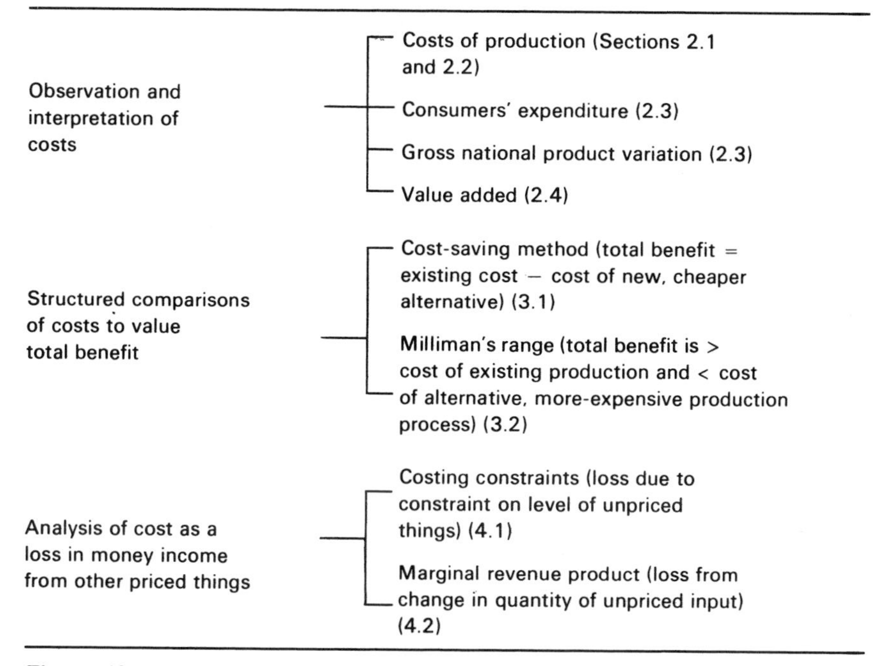

Figure 12.1. A classification of opportunity-cost methods for estimating monetary values

New Mexico State University. Particularly useful are the linear programming analysis and the study of recreation demand for the Ruidoso Ranger District (Gray and Anderson, 1964a and 1964b). This example provides a realistic theme for our review of the opportunity-cost methods.

The Ruidoso Ranger District of the Lincoln National Forest occupies 178,000 acres. Although only 5000 persons lived within the district, there were 300,000 visitors in 1960. These recreationists were competing among themselves for the use of the resources and also against the farmers and sawmillers. There was a clear need for the U.S. Forest Service to allocate its land among the competing uses in some rational manner.

1.1. The Available Resources

The resources (land, capital, and labor) available to managers of the Ranger District are shown in Table 12.1. Some land can be used for two or more purposes simultaneously. These lands are included in more than one use category, and the total resource area therefore shows as 297,000 acres rather than the actual area of 178,000 acres. Most of the land is forested

Table 12.1. Natural and Economic Resources in the Ruidoso Ranger District

Resource	Quantity
Land for camping and picnicking (acres)	1,403
Land for hiking (acres)	19,200
Land for hunting and fishing (acres)	71,000
Land for grazing (acres)	35,160
Land for producing timber (acres)	169,000
Land for cabins or homesites (acres)	148
Land for skiing (acres)	1,000
Total land resource (acres)	296,911
Surface water (acre-feet)	9,733
Groundwater (acre-feet)	7,210
Public capital (dollars)	121,875
Private capital (dollars)	12,600,000
Public labor (man-days)	4,270
Private labor (man-days)	25,530

Source. Gray and Anderson (1964a), Table 2.

(169,000 acres), but local administrators regard the district as mainly suitable for watershed protection and recreation.

The data on surface water resources are median annual net streamflow from nine years' records. The groundwater resource is assumed to be equal to the quantity that farmers pump from the ground. The quantities of labor and capital are defined as the amounts actually used in 1962.

1.2. The Competing Uses

Eight different land uses or activities (Table 12.2) were competing for these resources. Visitors engaged in four forms of recreation—camping and picnicking, cabin ownership, hunting and fishing, and skiing. Local residents were employed in the three activities of timber production, grazing, and orchard management. The eighth land use was production of water.

The requirements of each land use for each kind of resource (the input-output coeficients) were defined by Gray and Anderson (1964a, Appendix C). The hiking land resource provided mainly for the camping/picnicking activity. Because orchard management was equally suited to all the land resources, there was no separate orchard land resource.

1.3. Problem Formulation

In analytical terms, decision makers must determine the combination of land uses that meets the resource constraints of Table 12.1 and optimizes some specific objective. We have followed Gray and Anderson in specifying an objective of maximum social value, and in defining social value. The term *society* is implicitly equated to those who live in, work in, or visit the district or who use its products. Like Gray and Anderson, we have assumed that social benefits are equal to the market prices or consumers' expenditure for the various goods and services. The benefits of all land uses are therefore priced, and we can concentrate on reviewing the opportunity-cost methods. The variable costs of providing the goods and services were deducted from these prices to give a net benefit. The market prices, variable costs, and net benefits are listed in Table 12.2. The policy objective can be defined as maximization of these net benefits for all land uses together.

Linear programming is an effective procedure for analyzing this kind of allocation problem and for providing opportunity-cost information. Gray and Anderson (1964a) and many others present formal descriptions of this mathematical technique. Its usefulness to us rests on two of its characteristics. First, the technique determines the levels of those activities that maximize (or minimize) a given objective, subject to given constraints, and thus "solves" our policy problem. Second, additional information can readily be obtained on losses in monetary income that result from changes in activity or input levels, and this is useful opportunity-cost information. We repeated the linear programming analysis of Gray and Anderson to obtain the optimal land use pattern of Tables 12.3 and 12.4. This compares with the

Table 12.2. Market Prices (Total Benefits), Variable Costs, and Net Benefits for Eight Land Use Activities

Land Use Activity	Units	Market price[a] ($/unit)	Variable costs of production ($/unit)	Net Benefits ($/unit)
1	2	3	4	5[b]
Camping/picnicking	10 man-days	112.20	11.20	101.00
Grazing	100 lbs beef	23.00	5.70	17.30
Timber production	1000 board feet	7.50	1.90	5.60
Orchards	10 bushels	26.00	6.50	19.50
Cabin Ownership	5 man-days	64.00	8.00	56.00
Hunting/fishing	10 man-days	102.00	0.00[c]	102.00
Skiing	5 man-days	60.00	0.00[c]	60.00
Water production	acre-feet	1266.00	253.00	1013.00

Source. Columns 1, 2, and 3 are taken directly from Gray and Anderson (1964a) Table 5. Column 4 is provided by the present authors.

[a] Timber prices are on the stump; beef and apple prices at the farm gate.

[b] Column 5 = column 3 − column 4.

[c] For convenience we assume that hunting/fishing and skiing can be undertaken with no extra marginal costs to the producer.

Table 12.3. Optimal Land Use in the Ruidoso Ranger District—The Optimal Mix of Activities

Activity[a]	Units	Optimal Activity Level (number of units)	Net Benefit ($1000)
Camping and picnicking	10 man-days	91,240	9,215
Hunting and fishing	10 man-days	8,218	838
Skiing	5 man-days	13,998	840
Water supply	acre-feet	9,701	9,827
Total net benefit			20,720

[a] Grazing, timber production, orchards, and cabin ownership are not in the optimal mix of land uses.

actual patterns of land use shown in Table 12.5. We then extended the analysis to provide information for the rest of this chapter.

2. OBSERVATION AND INTERPRETATION OF COSTS

In a perfectly competitive economy, prices are a function of both consumers' willingness to pay and suppliers' willingness to produce. Willingness to produce is, in turn, a function of opportunity costs, which measure the sacrifices required to produce things. So in a competitive economy, prices depend on opportunity costs, and this provides the rationale for this group of methods.

Three interpretations of cost have been used in valuations: costs of production, expenditures by consumers, and net cost or value added. We now consider these interpretations in turn.

Table 12.4. Optimal Land Use in the Ruidoso Ranger District—Allocation of Land for the Optimal Activities

Land Resource	Total Available[a] Acres	Total Used in Optimal Mix
Land for camping and picnicking	1,403	1,105
Land for hiking	19,200	5,526
Land for hunting/fishing	71,000	50,742
Land for grazing	35,160	21,447
Land for timber production	169,000	169,000
Land for cabins	148	1
Land for skiing	1,000	1,000

[a] From Table 12.1.

Table 12.5. Actual Land Use in the Ruidoso Ranger District in 1962

Land-Use Activities	Units	Quantity of Use	Net Benefit ($1000)
1	2	3	4
1. Camping/picnicking	10 man-days	90,000	9,090
2. Grazing	100 lbs beef	4,480	78
3. Timber production	1000 board feet	367	2
4. Orchards	10 bushels	8,397	164
5. Cabin ownership	5 man-days	981	55
6. Hunting/fishing	10 man-days	9,200	938
7. Skiing	5 man-days	14,000	840
8. Water yield	acre-feet	3,696	3,744
Total net benefit			14,911

Source. Column 3 is taken from Table 7 in Gray and Anderson (1964a). Column 4 is obtained by multiplying the net benefit per unit from column 5 of Table 12.2 by column 3 of this table.

2.1. Production Costs as Benefit Indicators

Output will continue so long as the benefits exceed the costs of production. Actual production costs are therefore a minimum estimate of the total benefit. Several studies in the 1950s and early 1960s followed this simple method. For example, the U.S. Bureau of Reclamation estimated the monetary costs of projects and then assigned an equal sum to benefits (Trice and Wood, 1958). Secondary benefits were assumed to equal primary benefits, and primary benefits were themselves set equal to costs. As a result, all projects were desirable, and all had a benefit-cost ratio of 2:1.

A variation for public agencies is to use private costs as surrogates for missing public costs. The U.S. National Park Service advocated the use of private costs for similar facilities if public agencies lacked data (Robinson and Tanzi, 1962). In this way a value of $1.60 was estimated for the benefit of a man-day of recreation.

This method has many critics, and Coomber and Biswas (1973) dismiss it unconditionally. It measures disutility not utility, and thus it ignores a fundamental object of valuation. A second objection concerns the inadequacy of the information. If benefits are equated to costs, all projects will have the same net benefit, namely zero. Such information cannot assist choices. However, production costs can be made useful through the structured comparisons of Section 3 or by the procedures we now turn to.

2.2. Production Costs for Decision Information

The following three procedures develop ways of using production costs to guide decisions.

2.2.1. Cost Minimization. Some decisions specify that a given benefit must be achieved at least cost. In this case the unpriced benefit does not need to be valued but can just be specified as things to be exchanged. Production costs can then be estimated, and the least-cost combination of production techniques can be chosen.

This procedure is a direct application of the general valuation model (Equation 3.5)

$$\text{value} = \text{utility} - \text{disutility} \tag{12.1}$$

The amount of utility is fixed because the level of benefits are given. The alternative of highest value is therefore the one with the lowest disutility or cost.

Gray, Fisk, and Mathews (1974) applied this procedure to analyze pollution control strategies. The heavy recreation use of the Sandia Mountains of New Mexico caused pollution through noise, dust, garbage, and smoke. Permissible pollution levels were specified. Then linear programming identified the recreation activities and control techniques that minimized the costs of meeting these pollution levels. This procedure provided information on changes in costs, activities, and techniques to meet various levels of pollution control.

2.2.2. Cost of Replacement. Unpriced things can sometimes be valued or accounted for through the cost of replacing or maintaining them. For example, many writers have suggested that the benefits from flood and fire protection are equal to the replacement costs and damages that are avoided. Marstrand (1973) extends this valuation suggestion to the case in which replacement or maintenance costs can be assumed to be optimal. The marginal costs now equal the marginal benefits of monetary damage and unpriced costs avoided:

$$\text{marginal cost} = \text{monetary damage} + \text{unpriced costs} \tag{12.2}$$

Rearranging and transposing terms gives:

$$\text{unpriced costs} = \text{marginal cost} - \text{monetary damage} \tag{12.3}$$

which is a way to value the unpriced cost.

Expenditures to maintain or replace unpriced things are sometimes termed "defensive expenditures". They can be deducted from the other net benefits to account for unpriced things. Kneese (1977) discusses the use of this procedure to adjust national statistics to allow for maintaining environmental quality. At a project level Schwartz (1973) considers the psychic costs of the loss of family and friends through migration. This unpriced loss can be accounted for by including the costs of the future visits that will be needed to maintain these contacts.

2.2.3. The Supply Curve. Production costs are usually estimated for a specific output level for a particular project. Choices may sometimes be improved if a range of costs and associated output levels are available. The supply curve meets this need by showing marginal costs of production over a range of outputs. We now illustrate this application for an activity in the Ruidoso Ranger District.

A supply curve for the camping/picnicking activity was derived with a linear program by varying price and observing the quantity produced in the optimal mix. The curve (Figure 12.2) shows that marginal cost (equal to price in the program) is constant at $9.80 for the first 894,000 days. The curve rises in stepped fashion to 1,053,000 days, at which point it becomes infinitely inelastic. No further increase in price would increase the quantity supplied.

Choices on the optimal quantity of the activity can now be made, as we illustrated in Chapter 2. If there were a market price, the optimal quantity could be read from the curve. In a profit-maximizing situation, no quantity would be supplied if price were less than $9.80. At a price of $9.80, any amount up to 894,000 man-days would be supplied. Further price rises would bring forth increases in quantity up to 1,053,000 man-days.

This approach can provide helpful information even when benefits are

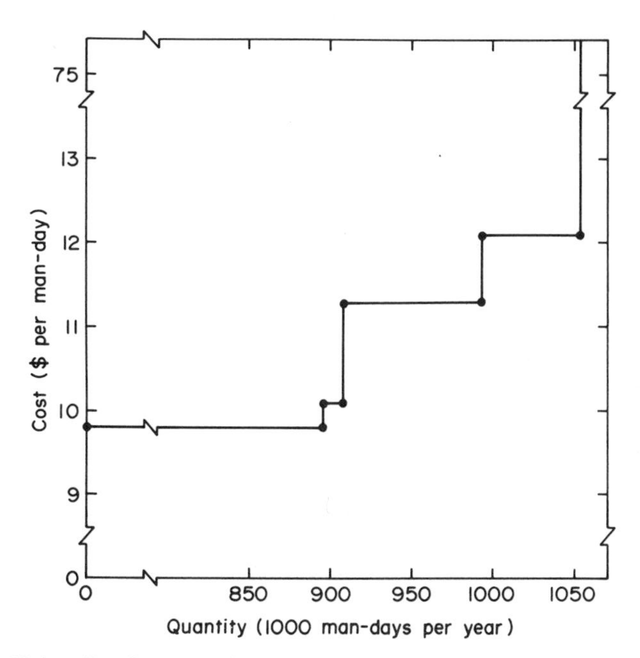

Figure 12.2. Supply curve for camping/picnicking on the Ruidoso Ranger District.

not valued. For example, the existing resources limit output to 1,053,000 man-days. Current (1962) use was 900,000 man-days (Table 12.5). Thus immediate choices about extra quantities are restricted to amounts between these limits. A decision might, for example, concern a fee to cover production costs. The supply curve indicates that such a fee would have to be at least $9.80 per man-day to increase the supply. This might be sufficient to deter many users. This approach can help define limits for choices and indicate specific problems.

2.2.4. The Procedures in Context. Only the structured form of the replacement cost procedure (Equation 12.3) estimates values. However, all three procedures can provide useful information for decisions. Cost minimization and supply curves may permit choices without any valuation of unpriced things.

2.3. Consumers' Expenditure

Expenditure data are often used to illustrate or promote a particular viewpoint. For example, Wallace (1956) reported that $96 million was spent annually on fishing and hunting in Washington. This large figure led him to conclude: "Wildlife is a natural resource of substantial magnitude, comparable in money value with many other important economic activities."

In the Ruidoso Ranger District in 1962, campers and picnickers spent an average of $11.20 per man-day. Of this total $4.80 was spent on transportation and $2.70 on food and lodging. With a total of 900,000 man-days, the gross expenditure on camping and picnicking was $10.1 million. This sort of information has been used for valuations, as we now describe.

2.3.1. The Nature of the Method. This method simply equates total benefit to the consumers' expenditure on acquisition and use. Burton and Wibberley (1965) applied the method to compare recreation and agriculture in the Ashdown Forest in Sussex and the Black Mountains in Wales.

The benefits of recreation were equated to the costs incurred by the consumers. Social value was then estimated as these benefits less the costs of supplying the recreation opportunities. The value of the same land in agriculture was estimated from potential monetary profit. The comparative values per acre per year were

	Agriculture	Recreation
Ashdown Forest	$21.80	$19.60
Black Mountains	$5.00	$4.20

On this basis there was little difference between the uses in a given location. By contrast, there was considerable difference in value between locations for a given use.

2.3.2. The Gross National Product Variation. Gross national product (GNP) is the monetary value of all final goods and services produced by a nation in a given period. This is consumers' expenditure on a national scale and for all things in aggregate. These data can be applied as we have just illustrated and with the same rationale: that benefits must at least equal costs or the expenditure would not have been incurred. They can also be used to estimate the benefit from a project as the associated change in GNP, as we show in the market price methods of Chapter 13.

2.3.3. Arguments against the Method. Coomber and Biswas (1973) aptly summarize the difficulties with the method

> Normally this method is adopted to impress possible investors in the size of gross consumer expenditures, but it is not an adequate investment criterion because: (a) it does not reflect net benefits, and (b) it reflects secondary benefits in addition to primary by including expenses incurred at nearby retail outlets.

The method fails to measure net benefits correctly. Because consumers' surplus is ignored, total benefit is underestimated. And disutility is not recognized, because consumers' expenditures cannot be deducted. If these expenditures were deducted, net benefit to consumers would always be zero.

Although the method reflects secondary benefits, it can fail to measure accurately contributions to local business activity. For example, 40 percent of the expenditures by the Ruidoso District recreationists were on transportation, but much of this was spent outside the region. Such external expenditures must be deducted for an accurate measurement of local impact.

Lewis (1965) noted an implication of the method: because protected species cannot be hunted, their value must be zero. Wennergren (1964) noted a related anomaly: if everything else is equal, economic efficiency requires things to be provided at the sites of highest profit. With the consumers' expenditure method, the most inaccessible sites have the highest benefit, and therefore, recreation should apparently be provided in the most inaccessible areas.

2.3.4. The Method in Context. Are the objections sufficient to rule out the method completely? Or are there some roles in which it can be useful? Although it underestimates total benefit, it may well be useful in comparisons of similar activities in different situations. This was the purpose for which Burton and Wibberley (1965) used it.

Gray and Anderson (1964a) illustrate a second kind of application, which we have followed in Table 12.2. We noted in Section 2.5.1 of Chapter 2 that net social benefit is equal to consumers' expenditure minus producers' costs plus consumers' surplus. The net benefit figures in column 5 of Table 12.2 therefore underestimate net social benefit, because they do not include consumers' surplus. However, the same measure is used for the priced goods—beef, timber, and water—that have market prices as for the unpriced goods—various forms of recreation—whose prices are estimated from consumer expenditures. This measure of net benefit can at least be applied consistently to all land uses in the analysis.

The potential of the method for demonstrating economic importance and overall contribution to business activity is illustrated by Payne and DeGraaf (1975) for nongame birds. Enjoyment of birdlife involves expenditures on birdseed, feeders, and books. Total direct expenditure in 1974 in the United States was at least 500 million dollars, which the authors noted is an impressive indication of the importance of nongame birds. Methodologically, this role provides a start toward valuing "passive" benefits like knowledge and the appreciation of things preserved from destruction.

In summary, the method has a potentially useful role in specific circumstances. But for general use, a net concept must be substituted, and this is the aim of the value-added approach, which we discuss next.

2.4. The Value-Added Method

Value added is the difference between consumers' expenditure and the costs of inputs that must be purchased from outside the local area. The difference is the value added by the local resources of land, labor, and capital. Value added is an improvement over consumers' expenditures because it localizes the business impact. The concept can readily be applied to all land-use activities, so that data from different activities can be compared and added.

2.4.1. The Method in Practice. The value-added approach has an obvious application in comparing the contributions of different projects to local business. For example, in a study of water allocation in New Mexico, Wollman, Edgel, Farris, Stucky, and Thompson (1962) developed the method for both primary and secondary rounds of purchases. Primary value added was defined for the farms and factories to which water was allocated. Secondary value added arose from the purchase of materials and services by these primary users. Wollman's study suggested that in the northern part of

New Mexico the value added by sport fishing was as great as that by agriculture. The authors went on to combine the estimates of value added by agriculture, recreation, and industry into an estimate of gross state output.

A comparison by Hughes (1965) of the potential value added by timber production and that added by existing wilderness use provided a ratio of 17:1 in favor of timber. But Hughes noted "... this is not interpreted to mean that there has been a misallocation of resources, but simply that society has been willing to pay this 'price' to have the wilderness thus far established." Estimates of value added do not imply that wilderness, for example, can be valued solely in these terms. But they do put problems in perspective, and they can assist in the selection of alternatives.

2.4.2. The Method in Perspective. If the objective of a project is to stimulate local business, value added is an appropriate method. Despite this useful role, however, the method is weak, because it ignores consumers' surplus and does not measure producers' surplus. As Clawson (1959) notes in a recreation context, expenditures reflect only the provision of facilities, goods, and services and not the value of the recreation. The value-added method does not measure the value or net benefit of the activity itself.

2.5. Overall Assessment of the Methods

The methods based on observed costs can have a useful role in measuring contributions to business activity and in providing information for choices. But they do not all measure value as a net concept. The consumers' expenditure method can be used to estimate total benefit, but the result is always a minimum value. The methods to which we now turn are structured comparisons of these same costs. They are simple extensions of the present methods and do estimate values.

3. STRUCTURED COMPARISONS OF COSTS

These methods provide monetary values for benefits from structured comparisons of opportunity costs. Net benefits can then be estimated by deducting the related expenditures. The cost-saving method which we consider first applies when a new production process would lower costs. Milliman's range method applies when the next-best process would have higher costs.

3.1. The Cost-Saving Method

A new technique, delivery system, or alternative source of inputs may become available at lower cost. The cost-saving method can then be used to value the benefit from this new technique.

3.1.1. Nature of the Method. The essence of the method was summarized by McKean (1958) in his consideration of the benefit of technological progress. One way to value this benefit is to estimate how much it would save:

$$\text{value of benefit} = \text{cost with the present method} - \text{cost with the new method} \tag{12.4}$$

The relative ease of cost assessment and the possibility of valuation without willingness-to-pay estimates are very real advantages of the method according to Steiner (1966) and Herfindahl and Kneese (1974).

3.1.2. The Formal Method. The fundamentals of the method are conveniently illustrated by the formal model presented in Figure 12.3. Suppose a new production process would shift the aggregate supply curve from CC' to AA'. If the industry demand curve is DD', output will increase from OI to OJ.

Consider, first, the suppliers' decision about adopting the new technology (Figure 12.3*a*). If B is the benefit from the new technique, C_e is the total cost with the existing process, and C_n is the total cost of the same output with the new technology:

$$B = C_e - C_n \tag{12.5}$$

In Figure 12.3*a*, C_e is depicted by $OCFI$ and C_n by $OAMI$, thus

$$B = OCFI - OAMI \tag{12.6}$$

This cost saving is the crosshatched area in Figure 12.3*a*.

This simple formulation must be modified for the extra costs and revenue from the extra output (IJ). The dotted area LGM is the excess of extra revenue over the extra costs, that is, the extra producers' surplus. The full effect to the suppliers therefore is

$$B = OCFI - OAMI + LGM \tag{12.7}$$

or with ΔPS for the change in producers' surplus

$$B = C_e - C_n + \Delta PS \tag{12.8}$$

Now consider the case of consumers or intermediate processors, as shown in Figure 12.3*b*. An intermediate processor is, in his economic reactions, a consumer of the raw materials he must buy for his processing. For ordinary final consumers, the demand curve DD' shows how much they would be willing to pay for various quantities of the good in question. For intermediate processors, the demand curve DD' shows the revenue they could obtain per unit from sales of various quantities of their product, net

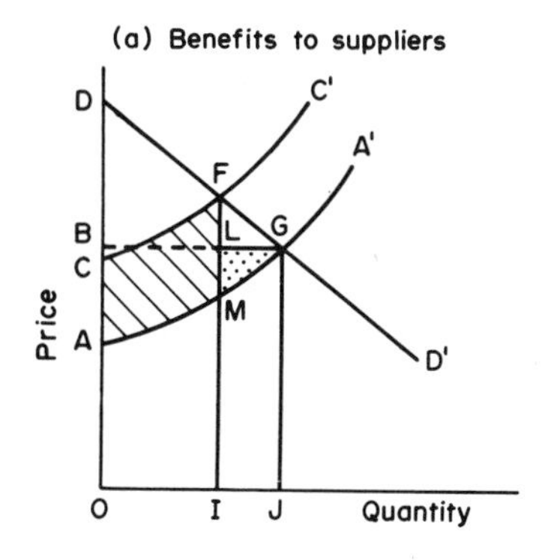

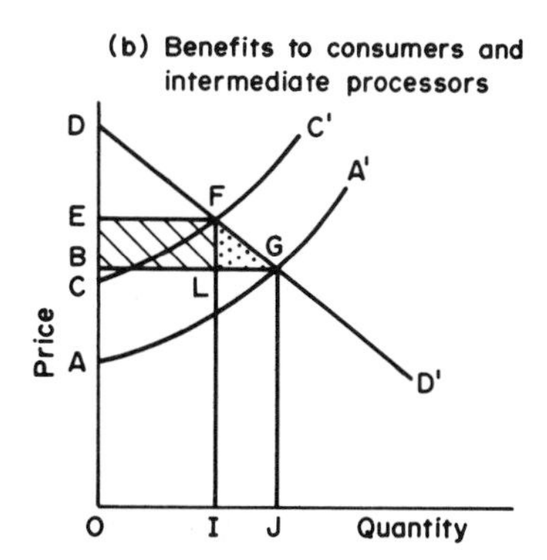

Figure 12.3. ***The formal model of the cost-saving method. (a) Benefits to suppliers. (b) Benefits to consumers and intermediate processors.***

of all processing costs except raw material. The supply curve CC' shows the marginal costs of the producers of the consumer good or raw material. In a purely competitive market, the quantity exchanged will be OI and the price will be OE. The consumer—or the primary processors, as the case may be—will have to pay the same price OE for all the units they buy. Because of the shape of the demand curve, these consumers or intermediate processors will enjoy a consumers' surplus of EFD when they buy OI units at a price of OE.

Let us now analyze the effects of a change on intermediate processors (the analysis is the same as for consumers). Suppose a technological change in transportation equipment has lowered the marginal costs of the raw material producers over all outputs so that the raw material supply curve shifts from CC' to AA'. If we assume that demand remains the same, the quantity exchanged will increase to OJ and the price of raw material will drop to OB. The benefit to the intermediate processors (B') from the lower price of the quantity of raw material they already were buying will be

$$B' = C_e - C_n \qquad (12.9)$$

or in terms of Figure 12.3*b*

$$B' = OEFI - OBLI = BEFL \qquad (12.10)$$

which is the area crosshatched in the figure.

This simple formulation must again be extended to take account of the extra costs and revenues of the increased output (IJ). The dotted area LFG in Figure 12.3*b* is the additional consumers' surplus realized by the intermediate processors from the additional output. Expressing this as ΔCS, the total benefit to the intermediate processors from the technological change is

$$B' = C_e - C_n + \Delta CS \tag{12.11}$$

This is the same formulation as in Equation 12.8, although the terms are measured differently, as seen in Figure 12.3.

Finally, the social value (net benefit) of the technological change can be determined by deducting the costs of developing and adopting the new technology from the benefits estimated above.

3.1.3. An Example: The Value of Convenience. The cost-saving method can sometimes be applied with cost expressed in other units, such as time, instead of money. Foster and Beesley (1963) sought to value the convenience of a seat on a commuter train as compared to the inconvenience of standing and holding to a strap. They observed passengers choosing between a slow train with an assured seat and a fast train with a virtual certainty of having to stand.

Some riders were indifferent as to which train they took. For them, the value of the convenience of a seat on the slow train was apparently the same as that of the time saved on the fast train. Those who always took the slow train apparently considered the value of an assured seat to be greater than the value of the time they could have saved. The benefit of a program that increased the number of available seats on fast trains could therefore be estimated from the time that would be saved by the present slow-train riders who in the future would ride the new train.

3.1.4. The Method in Practice. Cost saving has certain strengths and weaknesses as a measure of benefit. It is often relatively easy to assess both existing and new costs and to obtain an estimate of benefit. There is, however, a problem in that the estimates of C_e and C_n refer to the existing quantity (output OI in Figure 12.3). This quantity will increase to OJ, and it is difficult to estimate the effect of this increase on producers' or consumers' surplus without information on the elasticities of supply and demand.

The formal model shows that a mere comparison of existing costs with new costs ignores the change in producers' or consumers' surplus. Other things being equal, this method can be expected to underestimate true benefits. It is most useful when changes in quantity are small and the main effects are cost reductions. These conditions were present in Krutilla and Cicchetti's (1972) application of it to value the location benefits of a new site for power generation. They are implied in Marstrand's (1973) use to value the benefits of water pollution control. Since pollution control decreases other costs to water users, control is desirable because the benefits through cost savings exceed the expenditures on control.

3.2. Milliman's Range Method

Milliman (1962) advanced the following propositions: "As a *minimum* the intangible must be worth as much as it costs in terms of alternatives sacrificed. . . . it is often possible to place a *maximum* value on the intangible if it can be produced by alternative means."

If these minimum and maximum costs can be identified, we have a range for the value of an unpriced benefit. Data on camping and picnicking in the Ruidoso Ranger District are now used to illustrate this method.

3.2.1. Opportunity Cost as a Minimum. If people undertake a project, they must believe that the benefits from it are greater than its costs. The opportunity cost therefore provides a minimum estimate of the benefits of the project

$$\text{total benefits} \geq \text{opportunity cost} \tag{12.12}$$

The total costs of the 900,000 man-days of camping/picnicking were \$10.1 million or \$112.20 for each 10 man-days (Table 12.2). So we have

$$\begin{array}{c}\text{total benefits from}\\ \text{900,000 man-days}\end{array} \geq \$10{,}100{,}000 \tag{12.13}$$

3.2.2. Cost of the Alternative as a Maximum. The maximum value of a benefit must be less than the cost of the cheapest alternative means of obtaining the same benefit or people would use the alternative. Thus we can say

$$\text{total benefit} \leq \begin{array}{c}\text{total cost of the cheapest}\\ \text{alternative way of obtaining}\\ \text{the same benefit}\end{array} \tag{12.14}$$

If this total cost were \$14.4 million for the 900,000 man-days we would have

$$\text{total benefit} \leq \$14{,}400{,}000 \tag{12.15}$$

3.2.3. A Range for the Benefit. The minimum and maximum estimates of equations 12.12 and 12.14 can now be combined

$$\begin{array}{c}\text{total cost of}\\ \text{alternative}\end{array} \geq \begin{array}{c}\text{total}\\ \text{benefit}\end{array} \geq \begin{array}{c}\text{opportunity}\\ \text{costs}\end{array} \tag{12.16}$$

With the data of equations 12.13 and 12.15 the total benefit value for camping/picnicking can be bracketed

$$\$14{,}400{,}000 \geq \begin{matrix}\text{total}\\ \text{benefit}\end{matrix} \geq \$10{,}100{,}000 \tag{12.17}$$

The range for total benefit can be reduced to a range for net benefit by assuming that there is no consumers' surplus in the present use. As a minimum, the total benefits would then equal the total costs of $10,100,000. Equation 12.17 can therefore be converted to net benefits by deducting $10,100,000 from each side, giving

$$\$4{,}300{,}000 \geq \begin{matrix}\text{net benefits for}\\ \text{900,000 man-days}\end{matrix} \geq 0 \tag{12.18}$$

3.2.4. Discussion. This otherwise attractive method lacks the built-in validation check of other opportunity-cost methods. Because recreationists actually incurred costs of $10.1 million, we know they believed the total benefits were above this figure. But we have no check on the maximum, because we do not know whether they might have taken a higher-cost alternative. The only alternative might be so expensive that no rational people would take it, and the maximum would, in fact, remain undefined.

3.3. Comparison of the Methods

The choice between these methods rests on a simple distinction. The Milliman method requires that the cost of the alternative be higher, and the cost-saving method requires that it be lower. The information they provide also differs, because the cost-saving method should lead to a precise estimate, whereas the Milliman method can, at best, provide a range.

4. COST AS A LOSS IN MONEY INCOME

The term *cost* can be interpreted as loss in net money income as well as money outlay or opportunity cost. Two methods are reviewed here. The first rests on the loss in net monetary income from priced things, and the second on estimates of changes in income from a priced output for changes in an unpriced input. The methods therefore involve the estimation of changes in money income from priced things and provide a transition to the market price methods of Chapter 13.

4.1. Costing Constraints

An increase in, or constraint on, the production of unpriced things may lead to a loss of income from priced things. The procedure of costing constraints formalizes the estimation of this loss in income.

4.1.1. Application to the Land-Use Example. Changes in land use in the Ruidoso Ranger District illustrate how this procedure can often provide useful information. In 1962 all eight land-use activities were undertaken for a total net income of $14.9 million (Table 12.5). Suppose the district were to be declared a National Recreation Area. Land use would now be constrained to camping/picnicking, cabin ownership, hunting/fishing, skiing, and water collection. The exploitive uses of grazing, timber, and apple production would be excluded. The exclusion of these three uses would, if everything else remained the same, lower net money income. This loss can be calculated from Table 12.5 by finding the total net income without these three activities. The reduced total would be $14,667,000. Thus the loss in income is $244,000 per year, which would be the annual cost of this constraint on land use.

The procedure has a simple and effective role in decisions. If the district had already been declared a National Recreation Area, those making that decision must have valued the net benefits from the additional unpriced things at more than $244,000.

4.1.2. Costing a Range of Small Changes. Decisions may involve a range of marginal changes from the existing or optimal land-use pattern, rather than a single large change. Losses in net income through small changes from the optimum can be readily calculated with a linear program. The analysis of land use in the Ruidoso Ranger District was therefore extended to illustrate this use of value information.

The optimal mix of uses for the district comprises camping/picnicking, hunting/fishing, skiing, and water supply. Together these activities generate a net income of $20,720,000 per year (Table 12.3). The loss in net income that would result from a one unit increase in each of the excluded nonoptimal activities is $22.90 for grazing, $21.90 for timber, $642.90 for orchards, and $1.50 for cabin ownership. If policy makers wish to introduce one unit of grazing, they must be prepared to forego $22.90 of net income for the first 100 pounds of beef output. Or put another way, a rise in the market price of beef by $22.90 per 100 pounds would be sufficient to introduce one unit of grazing into the optimal land use mix.

Introduction of these nonoptimal activities into the land-use plan would create a cost for either the producers or the consumers. In our example, the cost would be very high ($642.90) for one unit of orchard production, but trivial ($1.50) for one unit of cabin ownership. In other words, it would be relatively cheap to introduce cabin ownership into the optimal mix of activities, and consumers might readily pay $1.50 for 5 man-days of occupancy. By contrast, consumers would have to pay $642.90 for every 10 bushels of apples if orchards were to be in the optimal mix. Or, if people insist on raising apples in the district, the unpriced benefits from doing so must be worth at least $64.30 per bushel.

In this same way a whole range of income losses can be calculated to show the effects of changing an activity level by successively greater quantities. Figure 12.4 shows the maximum obtainable net income from the district as the annual quantity of camping/picnicking is increased or reduced from the optimum quantity of 912,400 man-days. Such a reduction might result from a decrease in the amount of the particular land resource available. An increase could result from a policy decision to make more camping space available.

Figure 12.4 shows that an increase in camping/picnicking from 912,000 to 1,000,000 man-days would be associated with a $9.8 million drop in total net income. A 10 percent increase in use is associated with a 47 percent decrease in net income, which is a high sensitivity to this particular change. The benefits from increased activity are hard to determine, but they would clearly have to be large to offset the associated loss in net money income.

4.1.3. An Index of Recreation Value. A practical application of the costing constraint procedure provided a simple criterion for allocating land

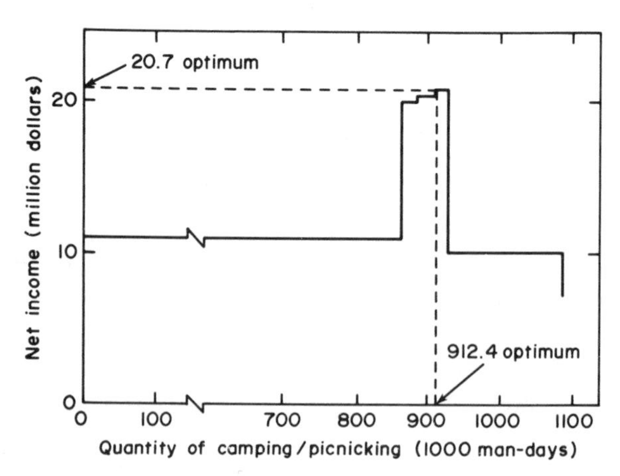

Figure 12.4. Maximum net income realizable by the Ruidoso Ranger District for a range of quantities of camping/picnicking.

between recreation and timber (Atkinson, 1956). The criterion was: if loss in net income from timber would exceed X dollars per man-day of recreation, the land should be allocated to timber. The basis and level of the dollar figure were derived as follows.

The existing uses of 34 tracts of forest land were observed. In all cases the land was of similar quality and suitable for both timber and recreation, but the actual combination of outputs varied with ownership. Tracts owned by timber companies were managed mainly for timber, but state parks were managed mainly for recreation. The following calculations were made for each tract:

(**a**) The value of the timber output and the number of man-days of recreation per year were observed. In the state parks, annual timber output was calculated as the potential output if managed for this purpose.

(**b**) The ratio of the net timber income in dollars to quantity of recreation in man-days was calculated.

(**c**) An assumption that land-use decisions follow consistent criteria was introduced. It was assumed that land allocation always seeks to maximize net benefits and that all owners place a similar value on recreation.

(**d**) The ratios of timber income to recreation output were ranked for all tracts, and the break-even point was noted. The major use changed from timber to recreation at a ratio of $730 per man-day. All land dedicated to timber production had higher ratios and all parklands had lower ratios.

The ratio of $730 per man-day is the "index of recreational value," to use Duerr's (1960) term. Such an index can be used as follows. Consider the land acquisition program of a state park agency. Expected timber values are compared to expected recreational use for each potential acquisition, and their ratio is calculated. Tracts should only be acquired if the ratio, or loss in net income per man-day of recreation, is less than the index of recreational value that has been determined independently for the particular state and time period.

4.1.4. Discussion. Estimation of lost money income is not a method of valuation as such. But the information defines the trade-off for unpriced benefits and, as Milton (1975) argues in the case of timber and wilderness use, can materially assist choices. Horner (1975) used linear programming to estimate the optimal incomes under existing use without pollution control and under two different control strategies. The loss from the existing income is the cost of control. Such losses would normally be an important aid in decisions.

4.2. Marginal Revenue Product

Marginal revenue product is the economist's term for the change in total income resulting from a one-unit increase in input. The related increase in total net income is the marginal revenue product less the marginal change in cost.

Let us consider the acquisition of more land in the Ruidoso Ranger District. Marginal revenue product is the contribution a marginal unit would make to total income. For a profit-maximizing firm, it is the maximum amount that can be paid for an extra unit of land. Skiing is in the optimal mix of activities for the district at 69,990 man-days (13,998 units of 5 man-days each in Table 12.3). At this output all acres of skiing land are used (Table 12.4). More skiing would require more land for ski lifts, which raises two related questions. How much land should be purchased, and how much should be paid for it?

The level of any constraint in a linear program can be varied to obtain a new optimal mix of activities and a new net income. Systematic changes in the quantity of skiing land provided a series of new net incomes. For completeness, the resource of 1000 acres (Table 12.1) was systematically reduced to zero and increased to 5000 acres. The difference in net income resulting from a change in land area is the marginal revenue product from the extra land. Capitalization of the differences in income gives the maximum that can be paid for each extra acre.

The marginal revenue products for skiing land are shown in Figure 12.5 as annual amounts. The first additional acre would add $77 to net income.

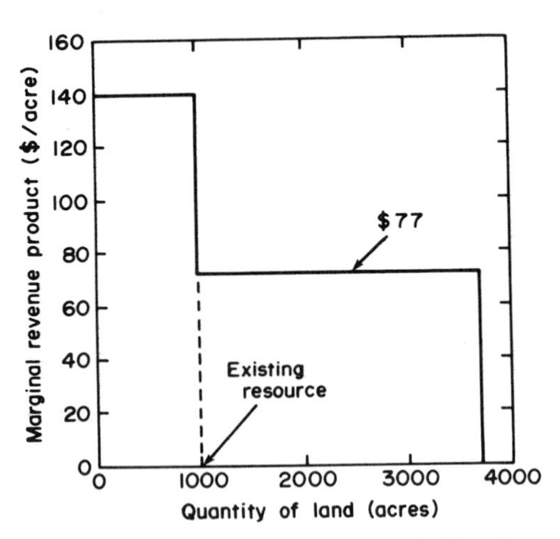

Figure 12.5. Marginal revenue products from additional amounts of skiing land in the Ruidoso Ranger District.

Thus at a 10 percent discount rate, up to $770 could be offered for this acre. The marginal revenue product remains $77 up to the 3599th acre. The 3600th acre would yield a marginal revenue product of zero and is not worth purchasing.

4.3. Discussion

The relative ease of measuring net incomes from priced things and the usefulness of the information for decisions promotes the use of these two methods. In our National Recreation Area example of Section 4.1, the trade-off information might be posed to the decision maker as follows: The loss in net income will be $244,000 if you exclude timber production, grazing, and orchards. Do you believe the value of the additional unpriced benefits will exceed this loss?

Information on trade-offs, or lost income, can be expressed in three ways. The net income traded for more unpriced things was illustrated in Section 4.1. Major (1969) extends this method by providing the decision maker with a schedule of net money incomes against associated levels of unpriced things. Marginal revenue product is a second way of expressing trade-offs when an unpriced input can be valued through its priced products. Lynne and Castle (1975) note a third trade-off—the sacrifice in income from a priced product for more of an unpriced product.

5. DO INCREASES IN EXPENDITURE INCREASE UTILITY?

The opportunity-cost methods in general, and the producers' and consumers' expenditure methods in particular, rest on the assumption that increases in expenditure lead to increases in utility. But is this generally true? And in what situations can larger expenditures be expected not to increase utility? We draw on the detailed discussions of the interpretation of GNP data by Samuelson (1950) and others for help in considering these questions.

5.1. A Theoretical Framework

Consider two goods and a consumer who has the preferences indicated by the indifference map of Figure 12.6. The budget line *BL*1 shows the maximum quantities of each good that can be bought for an initial expenditure and given prices. Budget line *BL*2 shows the combinations that can be bought with a higher expenditure at the same prices. The expenditure methods imply that higher expenditures (*BL*2 rather than *BL*1) are

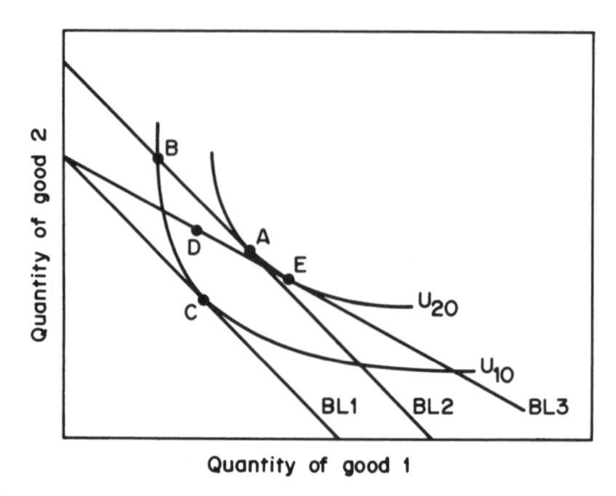

Figure 12.6. A model for explaining failures of consumer expenditures to indicate comparative utilities accurately.

associated with higher utilities (say U_{20} instead of U_{10}). Figure 12.6 allows us to examine this implication and some difficulties of making inferences from market data.

The following observations are based on the kind of aggregate data that are readily obtained—like those of Wallace (1956), for example—and that are often used.

(**a**) The consumers' expenditure method will correctly assess point *C* as being inferior to *A*.

(**b**) Point *B* has a lower utility than *A*, but the method will assess *B* as equal to *A*.

(**c**) Point *D* will be incorrectly assessed as being inferior to *B*. The combination of goods at *D* has a higher utility than does the combination at *B*.

The two anomalies in b and c arise because expenditures have not been allocated for maximum utility. If they had, the consumer would be at point *A* and never at point *B*, and the anomalies would not occur.

Imagine now that the price of good 1 has dropped to give a new price ratio, and *BL*3 is the new budget line. Points *D* and *E* now lie on the same budget line. Before the price change, point *E* was superior to point *D*, according to both the utility and the consumers' expenditure criteria. After the price change, the expenditure criterion will rate *D* and *E* as being equal, but their utility ordering has not changed. This third anomaly can occur when different market situations with different price ratios are observed and compared.

5.2. Practical Implications

These anomalies can be avoided if data collection follows two rather strict conditions. First, all situations in which data are collected must have the same relative prices. Second, individuals must be utility maximizers and must be in economic equilibrium.

These conditions are relevant to the consumers' expenditure method, but they also apply to the producers' costs method, the cost-saving method, and Milliman's range method. Because they are unlikely to be met in practice, how can an analyst overcome this difficulty? One conventional procedure is to restrict comparisons to similar things in similar situations. The biases may then be uniform, and the relative results may still be useful.

Another procedure is to restrict comparisons to simple, small decisions. After the price change shown in Figure 12.6, the consumers' expenditure method will rate positions D and E equally. However, E is actually preferred to D by the amount $(U_e - U_d)$ where U_e is the utility of position E and U_d is the utility of D. The error of the consumers' expenditure method can therefore be measured by $(U_e - U_d)$. The geometry of Figure 12.6 indicates that the size of this error can increase as (a) the price change increases for a given budget or (b) the budget increases for given prices. The consumers' expenditure method seems least applicable when price or budget changes are large and if there are many alternatives to choose between. Large, complex decisions may have to be analyzed by other kinds of methods. But the method may be suitable for small decisions with few alternatives. The choice of method once more depends on the nature of the decision.

6. DISCUSSION

In conclusion, let us summarize the usefulness of the opportunity-cost methods.

6.1. Disadvantages of the Methods

Critics seem to agree on several disadvantages.

(a) The methods measure the costs of obtaining the products, services, or access associated with unpriced things. But they do not all measure the utility of the unpriced good or service. They thus ignore the basic rationale of valuation.

(b) The methods implement the proposition that benefits must be at least equal to the costs incurred. They therefore provide minimum estimates of benefits.

(c) Methods like the simple interpretations of Section 2 wrongly imply that higher (lower) costs always mean higher (lower) benefits.

These criticisms must be accepted for valuation. But they may not be valid at all if we are interested in making decisions rather than valuing benefits.

6.2. The Methods in Context

The usefulness of the methods for decisions depends on (a) the similarity between the objectives of the decision and the parameters measured by the methods and (b) the ways in which the problem can be structured. We consider these points in turn.

Specific Methods for Specific Objectives. The methods fall into three groups when defined by the objective they measure (Table 12.6). Each of the groups can provide useful policy information for the objective it actually measures. Unlike the methods of Chapter 11, the opportunity-cost methods are not substitutes for each other. They measure different things and are suitable for different decisions. Much of the criticism of the methods seems to arise from rather illogical attempts to use, for example, an impact-estimating method to estimate values.

Decision Making or Benefit Valuation? The analysis of land use in the Ruidoso Ranger District indicated certain roles for the methods in decision making. The roles and the information they provide, are summarized in

Table 12.6. The Role of the Opportunity Cost Methods: Different Methods for Different Objectives

Objective	Methods
1. To estimate impact on business activity	Consumers' expenditure, producers' expenditure, value added
2. (a) To estimate consumers' surplus	Cost savings, Milliman's range
(b) To estimate total benefit	Marginal revenue product, Milliman's range, cost savings
3. To select the least-cost way of achieving a given goal or benefit	Cost minimization procedure, costing constraints, marginal revenue product

Table 12.7. The Role of the Opportunity-Cost Methods: Decision Making Rather than Valuations[a]

Method	Policy Information That Can Be Derived
	The Effect of
1. (a) Estimate a supply curve from production costs	A range of potential benefit values on optimal quantities of output
(b) Adjust by costs of providing same benefits	Replacing or maintaining environment or income
	Income Foregone by
2. Net income foregone	Adopting a project that is suboptimal
3. Marginal revenue product	Changing resource level by one unit
4. Costing constraints	Restricting a priced activity to a non-optimal quantity
	Identifies the Alternative
5. Cost minimization	that provides a given benefit at least cost

[a] The term *optimal* refers to the combination of land uses that gives the highest monetary net benefits. For convenience this is taken as a norm. This table can then refer to the analysis of land uses in the Ruidoso District in this chapter. In practice, any other norm could be used.

Table 12.7. The methods do not estimate values in any of these roles, but in each role they provide useful information for decisions. This kind of information seems useful for most policy decisions and not just for our example. The opportunity-cost methods are generally worth considering for these roles, despite their other disadvantages.

CHAPTER 13

Estimation of Monetary Values—Interpretation of Market and Land Prices

A market price is usually the best single indicator of comparative value, but it is just an indicator, because it does not measure value as such. Furthermore, market prices are very specific indicators and refer only to marginal units and to the places, times, and persons actually involved. Sometimes market prices can provide a basis for demand and supply schedules for estimating true social values, as we show in Chapter 15. This chapter shows how market prices can be used to estimate net monetary benefits or interpreted to provide values for unpriced things.

The first step in using market prices is to determine whether they are truly competitive. A competitive market must have freedom of exchange and many willing sellers and buyers. The prices themselves must meet two other tests. First, they must measure the opportunity costs of the marginal unit exchanged and thus the social cost of that unit. Second, they must equate supply and demand. An acceptable price measures the willingness of those involved to exchange the marginal unit.

Market prices can be divided into three main classes, as shown in Figure 13.1. In one group (class A) are truly competitive market prices. These can be used to determine values in the conventional manner of economic theory, and they are discussed briefly in Section 2 as a "base point" for this chapter.

A second group of prices (class B) form in markets that are not truly competitive. However, the factors that distort the markets can be identified, and it is possible to adjust the prices for them. This is also discussed briefly in Section 2.

Market prices do not exist at all for things in the third group (class C). However, competitive market prices do exist for some related things which can be used to estimate monetary values for the things in question. These related things may be of three kinds, as shown in Figure 13.1: (a) a subsequent output for which the thing being appraised is an input, (b) something that aggregates the thing being appraised with other things, or (c) a

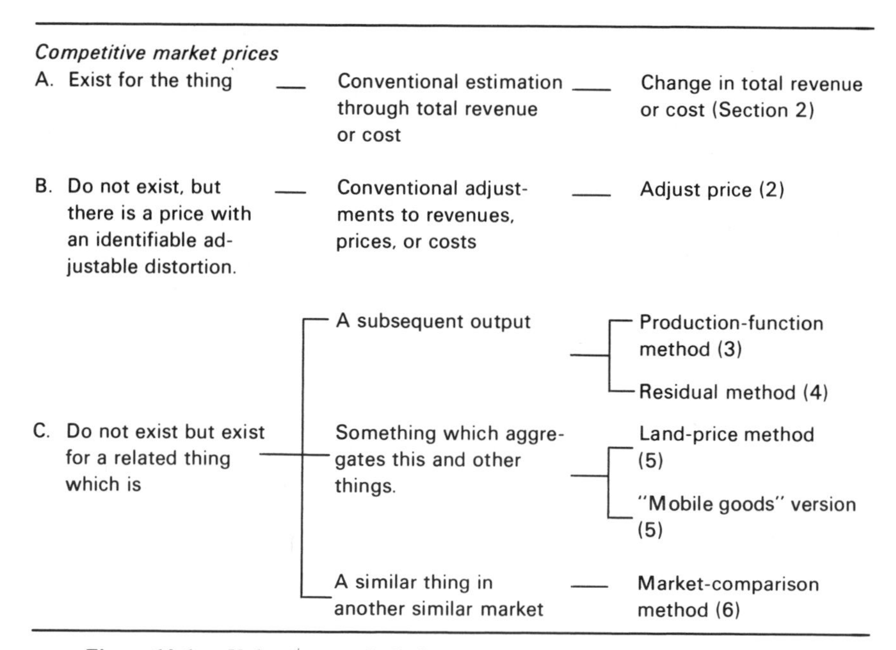

Figure 13.1. ***Valuation methods for various market price situations.***

similar thing in another similar market. The methods for using the prices of these related things are shown in Figure 13.1 and are keyed to the subsequent sections where they are described.

1. AN ENVIRONMENTAL POLICY EXAMPLE: PEST CONTROL

The methods of this chapter adapt the basic model of exchange to various situations. As usual, we use a single example to illustrate the different methods. But since each method is designed to handle a different kind of market price situation, the valuations produced by them cannot be directly compared, as they were in Chapter 9. The example therefore serves a slightly different function in this chapter.

There is a temptation to consider all monetary values as comparable and to add them for total values. The methods of this chapter all produce monetary values, but they have different tendencies to overestimate or underestimate net monetary and social benefits. Using a common example will let us compare these different biases when we get to Section 7.1.

Our example concerns decisions about the control of an insect pest. The decision maker needs information about the value of the damage that might be prevented by control. For simplicity, we refer only to the gross benefits of pest control. A full analysis would, of course, require the costs of control to be deducted. The example combines analyses of the gypsy moth problem in northeastern North America (McCay and White, 1973; Payne et al., 1973) and of pest damage to apples in eastern Canada (Fischer, 1968 and 1970). The pest in our hypothetical example is reducing apple production and timber production, and is also defoliating trees in residential areas.

Losses in Apple Production. We assume that apple orchards occupy 5800 acres and directly support 756 families. Annual production of 6.3 million bushels at a price of $1.20 per bushel at the farm gate yields a gross annual income of $10,000 per farm family. This output and income are achieved despite the loss of part of the yield to the pest.

Several policy questions are raised by the pest situation. Is it technically feasible to reduce the crop loss? How would the total revenue to all apple producers change if output were increased? Are control techniques profitable to individual farmers? We assume that these questions warrant analysis and that family income is important enough to encourage analysis with a view to action.

Losses in Land Value. Like many environmental goods, trees on residential property are not themselves exchanged in markets. But they provide benefits of shade, aesthetic enhancement, and privacy that add utility to a home and may be reflected in its market price. Payne, White, McCay, and McNichols (1973) estimated that trees add an average of 7 percent to property prices in Amherst, Massachusetts. We assume that the pest defoliates trees sufficiently to affect property values. The state agencies need to know if the resulting losses are serious enough to warrant action.

Losses in Timber Production. Like the gypsy moth, our pest is defoliating trees in the forest as well as in town. But the forest problem is different, because timber is an input to further processing for lumber, which is sold in a competitive market.

2. CONVENTIONAL MARKET-PRICE METHOD

A decision may involve a change in the quantity or quality of a consumer good or input. When these are priced, conventional economic analysis can be used to value the benefits and costs. Total consumer expenditure (market price $\times$ quantity) is a measure of total benefits. The change in total expenditure resulting from a decision can therefore be used as a measure of the total benefit of the outcome.

2.1. For a Change in Quantity

Apples are a final consumer good. Control of the pest will lead to increases in production and sales. But will an increase in consumption lead to greater consumer expenditure and producer revenue? In a competitive market an increase in total consumption will only occur with a decrease in price, unless demand has increased. In our simple example we have assumed that the demand schedule is constant. The additional total revenue to the whole industry would therefore be overestimated if the extra quantity were multiplied by the existing price. A new equilibrium price must be estimated.

2.1.1. Application to the Example. The benefit from pest control can be estimated in terms of the basic model of exchange. With an output of OQ_1 and a price of OP_1 in Figure 13.2, total revenue is indicated by the area OP_1AQ_1. At the existing market price of \$1.20 per bushel and at current sales of 6.3 million bushels, total revenue is \$7.56 million. According to Fischer (1968), insects and diseases cause an average loss of 15 percent of the Canadian apple crop. Adequate, well-timed, and careful treatment could apparently reduce the loss to 4 percent. We therefore assume that pest control would result in a new total production of 7.1 million bushels (OQ_2 in Figure 13.2).

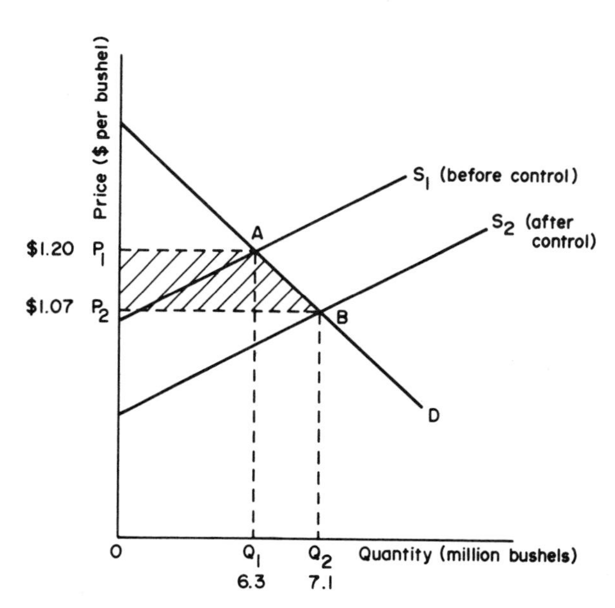

Figure 13.2. Measuring benefits of pest control in apple orchards.

This estimate of the new quantity must be supplemented with an estimate of the new price. We use Fischer's estimate of -1.21 for the price elasticity of demand for fresh apples. The elasticity formula of Equation 2.12 in Chapter 2

$$\text{elasticity} = \frac{\text{change in quantity}}{\text{original quantity}} \div \frac{\text{change in price}}{\text{original price}} \tag{13.1}$$

can be rearranged to solve for the change in price

$$\text{change in price} = \frac{\text{change in quantity}}{\text{original quantity}} \times \frac{\text{original price}}{\text{elasticity}} \tag{13.2}$$

The data on apple production can now be inserted

$$\text{change in price} = \frac{+0.8}{6.3} \times \frac{1.20}{-1.21} = \frac{0.96}{-7.62} = -0.13$$

And the new price $(OP_2) = 1.20 - 0.13 = \$1.07$.

The total revenue after pest control would be 7.1 million bushels at \$1.07 per bushel, or \$7,597,000. The result of a decision to control the pest would be

$$\begin{array}{c}\text{benefit from}\\ \text{pest control}\end{array} = \begin{array}{c}\text{total revenue}\\ \text{with control}\end{array} - \begin{array}{c}\text{total revenue}\\ \text{without control}\end{array} \tag{13.3}$$

$$= \$7{,}597{,}000 - \$7{,}560{,}000 = \$37{,}000$$

The total benefit would be \$49 for each of the 756 farms, or \$6 for each of the 5800 acres involved.

A different elasticity of demand would result in a different total benefit. If the elasticity of demand were -1.50, the change in price would be -0.10 and the new total revenue would be \$7.81 million. The total benefit from pest control under those conditions would be \$250,000, or \$331 per farm.

2.1.2. Relation to Net Social Benefits. Various people are involved in any economic activity. The pest control program involves the producers as a group, the producers as individuals, and the consumers as a group. It may also involve the government in promotion or regulation activities. Does this market-price method measure the benefits and costs to all of these groups?

The market-price method gives an accurate estimate of net benefits to the producers, but it does not measure the total net benefits to society because it ignores the change in consumers' surplus shown by the shaded area (P_2P_1AB) in Figure 13.2. The market price method underestimates value to society as a whole.

2.2. For a Change in Quality

2.2.1. Adapting the Basic Model. A change in a characteristic of a good makes it a different good for choices and exchange. When consumers perceive the change as a decrease in quality, the demand curve will shift to the left. When the change is an increase in quality, the curve will shift to the right, and if production costs are constant, the market price will rise. Similarly, a deterioration (improvement) in a characteristic of an input will shift the supply curve to the left (right). If demand is constant, this change will lead to a rise (fall) in market price. The benefit or cost of a change in quality is therefore reflected in movements of the market price. We now illustrate the valuation of such a change through market prices.

2.2.2. An Example: Wage Differences to Value Environmental Changes. Wages are the market price of labor and form as a response to demand and supply. Many factors affect the supply of labor, including the quality of the working and living environment. Changes in wages can be used to measure changes in characteristics of these environments. Using the with-and-without approach of Equation 13.3

$$\begin{matrix}\text{benefit from} \\ \text{change}\end{matrix} = \begin{matrix}\text{market price} \\ \text{with change}\end{matrix} - \begin{matrix}\text{market price} \\ \text{without change}\end{matrix} \qquad (13.4)$$

In a competitive market the marginal worker is indifferent to the same kind of employment in the city or in the country. The higher wages in the city must just compensate for the unpriced disadvantages of city life. Using Equation 13.4, the benefits from changes in an environment can be valued at the difference in wages. Nordhaus and Tobin (1972) used this method to value the environmental costs of city growth. Rothenburg (1967) used total wage costs to value the benefits of police protection. Costs of police services in different neighborhoods were compared. Then

$$\begin{matrix}\text{benefit from} \\ \text{extra protection}\end{matrix} = \begin{matrix}\text{nonslum} \\ \text{police costs}\end{matrix} - \begin{matrix}\text{slum police} \\ \text{costs}\end{matrix} \qquad (13.5)$$

The extra costs in the richer area indicate the willingness to pay for benefits from extra protection.

The concept of valuation on the basis of price changes has often been applied to education and health. The interpretation of land prices, which we discuss in Section 5, also rests on the same principle. Two of the difficulties—the isolation of price effects from other effects and the influence of elasticities—are discussed under land prices.

2.3. Adjustment of Distorted Prices

An analyst who works for a private individual, firm, or local authority may ignore gains and losses that fall outside his own organization. But an analysis that concerns a nation as a whole must include all benefits and costs. A social analysis may have to adjust benefits and costs that are estimated with market prices to overcome distortions resulting from taxes, subsidies, or tariffs. Fuller discussions of the necessary adjustments are provided by Mishan (1971) and Prest and Turvey (1965). A few of these adjustments are as follows:

(**a**) Subsidies to producers are excluded, even though they add to producer revenue.

(**b**) Revenues to producers are measured before taxes are deducted.

(**c**) All benefits are valued gross of tax. Taxes that are included in payments by consumers, such as sales taxes, are included, because the payments were made in full knowledge of the tax.

(**d**) A social cost-benefit analysis is national in scope. Any benefits from overseas projects are valued net of overseas taxes, because only the net benefit can be remitted.

(**e**) The cost of unemployed or underemployed resources is measured by their opportunity cost, which is generally lower than market price.

2.4. Discussion

The existence of market prices may permit an analyst to measure value as net monetary benefits or profit. But monetary profit will generally underestimate net social benefit.

Rothenburg (1967) demonstrated that the conventional market price method can be applied in such a way as to make net monetary benefit equivalent to net social benefit. His case concerned urban renewal with a government agency acting explicitly as the market place. The agency bought land in the competitive market, where land prices could be expected to equal true opportunity costs. Improvements involved the costs of labor and materials, both of which should represent true opportunity costs at the margin.

The benefits of urban renewal can be captured in higher land prices, as we see in Section 5. A government—or any monopoly seller—may be able to extract the entire willingness to pay from a buyer. As Rothenburg notes, if the agency is selling to private firms, the willingness to pay represents the private market's assessment of opportunities. The selling price could therefore include the entire consumers' surplus. Because of the activities of the government agency, the result may equal net social benefit.

3. PRODUCTION-FUNCTION METHOD

In some situations, a competitive market price does not exist for the object of a decision but does exist for a subsequent product that the thing under consideration helps to produce. For example, the water used by an industry does not usually have a competitive market price. But if it is used in the manufacture of some product like paper, whose selling price is established in a competitive market, the value of the water can be estimated from the value of the marketed product.

Demand for an input is a derived demand, and the benefits from its use are measured by its contribution to gross income. The contribution produced by an additional unit of the input (when all other inputs are held constant) is its marginal value product. The demand for an input is a schedule of these marginal value products. The marginal value products may be calculated in three different ways:

(1) Production function analysis rests on the derivation of an empirical production function (Section 2.2.3 in Chapter 2) and marginal physical products. Marginal value products are then calculated from the marginal physical products. We illustrate this method here for pest control in apple production.

(2) Budgeting provides a less-formal approach. Payments to all priced inputs are deducted from gross income to give the net income, or value, of the unpriced inputs. This method is illustrated in Section 4.

(3) Linear programming is a systematic budgeting procedure. When all other inputs are priced, marginal value products can be calculated for each limiting unpriced input. This method has been illustrated in Chapter 12 (Section 4.2).

3.1. Calculating the Production Function

A production function shows the outputs (Q) that can be produced from various quantities of a given input (I) when all other inputs are held constant:

$$Q = f(I) \tag{13.6}$$

Because output would usually be zero if only one input were used, the level of other inputs must also be recognized:

$$Q = f(I_1, I_2, \cdots, I_n) \tag{13.7}$$

Various algebraic forms of this equation can be used to calculate production functions from actual data. Heady and Dillon (1961) provide a comprehensive discussion of the range of forms and their application. We illustrate two common forms—the quadratic and the Cobb–Douglas.

Miller, Boersma, and Castle (1965) used both forms to estimate the value of irrigation water in corn and bush-bean production in the Willamette Valley, Oregon. A factorial experiment laid down to estimate the relative effects on corn output of water, nitrogen, and number of plants, produced the quadratic function:

$$\text{Output} = 0.50 + 11.6W - 0.49W^2 + 0.41N - 0.002N^2 + 0.00008WP + 0.0000007WNP \quad (13.8)$$

where W and N are the quantities of water and nitrogen input per acre and P is the number of plants per acre.

The Cobb–Douglas function has the multiplicative form

$$Q = aI_1^{b_1} \times I_2^{b_2} \times \cdots \times I_n^{b_n} \quad (13.9)$$

where a and b_i are the usual regression parameters to be estimated by applying the model to actual data. This nonlinear function can be changed into a linear form by taking the logarithms of both sides. Miller, Boersma, and Castle used this function in its logarithmic form to estimate the value of irrigation water. We illustrate it subsequently for pest control.

3.2. Calculating Marginal Value Products

The marginal physical product is derived from the production function. Then the marginal value product is calculated by multiplying marginal physical product by the price of the product. The marginal physical product of irrigation water is the partial derivative of output with respect to water in Miller, Boersma, and Castle's quadratic equation. At an application rate of 6 inches of water per acre, they estimated the marginal physical product of an extra unit of water to be 7.6 bushels of corn per acre. With a product price of \$1.40 per bushel, the marginal value product is \$10.60 per acre. An extra unit of water should be applied if its cost is less than \$10.60.

When the change in output arises from a change in only one input, marginal physical products are calculated from the Cobb–Douglas model as follows:

$$MPP_i = \frac{b_i \times \bar{Q}}{\bar{I}_i} \quad (13.10)$$

where MPP_i is the marginal physical product of input i, $\bar{Q}$ is the mean output, and $\bar{I}_i$ is the mean level of input i. The most reliable estimates of

MPP are obtained when output and input levels are set at their means. In the logarithmic form, geometric means must be used rather than arithmetic ones.

3.3. Estimating the Benefits of Pest Control

The production function is sometimes formulated entirely in monetary terms. Output is measured as gross money income and inputs as their gross cost. The marginal value product is then calculated in a slightly different manner, as illustrated by Fischer's (1970) analysis of pest control.

The Cobb–Douglas model was applied to survey data from 25 farms and gave the equation

$$\text{Log output} = 0.40 + 0.72 \text{ Log } I_1 + 0.23 \text{ Log } I_2 + 0.12 \text{ Log } I_3 \quad (13.11)$$

where output is gross income from apple production, I_1 is pest control costs, I_2 is cost of other inputs, and I_3 is capital investment in machinery and equipment. The coefficient of determination was reported as .75. Data were expressed in a monetary unit to aggregate related items into a single input variable. For example, the pest-control variable, I_1 consisted of pesticides, depreciation on special spraying machinery, and labor used in control procedures.

Marginal value product (*MVP*) can be calculated from a production function in monetary terms in the same way that marginal physical product is calculated from a function in physical terms

$$MVP_i = \frac{b_i \times \bar{Q}}{\bar{I}_i} \quad (13.12)$$

For the marginal value product of the pest-control costs (I_1), we use 0.72 for the regression parameter b_1 from the equation above and the observed mean output and input shown in Table 13.1:

$$MVP \text{ for pest control} = \frac{0.72 \times 10{,}000}{1393} = \$5.17 \quad (13.13)$$

At the margin, another dollar invested in pest control yields $5.17 in benefits.

The marginal value products for the pest-control input (I_1) and all other-noncapital inputs (I_2) are shown in Table 13.1 for two different areas. They may be interpreted as follows. For apple growers in area *A*, more pest control has greater comparative value than more other inputs because its *MVP* per dollar invested is higher (5.17 compared to 0.67). Because the *MVP* of the extra pest control is over five times as large as its cost, more pest control would clearly increase net income. In area *B*, the *MVP*s of more pest

Table 13.1. Marginal Value Products for Pest Control and Other Inputs

Variable		Mean[a] (Geometric)	Marginal Value Products per Dollar Invested	
Symbol 1	Name 2	3	Area A 4	Area B 5
Q	Output (Gross Money Income)	$10,000		
I_1	Pest control inputs	$1,393	$5.17	$2.34
I_2	Other inputs	$3,433	$0.67	$1.53

Source. Columns 4 and 5 from Fischer (1970), column 3 by present authors.
[a] Data for area *A* only.

control and more other inputs are much closer (2.34 compared with 1.53), and the greater value of pest control is not so obvious.

3.4. Discussion

Marginal value product information can assist with a variety of decisions about the quantity and mix of inputs. But the nature of the data influences the role of the method. On one hand, there may be data for specific single inputs, such as the quantity of water and nitrogen fertilizer in Equation 13.8. Specific data permit recommendations on specific inputs. On the other hand, data for separate inputs may be aggregated into a single input class as in Equation 13.11. This aggregate approach is typical for studies of the firm as a whole rather than for studies of single crops in single fields. The marginal value product information now refers to aggregate input classes. It may give a general indication of whether returns to each aggregate input exceed some composite price or whether there are large differences in *MVP* for a single input class between firms or between regions. But information on single inputs within the aggregate class is not available.

The availability of inputs, particularly capital, also affects the use of *MVP* information. Many firms face a capital constraint, and increases in the amount of one input would necessarily require decreases in another. Instead of comparing *MVP* with price for each separate input, the problem must be rephrased as: how much can profits be increased if present capital is reallocated among the inputs? Those inputs for which *MVP* is relatively high should be increased, and the others should be decreased. This constrained optimization approach is particularly suitable for whole firms as compared with single inputs in single situations. Decisions on reallocation of existing capital and expenditure can then be between broad classes, such as the pest-control, machinery and equipment, and other inputs of our pest-control example.

The production-function method requires a large amount of specific data for precise estimates of marginal physical product. It also requires careful statistical estimation of the production functions themselves. By contrast, the residual method, which we consider next, usually estimates extra output without this statistical precision and without specific production functions. The production-function method may therefore be more suitable for small projects with large amounts of specific data and the residual method for larger projects where less-precise estimates may suffice.

4. RESIDUAL METHOD

This method falls in the same category as the production-function method (Figure 13.1) in that a competitive market price does not exist for the thing being appraised but does exist for a subsequent output. With the residual method the total gross income from the subsequent output is estimated, and the costs of all priced inputs are deducted. The residual is the return to—or value of—the unpriced input(s). The nature of the method lends itself to simple budgeting techniques, and it is sometimes called the *budgeting method.*

In industrial and agricultural applications the unpriced inputs most frequently studied have been education and technology. In the environmental area the method is often applied to "mispriced" resources as well as to unpriced ones. Publicly owned water, for example, is usually exchanged at administratively determined prices rather than at market prices, but it can be valued by the residual method. Publicly owned timber is frequently priced and sold by some version of the residual method.

4.1. Adapting the Basic Model

The residual method is a direct application of the theory of derived demand. It starts with the price of a final product in a competitive market. The full costs of producing, processing, and marketing the product are estimated at their opportunity costs and deducted. The residual income is the return to—or benefit of—the one input not included in the costs. This residual is sometimes known as economic rent. As an application of the basic model of exchange, the method is simple, appropriate, and straightforward. In practice, it is imprecise and complex, but it can still be appropriate.

4.2. Application to the Pest-Control Example

The insect pest in our example is defoliating forest trees and reducing timber growth. What is the value of the wood harvest that is lost because of the pest?

The market for lumber is competitive, but the market for the logs used to manufacture lumber is usually not. On the selling side there may be only one supplier, such as a government forest service. On the buying side there are often only two or three sawmills within economic distance of a forest. There is no chance for competition among large numbers of sellers and buyers to produce a competitive price for the logs. Some other way is needed to determine price, and the residual method is often used.

Suppose the timber on an average acre could be converted into lumber that would bring a gross revenue of $2000 in the competitive lumber market. Suppose also that the costs of extracting the timber from this average acre, transporting it to a sawmill, and manufacturing and distributing the lumber from it would total $1600. This would leave a residual of $400. If the costs of the sawmill operator include a normal profit for himself, he could pay $400 for the standing timber. This residual stumpage price represents the derived demand for this timber and therefore its social value as it stands in the woods.

This stumpage value can now be used to assess the pest damage. The slower growth resulting from defoliation will accumulate and be felt in the future when the timber is sold. In their study McCay and White (1973) assumed that the timber would be ready for harvest in 10 years. They estimated that defoliation would cause volume losses of 25 to 30 percent during that decade. It was therefore necessary to predict what the future harvest would be with and without the insect damage. They made three projections of total future income per acre to allow for uncertainties about future growth and prices. These projections are shown in Table 13.2, along with the estimated money loss from defoliation.

For current decisions about pest control, the present worth of future loss is needed. McCay and White discounted the projected future losses at 7 percent, as shown in Table 13.2. Their best estimate of the expected future loss without pest control was $59.00 per acre.

Table 13.2 Estimation of Pest Damage to Future Timber Revenues[a]

	Total Income 10 Years from Now		Money Loss	
Projection	Without Damage	With Damage	In Year 10	Discounted to present @7%
Low	294	219	75	38
Expected	400	285	115	59
High	653	458	195	99

Source. McCay and White (1973).
[a] Revenues in dollars per acre.

4.3. Extensions to the Budgeting Approach

The simple budgeting approach has been extended in two ways, both of which attempt to identify and determine the costs of more inputs, and thus leave fewer items for the residual. As a first extension, assumptions may be made about some of the inputs. For example, Solow (1957) made explicit assumptions about the nature of the underlying production functions between output and some unpriced inputs. A second extension involves estimating the monetary contribution of some inputs by other methods, thus leaving less for the residual. Denison (1962) studied factors affecting economic growth in the United States, but instead of leaving education in the residual, he estimated the returns to it by the conventional market-price method and deducted them.

The pro-rata method used to value land in agriculture is another version of the second extension. Gross income is calculated, and monetary costs are deducted. The residual income is the contribution of all unpriced inputs, such as family labor, management, land, and owned equipment. As many of these unpriced inputs as possible are then valued at the rate at which they can be rented to others. When these input costs are deducted, the residual refers to fewer and more-specific inputs.

4.4. Some Applications of the Method

The basic ideas of the residual method are (a) to find a competitive market that will furnish an appropriate money price for estimating gross income and (b) to calculate the value of the unpriced input(s) as gross income less the opportunity cost of all priced inputs. These ideas have been applied to a variety of valuation problems, of which we give two examples.

4.4.1. Valuation of Noise. Walters (1975) studied the costs of airport noise to nearby residents. One approach was to assume that noise occurs in two discrete identifiable classes and to divide the housing market into noisy houses and quiet houses. The money value of noise was then derived as follows:

$$\begin{matrix}\text{value (cost)} \\ \text{of noise}\end{matrix} = \begin{matrix}\text{price of} \\ \text{quiet house}\end{matrix} - \begin{matrix}\text{price of noisy} \\ \text{house}\end{matrix} \tag{13.14}$$

Data were collected on the distribution of house prices and on other house characteristics to implement the equation and check that the difference in price was indeed due to noise. In this case the price of a noisy house indicates the value of quiet as a benefit, and therefore of noise as a cost.

4.4.2. Benefits of Urban Renewal. Among the benefits of urban redevelopment are opportunities for firms to relocate and more productive use of land. Rothenburg (1967) discusses the way in which these benefits and their associated costs can be captured in land prices, as we show in Section 5. The effects of improved location and improved productivity are lumped together in the new price, and the problem for valuation is to separate them. This may be achieved by finding a priced surrogate for one. Because the increase in land value is an observed money price, deducting the price of the surrogate will leave a residual value that must be due to the other factor.

4.5. Discussion

The difficulty with this method is the residual nature of the residual. Total income is a result of all inputs, and the budgeting procedure only deducts the effects of some of them. The residual income is due to all remaining inputs. In farm irrigation, for example, the residual may be a composite value of water and unpriced inputs such as management and family labor.

Analyses over time or among economic units require comparisons of the capital and labor used. But the quality of an input may differ over time or among firms. For example, the quality of machinery and the health and education of labor have tended to rise over time. Such quality differences can cause inconsistencies in comparisons over time or among firms. Iden's (1964) wide and unexpected variations in residual values for agricultural land in the United States between 1930 and 1961 may well be due to such causes.

The residual method is frequently used to set the price of timber, but controversies between government forest services and buyers are frequent. Input costs for equipment and allowances for roads are difficult to estimate. And as Weintraub (1959) noted, there may be two unknowns—profits to logger and return to timber—but only one residual equation.

Despite such difficulties, the applicability of the method is demonstrated by its widespread use. Forest services have solved the problems to a sufficient extent that the method is used to price timber the world over. Federal agencies in the United States also often use it to value irrigation water.

5. THE LAND-PRICE METHOD

In a conceptual sense, land can be viewed as a bundle of characteristics that together provide a flow of income or utility. When land itself is priced but some specific characteristic is unpriced, analysis of land prices can sometimes provide values for the unpriced characteristic.

5.1. Adapting the Basic Model

The market price of a fixed asset such as land can capture the flow of net income from the asset and express it in monetary terms. For priced goods the costs of variable inputs can be deducted from gross income to determine the return to land. The flow of annual returns can then be capitalized to determine a value for the land. The arithmetic of the capitalization process was set out in the present worth formula of Equation 2.22 in Chapter 2:

$$\text{land value} = B_1 + B_2WT_2 + \cdots + B_tWT_t \qquad (13.15)$$

where B_i is the net income in year i and WT_i is the appropriate weight or discount factor. The generality of this process has led to the name *income capitalization method* as an alternative to *land price method.*

The flow of utility from all land characteristics is aggregated in the price of land. Demand for land recognizes all the characteristics from which consumers derive utility. Supply of land recognizes the opportunity costs of providing land that has these characteristics. A change in land price can therefore result from a change in any one of its characteristics.

5.1.1. Complete or Partial Capture. The effect of a change in a land characteristic may not all be captured in the change in price. The price change may underestimate the value of the change in the characteristic. If the supply of land is not affected by a change in one of its characteristics, any change in land price must be a result of some change in demand. But the magnitude of the price change will be partly determined by the nature of the supply.

Take, for example, the effect of insect defoliation and the resulting death of trees on residential land. The insect causes a change in the land characteristic of "woodedness." If potential home builders consider woodedness an important characteristic, destruction of the trees will change the product being offered for sale. The determinant of market price will now be the demand for lots with few or no trees instead of the demand for wooded lots. People who have a preference for wooded lots will not be willing to pay as much for lots without trees. The demand for land after the defoliation will therefore be less (curve D_2 in Figure 13.3) than it was before (curve D_1).

If the supply of land is completely inelastic, as shown in Figure 13.3*a*, the entire effect of the change in the land characteristic will be captured in the land price change. The difference between P_1 and P_2 is the difference in what buyers are willing to pay for a house lot with trees compared to one without them.

If the supply of land is somewhat elastic, as shown in Figure 13.3*b*, the defoliation will cause a change in both the price and quantity of land exchanged. The demand for land without trees will be less, but the suppliers will not be willing to sell the same amount of land at a lower price. A new price of P_3 will develop at which the smaller quantity Q_2 will be exchanged. The market price of land will fall from P_1 to P_3. But this change in price does not represent the difference in willingness to pay for the same marginal units of land. At a total quantity of Q_2, buyers would have been willing to pay P_4 for the marginal lot if it were wooded, giving a difference in willingness to pay of $P_4 - P_3$. The difference in willingness to pay at a total quantity of Q_1 would be $P_1 - P_2$. The difference in market price ($P_1 - P_3$) therefore tends to underestimate the value of the shade trees. The more elastic the supply of land is, the greater will be the size of the underestimate.

5.1.2. Interpreting a Land-Price Model. A general function to describe variations in quantities consumed is given by Equation 2.4 in Chapter 2 as

$$Q_i = f(P_i, P_n, Inc, X_n) \tag{13.16}$$

To analyze variations in price, this function can be rearranged

$$P_i = f(P_n, Inc, X_n) \tag{13.17}$$

where the observations now refer to a specific quantity of the good i, usually a single unit such as a block of land. The other factors denoted by X_n can include the characteristics of the land. The prices of other goods (P_n) and buyer income (Inc) must still be recognized, as well as other characteristics of the buyers and sellers that are included in the other factors. Richardson, Vipond, and Furbey (1974) incorporate seller types as dummy variables in

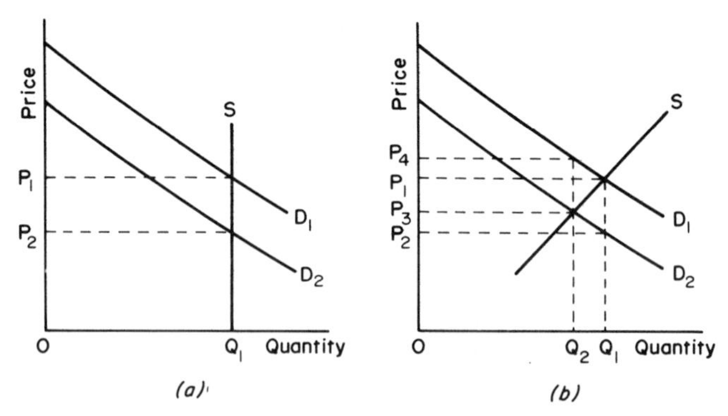

Figure 13.3. Influence of elasticity of supply on the change in price with a change in demand. (a) Supply is perfectly inelastic. (b) Supply is elastic to some degree.

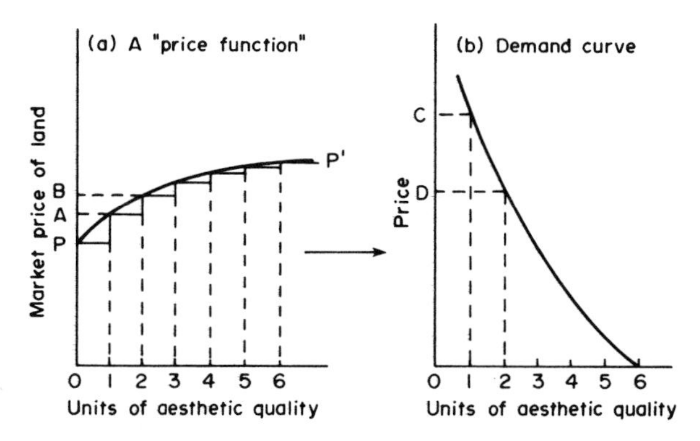

Figure 13.4. Derivation of a demand curve for aesthetic quality from the relationship between market price of land and aesthetic quality of land.

this model, coding them to distinguish between government, private, and farmer sellers.

Let us now assume that this model is being used to investigate the relationship between land price and some specific characteristic, such as aesthetic quality. We will also assume that a positive relationship has been established. If buyers obtain diminishing marginal returns from this characteristic, the relationship will be like PP' in Figure 13.4a. Land would sell for OP if it had no aesthetic quality. One unit of aesthetic quality would add PA to house price. A second unit would add AB, but a seventh would add nothing. The increments in house price provide points for a downward-sloping demand curve, as shown in Figure 13.4b. OC in Figure 13.4b = PA in Figure 13.4a, and OD in b = AB in a.

Empirical analyses usually set the price function (Equation 13.17 and Figure 13.4a) in the context of a representative house or representative block of land. A pest-control program may change the aesthetic quality of a number of blocks of land (n). The total benefit from the program can be calculated by aggregating the benefits from the individual blocks. If ΔP_i equals the change in price of block i resulting from the change in the characteristic,

$$\text{total benefit} = \sum_{i=1}^{n} \Delta P_i \tag{13.18}$$

There are several difficulties with this aggregation procedure. For strict accuracy, all individual buyers must have the same demand. Furthermore, an empirical analysis will provide only one point on the price function in Figure 13.4a. Only programs that make marginal changes away from this point can be assessed. Freeman (1974) presents potential statistical procedures for overcoming these problems, and we consider them later in this section.

5.2. Application to the Pest-Control Example

We follow the approach used by Payne, White, McCay, and McNichols (1973) in their study of the contribution of trees to residential land prices in Amherst, Massachusetts. To make our example complete, we use hypothetical data for some variables.

Let us assume there is a city in the affected area and that 500 house lots are sufficiently wooded to be attacked by the pest. Historical statistics indicate that the average family moves every 10 years. One-tenth of the houses—including 50 of those on wooded lots—will be on the market at any one time. We assume that the effects of defoliation on price are not large enough to change the number of lots offered for sale. The supply of affected houses is therefore completely inelastic.

The price model of Section 5.1.2 is implemented as follows:

(**a**) Data are collected on the prices (P_i) at which properties (i) have recently changed hands and on the characteristics (j) of these properties (X_{ij}).

(**b**) Two variables are included in the model to reflect our beliefs about the nature of the tree/price relationship: X_1 allows people to prefer more trees to less or vice versa; X_1^2 allows for changing marginal utility from extra trees. These two variables permit a curvilinear relationship like Figure 13.4*a* which can extend to a downward trend at large numbers of trees.

(**c**) Appropriate statistical methods are used to estimate the necessary coefficients and the constant for the model. The nature of the result may be summarized as follows:

$$P_i = f(X_{i1}, X_{i1}^2, X_{ij}) \tag{13.19}$$

(**d**) The model is now simplified for a standard house lot and for the two variables of interest. For a standard lot of 20,000 square feet, all X_i variables other than X_1 and X_1^2 are set at their means and added to the constant. The following regression is obtained:

$$P = 32{,}000 + 300\,X_1 - 5.2X_1^2 \tag{13.20}$$

This indicates that a property with no trees ($X_1 = 0$) can be expected to sell for \$32,000. Properties with 17 and 29 trees, but otherwise identical, may be expected to sell for \$35,600 and \$36,300, respectively.

(**e**) The formula

$$\begin{matrix}\text{value of change} \\ \text{in quality}\end{matrix} = \begin{matrix}\text{price before} \\ \text{change}\end{matrix} - \begin{matrix}\text{price after} \\ \text{change}\end{matrix} \tag{13.21}$$

may now be used to estimate the loss due to defoliation. If the number of living trees were reduced from 29 to 17 on the average lot,

$$\begin{aligned}\text{value of change} &= \$36{,}300 - \$35{,}600 \\ \text{in quality} &= \$700 \text{ per house}\end{aligned} \tag{13.22}$$

The total loss would be $35,000 for all 50 houses.

Using this model in this way, Payne, White, McCay, and McNichols found trees on residential lots in Amherst contributed as much as $290 each to land price.

5.3. Application to Other Problems

5.3.1. Valuation of Scenic and Aesthetic Benefits. The price of a tract of land can incorporate the scenic quality of the surrounding area. Isolation of the value of the scenic component poses difficulties, particularly in defining and measuring scenic quality. A simple procedure is to record 1 if there is a view from the land and 0 if there is not. The following study takes a slightly different and more-detailed approach.

Armstrong (1974) set out to quantify the amenity values of forests in Vermont, and particularly to identify the characteristics of forest land that contribute to market price. He collected information on actual and potential market prices from real estate agents and on characteristics such as lot size, distance to major ski areas and highways, presence or absence of electricity, elevation, access, and aesthetic quality. (The latter was coded from 2.55 for good quality with frontage on a trout stream in a quiet remote locality down to 2.00 for poor quality with a view only if trees were cut.)

His model to explain variations in price per acre for Addison and Orange Counties was

$$\begin{aligned}P = {} & -1520.1 + (4387/\text{area}) + 264\,(\text{aesthetic factor}) \\ & +1102\,(\text{electricity factor}).\end{aligned} \tag{13.23}$$

The coefficient of determination was .55. The estimated price per acre for a 100-acre tract with electricity but with the lowest scenic quality rating is

$$P = -1520 + 44 + 528 + 1366 = \$418 \tag{13.24}$$

The same size lot with electricity and the highest aesthetic quality, has an indicated price of $563 per acre. The value of the difference in aesthetic quality is $145 per acre.

Characteristics that contribute to aesthetic quality of land can sometimes be measured objectively on a continuous scale. The number of trees per 20,000 square feet provided an objective quantitative measure in the pest-control example of Section 5.2. The percentage of dwellings in a dilapidated state was used as a measure of environmental quality in Downing's (1973) study of commercial land values in Milwaukee.

5.3.2. Valuation of Improvements in Air Quality. The price of land, and particularly residential land, is influenced by the quality of its environment. Informal comparisons of changes in property value in 1962 suggested that house prices in St. Louis dropped by $1000 following air pollution from a new metal factory (Bach, 1972). Since the late 1960s several successful studies have related changes in land prices to changes in air quality (Waddell, 1974). We use them as examples of the difficulties involved in applying results from specific land-price studies to policy problems over larger areas.

Different problems may require different ways of measuring air quality as the independent variable for the land-price model. A chemical variable is indicated where the damage is due to chemical pollution. Ridker and Henning (1967) defined one of their variables as the presence of sulfur dioxide and trioxide, hydrogen sulfide, and sulfuric acid compounds. For other policy problems a physical variable may be indicated. Jaksch and Stoevener (1970) in analyzing the effects of pollution from a pulpmill on house prices in Toledo, Oregon, defined the air quality variable as weight of dustfall per unit area per unit time.

Air pollution imposes other costs besides lowering house and land prices. Sulfur-based chemicals not only damage paint, corrode metal and stone, and soil exposed surfaces, but also damage health and vegetation. Analyses of land prices may identify the costs to land and houses but will not identify other costs. These other costs must be analyzed separately, using the same kind of basic model but with medical costs (Jaksch and Stoevener, 1974) or state of health (Lave and Seskin, 1970) as the dependent variable.

Positive analytical results with the land-value method have been reported by Anderson and Crocker (1971, 1972), Ridker and Henning (1967), and Jaksch and Stoevener (1970). Freeman (1974), by contrast, reports two studies that showed no significant relationship between air quality and land prices. Ridker and Henning (1967) suggest that the effect of air pollution on land price is likely to be small relative to such other factors as buyer income.

Difficulties can arise in aggregating the values from an empirical study with a cross section of data. For example, Ridker and Henning found that a decrease in sulfur pollution level in St. Louis was associated with a price increase of $245 per house. As a guide for policy decisions, they multiplied this value by the number of houses that would benefit from a pollution control program. The total increase in property values over all St. Louis apparently could have been as much as $82,790,000, or an annual equivalent of $8 million at 10 percent interest. The annual cost of a shift to low-sulfur fuels was estimated at $10 to $15 million, indicating that a control policy would be marginally unprofitable.

Freeman (1971) argued that this aggregation procedure fails to recognize the marginal and specific nature of a cross-sectional survey. The $245 per house may be appropriate for a marginal change in the representative property in the sample, but it assumes constant conditions outside the sample. An air-improvement program for a whole city may involve nonmarginal changes and will certainly change conditions outside the sample. The value of $245 does not refer to such a major program and cannot be aggregated in this manner unless some more-general model is available for the whole city. However, individual values can have a broader role if there is precise specification of the assumptions, as Freeman (1974) showed in detail. There also can be a difficulty in separating supply from demand factors in the determination of price. This difficulty is discussed more fully by Kalter and Gosse (1970).

5.3.3. Valuation of Nonuser Benefits of Preservation. The benefits from preservation for historical, educational, cultural, scientific, or ecological purposes are difficult to value. All of them can arise without the consumer actually consuming a physical good or even using the resource. They are therefore sometimes known as *nonuser benefits.* Most of these benefits will accrue to people only in the future, and many are very hard to identify and estimate. Nevertheless, decisions about preservation are made and comparative values for different uses are assessed in the process. Because these decisions often involve the purchase of land explicitly for preservation, the prices paid for such land should help us quantify these informal comparative value judgments.

Gupta and Foster (1975) used the land-price method to estimate the social benefits from wetlands preservation in Massachusetts. Recent land purchases by government agencies were observed, purchase prices were recorded, and the quality of representative tracts for wildlife, cultural, and aesthetic benefits was estimated on a percentage scale. Experts observed the species richness, water chemistry, vegetation diversity, and other characteristics of each acquisition, scored each characteristic on a simple one-to-five scale, and assigned each a weight. A total percentage quality score for each wetland was calculated as a sum of the weighted scores of all these characteristics.

The highest price that had been paid for each class of land was determined. The highest price paid by the Division of Fisheries and Game for land for wildlife purposes, for example, was $1300 per acre. Assuming that the highest price was paid for the best land, $1300 is a monetary estimate of the wildlife benefits per acre from the best habitat.

The maximum money value and the quality score were then combined to provide a criterion for new preservation decisions:

$$\text{total benefit of new area} = \$1300 \times \text{percentage quality score of the new area} \tag{13.25}$$

For example, a potential acquisition might have a quality score of 60 percent, giving a total estimated benefit of \$780 (1300 × .60). This value of \$780 is compared to the market price of the wetland. If the market price is less than \$780, the social benefits would exceed the cost of acquisition, and the wetland should be acquired and preserved. Gupta and Foster (1975) and Foster (1977) discuss similar valuations for water-supply purposes, aesthetic purposes, and combinations of purposes.

The rationale behind land value as a measure of benefit is simple and appealing. In the wetland example purchases were made by government agencies in their capacity as trustee for the public. Presumably, these politically established agencies reflect the views of the people in their estimates of social benefit. Other land with the same characteristics should provide the same benefits, if everything else is equal, and should therefore be of the same value as that acquired in the past.

5.4. Application to "Mobile Goods"

In a conceptual sense all goods, services, and activities are composed of different characteristics that provide utility and thus contribute to total value. The method described in this section is most frequently used with the fixed good of land. But it is quite general and can be used equally well with "mobile goods."

Bishop and Cicchetti (1975) proposed its application to mobile goods under the name "characteristic or hedonic approach." They report two attempts to implement the method. In one, data were collected on willingness to pay for wilderness visits with different characteristics of trip length (X_1), quality of trails (X_2), numbers of encounters (X_3), and types of encounter (X_4). With willingness to pay as the measure of price (P_i), the data were analyzed with the conventional equation

$$P_i = f(X_1, \cdots, X_4) \tag{13.26}$$

Analysis in the manner shown in Section 5.2 provided values for each of the unpriced characteristics.

The method was also applied by Cowling and Cubbin (1972) to isolate the effect of changes in standard automobile models on price. The prices and characteristics of established models were observed in each year from 1956 to 1968. The characteristics included horsepower, car length, fuel consumption, and passenger space. Analysis of these time series data provided information on the contribution of each characteristic to total change in price.

5.5. Discussion

5.5.1. Actual Transaction Evidence Unnecessary. Payne, White, McCay, and McNichols (1973) say this method can be used when prices from actual sales are not available. They comment on three alternative sources of information: (1) Obtaining estimates from local real estate appraisers gives the best results. (2) Interviewing homeowners is more expensive and gives less consistent results. (3) Using values from the property assessment list maintained by local government for tax purposes gives generally poor estimates of current market values.

5.5.2. Land Prices May Not Reflect Total Benefits. The aggregation of changes in land price does not usually provide an adequate estimate of the total change in net benefits. We noted in Section 5.3.2. that improvements in air quality not only increase land prices but also improve health.

Property taxes become capitalized into the price of land. Potential buyers consider the tax burden as well as the price in purchase decisions. Proximity to a park may increase land price, but this in turn will normally increase the assessment and property tax. If a potential buyer is willing to pay an extra amount for proximity to a park, part of this will be absorbed by the higher tax. McMillan (1975) shows that land price based estimates of the benefits from an environmental improvement may be too low because they exclude the willingness to pay the extra tax. He suggests that errors as large as $500 are possible on a market price change of $2000.

Properties may provide benefits to persons other than the owners or purchasers, such as aesthetic benefits to passersby. These only influence the land price if the owner can sell or charge for them. When this is impossible, the external benefits or costs must be estimated in some other way and added to the change in land price.

6. MARKET-COMPARISON METHOD

This method values things at the known or recognized value of comparable things. Because no two things and no two exchanges are exactly alike, comparable situations are always hard to find. Because there are no general formal procedures for identifying comparable situations, reliable use of this method depends on careful and consistent analysis. The method is sometimes known as the *judgment method* (Robinson and Tanzi, 1962) because of the care and judgment needed.

6.1. Application of the Method

Clawson and Knetsch (1966) refer to this as the "market value method" and note that it was once the most common method for valuing recreation benefits of public projects. In 1957 the U.S. National Park service observed entrance fees on private recreation areas. Visitors were found to pay an average of $1.60 per day, and this was adopted as the value of the "average" benefit per recreation day in national parks (Robinson and Tanzi, 1962). It has been widely advocated for valuations in the development of water and related land resources in the United States.

6.2. An Extension of the Method

The "market value of fish" procedure (Clawson and Knetsch, 1966) tries to extend the method by assumption. It assumes that benefits in an activity with a given product (fish) are equal to the benefits in a different activity that has the same product. The benefits from sport fishing might therefore be estimated from the dockside value of the commercial fish catch. However, fish are the main object of commercial fishing, whereas sport fishing usually has other important objectives and other benefits, such as recreation. This extension to rather dissimilar things tends to underestimate value by ignoring such other benefits.

6.3. Discussion

Although the method appears straightforward, it involves several conceptual issues in addition to the practical problem of finding comparable markets. Consider an application of the method to the benefits of recreational use in a national park. Some comparable fee, such as $1.60, is obtained and multiplied by the estimated attendance to obtain total value. But if such a fee were to be introduced where none had existed before, the number of visitors might be reduced. The method could therefore overestimate the total willingness to pay.

There is also a paradoxical element of circularity in the method. It assumes that the best estimates will come from directly comparable things, that is, from things that are very good substitutes. But if they are such good substitutes, consumers will have difficulty choosing between them, and consumer choice may depend entirely on price, which is the value indicator to be estimated. The best sources for comparison may therefore create the most difficulties.

Despite these problems, the rationale of the method is sound, because it rests on consumer willingness to pay. It is widely used for taxation and legal purposes by setting the value of the land in question equal to the market price of a comparable tract in a comparable situation. The "comparison method" as it is known in Austrialia, establishes the price of farmland as the market value of other blocks of comparable soil productivity.

Because it uses past prices for present problems, the method may work reasonably well in times of relative price stability. But during booms market values change rapidly and may fluctuate widely, and during economic recessions price falls are inconsistent.

7. DISCUSSION

A choice between the market-price methods must consider the situation and role to which each applies. Let us review these situations, particularly with regard to possible biases in the superficially similar monetary values that the methods produce.

7.1. Possible Biases

Each of the methods refers to a slightly different situation, as shown in Figure 13.1. So their numerical results cannot be compared to expose differences in the methods, as we did in Chapter 9. However, we have noted some possible biases as the chapter progressed, and we now summarize them.

The conventional market-price method (Section 2) underestimates net social benefit, because it ignores consumer's surplus. The underestimate is smaller when demand is elastic, because the consumer's surplus is also smaller.

The directions of the biases of the land-price and market-comparison methods are indeterminate. Because the land-price method ignores consumer's surplus, it can be expected to underestimate net social benefit. But if supply is at all elastic, a decrease in demand will not only cause a lower price but also a reduction in quantity. By incorrectly assuming an inelastic supply, the land-price method can overestimate the true change in net monetary and net social benefits. The nature of the demand and supply curves in Figure 13.3*b* suggests that if both demand and supply are highly elastic, the land-price method can produce an estimate that is higher than the true change in net social benefit.

The market-comparison method may overestimate net monetary benefits, as we discussed in Section 6. Because it ignores consumer's surplus, it may also underestimate net social benefit. However, even this is uncertain, because if the demand were sufficiently elastic, the resulting overestimate of net monetary benefits could cause an overestimate of the change in net social benefits.

7.2. Roles of the Various Methods

The different methods measure different kinds of benefits. Although this distinguishes their potential roles, it also suggests that a combination may be useful for some problems. For example, the market-comparison method can only value benefits to actual users or purchasers of traded things. By its nature it ignores any benefits to persons who never visit the area or consume the good. By contrast, the land-price method can be expected to capture such nonuser benefits, as we discussed in Section 5. The residual method has been widely used for valuation of unpriced inputs, and its basic principles have had even wider application. The production-function method, with its marginal value product information, refers only to inputs. The different methods might be used for different aspects of a complex valuation problem.

CHAPTER 14

Estimation of Monetary Values—Direct Questioning

There is great intuitive appeal in asking a person the simple question: How much are you willing to pay for thing *A*? The response presumably will be an estimate of the total benefit the person expects from thing *A*, and subtracting the appropriate costs should provide an estimate of value.

This kind of method has been applied to many environmental problems, including air pollution (Barrett and Waddell, 1973) wildlife management (Hammack and Brown, 1974), and water resources (Gluck, 1975). The widespread application of the methods is due largely to the relevance for valuation of the willingness-to-pay concept, the flexibility of the methods, and the possibility of collecting useful data when no other information exists.

All these methods use direct questions and provide monetary estimates of total benefit. But they rest on somewhat different interpretations of the model of demand (Figure 2.1), as we discuss in Section 10 and Chapter 16. The methods estimate total benefit in two different ways (Figure 14.1). Methods in the first group have explicit questions on willingness to pay and provide total benefit data directly. These methods range from the unstructured single direct question of Section 3, through the simple developments of converging questions and budget allocation in Section 4, to the formal structured trade-off games of Sections 5 and 6.

Methods in the second group ask questions about quantities consumed, from which the analyst infers the willingness to pay. Oné method in this group (Section 7) bases the inferences on simulated choices in an actual market and on some enabling assumptions. The other two simulate a perfectly competitive market and base the inferences on characteristics of that market. The priority evaluator technique (Section 8) is based on the characteristic that the total utility of the marginal unit of each good equals the price of the good when the market is in equilibrium. The indifference-mapping method (Section 9) uses quantity information to provide a map from which a demand curve is derived.

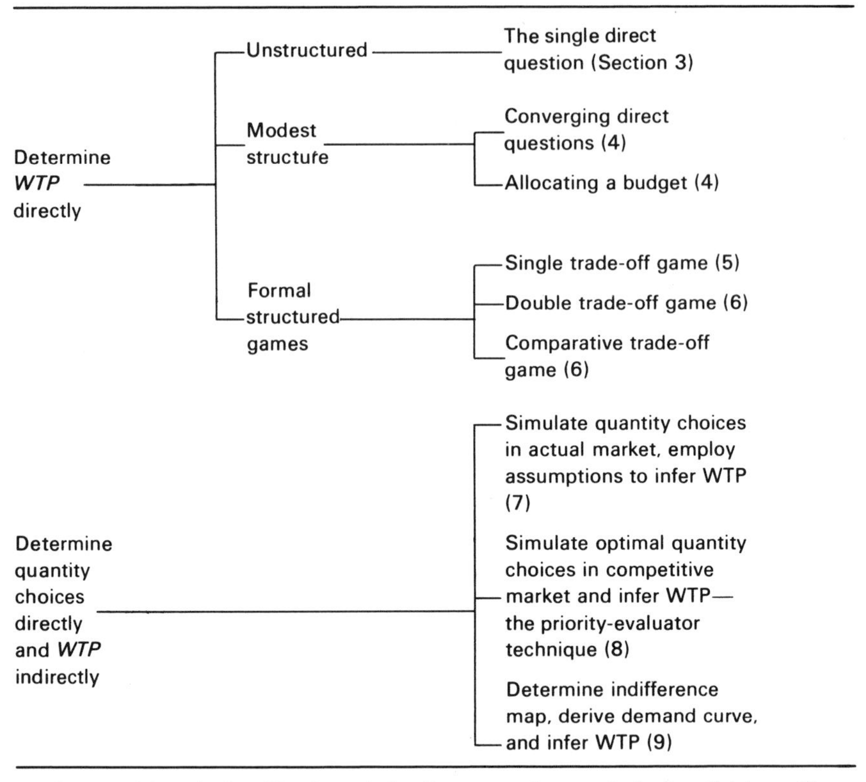

Figure 14.1. A classification of the direct-question methods for eliciting willingness to pay (WTP).

1. APPLYING THE BASIC MODEL OF EXCHANGE

1.1. Marginal and Total Willingness to Pay

These methods, particularly the first group, are direct applications of the basic model of exchange. Willingness to pay is an estimate of total benefit (consumer's surplus + consumer's expenditure) and provides a point on a demand curve. A *WTP* of $8 for the first unit is an estimate of the total benefit from this unit (point *A* in Figure 14.2). Estimates for successive units can then identify the downward-sloping demand curve (*AB*).

A demand curve defines the border between areas of possible choice and impossible choice. If the price for the first unit were above *A* in Figure 14.2, the consumer would not make the purchase. Any point above the demand curve denotes a price above willingness to pay for that unit and is in the area of impossible choice. Any point below the curve denotes a price below

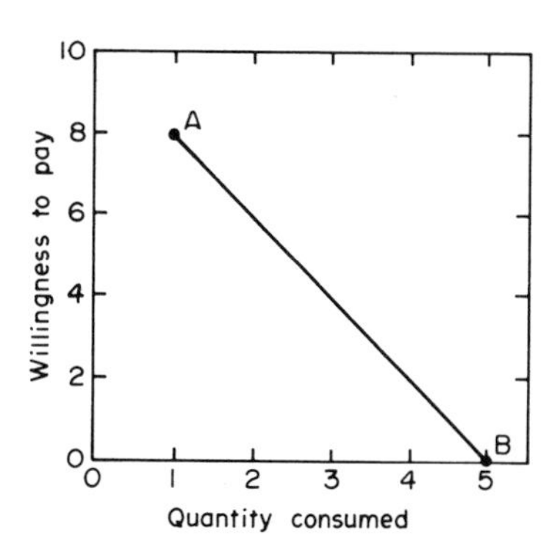

Figure 14.2. Willingness to pay for the marginal unit expressed as a demand curve.

willingness to pay and is in the area of possible choices. The demand curve represents a maximum, and the questions must search for maximum willingness to pay.

Willingness to pay is sometimes expressed as payment for a total quantity rather than a marginal unit. The data for the marginal units (Figure 14.2) may be expressed in a total benefit curve (Figure 14.3). This curve is an outward expression through exchange of the total utility curve (Figure 2.6). As background for the policy example in Section 2, the horizontal axis of Figure 14.3 can be defined for air quality. If extra units of clean air are associated with diminishing marginal utility, the total benefit curve will be shaped as in Figure 14.3. The subject is willing to pay $8 for the first unit of clean air (point *R*) and $14 for the first two units (point *S*). In the marginal terms of Figure 14.2, the willingness to pay is $8 for the first unit, $6 for the second, and so on down to $0 for the fifth.

1.2. Willingness To Pay or To Sell

Policy problems can involve two kinds of exchanges. Most decisions are about the possibility of obtaining extra quantities of a good, and the rele-

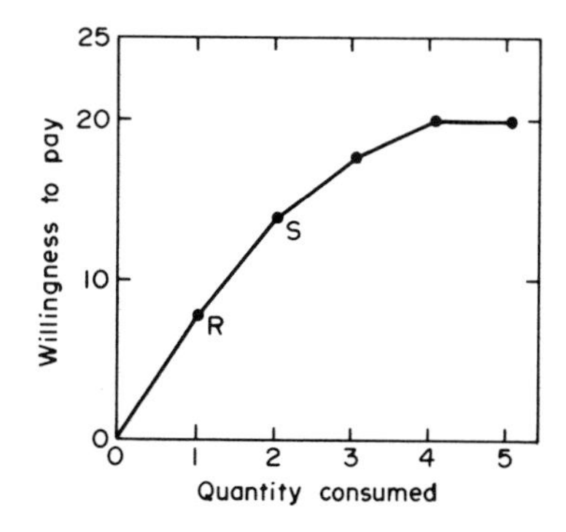

Figure 14.3. Willingness to pay for all units purchased expressed as a total benefit curve.

vant questions concern the willingness to pay for these extra amounts. However, some decisions may reduce the existing quantity of a good. Air-pollution decisions, for example, may involve a decrease in air quality. The relevant question would be: For how much are you willing to sell your right to clean air?

The two situations require different qualifications to the basic questions. The benefits from extra consumption are related to the maximum willingness to pay. The questions must seek for the maximum amount the person will pay. When goods are sold or the right to consume is withdrawn, the question must seek for the minimum amount the person will accept.

1.3. Scope and Objectives of the Chapter

The use of these methods involves some general problems and some problems that are specific to the methods. A general practical problem is the need to minimize the hypothetical nature of the questions. The general theoretical problems include aggregation and the choice between different interpretations of demand models. These general problems are discussed in other parts of this book. We concentrate here on providing an understanding of the methods, their theoretical background, and their specific problems.

2. AN ENVIRONMENTAL POLICY EXAMPLE: AIR-POLLUTION ABATEMENT

Consider a city with 125,000 households, 600,000 inhabitants, and a poor public-transportation system. Commuters must travel mainly by automobile, which creates air pollution. The main industries are chemical manufacturing, light shipbuilding, and paper making. A coal-fired power station serves the city and part of the state. Frequent temperature inversions combine with these factors to create a serious air-pollution problem.

The inhabitants are affected in various ways. Visibility is reduced, and buildings are dirty. The new paper factory has introduced an unpleasant smell. Sulfur oxides from the power station have an unpleasant odor and can cause lung damage. Oxidants from a number of sources irritate the eyes and throat and reduce the level of community health. Taken together, these sources, pollutants, and effects make for poorer health and a lower quality of life for the city's residents.

2.1. Framing the Problem

The city has been contemplating ways to reduce air pollution, and the additional new pollution has provided the necessary stimulus to define and compare alternative control measures. The analyst must make an assessment of the comparative values of the alternative control possibilities.

Techniques for measuring the quantities and safe limits for each pollutant are generally known. Techniques to aggregate the measurements into a pollution index are available (Babcock and Nagda 1972) and largely follow the methods of Chapter 9. For our purposes we assume that the standards can be expressed as follows. If pollutants exceed the standard, the air is "dangerous," and the inhabitants suffer irritations to eyes, nose, and throat and notice reduced visibility. If pollutant levels are below the standard, the air is "safe," and none of these effects is perceived.

The inhabitants are highly sensitive to the air pollution, and the number of "dangerous days" per week or year has meaning for them. The same parameter is useful for policy, because it combines frequency of occurrence with specific standards for the pollutants. Each pollutant can be related to its source, and specific policies for abatement can be identified and defined and their costs determined. The benefits of the alternative policies must be assessed through the direct-questioning methods. The willingness to pay questions can be framed in terms of the number of dangerous days.

2.2. The Example in the Chapter

Each method is applied to estimate the total benefit of some simple abatement programs. For the purposes of this chapter, just 10 inhabitants of the city are interviewed with the methods. They represent 10 households from the same suburb. Each household is subject to the same level of pollution—four out of five weekdays with dangerous air. Each household also has a similar annual income. The results are listed in Table 14.1. The results for a given method (along a row) reflect different benefits to each subject. But different benefits, in total or on the average, for a given subject (down a column) reflect differences between the methods.

To encourage consistency, all the methods were applied to a given subject in one interview. The previous results were hidden as the next method was applied. The two more complicated methods of Section 8 and 9 are not applied here. We draw on our experience elsewhere to discuss these two methods.

3. THE SINGLE DIRECT QUESTION

The simplest method of this group is the single direct question: How much are you willing to pay for thing *A*? We now apply this method to the air-pollution example and review some other applications of it.

Table 14.1. Estimates of Willingness to Pay in Dollars for 10 Subjects by Six Methods[a]

Method		Subject 1	2	3	4	5
Single direct question[b]		800	1000	500	4000	500
Converging questions[b]		900	1200	300	5000	500
Budget allocation[c] with budget of	$ 500	200*	50	10	—	50*
	1000	500	100*	25*	500	100
	1500	800	100	50	—	—
	3000	—	—	—	—	—
	5000	—	—	—	3000*	—
	15000	—	—	—	—	—
Single trade-off game	1sd to 2sd	350	300	25	500	50
	to 3sd	600	600	40	1000	100
	to 4sd	750	900	50	2000	200
	to 5sd	900	1100	50	3000	300
Comparative trade-off game	1sd to 3sd[e]	400	500	20	500	10
	to 5sd[e]	700	1000	30	2500	50
	3sd to 5sd[f]	300	100	600	100	100
Costless choice		>1900	<650	<650	>2500	>3000

[a] The first three methods and the sixth refer exclusively to the change from one safe day (1 sd) to five (5 sd). The single and comparative trade-off methods refer to this change as well as to others.
[b] Recorded to the nearest $100.
[c] * Actual budget for the subject.

3.1. Application to the Air-Pollution Example

All direct-question methods must be specified carefully. We gave the following introduction to each of our subjects:

> Consider your present family situation, number of dependents, home location, and financial situation. Consider also the current air-pollution situation, with dangerous air on four out of five weekdays causing irritation to the eyes, throat, and lungs and reduced visibility. The city is proposing a control program that would give five safe weekdays. Now, consider a once only donation to help finance this program. What is the maximum amount you are willing to pay toward the cost of the program?

The answers for our 10 subjects are listed in Table 14.1. The average willingness to pay was about $2400, and the range was from $500 to $10,000. If this were a representative sample of the city, the program would produce a net benefit if the total costs were less than $2400 per household.

Subject					Total *WTP*	Average *WTP*
6	7	8	9	10		
10000	2000	3000	600	2000	24,400	2440
12000	2000	3000	600	3000	28,500	2850
—	—	—	50	—		
50	900*	700	100*	500*	3,475	350
—	—	—	200	—		
—	2700	2400*	—	2000		
—	—	4000	—	2000		
1000*	—	—	—	—	8,275[d]	830
50	350	300	200	500	2,625	263
200	500	500	400	800	4,740	474
400	800	600	500	900	7,100	710
500	1350	700	600	1000	9,500	950
300	200	100	0	500	2,530	250
500	500	150	100	1500	7,030	700
200	200	100	50	200	1,950	195
<800	>5000	>6000	>1800	>5000	27,300	2730

[d] This total refers to the actual or "realistic" budgets, that is, the total for the data with asterisks. To save space results for nonstandard or nonrealistic budgets have been omitted for subjects 4, 5, 6 and 7. These budgets were $250, $2000 and $10,000.
[e] Over a base of $500.
[f] Over a base of $800.

3.2. Other Applications of the Method

The simplicity and relevance of the method has led to a variety of applications. Barrett and Waddell (1973) report three examples for air pollution. Ridker (1967) asked people their willingness to pay to prevent soot damage, and then estimated the costs of cleaning up the damage. All subjects were willing to pay at least as much as these costs, the excess being consumers' surplus. Erskine (1972) reports a variety of single direct questions from public opinion polls on a range of environmental problems.

The following two examples show how the method can also be used to measure willingness to sell and illustrate another way of isolating consumer's surplus from total willingness to pay.

3.2.1. Valuation of Sport Fishing. Willingness-to-pay questions are usually hypothetical, because the subjects are rarely asked to pay the amount they name. But their hypothetical nature can lend flexibility, as shown by Gluck's (1975) attempt to value sport fishing in New Zealand.

Irrigation proposals for the Rakaia River would destroy the existing sport fishery. Present fishermen may have a right to the water, either because of custom or because they are there now. Potential irrigators may have to buy the right to the water from the fishermen. The direct question for the fishermen was phrased as follows: "What is the smallest amount you would be prepared to take to [sell] your right to . . . fish the Rakaia River in the 1973/74 season." (Gluck, 1975).

The average willingness to sell was $609 New Zealand. The usual direct question was then asked to estimate the maximum willingness to pay to maintain fishing rights for the next season. The average willingness to pay was $68 per fisherman. Their minimum willingness to sell something they already had was apparently 10 times as large as their willingness to pay for more of the same thing.

3.2.2. Valuation of Duck Hunting. The direct-question method can readily be used to estimate consumer's surplus rather than total willingness to pay. In their mail questionnaire on duck hunting, Hammack and Brown (1974) asked people what their total hunting costs had been for the season. Then they asked what maximum additional cost these people would have paid and still gone hunting. The answers should be extra willingness to pay over total expenditure, or total consumer's surplus for the season. The mean consumer's surplus was approximately $250 compared with the mean actual expenditure of about $320.

3.3. The Threshold Variation

Sometimes only one alternative is involved, and the question is simply whether benefits cover costs. The threshold variation is useful in such situations. The subject is asked if he is willing to pay more than $\$X$ for thing A. The analyst seeks to determine whether willingness to pay is greater than some threshold ($\$X$) rather than to determine maximum willingness to pay.

The threshold can be set at the cost of supplying the thing, as in Shafer's (1964) survey of choices of recreation facilities. The total costs of developing and maintaining a facility can be estimated and divided by the expected number of visitors. This cost per visitor is the relevant threshold. If all subjects are willing to pay this amount, benefits would at least equal the cost of the proposed facility.

3.4. Discussion

The design and wording of survey questions is the subject of many texts, such as those by Bennett and Richie (1975) for medicine and Burton (1971) for recreation. We restrict our discussion to aspects that are of special interest for valuation, particularly the kind of payment simulated in the question and the problem of validation.

3.4.1. What Kind of Payment? A great variety of payment systems have been used, and the Auburn University (1971) survey on air pollution illustrates many of them. For reduction in automobile pollution subjects were asked how much they would be willing to pay in the forms of higher gasoline prices, bus fares, and reduced salaries to live in a pollution-free area. For reductions in water pollution subjects were questioned about increases in monthly water bills and user fees at recreation sites. Other studies have used questions about extra sales tax on local purchases, higher prices for specific products, and increases in the monthly electricity bill.

When government undertakes a project, most potential users will pay something through general taxes. They may also pay directly through user fees. Romm (1969) recognized these two kinds of payment and asked a pair of questions. The first concerned the size of the government budget for recreation facilities. The second asked how much the subject was willing to pay directly in excess of this. Helliwell (1973) also recognized the joint contribution of the government and private sectors when he asked what percentage of gross national product should be allocated to the environment.

Because people are not accustomed to paying for unpriced benefits, the selection of an appropriate kind of payment is critical. Some payment systems suit some kinds of problem better than others. Gasoline prices and bus fares suit transport problems, but entrance fees are more suitable for recreation. The payment system should be realistic for the problem, and it should be one already familiar to the subjects.

3.4.2. Are the Responses Honest? Direct questions are easy to ask and, as Table 14.1 shows, some monetary estimates can usually be obtained. But do the responses measure true willingness to pay? As the chapter proceeds, other methods will be applied to the same subjects, and we will see that different methods lead to widely different responses. Without one of the formal validation tests of Chapter 7, an analyst must defend his results on the basis of his own interview technique and the conceptual soundness of the question, and argue that the subjects carefully considered each response. Despite such a defense, doubts will remain, and a weak validation test may be better than none at all.

The single direct question is the basis of all the methods presented in Sections 3 to 7. The following methods are refinements of this useful approach.

4. DEVELOPMENTS OF THE SINGLE DIRECT QUESTION.

The two methods that we discuss next are direct developments of the single direct question. The involve a series of questions to converge on maximum willingness to pay (Section 4.1) and a budget to constrain willingness to pay (Section 4.2).

4.1. Converging Direct Questions

The single direct question may readily be developed into a series of converging questions. These simultaneously move up from a low monetary figure and down from a high figure to converge on maximum willingness to pay.

4.1.1. Application to the Air-Pollution Example. To implement this method the analyst needs some prior estimate of maximum willingness to pay. He can then select lower and higher figures to ensure that the questions actually converge. A rough estimate may suffice, because the initial figures can readily cover a wide range. For our first subject we selected a low of $200 and a high of $2000 and proceeded as follows (the responses are shown in parentheses):

Question 1 Are you willing to pay $200 for the four additional safe days? (Yes)
Question 2 Are you willing to pay $2000 for these safe days? (No)

We have verified that maximum willingness to pay is between $200 and $2000, and will narrow the gap with subsequent questions.

Question 3 Are you willing to pay $400 for these safe days? (Yes)
Question 4 Are you willing to pay $1800 for them? (No)

In a series of further questions, the yes answers converged to $900 and the no answers $950. This cutoff point between $900 and $950 brackets the maximum willingness to pay. Further questions could define the point more closely. Darling (1973) uses the precise midpoint, which in our example would be $925. We have rounded off to the nearest hundred dollars and use $900 for subject 1. The results for all 10 subjects range from $300 to $12,000, with an average of $2850 and are recorded in Table 14.1.

4.1.2. Discussion. The converging direct-question method is simple and often used. Knetsch and Davis (1966) applied it to value forest recreation in Maine and validated their results with an internal consistency test.

Beardsley (1970) reported that it gave estimates of the total benefit from a single recreation day similar to those produced by two variations of the travel-cost method (Chapter 16). Randall, Ives, and Eastman (1974) and Brookshire, Ives, and Schulze (1976) used it to value the aesthetic benefits from reduced air pollution. Both studies justified their results by noting similar valuations from similar studies with the same method.

Sinden (1973) attempted to estimate the comparative values of different landscapes in Oregon. The monetary results, in the form of willingness to pay extra costs to visit various other landscapes as compared with a base landscape, failed a prediction test of validation. But results elicited in the form of extra travel time passed the same strong validation test.

The need for some prior estimate of maximum willingness to pay seems to present little difficulty. But the converging method can only be successful in face-to-face interviews, whereas single direct questions can be used in mail questionnaires. Compared with the single direct question method, the greater intensity of the interviews and the converging nature of the questions may increase accuracy. Money is an obvious yardstick for the willingness-to-pay questions, but time or distance can also be used.

4.2. Allocating a Budget

Another simple development is to ask the subject to allocate a budget among specific alternatives so as to maximize his expected utility. The method, as we will apply it to our example, explicitly omits prices for the alternatives. A variation with prices is also considered here, but the methods with prices are presented in more detail in Sections 7 and 8. When prices are omitted, the allocation gives the maximum benefit attainable with the given budget and alternatives.

4.2.1. Selecting Budgets and Alternatives. Reliable results require a realistic budget and a realistic set of alternatives for each subject. The selection of a budget can be based on the following principles: (1) The same budget can be used throughout to try to standardize the results and remove any bias toward subjects with high incomes. (2) An arbitrary budget can be used throughout and the results pegged to some known value. Some procedures for pegging are discussed in Section 8 for the priority-evaluator technique. (3) Budgets can be selected to fit the financial situation of each subject. We use this principle, but supplement it with the next. (4) A number of budgets can be used. One can reflect the financial situation of each subject and the others can provide a range around this. The budget must always be defined for a realistic time span.

The alternatives must be real and must include the thing whose value is being estimated. Ideally, some of the alternatives should provide benefits simlar to those from this thing. Abatement of air pollution will benefit the home and general life of the family. So would replacement of furniture and new clothing. Other real alternatives for our 10 families include a holiday or trading for a new family car. After discussion with the subjects through a short pilot survey, the five alternatives of Table 14.2 were selected.

4.2.2. Application to the Air-Pollution Example. The five alternatives and a standard budget of $1000 were presented to each subject in the following manner:

> Consider that you have a budget of $1000 to spend on these five things. The budget must all be spent but you do not have to spend something on every alternative. Consider your present family situation and what it will be over the next six months. How would you allocate the $1000 among these alternatives?

The results for subject 1 are recorded in column 3 of Table 14.2. The question was repeated with two more budgets. Each subject was asked to select a realistic budget to reflect his present financial situation. Subject 1 selected $500, and his allocation of this amount is shown in column 2. We selected the third budget to bracket the realistic budget and to widen the range of the budgets. The third budget results for subject 1 are shown in column 4 of Table 14.2.

The average willingness to pay for all 10 subjects was calculated for the standard budget of $1000 and for the realistic budgets. The average was $350 for the former (Table 14.1) and $830 for the latter.

Table 14.2. Allocation of Different Budgets between Alternatives by Subject 1

	Budget (dollars)[a]		
Alternatives	500	1000	1500
1	2	3	4
Abatement of air pollution[b]	200	500	800
A new family car	0	0	0
New clothes for the family	100	100	200
A new room of furniture	50	100	100
A family holiday	150	300	400

[a] $1000 is the standard budget, $500 is the budget that best reflects this subject's financial situation, and $1500 arbitrarily increases the range of budgets.

[b] This alternative had already been specified as the increase from one to five safe days per week.

4.2.3. A Variation to Assist Choices. The budget-allocation method sets out to simulate the actual choices of a household or other decision-making unit. Hardie and Kirkley (1975) adapt the method to help analyze choices by the Maryland State Park Service for recreation facilities in the state parks. In recognition of the management/policy level of the choices and the fact that the subject "solves" the agency's problem, they call it "the managerial simulation method." Their variation produces results in quantities instead of money.

Prices are provided for each of five recreation alternatives, which represent their costs to the government. Random groups of subjects choose the quantities of each alternative that would meet a budget and maximize their own expected utility. The information produced is bundles of goods rather than monetary willingness-to-pay. The authors discuss how their results can be used in state-wide management and policy decisions. What the decision maker ultimately needs is the desired alternatives (which the method provides) rather than willingness-to-pay data as such. This kind of variation, providing quantity data for alternatives, simulates actual management/policy choices. The priority-evaluator technique, which we discuss in Section 8, develops this variation.

4.2.4. Discussion. The budget-allocation method can be expected to increase the reliability of results over those from the single direct question, providing the budgets and choices are realistic. Our subjects found the method simple and even enjoyable to follow. Little extra time was needed to explain the method, although careful responses did require noticeably more time than did either of the previous methods. The promise of extra reliability is obtained at little extra cost.

This method gave quite different numerical results from those of the two previous methods (Table 14.1). The results were much lower for all subjects and for both the standard and realistic budgets. The results for the realistic budget ranged from only 5 percent (subject 3) to 80 percent (subject 8) of the results obtained with the single direct question method.

Several variations of the method are possible. The constraint to spend all the budget can be relaxed, or a free choice can be added to cover all possible expenditures. The Hardie/Kirkley variation illustrates the flexibility of this kind of method. Their variation seems promising when all relevant choices can be considered, when the subjects will recognize all benefits and costs, and when choices can be a combination of several alternatives.

5. THE SINGLE TRADE-OFF GAME

The next three methods of this chapter (Sections 5, 6.1, and 6.2) are trade-off games. Subjects are asked to express a preference among groups of things, one of which can conveniently be money. The games never pose direct questions on willingness to pay, and this may increase subject involvement and reduce bias. But these advantages are obtained at the cost of a more formal structure to the method. We consider the general nature of these games before turning to the single trade-off game itself.

5.1. The Nature of Trade-Off Games

Subjects are asked to express a preference between two possible outcomes, each of which usually contains two things (Table 14.3). One object in one outcome is systematically varied until the subject is indifferent between the outcomes. The outcomes are then interpreted for willingness to pay (or in this case, willingness to trade off). We vary the thing in position c in Table 14.3.

These games are closely related to the models of utility estimation presented in Chapter 11. Indeed, the Ramsey model of Table 11.9 looks like the game of Table 14.3, except for the probabilities in the Ramsey model. The term *prospect* is used in the utility models to denote the uncertainty implied by the probability. When prospects are obtained with certainty, as in the trade-off games, they can be called *outcomes*.

5.2. Application to the Air-Pollution Example

The two objects for the game are selected first. Because we wish to obtain monetary data on willingness to pay for improvements in air quality, money must be one object and specific levels of air quality the other. The level of air quality is again defined as the number of safe days per week, and money is defined as a specific, one-time donation by the subject.

The analysis of the example is now extended to valuing the benefits from one, two, three, and four extra days of safe air. For simplicity, we start the game by comparing the existing situation (one safe day) to the smallest

Table 14.3. A Single Trade-Off Game[a]

Object	Outcomes I	Outcomes II
1	2	3
Money donation ($)	(a) 0	(c) n[b]
Air quality (safe days per workweek)	(b) 1	(d) 2

[a] The notations (a) to (d) denote the four positions in the table.
[b] This figure is varied until the subject is indifferent between the outcomes.

improvement (to two safe days). These situations are shown in outcomes I and II in Table 14.3. The existing situation (*a*) involves no money donation. To start the game, an arbitrary initial donation of $100 is entered at c in Outcome II. The game begins by asking the question: Do you prefer outcome I, outcome II, or are you indifferent between them?

The next step depends on the response to this question, as in the models of utility estimation. If outcome II is preferred, the sum of money in position c is raised, and the question is repeated. If outcome I is preferred, the sum is lowered, and the game is repeated. This process is continued until the subject is indifferent between the outcomes.

At indifference, the trade-off information can be derived as follows (using the logic of step 6 of Section 5.2.1 of Chapter 11). Let us assume the donation in outcome II at indifference is $350. We now know that the benefit of the additional safe day (from one to two per week) is just worth, or is exactly balanced by, the extra cost of $350. Subject 1 is just willing to trade off $350 for one extra safe day.

The game was repeated to value the improvement from one to three safe days with the following initial structure: $a = 0$, $b = 1$, $c = n$, and $d = 3$. At indifference the trade-off was $600. In a similar way, trade-offs of $750 and $900 were obtained for the improvements to four and five safe days. These four games (for the four trade-offs) were played with each subject. The results are recorded in Table 14.1. The average willingness to trade off for the full five safe days was $950, and the range was from $50 to $3000.

5.3. Variations in the Method

The basic concepts of the bidding game are the use of outcomes that consist of bundles of things and the search for an indifference judgment. We now consider two variations that adapt the method to slightly different situations.

5.3.1. For Things with "Humped Utilities." The utility derived from the two factors of Table 14.3 is unidirectional over the range of the data. More money is always preferred to less, and less air pollution is always preferred to more. Fishburn (1967) provides a variation for "humped utility" situations, in which more is preferred to less (or vice versa) up to some quantity, but beyond that quantity less is preferred to more.

Consider the example of a man who is about to change jobs and whose main concerns are salary and commuting time. He enjoys some travel and sets his optimal time at 15 minutes. This object is "humped," because either more or less time would decrease his total utility from travel.

This variation requires special definition of the outcomes. The optimal level of the humped factor (15 minutes) is sought and noted. The likely salary range of the new job is also noted. Let this be $20,000 to $25,000. An outcome is now defined with the optimal travel time and the lowest of these likely salaries (outcome I in Table 14.4). Different levels of travel time are specified for various outcomes II (II*a* to II*d* in the table). Each outcome II is combined separately with outcome I in separate games. The salary in outcome II is varied until the subject is indifferent between the outcomes. The resulting salaries at indifference are shown in Table 14.4 and provide the following value information. The subject is willing to trade off a reduction of five minutes of travel below the optimum for an extra $1000 per year (II*a*). He would trade off an increase of five minutes for $2000 per year (II*c*).

5.3.2. Using Preference Rather than Indifference Judgments. The single trade-off game is based on a search for an indifference judgment. Rather than varying the level of one of the things, MacCrimmon and Toda (1969) accept the first preference judgment and interpolate for indifference. They express their results as indifference curves based on the outcomes, as illustrated in Figure 14.4. Because outcomes I and II contain the same quantity of X_2 but different quantities of X_1, outcome I will be preferred to outcome II, and an indifference curve must pass between them. Another outcome (II*a*) is specified, and the preference judgment is elicited. If outcome I is also preferred to II*a*, the same indifference curve must also pass between I and II*a*. A series of preference judgments will give the approximate position of the curve.

Monetary valuations can readily be made if one good, say X_2, is money. The indifference curve can show the maximum amount of money the subject is willing to give up for some extra amount of X_1. In Figure 14.4 the subject is willing to trade off $*AB* for a gain of *CD* in X_1 and is as satisfied after the exchange as before. A larger monetary cost would push the subject to a lower indifference curve and be more than his maximum willingness to pay.

Table 14.4. Results of Four Applications of the Single Trade-Off Game[a]

	Outcomes				
Object	**I**	**II*a***	**II*b***	**II*c***	**II*d***
Salary ($1000)	20	21	23	22	24
Travel time (minutes)	15	10	5	20	25

[a] Data for outcomes II*a* to II*d* at indifference.

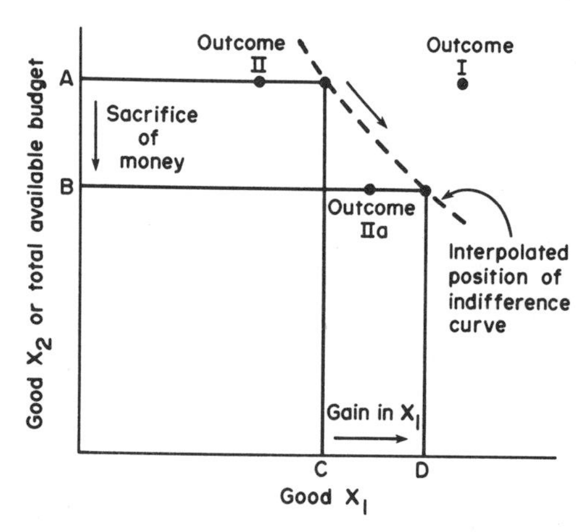

Figure 14.4. Use of preference judgments to derive an indifference curve for trade-off estimates.

5.4. Discussion

The single trade-off game is the basis of several other methods, as well as being a useful method itself. Like the models of utility estimation, this method rests on an assumption of additive utilities, although the assumption can be tested. We have discussed the problems created by the assumption of additive utility in Chapter 11.

6. DEVELOPMENTS OF THE SINGLE TRADE-OFF GAME

In Section 5 we considered the basic trade-off game and some direct variations of it. We now consider two modifications of the method to allow for more difficult preference situations (the double trade-off game) and for the valuation of differences between projects (the comparative trade-off game).

6.1. The Double Trade-Off Game

The single trade-off game is suitable when subjects can visualize and choose between outcomes that both contain money and the thing to be valued. The double trade-off game may be suitable when a subject has difficulty visualizing such choices. This method requires subjects to visualize outcomes that contain the thing being valued and a third item and other outcomes that contain money and the third item. The method proceeds as follows:

(**a**) The first step is to determine what outcomes the subject can visualize, and whether these outcomes will provide the necessary information. For our problem let us assume that subjects are willing to increase commuting time to move to a suburb with cleaner air and can visualize outcomes containing air quality and commuting time (the third item). We also assume that the price of land for houses varies inversely with commuting time and that subjects can visualize outcomes containing land price (money) and commuting time (the third item). These three objects are suitably paired to provide the necessary information.

(**b**) A first set of trade-offs is made. We take air quality and commuting time as the first pair, although the order of the pairs is not important. Outcome I is specified as the existing situation with 10 minutes commuting time each way and one safe day as the level of air quality. The air quality for outcomes II*a* to II*d* are fixed at the levels shown below. Then the single trade-off game is applied with II*a* to II*d* used as outcome II in four separate runs. In each game we seek the commuting time for which the subject is indifferent between outcome I and the respective outcome II. The following information was obtained for subject I:

	Outcome				
Object	I	II*a*	II*b*	II*c*	II*d*
Commuting time (minutes each way)	10	30	45	55	60
Air quality (safe days per week)	1	2	3	4	5

These results can be interpreted like those of Table 14.4. Outcomes I and II*d* indicate that the increase of four safe days (from 1 to 5) is worth an extra 50 minutes commuting time.

(**c**) The other pair—land price and commuting time—is now considered in the same way. The following information was obtained for subject 1, with outcome I representing the existing situation:

	Outcome			
Object	I	II*a*	II*b*	II*c*
Land price ($1000)	8	7.5	5	2
Commuting time	10	20	40	60

Outcomes I and II*c* indicate that an increase of 50 minutes in commuting time is compensated for by (or is equal to) a $6000 reduction in land price.

(d) The two sets of indifference data are now combined as follows. Consider the value of the improvement in air quality from one to five safe days. From step b we know that the utility from this improvement is equal to the cost of an extra 50 minutes of commuting time. From step c we know that this same cost in commuting time is exactly compensated by a reduction in land price of $6000. Subject 1 has indicated that he would be willing to pay $6000 for the improvement in air quality from one to five safe days.

This method was not applied to the other nine subjects and is not entered in Table 14.1.

6.2. The Comparative Trade-Off Game

This simple development derives value information for the difference between projects, and is suitable when one of several similar projects must be chosen. Consider the following two pollution-abatement projects:

Project	Benefit (safe days per week)		Total cost
	Total	*Extra*	
A	3	2	$100,000,000
B	5	4	$160,000,000

We consider the choice between the projects for a single decision maker and then, in a slightly different form, for our 10 subjects.

6.2.1. For a Decision Maker

(a) The two outcomes of the game are specified as in Table 14.3. Outcome I is defined as project A with $a = \$100{,}000{,}000$ and $b = 3$. Outcome II is defined as project B with $c = n$ and $d = 5$.

(b) The single trade-off game is played to find the figure for n at indifference. Let this be $140,000,000.

(c) This result may be interpreted as follows. The extra benefit from the two additional safe days would exactly compensate for an extra cost of $40,000,000. If project B cost less than $140,000,000, it would have the higher net benefit. If project B cost more than $140,000,000, project A would have the higher net benefit.

Fishburn (1967) discusses this method in the context of choosing industrial sites in different states, where the unpriced benefits arise from the different locations.

6.2.2. For the Individual Subjects. We applied the method to our subjects to obtain comparative values for an improvement in air quality from three to five safe days. A cost of $100,000,000 to the city is equal to a cost of $800 for each of the 125,000 households. Outcome I was defined as an $800 tax in position *a* and 3 safe days in position *b*. Outcome II was defined as $*n* tax in position *c* and five safe days in position *d*. The figure for *n* at indifference was found in the usual way.

The comparative values for the improvement from three to five safe days are shown in Table 14.1 for all 10 subjects. They range between $50 and $600, with an average of $195. The subjects are willing to pay an extra $195 on the average for this air quality improvement.

6.2.3. Relation to the Single Trade-Off Game. The comparative trade-off game merges into the single trade-off game if the existing situation is included as a project. To derive more data from our subjects, we set up outcome I as the existing situation, with one safe day and $500 once-only tax. Outcome II was defined successively as three (II*a*) or five (II*b*) safe days and $*n* tax. The method gave the following results for *n* at indifference for Subject 1:

	I	II*a*	II*b*
Property tax ($)	500	900	1200
Number of safe days	1	3	5

Subject one is telling us that an improvement to three safe days is worth an extra tax of $400, but an improvement to five safe days is worth an extra $700. The average figures for all 10 subjects were $250 for three days and $700 for five safe days.

7. THE COSTLESS-CHOICE METHOD

We now move to the methods that use direct questions to derive quantity data and then infer willingness to pay. All of them involve simulations of the quantity choices. The costless-choice method is the first and simplest of the group. It follows a suggestion by Romm (1969) that involves "costless" choices for the subjects.

7.1. Nature of the Method

This method is based on a simple, logical comparison. Consider a choice between a gift of money and a gift of an unpriced good, such as one more day of safe, clean air. If the subject chooses the good, the total benefit from the good must be at least as great as that from the sum of money. The simulated choice has provided a simple minimum valuation, using the principle of the consumers' expenditure method of Chapter 12. The present method is, in fact, a simulation of the consumers' expenditure method through the formal structure we now illustrate.

7.2. Application to the Air-Pollution Example

The method proceeds as follows:

(**a**) A group of things is selected as alternatives for the choices. The things we used for the budget allocation method (Table 14.2) are relevant to our pollution-control example and realistic for our subjects. To give a wider range of alternatives, we add to them a new swimming pool for the backyard. Ideally, these should all be things that the subject would purchase if he had enough money. The unpriced good—abatement of air pollution—is excluded from the alternatives in this method, because it is incorporated through the question in step c below.

(**b**) The cost of each alternative is carefully estimated for each subject. (The things must be defined previously with each subject.) The costs for subject 1 are shown in Table 14.5. The cost of the swimming pool will be the same for all subjects, but the costs of the other alternatives differ between subjects.

(**c**) The choices are simulated through the following question: If all of these things are free, which ones do you prefer to cleaner and safer air? We defined our unpriced good as the improvement from one to five safe days a week. The responses of subject 1 are shown in column 3 of Table 14.5, with other possible responses in columns 4 through 7.

Table 14.5. Possible Responses in the Costless Choice Method[a]

Alternatives	Cost ($)	Possible Sets of Responses[b]				
1	2	3	4	5	6	7
New family car	1900	$<A$	$>A$	$>A$	$>A$	$<A$
New swimming pool	1600	$<A$	$>A$	$>A$	$>A$	$<A$
Family holiday	1000	$<A$	$>A$	$>A$	$<A$	$<A$
New room of furniture	850	$<A$	$>A$	$<A$	$<A$	$>A$
New clothing for family	650	$<A$	$>A$	$<A$	$>A$	$>A$

[a] Costs in column 2 and responses in column 3 are for subject 1. Columns 4 through 7 show other possible responses.

[b] Notation $>A$ means the alternative is preferred to pollution abatement; $<A$ means abatement is preferred.

(**d**) The responses are interpreted as follows: If abatement is preferred to all of the alternatives (as in column 3), the total benefit from abatement is worth at least as much as the highest cost alternative ($1900 in this case). If all the alternatives are preferred to abatement (as in column 4), the benefit is worth less than the lowest cost alternative ($650 in this case). The subject may prefer only some alternatives to pollution abatement. The choices of column 5 show a consistent pattern with a change in preference between $850 and $1000. With this sort of consistent pattern, the benefit can be valued at the break. In this case, the value of abatement is more than $850 but less than $1000. Inconsistent choices, as in column 6, and reversed choices, as in column 7, cannot be interpreted.

We helped avoid inconsistent and reversed responses by ensuring that the subjects would purchase all the alternatives if they had enough money. The benefit figures for all subjects are shown in Table 14.1. They range from $650 or less to $6000 or more.

7.3. Discussion

The costless-choice method extends Romm's (1969) suggestion that simulated choices could provide the same information as actual choices. Actual consumer expenditures indicate minimum levels of total benefit. With our interpretation procedure in step d of the preceding section, the costless-choice method indicates the same minimum level when the thing in question is preferred (or "bought") as would an actual expenditure. With our simulation procedure the method also indicates the maximum level of total benefit when the thing is not preferred.

The choices in this method are preferences and not indifference judgments. This can lead to some difficulty in interpretation, for only minimum and maximum figures are obtained. However, inclusion of more alternatives at different costs can help narrow the range within which the desired figure falls.

8. THE PRIORITY-EVALUATOR TECHNIQUE

This market simulation game was pioneered by Hoinville and Berthoud (1970a) of the Social and Community Planning Research Group of London. The priority-evaluator technique (PET) simulates choices in a perfectly competitive market. It incorporates a procedure to adjust initial prices set by the analyst toward the prices that would develop in a competitive market. Value information is then inferred from these competitive prices. We discuss the nature of the method first, and then we apply PET to our pollution-control example in a general way to show how the values are inferred.

8.1. Nature of the Method

The indifference-curve approach to consumer choice described in Section 3.2 of Chapter 2 indicates that a consumer will maximize the utility he can obtain from a given budget when the following two conditions are met. (1) He must spend all his budget. In terms of the diagram shown in Figure 2.7 of Chapter 2, he must be on a budget line such as FF'. (2) His combination of purchases must provide the maximum possible utility. In terms of Figure 2.7, he must be on the highest indifference curve, such as U', that can be reached with his budget.

The consumer will therefore be at the point of tangency of an indifference curve and the appropriate budget line (point D in Figure 2.7). At this point the slope of the budget line (i.e., the ratio of the prices P_i) is the same as the slope of the indifference curve (i.e., the ratio of the marginal utilities MU_i). The marginal utility obtained from a dollar spent on any one good will therefore equal the marginal utility from a dollar spent on any other good (Section 3.1.2 of Chapter 2). In mathematical terms

$$\frac{MU_1}{P_1} = \frac{MU_2}{P_2} = \cdots = \frac{MU_n}{P_n} \qquad (14.1)$$

where there are n goods.

Most survey approaches succeed in satisfying the first condition. It is easy to check whether subjects have spent a given budget. But it has proved relatively difficult to make the second condition operational. The contribution of PET lies in implementing this second condition through a simple questionnaire approach.

When the second condition (Equation 14.1) is satisfied, the market price of the ith good will equal the marginal utility of the ith good for the representative individual in the market. At this point this individual will be indifferent to further trade-offs among goods 1 to n. Hoinville and Berthoud extend this concept and observe that such further choices can be expected to follow a random pattern, constrained only by prices and the budget.

This idea can be converted into a simple test. When the second condition is satisfied, the observed frequency of choice of good i should be equal to the expected (random) frequency of choice of good i. Therefore if

$$\frac{\text{observed frequency of choice } (O) \text{ of good } i}{\text{expected frequency of choice } (E) \text{ of good } i} = 1 \qquad (14.2)$$

the market is in equilibrium, and utility is maximized. More specifically, when this condition is satisfied for all goods, MU_i must equal P_i for all goods taken by the representative user. Under these conditions, observed prices are money estimates of marginal utilities.

The analyst must first calculate the frequency of choice of each alternative good that consumers can be expected to make with a given budget—given specific initial prices for each good. A questionnaire is then devised that will simulate actual choices, and the choices made by a number of subjects with the given budget are observed. The observed frequencies of choices are compared to the expected frequencies. If the observed frequencies are identical with the expected frequencies, the specified set of prices satisfies the condition of Equation 14.1 and the test of Equation 14.2.

If the observed frequencies are not the same as those expected, the prices must be changed and the subjects must be resurveyed. The ratio of the observed to the expected choices (Equation 14.2) indicates the direction in which the prices should be changed. When the prices are too high, the O/E ratio will be less than 1, because in a competitive market a higher price will lead consumers to choose the good less often. Similarly, an O/E ratio above 1 indicates that observed choices exceed the expected number, and the price must be too low. This price should be raised because it is lower than the marginal utility to the representative user. The price adjustments require experience and judiciously applied statistical tests.

8.2. Application to the Air-Pollution Example

We now illustrate the method for the pollution-control example but do not follow through to specific results. In Chapter 20 we apply the method fully and quote O'Hanlon and Sinden (1978). The initial step is to select the goods for the subjects to choose between. The number of goods must be large enough for a useful analysis but small enough to avoid confusion. All the previous applications (Hoinville and Berthoud, 1970a; Pendse and Wyckoff, 1974a and 1974b) use five different things and three different quantities of each to give 15 alternative purchases in all. For convenience, we term each of these purchases a *good*. Table 14.6 shows part of the 15 alternative goods for our pollution-control example.

The three quantities of each of the five things can be defined to fit the particular problem being analyzed. Good 1 in Table 14.6 is defined as one day of safe air quality per week to correspond to the existing situation. Goods 2 and 3 denote possible improvements in air quality. To simulate a competitive market, the five things selected must be independent of each other in production. They must be continuously variable in both production and consumption. And the utility consumers receive from them must be

Table 14.6. Application of the Priority-Evaluator Technique to the Pollution-Control Example

	Initial survey			Resurvey		
Goods[a]	Prices ($)	O/E Ratio	Direction of Price Change	Prices ($)	O/E Ratio	Direction of Price Change
1	2	3	4	5	6	7
A. Air quality						
1. One safe day	1	1.13	↑	100	1.10	↑
2. Three safe days	500	1.43	↑	600	1.20	↑
3. Five safe days	1000	0.12	↓	800	0.80	↓
B. Furniture						
4. One new room	850	1.02	↑	900	1.00	—
5. Two new rooms	1700	1.17	↑	1800	1.10	↑
6. Three new rooms	2550	0.98	↓	2400	1.05	↑
. .	.			.		.
. .	.			.		.
. .	.			.		.
E. New clothing						
13. Small quantity	650	0.14	↓	500	0.80	↓
14. Medium quantity	1200	1.45	↑	1500	1.40	↑
15. Large quantity	1800	1.75	↑	2000	1.60	↑

[a] Each good (1 to 15) is a specific quantity of a particular thing (*A* to *E*)

independent of any other consumption, that is, be separable and nonadditive.

8.2.1. Procedure. Once the goods have been chosen, the method proceeds as follows:

(**a**) Each of the 15 goods is identified for the subjects by written and oral description and perhaps by drawings. This important first step may create problems, because the identification must be general enough and quick enough to interest all subjects but specific enough to inform them.

(**b**) An initial price for each good can be calculated as the total social cost of supplying it divided by the likely number of purchasers. They are the prices for the initial survey (column 2 of Table 14.6).

(**c**) A budget is now selected. The budget must be high enough to allow a selection of all five things at some level but not large enough to buy the maximum level of all five. Subjects are asked to allocate the budget over all 15 possible goods but to choose only one quantity of each thing and to choose each thing only once. The choices are recorded and inspected. Some possible ratios of the observed to expected choices are shown in column 3. These O/E

ratios vary from 0.12 to 1.75, and none is equal to 1.00. Some adjustment of prices is necessary.

(**d**) The O/E ratios show the direction in which prices should be adjusted to make the ratio approach 1.0. The ratio for five safe days is 0.12. It it less than one because there were too few observed choices of this good. If the price were lowered and the subjects were resurveyed, the ratio should rise. The price of $1000 for the initial survey was lowered to $800 for the second survey. If the O/E ratio is over 1.0, the price must be raised. In this way all the prices of column 2 were adjusted to those of column 5.

(**e**) The same subjects are resurveyed with the new set of prices and the same budget, and a new set of O/E ratios is calculated (column 6).

(**f**) Because only one of the O/E ratios in column 6 is exactly equal to 1.0, the question arises of how close to 1.0 the set of ratios is as a whole. The chi-square test is one suitable way to test for a significant difference from 1.0 because it compares an actual set of numbers (the actual O/E ratios) with an expected set. Equation 14.2 shows that each number in the expected set of ratios is 1.0. The chi-square statistic can now be calculated for the ratios in columns 3 and 6. If the set of actual O/E ratios is not significantly different from the expected set (all 1.0s), the prices represent marginal utilities, and the second condition (equation 14.1) is met. The data can then be interpreted as below. However, if the sets are significantly different, steps d, e, and f must be repeated.

8.2.2. Interpretation. A set of prices that meets the second condition of Equation 14.1 gives the relative values of the marginal utilities. The budget must now be checked and relative figures converted to actual figures. The value information can then be extracted.

The budget may be the actual income that the representative subject has available for these goods. In this case the prices can be interpreted directly. Or the budget may have been set arbitrarily by the analyst. In this case, O'Hanlon and Sinden (1978) have pegged the final prices (such as those of column 5 in Table 14.6) to a known benefit before interpretation. For example, suppose the willingness to pay for a single room of furniture had been estimated with some other method at $1200 instead of the $900 in row 4. Twelve hundred dollars is the monetary value of the marginal utility of this amount of this good and provides the necessary peg against which to adjust all the other prices. We must multiply all prices by 1200/900, or 1.33. We illustrate this pegging procedure again in Chapter 20.

Suppose the prices of column 5 are acceptable and the budget is the actual available income of the representative user. Then the value of the benefit from one safe day is $100, from three safe days is $600, and from five safe days is $800. If the budget were not the actual available income, and if pegging indicated the above multiplier of 1.33, the values of the benefits would be $133, $800, and $1064, respectively.

8.2.3. Some Details of Application. Because the initial prices are adjusted once, and perhaps twice, a degree of arbitrariness can be tolerated in the initial set. This simplifies the problems of selecting the appropriate initial prices for step b. The amount of the price adjustment is a matter for experience, because the method provides guidelines only for the direction.

A dummy factor for "all other goods" could be inserted. Subjects would then have an opportunity to spend the budget on other things, and truer responses might be elicited.

Hoinville and Berthoud (1970a) developed the method from steps a to d. The use of resurveys and the statistical test were introduced by O'Hanlon and Sinden (1978) because none of the original O/E ratios in their application were near unity.

8.3. Discussion

The priority-evaluator method simulates a competitive market and provides average values for the representative individual. The success of the simulation can be judged by the set of O/E ratios, which provides a built-in test for consistency. The likelihood of success depends on an ability to resurvey the same subjects once or perhaps twice and on the analyst's ability to choose new prices to move the ratios toward unity. Hoinville (1976) notes that different subjects may make widely different choices, and each may require a different kind of adjustment. A given change in price might favor some but disadvantage others and thus lead to no improvement in the O/E ratios, which are calculated as an average for the representative user. This difficulty may be minimized by interviewing different groups that are more homogeneous than the total population. O'Hanlon and Sinden (1978) report apparently successful applications of the method to separate groups of conservationists, farmers, environmental planners, and professional foresters, but a less-successful application to a random sample of the population.

9. THE INDIFFERENCE-MAPPING METHOD

Indifference maps depict preferences for different quantities of different goods (Figure 2.7), and can be derived without reference to willingness-to-pay questions. Existing observable prices and available budgets can be introduced separately to derive a demand curve. The appropriate area under the curve can then be treated as the willingness-to-pay data. The use of actual prices and actual budgets with the map allows these data to be inferred without asking the direct question: How much are you willing to pay for thing *A*? The following three examples illustrate the potential of the method.

9.1. Estimating the Benefits of Recreation

Empirical procedures to derive indifference maps were reviewed by Sinden and Wyckoff (1976). The only procedure that provides entire maps, with the necessary scaled utility intervals, is the Ramsey model of utility estimation, which we described in Chapter 11. The Ramsey model provides utility functions (in the form of Equation 2.1) that can readily be interpreted as indifference maps. The maps refer to the choices of one subject, and a separate utility function must be derived for each.

The Ramsey model was used to obtain utility functions for recreation activities at a state park in Oregon (Sinden 1974). Each function was interpreted for an indifference map, and actual prices and budgets were introduced through the budget line to provide a demand curve for each individual. The total willingness to pay for subsequent days of recreation at the park was estimated as the appropriate area under the curve. The benefit values for the first extra day ranged from $1.80 to $6.00 for the five subjects and were validated in a back projection test.

9.2. Investigating the Disutility of Crowding

The method may be most suitable for small problems, because much time and skill are required for the interview with the Ramsey model. Sanderson (1974) applied the method through this model to the effects of crowding on utility. The empirical indifference maps provided information on crowding as a rationing device and on the optimal level of crowding at recreation sites in New South Wales. Sanderson succeeded in reducing the interview time from Sinden's (1974) three hours to less than two hours.

9.3. Valuing the Rural Way of Life

The intensive interview procedure for the utility functions can sometimes permit the estimation of more elusive values. For example, Liesch and Sinden (1976) used the method to value the rural way of life. Governments often purchase rural land and have to estimate appropriate purchase prices. Characteristically, they calculate the income potential of the land and offer a lump-sum equivalent to the farmer. Equally characteristically, the farmer refuses, and his refusal indicates there are unpriced benefits not recognized by the income equivalent. These include the benefits of a family home and relationships with nearby friends, which may be grouped as the rural way of life.

The Ramsey model was applied to derive indifference maps for two goods. One was the rural way of life. The second good was overseas trips, because this is a good most coveted by the farmers and the one most unavailable at their present low incomes. The benefit of the rural way of life was estimated as a compensation value (Chapter 5). The number of trips required to exactly compensate farmers (or leave them on the same indifference curve) for the loss of the rural way of life was observed from the map. The cost of these trips was the compensation value.

9.4. Discussion

The need for two to three hours per interview and for skilled interviewers results in an expensive method. This weakness can at the same time be a strength, because the detail of the interview and the approach through quantity comparisons permit the estimation of more elusive values.

10. DISCUSSION

Willingness to pay and the associated quantities consumed are the behavioral expressions of basic attitudes and preferences. The methods of this chapter all attempt to measure and use these outward expressions of underlying preferences.

10.1. Variation in Results

The empirical results of Table 14.1 are disturbing. Even though each method was applied with the usual care and the usual interview procedures, the results vary widely. Average willingness to pay for the change from one safe day to five varies from $350 (budget allocation with $1000 budget) to $2850 (converging direct questions). The results from individual subjects also varies widely, with subject 6 showing a range from $50 to $12,000, depending on the method used.

This variation results partly from the hypothetical nature of the questions and partly from differences in the methods. All the methods use hypothetical questions, and all of them were applied to the same example. But they differ in their concepts of demand and in their ability to elicit true responses.

All the methods estimate total benefit, but they employ different interpretations of the model of demand. These different interpretations include movements along indifference curves or budget lines, use of fixed or variable quantities, simulation of market price and quantity data, and estimation of lump-sum payments. We briefly review the methods for their interpretations because, as Hardie (1977) points out, differences in them may lead to different values.

The trade-off games rest on movements along indifference curves because the subject must be equally satisfied with both outcomes. But the budget-allocation method and its variations rest on movements along a budget line. Figure 2.7 in Chapter 2 shows that these two movements may not give the same change in one good (such as money) for a given change in another good (such as air quality).

The costless-choice and indifference-mapping methods and priority-evaluator technique, all fix a price and allow the subject to choose his own quantity to consume. But the single-direct-question and converging-direct-question methods fix a quantity and allow the subject to state his willingness to pay.

The priority-evaluator technique and the single- and converging-direct-question methods most nearly simulate the marketplace. Benefits are estimated from observed prices and quantities. But the trade-off games estimate lump-sum amounts that leave the subject as satisfied after the change as he was before. In Section 5 of Chapter 16 we consider further the differences in value that may arise from these particular differences in interpretation.

Such differences are likely to lead to different estimates of benefit. The analyst should select the interpretation that suits his problem. But this correct procedure is often hard to follow. Thus he must select on the basis of ability to promote true responses and to be validated.

10.2. Checking the Results

The two simplest—and the two weakest—validation tests are the arguments that the questions are relevant and the interviews were careful and that these results are comparable with other results for similar problems. There are other stronger tests, as discussed in Chapter 7, and we used one of these to check the consistency of our results. We believe that willingness to pay for environmental improvements should rise with income and education. So we collected data on family income and years of college education and calculated simple correlation coefficients for the results of each method against income and education. The results are shown in Table 14.7.

The tests were performed as follows. An acceptable set of results should follow our belief and have a positive correlation coefficient. The most acceptable results are those with the highest coefficients, and any with coefficients less than .40 are rejected as showing insufficient consistency. A

Table 14.7. Correlation Coefficients between Characteristics of Subjects and Their Responses for Six Methods

Method	Income[a]	Education[a]
1	2	3
Single direct question	.42	.41
Converging direct questions	.48	.42
Budget allocation		
$1000 standard budget	−.15	.68
"Realistic" budget	.27	.60
Single trade-off game[b]	.61	.57
Comparative trade-off game[b]	.80	.55
Costless choice	−.34	.36

[a] The simple correlation coefficient between income and education was .25.
[b] The results used are those for the improvement from one to five safe days to be comparable with other methods.

method that has a high coefficient for both income and education is better than one that has this for only one characteristic. Despite the small number of subjects, the coefficients of Table 14.7 provide some interesting implications for choosing a method.

10.3 Making the Choice

Based on the empirical results of Table 14.1, the tests reported in Table 14.7, and our own experience, we offer the following comments on the choice of a method.

(**a**) The single direct question and converging direct question methods are the least structured of this group and have no built-in checks. These two methods produced the highest willingness to pay figures ($2440 and $2550). Both of them just meet the two validity tests of Table 14.7.

(**b**) The converging-direct-question method has failed twice in our previous applications. Monetary data for willingness to pay for different landscapes in the Cascadia study (Sinden, 1973) failed a back-projection test. Data in an unpublished study of preservation of a rare natural resource failed the internal consistency test.

(**c**) The budget-allocation method introduces more formality and structure to the questions. Perhaps as a consequence, the average willingness-to-pay figures are lower than those from the direct-question methods. But the method failed the income-consistency test in Table 14.7. The test with income for the budget-allocation method with a standard budget has a confusing negative sign. This supports our experience that the artificial standard budget does not elicit supportable results, particularly when the standard budget departs greatly from the subject's real one.

(d) The costless-choice method failed both of the tests in Table 14.7. Both coefficients are less than .40, and one has a confusing negative sign. This result may not indict the method, however, because the willingness-to-pay data for the test were taken from imprecise inequalities.

(e) The trade-off games are the most formal and highly structured of the direct approaches to willingness to pay. The two versions of the game performed best in the tests of Table 14.7. The single trade-off game and the comparative trade-off game passed both the income and education consistency checks well above the 40 percent limit. Our subjects found the games simple to play. Their relative simplicity and the promise of high consistency in the results makes these the most favored methods.

The variation in results in Table 14.1 and in the tests of validity in Table 14.7 indicate that a method must be chosen with great care. A more-structured method may generally be preferable to a less-structured one. At the very least, the analyst must check his results with the strongest possible validation tests before using them for policy advice.

CHAPTER 15

Estimation of Net Social Benefit—Direct Methods

Our starting point in this book was the general definition that the value of a thing is the utility derived from its possession or use less the disutility involved in its production and acquisition. In Section 2.5.1. of Chapter 2 this conceptual definition was given operational content in terms of consumers' surplus, producers' surplus, and net social benefit. These economic concepts enable us to make empirical measurements of value as the net utility from the consumption and production of particular things.

1. NET SOCIAL BENEFIT AS AN IDEAL FOR VALUATION

The utility concept of value embraces benefits to both consumers and producers. Consumers' surplus is the difference between the price consumers are willing to pay and the price they have to pay. Graphically, it is the area between the demand curve, which shows maximum willingness to pay, and market price (Figure 2.5 in Chapter 2). Producers' surplus is the difference between the price producers are willing to accept and the price they actually receive. It is the area between market price and the supply curve, which shows the cost of production. Total net benefit to society is the sum of producers' and consumers' surplus. Any decision that concerns net benefits and society as a whole can be formulated in these terms and analyzed with these concepts.

1.1. Practical Methods for a Theoretical Model

The basic notion of consumers' surplus was originally expounded by Dupuit in 1844 (Peacock et al., 1952) and elaborated by Marshall (1890). Over the years it has been supported by such economists as Hicks (1941, 1943) and Mishan (1960, 1971) and criticized by Little (1950) and others. The debate has been abstract and theoretical but seems to have sharpened rather than prevented empirical application.

The basic notions have been used in environmental decisions about water resource investment, recreation facilities, agricultural policies, and transport and engineering projects. Nevertheless, to judge from the literature, there have been fewer practical applications than discussions of theory. There are three possible reasons for the relatively limited application up to now. (1) The models may be difficult to grasp, and because they have been developed primarily in economics, general knowledge of their existence and applicability may be limited. (2) It is often difficult to formulate particular decisions in the general framework of Figure 2.5. (3) The methods for implementing the models require very specific data that have often proved difficult to collect. The problems of data collection must be solved in the field by individual analysts, so this chapter will focus on the first two reasons—lack of knowledge of the concepts, and methods and difficulties of formulating decisions.

The various methods of calculation are discussed in terms of a single environmental policy example. As each method is discussed, other applications are also considered to show how it has been applied and how decisions can be formulated in practice.

The focus on formulation and application has kept us from dealing fully with certain topics. In our examples, all estimates of price and quantity are taken as single values, and probability distributions are ignored. But the problem of uncertainty has been discussed at length by Raiffa (1968) and others. We also cannot discuss the theoretical questions that have been the subject of debate ever since Dupuit's original work. A good survey of this debate is provided by Currie, Murphy, and Schmitz (1971).

1.2. Methods of Calculation

We have grouped these methods together in Chapters 15 and 16 because they all base monetary values on the same notion of net benefit. But there are two distinct approaches to the calculation of monetary values, as shown in Figure 15.1.

If sufficient data are available, a direct approach has been used. Analysts have attempted to calculate the consumers' and producers' surplus directly by measuring the relevant areas under the curves. If all necessary data are available, a unique estimate of net social benefit is possible. The critical data are the price elasticities of demand and supply. If no elasticity data are available, the whole possible range of values or some average point estimates have been used. When one elasticity is known, or known within some

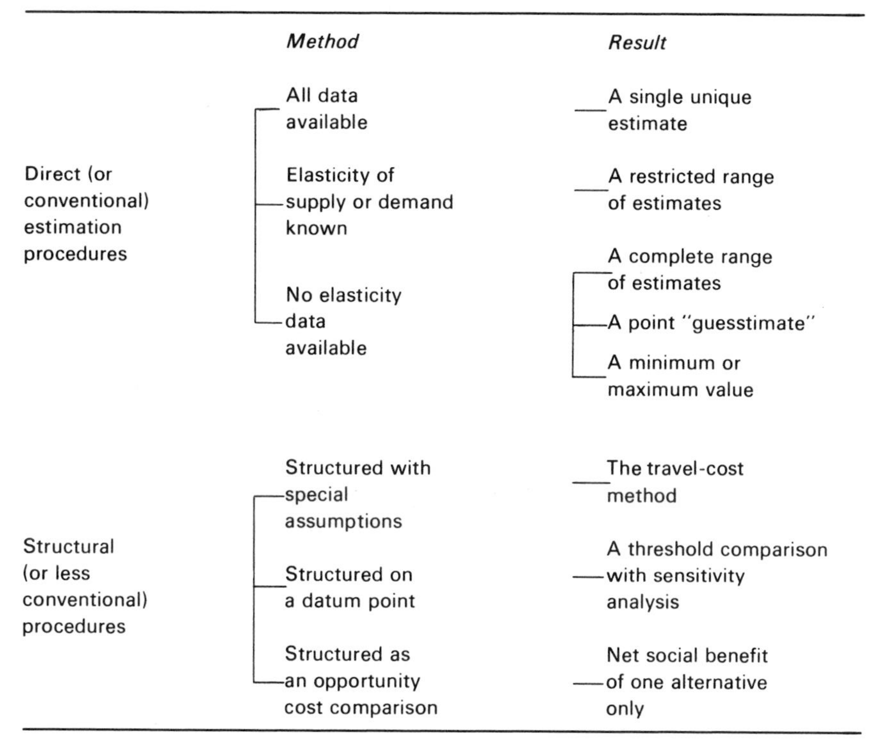

Figure 15.1. A classification of methods of calculating net social benefit.

defined range, a restricted range of estimates can be made. These direct approaches are considered in this chapter.

If sufficient data are not available, a structured approach can be used. These structured procedures are considered in Chapter 16. At the end of that chapter, we present our conclusions about all of the net social benefit methods of both chapters.

2. AN ENVIRONMENTAL POLICY EXAMPLE: MAINTENANCE OF WILDLIFE HABITAT

We use a single environmental policy example to illustrate the various methods presented in this chapter. Each of them provides a different way of estimating net social benefit, and the example serves as a theme to give continuity to our explanations. A variety of other examples are also used to illustrate the application of individual methods.

This example differs somewhat from those in earlier chapters in that we will present a detailed partial analysis of the problem in this section before using it with any of the methods. All of these methods start with some information about supply and demand, and calculate or estimate net social benefit from it. A first step must be to acquire this basic information. Since the procedures for estimating supply and demand are accepted techniques of economic analysis, we will show this first step only once rather than with each method.

As shown in Figure 15.1, the difference between the methods lies in the completeness of the basic data available. An analyst must first determine how much information he can acquire about supply and demand and then choose a method that will give usable estimates of net social benefit with this available information.

In this section we develop complete basic supply and demand information for the wildlife habitat situation. This permits the use of the first method—the direct-estimation procedure with all data available. By assuming that various parts of this information are not available, we are then able to illustrate the situations to which the other methods apply.

2.1. The Breeding Grounds of Ducks in North America

The ponds of the North American prairies are the breeding grounds of this continent's most sought-after ducks (Munro, 1969). These ducks are migratory, breeding mainly in Canada and wintering in Central America. Most of the hunting takes place in the United States.

The breeding habitat is threatened because the ponds are mostly on farmland, and the farmers have been filling them to increase grain production. Elimination of these breeding grounds would severely reduce the duck populations and perhaps lead to the extinction of some species. Competition between these two land uses will intensify in the future. Pressures for wildlife preservation and hunting are increasing, but economic pressure on the farmers to fill the ponds is also increasing. Hedlin (1969) summarizes the problem in the question "What does the wildlife manager have to offer to correct the economic disutilities of having potholes in the middle of a farmer's field?"

The free market does not generate appropriate prices to guide the allocation of land to these alternative uses. The market is complicated by the international nature of the wildlife resource. But even if the ducks were not migratory, there would be a serious divergence of social from private values, because the costs are borne by one group—the farmers—and the benefits accrue to other groups. Attempts by the governments to equalize farmers' incomes by subsidies further distorts the market price from the comparative social value.

The unpriced values of the wildlife resource originate in nonconsumptive benefits from bird watching, photography, and knowledge that the wildlife exists and in consumptive benefits from hunting. Following Crissey (1969) and Hammack and Brown (1974), we assume that the value of the nonconsumptive benefits is not affected by the total size of the duck population. The problems with nonconsumptive uses arise from the distribution of the duck population rather than from its size. Decisions about the size of the duck population and the pothole habitat depend, therefore, on the benefits from hunting and the costs of habitat maintenance.

The net benefits from hunting vary with the size of the total duck population and consequently with the size of its breeding habitat. The important questions for policy are: What is the optimal number of ducks and of ponds, and would marginal increments in duck and pond numbers produce net benefits for society? Goldstein (1971) and Hammack and Brown (1974) analyze these problems of resource allocation in detail. We limit our example to the question of increments in the size of the duck population and in the number of ponds.

2.2. Interactions among Habitat, Duck Population, and Hunters

The first step in an analysis is the definition of policy alternatives. Because the habitat problem can be expressed in terms of alternative quantities of ducks killed, we need a model of the interactions among habitat, duck population, and hunters. A simplified version of Hammack and Brown's model is presented in Figure 15.2.

Our first simplification is an assumption that management for a constant number of breeders is both possible and actually achieved. We set this number at 9.354 million, which was the average number of breeding ducks between 1955 and 1968. These breeders and the number of available ponds are the two inputs in the production process. The output of immature ducks in September (QI) will vary with the number of ponds, because the number of breeders is being held constant. Hammack and Brown give a 95 percent survival for breeders between May and September and an 84 percent survival for the whole fall flight until the following May. At this survival rate, 11.136 million birds must exist in the fall to provide 9.354 million breeders the following spring. Any birds in excess of 11.136 million in the fall can be taken by hunters (QK). The number of ducks available for hunters is

$$QK = (9.354 \times 0.95) + QI - 11.136 = QI - 2.250 \qquad (15.1)$$

where both QI and QK are measured in millions.

Another simplification in this model concerns natural mortality. In their

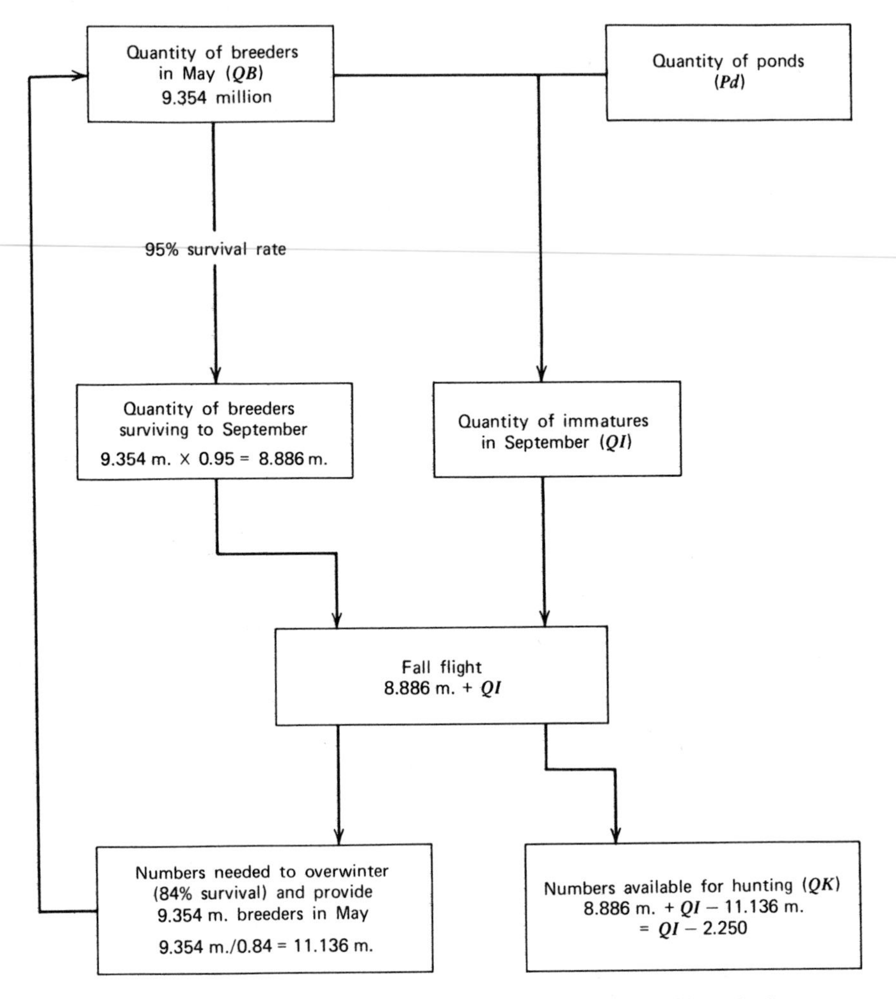

Figure 15.2. A simplified model of the interactions among habitat, duck population, and hunters.

full model, Hammack and Brown permit mortality to vary independently. We assume that annual mortality always equals the sum of the 5 percent mortality between May and September, the 16 percent mortality between September and May, and the annual hunters' bag. We also assume that all ducks available for hunting (QK) are both killed and retrieved.

The model must now be given empirical content by deriving a production function and demand and supply functions.

2.3. The Production Function

A production function relates the quantity of output to the quantity of variable inputs. The function for our example has been specified in an informal way in Figure 15.2, where the output is number of immatures and the inputs are quantity of ponds and quantity of breeders. This gives the following relationship

$$QI = f(QB, Pd) \tag{15.2}$$

where QI is number of immatures, QB is number of breeders in May, and Pd is number of ponds.

Hammack and Brown derived a quantitative expression for this equation from time-series data for the period 1955 to 1968. One of their preferred models was

$$\ln QI = 1.36 + \underset{(0.168)}{0.269} (\ln QB) + \underset{(0.068)}{0.460} (\ln Pd) \qquad (15.3.)^*$$

with the three variables expressed as natural logarithms. The coefficient of determination was .83, and the standard errors are in parentheses. We use this as our production function. Because the number of breeders has been set at 9.354 million, Equation 15.3 can be reduced by substituting the natural logarithm of 9.354, which is 2.236.

$$\ln QI = 1.36 + 0.269\,(2.236) + 0.460\,(\ln Pd) \tag{15.4}$$

and the final production function is

$$\ln QI = 1.96 + 0.460\,(\ln Pd) \tag{15.5}$$

Equation 15.5 shows how the number of immatures changes as the number of ponds changes when the number of breeders is fixed. This production function provides the basis for the supply curve.

2.4. The Supply Curve

Supply curves show the quantities of given things that producers are willing to produce over a range of prices. A supply curve for the quantity of ducks killed was calculated in the following manner:

(a) The function for the production of immatures (Equation 15.5) was solved for a range of number of ponds from 0.25 to 5.0 million. The numbers of immatures are shown in column 2 of Table 15.1 for the range up to 1.5 million ponds.

* Equations 15.3 and 15.8 are from *Waterfowl and Wetlands: Toward Bioeconomic Analysis*, by Judd Hammack and Gardner Mallard Brown, Jr., published by Resources for the Future, Washington, D.C. 1974.

Table 15.1. Derivation of the Supply Curve of Ducks Available for Hunting

Number of Ponds *Pd*	Number of Immatures *QI*	Quantity Killed *QK*	Change in *QK*	Mean Level of *QK*	Change in Total Cost ($)	Change in Total Cost per unit Change in *QK*
1	2	3	4	5	6	7
			Millions			($ per duck)
			1.55	0.78	3	1.94
0.25	3.8	1.55				
			1.40	2.25	3	2.14
0.50	5.2	2.95				
			1.90	3.90	6	3.16
1.00	7.1	4.85				
			1.50	5.60	6	4.00
1.50	8.6	6.35				

(**b**) The number of ducks available for killing (QK) was calculated from the data of column 2 and Equation 15.1. For example, at 0.25 million ponds there are 3.80 million immatures, so that the number available for hunters is 3.80 − 2.25 or 1.55 million.

(**c**) The changes in QK for each increment in number of ponds were calculated (column 4).

(**d**) The mean levels of QK for each increment were determined (column 5). For example, the second increment in QK is from 1.55 to 2.95. This increment of 1.40 takes place over a mean level of $(2.95 + 1.55)/2$ or 2.25.

(**e**) The annual cost of each pond, as an annuity equivalent, was set at $12. This is the approximate annual opportunity cost of a pond devoted to wildlife habitat. Preservation of 0.25 million more ponds would have an annual cost of $3 million. The increases in total cost are shown in column 6.

(**f**) The marginal cost of an additional duck was calculated by dividing the change in total costs (column 6) by the change in number of ducks killed (column 4). At a mean level of 0.78 million, the marginal cost is 3/1.55 or $1.94 per duck.

(**g**) The total quantities produced (column 5) were expressed as a mathematical function of their respective marginal costs (column 7). Conventional economic theory says the quantity supplied is a function of market price because, for efficient production, marginal cost will be equal to market price.

$$QK = f(MC) \tag{15.6}$$

The quantitative model we developed from the data in Table 15.1 is

$$QK = -1.29 + 1.60\,MC \qquad (15.7)$$
$$\qquad\qquad (0.07)$$

The standard error is in parentheses, and the coefficient of determination is .98.

This supply curve can be interpreted in our policy example as follows. The supply of ducks is provided by default. If the farmers tolerate various opportunity costs, they permit various numbers of ponds to persist, and thus permit various quantities of ducks (QK) to be "produced." The supply curve from Equation 15.7 is presented in Figure 15.3. It slopes upward because the total number of breeders is fixed, which causes the marginal product of additional ponds to diminish.

2.5. The Demand Curve

Our wildlife problem has arisen because the market has failed to guide resource allocation. One cause of this failure is the physical and institutional difficulty of getting consumers (hunters) and producers (farmers) together in an exchange situation. This difficulty provides a modest advantage for our analysis. Because the consumers are separated in space

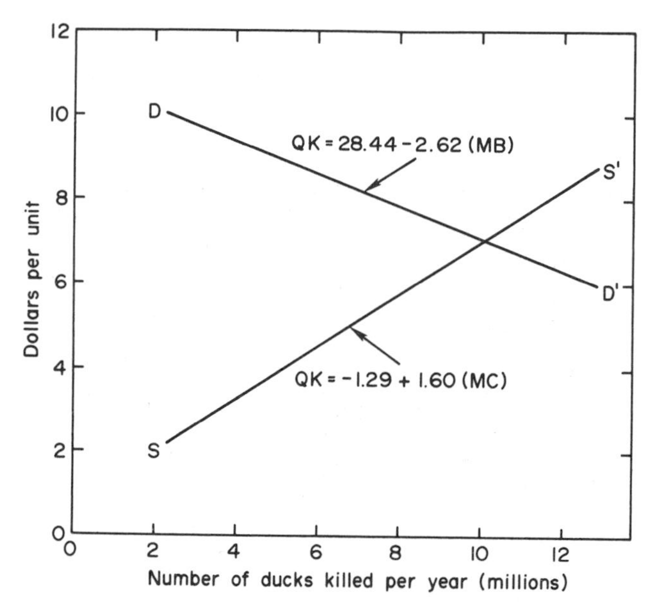

Figure 15.3. Demand and supply curves for ducks for hunting.

and time from the producers, demand is independent of supply, and a demand curve can be derived separately from the supply curve.

Information for a demand schedule was obtained by Hammack and Brown (1974) through questionnaire surveys of hunters' willingness to pay for the number of waterfowl bagged. Total willingness to pay (or total benefit) was related to the number of ducks bagged per season and to certain socioeconomic characteristics of the hunters. One of Hammack and Brown's preferred models, with a coefficient of determination of .22, was

$$\begin{aligned} \ln TB = 1.54 &+ \underset{(0.053)}{0.443} (\ln \text{income}) + \underset{(0.037)}{0.163} (\ln \text{number} \\ &\text{of seasons hunted}) + \underset{(0.027)}{0.149} (\ln \text{cost per season}) + \underset{(0.032)}{0.409} (\ln QH) \end{aligned} \tag{15.8}$$

where TB is total benefit or total willingness to pay in dollars and QH is number of ducks killed per hunter in a season. This model was reduced to a simpler form like Equations 15.4 and 15.5 by setting at their means the income at $12,100, the cost per season at $322, and the number of seasons hunted at 16.2. Equation 15.8 then reduces to

$$\ln TB = 3.95 + 0.409 (\ln QH) \tag{15.9}$$

A demand schedule was derived from this total benefit function as follows:

(a) The total benefits for a range of kills (QH) from 0 to 28 were calculated from Equation 15.9. Table 15.2 shows only the range between 4 and 10.

(b) The increments in total value were calculated and inserted in column 3. (The marginal per-duck values of column 4 were obtained by dividing the per-two-duck data of column 3 by two.)

(c) The mean of the numbers killed per hunter was calculated as the average of each pair of values in column 1 and recorded in column 5.

(d) The total number of ducks killed was the product of the number of hunters and the mean kill per hunter. We took Hammack and Brown's estimate of 1.7 million hunters in the United States as our total number of hunters. The total kill figures of column 6 were obtained by multiplying the mean bag figures of column 5 by 1.7 million.

(e) The data in columns 6 and 4 were those needed for an aggregate demand curve. Data for the complete range of QH values from 0 to 28 were obtained. Those within the decision-making range (QK = 5 million to 12 million) were generalized into the following linear equation (the coefficient

Table 15.2. **Derivation of the Demand Curve for Ducks for Hunting**

Number Killed per Hunter per Season *QH*	Total Benefit per Hunter *TB*	Change in Total Benefit for an Additional		Mean Number Killed per Hunter	Total Number Killed (millions)[a] *QK*
		2 ducks	1 duck		
1	2	3	4	5	6
4	92				
		16	8	5	8.5
6	108				
		14	7	7	11.9
8	122				
		11	5.5	9	15.3
10	133				

[a] With 1.7 million hunters, column 6 = column 5 × 1.7.

of determination was .98, and the standard error is in parentheses):

$$QK = 28.44 - \underset{(0.13)}{2.62}\,(MB) \qquad (15.10)$$

The negative regression coefficient indicates that the marginal benefit (*MB*) of the additional duck diminishes as the number of ducks bagged increases. This equation provides the required demand curve, which is shown in Figure 15.3, and slopes downward as expected.

2.5.1. Other Procedures for Deriving Demand Curves. Less-formal procedures can sometimes be used to estimate demand curves. Analyses of cross-sectional data usually assume that single observations for single individuals can be analyzed as if they were different observations for the representative user in the market. With this conventional assumption, any of the sets of observations or results in Table 14.1 of Chapter 14 can be used to derive a market demand curve. This procedure was used for just this purpose by Knetsch and Davis (1966) and Beardsley (1970) in recreation and for air pollution by Barrett and Waddell (1973).

Frank and Heiss (1968) were interested in the social benefits of using satellite photography in the management of grazing lands. They were able to observe two price/quantity points and to estimate a third. The Bureau of Land Management (BLM) had photographed 11,400 square miles at a cost of \$3.50 per square mile. This cost could be considered as equivalent to a market price that BLM was willing to pay. The Forest Service had photographed a larger area at a somewhat lower cost. Frank and Heiss combined the BLM and Forest Service data to obtain a second quantity of 70,000 square miles at an average cost of $2.50 per square mile. They then made a best estimate that the agencies would have photographed 700,000 acres if the cost had been zero. This gave three points for a demand curve. Assuming away the identification problem, they took the total area under the demand curve at a zero price as a measure of total social benefit.

If such less-formal procedures are used carefully, they may provide usable estimates of demand curves. However, if they are used naively or crudely, the results may be very misleading.

2.6. Assumptions underlying the Example

We do not seek to solve the wildlife policy problem in any conclusive way, but merely to use it for illustration of the methods. This use of the example involves certain assumptions. Because we follow Hammack and Brown's analysis, we accept their following assumptions:

(**a**) Society is able through suitable institutional arrangements to set up a market in which consumers and producers can interact.

(**b**) The demand and supply curves are representative of their particular section of the market.

(**c**) There are no externalities or economies of scale. (This assumption may be innocuous in the present example but could be important in other applications.)

(**d**) Hammack and Brown built and accepted their economic models according to standard methods. As usual, they combined subjective judgment with the objective criteria of economics and statistics. Our use of their models means that we have accepted their standards, such as the coefficient of determination of .22 for Equation 15.8. We prefer higher levels of accuracy, but their models are useful for our purpose.

We also make the following assumptions of our own:

(**e**) The supply and demand curves are linear. Curvilinear relationships would not affect the principles but would complicate the arithmetic. We felt that the benefits of simplicity were greater than the cost of some loss of reality.

(**f**) The present ponds remain because their marginal cost is below the equivalent of $3.83 per duck bagged.

(**g**) Management can shift between any pair of points on the supply curve.

(**h**) We ignore the implications of the negative constant of Equation 15.7. It results from our linear approximation rather than from the true nature of the production process.

The first four assumptions did not seem to restrict Hammack and Brown's original analysis. The magnitude and direction of their results were insensitive to these particular assumptions. Similarly, the second four assumptions do not seem to restrict our use of these data and this problem for our purposes.

3. DIRECT METHODS FOR CALCULATING NET SOCIAL BENEFIT

Which of the various direct (or conventional) methods listed in Figure 15.1 is best to use for calculating net social benefit depends on the particular decision involved and on the data that are available. Because the main obstacle to the use of these methods is lack of data, we consider this problem first. For ease of presentation, we confine ourselves to one kind of decision here. Section 4 considers different kinds of decisions. We briefly discuss the kind of data needed and then look at the three classes of direct methods.

3.1. Data Needed for Decisions

We can illustrate the kinds of data needed for the net-social-benefit methods with the duck-habitat example. The decision question is whether to expand the area of habitat by preserving 10 percent more ponds. Let us assume that there are 1 million ponds at present. The production function (Equation 15.5) shows that an annual output of 7.10 million immatures would result from an input of 1 million ponds. Allowing for maintenance of the breeding stock, this would leave 4.85 million birds available for hunting. This is the quantity Q_1 in Figure 15.4. A 10 percent increase in the number of ponds would raise the number of immatures to 7.43 million and the number available for hunting to 5.18 million. This is the quantity Q_2 in Figure 15.4.

The marginal costs associated with these quantities can be calculated from the supply model (Equation 15.7). A quantity of 4.85 million is associated with a marginal cost of $3.83, and a quantity of 5.18 million with a marginal cost of $4.04. The marginal benefits resulting from these quantities can be calculated from Equation 15.10. The 4.85 millionth duck killed provides a marginal benefit of $9.00 ($MB_1$), and the 5.18 millionth duck, a marginal benefit of $8.88 ($MB_2$).

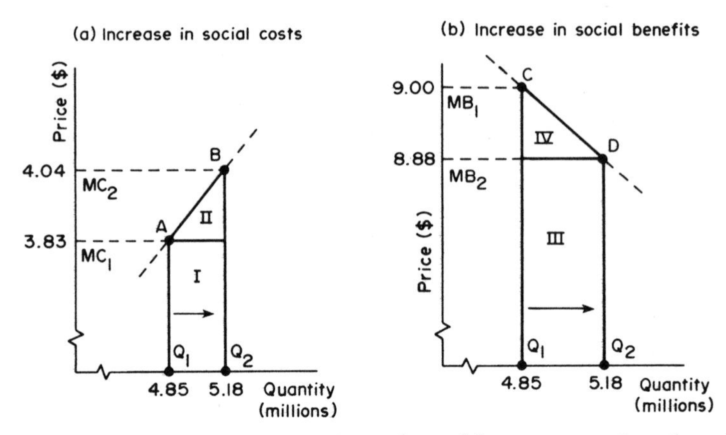

Figure 15.4. Use of the net-social-benefit model to measure the value of an increase in quantity.

These are the data necessary to calculate the net social benefit that would result from this policy change. They can be summarized and generalized by item as follows:

Item	Before the Change	After the Change
Total quantity consumed	4.85 million	5.18 million
Benefit from marginal unit	9.00 dollars	8.88 dollars
Cost of marginal unit	3.83 dollars	4.04 dollars

If Parts *a* and *b* of Figure 15.4 were plotted on the same graph, the demand and supply curves would intersect somewhere to the right of Q_2. An increase in quantity from Q_1 to Q_2 would be a movement toward the equilibrium of supply and demand. In the situation shown in Figure 15.4 the social benefit from an increase in quantity is greater than the related social cost, and increasing the quantity will produce a net social benefit.

If Q_1 were to the right of the intersection of supply and demand, an increase to Q_2 would be a movement away from equilibrium. The increase in quantity would have a social cost larger than its social benefit, and increasing the quantity would produce a net social loss. In this situation (to the right of the equilibrium point), if the present quantity were Q_2, a reduction in output to Q_1 would produce a net social benefit.

This example involves movements along existing demand and supply curves. An action that would change demand or supply (that is, move the whole curve) can still be analyzed in this same way. An example of this is presented in Section 3.3.2.

The concept of elasticity provides a useful way to summarize and relate the changes in price and quantity. The price elasticity of demand (e_d) is the percentage change in quantity consumed for a 1 percent change in price. The price elasticity at any point on the demand curve of Figure 15.4 can be calculated from the demand function of Equation 15.10 and the basic elasticity formula of Equation 2.12. The regression constant (−2.62) in Equation 15.10 shows the change in quantity for a one-unit change in price (marginal benefit), and incorporates both of the change terms in the basic formula. At point C we have

$$e_d = \frac{-2.62 \times 9.00}{4.85} = -4.87 \tag{15.11}$$

Similarly, the price elasticity of supply is the percentage change in quantity supplied resulting from a 1 percent change in price. With the use of the regression coefficient, which shows the increase in quantity for a one-unit rise in price, elasticity can be expressed as

$$e_s = \frac{b \times \text{the specific price}}{\text{the specific quantity}} \tag{15.12}$$

where the term b is the coefficient from the supply model (Equation 15.7). At A in Figure 15.4 the price is \$3.83 and the quantity is 4.85 million. The elasticity of supply is then

$$e_s = \frac{+1.60 \times 3.83}{4.85} = +1.26 \tag{15.13}$$

These elasticities provide measures of the slopes of their respective curves at specific points. They are used in the remainder of this chapter as convenient "pegs" for describing the data.

3.2. Method Using All Necessary Data

Sometimes all three data items—the total quantity consumed, benefit from marginal unit, and cost of marginal unit—are available for both before and after the proposed change. When this is so and the trends are linear, a simple arithmetical calculation can determine the net social benefit from the change. We can illustrate this with the duck-habitat example.

In Figure 15.4*a* we see that when output is increased from Q_1 to Q_2 the total social costs increase by the area ABQ_2Q_1. This total consists of two parts: rectangle I, which shows what the additional units would cost if the marginal cost stayed the same as before the change (MC_1), and triangle II, which shows the extra cost of these units that results from the increase in marginal cost to MC_2. For the increase of 330,000 ducks killed, the total increase in social cost would be:

$$\begin{aligned}\text{value of rectangle I} &= (\text{change in quantity}) \times \$3.83 \\ &= \$1.264 \text{ million}\end{aligned} \tag{15.14}$$

$$\begin{aligned}\text{value of triangle II} &= \tfrac{1}{2}(\Delta Q \times \Delta P) \\ &= 0.5(330{,}000 \times \$0.21) \\ &= \$0.035 \text{ million}\end{aligned} \tag{15.15}$$

$$\begin{aligned}\text{total change} &= \text{rectangle I} + \text{triangle II} \\ \text{in cost} &= \$1.299 \text{ million}\end{aligned} \tag{15.16}$$

The change in social benefits (CDQ_2Q_1) can be calculated in a similar way (Figure 15.4*b*):

$$\begin{aligned}\text{value of rectangle III} &= (\text{change in quantity}) \times \$8.88 \\ &= \$2.930 \text{ million}\end{aligned} \tag{15.17}$$

$$\begin{aligned}\text{value of triangle IV} &= \tfrac{1}{2}(\Delta Q \times \Delta P) \\ &= 0.5\,(330{,}000 \times \$0.12) \\ &= \$0.020 \text{ million}\end{aligned} \tag{15.18}$$

$$\begin{aligned}\text{total change in} &= \text{rectangle III} + \text{triangle IV} \\ \text{benefit} &= \$2.950 \text{ million}\end{aligned} \tag{15.19}$$

The total change in net social benefit resulting from the decision would then be:

$$\begin{aligned}\text{change in } NSB &= (\text{change in benefit}) - (\text{change in cost}) \\ &= \$2.950 \text{ million} - \$1.299 \text{ million} \\ &= \$1.651 \text{ million}\end{aligned} \tag{15.20}$$

This result indicates that in this example a decision to preserve 10 percent more ponds would have a positive social value.

This same method was used by Buxton and Hammond (1974) to estimate the social value of a proposed government program to support milk prices in the United States. Although they were concerned with a priced commodity, their procedure was analogous to that used in our example.

3.3. Methods Using a Range of Elasticity Data

In many cases only part of the data are available, and net social benefit cannot be calculated by the simple method described above. To judge from our experience and the literature, the most elusive data are the elasticity coefficients. Without slopes for the supply and demand curves, it is difficult to estimate what prices and quantities will be after a proposed change. However, it can often be determined that the slopes must be within some limits, and it is then possible to calculate a range of possible results.

The following two sections show how net social benefit can be estimated when only a range of elasticity information is available for supply or demand. We present two examples to show how the procedure can be applied to situations in which demand-elasticity information is lacking or in which supply-elasticity information is lacking.

3.3.1. Supply Elasticity Known But Only a Range of Possible Demand Elasticities. We can illustrate this situation with the duck-habitat example. The problem is to estimate the net social benefit of preserving 10 percent more ponds.

Suppose we know that the elasticity of supply of ducks is +1.26. The change in social cost from preserving the additional habitat would then be $1,299,000 as calculated in Section 3.2.

To determine the net social benefit, we must know the gross social benefit that would result from having 330,000 more ducks available for hunting. Suppose we do not know the elasticity of demand for ducks but believe that its upper limit is not higher than −4.87 and its lower limit not lower than −1.00. We can proceed as follows:

(a) The available data are: a present price of $9.00 per duck (point *C* in Figure 15.4*b*), a present consumption of 4.85 million ducks killed per year, and a proposed increase in consumption of 0.33 million ducks per year.

(b) These data are inserted into the general elasticity formula of Equation 2.12

$$\text{elasticity} = \frac{\text{change in quantity}}{\text{original quantity}} \div \frac{\text{change in price}}{\text{original price}} \tag{15.21}$$

and the formula is rearranged to solve for change in price, as in Equation 13.2:

$$\Delta P = \frac{0.33}{4.85} \times \frac{9.00}{e} \tag{15.22}$$

where ΔP is change in price and e is elasticity of demand.

(c) The changes in price are calculated with Equation 15.22 for the assumed upper and lower limits of elasticity, giving

Elasticity	Change in Price
−4.87	−$0.12
−1.00	−$0.61

(d) The new prices, at point *D* in Figure 15.4*b*, are calculated by adding the changes in price to the original price of $9.00.

Elasticity	New Price
−4.87	$8.88
−1.00	$8.39

(e) The total change in social benefit is calculated as described in Section 3.2. Total change in benefits = area rectangle III + area triangle IV. For the assumed upper and lower limits of elasticity this gives

Elasticity	Change in Benefits
−4.87	2.930 + 0.020 = $2,950,000
−1.00	2.768 + 0.101 = $2,869,000

(f) The change in net social benefit is then calculated by subtracting the previously determined change in social cost of $1,299,000 from these estimated changes in social benefit:

Elasticity	Change in Net Social Benefit
−4.87	2.950 − 1.299 = $1,651,000
−1.00	2.869 − 1.299 = $1,570,000

This example shows that if an analyst can estimate the possible range of demand elasticity, he can produce useful information about the effect of a decision on net social benefit. Although the range of elasticities in our example is very large, two useful pieces of information are obtained: (1) increasing the number of potholes preserved by 10 percent would have a positive effect on net social benefit and (2) the resulting change in *NSB* is not likely to be larger than $1,651,000 nor smaller than $1,570,000. Decision makers can compare these values with the estimated net social benefits that would be produced by alternative uses of the pothole area.

3.3.2. Demand Elasticity Known But Only a Range of Possible Supply Elasticities. We can illustrate this situation with a study by Griliches (1958) of research on hybrid corn. Griliches set out to determine what net benefit had accrued to society as a result of this research. He used the same conceptual model as Figure 15.4*b* except that he assumed supply and demand were in equilibrium without the research and also with it. He reasoned that the hybrids developed by research had increased corn output at all levels of cost. That is, the research had changed the supply schedule (shifted the curve to the right). Griliches defined the benefit from research as the value of the corn that would not have been produced if the hybrids had not been developed.

Evidence was available that the price elasticity of demand for corn was −0.5. Because Griliches knew much less about the supply elasticity of corn, he explored the consequences of two extreme situations—an infinitely elastic supply and an infinitely inelastic one. These extreme situations are pictured in Figure 15.5.

If the supply of corn were infinitely elastic, as in Figure 15.5*a*, the marginal costs would be constant. The area under supply curve S_2 shows the total cost of producing the quantity (Q_2) that would have been produced and sold at price P_2 if there had been no research. The research reduced costs and shifted the supply curve downward to S_1. The area under this new supply curve shows the total cost of producing the quantity that was produced and sold at price P_1 as a result of the research. The shaded area shows the amount added to consumers' surplus as a result of the research. The change in net social benefit was equal to the combined areas of rectangle III and triangle IV.

If the supply of corn were infintely inelastic, as in Figure 15.5*b*, the area under the demand curve to the left of supply curve S_2 would consist of consumers' surplus above the price line P_2 and producers' surplus below it. This is the net social benefit from corn production if the hybrid had not been developed. The research shifted the supply curve to S_1. Triangle IV shows the amount this added to consumers' surplus and rectangle III the amount it added to producers' surplus. The shaded area shows the change in net social benefit as a result of the research.

Griliches (1958) calculated the net social benefits under these two extreme situations. He found that with his demand elasticity, net social benefit would be less if supply were infinitely elastic than if it were infinitely

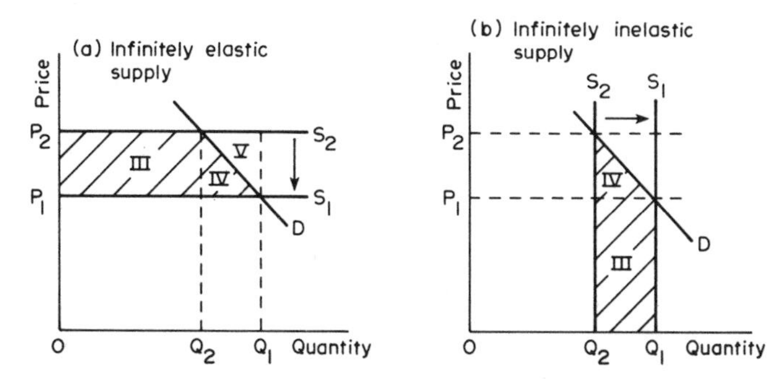

Figure 15.5. A simple model to measure the benefits from research or innovation.

inelastic. Using this most-conservative assumption, he estimated that the net social benefit from hybrid corn research had been at least $341 million per year.

3.4. Methods Usable When No Elasticity Data Are Available

Two approaches can be taken to calculate changes in net benefit when there is no information about the slopes of the curves. One is to assume that present prices and costs will remain constant despite the increased output. The other is to use point estimates of new prices and quantities.

3.4.1. Assuming Constant Prices and Costs. When demand, supply, or both could be anywhere between perfectly elastic and perfectly inelastic, the outcome might be anything from a net social loss to a net social benefit. If either demand or supply is perfectly inelastic, consumption cannot be increased, and any attempt to do so must result in a net social loss. If demand and supply are both perfectly elastic, the net social benefit from an increase in output will be as large as it possibly can be, and sometimes this is enough to guide decisions.

If demand and supply are perfectly elastic, present prices and costs will remain the same when output is increased. The maximum possible net social benefit can therefore be estimated by assuming constant prices and costs. At the present output of 4.85 million ducks in Figure 15.4, the marginal benefit (price) is $9.00, and the marginal cost is $3.83. If we assume that these remain constant, we can estimate the net social benefit from producing 330,000 more ducks as

increase in total benefit	= 330,000 × 9.00 =	$2,970,000
increase in total cost	= 330,000 × 3.83 =	$1,264,000
Net increase in social benefit	=	$1,706,000

We will not illustrate this procedure with another empirical example because increases in output usually raise marginal costs and lower marginal benefits, and an actual case of constant costs and prices is unlikely. This procedure will inevitably overestimate net social benefit. However, if the decision maker in the example above knew that some alternative use would produce a net social benefit of more than $1,706,000, he could be sure that preserving the area for duck habitat would not be the most valuable use.

3.4.2. Using Point or Average Estimates of Money and Quantity Data. Rather than using an unrealistic assumption of constant prices and costs, a well-informed analyst may prefer to make single or point estimates of the new marginal costs and prices. Two versions of this procedure have been used.

Extreme New Figures. One version is to estimate the extreme possible change in net social benefit and then modify this figure to arrive at a more realistic estimate. Schmitz and Seckler (1970) took this approach in their study of the development and introduction of mechanical tomato harvesters. They knew the current tomato output after introduction of the harvesters (OQ_1 in Figure 15.5*a*) and estimated the amount by which the harvesters had reduced per-unit costs ($P_2 - P_1$). They then calculated the net social benefit as the cost saving multiplied by the total output. They recognized that this overestimated net social benefit by the amount in triangle V and modified their values to allow for this.

Single "Best" Estimates. The other version is to make as good an estimate as possible of the new marginal cost and marginal benefit that will exist after the change. We can illustrate this approach with the study by Anderson and Auster (1974) of road salting.

The application of salt has been perceived as a cheap and efficient way to clear snow and ice from roads. Its use in the United States has increased eighteenfold in the last 20 years, and the total expenditure on road salting in 1970 was $100 million. Anderson and Auster set out to estimate the unpriced benefits and costs of salting. They estimated the benefits from changes in highway safety and travel time, and the costs of damage to vehicles, water supplies, and vegetation.

Data were available on current quantities, costs, and prices but not on elasticities, nor on what the quantities, costs, and prices would have been without salting. Anderson and Auster made no attempt to estimate the elasticities of demand or supply of journeys or passenger miles. They noted that the number of miles traveled each winter was about 80 billion. That is the present output OQ_1 in Figure 15.5*a*. It includes business travel and travel to work. The demand for these two kinds of travel is likely to be fairly inelastic, with the journeys being undertaken whether roads are salted or not. It also includes leisure travel, the demand for which is probably highly elastic.

The effect of salting is to reduce the real costs of travel. Anderson and Auster estimated the total reduction at 1¢ per mile. If the demand for all types of travel were completely inelastic, the annual cost reduction would be 80 billion miles × 1¢, or $800 million. All other things being equal, this is the maximum possible benefit. If the demand for any of the three kinds of travel is at all elastic, the without-salting quantity of travel (OQ_2) would be less than the with-salting quantity (OQ_1). The overestimate of the benefit would be shown by triangle V. Anderson and Auster argue that the more elastic the overall demand is, the greater will be the overestimate of net social benefit.

Another example of the single-best-estimate approach is Foster and Beesley's (1963) benefit-cost analysis of a new underground railway in London. The total cost of the new railway between Victoria and Walthamstow was estimated to be £ 48 million. This cost would be associated with an increase in the total number of railway trips between points served by the line, as shown in Figure 15.6. There are important indivisibilities in this situation. Either the whole line is built, or nothing is built. If it is built the resulting increase in quantity will be ($OQ_2 - OQ_1$). The marginal cost of a trip is therefore constant over the whole range from OQ_1 to OQ_2.

The new underground railway would generate two kinds of benefits, which are illustrated in Figure 15.6. The first kind would accrue to present travelers on the route. They are now traveling above ground, and their total cost includes cash fares, time costs, and other unpriced costs, such as those due to congestion. The combined marginal cost of all these items is measured on the monetary axis of Figure 15.6. The new railway will reduce cost to these present travelers from OP_2 to OP_1 The total value of these decreased costs is represented by rectangle III.

A second kind of benefit is the consumers' surplus to new travelers who are attracted by the new line. This extra traffic is shown by the increase in trips from OQ_1 to OQ_2. The additional net social benefit to these new users is represented by triangle IV.

The total value of each of these kinds of benefits was calculated as the product of the estimated amounts of travel and single-point estimates of the average changes in cost to the consumers. An example is new traffic generated by the railway. The total number of new journeys was estimated at 30,000 per day or 9 million per year. By transferring to rail travel these

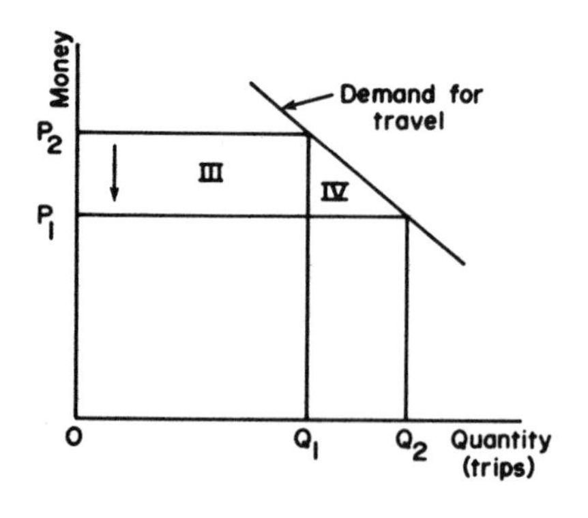

Figure 15.6. Measuring the net benefits from a new railway line.

people would save an average of 5 minutes on the trip. Using an average value of £ 0.128 per hour for time, Foster and Beesley estimated the time saving to be worth £ 96,000 per year. The saving in fares was calculated to be 1.7 pence per trip, or £ 63,000 per year. The total saving of time and money was £ 159,000 per year (the value of triangle IV in Figure 15.6). This point-estimate approach rested on a calculation of the average net benefit for each unit of a known change in quantity. Foster and Beesley valued both kinds of benefits in this manner. The net social benefit of the underground line proved to be positive over a wide range of discount rates and assumptions about other data.

3.5. The Methods as Approaches to Data Deficiencies

We have discussed a number of direct methods for calculating changes in net social benefit. They are all variations on the same theme, and the choice among them depends on the availability of data. All implicitly assume that present output and present price are known. If present output is not the equilibrium output (as it is not in Figure 15.4), the methods also require that both present marginal cost and present marginal benefit be known.

At the very least, one more data item must be available. This is usually the change in quantity or the change in price. When this is all that is available, the methods of Section 3.4 can be used to estimate the extremes of possible net social benefit. Various modifications of this method involve the use of point estimates and maximum (or minimum) estimates.

The precision of the estimate of net social benefit can be improved if more data are available. It is common for one elasticity to be known but not the other. With this additional information an analyst can use the methods of Section 3.3 rather than those of 3.4. Occasionally, all data are available, and the method of Section 3.2 can be used.

An analyst should start by trying to find a complete set of data in order to use the method of Section 3.2. If he is unable to find all the data, he can move to the less-precise methods of Section 3.3 or even 3.4.

4. APPLICATION TO VARIOUS KINDS OF DECISIONS

In the introductory section of this chapter we discussed reasons why there has not been more use of the net-social-benefit methods. One reason appears to be lack of knowledge of the methods and another the difficulty in formulating decisions in the appropriate framework. Section 3 has discussed and illustrated the methods, mainly, in the context of a specific decision about expansion of wildlife habitat. We now consider some other kinds of decisions to show how they can be formulated in the appropriate framework.

4.1. Measuring Benefits from Improvements in Management

4.1.1. Formulation of the Model. Technological and managerial advances lower costs of production and therefore shift supply curves downward and to the right. In Section 3.3.2 we discussed Griliches' (1958) valuation of the benefits of research on hybrid corn. Because his analysis was ex post, he knew the quantity of output resulting from the research, but he had to estimate what production and price would have without it. We can use the duck-habitat case as an example of improvement in management.

Let us follow the procedure of Ryan (1975) and assume that we wish to value the net benefits of introducing a change in habitat management that would increase the number of breeding ducks. For any given number of ponds, this improved management would increase the number of ducks available for hunting. The supply curve in Figure 15.7 will move to the right, indicating a lower marginal cost for any given quantity and a greater number of ducks for any given marginal cost. Assume that the policy objective is still to increase the total bag from 4.85 to 5.18 million ducks per year. The value of the resources saved by this managerial advance is shown by the shaded area in Figure 15.7. The net benefit to society is equal to this saving in resources, less any costs for research or extension that are necessary to obtain the increased output.

4.1.2. Application to the Duck-Habitat Example. Let us assume that the improvement in duck-habitat management increases the number of mallard breeders by 10 percent or from 9.354 to 10.289 million. The figure entered for QB in Equation 15.3 will now be 10.289 instead of the 9.354 shown in Section 2.3. Equation 15.4 becomes

$$\ln QI = 1.36 + 0.269\,(\ln 10.289) + 0.460\,(\ln Pd) \qquad (15.23)$$

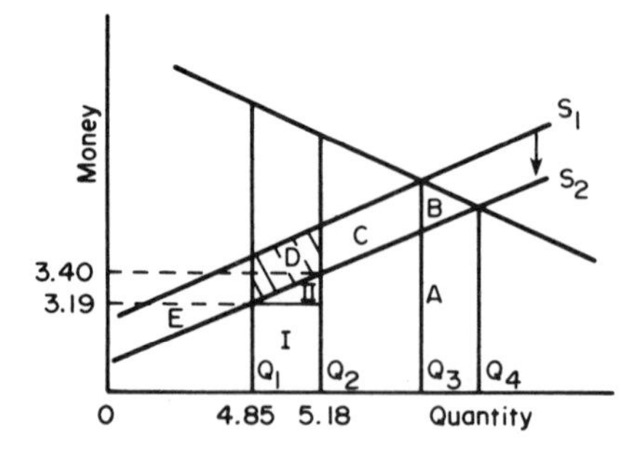

Figure 15.7. Measuring the net benefits from an improvement in management.

Collecting terms, we have

$$\ln QI = 1.99 + 0.460 (\ln Pd) \tag{15.24}$$

Equation 15.24 and its predecessor (15.5 in Section 2.3) differ only in their constants. The change in the constant from the original one in Equation 15.5 is 1.99 − 1.96 or 0.03. Because Equation 15.24 is a function in natural logarithms, the arithmetical value of this change is the antilog of 0.03 or 1.03. This indicates an increase of 1.03 million immatures, which is a fixed increment to all levels of output in Table 15.1. The supply curve equation (15.7) can be rewritten as

$$QK = 1.03 - 1.29 + 1.60\,MC$$
$$QK = -0.26 + 1.60\,MC \tag{15.25}$$

This new equation can now be applied in the manner of Section 3.2 to calculate the increase in social cost that will accompany the required increase in output under the new supply conditions. The procedure can be summarized as follows:

(**a**) The new marginal costs are calculated first. We can rewrite Equation 15.25 as

$$MC = \frac{QK + 0.26}{1.60} \tag{15.26}$$

By solving Equation 15.26 for different levels of QK, we find the marginal cost at an output of 4.85 million ducks is $3.19, and at an output of 5.18 million is $3.40. These costs are shown in Figure 15.7.

(**b**) The total increase in social costs equals rectangle I plus triangle II in Figure 15.7:

$$\begin{aligned} \text{value of rectangle I} &= (\Delta Q \times \$3.19) \\ &= \$1{,}053{,}000 \\ \text{value of triangle II} &= 0.5\,(\Delta Q \times \Delta P) \\ &= \$35{,}000 \\ \text{total increase in social cost} &= \$1{,}088{,}000 \end{aligned}$$

(**c**) The total social cost for the same increase in quantity under the original supply curve S_1 was $1,299,000. The value of the savings in resources is therefore 1.299 − 1.088, or $211,000 per year. The net social value of this improvement in habitat management is $211,000, less any costs of invention or adoption.

4.1.2. Generalization. Ryan's (1975) study assessed the net social benefits from an improvement in the management of herds of cows rather than flights of ducks. But the methods are quite general and therefore applicable to all similar problems. If a particular industry is in competitive equilibrium, an improvement in management will lower production costs and increase the optimal output from Q_3 to Q_4 in Figure 15.7. This will shift resources into this sector of the economy and raise total production costs by area A (Figure 15.7). The increased output will increase total benefits by areas $(A + B)$. The reduction in the production costs of the previous output (OQ_3) as a result of the shift in the supply curve is shown by areas $(C + D + E)$. The net social benefit from the improvement in management can be summarized as follows:

$$\begin{aligned}\text{net benefit} &= \text{total benefit from extra output } (OQ_4 - OQ_3) + \text{resource savings on original output } (OQ_3) - \text{extra costs of extra output} \\ &= (A + B) + \text{resource savings on original output} - A \\ &= B + \text{resource savings} \\ &= B + C + D + E \end{aligned} \tag{15.27}$$

4.2. Choosing between Alternative Policies for Expanding Output

4.2.1. Formulation of the Model. The concept of net social benefits has proved particularly useful in measuring and comparing the effects of production policies. This is perhaps the most-general application of the methods. In this section we show how the model can be formulated and applied to a choice between alternative means of achieving a desired increase in output.

Assume that a decision has been made to increase the number of ducks available for hunting from 4.85 to 9.98 million per year. The increase in

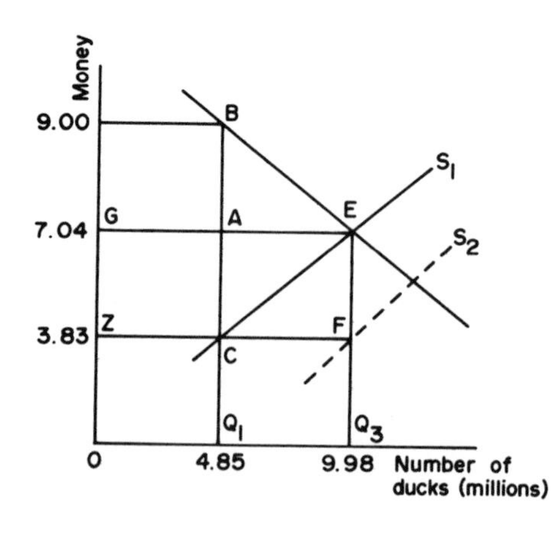

Figure 15.8. A model for choosing between alternative policies for increasing ducks for hunting.

total social benefit is shown by area Q_1BEQ_3 in Figure 15.8. Assume also that the choice is between a policy of paying landowners an annual sum for every duck produced and one of buying the ponds outright. The social cost of buying the ponds is shown by area Q_1CEQ_3.

A subsidy of EF per duck would lower the supply curve from S_1 to S_2. The marginal cost to the farmer for the 9.98 millionth duck would then be \$3.83. In view of the figures developed earlier in this chapter in the wildlife-habitat example, it appears that if the opportunity cost of leaving the ponds is less than \$3.83 per duck, farmers will leave the ponds, and the ducks will be produced. A subsidy of EF would lower the farmers' cost to the level required to get the desired results. The social cost of the required annual payment is shown by the area $GEFZ$.

The salient features of this formulation are as follows:

$$\begin{aligned} \text{total benefit} &= Q_1BEQ_3 \\ \text{total cost of purchase} &= Q_1CEQ_3 \\ \text{total cost of subsidy} &= GEFZ \end{aligned}$$

4.2.2. Application to the Duck-Habitat Example. The data for the wildlife example have all been calculated earlier in this chapter and are shown in Figure 15.8 as annual figures. Social cost and benefit for an increase from 4.85 to 9.98 million ducks can be calculated as follows:

$$\begin{aligned} \text{total benefit} &= Q_1BEQ_3 \\ &= Q_1AEQ_3 + ABE \\ &= (7.04 \times 5.13) + 0.5\,[(9.00 - 7.04) \times 5.13] \\ &= \$41{,}143{,}000 \end{aligned} \tag{15.28}$$

$$\begin{aligned} \text{total cost of purchase} &= Q_1CEQ_3 \\ &= Q_1CFQ_3 + CEF \\ &= [3.83 \times 5.13] + 0.5\,[(7.04 - 3.83) \times 5.13] \\ &= \$27{,}882{,}000 \end{aligned} \tag{15.29}$$

$$\begin{aligned} \text{total cost of subsidy} &= GEFZ \\ &= 9.98 \times (7.04 - 3.83) \\ &= \$32{,}036{,}000 \end{aligned} \tag{15.30}$$

These figures indicate that the purchase policy would be cheaper than the subsidy policy. Irrespective of any other advantages of purchase over subsidy, the purchase policy is preferable on social-cost grounds alone. Furthermore, because the total benefits from purchase (\$41,143,000) would be greater than the total costs of purchase (\$27,882,000), the purchase policy would lead to a net increase in social benefit. The value of the purchase policy would be positive and can be estimated at \$13,261,000.

4.2.3. Generalization. This application of this method to compare the social costs of alternatives can be traced back to Dupuit's (1844) original discussion of the effects of sales taxes on consumers' surplus. Marshall (1890) extended the theory to include producers' surplus. The importance of the concept of net social benefit in this context rests on its role as a measure of change in utility. Tweeten and Tyner (1966) claim it is generally applicable for measuring changes in utility to society because it incorporates changes in both producers' and consumers' surplus and acknowledges changes in both output and price.

4.3. Measuring the Social Cost of Decisions That Decrease Utility

Sometimes it is necessary to estimate the social cost of a decision that would have as one result a decrease in the utility people have been receiving. An example is the increase in noise that would accompany the establishment of an airport. The social cost of this change in environmental quality might be indicated by a lower demand for houses in the newly noisy area.

Paul (1971) reports that Wise estimated the social costs of noise from Gatwick Airport near London. By using point estimates of money and quantity, he extended the land-price method of Chapter 13 to measure net social benefit. In his model, which is shown in Figure 15.9, Wise assumed an inelastic supply curve (*RD′*). He also assumed that the demand curve for houses was linear and that the disutility from increased noise would cause the demand for houses in the affected area to shift downward from curve *DD′* to curve *AB*.

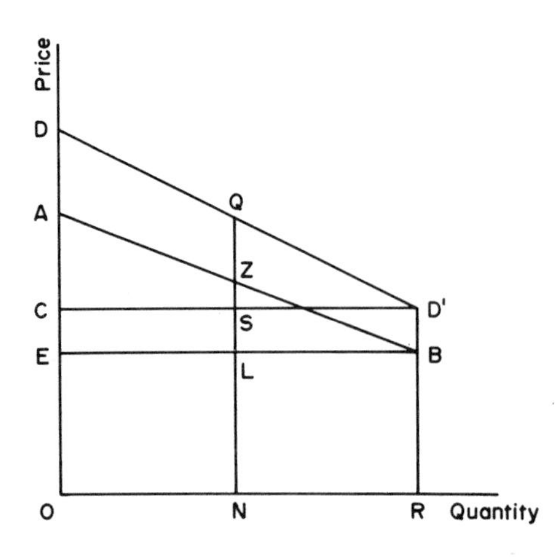

Figure 15.9. Model for estimating the social cost of a decision that decreases utility. (After Paul, 1971).

Wise observed the total number of houses exchanged (OR), and the market price of houses before the airport construction (OC or RD') and afterward (OE or RB). The average decrease in house price is shown by BD'. If the elasticity of demand were known, the social cost could be calculated as the area $ADD'B$.

He was able to obtain information on the median consumers' surplus on houses purchased before airport construction and on those purchased afterward. If it is assumed that the OR houses exchanged are arranged in Figure 15.9 in order of decreasing consumers' surplus from left to right, the house with the median consumers' surplus will be located at point N. The consumers' surplus for this median house can then be plotted as QS above the price line CD' which existed before the airport and as ZL above the price line EB which would exist after airport construction. With points D' and Q known, the "before" demand curve DD' can be plotted, and with points B and Z, the "after"curve can be plotted. Because the slopes of the demand curves are now known, the value of area $ADD'B$ can be calculated to determine the total loss in consumers' surplus resulting from the airport noise.

The difficulties inherent in this approach—and the importance of the assumptions—are discussed by Paul (1971). One of the difficulties lies in the need to establish a causal relationship between increased noise and change in market price. However, the method shows the appropriate orders of magnitude and gives an indication of what people would pay to buy back the lost quiet. This estimate of social loss may be useful in determining compensation.

5. SUMMARY

In this chapter we have presented various methods that can be used to make direct estimates of net social benefit. The choice among them depends on the amount of data available. In Section 4 we also show how appropriate methods can be selected for various kinds of decisions. Chapter 16 presents some structured, or less conventional, methods that have been developed for use when the necessary data cannot be obtained for the direct methods. Because the methods of Chapters 15 and 16 all aim to produce estimates of net social benefit, we postpone a general discussion of this kind of method until the end of Chapter 16, where we can consider all the methods together.

CHAPTER 16

Estimation of Net Social Benefit—Structured Methods

In Chapter 15 we saw that the net-social-benefit model can be an accurate way of estimating social value when all necessary data are available. And we saw that it is possible to modify the direct procedure and obtain usable results, even when all necessary data are not available. In many decision situations, however, very little or perhaps none of the data needed for the direct approach are available. Studies have demonstrated that even under this condition, usable estimates of comparative value can often be obtained by using a structured rather than a direct approach to determining net social benefit.

Figure 15.1 divided the net-social-benefit methods into direct procedures, which have been covered in Chapter 15, and structured procedures, which are covered in this chapter. Three different ways of structuring the procedure have been shown in Figure 15.1. These methods sometimes give estimates of value in relative rather than absolute terms.

The first procedure—the travel-cost method—involves restrictive assumptions but can still give usable estimates of net social benefit. Because of the assumptions, however, the estimates can only be compared with other estimates with similar structures. The second procedure involves a threshold datum point. A "massive" sensitivity analysis can be undertaken to estimate net social benefits in relation to this datum. An absolute value cannot be obtained, but a comparative decision can be made. The third procedure is an opportunity-cost comparison. It is a measure of the value foregone if the action is (or is not) taken. A decision is possible if the decision maker has some estimate of the value of the alternative.

I. THE TRAVEL-COST METHOD

The travel-cost method was originally developed to assist in making policies about outdoor recreation. The idea was apparently first suggested by

Hotelling in a letter to the National Park Service, as reported in Prewitt (1949) and has been used and developed by many workers since that time. The central theme of the method is that the cost of traveling to a place influences the number of visits made to it. This can be expressed as a demand function

$$QV = f(TC) \tag{16.1}$$

where QV is the number of visits and TC is the cost of travel.

The method is appropriate for any problem in which all benefits accrue from visits, the number of visits varies with travel cost, and the structural features or assumptions of the method can be accepted. There are two forms of the method. One values the "whole experience" as described in Section 1.2, and the other the "on-site experience" (Section 1.3). There is one major variant that uses distance as a proxy for price (Section 1.5), and a number of developments which are discussed in Section 1.6.

1.1. Structural Features of the Method

The travel-cost method is based on conventional demand functions of the following form

$$Q_i = f(TC_i, X_1, \cdots, X_n) \tag{16.2}$$

where Q_i is the quantity of activity i taken per unit of time by a given sample of people, TC_i is the travel cost in activity i, and X_1 to X_n are income and other explanatory variables. A demand curve for i is derived by plotting Q_i against TC_i for a range of travel costs. All other variables are held constant at their means.

The marginal user is the most distant one who engages in activity i at this site. People who live farther away will not use the site at all. The basic principle for valuation is that the consumer's surplus of user j is equal to the travel cost of the marginal user minus the travel costs of user j

$$CS_j = TC_m - TC_j \tag{16.3}$$

where CS_j is the consumer's surplus enjoyed by j, TC_m is the travel cost of the marginal user, and TC_j is the travel cost of j.

To apply this principle, the following restrictive assumptions must be made:

(a) All users obtain the same total benefit, and this is equal to the travel cost of the marginal (most distant) user.

(b) The consumer's surplus of the marginal user is zero.

(**c**) Travel cost is a reliable proxy for price. This, in turn, rests on an assumption that the disutility of overcoming distance derives from monetary costs alone.

(**d**) People in all distance zones would consume the same quantities of the activity at given monetary costs. That is, the demand curves for all distance zones have the same slope.

Assumption d is a feature of all cross-sectional demand studies. The validity of this assumption is measured by the coefficient of determination of the pooled regression of quantity against travel cost (Equation 16.2) for people in all zones. If coefficient of determination is high, the assumption can be accepted as being generally true.

1.2. A Method for the "Whole Experience"

This method develops the data for a demand curve by measuring the number of visits to the thing being valued and the travel cost of those visits. Assumption c of the preceding section permits the analyst to substitute travel cost for price. A demand curve can then be plotted, and net social benefit can be derived in the usual way. Assumption a allows travel expenditures to be used as a measure of benefits. When all costs are included, these benefits refer to the "whole experience," to use the terminology of Clawson and Knetsch (1966).

We illustrate this method with the example of the gorgelands area of New South Wales (Chapter 8), even though the data for number of recreation visits and population are approximate. The method proceeds as follows:

(**a**) Data are collected on the quantities and marginal travel costs of visits to the site and on the population of the area from which visitors come.

(**b**) The area of visitor origin is divided into zones of increasing travel cost. For illustration, we will use the five zones shown in Table 16.1.

(**c**) The population of each zone is noted. We use number of families as our measure of population because it is more significant than number of individuals for recreation visits.

(**d**) The families in the visitor survey are allocated to their zones, and the number of family visits from each zone is recorded (column 3).

(**e**) The number of family visits from each zone is divided by the total number of families in the zone to give the average number of visits per family for the whole zone population (column 4).

Table 16.1 Estimation of Value with the Travel-Cost Method for the "Whole Experience"

Zone	Population (Number of Families)[a]	Number of Family Visits[b]	Average Number of Visits per Family[c]	Average Cost per Family Visit ($)	Consumer's Surplus per Visit ($)	Total Consumers' Surplus ($)
1	2	3	4	5	6	7
1	2480	14,880	6	0.5	11.0	163,680
2	6184	30,920	5	4	9.3	287,556
3	2480	7,440	3	12	4.7	34,968
4	1240	2,480	2	15	3.2	7,936
5	2480	2,480	1	19	0	0
Total		58,200				494,140

[a] From census records.
[b] Derived by survey.
[c] In each zone, so column 4 = column 3 ÷ column 2.

(f) The average cost per family visit is calculated for the families in each zone (column 5).

(g) The average number of visits per family is plotted against the average travel cost per family for each zone. A demand curve is then fitted to these zone-average points, as shown in Figure 16.1.

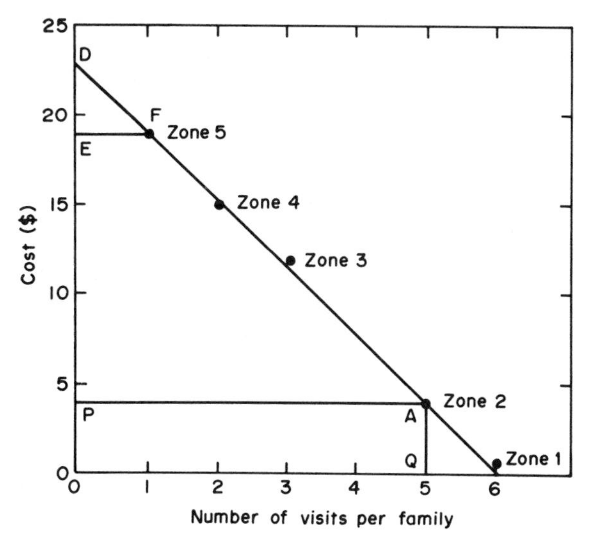

Figure 16.1. Demand curve for the whole experience.

(**h**) Consumers' surplus is calculated from the demand curve in the usual way and is shown in column 6. For example, zone 2 has an average quantity of five visits per family (*OQ*) and an average travel cost of $4 per visit (*OP*). The consumer's surplus of families in zone 2 would normally be measured as triangle *PDA*. But point *D* is undefined because families from zone 6 do not actually visit the area and their travel costs cannot be observed. We therefore must call on assumption a of Section 1.1 that all users obtain a total benefit equal to the travel costs of the marginal user (in zone 5) and assumption b that the consumer's surplus of the marginal user is zero. These assumptions permit us to ignore triangle *EDF* (the consumer's surplus of the marginal user), and to measure the consumer's surplus of five family visits from zone 2 as the area *PEFA*. The error introduced by ignoring *EDF* is often very small. The average consumer's surplus per visit for the families of zone 2 is the area *PEFA* divided by 5, or $9.30 (column 6). The average consumer's surplus for the other zones is calculated in the same way.

(**i**) The total consumer's surplus for each zone (column 7) is calculated as the product of the average consumer's surplus per visit (column 6) and the total number of family visits (column 3).

(**j**) The net social benefit provided by the area being valued is indicated by the sum of the consumers' surpluses in all zones. For our example, the net social benefit from the gorgelands area is $494,140 (column 7), or $8.49 per family visit.

This method—and its adaptations in the following sections—is called the travel-cost method because it was developed for valuation of outdoor recreation, where the main cost is usually travel. However, in practice, all marginal costs of visits are included whether they are for travel or not.

1.3. A Method for the "On-Site Experience"

The preceding method for the whole experience can only estimate the minimum value, because it assumes that users from the most distant zone obtain no consumers' surplus, and there is usually no opportunity for visitors to demonstrate their maximum willingness to pay for the site itself. Clawson (1959) extended the whole-experience method to overcome the second problem and to value the on-site experience.

The extension rests on a belief that a family in one zone would behave the same as a family in another zone now does if the first family's costs were the same as those of the second. This belief is conventionally expressed as an assumption (d in Section 1.1), although it can be validated in the analysis. The difference in costs between one zone and those for a higher-cost zone can be used to simulate an entrance fee for people in the first zone and to estimate how they would behave if such a fee existed at the site.

At present, no entrance fee is charged to visit the gorgelands area. The 58,200 family visits in Table 16.1 are being made at an extra cost of zero dollars above the travel costs. This information lets us plot point *A* in Figure 16.2. The remaining points for the demand curve are calculated as follows:

(**a**) The information contained in Table 16.1 and Figure 16.1 is first obtained.

(**b**) An extra cost of, say, $1 (equivalent to an entrance fee at the site) is added to the cost per family visit figures in column 5 of Table 16.1 to give the new cost per family visit shown in column 2 of Table 16.2.

(**c**) The new average numbers of visits per family are read from Figure 16.1 for each new cost and entered in column 3.

(**d**) The new total number of visits for each zone is calculated by multiplying the new average number per family by the number of families in the zone and is entered in column 5.

(**e**) The sum of the new numbers of family visits for the five zones gives a new total of 52,499 visits after the imposition of an extra cost of $1. This is entered as point *B* in Figure 16.2.

(**f**) Steps b to e are repeated for a range of extra costs, and the results are

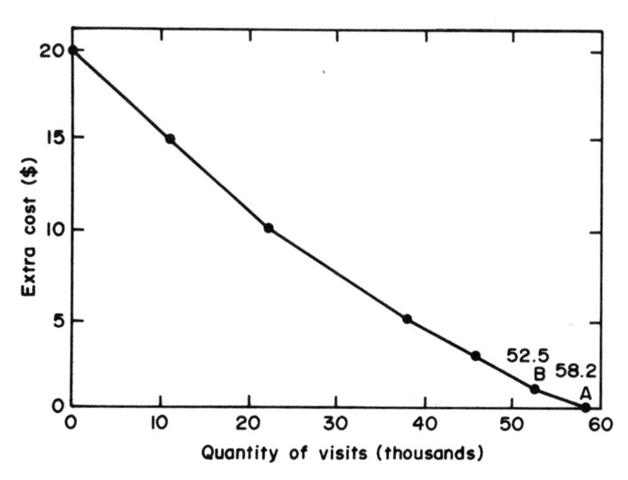

Figure 16.2. Demand curve for the on-site experience.

Table 16.2. Estimation of Value with the Travel-Cost Method for the "On-Site Experience"[a]

Zone	New Cost per Family Visit ($)	New Number of Family Visits	Number of Families[b]	Total Number Of Visits
1	2	3	4	5
1	1.5	5.7	2480	14,136
2	5	4.8	6184	29,683
3	13	2.6	2480	6,448
4	16	1.8	1240	2,232
5	20	0	2480	0
Total				52,499

[a] First step for an extra cost of $1.
[b] From column 2, Table 16.1.

plotted to give a demand curve. Figure 16.2 shows the result of calculating the quantities of visits for extra cost of $3, $5, $10, $15, and $20 in our example.

(g) The total consumers' surplus is calculated from the area under the demand curve. In our example the total consumers' surplus for the 58,200 visits made at zero extra cost (no entrance fee) is $520,000, or $8.93 per on-site visit.

The on-site experience method estimates maximum willingness to pay by simulating what people would pay for use of the site itself after having paid the travel cost of getting to it. The $8.93 value for the on-site experience is slightly larger than the $8.49 value for the whole experience, which was based only on travel cost. The same relative magnitudes were found by Clawson and Knetsch (1966). The relative magnitudes depend partly on the shape of the demand curve for the whole experience (Figure 16.1). The more concave the curve, the larger the relative size of the on-site value.

1.4. Examples: Wildlife Management and Medical-Facility Location

Because of the structural assumptions underlying its analysis, the travel-cost method is limited to estimating minimum values and comparative values of similar things. We illustrate its use for minimum values in Chapter 20. In this section we give two examples of its use to compare similar things.

Wildlife Management. Garrett, Pon, and Arosteguy (1970) needed the value of the effects on deer as part of their economic analysis of two range-improvement practices—seeding to improve pasture and controlling pinyon-juniper brush. They sent questionnaires asking for hunting-trip costs, to all who had hunted deer in Nevada in the 1967 season. The respondents were then divided into 20 zones of origin based on distance from several wildlife management areas. A regression equation relating the average number of trips per hunter to the marginal costs per trip for each zone was calculated to give a demand curve for each wildlife management area.

Based on Pearse's 1968 study, which found that hunting was the sole purpose of 95 percent of all hunting trips, Garrett, Pon, and Arosteguy assumed that the entire benefit obtained by the Nevada hunters was due to hunting. The consumers' surplus calculated from the demand curves was therefore an estimate of the annual value of deer hunting in the management areas. Dividing this consumers' surplus by the number of deer in the area and then by 365 days gave an estimate of the value of a deer-day unit.

A program of seeding crested wheatgrass improves pasture for livestock but decreases the available forage for deer. This decrease was estimated and multiplied by the deer-day value for the particular area. This monetary loss was then included with the other seeding costs for a more complete estimate of the cost of the project. A program of controlling pinyon-juniper brush by chaining often increases range use by deer. The estimated increases in deer-days of use were multiplied by the deer-day values for the particular areas and included in the benefit estimates for the program.

Location of Medical Facilities. Christianson (1976) wished to compare the social values of alternative locations for satellite medical facilities. He calculated travel costs to the various locations and used them as a proxy for price in the whole-experience method. He also incorporated probabilities of use and pessimistic and optimistic ranges into his demand functions.

The basic demand function was derived from information on actual travel to an existing clinic. Various proposed locations for satellite clinics were then analyzed, using estimated travel costs and number of visits from various distances. The apparent willingness to pay, based on a consumers' surplus calculation similar to that in Table 16.1, ranged from $400,000 for the location with the highest rank to $42,000 for the one with the lowest. Many objectives influence decisions about locating medical facilities, and these consumers' surplus figures are but one criterion. However, they do indicate the comparative social values of different locations for similar medical facilities.

1.5. Distance as a Proxy for Price

In some cases quantity of use may be related not to monetary travel costs but to travel distance. Sinden (1974) found that travel costs were not a statistically significant variable in explaining recreation use in Oregon but that use did vary with distance. Distance may sometimes act as a rationing device for outdoor recreation in the same way that price does in a competitive market. When the monetary costs of travel are small, distance may be a logical proxy for price in the travel-cost method. Merewitz (1966) and Mansfield (1971) used distance in their studies of recreation benefits in the same way that we used travel cost in Sections 1.2 and 1.3.

A problem with distance as a proxy for price is the meaning of the resulting value estimate. The unit must be something like miles per visitor day, which cannot be compared directly with monetary values. Some writers have converted distance units to monetary units by a cost-per-mile multiplier. Smith and Kavanagh (1969) used 3.8 old pence per mile in a study of trout fishing in England. Such a procedure assumes that the marginal disutility of time is constant and that all users incur the same monetary costs per mile. However, it can be useful for comparing similar things.

1.6. Developments of the Travel-Cost Method

One of the earliest applications of the travel-cost method was the study by Trice and Wood (1958) of recreation benefits in California. The next chronological development was Clawson's (1959) distinction between benefits derived from on-site activities and those involved in travel to and from the site. A number of other developments have taken place in an effort to overcome weaknesses in the method. We briefly review the most important of them.

Intervening Recreation Opportunities. One problem with dividing users is that the farther a zone is from the site being evaluated, the greater is the likelihood of there being attractive substitute sites in the intervening distance. Brown, Singh, and Castle (1964) added a distance variable to their demand function to account for these intervening opportunities. Boyet and Tolley (1966) and Burt and Brewer (1971) dealt with this problem more directly by including the quantities of use at the alternative opportunities as variables in their demand functions

Effect of Income on Valuation. Seckler (1966) pointed out that the slope and position of demand curves are affected by the incomes of the consumers as well as by the utility they obtain from a recreation experience. The points obtained from different zones might be on different demand curves representing users in different income classes. Or differences between demand curves (and consumers' surplus) for various recreation areas might result more from differences in incomes of the users than from differences in utility. Stoevener and Brown (1967, 1968) showed how demand curves from this method could be adjusted to correct for income effects. Sinden (1974) found that income affected some recreation activities but not others. An analyst must therefore consider the kind of thing being valued and determine whether income may have a significant effect on his results or not.

Time Bias. Cesario and Knetsch (1970) suggested that there may be a consistent bias in the demand curve resulting from the assumption that the disutility of overcoming distance is solely a function of money costs. They felt that time costs were also important.

The travel-cost method assumes that it is possible to deduce from the behavior of user *B* the effect that an increase in travel cost will have on user *A*. For example, user *A* may be making four visits per year to a recreation area at an average cost of $1 per visit. User *B*, who lives farther away, may be making only two visits at a cost of $3 per visit. The method assumes that if the costs of user *A* were increased to $3, he would also make only two visits. Cesario and Knetsch agree that the number of *A*'s visits would probably decrease at the higher cost. But because *A*'s travel time would remain the same, his total costs (money + time) would not be as high as *B*'s, and the number of visits he makes might therefore not fall to the same level as *B*'s.

This problem can be overcome, at least in theory, by observing actual trade-offs between time and monetary costs. A new cost variable can then be obtained as a function of both time and money.

Individual Variation. Brown and Nawas (1973) note that the aggregation of data by zones masks individual differences in behavior. This effect is beneficial for prediction or projection of aggregates, because the coefficient of determination figures are higher and the models behave more predictably. But individual unaggregated data are preferable for investigation of the effects on behavior of variables like income or a quality characteristic.

Pearse (1968) proposed a way of avoiding aggregation into zones and the assumption that all individuals from the same zone behave the same way. He used travel-cost data to analyze the same kind of problem but without using demand curves, as follows:

(a) Subjects are divided into income groups.

(b) The marginal costs of all subjects are considered, and the highest one in each income class is noted.

(c) The consumer's surplus for each subject is calculated as the highest marginal cost in his income class minus his own marginal cost.

(d) Consumers' surplus for all subjects is totaled to give the estimate of value.

1.7. Role of the Method

The travel-cost method is usable whenever travel cost is a significant determinant of use and the assumptions listed in Section 1.1 can be accepted. The analyst must make the additional assumption that all travel costs were incurred specifically to visit the site being valued, or else he must separate out the costs that were incurred for that purpose from other costs that are not relevant to the valuation. Finally, the travel-cost method and the variant that uses distance as a proxy for price are most useful for comparisons of similar things because the estimates obtained are always minimum values.

2. THE STRUCTURED SENSITIVITY ANALYSIS

A second way of structuring the procedure is to determine a threshold datum point, and then determine net social benefits relative to this datum and do a sensitivity analysis. We illustrate this approach with a study by Krutilla and Cicchetti (1972).

2.1. Nature of the Method

Krutilla and Cicchetti set out to compare the net social benefits of two alternative uses of Hells Canyon on the border of Oregon and Idaho—construction of a dam to generate hydroelectric power or preservation of the canyon for recreation. Because adequate data were available for the development alternative, the authors could estimate the present worth of the net social benefits from constructing a dam and generating power. Data on the net benefits from preservation for recreation were more difficult to obtain.

Krutilla and Cicchetti therefore performed an extensive sensitivity analysis and made a threshold comparison that was structured as follows. If the present worth of the net social benefits from preservation (*NPWP*) is greater than that of the net social benefits from development (*NPWD*), the canyon should be preserved. Alternatively, if *NPWD* is greater than *NPWP*, the canyon should be developed. The net benefits from development thus provide a threshold for the decision. The analyst does not need a precise valuation of *NPWP*, although he does need a reliable valuation. All he has to show is the size of *NPWP* relative to the threshold.

2.2. Structural Features of the Method

The net social benefits from preservation for recreation had to be estimated. Krutilla and Cicchetti structured the problem as in the net-social-benefit model of Figure 16.3. The necessary data were "collected" by *a priori* reasoning of the following nature. The things exchanged are visits to the canyon per year. Krutilla and Cicchetti argued that the supply of a given quality of this benefit cannot be increased. The supply curve is therefore completely inelastic, and the quantity *OS* is the maximum that can be supplied in any one year, no matter what the demand is. The authors estimated *OS* in terms of the carrying capacity of the site.

Changes over time in the slope of the demand curve (*AB*) were also estimated by *a priori* reasoning. The rate of shift of each end of the curve was related to a parameter with a known rate of change. The rate of shift from *A* up the price axis in Figure 16.3 was related to the projected growth in real per-capita income. Growth rates of 4, 5, and 6 percent were considered. The rate of shift from *B* along the quantity axis was set equal to the recorded growth in visits to the site, but was dampened to equal the rate of population growth. Over time, these two rates of shift (from *A* and *B*) will produce new demand curves of changing slope and position.

By considering the alternatives to power production and to recreation at the canyon, and by using the principles of the cost-saving method of Chapter 12, user costs of visiting the site can be dropped from the model. In year 1 the net social benefit of preservation for recreation is the area *OAB*. In year *t* the net social benefit will be *OCDS*.

Only one piece of information is now missing—the position and slope of the demand curve in year 1. Krutilla and Cicchetti let the first year's net

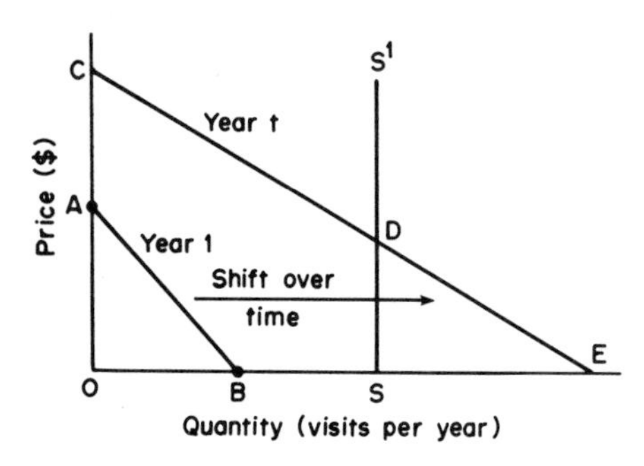

Figure 16.3. Measuring the net benefits of preservation.

benefits from preservation B_p (area OAB in Figure 16.3) be an unknown. The growth of the net social benefits over time could be calculated with the assumptions about the rates of shift of A and B and the position of the supply curve at S. If G_p is this growth rate for a specific set of assumptions, appropriate discounting procedures give the identity

$$B_p \times G_p = NPWP \tag{16.4}$$

At the threshold, $NPWP$ equals $NPWD$, by definition. This equality can be combined with Equation 16.4 to give the following equation for the threshold situation:

$$B_p \times G_p = NPWD \tag{16.5}$$

All other things being equal, society would be indifferent to a choice between preservation and development in this situation. Equation 16.5 can be rewritten for the threshold situation as

$$B_p = \frac{NPWD}{G_p} \tag{16.6}$$

Because $NPWD$ is known and a given set of assumptions provide a given figure for G_p, this equation can be solved for B_p. With realistic assumptions for G_p, the necessary value of B_p at the threshold worked out to $80,000.

The threshold comparison states that if B_p is greater than $80,000, preservation is more desirable, but if B_p is less than $80,000, development is preferable. Krutilla and Cicchetti estimated the actual value of B_p to be $900,000. This was so much larger than $80,000 that preservation for recreation was clearly the more desirable alternative.

2.3. Role of the Method

When can this method be applied to other decisions? The procedure rests on three data items: (1) a datum or threshold level, (2) estimates of changes over time in the net social benefit being valued, and (3) an estimate of net social benefit from this alternative in the initial year. These three items are related in Equation 16.6.

The suitability of this method for other similar decisions depends on the availability of these data. The method can be applied when all of the following conditions are met:

(a) There are two mutually exclusive alternatives.

(b) The net social benefit from one alternative can be valued in money.

(c) A priori reasoning or actual data are available to estimate either the growth factor or the initial year's benefits for the other alternative.

(d) Some approximation is available for the other item in condition c.

The contribution of this method, and its potential for use elsewhere, depends on a careful structuring of the threshold and the sensitivity test. The method does not provide estimates of value as such, but it may provide enough information for a decision, as in the Hells Canyon case.

3. THE OPPORTUNITY-COST PROCEDURE

The structured sensitivity analysis method of Section 2 requires some information on both of the alternatives being considered. In Krutilla and Cicchetti's comparison of preservation and power development, the net present worth of development was known and the net present worth of preservation was available within certain subjective and rather wide limits. The situation can often be that there are no data at all for one alternative. It is usually the environmental alternatives for which data are lacking. If no data are available for the value of preservation, the best an analyst can do is to make careful estimates of the value of development and present these to the policy makers. These are the opportunity costs of preservation. The reason they are considered here rather than along with the monetary opportunity costs in Chapter 12 is that the value of development is calculated as a net social benefit with full recognition of consumers' and producers' surplus. Because the features of the opportunity-cost methods have been discussed in Chapter 12, we simply present two examples here.

3.1. The Social Cost of Preserving the Great Barrier Reef

The question whether to drill the Great Barrier Reef for oil or preserve it for other uses has concerned the Queensland state and Australian federal governments for some time. To aid in an objective decision, Cochrane, Fitzgibbons, and Hendrikx (1971) prepared a benefit-cost analysis of drilling for oil. The results were estimates of the net present worth of development, which is the social opportunity cost of preservation.

Future oil prices were set equal to present prices, and the elasticity of supply of oil was estimated, with particular reference to capital availability. The critical information for this study was the future-output level, because considerable uncertainty surrounded both the rate at which drilling would locate oil and the amount of oil at each strike. The authors therefore estimated the probability of given quantities of oil at specific times and then expressed the estimates of net social benefit in terms of probabilities. There was a 5 percent chance that the capitalized value of the net social benefits from drilling would be greater than $170 million and a 5 percent chance that it would be less than $13 million. There was thus a 90 percent chance that the value from drilling would be between $13 million and $170 million. These estimates of the social opportunity costs were presented to the state and federal governments. Their problem was thus narrowed to deciding whether the net social benefits from preservation would exceed $170 million.

3.2. The Social Cost of Preserving the Cooloola Colored Sands

A large proportion of the world's titanium and paint pigment comes from the sand dunes of Australia. The dunes of the Cooloola Region in Queensland are particularly rich in rutile, zircon, and ilmenite ores. This region is also highly valued by environmentalists because it is accessible and the rainbow coloring of the sands is spectacular and rarely seen elsewhere. A policy decision whether to preserve the Cooloola sands or to mine them was needed.

Fitzgibbons and Hendrikx (1970) attempted to assess the net social benefit from mining the sands as an indicator of the social cost of preserving them. The capital and labor inputs to mining could all be valued at their social opportunity costs. The problem lay in determining the price that might be obtained for the ores. Fitzgibbons and Hendrikx were convinced that the demand for rutile and zircon was inelastic, but they could not derive a more precise estimate. They therefore performed a sensitivity analysis.

It showed that if the elasticity of demand were 1.83, the net present value from mining would be exactly zero. That is, mining would only produce positive net social benefits if demand were more elastic than 1.83. If demand were less elastic than this, the additional output would depress the price to a point where it was below the cost of production. If the elasticity were 1.0, the net present worth of mining the sands would be −$7,200,000. Because demand is thought to be inelastic (less than 1.0), the best possible outcome from mining would appear to be a social loss of $7.2 million. In this case, it was not necessary to estimate the value of preservation. The decision could be based solely on the social effects of the other alternative.

4. ADJUSTMENTS TO THE ESTIMATE OF VALUE

Throughout Chapters 15 and 16 we have implied that decisions depend entirely on changes in net social benefit. Accordingly, the methods and examples have concentrated on the measurement of changes in net social benefit. We have also implicitly assumed that perfect competition exists, that there are no externalities, and that all real costs are included in the estimates of marginal cost. An analyst may wish to adjust the net-social-benefit estimates to allow for the effects of imperfect markets. Such adjustments have been made in two ways. The net social benefit may first be estimated and then adjusted, or specific adjustments may be incorporated directly into the model as it is formulated and as the estimate is calculated.

5. DISCUSSION AND CONCLUSIONS

We noted at the beginning of Chapter 15 that although both it and Chapter 16 present methods for calculating net social benefit, they differ in the amount of information available to the analyst. For this reason, we postponed a discussion of the net-social-benefit methods until we could talk about both chapters at the same time.

There has been much controversy over the formulation and use of the consumers' and producers' surplus concepts. Currie, Murphy, and Schmitz (1971) reviewed 191 journal articles and books on this issue. They found general agreement that the net-social-benefit concept provides a useful fundamental model for analysis. However, there are several basic difficulties with the model.

Interpretations of Consumers' Surplus. There are two alternative ways of implementing the net-social-benefit model. The need to reconcile and choose between them is something of a disadvantage. The traditional Marshallian definition was the surplus to consumer and producer, as depicted in Figure 2.5 in Chapter 2. The operational procedure here rests on the derivation and use of demand and supply curves. We have discussed this procedure in these two chapters.

An alternative view was presented by Hicks (1941, 1943, 1956). It recognizes a need to ensure that the individual is on the same indifference curve before and after consumption. The operational procedure is to estimate lump-sum payments that would make the individual feel as satisfied after consumption as he was before. Practical methods for this kind of value estimate have been discussed in Chapter 14. It is possible to apply the methods of Chapter 15 to obtain this second kind of value estimate, but the demand curves must be adjusted to compensate for the lump-sum transfers. This kind of demand curve is known as an income-compensated demand curve.

Two practical implications arise from these different formulations of the basic model. First, how large and in what direction are the biases? Mohring (1965) summarizes the situation as follows. Net-social-benefit computations based on observed prices and quantities (the Marshallian approach) tend to underestimate values developed by the Hicksian approach. But the inaccuracies tend to be small if (a) the income elasticity of demand for the thing is small, (b) it makes up a small part of the individual's budget, or (c) it has close substitutes. If all these conditions are met, the two methods will provide similar values, and the difference in interpretation can be ignored. Otherwise, both interpretations must be considered.

The second practical implication concerns the precise definition of consumers' surplus. The Hicksian approach leads to various definitions among which an analyst must choose. Different definitions apply, depending on the direction of the change in consumption (increase or decrease), on whether price or quantity changes, and on whether the supply or demand curve shifts.

The definitions of consumers' surplus and net social benefit that we have used in Chapters 15 and 16 appear satisfactory for the kinds of decisions for which the valuation methods in this book are intended. Only broad social decisions that justify a high expenditure for the information seem to warrant the use of more elaborate conceptual models.

Aggregation. A further difficulty involves aggregation of information for various people. The direct aggregation of producers' and consumers' surplus into an estimate of net social benefit implicitly assumes that a monetary gain of one unit to consumers has the same weight as a one-unit gain to producers and taxpayers. Furthermore, there is an implicit assumption that gains within any of these groups are of equal weight regardless of the individuals to whom they accrue. If this assumption is false, the error can be overcome in comparisons between groups by simple adjustments to the figures. The error can also be offset by the decision maker, who can always decide that a change that shows a positive total net social benefit would still be undesirable for distribution or other reasons.

Transfers from taxpayers to either consumers or producers invoke assumptions about the marginal utility of money, especially if transfers are large. If the marginal utilities to the taxpayers and the beneficiaries are the same, net social benefit is a true measure of value. However, if marginal utility is higher or lower for the taxpayers, the net social benefit will overstate or understate the value of a program.

Are the Methods Useful? An analyst will have to answer the following procedural questions for himself in deciding whether to use the methods. If a wide range of estimates would be the best possible result, are the methods worth using? If he is unfamiliar with the methods, is it worthwhile spending the extra time and effort on them? Are these methods any better than those of the other chapters? Are the likely advantages of an improved conceptual basis and the possible advantage of a reliable monetary value greater than the disadvantage of the extra effort required?

Our experience and the application to the wildlife example suggest that these methods are no more difficult to use than those of the other chapters. The important question is how useful monetary estimates of value are likely to be. Their usefulness can be summarized in the following propositions:

(**a**) The methods can only be applied to homogeneous goods and services. For some things, like road or recreation sites, the quality of the benefit may change as more people use them.

(**b**) The use of a range of data will provide a range of estimates for net social benefit. This poses no difficulty for a decision if the net social benefit of the other alternative falls outside the limits of this range of estimates.

(**c**) The use of ranges of data can fail completely if the value of the other alternative falls within the range of estimates of net social benefit.

(**d**) Estimates of net social benefit include consumers' surplus as well as monetary profit to the producer (producers' surplus). They cannot be compared with estimates of net benefit from monetary profit alone. Monetary profit and net social benefit are different concepts of value, and comparing estimates based on the two concepts is not legitimate.

(**e**) Following from the previous point, the values from a structured approach can only be compared with other values derived from the same approach. For example, travel-cost estimates can only be compared with other travel-cost estimates.

Theory and Practice. Two questions now arise. What has been achieved by the extensive theoretical discussion in the literature, and how do the theoretical problems affect practical application? Theoretical soundness and precision are desirable goals in themselves, and a practitioner certainly needs to be aware of these debates. But many authors have recognized that their contributions have little practical relevance. At an early stage in the debate Mishan (1947–48) wrote "Since the rehabilitation of consumers' surplus by Professor Hicks, several attempts have appeared to establish the most appropriate money measures of this concept, attempts accompanied by apologies for introducing into the concept refinements which are apparently of little practical significance."

It seems to have been easy to raise theoretical objections about the concepts of consumers' and producers' surplus. But these have not damaged the general usefulness of the concepts in providing an appropriate framework for analyzing and describing the effects of decisions, and for determining the direction and magnitude of social benefits. Applications can never be precise, because some assumptions will always be violated and because data and estimating techniques will always be imperfect. But the concept and methods do give estimates of value that are useful for policy. As Tintner and Patel (1966) say, the concept of net social benefits provides a better idea about the utility and value aspects of policies than any other proposed concept.

CHAPTER 17

Estimation of Social Values

The preceding chapters in Part II dealt primarily with individual values and with situations in which social value is equal to the sum of individual values. However, social value cannot always be estimated so simply. There are situations in which (a) separate group values exist in addition to individual values, (b) all individual values do not have the same weight in determining social value, and (c) effects on the group are not fully recognized by individual members. This chapter considers how to estimate social value in such situations.

1. THE FORMATION AND ANALYSIS OF SOCIAL VALUES

Comparative social values must be based on the differences things would make to the life of a group of people. "Life of the group" may be interpreted in various ways, as shown in Table 17.1.

Any group that is more than just a temporary assembly of people has a group life distinguishable from the individual lives of its members. This group life is reflected in utilities like national pride and family honor. A family may protect its name at considerable personal cost to individual members. Although people might not remain in such groups if they felt they received no personal benefit, these kinds of group values are not aggregates of individual values. They are values that accrue to the group as a whole, and they are produced by individuals acting for the good of the group. Situation 1 in Table 17.1 involves only this kind of social value.

A second kind of situation involves combinations of individual and group values (situation 2 in Table 17.1). The social value of disease control, for example, is more than individual lives saved and individual suffering reduced. It includes survival of a strong and vital race or nation, and health programs are often supported on this ground alone. To analyze decisions in such situations, an analyst must estimate and combine both individual and group values.

Table 17.1. Formation and Analysis of Social Values

Situation	Makeup of Social Values	Method for Estimating Social Value
1.	Only group values, no purely individual benefits and costs	Estimate group value as seen by the group as a whole (group valuation of group things)
2.	Both group and individual values exist and are included in social value	Estimate and add group and individual values
3.	No separate group values. All benefits and costs are fully recognized by individuals. Social value is the sum of individual values with appropriate weighting	Estimate both weights and individual values to derive a weighted aggregate value
4.	No separate group values, but benefits and costs are not full recognized by individuals (e.g., external effects; future benefits)	Estimate all benefits and costs, including those which individuals do not recognize (group valuation of individual things)

In other situations there is no separate group value. The people who happen to be riding in the same bus form an assemblage of individuals that has no group life of its own. In summer, an air-conditioning unit has value to these people, but the social value consists entirely of individual values. There is no group value of the kind described in the preceding paragraphs, and the analyst's task is simply to aggregate individual values in the appropriate way (situation 3).

A fourth situation involves only individual values, but these are not fully recognized by members of the group (situation 4). Two examples are external effects and streams of benefits and costs over time. In both cases, society usually recognizes all costs and benefits, but individuals usually do not. What appears to be a group value really consists of unrecognized individual values. Consider, for example, a coal-fired power plant that produces both electricity and smoke. The money costs of power generation are recognized, but the external costs of air pollution are often ignored. Social value must be an aggregate of the value to the power company and the disutilities to those affected by the smoke.

Benefit-cost analyses are social in nature and should recognize all four situations in Table 17.1. But they often have concentrated on the fourth situation, in which true social values are not fully recognized by individuals or the existing market. We have differentiated the four situations of Figure 17.1 in an effort to provide a more comprehensive analytical framework.

1.1. Some Necessary Subjective Judgments

Estimation of group and social values involves some difficulties that do not arise in individual decisions or when all individuals are treated equally. There is the relatively-straightforward question of which values are to be included, and the less-straightforward questions of how the group decision is to be made and who is to make it. The latter questions concern the judgments implicit in all group decisions. The subjective nature of these judgments must be accepted by the analyst. His task is to make them explicit.

1.1.1. Which Values Should Be Included? Discussions of environmental policy raise questions about including the preferences of future generations and benefits to people who never use a resource but care about its preservation. The answer is simple: A decision made on behalf of society must include all values.

The most important distinction for valuation is between group values and individual values. Three kinds of values must be included: group values for group things, individual values for individual things, and group values for individual things. In some situations the group value of a thing will differ from its individual value. The main examples are external effects and values to future generations. Whenever the group and individual values differ, the group value must be chosen. We can set this out as follows:

$$\text{social value} = f(\text{group values of group things, group value of individual things}) \qquad (17.1)$$

The f indicates that it may not be possible to add the two groups values directly. We explore this aggregation problem as the chapter proceeds.

The problem in estimating group values is to obtain estimates from people who are acting in pursuit of social objectives rather than personal ones. Methods from the preceding chapters may be used with a group setting for the questions and analysis.

Chapter 4 showed that different groups may have different goals, moral attitudes, and characteristics. The analytical methods must be consistent with these, because different groups will place different values on the same things. The same kind of value data will be collected for each group, but they may be treated differently. The difference in treatment mainly concerns whose values are recognized and how they are combined.

1.1.2. How Are Values Combined? Once data on group and individual values have been estimated, they must be combined into social value. The aggregation is a subjective group decision, which the analyst must accept (although he may try to influence it). This is something of a mixed blessing for valuation. On the one hand, it may simplify data collection, because the analyst can ask the decision makers for the necessary judgments. On the other hand, these judgments are sometimes conflicting and often inadequate, and the analyst may need to spend much time clarifying them.

The subjective judgments about aggregating values may involve weighting. Equation 17.1 can be rewritten as

$$\text{social value} = [(WT_1 \times \text{group value of group things}) + (WT_2 \times \text{group value of individual things})] \quad (17.2)$$

Decision-making procedures may range from a referendum, in which each person's value is treated equally, to a dictatorship. The analyst needs to obtain information about the procedures and weights, but he should accept the judgments involved and make his analysis consistent with them.

1.1.3. Whose Values Should Be Included? Effective decision makers may be everyone in the group, a panel of experts, elected representatives, elected leaders, or a dictator. The analyst must try to identify the actual decision maker and apply the methods to him. We leave this important and difficult task of identification to others and concentrate on valuation.

1.2. Objects and Scope of this Chapter

The overall object of this chapter is to examine the special difficulties of social decisions and some of the methods that can help with them. We have set out the four situations in which social values can form in Table 17.1. Now we consider the new data that are needed for group decisions, as shown in Figure 17.1. The chapter concentrates on methods for estimating the data required.

This chapter does not attempt to examine the conceptual foundations of group or social organization. These have been the subject of other books, such as those by Buchanan and Tullock (1962) on the economics of decision making and by Haefele (1973) on environmental management. We seek only to review and set in context the methods by which social values can be assessed.

2. ADAPTING STANDARD ECONOMIC PRINCIPLES

Social valuations differ from individual valuations in their recognition of group values of group things, group valuations of individual things, and the aggregation of individual and group values. Our task in this chapter is to

New Data required[a]	(1)	Group values for group things
	(2)	Group values for individual things—true values for: (i) Things recognized by individuals (ii) Things not recognized by individuals
	(3)	Relevant aggregation procedures (i) Weights for individual values (ii) Knowledge of group's decision procedure
Methods	(1)	Adapting standard economic principles (i) To elicit group data on values and weights (ii) Relating aggregation procedures to group characteristics (Section 2)
	(2)	Forming a group consensus on a data item (Section 3)
	(3)	Analysis of past decisions for value and weight data (Section 4)
	(4)	Analysis of past behaviour (Section 5)
Estimate comparative values	(1)	By aggregation with weights (Section 6)
	(2)	With other kinds of values (Section 7)

[a] In addition to individual values for individual things collected with the methods of Chapters 9 to 16.

Figure 17.1. Data and methods for group valuation and decision.

apply the economic principles of Chapter 2 to the estimation of group values. We must consider the utilities and disutilities that are involved, the things that are exchanged to generate these utilities, and the participants in the exchange.

Group survival and cohesiveness are benefits that accrue to a group as a whole. National pride, prestige, and heritage are utilities that accrue to national groups. Such benefits are generated in the normal way by using resources to satisfy wants. Their special feature is that the wants are those of the group as a whole. The new task is to obtain access to the group leaders to find out how benefits and costs are aggregated into group values.

2.1. Obtaining Values for Group Benefits from Leaders

Group wants are satisfied by the same kind of exchanges as individual wants. All groups possess limited resources and have relatively unlimited wants. Exchanges take place to convert the resources into things that satisfy wants. They follow the principle of utility maximization, but it is group utility that is maximized and the decisions are made by group leaders. The requirements for estimation are:

(a) Units of the things being valued must be identified clearly enough to measure the current production (Q_1) and the quantity that would result after the decision (Q_2). This will define the increase in output ($Q_2 - Q_1$) in Figure 17.2.

(b) The group leader(s) must provide an estimate of the social benefit from the increase in output. This increase in total utility is shown by the shaded area in Figure 17.2. Any of the methods in Chapters 9 to 16 can be used. The only requirement is that the leader must state his estimate of the utility to the group and not to himself. This is illustrated in Figure 17.2 by two demand curves for the same individual, one for the benefits to himself

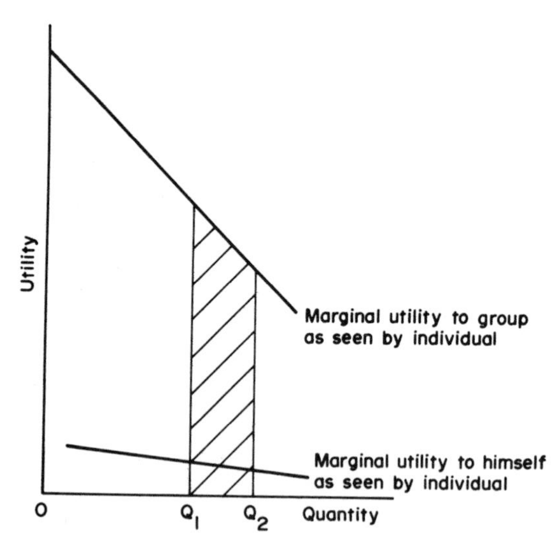

Figure 17.2. Adaptation of the standard benefit model to measure group benefits.

and the other for benefits to the group. The individual benefits are much smaller than the social benefits in this case.

(c) The costs and benefits must be brought together. This may require the estimation of utility in money or a structured comparative assessment such as we outlined in Chapter 6 and discuss more comprehensively in Chapter 18.

2.1.1. An Example: Value of Group Image. A simple example shows how the basic economic principles can be adapted to estimate group value. Let us assume that the image of a town is directly dependent on the appearance of its public buildings. (We also make the reasonable assumption that appearance and efficiency in use are quite unrelated.) The current program of building restoration allows for Q_1 buildings to be restored, cleaned, and painted each year. The town council has before it a proposal to increase the restoration program to Q_2 buildings next year.

Each group leader must be asked to consider the improvement in the town's image that would result from restoring the extra $(Q_2 - Q_1)$ buildings. This is the group benefit. There may be some benefits to individual citizens, but the leaders are asked to consider only the group benefits. The council's task is to allocate its current budget among competing uses this year or to consider an increase in taxes for restoration next year. The benefit from the improved image must be compared with the benefits from other ways of spending the current budget, or it must be compared with the dissatisfaction that would result from increased taxes. In either case a decision will be reached without a direct money valuation of the improvement in image.

2.1.2. Difficulties in Applying Economic Principles. The success of this procedure rests on the ability of leaders to answer questions from the viewpoint of society as a whole. They must distinguish group benefits from individual benefits and estimate the utility of extra output to the group and not to themselves.

A related difficulty is obtaining access to leaders of the group. This may require simulation of the leader's role by other, more-accessible members of the group. Keeney (1973) apparently gained access to heads of government departments in Mexico City to assess the net benefits of a new airport, using some methods from Chapter 11.

If data are obtained from various individuals, it may be necessary to reconcile differences. This is the consensus problem that is considered in Section 3.

2.2. Relationship between Group Characteristics and Aggregation Rules

Whenever two or more individuals are involved in making one decision, the nature and structure of the group will affect the decision. The most important structural feature is the procedure through which separate values are aggregated into a group value.

We suggested that newly formed, voluntary, and specific purpose groups are likely to have goals and attitudes close to individual goals and attitudes. By contrast, older, compulsory, and general groups may have group goals and attitudes that differ widely from individual ones. The characteristics of various groups can cause differences in final aggregate group values because they lead to slightly different aggregation rules. The aggregation rules range from majority rule with equal weights for all individual members to dictatorial rule with only one person's weights considered. We have considered ways to elicit weights in Chapter 8 and 11 and consider the effects of weighting in detail later in this chapter.

3. FORMING A CONSENSUS

In any group decision there will be differences of opinion that imply differences in individual assessments of value. How can such differences in value data be resolved? One way would be for a major decision maker to combine the data himself. Another way is to use some weighting procedure. We discuss the implications of such procedures in Section 5. A further possibility is to get individuals together to form a consensus among themselves. Three procedures for doing this are discussed here. They are not valuation methods as such, but procedures for reducing differences in data obtained with the methods of Chapters 10 through 16. These procedures all involve reassessments through feedback or through higher-order subjects.

3.1. Reassessment by the Same Individuals

Turban and Metersky (1971) applied a rating method to weight different objectives in the choice of a defense system. Although they carefully selected well-qualified experts as subjects, they noted large differences in the weights obtained. They adopted the following procedure to overcome this:

(a) Each subject first made his own independent estimate of the utilities.

(b) A statistical test was made of the differences between estimates. If the differences were not significant, the individual estimates were accepted and averaged. If they were significant, the following further steps were taken.

(**c**) The overall results of the test were sent back to each subject, who was asked to reassess his own response.

(**d**) If the differences remained large, the subjects were brought together. The utility data were displayed, promoted by their advocates, and discussed. The subjects were then asked to provide another set of utility data in the hope that more consistent scores would result.

An anonymous feedback or reassessment procedure (Section 3.3) may be used to supplement this approach. Steps a to d may be suitable for modest differences of judgment, and anonymous feedback may be added for cases of considerable disagreement. The anonymous procedure may be appropriate for cases of opinion, and open discussions more suitable for cases of technical facts.

3.2. Reassessment by Higher-Order Individuals

In his study of decision making in the National Aeronautics and Space Administration, Edwards (1972) confronted the consensus problem. These decisions required an estimate of weights for various objectives similar to the weights derived in the pollution-control example of Chapter 11. Once a set of weights has been obtained from each subject, Edwards' procedure is as follows:

(**a**) The subjects are brought together to argue. One subject may have special information to offer, another may understand the problem better, and a third may be more persuasive. In the discussion some or all of the disagreement may disappear.

(**b**) If this face-to-face discussion does not resolve the disagreements, several sets of data are used to analyze all alternatives. This sensitivity analysis should highlight specific areas of disagreement. It might show that the points of the disagreement have no effect on the outcome of the choice. If so, the problem is solved; if not, the analyst must proceed further.

(**c**) At this stage, the best approach is to appoint a higher-order group of subjects. They are usually the immediate superiors of the first group. Step a and perhaps step b are repeated. The higher-order experts may have extra information or may be able to take executive decisions that lead to agreement.

(**d**) If the higher-order experts cannot resolve the disagreement, a final step is to replace them with elected political representatives or with members of the board of directors in a private firm. This final set of persons will ultimately have to resolve the disagreement anyway. Incorporating them in the analysis may make explicit the utilities and disutilities on which the decision will finally be based.

3.3. Anonymous Reassessments by the Same Individuals—the Delphi Method

The Delphi method originated through the work of Dalkey and Helmer (1963) at the Rand Corporation. The general procedure is to ask each person in a group for data, and then through successive rounds of feedback to encourage them to revise their data toward a group mean. Direct face-to-face confrontations are deliberately avoided through the use of mail questionnaires.

The successive rounds are as follows: (1) Data from all individual subjects are collected and summarized. The results are charted with displays of the means and the lowest and highest quartiles. (2) These results are sent back to each subject. Those with data in the extreme quartiles (or more generally with data widely different from the means) are asked to explain their estimates and to revise them if they wish. (3) The new results are again sent to the subjects and they are again invited to explain and revise. Further rounds may be undertaken until a reasonable consensus has been obtained or the possibility of consensus has been ruled out.

Although the method was developed primarily for the purpose of forecasting, it can be applied in a number of ways. Pill (1971) says ". . . the Delphi technique is a method of combining the knowledge and abilities of a diverse group of experts to the task of quantifying variables which are either intangible or shrouded in uncertainty . . ."

The Delphi method embodies the best characteristic of committee decisions—the availability of opinions and reasoning to all—but avoids the social compromises that inevitably occur in committee decisions. It also allows experts to consult with colleagues outside the panel of experts. However, the method has weaknesses that are common to other methods of group decision. Some expert's views are bound to be more reliable in certain areas than those of others. The solution to this problem is to weight the responses, as we see in Section 5.

4. ANALYSES OF PAST DECISIONS

The basic philosophy of this book is that values are estimated in order to make decisions. If we state this in reverse, past decisions should imply relative values. Such reverse reasoning is the justification for the case-history method of teaching (Smith, 1954).

4.1. A Potential Source of Value Data

A simple example may help illustrate the general idea. Over the years, the Dutch government has invested in land reclamation on a relatively large scale. This has consisted of constructing dikes and draining the low lying areas of land. The Dutch Agricultural Investment Commission (1960) assessed the profitability of a representative reclamation project, Eastern Flevoland in the Zuider Zee.

The investment was analyzed from the viewpoints of a private investment and a social investment for the nation as a whole. In the latter analysis, the net social benefits were calculated for the priced benefits and costs. These were expressed as percentage rates of return by dividing the average annual net benefit by the total social capital invested. On this basis the Eastern Flevoland project returned 1.6 percent at 1955 prices but had to meet capital repayments of 3.5 percent. The project was therefore not profitable in monetary terms. For it to have broken even, there must have been unpriced benefits that raised the rate of return by 1.9 percent.

These unpriced benefits included more space for housing, more recreation facilities, improvement in traffic flows, stimulation to science, and an increase in food supplies. The value of these unpriced benefits can be estimated as follows. If investment in reclamation continues in full knowledge of the monetary returns, the unpriced benefits must be worth at least as much as the financial deficit. In the Eastern Flevoland, these benefits must have a minimum value of 268 guilders per hectare per year, because that would raise the annual return on capital to the 3.5 percent required for the project to break even.

4.2. A General Systematic Approach

A general approach to the analysis of decisions was proposed by Weisbrod (1968). He was attempting to improve future government decisions by clarifying the impacts of past decisions, with particular reference to distribution of income and economic efficiency. Weisbrod's general philosophy was that analysis of past decisions can, at worst, provide some insight on the relative values actually ascribed to different things. At best, it can provide useful information or specific values to assist and guide future decisions in the same policy area.

Weisbrod started from the observation that in the past some projects with low benefit-cost ratios had been undertaken in preference to others with higher ratios. This ratio is a conventional measure of economic efficiency. He then analyzed past decisions to determine the relative values or weights ascribed to given benefits when they accrued to different groups. (He defined groups by income, age, race, and location.) For example, $1 of benefits to high-income whites might have had a "social or group value" of only one-fifth as much as $1 to low-income blacks. In this example the weights must reflect the marginal utilities of income to each kind of person as perceived by the politicians, who presumably were acting for the group as a whole. Such a set of weights can indicate the marginal utility of a thing to different kinds of people.

4.2.1. Procedure. The steps in Weisbrod's procedure are:

(**a**) The characteristics (K_i) of interest are identified for each project (j). These characteristics are symbolized by K_{ij}. In Weisbrod's example the characteristics are the benefits to different groups in society. In other analyses the data would relate to other characteristics, such as features of trees and woodland.

(**b**) Some measure of the relative preference for projects is obtained. These preference data must reflect the overall value of the project as perceived by the decision makers. If it is believed that the benefit-cost ratio reflects these preferences, the ratio itself can be used. If projects are undertaken in an order of preference, the order number (1, 2, . . ., n) can be used. In a subsequent example, monetary costs of preservation will be used for this measure of value. Weisbrod discusses various ways of deducing these preference data and of adapting benefit-cost ratios to show such preferences. These value data can be symbolized by V_j.

(**c**) The basic relationships can now be established. Weisbrod makes the general hypothesis that the total value of project j is a function of its particular characteristics

$$V_j = f(K_{ij}) \tag{17.3}$$

(**d**) A statistical model is now selected for deriving an empirical estimate of Equation 17.3. Weisbrod selected the simple model

$$V_j = a + b_1K_{1j} + b_2K_{2j} + \cdots + b_nK_{nj} \tag{17.4}$$

(**e**) The data are inserted into the selected model, and it is solved to give the coefficients (b_i). These coefficients are the required information on the contributions to value of the various characteristics.

4.2.2. Discussion. Weisbrod acknowledged the difficulties in obtaining and interpreting some data items. Despite these difficulties, Weisbrod promoted this approach as a means of discovering the relative values that a group has placed on given things. The results can (a) help make explicit the informal and implicit valuations in past decisions, (b) assist with future decisions by providing weights for aggregating individual values, and (c) test for differences between group values and the aggregate of individual values.

4.3. To Derive Equity Weights

An empirical attempt to discover the equity weights that were implied in group decisions at the national level is reported by Haveman (1965). His approach followed the same general procedure as Weisbrod's. He wished to analyze public investments in water resources in terms of their contribution to two objectives—economic efficiency (national income) and equity (the distribution of income). The weights obtained express the value of gains and losses in terms of utility rather than money. Because the same benefit may be valued differently by a group if it accrues to different persons, a benefit-cost criterion may be met in these utility terms, even though it is not met in monetary totals.

Haveman proposed the following philosophy. Personal income-tax rates are structured on the principle of equimarginal sacrifices. An estimate of the marginal utility of an extra dollar to a person in a given income class can therefore be derived from the tax schedules that have been approved by the legislature. A set of weights to reflect the relative marginal utilities can then be calculated.

These weights can be used in an analysis. The criterion of economic efficiency can be formulated in terms of the standard benefit-cost ratio. The effect of each alternative project on income distribution can then be measured in terms of an "empirical gauge." This gauge, in Haveman's study, was the weights that directly reflect the diminishing marginal utility of money as perceived by the group.

4.3.1. Procedure. We illustrate the procedure with the data from Haveman's 1965 study shown in Table 17.2. Although these income figures are out of date, they will serve for illustrative purposes. The procedure is as follows:

(**a**) The basic data are assembled. The marginal tax rate for each income class is shown in column 2 of Table 17.2 and the percentage of the marginal dollar that may be retained is shown in column 3.

(**b**) A base income level is selected. It is convenient to set this at the average annual income, which is $3000 in our example. This becomes the standard against which to judge the marginal utility to individuals of other incomes.

(**c**) The weights are calculated by dividing the percentage of the marginal dollar retained by each income group (column 3) by the percentage retained

Table 17.2. Derivation of Equity Weights to Show the Relative Utility of a Marginal Dollar to Various Income Groups

Adjusted Gross Income ($)	Marginal Tax Rate (%)	Marginal Dollar Retained (%)	Equity Weights
1	2	3	4
600	0	100	1.11
1,000	5	95	1.06
3,000	10	90	1.00
10,000	20	80	0.89
25,000	30	70	0.78
38,000	40	60	0.67
100,000	50	50	0.56

Source. The figures in columns 1 and 2 were read from Figure 4 in Haveman (1965).

at the base income level (90). The results in column 4 are the desired weights.

4.3.2. Application. Water-resource projects were examined by Haveman for which the monetary benefits and costs had already been defined and compared by benefit-cost ratios. He identified the actual beneficiaries and losers and their current income levels. The benefits and costs were then multiplied by the appropriate weights to adjust for differences in the marginal utility of income to these people.

For example, a benefit of $100,000 that all accrued to people in the lowest income class was multiplied by a weight of 1.11 to give an adjusted benefit of $111,000. Similarly, a cost of $50,000 would be multipled by 0.78 if the funds were all obtained from taxes paid by people with incomes of $25,000 per year. The adjusted cost would be $39,000. The unadjusted benefit-cost ratio would have been 100,000/50,000, or 2.0. The weighting changes it to 111,000/39,000 or 2.85. This reflects the fact that the benefits accrue to people with lower-than-average incomes and the costs are borne by people with higher-than-average incomes.

4.3.3. Discussion. Throughout his analysis, Haveman was conscious of the problems of analyzing group decisions. Although the analysis appeared straightforward, he noted that in reality it was "problematic." With regard to the consistency of values over time he said ". . . there is no single policy-maker who is both rational and consistent, but rather a transient group of policy-makers, who, acting as a group, are neither rational nor consistent, [thus] any attempt to secure an estimate of their evaluation must rest on evidence which is largely inadequate . . ." Nevertheless, Haveman noted that there was substantial evidence to show that Congress does place different values on income flows to persons of different incomes.

4.4. To Derive Weights for Characteristics

The two previous examples involved the derivation of weights, or relative values, for monetary benefits to particular groups. Weights may also be needed to assess and help aggregate characteristics of the environment. In this section we consider two forestry examples that attempt to derive the weights groups have assigned to different characteristics. The first is an analysis of local government actions and the second an analysis of court decisions. In both cases the analysts follow Weisbrod's general approach to derive the contribution of each relevant characteristic to the total value given in the decision.

4.4.1. From Decisions by Local Government. The relative values that a group places on characteristics can sometimes be determined from a number of group decisions. If specific values and patterns can be discovered, they can be generalized for use in future planning. Helliwell (1967) used this approach to derive the values implied by certain groups in decisions to preserve trees and woodlands. These groups were county councils and other local government bodies that had incurred extra costs to preserve trees and woodlands instead of clearing them for development. Helliwell's procedure was as follows:

(a) Data were collected on the extra costs (Y) and on the characteristics (K_n) of each tree or woodland. In the study on individual trees, seven characteristics were observed: crown area, life expectancy, importance of position in landscape, presence of other trees, form, species, and special or historical value.

(b) The numerical measurement of each characteristic (K_n) was converted to a utility score (X_n), which ranged from 1 to 4. Specific relationships were postulated, with an assumption of diminishing marginal utility, to convert measurements of the characteristics to utilities. The conversion for the characteristics crown area and life expectancy are shown in Figure 17.3.

(c) The scores (X_n) for the characteristics were aggregated in a multiplicative model

$$\text{aggregate score} = (X_1 \times X_2 \times X_3 \times X_4 \times X_5 \times X_6 \times X_7) \quad (17.5)$$

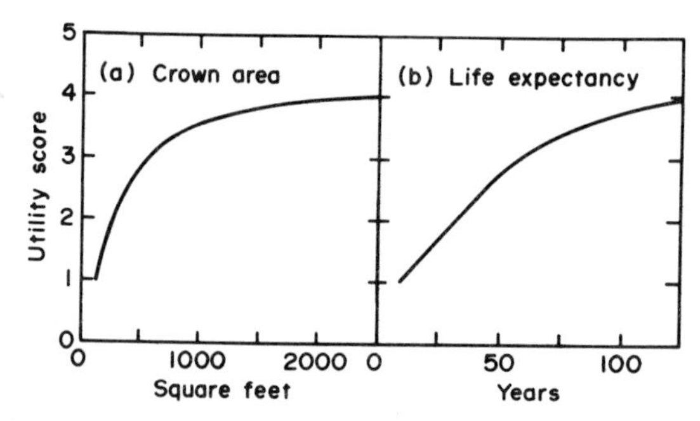

Figure 17.3. Conversion of physical characteristics of trees to utility scores. (a) Crown area. (b) Life expectancy.

(**d**) The final step was to convert these aggregate scores to monetary values. By observation and the use of regression methods, Helliwell derived a value of £0.2 per score unit of 1, giving

$$Y = 0.2 \text{ (aggregate score)} \tag{17.6}$$

The full valuation model can be expressed as

$$Y = 0.2\,(X_1 \times X_2 \times X_3 \times X_4 \times X_5 \times X_6 \times X_7) \tag{17.7}$$

where Y is a monetary value in pounds and X_n are the scores for each observable physical characteristic.

Helliwell's reasoning is "the price which a local authority is prepared to pay to prevent the felling of trees and woodlands should . . . be an indication of the value placed on these by the community at large." The "price" is the extra cost that the trees impose.

4.4.2. From Decisions by Courts. The problem of valuation of individual trees occasionally comes before the courts. Kielbaso (1971) found that through time and many appealed cases, two principles have emerged. Most monetary values are based on the difference in property value with and without the tree. In some cases, valuation is based on the cost of replacement with a resonable substitute tree.

Peters (1971) made a systematic analysis of legal decisions to find a pattern in past valuations that would improve future valuations. Data from 24 decisions were systematized into a simple explanatory model. The procedure was to relate property values to the characteristics of each tree. The final model contained three independent variables: size, species, and condition of the tree:

$$\text{value of tree} = f(\text{size, species, condition}) \tag{17.8}$$

Size was defined as the cross-sectional area of the tree at 4.5 feet above ground. The species variable was defined as a percentage. Various species were allocated relative percentages on the basis of previous court valuations. In Table 17.3 live oak is set at 100 percent and black willow is allocated 20 percent. The condition variable was also defined as a percentage. Items such as location, age, and disease affected the assessment of condition. Equation 17.8 was then implemented by introducing a monetary value. In this example, a value of \$9 was introduced as follows:

$$\text{value of tree} = \$9 \times (\text{size variable} \times \text{species variable} \times \text{condition variable}) \tag{17.9}$$

On this basis the live oak is valued at \$1590 and the black willow at \$64. The multiplier value of \$9 refers to urban residential areas. A multiplier of \$3 to \$5 was suggested for rural residential areas. The final monetary values will vary with both place and time. Peters' example illustrates an explicit and apparently successful attempt to analyze a series of legal decisions and to derive the pattern of implied values.

References in the literature to attempts at deriving patterns from past legal decisions are rare. Walters (1975) reports that compensation awards for aircraft noise have been assessed at the change in market value of properties. Waddell (1974) reports on a study by Havighurst (1969) of air pollution in the Philadelphia region. The study examined all litigation that might help place values on the damages of air pollution. Only a few such court cases were discovered, and the number was too small to allow a systematic analysis.

4.5. Discussion

The difficulties in deriving relative values from past decisions can be summarized as follows:

Table 17.3. Valuation of Two Shade Trees

Species	Size Variable (square inches)	Species Variable (%)	Condition Variable (%)	Product[a]	Value[b] ($)
1	2	3	4	5	6
Live oak	176.7	100	100	176.7	1590
Black willow	176.7	20	20	7.1	64

Source. Peters (1971).
[a] (Column 2 × column 3 × column 4)/10,000.
[b] Column 5 × \$9.

(**a**) The analysis inevitably assumes that the decisions were made in full knowledge of the consequences or characteristics analyzed. This is not likely to be true, but the analysis imputes the full values to these characteristics. Because administrative decisions are based on all sorts of considerations, the residuals must contain these elements as well as those inferred in the analysis. And an element of randomness may be involved in any group decision.

(**b**) The decisions usually provide average values for existing things. But because the future is concerned with marginal changes and additional output, it is marginal values that are needed.

(**c**) The method assumes that the decision makers made all their decisions in a rational manner.

Past decisions always imply comparative valuations. There may be complaints that too much is spent on computers and too little on salaries. This suggests that the utility from the last dollar spent on hardware is too low and that from the last dollar spent on personnel too high. Trade-off data are clearly indicated, but deriving implications is difficult.

Decisions by different agencies may give different values. The cause of unpricedness is the lack of a market in which all agencies can adjust their activities to give the same values. If all life-saving policies were adjusted until the cost of saving the marginal life was the same in all policies, it might be possible to save more lives for the same budget.

Because of difficulties in analyzing past decisions, we may question whether the effort is worthwhile. Haveman (1968), in discussing Weisbrod's attempt to derive weights, concluded ". . . Although the problems are conceptually difficult and empirically sticky . . . the expected social returns from improved analysis surely justify the expenditure of substantial efforts in this area. . . ." The apparent success of some of the examples we have discussed in this section leads us to similar conclusions.

5. ANALYSES OF PAST BEHAVIOR

Past behavior implies decisions, and these in turn imply comparative valuations. Comparisons of such behavior should therefore provide information on values. Behavior can be observed in the forms of quantities consumed or the levels of characteristics chosen. If all other things are equal, larger quantities and more-favorable levels indicate higher values. The ways of implementing these comparative valuations are shown in Figure 17.4. Behavior may be observed for the same thing at different times or for similar things at a given time. Or the observed quantity may be compared with some subjective norm. We review these methods before discussing their assumptions and applications.

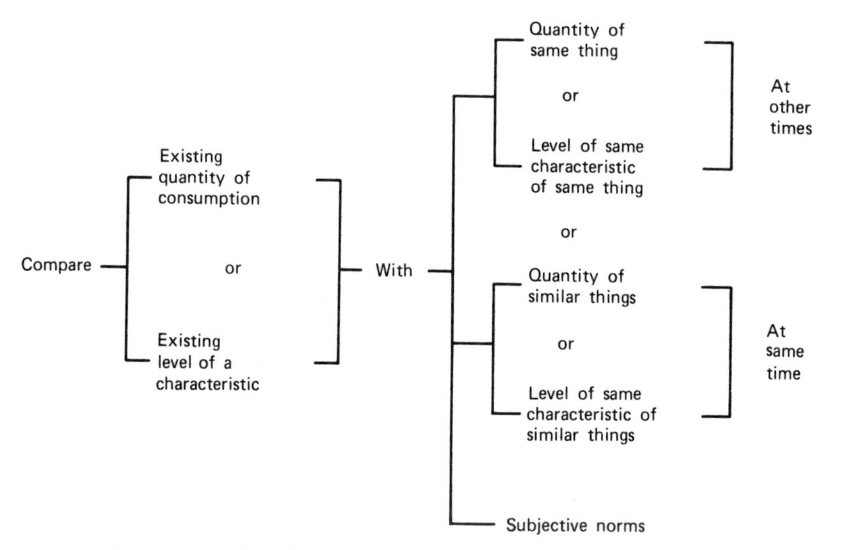

Figure 17.4. Possible comparisons in analyses of past behavior.

5.1. Based on Observed Quantities

Comparisons with Same Thing at Other Times. Trends over time are common indices of success and a basis for decisions. Doolittle, Kootsher, and Mercer (1975) measured effectiveness of fire prevention as the ratio of the number of fires in 1971–1972 to the number that had occurred in 1968–1969. These ratios were calculated for various regions and related to the characteristics of the regions and their personnel.

Comparison with Similar Things. Comparisons with the consumption of similar things can form a basis for estimates of relative benefit. Quantities of consumption were used as a benefit measure in recreation analyses by Lime (1971) and Cordell and James (1972). Coomber and Biswas (1973) call these indices "attractivity models." Cesario (1969) used the method to compare the attractiveness of parks. At any given distance from population centers, the parks with more users must be more attractive and therefore have higher comparative values.

Comparison with a Subjective Norm. Consumers or decision makers can provide the subjective norms with which to compare the quantities consumed. Brewer and Gillespie (1967) counted the numbers of recreationists in different activities and asked them to name their preferred activities. Their "satisfaction index" was the ratio between the number of people who named an activity as preferred and the number who engaged in it.

The system of merit-weighted user days, which is described in Section 6.2.2, obtains the subjective norm from decision makers. The desirable quantity of use is a subjective estimate based on population density, alternative opportunities, access, and income. The merit weight is the ratio of desirable quantities to actual quantities of use.

5.2. Based on Observed Levels of Characteristics

Because it is the characteristics of things that provide utility, they are a logical basis for a comparative value index. The methods of Chapter 9 aggregated and compared data on various characteristics. We now consider a simpler version of the same concept here.

Wennergren (1968) suggested that the surface area of a water body and its distance from home are the important characteristics for water-based recreation. The utility of a site can be assumed to increase with area and to decrease with distance. An index of comparative benefit can be calculated by dividing the area/distance of a particular site by the sum of the area/distance for all sites.

5.3. Discussion

These methods rest on the assumption that all units of consumption, or all unit changes in a characterisitc level, provide the same net benefit. This assumption ignores diminishing marginal utility and increasing marginal cost. A related implication concerns interpersonal comparisons. Do four units consumed by one person provide the same total utility as one unit each consumed by four persons? This assumption and the implications are hard to accept.

The simple indexes that compare quantities also ignore costs. But since Wennergren's (1968) more complex index has terms for area and distance, the distance could serve as a proxy for cost and thus incorporate it into the comparative value.

The above problems restrict these methods to comparisons between alternatives with similar quantities, given populations, and constant costs. Within these restrictions, the built-in validation of observed data makes these methods useful.

6. WEIGHTING THE COMPONENTS OF SOCIAL VALUE

Social value is a composite of value to individual members and group value to society. When it consists entirely of individual values, the analyst's problem is to find an appropriate way to weight and aggregate these values. Section 4 considered the derivation of weights from past decisions. In this section we consider some other ways to derive weights and the social bases for selecting weights.

6.1. An Example: Choice between a Reservoir and a Natural River

The decision to construct a reservoir on a natural free-flowing river will depend in part on the values of the various uses of the reservoir compared to those of the river. One objective of a study of the South Santiam River in Oregon (Sinden, 1973; Pendse and Wyckoff, 1974b), was to obtain the relative values of different landscapes. A further objective was to incorporate these values into estimates of the net social benefits from different kinds of recreation in the two water environments.

6.1.1. The Basic Data. Data were collected from household groups on their socioeconomic characteristics and their relative valuations of different landscapes. The value data were in the form of responses to landscape drawings representing five water-resource environments, as described in Section 1.1 of Chapter 10. The full procedure is described in Sinden (1973). Each household head was asked the following question: "Assume that you can engage in the same recreation activities at each of the five sites shown in the drawings. Consider now your choice of a recreation site for next weekend. How much extra time would you be willing to travel to reach site *B* rather than to stay at *A*?" This question was repeated for the other three sites.

The responses were a measure of the value of the four other sites relative to that of site *A*. For illustration, we use only the data on campers and sites *B* and *C*, which were a lake in a natural setting and the natural free-flowing river. The decision criterion is:

$$\text{total value of site}_i = \Sigma V_{ij} \qquad (17.10)$$

where V_{ij} is the value of site i to household j. If weights are involved, the criterion can be rewritten as

$$\text{total value of site}_i = \Sigma(V_{ij} WT_j) \qquad (17.11)$$

where WT_j is the weight assigned to household j.

6.1.2. Using Equal Weights. When no group values exist, the simplest procedure is to add the individual values. Suppose we wish to compare the social values of a park on the natural river and one on the reservoir. Let us assume that admission fees are charged at both parks. Because the people who use these parks must feel the value obtained is at least as great as the admission fee, the social values of the parks can be estimated by adding all the admission fees paid during a season. The park with the greatest total receipts should have the greatest social value.

If the admission fees were the same, the total numbers of visitors alone would indicate the comparative social values. If no admission fees were charged, the total numbers of visitors would still indicate comparative values. But the indicator would be weaker, because there is no direct measure of willingness to pay. All we would know is that the parks are worth visiting and that more people prefer one to the other.

In the South Santiam case, fees were charged at the state park but not around the reservoir. However, the simple, unweighted approach can be used by measuring the comparative values in terms of willingness to travel extra hours. The data will be analyzed for the representative user and then be combined with estimates of the number of users. The value equation for the representative user is adapted from Equation 17.11:

$$\text{total value of site}_i \text{ to representative user} = \frac{\Sigma(V_{ij}WT_j)}{\Sigma WT_j} \qquad (17.12)$$

In this simple example the weights are all equal to 1. The results for each site are shown in row 1 of Table 17.4 for reservoir users and river users. (Reservoir users are those who spent a major part of their time at reservoirs and river users those who spent their time along the river.) The representative reservoir user preferred site *C*, but the representative river user preferred site *B*.

6.1.3. Weighted by Length of Stay. Park visitors do not usually all stay for the same length of time. If visitors to one park stayed an average of 1 hour, but those who visited another park averaged, 4 hours, the same number of visitors should indicate a greater social value at the second park than at the first. We might therefore not just add up the number of visitors but give each visitor a different weight based on time spent in the park. This would use hours of attendance as an indicator of value to the visitors. A person who stayed 4 hours would be assumed to get twice as much value as one who stayed only 2.

The data on relative values in the Santiam study were weighted by length of stay. Each user's willingness to travel (V_{ij}) was multiplied by the length of time the family had spent at the reservoir or on the river in the last year. The results are shown in Table 17.4. Weighting changes the ranking of sites by the reservoir users, and site *B* is now preferred to site *C*.

6.1.4. Weighted by Intensity of Preference. Intensity of preference may be used as a basis for aggregation. The argument is that different

Table 17.4. Comparative Values of Two Recreation Sites to Two Kinds of User[a]

Weights	Reservoir Users		River Users	
	Site *B*	Site *C*	Site *B*	Site *C*
1. All weights = 1	3.4	3.7	4.0	1.1
2. By length of stay[b]	3.6	3.2	7.9	2.9
3. By distance of travel[c]	5.6	4.0	5.7	2.0
4. By equity weights set I	3.4	3.7	6.7	1.7
5. By equity weights set II	3.5	3.8	7.0	2.8

[a] Value is measured as willingness to travel extra hours to reach site *B* or *C* rather than stay at site *A*.
[b] As number of hours per family member per year.
[c] As miles of travel (single trip) from home.

benefits should be weighted according to the intensity with which they are felt. The analyst's task is to identify and derive a set of weights that reflect this intensity. In our example, one possibility is to use distance of travel as the weight. Other things being equal, families that travel farther are indicating a stronger preference, and their views should be given more weight.

The individual values for the two sites were weighted by distance of travel and the results are shown in Row 3 of Table 17.4. Again, the weighted ranking of sites by the reservoir users is different from the unweighted ranking.

6.1.5. Weighted by Equity Considerations. Traditional reasons for weighting are to achieve equity or to allow for differences in income. Individual incomes are often used as a basis for weights, and Section 4.3 discussed one method for deriving them. We apply a simple set of weights here on the premise that benefits to low-income users should be given more weight than benefits to high-income users.

Before-tax incomes of visitors to the South Santiam Valley ranged from $2000 to $20,000 per year. For a first set of weights (set I), the weight for $2000 was set at 1.0 and that for $20,000 at 0.55. Intermediate incomes were scaled in proportion. For a second set (set II), the weight for $2000 was again set at 1.0, but that for $20,000 was set at 0.1, and intermediate incomes were scaled accordingly. This second set gives a lower weight to high incomes than does the first.

The value of each site to each kind of user was calculated with Equation 17.12, and the results are shown in Table 17.4. The ranking of sites by both equity sets is the same as the original unweighted ranking. The reservoir users prefer site *C* while the river users prefer site *B*.

Equity weights are often used, but their form and derivation differ. The weights derived by Haveman (1965) were based on the political judgments built into tax schedules. Foster (1966) advocated a procedure based on actual monetary incomes. He felt that individual benefits should be weighted by the mean income in the community divided by the income of the beneficiary, and that costs should be weighted by the mean income in the community divided by the income of the loser. These ratio weights have the effect of lowering benefits to high-income persons and raising them to low-income persons.

6.2. Some Other Weighting Systems

We have seen that individual values can be weighted by amount of use, intensity of preference, and equity considerations. This section considers three other bases for weighting.

6.2.1. By Market Values. One of the advantages claimed for market values is that they serve the weighting function. Take, for example, the total social cost of requiring two individuals to spend one day in some public service. If one is an unskilled worker who usually earns $30 per day and the other a professional who earns $100 per day, the total social cost of the day of public service can be estimated at $130. The social cost is here measured as an opportunity cost. This is more informative than two man-days, and a truer value than the $80 that would be obtained by using the average area wage rate of $40 per day.

The weighting provided by market values may not always be acceptable, however. Suppose that because of an economic recession, these two people were working only 80 percent of the time. And suppose the government is considering two alternative employment programs, one of which would provide additional work for the unskilled person and the other for the professional. Which would have the greater social value? If these people were paid at their usual wage rates, additional days of work by the unskilled person and professional would appear to be worth $30 and $100, respectively. But an additional $30 might have much greater marginal utility to a family with an income of only $6300 than an additional $100 would have to a family with a $21,000 income. The relative market prices of labor seem to weight the comparison in the wrong direction.

It would appear better to measure the outputs of the two programs in days of work and to arbitrarily give higher weight to a day's work for a poor person than for a wealthier person. If the purpose of the programs is to increase total welfare, individual values must be measured and weighted in such a way that when they are aggregated, the resulting value estimates will be valid comparisons of contribution to total welfare.

6.2.2. By Merit. Choices between things may involve some perception of the "merit" of those things. Decision makers might decide, for example, that minority activities, such as backpacking, have more merit than mass activities, such as picnicking. Or they might decide that recreation activities based on natural environments have more merit than those based on man-made developments. Some things and activities are commonly judged to be more worthy than others and therefore receive more weight in valuations.

Quantitative procedures for deriving merit weights have been discussed by Mack and Myers (1965) and Craine (1965). Craine suggested that merit weights should be based on utility estimates and should be responsive to the views of the whole group. Mack and Myers argued that the use of weights is one way of overcoming some of the problems caused by lack of prices. Money prices are usually least suitable and least available at the point where they are needed most—for the allocation of investment among programs.

Mack and Myers reviewed some of the methods for estimating values and found them unsatisfactory. To fill the gap, they advocated a system of "merit-weighted user days," which substantially met fourteen ethical criteria. The system was based on attendance at recreation facilities. The recreationists' area of origin was divided into zones, and the average attendance was calculated for each zone. Then factors of distance, alternative facilities, and socioeconomic characteristics were used to estimate the expected or desirable number of visitors. The merit weight was obtained as follows:

$$\text{merit weight} = \frac{\text{expected number of visitors from zone } i}{\text{actual number of visitors from zone } i} \qquad (17.13)$$

6.2.3. By Self-Determined Weights. Subjects can be asked to rate their own competence to answer particular questions or to provide certain data. This is appropriate when answers from some are believed to be more relevant or useful than those from others. They can be asked to leave questions blank when they feel they have no expertise. Wills, Wilson, Manning, and Hildebrandt (1972) suggest that subjects be asked to rate their competence on each question on a scale of 0 to 10. These ratings can then be used as weights.

Self-determined weights may be useful when technical data or forecasts are involved. These are usually elicited from experts, and the views of some experts are likely to be more useful on some questions than on others. However, there would be no justification for using this procedure in our reservoir example, because the weights must be indicated by the group as a whole or by its elected leaders.

6.3. Discussion

The preceding sections have discussed ways of weighting the values of representative individuals before aggregating them into social value. Several aspects of the aggregation process deserve further consideration.

6.3.1. The Welfare Basis for Aggregation. The welfare economics literature warns of the dangers inherent in making comparisons between persons and adding value data for different people. It is often stated that such interpersonal comparisons are impossible. But the decisions for which valuations are actually made do not attempt to produce optimum outcomes. All they seek is the better alternatives in specific situations. These are usually existing situations that are known and identifiable. If the objectives of decisions and the consequent purpose of valuation are kept clearly in mind, it should be possible to decide how much relative weight should be given to the different people and the various benefits that make up the total social value.

The choice of a system of weights will always be subjective. Nash, Pearce, and Stanley (1975) note in the context of overall benefit-cost analysis that there are many different ways of aggregating data and that each is logically consistent with a particular set of moral or ethical judgments. Various sets of weights can be justified by reference to different sets of moral judgments. When aggregation is necessary, an analyst has three possible approaches: (1) He can present his data in a disaggregated form, with the incidence of all benefits and costs clearly displayed. (2) He can use equal weights and explicitly say so. (3) He can derive a set of weights to match the appropriate ethical judgments. In this case he must first search for the ethical judgment and then for the weights.

6.3.2. Weights for Individual and Group Values. We must now return to those social valuations that include group as well as individual values. Two extreme cases exist. In one the group value is of such overriding importance that it determines the social value, regardless of the individual values involved. Examples are cases in which the survival, independence, or stability of the group is at stake. At the opposite extreme, group values are so minor or so closely correlated with individual values that social value consists almost entirely of individual values.

In cases between these extremes an attempt must be made to weight the group and individual values. The purpose of the valuation will have a major influence on the logic of weighting. Sensitivity testing is often helpful. If the order of comparative values remains the same despite large changes in weights, a crude weighting system is adequate. But if comparative values are very close and a small change in weights changes their order, it may be necessary to devote considerable time to the development of valid weights.

7. DECISIONS IN WHICH INDIVIDUAL VALUES ARE NOT FULLY RECOGNIZED

When social values derive entirely from individual values, the individual values may all be fully recognized or they may not. In the first case an estimate of social value only requires the aggregation of individual value data, as we discussed in Section 6.

In the second case the failure to recognize fully all of the individual values may be due to externalities or to a lack of appropriability. The following discussion focuses on how the values can be fully recognized and how decisions are made in such situations.

7.1. Externalities

Social values will differ from the aggregate of individual values whenever externalities are present. In terms of costs:

$$\text{social cost} = \text{individual costs} + \text{external costs} \tag{17.14}$$

This relationship has long been recognized, but empirical attempts to measure external costs are quite recent.

Horner (1975) analyzed the external costs of water pollution by nitrogen from fertilizers used in the San Joaquin Valley of California. Sokoloski (1967) studied the external costs of damage to fisheries, tourism, and recreation caused by wastes from a pulpmill at Toledo, Oregon. And Gray, Fisk, and Mathews (1974) investigated the external environmental costs resulting from recreational use of the Sandia Mountains in New Mexico.

These three studies used different methods to place values on the unpriced external effects. The replacement-cost method, opportunity-cost method, and a version of the gross-expenditure method were used. None of these analysts attempted to measure the individual disutilities that might arise from nitrogen pollution or from recreation in a polluted estuary. These true external costs were never calculated. Decisions were made in terms of the control cost, and the various opportunity-cost methods apprently provided sufficient information for them. All unrecognized values may not need to be estimated but only those that are vital to the decision.

7.2. Public Goods

Public goods can be enjoyed by everyone at the same time because the amount consumed by one person does not affect the quantity available for others. No market price can exist because the producers cannot appropriate them and prevent others from enjoying them. The difficulty for valuing public goods is that consumers do not have to express their willingness to pay.

Because individual choices cannot be observed, some form of direct question or bidding game must be used to elicit values. But when individuals cannot be excluded from enjoying the benefits, they have no incentive to give true responses to the questions and tend to act like "free riders." How then can these values be estimated? The conceptual model indicates that individual demand curves should be aggregated vertically in this situation. But this piece of theory seems rather barren unless empirical data on demand can be collected. There have been some attempts to do this.

Randall, Ives, and Eastman (1974) estimated the social value of eliminating the aesthetic disutilities created by a power station and its associated coal mine in the Four Corners area of New Mexico. Sinden (1973), in the example presented in Section 6.1, tried to obtain recreationists' willingness to pay for camping on reservoir or river sites. Bohm (1972) studied the willingness of television viewers to pay for specific programs on regular TV channels. All three cases involved public goods.

Direct-questioning methods and bidding games were used in these studies. The presence of public goods does not hinder the collection of data, but it does cast doubts on their validity. Randall, Ives, and Eastman structured their questions to encourage true responses. So did Sinden, but his results could not be validated. Bohm was careful to encourage responsibility and to ensure anonymity. Validation was successful in this case. These examples indicate that the problem of public goods can be overcome by careful analysis, the use of validation techniques, and the cooperation of respondents.

8. DISCUSSION AND CONCLUSIONS

Estimating the social value of something is clearly more difficult than estimating its value to individual people. Part of the difficulty may be overcome by resolving some apparent conflicts in individual responses. Individuals sometimes give two different appraisals of the value of the same thing, one based on what they prefer for themselves and the other on what they feel is appropriate for the group as a whole. People who would all select the same alternative if making individual choices may also differ on which alternative is best for the group.

We feel that if a decision is completely specified, such apparent conflicts will usually disappear. Table 17.1 presents four different situations in which social value may be formed. For a decision involving situation 1, individual values are not relevant, and the analyst needs people's estimates of value to the group. For a decision involving situation 3, group values are not involved, and the analyst needs only estimates of individual values. For a decision involving situation 4, group values are not involved. But there are individual values, such as benefits to future people, that are not recognized by individual respondents in their own valuations. In this situation, the analyst needs individual appraisals of the recognized values plus a group appraisal of the unrecognized values.

Decisions involving Situation 2 require the most complex valuations. Because both group and individual values exist, the approach must combine the approach used for situation 1 with those used for situations 3 or 4. The specific nature of the decision will determine the relative weights that must be given to the various components of social values.

One of the central theses of this book is that different decisions may require different concepts of value and different valuation methods. If an analyst will identify the specific characteristics of a decision, Table 17.1 will help in selecting the most useful approaches to estimating social value.

PART III

RATIONAL DECISIONS WITHOUT MARKET PRICES

CHAPTER 18

Why Decisions Involving Unpriced Values are Considered Difficult

In Part I we saw that comparative values have their bases in individual and social situations. They are only meaningful when they are specific and only useful in relation to specific choices or decisions.

In Part II we saw that investigators in many disciplines have used a variety of methods for estimating unpriced values. Our analysis showed that these methods—or combinations of them—can produce useful indicators of comparative value for their particular situations.

Why, then, do people still consider decisions involving unpriced values difficult or even impossible? We feel this attitude is often a result of some misconception of the problem. Such misconceptions include (a) a difficulty in distinguishing what is exchanged and a consequent emphasis on valuation of the wrong things, (b) an undue confidence in market prices and a lack of knowledge of other ways of deriving value information, (c) a lack of appreciation of the causes of unpricedness and an associated misdirection of analytical effort, and (d) an unnecessary emphasis on the determination of social values where decisions can be made without monetary values or even without values of any kind. If planners can avoid such misconceptions, we feel they can usually develop estimates of comparative values that will be helpful in their decisions.

1. DIFFICULTY IN DISTINGUISHING WHAT IS ACTUALLY EXCHANGED

Every decision involves some kind of exchange. The affected people receive something, but they also give up something. Social choices are complicated because the exchange often involves benefits to some and costs to others.

The comparative values of the things exchanged depend on the differences they make—or could make—to the lives of the affected people.

Estimates of these values can be obtained from willingness to pay, that is, from what the people are willing to give in order to obtain—or avoid receiving—the results of a decision.

Any appraisal of comparative values must therefore start with a determination of what would be exchanged in the decision. Three kinds of problems interfere with this determination:

(**a**) A tendency to try to value the basic resource rather than the activity involved in the exchange.

(**b**) A tendency to try to value the ultimate utility rather than the activity involved.

(**c**) A tendency to still think about tangible goods and services rather than activities as objects of exchange.

Let us see how these are related to the value formation process by identifying and analyzing the linkage between resources and utilities.

1.1. Identifying the Causal Chain from Resources to Utilities

A valuation problem arises when a decision has to be made about some resource. This resource may be anything from a coal deposit to a surgeon's skills. It is a resource because it has the potential of making a favorable difference to someone's life. It can provide utility, which in the cases of the above resources might take the forms of comfort and improved health.

Value formation always involves resources and utility, but the value actually arises in the activity of deriving utility from the resources. A surgeon always has the potential of providing great utility. But if we are in good health, he cannot make a favorable difference to our lives and is of no value to us. If we are stricken with appendicitis, we can realize the surgeon's potential value by undergoing an operation. The value actually arises in the activity of being operated on. We pay for an operation, not for good health nor for a surgeon.

To see why people find it difficult to distinguish what is exchanged, let us look more closely at the three parts of the causal chain: resources, use of resources, and ultimate utilities. Then in Section 1.2 we analyze this chain from a valuation viewpoint.

1.1.1. Resources. A resource is something that people can use to satisfy a need or desire. It must have potential utility. But by itself it has no value. People must be able to use it in some way that can make a difference to someone's life. The resource is essential, but value can only be realized through its utilization. Valuation must therefore focus on the activity of using resources rather than on the resources themselves.

We can recognize three broad categories of resources, which are summarized in Table 18.1. No attempt is made to present them in an order of importance. We are trying to show that there are many kinds of resources and that few of them can be used alone. The value of a resource usually depends on the possibilities of combining it with other resources in some form of use.

It is easy to see from Table 18.1 why there is a temptation to try to value directly the resources affected by decisions. Decisions involve choices between things like forests and highways, for example, and what are needed to guide such decisions are the comparative values of forests and highways. But the values of such resources derive from their use by people, and the valuation process must start from the activity of using them. "What is the value of a lake?" is a meaningless question. "What is the value of a lake as a place where people can swim?" is a question that can be answered by determining the value that people assign to the activity of swimming.

1.1.2. Ultimate Utilities. An ultimate utility is something that people feel affects the quality of life. Table 18.2 lists a number of things that fall in this category. We have not tried to list these in an order of importance and lay no claim to completeness. Our purpose is not to analyze the ultimate utilities that people seek but to show the role they play in valuations.

The basis of value is to be found in these ultimate utilities. Anything that can contribute no utility is of no value to people. It is tempting, therefore, to try to focus valuations on the utilities themselves.

But decisions seldom—if ever—involve choices between ultimate

Table 18.1. A Classification of Resources

Natural Resources	Cultural Resources	Human Resources
Soil	Structures:	Knowledge
Landforms	Buildings	Technology
Minerals	Dams, dikes	Skills
Natural vegetation	Transport facilities	
Wild animals	Machines	
Water bodies	Tools and equipment	
Air and wind	Domesticated animals and plants	
Sunlight	Stocks of goods	
	Collections	
	Books and other recorded information	
	Artifacts (including works of art)	

Table 18.2. A Classification of Ultimate Utilities

Physiological State	Emotional State	Social State
Health	Interest	Companionship
Physical	Diversity	Friendship
Mental	Excitement	Love
Safety from:	Sense of achievement	Acceptance
Disease	Pride	Self-confidence
Accident	Pleasure	Esteem
Death	Aesthetic appreciation	Status
Mistreatment	Freedom from:	Liberty
Freedom from:	Worry	Security
Pain	Fear	Power
Discomfort	Peace of mind	
Stress, tension	Satisfaction	
Fatigue	Fulfillment	
	Happiness	
Life expectancy	Sense of moral obligation fulfilled	

utilities. One may have to decide, for example, whether to work overtime or engage in a sport. By working overtime, he could obtain utility in the forms of freedom from discomfort, a sense of achievement, and security. By engaging in the sport, he could obtain utility in the forms of health, excitement, and companionship. "What is the comparative value of security versus health?" is not a question that will help make this decision. "How much security might I obtain by working overtime?" and "What benefits to my health might accrue from engaging in the sport?" are useful questions. They can contribute to estimating the values involved in deciding whether working overtime is worth more than participating in the sport. It is the comparative values people feel they would get from alternative actions that form the basis of rational decisions.

1.1.3. Activities That Derive Utility from Resources. The links in the causal chain between resources and ultimate utilities consist of human activities. An ultimate utility may be potentially important, but it can make no difference in anyone's life unless it is actually produced through human activity. A resource can have no value unless its potential utility can be realized through use.

Table 18.3 presents a summary of the activities through which people derive utilities. The relative difficulty of identifying and measuring these activities tends to increase from left to right in the table.

Productive Activities. These activities produce things that have utility. The activity is a means and not an end. People engage in it primarily for the products. There are cases in which people derive some utility from the activity itself as well as from its products. But one must look beyond the primary activity to understand fully how value is derived.

The product of such activity may be a producer's good that is used in further production of other things. The value of this product must be assessed in the light of the further activity. But even products that are consumers' goods must usually be used to derive utility from them. Production of some services, like medical care, may provide immediate utility. But what people receive from most services, such as education, must be used to derive utility.

Participatory Activities. These are activities from which people derive utility directly. The activity is an end in itself rather than a means to some other end. Many participatory activities, such as swimming, produce no tangible products at all. They ordinarily produce utility only for the immediate participants.

Other participatory activities like arts and crafts do result in tangible products. These are not the main reason for engaging in the activity, but

Table 18.3. Activities through which Utilities Are Derived

Productive Activities	Participatory Activities	Reception of Stimuli from the Environment
The product of the activity provides the utility; not the activity itself (Product may be a producer's good and serve further productive activities)	Participation itself provides the utility; any product of the activity is secondary in importance	Stimuli received from a person's environment provide some form of utility
Examples: Land management Manufacturing Construction Mining Medical services Protective services Entertainment services Education services Religious services News dissemination Research	Examples: Sports and games Hiking, mountain climbing Collecting Boating, flying Arts and crafts Camping Amateur drama and music Social dancing Racing	1. Active deliberate reception (including listening) a. Natural phenomena, such as scenery b. Cultural and historical artifacts, such as museums c. Human activities, such as theater, concerts 2. Passive reception Pleasant or unpleasant stimuli to senses of sight, hearing, smell, taste, feel

utility is often derived from both participation and the resulting products. Many actual situations lie in the borderline area between these categories.

Reception of Stimuli from the Environment. These are activities through which people receive stimuli that have utility for them. The activity is one of reception rather than production or participation.

The reception may be active, with people deliberately observing some phenomenon to derive utility from it. Observation may take many forms, such as looking or listening, and the utilities obtained may be of many kinds, such as interest or aesthetic appreciation. People also receive many stimuli passively from their environment. They are exposed to sights, sounds, and smells their sensory organs take in automatically. They derive utilities from pleasant environmental stimuli and suffer disutilities from unpleasant ones.

1.2. Analyzing the Causal Chain

Section 1.1 examined some of the links in the causal chain from resources through the activities that derive utilities from them to the ultimate utilities themselves. In this section we show how a value appraisal should approach this causal chain. We use as examples two hypothetical decisions, one involving a priced benefit and the other involving an unpriced one.

1.2.1. A Decision Involving a Priced Good. Let us assume a government reclamation agency has been given enough money to extend irrigation to one of two currently arid but potentially arable areas. Let us further assume that the cost of providing irrigation would be the same for both areas. The agency's problem is to decide which area to develop. As a guide in making this choice it needs estimates of the comparative social values of the alternatives. The question appears to be: What would be the comparative values of the land in the two areas after irrigation?

However, these lands will have no value of their own; any value must derive from the use made of them. Let us assume that the rational uses after irrigation would be growing corn on one area and beans on the other. Because these are both nourishing foods, they have the potential of producing utility by maintaining physical health. The question now appears to be: What would be the comparative values of the health utility that each area would produce?

But this utility will be derived in the process of consuming the corn or beans as food. The real question, then, is: What are the comparative values to future consumers of the opportunity to eat food produced from the corn grown on one area or from the beans grown on the other? Current consumers are indicating their estimates of these values by what they are willing to pay for corn and bean products in the market. How much they actually have to pay depends on what it costs all other farmers to put corn and beans on the market. Current market prices show the combined valuations of the marginal consumers and producers. They are usable estimates of the social values of the corn and beans that might be grown on this newly irrigated land. The area that will produce a crop with the greatest total market value is the one whose development would have the greatest social value.

1.2.2. A Decision Involving an Unpriced Good. Let us assume a government agency has been given enough money to acquire an extensive tract of wild land and preserve it as a wilderness. Let us also assume there are several suitable tracts that could be acquired and preserved at the same cost. However, the legislature has appropriated only enough money to acquire one. The agency's problem is to decide which tract to acquire and preserve. As a guide to this choice it needs estimates of the comparative values of the alternatives. The question appears to be: What will be the comparative values of these potential wilderness areas?

However, these wild lands will have no value in themselves. Any future value will derive from favorable differences that their existence will make to the lives of people. Wilderness areas are said to provide people with utilities in the forms of physical and mental health, interest, a sense of achievement, aesthetic appreciation, peace of mind, satisfaction, and companionship. The question now appears to be: What would be the comparative values of the health and other utilities provided by the alternative areas if they were preserved in wilderness condition?

These utilities will only be derived by people if they partake of a wilderness experience. We are aware that a wilderness experience can take many different forms, including for some people just a knowledge that it is there. However, to simplify the example, let us make an assumption that the only way people can partake of such an experience is by hiking in the wilderness. In this case the real question is: What is the value to future people of the opportunity to hike in each of these potential wilderness areas?

This differs from the example in Section 1.2.1 in that wilderness hiking is not an activity that is bought and sold in markets. There are no market prices to indicate how much people are willing to pay for a day of wilderness hiking. The planner must use one or several of the techniques described in Part II. If data are available on costs and quantities of hiking, the net-social-benefit methods of Chapters 15 and 16 might be used. If no data are available, a direct-questioning method from Chapter 14 or perhaps a total-utility method from Chapter 11 might be used to elicit estimates of willingness to pay for hiking. There may be problems in determining total values for each tract if the comparative values per unit cannot be quantified. But the important point is that what must be appraised is the comparative values of the wilderness experiences obtained through hiking in the areas and not the values of the wilderness areas themselves or of the ultimate utilities people will get from the experience.

These examples demonstrate the importance of distinguishing exactly what is being exchanged in a prospective decision. The tendency is to try to value the resources or the utilities. But decisions are made about the activities that derive utility from resources. One must decide whether to go forward with a proposed activity or, if a choice is involved, which activity to pursue. As the examples show, this is just as true of priced goods as of unpriced ones. Market prices are evidence of willingness to pay for certain activities. Where they do not exist, the necessary evidence can be obtained by other methods. If one concentrates on the activities, the estimation may be no more difficult for unpriced things than for priced ones.

2. LACK OF UNDERSTANDING OF ALTERNATIVE VALUATION METHODS

Value is often equated with the prices for which things sell. It is not surprising, therefore, that people consider it difficult to appraise the value of something for which there is no market price. But their opinion is based on the misconceptions that (a) market prices accurately measure relative values and (b) the only way to appraise relative value is to determine market prices. We discussed the first misconception in Chapter 2. Now we discuss the alternative valuation methods as means of determining comparative values.

2.1. What Is Required of a Method?

Market prices are useful value indicators, because they show the amounts people are actually willing to pay for goods and services. If a decision is being made in a situation similar to that in which market prices have developed, these prices may indicate the comparative social values of the alternatives being considered. A comparative valuation based on market prices tells a planner that if the people involved were making this decision themselves, their behavior in previous exchanges indicates they would choose a particular alternative. The alternative valuation techniques develop other kinds of information that also indicate the choices people would make if they had a chance to do so. These techniques seek reliable guides to social decisions rather than accurate assessments of social values as such.

2.2. What Do the Alternative Methods Measure?

Part II presents a variety of methods that take different approaches to the comparative valuation problem. They are grouped in chapters by the kinds of value estimates they provide. We consider them here in the same order. Some of their key features are shown in Table 18.4.

Multiple-Objective Methods (Chapter 8). These methods are used for decisions between alternatives that would produce more than one kind of output or would meet several objectives. These methods do not attempt to measure values but to provide an ordering of alternatives in terms of their value.

There are several ways to make decisions that involve multiple objectives. (1) One objective or dimension can be optimized, subject to constraints on all the others. (2) All objectives can be converted to a common measure, usually a monetary one. Opportunity-cost values can sometimes be calculated for all dimensions, even when net-social-benefit values cannot. Alternatively, the common measure may be deviations from a mean, as in the benchmark and goal-programming methods. (3) Weights

Table 18.4. The Role of Alternative Methods in Valuation

Method	What Is Measured	Information Provided	Suitable Problems
Multiple objectives	Various	Various	Those with many objectives
Characteristics of the environment	Aggregates of levels of characteristics	Dimensionless indices of comparative value	Selection from a group of similar things
Estimates of utility	Total utility (or disutility)	Relative utilities	Selection from similar things
Opportunity cost	Loss and change in utility	Little on net benefits; much for choices	Various
Interpretation of market prices	Net or total utility	Net benefits for unpriced thing	Problems requiring monetary values
Direct questioning	Willingness to pay	Monetary estimate of net benefit	Problems requiring monetary values
Net social benefit	Utility and opportunity costs	Monetary estimate of net social benefit	Problems requiring monetary values
Social and group valuations	Various	Various	Social and group valuations

can be calculated to permit the addition of different dimensions of utility or disutility. (4) A muliplicative model can be used to provide useful dimensionless indexes or relative values.

Value Indexes Based on Characteristics (Chapter 9). These methods do not attempt to measure values as such. In comparing the values of alternatives, they do not try to identify and measure the utilities that people would derive from them. Instead, they search for characteristics that people agree are critical in determining the value of the things being considered. For example, if people agreed that the characteristic of highway transportation most important to them was travel speed, a planner could choose the most valuable highway design from among identical-cost alternatives by merely comparing their average allowable driving speeds. It is clear that driving speed does not measure value, but it is a useful indicator of comparative value in this case.

These methods are useful when many characteristics are important because they can aggregate these into a single figure. The final number is a dimensionless index of comparative value. These methods are appropriate when the decision is a choice between similar things and all alternatives have the same cost or a total budget is given. They provide no monetary information.

Estimates of Utility (Chapters 10 and 11). These methods estimate the comparative total utilities people would receive from various alternatives. They seek the alternative from which people would obtain the greatest total utility regardless of cost. They do not measure willingness to pay, except in the sense of having to give up other possible alternatives to have the chosen one. If the costs involved in a decision are fixed, insignificant, or otherwise ignored, a measure of total utility may be all that is needed to guide the decision. However, net utility and comparative values can sometimes be obtained with these methods, as we illustrated with the theme example in Chapter 11.

These methods vary greatly in ease of data collection, reliability, and rigor. The expedient methods of Chapter 10 rely on a very small number of direct questions for each utility estimate. They are rapid and easy to use, but the responses may not reflect true preferences. The rigorous methods of Chapter 11 are slower and more difficult to apply because they use many questions for each utility estimate. But the reported applications of these rigorous methods indicate that they obtain valid responses. All provide the same kind of value estimate, but the cost of data collection must be balanced against the benefits of greater validity.

Opportunity-Cost Estimates (Chapter 12). These methods estimate the comparative total disutility in obtaining the alternatives under consideration. They do not measure willingness to pay, except in the sense that people are not likely to bear opportunity costs unless they consider the benefits to be at least as great as the costs. Opportunity costs should therefore indicate minimum values.

When the benefits from a decision are fixed or insignificant, the alternative with the lowest opportunity cost will produce the greatest net benefit. These methods can therefore give the necessary information for choosing between alternative means of achieving the same end. Actual expenditures can often be determined when there are no markets for the things being appraised. The expenditures may take other forms than market price, but they are still opportunity costs and can be interpreted in the same way.

These methods are of three kinds: (1) those that use net income foregone as a guide for decisions, (2) those that use structured comparisons of costs to estimate net benefit, and (3) those that are based on observations of monetary expenditures. The opportunity-cost methods do not measure value as such but can provide much comparative information about the alternatives.

Interpretation of Market Prices (Chapter 13). These methods estimate comparative net benefits by working from existing market prices. If the existing market price is not considered to be a valid measure of social value, one technique is to measure the amount by which the market price is distorted and to correct it. If market prices are considered reliable estimates of social value but only exist for related things, these methods attempt to measure the relationship between the thing being assessed and some priced thing and to derive a value from this relationship. When related market prices are available, these methods can give good estimates of comparative value.

Direct Questioning (Chapter 14). These methods estimate comparative net benefits by directly measuring willingness to pay. Through systematic questioning of the people affected by the decision, they extract information on maximum willingness to pay in monetary terms. Because they do not involve actual exchanges, these techniques do not depend on the existence of markets for the things being appraised.

Net-Social-Benefit Methods (Chapters 15 and 16). These methods estimate net social benefit directly. They approach this by developing demand curves for the products. Equilibrium price is estimated from the demand curve on the basis of total quantity exchanged, or a supply curve is also developed. In the latter case an estimate of the combined consumers' and producers' surplus is used as an indicator of social value. These techniques simulate a market exchange, but they do not require actual transaction evidence and can be used where there is no real market for the product.

The main difficulties with these methods lie in collecting the data and in structuring the model to fit specific decisions. Chapter 15 discusses various possible applications of the method in the face of sparse data. The travel-cost methods of Chapter 16 are applicable to any policy problem in which the costs of acquisition and consumption are mainly those of travel.

Social and Group Valuations (Chapter 17). These methods are not all restricted to group valuations but can assist with this problem. They include methods to promote a consensus to derive and use weights for aggregating individual values, and to analyze past group decisions and behavior. They do not all provide comparative values directly, but they can help derive data that may be used in estimating values.

Summary. The alternative methods all measure something that is correlated with or closely related to value. They do not all measure value as such, but neither do market prices, as we saw in Chapter 2. All of the valuation methods produce indicators of comparative value.

Monetary values are not the only common yardstick for comparison. Some decisions only require estimates of the utilities and disutilities of the alternatives. Other decisions can be based on other yardsticks, such as time or travel distance.

The real difficulties of valuation do not lie in a lack of methods or basic concepts. The fundamental difficulties are those of sampling, uncertainty, and cost of information. These difficulties are not limited to valuation or to environmental problems but are common to all of the sciences, particularly the social sciences.

2.3. How Can Unpriced Values Be Used in Making Decisions?

Valuations are means to an end—to provide comparative values as aids to decisions. If it were possible to estimate monetary values for all of the benefits and costs of a decision, the final comparative assessment could be a single, simple number for the value of each alternative. But analysts can seldom estimate all of the relevant values. And it is rare for there to be one single alternative that is best on all objectives. The final assessments will usually not be simple. But the analyst may be able to structure the comparisons or data so that decisions can be made with partial sets of values.

The preceding section summarized the methods with which values can be estimated. In this section we bring together various procedures for structuring and presenting value information.

A variety of procedures can be used for presenting comparative values and other information on unpriced benefits and costs. In a discussion of decision making in resource management, Alston and Freeman (1975) list five different techniques. In the context of national defense, Hitch and McKean (1960) present four procedures, only one of which is discussed by Alston and Freeman. We have combined these and other lists with the various procedures noted in Parts I and II into the following nine.

2.3.1. Describe and List Information. As Mishan (1971) says, the least an analyst can do is clearly reveal the area of ignorance. The simplest procedure is to describe and list the unpriced benefits and costs and the things exchanged. Whenever possible, the descriptions should be quantitative. The task of integrating these unpriced things and those with monetary values can then be undertaken by the decision maker. Rothenburg (1967) suggests that we can always list quantitative effects in their original dimensions, such as days of illness. This listing imposes minimal demands on analytical resources, and all benefits and costs should be capable of description. The environmental impact statement is an example of this procedure.

2.3.2. Concentrate on Quantities, Not Values. The goal of many decisions is to provide improved quantities of goods and services. A useful procedure is to concentrate on the choice between alternative combinations of goods or between alternative plans or project designs. There are various way of eliciting people's preferences for these alternatives.

Choice between Goods. A straightforward procedure is to elicit preferences for different combinations of goods and services through direct questions. These preferences must then be aggregated in a socially acceptable manner. Hardie and Kirkley's (1975) application to outdoor recreation was described in Chapter 14.

Choice between Plans. Hitch and McKean (1960) apply the same approach to alternative designs or plans for a project. The objective of and constraints on the project are fully specified. Then alternative plans are developed to meet the constraints and objectives. Unpriced things are incorporated as constraints or are otherwise included in the plan. The decision maker can then select one of the acceptable plans. Ackoff (1976) makes a similar proposal for measuring the quality of life. He suggests that social systems be designed to meet quality constraints and be displayed for public comment. The comments can then be transformed into a decision.

Value the Differences between Projects. A third procedure is to formalize and structure the implicit aspects of the two preceding approaches. The comparative trade-off game of Chapter 14 concentrated on the differences between projects, plans, or bundles of goods and services. It provides monetary estimates of the difference in total utility between projects. Such monetary estimates may be easier to aggregate for decisions than are preferences or public comments.

2.3.3. Use Rapid Monetary Estimates. Imprecise estimates of values may suffice for some decisions. The estimation can be rapid, and the least-demanding method can be used, even though more rigorous ones are available. This approach is satisfactory when the values of the alternatives differ by an order of magnitude or one benefit or cost dominates the choice.

The selection of a freeway route for Adelaide in South Australia illustrates both situations. One cost was the relocation of homes and families. Instead of estimating the associated loss in utility and the total monetary costs, Nairn (1971) estimated only the cost of replacing the homes. The cost of additional noise was estimated from the expenditure on soundproofing, with no attempt to value disutility, and the cost of street severance was estimated from the cost of a bridge to maintain access. These estimates were obtained quickly and, as Nairn acknowledged, may be notional at best. But a decision was possible because road-user costs were found to dominate all of these costs by an order of magnitude, and on this basis one route was clearly preferable. With this approach, a discussion of the choices can be inititated. The values can be refined later if necessary.

2.3.4. Make Sensitivity Analyses of the Values. An effective procedure is to estimate the sensitivity of total project values to changes in the individual benefits and costs. If total values prove to be insensitive to variation in the figures for benefits and costs that are hard to estimate, attempts to refine the values for these things can cease and the choice can be made. There are several ways to apply this approach.

For Break-Even Points. Key points in a decision can often be crystalized by calculating break-even points and their associated trade-off data. For example, under present circumstances project *A* may be the best means for achieving a given objective. But if some effort is devoted to educating the public, project *B* may achieve this same objective at a lower cost. The trade-off is education cost for project savings. If the costs of the education program are just equal to the cost saving, project *B* "breaks even" with project *A*. If the costs of the program are less, project *B* would be preferable.

For Unusually Large Benefits or Costs. Decisions may be dominated by certain benefits or costs. An unusually high cost may be reason enough for rejecting a project without valuing other things. Similarly, one unusually large benefit may justify a project without further valuations.

For Maximum and Minimum Values. Many of the methods can provide maximum or minimum estimates of values. Several of the methods for calculating opportunity costs (Chapter 12) and net social benefits (Chapter 15) can do this. Such extreme estimates may prove useful in a decision resting on one key value, or in a comparison of projects when one can be adequately valued.

For Orders of Magnitude. It is sometimes possible to identify very large differences in magnitude between individual benefits or costs. For example, in Nairn's (1971) study of alternative routes for the proposed Adelaide freeway, it was found that $740 million out of the estimated total cost of $880 million for the Sturt River route could be attributed to the monetary costs of road users. It was clearly better to refine the data on road-user costs than to devote more time to those costs making up the remaining $140 million. The expedient methods of Chapter 10 can often be used in rapid, large-scale surveys to provide rough estimates of orders of magnitude.

2.3.5. Combine Several Methods. Many writers advocate using several simple methods when an appropriate method is hard to apply. If two methods provide similar results, the common value appears to be strengthened. There are other advantages to combining methods in a formal or informal manner. For example, Waddell (1974) notes that the land-price method is suitable for air-pollution problems because land values reflect pollution effects and the method is easy to apply. But the characteristics method of Chapter 9 may provide more insight into the process by which disutilities arise from air pollution. The two methods give complementary information and may usefully be applied together.

But what does an analyst do if the values differ significantly? And, more fundamentally, is the procedure itself justified? Consider the attempt by the Dutch Agricultural Investment Commission (1960) to estimate the social cost of land that could be reclaimed by eliminating freshwater reservoirs. They decided that "The resulting loss can be assessed in various ways.

Firstly, one can calculate what returns the quantities of fresh water lost would have yielded. Secondly, one can calculate the cost of replacing the supply of water lost through reclamation."

In this case both methods happened to give similar values. But because the objective was to calculate the net social benefit from reclamation, the first suggested procedure—to calculate the loss in net social benefits—was the correct one. The second method—the replacement-cost principle—cannot ordinarily be expected to provide similar values. We noted in Chapter 12 that this procedure only gives the true change in net social benefit when the same quantity is consumed after the decision as before.

The method of valuation used must match the criterion or objective of the analysis. Combining different kinds of methods is not usually a logical procedure unless all of the methods fit the particular objective.

2.3.6. Use Structured Comparisons. Environmental benefits and costs can often be defined in quantitative terms even when they cannot easily be valued. We discuss four ways of using this.

Determining the Cost of Constraints. Many decisions about actions to reduce pollution involve the setting of constraints on allowable amounts of pollutants. Because these constraints can be defined in terms of technical data, it is often possible to calculate the losses in monetary income that would be associated with them. The opportunity cost of achieving an improved level of air or water quality can thus be estimated by determining the cost of the constraints involved.

Threshold Comparisons. It is sometimes possible to value one of the alternative projects adequately. This value provides a threshold or datum point to which other alternatives can be compared. A decision can then rest on evidence of the alternative project being more or less profitable. The net benefit of the alternative does not have to be valued precisely.

Changes in Cost. The replacement cost or the change in cost of providing a thing can furnish true estimates of value when the quantity and nature of the thing are held constant. For example, one freeway route in Adelaide would have destroyed a building of great historical interest. Although it was not possible to replace the building, it was possible to move it. The cost of moving this building elsewhere could serve as a proxy for its value. Because this cost would certainly have to be incurred, it is relevant to the decision.

Some projects would lower (or raise) the cost of acquiring particular things. The utility of these things may be hard to value, but the value of the project can be estimated from the change in cost, because the utility will be constant.

Cost Minimization and Benefit Maximization. A cost-minimization decision only requires an estimate of monetary costs. And benefit-maximization decisions can be made with any quantitative index of benefits. For these kinds of comparisons data are not needed on net utilities or values. However, both the cost-minimization and benefit-maximization procedures require that all costs or benefits be measured in the same units.

2.3.7. Use Nonmonetary Indexes of Relative Value. Many decisions do not require monetary estimates of value as guides. Three kinds of non-monetary value indexes are sometimes useful.

Characteristics of the Environment. Many decisions are choices among similar things. Chapter 9 discussed the use of indexes to identify the best and worst in groups of similar things. Workers in various disciplines have constructed indexes to measure relative quality or value. Such indexes avoid valuation in monetary terms but provide useful data for some kinds of choices.

"Exchangeable" Nonmonetary Units. Some decisions can be based on simple rankings of alternatives, provided the yardstick used has a common scale and common origin. Time can be a suitable yardstick when time is the limiting resource, as in outdoor recreation. Another suitable measure can be quantities of goods consumed, as was discussed in Chapter 17. The benchmark method of Chapter 8 can use any convenient environmental characteristic as a standard for choice.

Dimensionless Indexes. At several points in the book we have discussed dimensionless measures of relative value. Goal programming, multiplicative models, and the benchmark method of Chapter 8 are examples. This kind of method does not measure value in the sense of net utility but does provide useful guides for decisions.

2.3.8. Provide Opportunity-Cost Data. It is often possible to calculate the opportunity costs of a project, even when the benefits cannot be valued in monetary terms. For some decisions the opportunity-cost procedures of Chapter 12 can provide a true estimate of net social benefit. But even when these methods cannot be used alone, a comparison of opportunity costs will help with many decisions.

2.3.9. Two Final Procedures. There may be some decisions for which none of the preceding approaches are suitable. But an analyst still has two procedures to which he can turn. He can always use the direct-question methods of Chapter 14 to obtain missing information. And he can reallocate his resources to collect more technical or value data.

2.4. What Are the Limitations of the Alternative Methods?

All the methods presented in this book have limitations. None of them can give a perfect measure of value. In discussing the use of the various methods in Part II, we tried to define their specific limitations, and we do not repeat that here. But we wish to stress some major points that are essential to an intelligent use of the methods.

All these methods implement the basic value relationship

$$\text{value} = \text{utility} - \text{disutility}$$

The various groups of methods provide a variety of ways of applying this equation. But even within one group, individual methods often involve different interpretations of the value equation, because they are based on different assumptions or refer to different kinds of decisions.

The approach that is most helpful depends on the purpose for which the valuation is being made. Some of the methods are only suitable for certain kinds of decisions. We have tried to suggest how the methods that best fit the decision at hand can be selected. For more complex decisions the methods for dealing with multiple objectives and group values presented in Chapters 8 and 17 may be used to supplement or take the place of the more straightforward methods of Chapters 9 to 16. When some values are missing, the procedures for structuring decisions which we just discussed in Section 2.3 can help make the most of the available information.

Each method requires certain kinds of information. When this cannot be obtained, the methods cannot be used. If the relevant people are not willing to cooperate with a planner, for example, he cannot learn much with the direct-question methods. Even if they are willing to cooperate, the quality of the information obtained—and the consequent validity of the results—will depend on their attitudes toward participation.

Some of the methods are expensive or time consuming. If a decision has to be made quickly, the time required to interview enough people may rule out any method that obtains information through direct interviews. The rigorous techniques for estimating total utility and consumers' surplus are quite expensive. They can only be justified for decisions that involve large values or major policy issues.

All valuation methods, including market prices, must be used judiciously. They do not eliminate the need for judgment on the part of the planner. They are tools, and it is the way they are used that ultimately determines the usefulness of the results.

3. LACK OF APPRECIATION OF WHY SOME THINGS ARE NOT PRICED

Daily purchases of priced things lead many people to equate market price with value. Things that do not have market prices should therefore have no value. But since this is obviously not true, people tend to feel that unpriced things must have a different kind of value than priced ones. Because there does not seem to be any accepted way of measuring this different kind of value, people then think decisions about unpriced things must be difficult.

This is reflected in the reasons commonly given for why things are unpriced. Some things are said to be unpriced because they occur naturally or are free gifts of nature. Others are claimed to be unpriced because they are intangible. Still others are said to be of such an emotional or psychological nature that they are not susceptible to pricing. But none of these so-called reasons is sufficient to explain the lack of prices. The whole line of reasoning is based on a misunderstanding. These things do not lack prices because they have a different kind of value but because they have characteristics that prevent people exchanging them in markets where prices can develop. Let us analyze these characteristics more closely.

3.1. The Basic Reason Why Things Are Not Priced—Inappropriability

The real reasons why things are not priced all relate in some way to the exchange process. There may be some things for which it is impossible to develop prices, but we do not think many fall in this category. In most cases an inability to develop prices can be traced to conditions surrounding the value object or to circumstances of the people concerned with it.

Many things are not priced because there is no feasible way to make other people pay for them. It is not possible for someone to appropriate these things and exclude others from them. Consumers can get these things without going through an exchange. And without exchanges, there are no markets or market prices. The consumer still pays a price for these things in the form of opportunity costs, but he does not do it overtly where other people can observe how much he is paying.

Value objects may be natural things or human products. Those produced by people are usually priced because the producers can withhold them from other people by refusing to produce more. Some do not have prices for reasons we discuss later. Things not produced by people may or may not have prices depending on whether someone can get exclusive control of them. If a person can appropriate a thing by taking physical possession of it or by excluding people from it, he can force others to pay him for it. It then becomes a priced object.

There are some natural things that people cannot use because they are inaccessible. If a person supplies a means of access and has exclusive control of it, he may be in the same position as if he had produced the object itself and thus be able to charge a price for it. An example is a sea lion cave in coastal Oregon, a natural rock formation used as a resting and mating area by sea lions who spend most of their lives in the open ocean. The entrance is below normal tide levels and inaccessible to people who would enjoy observing the lions. An entrepreneur sank a shaft to a point where a window could overlook the cave and installed an elevator to carry people to that point. He is now able to charge an admission fee because although he does not own the animals, he has exclusive control of the access to them. Observation of sea lions is now a priced commodity.

3.2. Inadequate Incentive to Appropriate

Many things are unpriced because they cannot be appropriated or because the net benefit from doing so would not make it worthwhile. For example, it may be physically impossible, and therefore prohibitively expensive, to restrict access to some value objects. A thing may be so widely distributed that no one can appropriate more than an infinitesimal part of the total, as is usually the case with air. Or the possible means of access may be so numerous that no one can block more than a few of them. If sea lions could be observed in the sea at all times from any point on the Oregon coast, there would be no way of forcing people to pay, and sea lion observation would be an unpriced commodity.

In other cases the profit potential may not be sufficient to attract entrepreneurs. It might be entirely possible for a landowner to exclude people from entering his property and picking berries. However, there may be few pickers in the area and none willing to pay much for the right to pick berries. The landowner may therefore feel the income he could derive from selling berry-picking rights would not justify the effort. If other landowners feel the same way, berry picking will remain an unpriced activity.

3.3. Free or Forced Exchange for Social Reasons

It may not be possible to appropriate and charge a price for certain things because society feels it is not morally acceptable. It would not usually be possible to restrict access to lifeboats on a sinking ship and thus make a priced commodity of the opportunity to save one's life. Some things are unpriced because society feels it would be morally wrong for people to withhold them from others.

A social group may also feel it is not in the interest of the group as a whole for certain things to be withheld from some of its members. It may therefore take steps to prevent the exclusion of potential consumers and thus make it impossible for markets and prices to develop. Two kinds of things fall in this category. The first are merit goods—things that society feels are good for its members and which they should have, regardless of their preferences. An example is compulsory basic education. The second class are equity goods—things that are given special treatment with an aim of equitable distribution. Examples are emergency medical treatment and fire protection. These social goods are usually provided at public expense and without a direct price to consumers.

3.4. Free or Forced Exchange for Biophysical Reasons

The biophysical characteristics of some things make it possible for people to consume them without paying, or force people to consume them against their wishes. The first kind are partly public goods—things that automatically become available to other people if they are produced or paid for by one person. An example is highway beautification. This first class also includes external economies—beneficial effects of one person's actions that automatically become available to other people. An example is the reduction of flood damage downstream as a result of reforestation of headwater lands for timber production. The second kind are external diseconomies—negative effects of one person's actions that are borne by other people. An example is the deterioration of water quality downstream as a result of effluent discharge upstream. The downstream water users are forced to receive these disutilities which the effluent discharger did not impose on them intentionally.

3.5. Free Exchange for Individual Reasons

In some cases a producer desires to give his product away free. People voluntarily provide many kinds of services to others without compensation. Because no market exchange takes place, one cannot find market prices for the services of volunteer firemen and Red Cross volunteers. Analysts have been puzzled over the valuation of housewives' time. The services they provide are obviously of very high value to their families, but because they are not paid in money, no market prices develop. Finally, according to custom some things are given away free. People are expected to serve without compensation as officers of clubs and as local politicians. Such customs vary among countries and often among localities.

3.6. Indivisibility

Some things cannot be divided into exchangeable units. For example, a flood-control program cannot be divided into units that would make it possible for a person to buy just enough to protect himself. The affected social group must buy the whole program or none at all. There is not likely to be a market price for individual protection from floods.

3.7. The Common Theme

For a market price to develop, suppliers must be able to appropriate something that other people want and exclude them from it unless they pay a price for it. Some things do not have prices because there is not enough incentive for anyone to appropriate them. Others are not priced because society is not willing to allow individuals to appropriate them and exclude others from them or because society feels it is necessary to supply them as a social enterprise. Some cannot be appropriated for biophysical reasons or cannot be divided into marketable units. The inappropriability that is the common characteristic of all these situations is the real reason why unpriced things do not have prices.

4. INCOMPLETE CONSIDERATION OF THE DECISION SITUATION

Decisions involving unpriced values are often considered difficult merely because some things are unpriced or benefits and costs are measured in different units. But valuations are made to aid decisions. A rational decision requires a comparative valuation of the alternatives among which the decision maker must choose. Comparative valuation is a means, not an end. One cannot decide whether an unpriced value is difficult to estimate or not until one understands the decision in which it is to be used.

There are two broad types of decisions that require comparative valuations—compensations and choices between alternatives. In the following sections we see how they determine the kind of valuation needed.

4.1. Compensation

A compensation situation arises when something unfavorable has happened to someone and other people wish to offset the loss. The loss may have already occurred and someone has a contractual or legal obligation to compensate the injured party. Or an action may be under consideration that will damage someone and it is necessary to know the compensation involved to decide whether to undertake the action or not.

The objective of compensation is to return the damaged person to a state of well-being at least as good as he enjoyed before. Compensation must therefore be based on a comparison of the person's situations before and after the loss.

Chapter 17 discussed two examples of method used by Peters (1971) and Helliwell (1967) to systematize and analyze past decisions. Peters' analysis considered compensation specifically, and Helliwell's analysis can readily be applied to compensation decisions. In Figure 18.1, we present a classification of compensation decisions to aid in selecting appropriate methods. Compensation situations can be divided into those in which replacement in kind is possible and those in which it is not. Situations in which replacement in kind is not possible can be further subdivided into those in which data are available from previous compensation decisions and those in which no previous data are available. As shown in Figure 18.1, different methodological approaches are useful for each of these situations.

4.1.1. Replacement in Kind Possible. In some cases it is possible to compensate a person by replacing the object that was destroyed or lost. In such cases no appraisal of value is necessary. All that is needed to determine the amount of compensation is a physical inventory of the loss.

4.1.2. Replacement in Kind not Possible. Compensation in this case must consist of an equivalent value in some other form. The form most commonly used is money because it is readily exchangeable for a great variety of things. But this does not necessarily mean that there is a market price for the loss. The owner may be compensated by a sum of money large enough to buy things equivalent in value to that of the loss.

Sometimes, compensation in money is not satisfactory because the damaged person feels he will not be able to buy an adequate replacement. A farmer whose land has been taken may feel that the only satisfactory compensation would be in the form of land. It is usually impossible to replace one tract of land with another that is identical in all respects. It is necessary to find another tract that the farmer considers of equal value to him. If productivity is his criterion, it is necessary to find another tract of the same productive potential, even though it may be of a different size.

The compensation situation requires an exact determination of comparative values. Valuations for compensation are therefore likely to be more difficult than are those made for choices among alternatives. Even when they

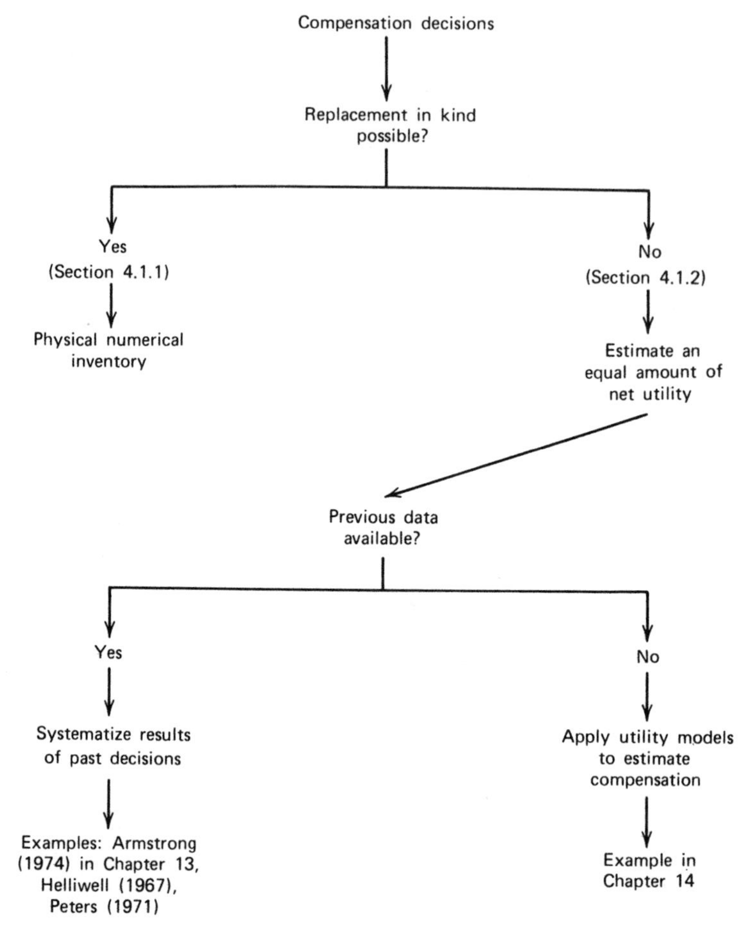

Figure 18.1. A classification of compensation decision situations to aid in selecting a valuation method.

exist, market prices may not be adequate for this purpose. The valuation problem for compensation is one of finding another object that the affected person feels has the same net utility. It may not be necessary to determine the value of either object if it can be established that this person would be indifferent to which he had.

4.2. Choice between Alternatives

Decisions always involve marginal changes from existing situations. They usually can be approached as choices among alternatives.

One kind of decision involves only two alternatives. This is the either/or decision. An example is a proposed flood-control dam. The two alternatives are to continue the status quo or to make a change by building the dam. The analyst must compare the value of the present situation with the value of the one that would exist if the dam were built. He does not necessarily have to know the value of the present situation. All he has to determine is whether the marginal change in social value brought about by building the dam would be positive or not. If it would be positive, society would be better off building the dam.

A second kind of decision involves various alternatives in addition to maintaining the status quo. If all alternatives would produce positive changes, the rational choice is the one that would produce the largest change. If the marginal change is measured in social value, this alternative will add most to total social value.

The situation in which the choice must be made determines the kind of value information needed. One can imagine a situation in which a decision maker has no constraints on his choices. Under these conditions, the number of alternatives would be very large. To make a choice, the decision maker would have to compare the value of one alternative against that of every other possible alternative. But this is clearly an imaginary situation. Any actual situation will have constraints on what the decision maker can do. He does not have to consider all imaginary alternatives, but only those that are actually possible in his situation. Figure 18.2 presents the three kinds of situations which a decision maker might face and shows how valuation can be tailored to them.

4.2.1. Neither Benefits nor Costs Fixed. A common situation is one in which neither costs nor benefits are absolutely specified but in which there are some constraints on available resources or on demand. Marginal costs of resource inputs will therefore rise with increasing production, and marginal utility will diminish with increasing consumption.

The decision maker must analyze each alternative as a marginal change from the existing situation. The value comparison takes the form

$$(MU_m - MC_m) \text{ compared to } (MU_n - MC_n)$$

where MU_m is the marginal utility resulting from alternative m and MC_m is the marginal cost of obtaining that utility. Only alternatives whose marginal utility would exceed their marginal cost need be considered in the decision.

This is the most difficult of the choice situations, because not only is MU_m likely to differ from MU_n and from the marginal utilities of other alternatives, but also MC_m is likely to differ from MC_n. It is therefore necessary to estimate the marginal utilities and marginal costs for each

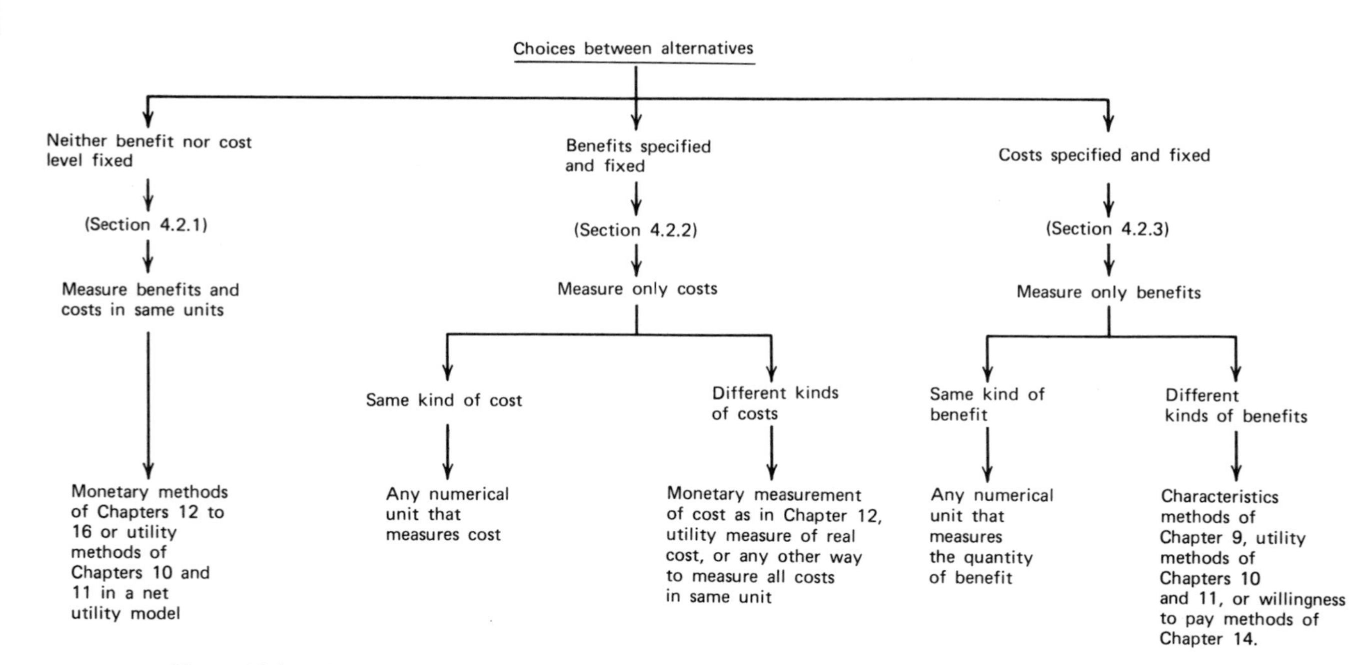

Figure 18.2. ***A classification of choice-between-alternatives situations to aid in selecting a valuation method.***

alternative and to somehow express the marginal net values in comparable terms.

4.2.2. Benefits Specified. In many situations the decision maker does not have to worry about which benefit to choose because that is specified for him. His problem is to decide how best to produce that benefit. The marginal utility of the benefit will presumably be the same regardless of how he decides to produce it. Any differences in marginal social value among the alternatives open to him must result from differences in their marginal costs. The best choice will, therefore, be the alternative that involves the smallest cost. The values comparison takes the form

$$(B - MC_m) \text{ compared to } (B - MC_n)$$

where B is the constant marginal utility of the benefit and m and n are two alternative ways of obtaining B. This reduces to

$$MC_m \text{ compared to } MC_n$$

In this kind of situation, a cost-minimization procedure will help to make the decision, even though it will not place a value on the benefit. The opportunity-cost methods of Chapter 12 and the travel-cost method of Chapter 16 are developed from this principle. They are most applicable to this kind of situation.

The kind of value estimate needed depends on the kind of costs involved. Let us consider what these might be.

Same Kind of Cost. The costs of all alternatives may be of the same kind. For example, there may be three alternative routes for reaching a waterfall. The cost of getting to the waterfall by any of the routes is a certain amount of walking time. Assuming there are no other differences, the most valuable route is the one that requires the least walking time. It is not necessary to place a value on a view of the waterfall or on a unit of walking time. When the costs are of the same kind, they can be compared in physical quantities.

Different Kinds of Costs. If the alternatives involve different kinds of costs, they cannot be compared in physical terms. Suppose a public-works director has been instructed to make certain improvements to a town park and to transfer the necessary funds from another part of his budget. He can see only two alternatives: take the road maintenance crew off that work long enough to improve the park or use the money he had budgeted for painting the municipal building to pay for the park work. The citizens will enjoy the same utility from the improved park in either case, but the net social benefit will depend on how much they have to sacrifice for it.

The director cannot choose the least-cost alternative by comparing man-hours of road crew time with dollars of painting budget. He might compare the wages that would be paid the road crew while they worked on the park with the painting budget. Both would be expressed in money and therefore would be comparable. But the real costs to the citizens would be having to travel for another year on poor roads or having to put up for another year with a shabby municipal building. The monetary costs would not accurately reflect these comparative sacrifices. What must be compared are the opportunity costs of the two alternatives: How does the marginal utility to the citizens of the road improvement compare with that of a freshly painted municipal building?

4.2.3. Costs Specified. In many situations a decision maker does not have to worry about what cost to incur because that is specified for him. His problem is to decide how to produce the greatest benefit from a fixed budget. (The budget may be in money or in resources such as labor or land.) The opportunity cost of the fixed budget will be the same regardless of what benefits are produced. Any differences in marginal social value between alternatives must result from differences in marginal utilities. The best choice is therefore the alternative that would produce the maximum utility. The value comparison takes the form

$$(MU_m - OC) \text{ compared to } (MU_n - OC)$$

where OC is the constant opportunity cost of the fixed budget and m and n are two alternative ways of using OC. This reduces to

$$MU_m \text{ compared to } MU_n$$

Same Kind of Benefits. All alternatives may produce benefits of the same kind. Suppose a state government has decided to allocate a certain amount of resources to a long-term program of reforesting idle lands in the state. Assuming that forest cover is of equal value on all idle land, the most valuable reforestation program will be the one that establishes successful plantations on the greatest number of acres. It is not necessary to place a value on an acre of reforested land or on the opportunity cost of the resources used. When benefits are of the same kind, they can be compared in physical quantities.

Different Kinds of Benefits. If the alternative uses of a fixed budget involve different kinds of benefits, they cannot be compared in physical terms. Suppose land has been acquired for a state park and the director has been allocated a certain amount of resources for its development. The two alternatives appear to be to develop part of the land intensively for playing fields or to develop the whole area extensively for hiking trails and picnic areas. The comparative social values of the alternative developments depend on the utilities they would provide the people of the state. Because there already are other recreation opportunities in the state, the value will depend on the marginal social utilities of the additional facilities. These will depend on how many people would use each new facility. The director must compare the additional utilities that would be enjoyed by the two groups of people who use the different developments.

5. CONCLUSION

We have demonstrated in this chapter that decisions involving unpriced values are not necessarily more difficult than those involving priced values. The analyst must first distinguish clearly what is being exchanged as a result of the decision. If he tries to place a value on the underlying resource or on the ultimate utility, he is not likely to produce information useful for the decision. Second, he must be aware of the weaknesses of market prices as value indicators and fully cognizant of what the alternative valuation methods can and cannot do. If he uses either market prices or alternative methods naively, he can make serious mistakes. Third, he must appreciate why the things he is dealing with do not have market prices. Which of the alternative methods can be validly used and how they can be used depends on why the things being valued are not priced. Finally, he must always approach valuation in the context of the specific decision. A clear understanding of the kind of value information needed for the decision will almost always make it possible to obtain helpful estimates of comparative values. The following chapter will show how useful information can be obtained for some things that are reputedly very difficult to value.

The purpose of comparative valuations is to assist in making rational decisions. The more accurate our estimate of comparative values, the more likely we are to choose the alternative that is really most valuable to us. But there are always costs involved in obtaining more information. Additional information is only justified if the benefits from having it exceed the cost of obtaining it. It is never justifiable to spend more on a value appraisal than is necessary for the decision. Even when a decision affects millions of people and involves very large values, a simple method may adequately determine comparative values. The more detailed methods of Part II of this book are only justified when a high degree of accuracy is essential to a rational decision.

CHAPTER 19

Reputedly Difficult Valuations—Analyses of Examples

Chapter 18 discussed a number of reasons why decisions involving unpriced values are considered difficult. We found that many apparent difficulties become less restrictive or disappear when decisions are analyzed fully and logically. This chapter applies that finding to some things people say are very difficult to value.

The basic valuation problem is to find out how people feel about the differences things make to their lives. Why should it be more difficult to get such information about unpriced objects? Chapter 18 suggested the difficulty often results from misunderstandings about what is being exchanged, why the objects in question are unpriced, or the nature of the decision itself. With this in mind, let us analyze some examples.

1. WHAT IS THE VALUE OF A REDUCTION IN NOISE?

Most noise problems center around noise reduction. Few people want more noise, but many desire to reduce it. Planners need to know the value of reducing noise, but have no market to which they can turn for a price.

1.1. Nature of the Valuation

People experience noise as a physical effect, and its disutility is less subjective than the utilities of many unpriced things. Noise can also be measured accurately in physical terms.

Objectionable noise is not a natural phenomenon. It is produced by people for personal satisfaction, as in the case of trumpet players and some motorcyclists, or as an external effect of some other activity, as in the case of power mowers and jet airplanes. The people involved do not intentionally produce noise and would be just as happy not to do so.

Objectionable noise is almost always a spillover effect of human activities carried on for other purposes. What people are asked to give up in noise abatement is not the opportunity to make noise but the opportunity to enjoy riding a motorcycle or to transport useful products in a truck. Such noisy activities have utility for those who engage in them, and in the aggregate they also have social utility. The valuation problem is to compare the social utility of noise reduction with the social utilities that will be lost by abandoning a noise-producing activity.

1.2. Nature of the Decision

Decisions usually involve reduction rather than elimination of noise. The result of a decision is a marginal decrease in the amount of noise. But there also will be a marginal decrease in social value as a result of the decreased physical output or increased cost of the noise-producing activity. For example, to reduce noise level at an airport it may be necessary to decrease the number of flights or to increase the cost of maintaining the same number. Either will lead to a marginal decrease in the social value of airport services. The decision maker must compare this with the marginal increase in social value resulting from noise reduction.

If it has already been decided for health reasons to reduce the general noise level by a certain amount it is not necessary to value noise reduction itself. The decision should choose the least-cost means of achieving the specified reduction. If a fixed budget has been allocated to a noise-reduction program, it again is not necessary to estimate the value of noise. The decision should choose that one of the possible actions that will achieve the greatest reduction.

The accuracy of noise measurement and the transferability of a noise index can assist decisions that require monetary estimates of net utility. Walters (1975) observed an inverse relationship between a physical index of noise and house prices around a London airport. He generalized this relationship into a simple rule for estimating the monetary noise costs of a new airport from its predicted noise index. The rule takes the same approach as in the example of the effect of trees on house prices in Section 5.2 of Chapter 13.

Many decisions concerning noise are of an either/or nature—should a particular action be taken or not? The criterion is whether the result of the decision will be a net increase in social value. Some decisions involve a choice among alternative programs which have different costs and would achieve different amounts of noise reduction. The analyst must estimate social benefits and costs in the same units to determine net social value.

1.3. Toward a Rational Approach

In a fixed-budget situation it is only necessary to rank alternatives in terms of noise reduction achieved. However, the total noise level may be composed of various kinds of sounds, some of which are more damaging, distracting, or annoying than others. It may be possible to rank or weight these in order of disutility. Then the methods of Chapters 9 and 11 may help aggregate the sounds into a single index for a decision. If alternative actions can be specified as to the kind of noise reduced, they can be ranked by one of the expedient methods of Chapter 10. If the negative effects of noise are recognized by the affected people, direct questioning or the trade-off games discussed in Chapter 14 may be the best means of ranking alternatives.

The single-direct-question method was used by the Roskill Commission to obtain a monetary estimate of the costs of airport noise in London (Paul, 1971). Subjects were asked to consider two houses that were identical in all respects including price except that one was affected by airport noise. The subjects were asked how much cheaper the noisy house would have to be before they would consider buying it. Fifty percent replied that no reduction in price would induce them to live close to a major airport. The responses of the others varied from zero to £7000.

In many cases it is possible to treat noise as a threshold problem. An example is a decision by timber harvesting firms whether to provide ear-protection equipment for woods workers. McDermid and McKnight (1975) report that a study in Louisiana found chain saws produced a mean noise level of 110 decibels. Under the Occupational Safety and Health Act, the permissible exposure to noise at this level is only one-half hour per day. The noise reduction achieved by ear-protection equipment would make it possible for loggers to work a full day. Most employers had little difficulty deciding that the utility of the additional working time plus the personal benefits to the workers exceeded the threshold cost of providing the equipment. Noise reduction had a net value to them.

When decisions cannot be based on comparative utilities or thresholds, it is necessary to make an estimate of net value. This should be expressed in monetary units. Four of the methods discussed in Chapters 12 through 17 are suitable for this and are presented in a simple example. Suppose the volume of traffic on a major highway is increasing and the people who live along it are complaining about the rising noise level. A plan has been proposed to construct buffer strips of trees, shrubs, and mechanical baffles to dampen the noise spillover. Would the resulting noise reduction have a net value after the cost of the buffer strip is paid?

One approach is through the opportunity-cost methods of Chapter 12. An engineering study can be made to determine the least expensive way of soundproofing the affected houses. The cost of this program indicates the social opportunity cost of reducing the noise. This and the cost of the proposed buffer strip can then be presented to the decision maker, who must decide whether to reduce the noise and, if so, by which method.

A second approach is through the interpretation of land and house prices, as discussed in Chapter 13. The market value of real estate in the noise zone and of equivalent houses in areas with noise levels approximating those to be achieved with the buffer strip can be determined from current transactions. The value of the buffer strip should be at least as great as the difference between the current value of real estate in the affected zone and the value it would have in a quieter area.

In the absence of sufficient transactions appraisals by competent local real estate dealers can be used. The Roskill Commission (1971) followed this approach in investigating the effect of noise from the third London airport on prices of nearby houses. Prices inside the noisy zone were found to be as much as 22.5 percent lower than those outside the zone. The decrease in price was correlated with the actual noise level.

A third approach is to use compensation awards by courts as indicators of the change in market price resulting from noise. The California Supreme Court found in favor of some 600 property owners in a suit against Los Angeles over damage from airport noise (Aaron vs. City of Los Angeles, 1970). Awards ranged from $800 to $6000. If noise levels along the highway approximated those near the Los Angeles airport, the utility of a buffer strip might be estimated to be in this same range.

Finally, one of the direct-question methods of Chapter 14 can be used to learn how much residents of the noise zone would be willing to pay to reduce the noise level to that which might be achieved with the buffer strip. A representative sample of residents would be interviewed and their responses aggregated to obtain the total willingness to pay of the noise zone population. The value of the buffer strip should be at least equal to this total willingness to pay.

One method may be enough if the benefit it indicates is much larger or much smaller than the estimated cost of the buffer strip. If the estimated benefit is very close to the cost, it would be desirable to make other estimates with other methods. Because all of the methods have weaknesses, a combination of methods could be most reliable.

2. WHAT IS THE VALUE OF A PERSON'S TIME?

Many decisions involve an exchange of time between users or between individuals and groups. Comparative values for the times and other things being exchanged are necessary for rational decisions.

2.1. Nature of the Valuation

Time is a flow resource whose value stems from the use made of it. It cannot be stored, and the potential yield is lost if it is not used. But time is measurable and can be exchanged. If a person does not have enough time of his own, he can often buy part of someone else's time. By hiring a baby-sitter, for example, parents can buy enough additional time to enable them to both attend a concert and watch over their children. In situations like this, time is usually a priced commodity. Baby-sitters give up some of their limited time in exchange for money, and the price they demand depends on how valuable their time is to them. This in turn depends on the utility they could derive by using their time in some other way.

It is not time itself that has value but what might be done during that time. The value of an hour is without meaning, but the value of an hour of surgery or of automobile use can have meaning. Even here, one must specify the kind of surgery and the circumstances in which the automobile is used. The value of time derives from the values of the purposes for which it is used.

The duration of time can be measured precisely, and most things affected by time can be specified objectively. A subjective aspect may arise in determining possible alternative uses. There is disagreement, for example, as to exactly what people obtain from leisure time. We are forced to spend a substantial part of our time sleeping, but most people also use additional time for an ill-defined purpose called "resting." The value of a coffee-break obviously depends on something more basic than coffee consumption.

2.2. Nature of the Decision

Time is sometimes viewed as a commodity to be saved. This is common in decisions about road construction, airport expansion, and other programs that make it possible for people to travel faster from one place to another. The decision criterion is whether the social value of the time saved by future travelers will be greater than the improvement costs.

Time is also viewed as a resource that people use to obtain benefits. This is common in decisions about preserving, developing, or improving sites for recreation. The decision criterion is whether the additional recreation opportunities will have a social value greater than their cost. The social value is indicated by the willingness of recreationists to pay. Because people must expend both time and money to use recreation opportunities, the time expenditure must be estimated in monetary units and added to the financial expenditure. The expenditure of time can be measured as the opportunity cost of using limited time resources.

Time is also seen as a resource and explicitly treated as a cost in decisions about committing resources to exclusive uses for periods of time. Competitive market prices are good estimates of opportunity costs for such decisions. The most serious exception is the time of housewives and others who are not regularly compensated at market wage rates. However, the time of housewives who hold other employment does have an explicit opportunity cost, and the use of time by their families is influenced by the wives' wage rates. Prochaska and Schrimper (1973) found that such families tend to eat out more than other families and that the frequency of eating out rises as the wife's wage rate increases. The allocation of the time resource to different ends is thus influenced by its value.

Finally, there are situations in which time has negative value. This is seen with elderly and handicapped people (and perhaps also children) who have difficulty filling their idle time. The social opportunity cost of having them do something is actually negative. Analysts must therefore be careful not to overestimate time as a cost. When volunteers provide the labor input, one must recognize that the time they work may represent a social benefit rather than a social cost. The travel time of elderly recreationists may provide utility because it fills otherwise idle time. And the time saved by a transportation improvement could have no value to people if they already have a surplus.

2.3. Toward a Rational Approach

Saving Time. For decisions that aim at saving time, there are four useful approaches. Let us use as an example a highway improvement program that would reduce the average commuter's round trip time. One could use the opportunity-cost methods of Chapter 12. The time of commuters might be valued at their wage rates. This is valid for commuters such as salesmen, who can use additional time to increase their incomes. People on fixed salaries or fixed schedules cannot do this and might value their free time at rates different from their wage rates. Cesario (1976) reports the value people place on nonwork travel time is between one-fourth and one-half of their wage rates.

A second approach is possible when people can be observed choosing among transportation forms that differ in cost and speed, as in Chapter 15. These choices can be considered as trade-offs between money and time. Those who select the higher-cost, faster forms apparently feel the time saved is worth the additional money. Their average additional expenditure is a rough estimate of the value of saved time. Those who use the slower modes do not consider the time saved to be worth the marginal cost of a faster one. Markham and O'Farrell (1974) found that the time and cost of train travel and the cost of car travel all affected Dublin commuters' choice between train and automobile. An analysis of actual choices suggested that a reduction in travel time of five minutes per trip would divert twice as many commuters to rail transportation as would making rail travel free. For these people, a time saving of five minutes was more valuable than a cost saving of thirty pence.

A third approach is to use the direct-question methods of Chapter 14. People can be asked to estimate the value of a proposed saving in commuting time. One of the original applications of the priority-evaluator technique discussed in Chapter 14 was to estimate the value of time savings to London commuters (Hoinville and Berthoud, 1970b). A time saving of 10 minutes was found to provide the same utility as a fare saving of 10 pence.

A fourth approach is to use real estate values, as discussed in Chapter 13. The prices of houses and other real estate usually vary inversely with distance from commercial and employment centers. Differences in values of similar houses in similar settings can be construed as the capitalized worths of differences in commuting time. Owen and Thirsk (1974) found a strong relationship between the level of residential development and the distance to the commercial center of Houston. Their finding that distance was the most important explanatory variable supports the valuing of time through its proxy of distance.

Time as a Cost. There are two useful approaches for decisions in which value is indicated by behavior and willingness to pay. The first is to use an opportunity-cost method from Chapter 12. One approach is to base value on a person's regular wage rate. In a study of social and recreational trips between Edinburgh and Glasgow, Watson (1974) found people valued time at an average of 67.5 percent of their wage rates. Cesario (1976) argues that because recreational travel takes place during nonworking periods, the appropriate opportunity cost is the value placed on time for leisure activities rather than on that for work. Direct-questioning techniques from Chapter 14 may be needed to extract these opportunity costs. However, the alternative to recreational travel for some people might be productive work. In this case the analyst should try to find the wage rate or, more generally, the marginal value product of the time units.

The second approach is to observe the trade-offs that people make between money and travel time when choosing recreation sites. For example, suppose there are two comparable camping areas—a nearby one that charges an entrance fee and a distant one that makes no charge. If all arriving campers are informed about both campgrounds, their choices will indicate the value they place on the time required to reach the second campground.

(A useful general review of the valuation of time is to be found in Harrison and Quarmby, 1972.)

3. WHAT IS THE VALUE OF OPEN SPACE?

The growing concentration of people and structures has reduced space to a point where many people feel crowded. Land-use planners must make many choices involving the creation or preservation of open space and need information about its social value.

3.1. Nature of the Valuation

Open space clearly does not mean empty space, but includes objects and their relative positions in this space. For many people the term implies some kind of natural cover or at least rural uses. For others it implies aesthetic characteristics that rule out things like open-face mines. The benefits people derive from open space are varied and quite subjective.

The physical aspects of open space are readily measured, but the utilities derived from them are more difficult to measure. Quality is an important determinant of value, but it varies with the surrounding areas and the availability of alternatives. Open-space value is specific to site and person. Similar areas have different values in different places and for different people.

Open-space benefits can only be appropriated to a certain extent. One can exclude people from entering on the land itself, but it is difficult to exclude them from looking at it or obtaining sensations of openness and space. Although open space is not a market commodity, its value may be incorporated in the values of appropriable things like houses and campgrounds.

Open space is usually a public good, because one person's enjoyment does not detract from that of others. Social utility is often greater than that enjoyed by individual owners, and social value may be poorly indicated by the private value of land for open space.

The exchange that takes place when open-space areas are preserved is not usually clear and neat. Only when people purchase an area specifically for preservation do we see an explicit appraisal of open-space value. When people decide to preserve open spaces, they do not get something new but prevent a loss. They receive the right to continue enjoying open-space benefits. This is often obscured by the fact that the people who will benefit in the future are not the same ones who have benefited in the past. Exchanges take place mainly in the public sector with governments or quasipublic agencies acting for consumers.

3.2. Nature of the Decision

Open space can be created by demolishing existing structures and rehabilitating the sites. An example is the creation of miniparks in urban areas. The decision criterion is whether the social benefit from open space (net of the rehabilitation costs) will be greater than the net social benefit from alternative uses. The decision is simplified if no alternative uses are attractive to private entrepreneurs. In this case the decision criterion is whether the social utility of open space will be greater than the rehabilitation costs.

A more common decision is whether an open area should be maintained or converted to a more-intensive use. The decision criterion is whether the net social benefit from the proposed use (after all conversion costs) will be greater than the present open-space value. When the quantity of land is fixed, a change in land price can give an accurate estimate of the change in net social benefit, as we discussed in Chapter 13. For example, the conversion of wetlands around San Francisco Bay to more intensive uses has raised land value by at least $47,000 per acre (Luken, 1974). The decision maker needs to know whether the social value of continuing this land in open space is greater than $47,000 per acre.

Finally, a decision may involve a choice between two open-space areas. For example, a school may have to be built in one of two open areas. If construction costs would be the same in either area, the decision must be based on which of the areas would represent the least social cost in terms of open-space values lost. A similar situation exists when only enough funds are available to acquire and preserve one open-space area. The choice must go to the area that will have the greatest social value.

3.3. Toward a Rational Approach

Creation of Open Space. When the only alternative to demolishing structures to create open space is to allow the present condition to continue, the decision can be approached as a threshold problem. The threshold is the cost of demolishing the structures and establishing satisfactory open-space conditions. This can usually be estimated accurately. The decision maker needs only to decide whether the social value of the proposed open space will be greater than this threshold cost. The direct-question methods of Chapter 14 can be used to estimate the minimum social value of the open space.

The threshold approach can also be used when there are alternative uses for the land. The social value of the best alternative use provides the base for the threshold. This may be estimated by soliciting bids for purchase of the land. If the land market is reasonably competitive, the highest bid should indicate the value of the land in its best alternative use. If the market cannot be used directly, the net annual income from the best alternative use can be estimated after allowing for all development costs, operating costs, and normal profit. This net income can be capitalized at the market rate of interest to obtain the value of the land in its present condition. The cost to society of creating open space would be the value of the land in the best alternative use plus the cost of rehabilitating the land into a satisfactory open-space condition. This total social cost is the threshold. If the maximum possible open space value is less than the threshold, the land should not be used for open space. If the minimum open-space value would exceed the threshold, rehabilitating the area for open space would be socially desirable.

The direct-question methods of Chapter 14 can assist threshold decisions to create open spaces. For example, Berry (1975) used the single-direct-question method to value the benefit from existing open-space parks in Philadelphia and the benefit from additional parks. The average annual household benefit from one existing park was estimated at $60. This average benefit would rise to $75 if the area of the park were doubled. The marginal benefit of $15 per household multiplied by the number of households can be compared to the cost of acquiring the additional land.

Preserving Open Space. This can also be set up as a threshold decision. The value of the land in the proposed new use can usually be determined from offers to purchase or by capitalizing estimated net revenues. The question is whether people feel the land has greater value as open space than it would have in the alternative uses. A good approach is direct questioning or a trade-off game, as discussed in Chapter 14. Additional information may be obtained from real estate prices if house lots near the open-space area can be compared with similar lots in areas without open space, This approach is described in Chapter 13 and illustrated with the Gupta and Foster (1975) study of wetland acquisition.

Choice among Open-Space Areas. This kind of decision requires an indicator of the comparative social values of the alternative areas. Precise values are not usually needed. If information can be developed on the open-space characteristics that people feel are most closely related to value, the areas can be compared as described in Chapter 9. For example, if open space is being acquired along highways to provide a pleasing environment for travelers, alternative areas might be compared primarily in terms of visibility.

One of the total-utility methods discussed in Chapters 10 and 11 may also be useful. Decision makers, representative groups, or the general public can be questioned as to the priorities they would assign to preserving various open-space areas. As Berry (1975) shows, the relative positions of different areas on this overall scale are good indicators of their comparative social values. In his study the relative priorities of different parks for different purposes were expressed on a simple percentage scale. The scale recorded the proportion of the people sampled who felt that a given purpose was important for a given park. The results obtained with an expedient method (Chapter 10) provided a basis for choice among different kinds of open space.

4. WHAT IS THE VALUE OF AN ENDANGERED SPECIES?

Of the animal species known to have been alive in 1600, some 130 are now extinct, and at least 307 others are in danger of extinction (Fisher et al., 1969). Many species of plants have also become extinct or are in danger. The apparent acceleration in this process has stimulated proposals to reduce further extinctions. The question arises of whether the social value of vanishing species justifies their preservation.

4.1. Nature of the Valuation

The significant characteristic of these species is that if their total populations fall below a critical number, the current declines will become irreversible, and the species will vanish. The value at question is not that of individual animals or plants but rather of the continued existence of species. Attempts are made to preserve representatives of vanishing species under artificial conditions. But the results are museum pieces whose value differs from that of animals and plants in the wild. We consider here only the value of preservation under natural conditions.

What people receive from successful preservation efforts is a knowledge that the species will continue to exist and a possible opportunity to see and study them. The utility is subjective and often emotional. The present population of a species can usually be measured fairly accurately, but population and trends in numbers are just indicators of what is happening and not measures of utility. Value depends only on whether the species survives.

Preservation of an endangered species is not ordinarily a market commodity. Except for occasional cases of individual philanthropy, exchanges take place in the public sector. However, preservation and valuation can sometimes be achieved through the market system, as in the case of the

California tule elk. Controlled hunting and maintenance of the herds have produced a situation in which the total willingness to pay for the limited number of shooting permits exceeds the total costs of preserving a species that was near extinction (Ciriacy-Wantrup and Phillips, 1970).

4.2. Nature of the Decision

Extinction is a part of evolution, and it is estimated that one-fourth of the known extinctions since 1600 resulted from natural, nonhuman causes (Fisher et al., 1969). The present rarity of 32 percent of the endangered birds and 14 percent of the endangered mammals is attributed to natural causes. Human actions are responsible for the danger to the majority of the species now threatened with extinction.

Decisions about endangered species become necessary when (a) a natural cause of threatened extinction might be offset or eliminated by human actions, (b) existing human actions detrimental to a species might be modified or eliminated to preserve the species, or (c) a proposed human action would threaten a species with extinction.

In the first case resources would have to be transferred from other productive activities into actions against the natural cause of extinction. The decision maker must decide whether the social benefits from preserving the species will be greater than the opportunity costs required.

The second situation requires a trade-off decision. If people continue present actions, the species will eventually be exterminated. To preserve it, people must change their practices or give up some actions altogether. Since present actions provide utility, changing or abandoning them will mean a sacrifice. The decision maker must decide whether preservation of the species will have social value greater than that being derived from the destructive actions that will have to be abandoned.

In the third situation the social loss that would result from extinction of the species plus the direct costs of carrying out the proposed action must be compared with the prospective social benefits from the action. The decision criterion is whether the proposed project would have a positive social value.

4.3. Toward a Rational Approach

All decisions about endangered species can be set up as threshold problems. What the decision maker must decide is whether the social benefits to be derived from preserving the species would be greater than the social costs involved.

In the case of offsetting a natural threat, the costs can usually be estimated quite accurately because they ordinarily consist of financial outlays.

Sometimes they are more complex, as in the case of the Dutch elm disease. Here it appeared possible to control the lethal fungus by destroying the insect that carried it. However, the pesticides used for this purpose also damaged birds and desirable insects. The threshold question is whether the social value of preventing extermination of the American elm is greater than the monetary cost of control plus the social costs of disrupting the ecosystem.

In the other two situations the human actions that would have to be foregone can often be appraised with market prices. This opportunity-cost approach was used by Goldstein (1971) to analyze the use of wetlands in central North America. At competitive market prices an acre of drained wetland provides a net annual income to a farmer of between $2 and $11. This income must be forgone if the wetland is preserved as a waterfowl breeding area.

When unpriced values, such as recreation benefits, are involved in the opportunity cost, the decision must be approached as a comparison between the value of species preservation and a bundle of other priced and unpriced values. If a species is threatened by environmental changes resulting from activities on which a substantial number of people depend for a living, comparative social values may be difficult to estimate.

In all these cases decisions must be made at a fairly high level in the social hierarchy. Reliable estimates of individual willingness to pay are usually difficult to determine, and market prices have little meaning. A comparative appraisal of social values must be made by someone in a position to act for the public. The analyst's job is to provide this person with as much information as possible about the alternatives.

Because a decision against preservation may be irreversible, it seems reasonable to place the burden of proof on the alternative actions. The decision question should be whether the social value of continuing present actions (or of instituting new actions) is greater than the value of preserving the endangered species. People can than be asked how large these other values must be before they would be willing to vote for permanent destruction of the species.

Many people have no opinion about preservation of endangered species because they lack knowledge or interest. Some would have difficulty making rational judgments even if information were provided. The direct-question methods of Chapter 14 will only be useful if the sample is selected from informed people in positions of responsibilty for social decisions.

Some historical information is available to indicate the relative magnitude of people's willingness to pay for the preservation of endangered species. An example is the hairy-nosed wombat in Australia. In 1967 one of the last three natural habitats of the wombat was about to be converted to agriculture. The owner was willing to sell the land at its market price, which presumably represented its social value in agriculture. An aggressive campaign by a preservation society raised the necessary $18,000 from people throughout South Australia in five weeks. Before the campaign ended the society had actually raised a total of $30,000. People in South Australia clearly felt that this particular tract of land had a higher social value as habitat for the endangered hairy-nosed wombat than as an agricultural resource. The analysis of past decisions and behavior, as described in Chapter 17, can provide useful information on the magnitude of the values involved. Such historical information can also be useful in testing the validity of the answers obtained to the hypothetical questions posed in the direct question methods.

5. WHAT IS THE VALUE OF GRADUAL CHANGE?

Many things change gradually over long periods of time. These slow changes may be imperceptible to people accustomed to thinking in days or years but may be significant for long-range planning. How can one place a comparative value on them?

5.1. Nature of the Valuation

Gradual changes may be positive or negative; they may represent increases or decreases in value. Their important characteristic is that their effects gradually accumulate until someone's life is measurably affected. The slower they occur, the less likely people are to be aware of them. Some changes, such as depletion of soil fertility, may occur so slowly as to go unnoticed during individual lifetimes, but are felt by society over generations.

The length of time it takes a gradual change to accumulate is important for valuation. Daily depreciation of an automobile is unnoticeable, but in 10 years most have depreciated to a point where they are no longer usable. Car owners are usually aware that depreciation is reducing the expected lifetimes of their vehicles. Because autombiles are priced commodities, depreciation is assessed in the market and expressed in the prices paid for cars of different ages. By contrast, the weathering of rock into soil is such a slow process that it is not considered at all in determinining the price of land.

It is only possible to measure change over time. Even so-called current change must mean change during the next hour or day. Current change differs from future change only in the length of time recognized. The value of change might be appraised from two viewpoints. (a) The value of the accumulated change at the future time when its impact will become measurable or realizable. This may also be expressed as the difference between the present value and the future value. (b) The value of the ongoing change during the period from now until it will become measurable.

Estimation of the future value of an accumulated change involves a large subjective element. This stems mainly from uncertainty, because none of the factors that will determine future value can be measured, or even positively identified, today. The problem is to estimate what might happen in the future to cause relative values to be different from what they are now.

The value of a gradual change during a future period can only be expressed as a rate per unit of time. For changes like automobile depreciation that take place over fairly short periods, the rate is usually expressed in units of one year. For very slow changes, longer periods such as decades or centuries might be needed to comprise measurable amounts. It seems questionable whether such slow changes can be expressed in the form of a rate that has meaning for human decision.

5.2. Nature of the Decision

Decisions involved with gradual change all seem to be of an either/or nature. Some decisions affect gradual changes that are already going on. These may be active increases or decreases in quantity or quality. Such decisions are concerned with whether some action should be taken that would stop, reduce, maintain, or accelerate an ongoing change. Other decisions would initiate gradual changes, which may be decreases or increases. The question in such decisions is whether an action should be taken that would start a gradual change in something.

Gradual decreases or increases may be desirable or undesirable, depending on the specific situation. They may show up as either costs or benefits in the outcome of decisions. Rational decisions require that they be treated like other costs and benefits in estimating the net value of a proposed action.

5.3. Toward a Rational Approach

Because gradual changes are imperceptible, there does not seem to be any way of asking people to place values on current changes. Even a professional forester is not able to "see" one year's change in the wood volume of a tree. It is necessary to assess a gradual change over a period long enough that it accumulates to an amount people can perceive in value terms. Because the actual impact of gradual change may be far in the future, it is best to value the accumulated impact as if it were effective today.

The proper procedure is to estimate the flow of benefits and costs with the gradual change and without it. The values of the two flows can then be compared in the usual ways. For example, all old European cathedrals have been gradually deteriorating since they were built. Suppose studies indicate that at the present rate of decay, a particular cathedral will be a complete ruin in 200 years. It is impossible to determine what value that cathedral would have to people living 200 years from now. The best approach is to use its present value as an estimate of future value. This value divided by 200 years provides an estimate of the annual decrease in the value of the cathedral. Any rational action to stop or offset this deterioration should have an annual cost of no more than this amount.

In the case of a depreciating asset, the information needed is the value today and the length of the period over which it will depreciate. If the asset is a priced thing, market price gives an estimate of present value. If it is an unpriced thing, the replacement cost or other opportunity-cost methods from Chapter 12 can be used. People's opinions about present value may also be solicited through the direct-question methods of Chapter 14.

In the case of an increasing change, future value must be simulated. A priced commodity, such as a stand of timber, can be appraised at present market prices. For unpriced things the direct-question methods of Chapter 14 can be used to determine people's valuation of similar things today. For example, if pollution of a river is increasing very gradually, people could be asked how much they would pay today to avoid having the river immediately polluted so badly that it could not be used for swimming and boating. This simulates the future loss that the gradual increase in pollution will lead to in, say, 30 years.

Sometimes a gradual change can be treated as a threshold problem. If the annual cost of preservation is known, people can be asked whether they are willing to pay this much every year to preserve the thing forever. This is probably the way many European cities decided to undertake continuous maintenance programs on their medieval monuments. They did not have to determine the value of an old cathedral, but only whether this value was greater than the necessary annual costs of preventing its deterioration.

6. WHAT IS THE VALUE OF HUMAN LIFE?

Situations arise in which proposed actions would affect the continued survival of some individuals. How can planners decide whether the benefits of an action outweigh the loss of lives it might involve or whether the costs of an action are justified by the lives it would save?

6.1. Nature of the Valuation

There are two senses in which a human life may be valued—the value to the individual himself of being alive and the value to other people of this person being alive. People's individual decisions about their own lives are beyond the scope of this book. We limit this discussion to the value of a human life to other people.

The value of another person's life may derive from two sources—the benefits that person provides to the evaluator and the knowledge that the person obtains utility from being alive. The first source underlies the protection of servants and employees; the second underlies efforts to rescue strangers. Most valuations of other people's lives rest on a combination of these sources. However, one may outweigh the other, as in efforts to prolong the lives of terminally ill patients whose further existence apparently benefits no one else.

The valuation of a person's life on the basis of utility to other people is reasonably straightforward. Because his death would terminate the benefits he produces, the level of the benefits measures the value of his continued existence. This principle is the basis of compensation awards by the courts. Buehler (1975) notes that courts are likely to award a widow the equivalent of the present worth of her late husband's earnings. The average award in 98 cases in the United States prior to 1975 was $167,000. This method does not measure all of the loss resulting from a death, but it provides a way to compensate for the loss of some of the benefits from another person's life. Dawson (1967) in a study of the cost of road accidents in Great Britain discusses the difficulties of analyzing past court decisions, and cites a valuation by Thedie and Abraham (1961). They derived an estimate for 1957 of £2150 sterling as the loss to others for each person killed in highway accidents.

The valuation of another person's life on the basis of the utility that person derives from being alive is subjective. However, it is apparent that people do not feel that the lives of all other persons are equally valuable. This can be traced to three subjective elements that presumably influence the individual value of being alive—the probability of dying, life expectancy, and the quality of life. If all other things were equal, we would expect a rational person to choose a life that presented a low probability of death, would normally continue for a long time, and would be of high quality.

Because ordinary people risk their lives in daily activities like driving automobiles, they apparently do not consider that a certainty of remaining alive has infinite value. However, people do demand much higher compensation for working in hazardous occupations. From society's viewpoint, the benefits a person might realize from something done for him, such as providing an education, depend on the probability of his remaining alive.

The expense and effort devoted to attempts to rescue another person usually vary with the probability of finding him alive.

There is little evidence that people with short life expectancies consider life less valuable than those with long life expectancies. But it is clear that other people usually consider children's lives to be more valuable than those of elderly persons. This is certainly affected by the utility that society expects to receive from these individuals, but it is also affected by the amount of utility these individuals are expected to enjoy during the remainder of their lives.

People living in misery do not generally seem more inclined to give up their lives than those who live pleasantly. Only a small minority of people feel life is so bad that they commit suicide. However, people do use quality of life as a criterion in assessing the value of another person's life. For example, society often devotes less effort to protecting the inhabitants of slum areas than the residents of wealthier sections.

6.2. Nature of the Decision

Decisions about other people's lives are of two kinds—those concerning actions aimed at preventing a loss of life and those concerning actions that might cause a loss of life.

Preventing a Loss of Life. This kind of decision involves a variety of actions, such as rescues, accident prevention, and the provision of life-support facilities in hospitals. The decision maker must decide whether the benefits from preventing a death will outweigh the costs of doing so. The value of the lives in jeopardy may be assessed in terms of the utilities they provide to society or the utility of life to the endangered person. This kind of decision may also involve choices among lives, as when only one of several people can be protected.

Causing a Loss of Life. This kind of decision involves actions that might result in the loss of someone's life. The decision maker must decide whether the social value of the end is greater than that of the lives that might have to be sacrificed to achieve it. Very few decisions involve a certainty that lives will be lost. Most actions present only some probability that participants might be killed. The decision therefore rests on a comparison of the value of the desired end and the probability that lives might be lost. The higher the probability of loss, the more important the valuation of the lives involved is to the decision.

6.3. Toward a Rational Approach

Decisions about other people's lives raise major moral issues. There is no way of determining absolutely what is right and what is wrong. But one cannot escape the moral problem by not making decisions. The decision maker must use all the information he can obtain. The methods of this book will not make the decision for him. They will not even tell him what the value of human life is. But we think they can provide comparative information that will help him make as rational a decision as possible.

Preventing a Loss of Life. Decisions about preventing deaths can be approached as threshold problems. The costs can usually be determined accurately. The question is whether the value of a life which might be saved is greater than this cost. In crises, the decision is often made by people voluntarily contributing money and assistance. This suggests that one means of determining value is to give the public an opportunity to contribute.

Longer-run decisions about accident prevention or installation of kidney dialysis machines in hospitals cannot be based on individual willingness to pay. Decisions must be made in the public sector by representatives of the general public. Because the lives that might be saved cannot be specified, it is a case of valuing lives of unidentifiable people. A guide may be obtained by using the direct-question methods of Chapter 14 to seek opinions of how much the public should spend to save some given number of lives per year.

A frequently used approach to longer-run decisions is to estimate the future earnings of those who would be saved and to capitalize them at the market rate of interest. This indicates future productivity and the contribution to society that would be lost if an individual died now. Because particular individuals cannot be identified, it is necessary to use average figures for annual earnings and years of future employment. This method underestimates social value because it includes no allowance for personal values. However, it does indicate a minimum social value of the lives that might be saved.

Valuation through estimating lost future earnings can assist in the general allocation of social resources to saving lives. Radtke (1974) valued the human capital of Pacific Northwest counties in terms of its financial productivity. Then the marginal value product of an extra doctor (additional lives saved) was estimated with the production function method of Chapter 13. The increase in human capital from these saved lives was estimated to be $35,511. Radtke applied this value information to the allocation of doctors and health facilities within and among counties. Buehler (1975) argues that allocation of resources to flood-mitigation should consider the monetary value of the lives saved. The estimated number of lives can be valued at future earnings and included in the analysis.

For actions that would protect the general public, a group-insurance approach may be taken. For example, if the probability of people needing the intensive care units of hospitals to survive coronaries could be calculated, their willingness to pay annual fees to ensure the availability of such services might be determined. People would, in effect, be placing values on their own lives, and these values in aggregate would indicate the annual social value of an intensive care unit.

A choice among lives is a very difficult problem. It is usually faced in crisis situations when there is no time for analysis. Most societies have developed cultural guidelines, such as "women and children first" and "protect the leaders." These suggest that social value ultimately rests on the utility of individuals to the group. A rational comparative valuation must be based on how essential or important various individuals are to the rest of society.

Causing a Loss of Life. A decision that might sacrifice lives can be approached as a threshold problem. The threshold is provided by the value of the ends that would be achieved. It can frequently be measured with market prices. For example, the organization and operation of a fire department involves some probability that firemen might lose their lives. The amount of property the department would save can be estimated and valued at market prices. The question is whether the social value of the minimum number of lives that could be lost would exceed the value of the property saved. The accuracy of the probability forecast is critical. Because everyone runs some risk of being killed in everyday activities, a low probability would indicate a commonly accepted risk. However, a high probability of fatal accidents would cast serious doubts on the proposal.

7. CONCLUSIONS

We have looked at some reputedly difficult valuation subjects and found that ways exist for dealing with them. Methods are available for the planner or analyst who must include unpriced benefits or costs in the information he assembles for decisions. Many people have worked on this problem in many fields, and we have consolidated their results in Part II. A planner still has to apply these analytical resources to his own valuation problem, and it may help if we summarize some points that we consider vital. Chapter 20 illustrates the application of these points to a large and complex valuation problem.

Because valuations are always made to guide decisions, the first step must be to define clearly the nature of the decision. This determines the kind of comparative value information needed. The kind of information, in turn, determines the kind of method that will be most useful. Only after the decision has been clearly defined should the analyst proceed to the specific value objects and the nature of their valuation.

Once the basic problem is clear, the analyst should review the literature thoroughly, because new ideas and approaches keep appearing. It is important that the analyst not limit himself to literature in his own field, such as recreation or transportation, because the ideas and techniques developed in one field have proven useful in other fields.

The analyst must remember that different methods fit different decisions. Many methods can be used in combinations. There is no perfect method, and an analyst must be prepared to experiment and innovate to find the method or methods most useful for his particular decision.

Finally, it is always possible to ask face-to-face questions about willingness to pay. This is often the best source of comparative value information. Other methods may be cheaper, and they should be used to the extent they can be. If they produce questionable results, however, the analyst must use his ingenuity in obtaining willingness-to-pay information.

CHAPTER 20

Complex Decisions Involving Unpriced Values—Analysis of an Example

Actual decisions are more complex than many of the examples we have considered so far. They usually involve many different things, some priced and some unpriced, some consumptive like steak and some nonconsumptive like scenic views. The benefits and costs of all these things must be considered, and the planner must develop a strategy to value, aggregate, and present the relevant information. In this final chapter we analyze a real decision to indicate some approaches to this complexity.

Analyzing an actual example also allows us to consider a persistent problem in valuation—the lack of appropriate data. A planner will never have adequate values—in money or another unit—or adequate quantitative data on benefits, costs, levels of characteristics, or things exchanged. How, then, is he to integrate money with nonmonetary values, ordinal with cardinal values, and qualitative descriptions with quantitative units?

We hope to show how complexity in decisions can be approached through systematic analysis. As in the rest of the book, we ignore risk and forecasting to concentrate on values and value information. An analysis tries to reduce the latitude for subjective judgment and thus to reduce controversy in decision making. Our objective is comparative values to guide choices rather than money values of perfect accuracy.

The valuation process is a series of steps ending in the estimation of value information and the final assessment of comparative values (Chapter 6). We concentrate here on the last two steps. These may be approached through monetary values alone, through nonmonetary values alone, or through a combination of nonmonetary and monetary values, as shown in Figure 20.1. Each approach consists of several stages, in each of which more value information is collected, assessed, and presented. At each stage the analyst and decision maker decide whether the information on comparative values is adequate for a choice. If it is not, the valuation process is carried further.

The initial stage in the analysis is problem formulation, which we

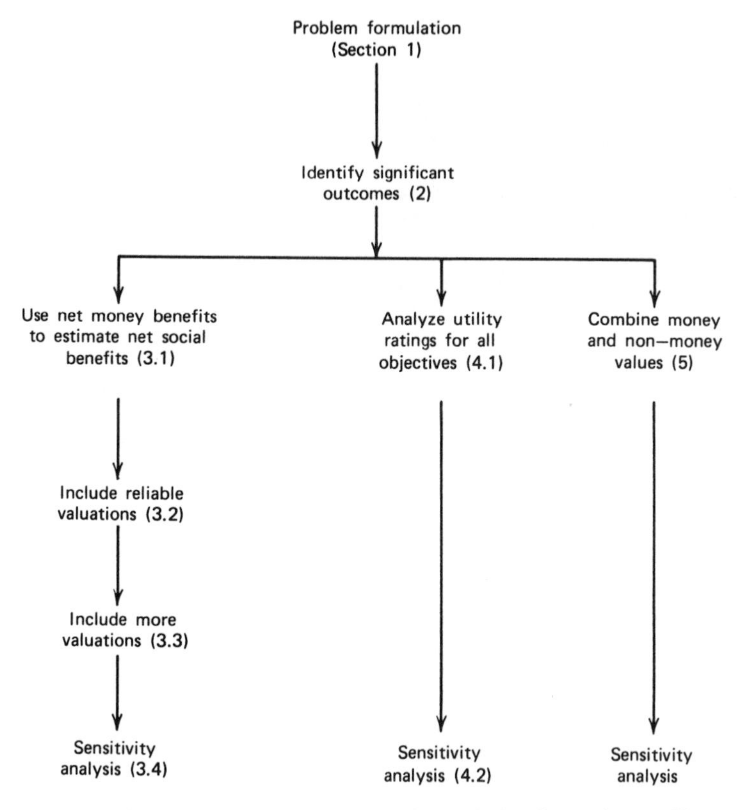

Figure 20.1. Three approaches to the analysis of complex problems.

consider in the next section. The second and very important stage for complex decisions—identification of the significant and insignificant outcomes—is considered in Section 2. The remainder of the chapter examines how the three approaches of Figure 20.1 can deal with complexity.

1. PROBLEM FORMULATION: A GORGELANDS NATIONAL PARK

The possibility of a gorgelands national park for New South Wales was introduced in Section 1 of Chapter 8. The park would preserve the habitat of an endangered kangaroo species and a rare eucalypt species, preserve the remaining natural landscape, and promote more natural vegetation on the rest of the landscape. The decision would be made by the state and federal governments in terms of several social objectives. We now define the land-use alternatives, the social objectives, and the nature of the decision.

1.1. Four Land-Use Alternatives

Four alternative land-use plans for the gorgelands area were outlined in Section 1 of Chapter 8. They are described in more detail in Table 20.1. The existing uses produce 1010 cattle and 25,000 tons of antimony ore annually. Alternatives *A* and *B* are intermediate between the existing condition and the complete park of alternative *C*.

In plan *A* all but one of the grazing leases would be purchased, but mining would be allowed to continue. The resulting park would substantially preserve the natural landscape for an acquisition cost equivalent to $74,000 per year. In plan *B* the last grazing lease would be acquired, raising the acquisition cost to $90,000. This additional acquisition would eliminate the monetary benefit from cattle but secure the kangaroo habitat. Plan *C* dif-

Table 20.1. The Nature of Four Land Use Alternatives for the Gorgelands Area[a]

Descriptive Item	Alternatives			
	Existing Use	*A*	*B*	*C*
1	2	3	4	5
Park size (1000 acres)	0	292	424	424
Number of cattle sold per year	1010	230	0	0
Net money benefit—cattle ($1000)	51	12	0	0
Annual mine output (1000 tons ore)	25	25	25	0
Net money benefit—mining ($1000)	455	455	455	0
Acquisition cost—farms ($1000)	0	74	90	90
Acquisition cost—mine ($1000)	0	0	0	455
Park operating cost ($1000)	0	100	100	100
Number of farm leases	32	1	0	0
Number of farm families wholly supported by area	8	1	0	0
Recreation (1000 family visits per year)	58.2	62.7	64.3	64.3
Number of major research projects	1	1	1	2
State of vegetation and landscape	Many thousand acres natural; several thousand cleared for grazing; rest grazed a little; mine workings	———	———→	Total area reverts to natural vegetation
State of preservation	All habitats subject to grazing; nothing preserved	———	———→	All habitats preserved

[a] The money data are present worths expressed as annuities at 10 percent.

fers from plan *B* in that the mine would be acquired to preserve the eucalypt habitat. We now assume that the permanent full park status of alternative *C* would encourage one additional research project. The policy problem is to choose one of these four alternatives.

1.2. The Social Objectives

Society recognizes many objectives. An important one is net social benefits. Cattle and mining produce priced goods and contribute net monetary benefits. The cattle prices form in a reasonably competitive market, but the net monetary benefits to the producer do not include consumers' surplus. The mining data are returns to the company and vary with the price of antimony. These net monetary benefits must be converted to net social benefits. Net social benefit is also affected by the acquisition cost and annual operating costs.

Society's objective of an equitable income distribution involves the farm families presently supported by the gorgelands area. Of the 32 lease properties, eight are wholly dependent on the area. Alternative *A* would displace all but one of them. We show outcomes for this income distribution objective as the number of families wholly supported by the area.

Objectives for the environment include recreation and preservation. The recreation objective is measured by the number of family visits per year. Preservation is recorded descriptively, as in Table 20.1. The research objective is measured as the number of projects.

1.3. The Nature of the Decision

In a national policy decision, like the gorgelands park case, neither the budget nor the benefit levels are fixed. Because the overall objective is to maximize net benefits, the simple criteria of cost minimization or benefit maximization (Chaper 5) are not adequate. The total utility and opportunity-cost methods are not suitable for the final decision, but they can assist in the analysis.

The analytical difficulties are increased by some significant externalities. Farmers clear the natural forest to promote pasture, and miners scar the landscape with their spoil dumps, access routes, and mine workings. These actions reduce the benefits to recreationists through the changes they make in the natural landscape. The external effects must be identified, valued, and included in the analysis.

The decision to purchase the land for the state will be viewed differently at different levels in the government hierarchy. Each level will use its own criteria and valuation methods. For example, the National Parks and

Wildlife Service will compare the biophysical characteristics of the gorgelands with those of other areas available for preservation. The methods of Chaper 9 are eminently suited to this purpose. Other government agencies will assess the comparative value for intensive recreation. These agencies can readily use the travel-cost method or other methods from Chapters 10, 12, or 14. Ultimately, the Department of Treasury and Planning must decide whether the benefits from a gorgelands park would be greater than the costs and whether the net benefits would be greater than those that could be produced with the funds in other projects.

2. IDENTIFYING THE SIGNIFICANT OUTCOMES

The next stage in the analysis, as shown in Figure 20.1, is to identify those benefits and costs that will have a negligible impact. These outcomes can then be ignored to reduce the complexity of the analysis and decision. Table 20.2 shows a complete list of benefits and costs for the proposed park alternatives. We now define two criteria that can be used to identify the less significant outcomes.

Criterion I. Is the Expected Change in Benefit (or Cost) Large or Is It Negligible? This criterion must be based on actual knowledge and can only be applied when knowledge is adequate. We define *negligible* as meaning no measurable change in the outcome through establishment of a park. Based on this criterion, as shown in columns 2 and 3 of Table 20.2, outcomes 11 to 14 are insignificant. There will be no measurable change in water quality, life of historical objects, or pest damage to cattle. The remaining benefits and costs (1 to 10) are now subjected to a criterion based on an expedient method of utility estimation.

Criterion II. Do People Rate the Utility of the Benefit or Cost Near Zero? This second criterion can be applied to outcomes that accrue mainly to the subjects questioned in a survey.

A random survey of the population of the largest nearby town (Armidale) was undertaken for 13 of the 14 outcomes in Table 20.2. The utilities were recorded on a 7-point Likert scale, from extremely satisfied (+3) to extremely dissatisfied (−3). As part of the survey the subjects were informed of the likely magnitude of the benefits and costs.

The incidence of each outcome is shown in column 4 of Table 20.2, with the average utility rating in column 5. The urban population surveyed rate the utilities of outcomes 7 to 10 between −0.3 and +0.4. These ratings are close to neutral, and we conclude that the population is unconcerned about these benefits and costs.

Table 20.2. Identification of Less-Significant Benefits and Costs[a]

Benefit or Cost	The Change		Local Population	
	Adequate Knowledge?	Expected Size	Bears the Outcomes?	Total Utility[b]
1	2	3	4	5
1a Cattle output	√	*L*	x	−0.2
b Mining output	√	*L*	x	−0.3
2a Acquisition cost	√	*L*	x	[c]
b Operating cost	√	*L*	x	[c]
3 Income distribution	√	*L*	x	−1.1
4 Recreation visits	√	*L*	√	1.1
5 Research projects	x		x	1.4
6 Preservation of:				
a Natural landscapes	x		√	1.7
b Kangaroo species	x		x	1.6
c Eucalypt species	x		x	1.6
7 Restriction of current activities (e.g., camping) in area	√	*L*	√	0.4
8 Restriction on new activities (e.g., chair lifts)	√	*L*	√	0.4
9 Educational benefit	x		√	0.2
10 Increased fire hazard through fuel buildup in park	x		√	−0.3
11 Increased life of historical objects	√	*N*	√	2.1
12 Lower cattle output outside park because of more pests from park (e.g., dingoes)	√	*N*	x	−0.9
13 Less antimony effluent in downstream water	√	*N*	x	1.9
14 Decrease in flood damage downstream	√	*N*	x	1.9

[a] *L* = large, *N* = negligible, √ = yes, x = no.
[b] On a 7-point scale from +3 = extremely satisfied to −3 = extremely dissatisfied.
[c] Not surveyed.

Outcomes 7 to 14 are shown by these criteria to be insignificant, and we can drop them from our analysis. The procedure has been to drop an outcome if technical knowledge is adequate and indicates no measurable change or the population that bears the outcome rates it as insignificant. Outcomes 1 to 6 cannot be excluded by either of these criteria and must be included in the analysis.

3. A MONETARY APPROACH

One obvious approach is to convert all benefits and costs to monetary values. We considered the merits of this approach earlier in the book, and we now consider its feasibility. The approach proceeds through the following stages.

3.1. From Net Monetary Benefits to Net Social Benefits

The net monetary benefits of Chapter 8 were net incomes to the producers based on monetary costs and market prices of the output. They must be recalculated as net social benefits to include consumers' surplus and to correct for any distortions in market prices or monetary costs.

The market for cattle in New South Wales is sufficiently competitive that the market price can be accepted as an indicator of social value. The elasticity of demand is known, but the elasticity of supply is not. We can therefore use the procedure of Section 3.3.2 in Chapter 15 to estimate the net social benefits from cattle as the extremes of the possible supply elasticities, following Griliches' (1958) example. This gives a maximum possible value of $150,000 for the existing cattle output and a minimum possible value of $30,000, compared to the best estimate of $51,000 for the net money benefit in Chapter 8. We use the minimum value of $30,000 in the rest of this analysis.

All the mining output is exported, and any consumers' surplus accrues outside Australia. The market price of the ore is a world price that forms in competition with many other suppliers. The price is competitive and represents the purchasing power for which ore can be exchanged. For these reasons, the net monetary benefit of $455,000 in Table 20.1 can be accepted as the net social benefit to Australia.

These net social benefits are entered in Table 20.3, where the monetary outcomes are defined.

3.2. Include Reliable Valuations of Unpriced Things.

The decision maker may consider the information in Table 20.3 and request further analysis. The analyst may feel that reliable monetary values can be obtained for some of the unpriced things and extend the analysis to these reliable valuations. For the gorgelands problem these items include income distribution, recreation, and research.

Income Distribution. A park will displace farm families, and the government will compensate them for their losses. Compensation should exceed the land purchase price by the value of the utility of the rural way of life. In Section 9.3 of Chapter 14 we estimated this compensation value for the gorgelands example. The indifference-mapping method gave a lump-sum compensation of $50,000 per family above the acquisition cost, or $5,000

Table 20.3. First Stage in the Monetary Approach—Net Social Benefits Replacing Net Monetary Benefits

Objectives	Alternatives			
	Existing Situation	*A*	*B*	*C*
1	2	3	4	5
With monetary outcomes[a]				
Net social benefit—cattle	30	7	0	0
Net social benefit—mining	455	455	455	0
Subtotal—net social benefit	485	462	455	0
Acquisition cost—farms	0	−74	−90	−90
Acquisition cost—mine	0	0	0	−455
Subtotal—acquisition cost	0	−74	−90	−545
Operating cost of park	0	−100	−100	−100
Total Money Value	485	288	265	−645
With Nonmonetary outcomes				
Income distribution (number of farm families wholly supported)	8	1	0	0
Recreation (1000 family visits)	58.2	62.7	64.3	64.3
Research projects (number)	1	1	1	2
Preservation of:				
Natural Landscapes	No	Yes	Yes	Yes
Endangered kangaroo	No	No	Yes	Yes
Rare eucalypt	No	No	No	Yes

[a] As present worths in thousands of dollars expressed as annuities at 10 percent.

per year as an annuity. This figure is close to similar compensations in the state of Victoria and was well validated in an internal consistency test. It is sufficiently reliable to use as the social cost for the income distribution objective. For the eight families displaced by alternatives *B* and *C* the total social loss is $40,000 per year.

Recreation. We estimated the net social benefit of the on-site gorgelands experience with the travel cost method in Section 1.3 of Chapter 16. This value was $8.93 per family visit. The assumptions of the method suggest that this must be a minimum value. An informal survey using the single-direct-question method of Chapter 14 indicates that this figure is about right and may even be the maximum value. We rounded this value to $9.00 and multiplied by the number of visits shown in Table 20.3 to obtain the net social benefits of recreation shown in Table 20.4.

Research. The stability of land use in a complete national park will encourage scientific research. Alternative *C* can be expected to result in one new research project in the area. This research would probably have been done anyway, but at a more costly location. Following the cost-saving method of Chapter 12, the saving in research expenditure can be used as a measure of the increase in net social benefit from alternative *C*. We estimate this saving at $100,000 and include it directly.

The values for income distribution, recreation, and research are entered as monetary outcomes in Table 20.4. The total monetary value for each alternative is now larger than in Table 20.3. The remaining nonmonetary outcomes are still described.

3.3. Further Valuation of Unpriced Things

Three things remain to be valued—the natural landscape, the habitat of the endangered kangaroo, and the habitat of the rare eucalypt. These three unpriced benefits can be presented to the decision maker in the form of trade-off questions. For example, the differences between existing use and alternative *A* are the higher total monetary value of existing use and the preservation of more natural landscapes under alternative *A*. With the information in Table 20.4, the choice between existing use and alternative *A* can be presented to the decision maker in this form: Is the increase in the

Table 20.4. Second Stage in the Monetary Approach—Reliable Valuations of Unpriced Things

Objectives	Alternatives			
	Existing Situation	*A*	*B*	*C*
1	2	3	4	5
With monetary outcomes[a]				
Net social benefit—cattle	30	7	0	0
Net social benefit—mining	455	455	455	0
Acquisition cost—farms	0	−74	−90	−90
Acquisition cost—mines	0	0	0	−455
Operating cost of park	0	−100	−100	−100
Income distribution—compensation	0	−35	−40	−40
Recreation—net social benefit	524	564	579	579
Research—net social benefit[b]	0	0	0	100
Total monetary value	1,009	817	804	−6
With nonmonetary outcomes				
Preservation of:				
Natural landscapes	No	Yes	Yes	Yes
Endangered kangaroo	No	No	Yes	Yes
Rare eucalypt	No	No	No	Yes

[a] As present worths in thousands of dollars expressed as annuities at 10 percent.
[b] As the cost saving on the additional project in alternative *C*.

amount of natural landscapes that would be preserved by dedicating 292,000 acres to a national park worth the $192,000 difference in annual money value?

Alternatives *B* and *C* differ only in the higher total money value of alternative *B* and the preservation of the rare eucalypt species under alternative *C*. The choice between a park like alternative *B* and one like alternative *C* can be presented to the decision maker in this form: Is the preservation of the rare eucalypt and its habitat worth the $810,000 difference in annual money value? If the decision maker does not feel that he can make a choice on the basis of these trade-offs, the analyst must try to provide more information about the values of the remaining unpriced things.

There were no data on physical characteristics, opportunity costs, market prices, or observable behavior for the preservation of the natural landscapes, the endangered kangaroo, or the rare eucalypt. Our approach was therefore restricted to the survey/questioning methods of Chapters 10, 11, and 14. We chose the priority-evaluator technique of Chapter 14 because it simulates a competitive market and produces monetary prices. The differences between these prices for existing use and for the area in a national park is a measure of the difference in consumers' surplus for the marginal unit of preservation. The results can therefore be added to the other net social benefit figures in Table 20.4. This method was applied to a random sample of the population of Armidale.

Because the subjects questioned with the priority-evaluator technique cannot usually handle more than 15 alternatives, we were only able to compare existing use with alternative *C*. Including alternatives *A* and *B* also would have made the total number of alternatives unmanageable. Because alternative *C* is the only one that would preserve landscapes, kangaroo, and eucalypt, one application of the PET method gave us an estimate of the values of preserving all three.

To provide a third alternative level on the opposite side of existing use from alternative *C*, we described an alternative of more development, in which the number of cattle would be increased and natural landscapes would be completely eliminated. The intensity of mining use would also increase. These three alternative levels of land use are shown in Table 20.5.

The utility of landscape preservation is derived through the activity of visiting sites for recreational purposes. The first good to be considered was therefore described as the naturalness of recreation sites. Because the endangered kangaroo and eucalypt are actually seen by very few people, the utility that most people obtain is from the knowledge that they still exist. The second good was therefore described as knowledge of the preservation of habitats for these endangered species. These first two goods are shown in Table 20.5.

For the priority-evaluator technique to function properly, there must be alternative goods among which the subjects can choose. We selected three that fit the gorgelands situation. The first was the probability of seeing a wildlife species. This would increase from left to right through the three levels of Table 20.5. The second was the external effects of cattle grazing; that is, the visual and other impacts of cattle grazing on people using the area. For a final good we chose the external effects of mining. This would include not only the visual impact of the mining operations themselves but also related effects like truck traffic on the roads. Both of these external effects would decrease from left to right in Table 20.5.

We applied the method as described in Section 8.2.1 of Chapter 14. An initial set of prices per visit was chosen as indicated by $P11$ to $P53$ in Table 20.5. Each subject was given a budget and instructed to spend it all by buying one level of each of the five goods. If the prices $P11$ to $P53$ accurately represented the marginal utilities per visit of the 15 things, the subjects would be indifferent as to which ones they chose to give a random selection of the 15 things.

The responses to the first survey did not give this theoretically expectable distribution. The ratio of the number of observed choices to the number of expected choices was therefore calculated for each good, and the initial prices were raised or lowered as indicated by the O/E ratios. The survey was then repeated with the same subjects. The prices were again adjusted, and a second survey was made. This time the O/E ratios were near enough to 1 to be acceptable.

The simulated market price for naturalness of recreation sites under existing use ($P12$) was $3.50. Under alternative C ($P13$) it was $6.00. This indicates a willingness to pay $2.50 per visit for the increased naturalness of

Table 20.5. Pattern for Applying the Priority-Evaluator Technique to Value Preservation of Landscapes and Endangered Species in the Gorgelands Example

Item	Level of Land Use		
	More Development	Existing Use	Alternative *C*
	1	2	3
1 Naturalness of recreation sites	$P11$	$P12$	$P13$
2 Knowledge of habitat preservation	$P21$	$P22$	$P23$
3 Probability of seeing a species	$P31$	$P32$	$P33$
4 External effects of cattle grazing	$P41$	$P42$	$P43$
5 External effects of mining	$P51$	$P52$	$P53$

alternative *C*. The relative sizes of *P*12 and *P*13 are acceptable, but their actual sizes would vary with the size of the budget the subjects had to spend. A separate survey with the converging direct-question method had indicated a willingness to pay of $4.00 per visit to the existing landscapes. This was used as a peg to adjust the values obtained with the PET method. Each price in the final set was multiplied by 4.00/3.50, or 1.14. This raised the willingness to pay for the increased naturalness of alternative *C* to $2.85 per visit. The 64,300 family visits under alternative *C* in Table 20.1 would therefore have a total additional value of $183,000, when rounded to the nearest thousand.

The simulated market price of knowledge of endangered species preservation was $2.50 per visit under existing use (*P*22). The much greater preservation under alternative *C* (*P*23) received a price of $9.00. This indicates a willingness to pay $6.50 per visit for the increased knowledge that the endangered kangaroo and rare eucalypt are being preserved under alternative *C*. Using the same peg as with naturalness above, we multiplied this value by 1.14 to obtain an estimate of $7.41 per visit. The 64,300 family visits would therefore have a total additional value of $476,000.

The method was also applied to a pro-park lobby group, a group of farmers' sons who were students at the university in Armidale, and to two groups of visitors who have seen the area once but will never see it again. Apart from the farmers' sons, these groups gave substantially the same values for increased naturalness and knowledge. The students, in the role of farmers, gave lower values for both things. But farm families around the gorgelands rarely visit the area for recreation. We feel the values of $183,000 for natural landscapes and $476,000 for increased preservation are representative of the visitors and local urban population.

These values can now be added to the total money value of the other benefits and costs shown in Table 20.4.

	Existing Use	Alternative *C*
Total of money outcomes from Table 20.4	$1,009,000	–$6,000
Natural landscapes	0	183,000
Species preservation	0	476,000
Totals	$1,009,000	$653,000

Two kinds of figures are combined in these totals. Some are actual net social benefits from the alternatives, such as those for cattle and mining. The others, like those for research and preservation, measure the differences in value between one alternative and another. The totals in the preceding paragraph (and those in Table 20.4) are not the real social values of the alternatives. They are comparative values and indicate the magnitude of the differences between the alternatives. The social value of the existing use of the gorgelands area is not exactly $1,009,000, nor would that of the proposed park in alternative *C* be exactly $653,000. But unless there are gross errors in the valuations, the proposed park would clearly have less social value than the existing use.

Although the limitations of the priority-evaluator technique prevented us from testing all four alternatives against each other, we can extract some information about alternatives *A* and *B* from the PET survey. Both of these proposed parks would provide about the same amount of natural landscape preservation as alternative *C*. We can therefore credit alternatives *A* and *B* with an additional value of about $180,000 for the landscapes they would preserve. We cannot follow this approach for the value of endangered species because our PET survey lumped the kangaroo and rare eucalypt together in one choice. Alternative *A* would preserve neither, but alternative *B* should receive some unknown amount of credit for the kangaroo habitat it would preserve.

If we add the $180,000 for landscape preservation to the total monetary values of the other benefits and costs shown in Table 20.4, we obtain total values of $997,000 for alternative *A* and $984,000 for alternative *B*. Both are very close to the total value of $1,009,000 for existing use, especially if alternative *B* is given some credit for kangaroo preservation. There seems to be little choice between existing use and a national park of the kind proposed in alternative *A* or *B*. This raises the question of whether this outcome could be a result of errors in our estimates of some of the individual components. The next section checks this possibility with sensitivity tests.

3.4. A Sensitivity Analysis

Some of the data that must be used in analysis will be poorly defined. In our example it was difficult to estimate the lifetime of the mine. The price of antimony is also uncertain because it fluctuates with the world market. Different figures could therefore have been used for the number of years that the mine will produce or for the price of antimony during those years. All the alternatives include very large figures for the net social benefit of recreation. There could be errors in the estimates of the number of family visits to the area or in the estimated consumer's surplus of $9.00 per visit. It is necessary to determine whether differences in any of these figures could change the ordering of the alternatives.

3.4.1. For Mine Lifetime. The net social benefit from mining of $455,000 per year was based on an expected 20-year lifetime. If the mine were to last for 40 years, the annual benefit would be $530,000. By contrast, if the mine were to last for only 15 years, the annual benefit would be only $410,000. Using a lifetime anywhere between these extremes has little arithmetic impact on the results and no effect on the ordering of the alternatives. The results of the analysis are insensitive to the mine lifetime used.

3.4.2. For Ore Price and Quality. The net social benefit of $455,000 per year used in our analysis was based on a price of $70 per ton of semi-processed antimony ore of 4 percent quality. If the quality should prove to be different or the world market price should change, the price could be higher or lower than $70. The effect of different prices on the net social benefit would be as follows:

Price per ton of ore ($)	50	53	60	70	80
Net social benefit ($1000)	0	50	200	455	700

Any decrease in the net social benefit from mining would have an identical effect on the total money values of existing use and of alternatives *A* and *B*. However, alternative *C* includes an acquisition cost for the mine equal to the net income from the mine. A decrease in the value of the mine would reduce this acquisition cost. This means that any decrease in the net social benefit from mining will increase the total money value of alternative *C* by the same amount that it decreases the values of existing use and alternatives *A* and *B*.

If the price of antimony ore were $53 instead of $70, the net social benefit from mining would be only $50,000. The total monetary value of alternative *B* in Table 20.4 would then be $399,000. Because the government would only have to pay $50,000 per year for the mine, the total monetary value of alternative *C* would also be $399,000. A change of $17 per ton in the price of ore would eliminate the comparative value difference between alternatives *B* and *C*. Because alternative *C* would also preserve the rare eucalypt, it would now be preferred over alternative *B*.

If the price of ore were $50, the net social benefit from mining would be zero. The total monetary value of existing use would now be $554,000 and that of alternative *C* would be $449,000, without any allowance for preservation of landscapes and the endangered species. The allowances from Section 3.3 and this decrease of $20 in the price of ore would make the complete national park of alternative *C* the preferred choice over existing use. The sensitivity of the ordering of alternatives to the price of ore raises a question of how much weight should be given to the mine in a decision about establishing a national park.

3.4.3. For Recreation Benefits. The difference in recreation benefits between the alternatives is small compared with the absolute number of visits. The social value of recreation is calculated in Table 20.4 with a consumer's surplus of $9 per family visit. For one of the proposed parks to have as high a total money value as existing use (Table 20.4), there would have to be a greater increase in the number of family visits than is shown in Table 20.1, or the consumer's surplus per visit would have to be more than $9.

For alternative *A* to have the same total monetary value as existing use, the recreation benefit would have to be $192,000 more than is shown in Table 20.4. If the increase in number of visits shown in Table 20.1 is correct, this would require a consumer's surplus of $52 per visit rather than the $9 used. If the $9 consumer's surplus is correct, the number of visits would have to increase over six times the number shown in Table 20.1. For alternative *B* to have the same total monetary value as existing use, the consumer's surplus per visit would have to be $43, or the number of visits would have to be over five times greater than estimated. No conceivable increase in consumer's surplus or in number of visits would suffice to make the total monetary value of alternative *C* equal to that of existing use. None of these changes are within the likely analytical error. The ordering of the alternatives is insensitive to errors in the recreation data.

3.5. A Reflection on the Monetary Approach

The elements of the monetary approach are (a) the elimination of insignificant things, (b) the use of established methods, such as the net-social-benefit and travel-cost methods, (c) the application of newer methods, such as the indifference-mapping method, and (d) the recognition of the comparative nature of valuation for such things as research. This approach proved feasible for the gorgelands problems, although we would have preferred more data and better validation for the values obtained.

This approach substantially improved the value information over that initially available in Table 20.1. A policy decision could probably be made at the stage of Table 20.4, where the choices are single trade-offs of a monetary value against one unpriced thing.

4. A UTILITY APPROACH

The utility approach requires weights (WT) for each objective (j), converts outcomes to utilities (U), and then derives an index of comparative value for each alternative (i) from its utilities and weights as follows:

$$V_i = \sum_{j=1}^{n} (U_{ij} \times WT_j) \quad (20.1)$$

where n is the number of objectives. We introduced this model as Equation 11.1 and discussed its application in Chapter 11. We will now apply it to the Gorgelands problem.

This procedure differs from the monetary approach because utility data (U_{ij}) are not directly observable, as are numbers of recreation visits, for example. Utility data must be collected for all alternatives and for all objectives. They can all be collected in a single survey with a single method and can therefore all be of equal reliability.

The weights for the objectives of Table 20.3 were derived in Section 6.2 of Chapter 8 and are repeated in column 6 of Table 20.6. We assign the same negative weight (−0.7) to operating costs as to acquisition costs. The weights for each objective refer to the whole range of outcomes for that objective and were obtained from a representative sample of the whole population. We can therefore apply the same weight to all levels of an outcome and to all decision makers. The next step is to convert the outcomes of Table 20.3 to utilities and to estimate the comparative values of the alternatives.

4.1. Estimation of Comparative Values

The utility ratings were derived by the ratio estimation method (Section 3.2 of Chapter 11). The subject was asked to consider a given objective and to give a rating of 10 to the least-preferred outcome. He then estimated all other utilities relative to this base. For example, suppose the subject feels he would derive 30 percent more utility from the landscapes in alternative C than from the existing landscapes. He would rate existing use at 10 and alternative C at 13 for this objective.

We simulated an application to three government decision makers—the Department of Treasury and Planning (here called the planner), the National Parks and Wildlife Service (parks officer), and the Department of Mining (miner). They present a representative range of preferences.

The set of utility ratings for the planner and the general weights are shown in Table 20.6. These data were inserted in Equation 20.1 to estimate the comparative values of the four alternatives to the planner. The ratings were then elicited from the two other subjects and their comparative values were calculated. The full set of values was

Decision Maker	Existing Use	Alternatives		
		A	*B*	*C*
Planner	90.5	83.4	97.1	36.3
Parks officer	82.6	80.7	109.4	68.4
Miner	100.2	87.3	91.1	15.5

The most-preferred alternative should have the highest comparative social value. The results indicate that the planner and the parks officer both prefer alternative *B*, but the miner prefers the existing use.

4.2. A Sensitivity Analysis

These comparative values rank the alternatives and suggest the approximate size of the utility differences between them. But we need to check through sensitivity analysis whether possible differences in any of the data might change the ranking.

4.2.1. For Intensities of Preference. The comparative values narrow the choice to existing use (ranked first by the miner) and alternative *B* (ranked first by the planner and the parks officer). All three of the subjects ranked these two above either alternative *A* or alternative *C*. We can now determine what changes in the data would be required to reverse the ranking of the two preferred alternatives.

Table 20.6. A Set of Utility Ratings by a Simulated Planner[a]

Objectives	**Ratings for Alternatives**				
	Existing Situation	*A*	*B*	*C*	Weights
1	2	3	4	5	6
Net social benefit	50	50	50	10	0.7
Acquisition cost	10	15	16	70	−0.7
Operating cost	10	16	16	16	−0.7
Income distribution	15	11	10	10	0.9
Recreation	10	11	12	12	0.3
Research	10	10	10	(12)	1.0
Preservation of:					
Natural landscapes	10	13	13	13	1.3
Endangered kangaroo	10	10	(20)	(20)	1.5
Rare eucalypt	10	10	10	12	1.5

[a] Net social benefit and acquisition cost refer to the respective subtotals in Table 20.3. The data in parentheses were the most difficult to estimate and are most susceptible to error.

The cost of the farms that would have to be acquired for alternative *B* is a reasonably firm estimate. We can therefore test how sensitive the rankings of the three subjects are to changes in this acquisition cost. The planner rates the value of alternative *B* 6.6 weighted units higher than that of existing use (97.1 – 90.5). Because the weight applied to acquisition costs is 0.7, this difference is equal to 9.4 unweighted units. To give equal ratings to the total utilities of the two alternatives, the planner would have to give acquisition cost for alternative *B* a utility rating of 25.4 instead of the 16 shown in Table 20.6. This would be a 60 percent change. If we assume that the utility of a dollar is constant, this would require an increase of $54,000 in the acquisition cost.

A change of 9.4 units in the utility ratings of the other objectives in Table 20.6 would also equate the total utilities of the two objectives. However, the net social benefit from mining is the same under both alternatives, and the other large item—net social benefit from recreation—is only $55,000 larger in alternative *B* than in existing use (Table 20.4). The planner would have to make a major change in some utility judgments before he would prefer existing use over alternative *B*.

The difference for the parks officer is even higher. It would require a change of 38.3 unweighted units of utility to equate the total utility of the existing use to that of alternative *B*. Assuming constant utility for money, this would require a change of about $230,000 in acquisition costs. The parks officer's preference for alternative *B* is so strong that it cannot be a result of errors in the data.

The preference of the miner for the existing use is similar in intensity to that of the planner for alternative *B*. The acquisition costs of alternative *B* would have to be $68,000 lower before he would consider the park to be worth as much as the existing use. The comparative values of the three kinds of subjects are supported by this test.

4.2.2. For Less-Reliable Utility Ratings. The ratings for the research project and preservation of the kangaroo were the most difficult to estimate. Minimum ratings for both were entered in Table 20.6 and used in the calculations. We must check to see whether higher ratings for these two objectives might have affected the comparative values.

The research project would only affect the comparison between alternatives *B* and *C*. The planner rates the value of alternative *B* 60.8 weighted utility units higher than that of alternative *C*. Because the weight assigned to the research project is 1.0, the unweighted utility rating for research in Table 20.6 would have to be increased by 60.8 to equate the total utility ratings of alternatives *B* and *C*. For the parks officer, the utility rating for research would have to be increased by 41.0 to equate the two alternatives.

It is not possible that the actual utility of an additional research project would be five times as large as the ratings given by these two people. This eliminates the only serious possibility that the planner and the parks officer might really prefer alternative *C*.

The miner rates the value of existing use 9.1 weighted utility units higher than that of alternative *B*. These alternatives differ in that alternative *B* would preserve natural landscapes and the habitat of the endangered kangaroo. Let us assume that if the miner rated preservation higher, he would increase the ratings of both by the same amounts. An increase of 4.55 units in the weighted ratings of both landscapes and kangaroo would equate the total utility ratings of existing use and alternative *B*. Because the landscapes have a weight of 1.3, their unweighted rating would be 3.5. The kangaroo, with a weight of 1.5, would have an unweighted rating of 3.0.

The miner's original ratings (which are not shown in Table 20.6) were 11 for landscape preservation and 14 for endangered kangaroo preservation under alternative *B*. It would only be necessary, therefore, to increase the rating for landscape preservation from 11 to 14.5, and for kangaroo preservation from 14 to 17.0 to equate the total utilities of existing use and alternative *B*. Because the original utility ratings for these objectives were less dependable than those for other objectives, increases of this magnitude could be within the limits of error of the original estimates.

The sensitivity analysis has eliminated any possibility that alternative *C* might be the preferred one. Alternative *A* was already eliminated because no change in utility ratings could make it superior to alternative *B*. The sensitivity test showed that the parks officer would not prefer the existing use under any conditions and that the planner would only prefer it under very unlikely conditions. Two of the three subjects definitely prefer alternative *B*. Finally, the tests showed that a reasonable increase in the utility ratings of the preservation objectives would be enough to offset the apparent preference of the miner for the existing use. The utility approach ranks alternative *B* first and existing use second in comparative value.

4.3. A Reflection on the Utility Approach

Unlike the monetary approach, this analysis requires access to the decision maker. The comparative values cannot be compared to those from other fields, such as transportation or education, unless they have been estimated in the same way and with the same objectives. These disadvantages for the utility approach are partly balanced by its ability to accomodate outcomes that are described quantitatively or qualitatively, in monetary units or non-monetary units.

A residual difficulty of this approach is the need for a final aggregation of the different viewpoints, such as those of the parks officer and the miner. Sensitivity tests help clarify the differences and may sometimes indicate negligible ones. By contrast, the monetary approach values all things in a common unit and aggregates them directly. The monetary procedure automatically incorporates different viewpoints through the common money unit.

5. A MIXED APPROACH

Several of the multiple objective methods of Chapter 8 aggregate monetary and nonmonetary values. We have just illustrated the use of the weighted additive method in a utility approach to analyzing values. We now turn to the maximin, maximax, and goal-programming methods to review their potential in the analysis of complex valuations.

5.1. The Maximin and Maximax Methods

The maximin method appears particularly suitable for complex problems because it formalizes the common decision-making procedure of identifying and considering the most significant negative outcome of each alternative. Together, the maximin and maximax methods formalize the investment criterion of selecting the project that will have the lowest loss if it fails (maximin) and the highest gain if it succeeds (maximax). We try to apply the methods together and avoid the need to decide whether the decision-maker is pessimistic or optimistic.

Our simulated planner considered the data of Table 20.3 and indicated these worst and best outcomes:

Alternative	Worst Outcome (maximin)	Best Outcome (maximax)
Existing situation	Kangaroo habitat not preserved	$485,000 net social benefit
A	Kangaroo habitat not preserved	$462,000 net social benefit
B	No farm families wholly supported	Kangaroo habitat preserved
C	$545,000 acquisition cost	Kangaroo habitat preserved

The maximin method uses the best of the worst outcomes as a criterion for the preferred alternative. Let us assume that an acquisition cost of $545,000 is considered worse than no families supported. Alternative *B* will then be preferred to *C*. The outcomes for existing use and alternative *A* are identical, but an outcome of no families supported is considered less bad than no kangaroo habitat preserved. Alternative *B* is therefore chosen by the maximin method, because the other alternatives have worse possible outcomes.

The alternative with the best of the best outcomes is chosen in the maximax method. If the planner believes that a net social benefit of $462,000 is preferable to preservation of a single species habitat, alternatives *B* and *C* will drop out. Existing use will be slightly preferred over alternative *A* because of its higher net social benefit. The results of these two methods contradict each other because maximin chooses alternative *B* and maximax chooses existing use. However, when used together, the methods act as an effective filter because they clearly eliminate alternative *C*.

5.2. A Version of Goal Programming

Goal programming selects the combination of alternatives that minimizes weighted deviations from specified goals. It combines alternatives into land-use plans and is more suited to a design problem than to a choice between mutually exclusive alternatives, like those in Table 20.3. The method follows the procedure of defining ideal outcomes for each objective and selecting the alternative that departs least from these ideals. Goal programming also provides a convenient arithmetical way to measure these departures and aggregate them into a comparative value.

Application. We applied the basic principles of goal programming to our problem as follows.

(a) The preferred outcome for each objective was selected as the goal. The goals are listed in column 2 of Table 20.7. The preferred outcome for net social benefit is the highest possible value, or $485,000. The goal for recreation is the highest possible outcome of 64,300 family visits. The preferred outcomes for the three preservation objectives are denoted by "yes, there is preservation." (We code this information as 1 = yes and 0 = no.)

(b) The deviations from these goals were calculated for each objective in each alternative. The complete set of deviations for alternative *B* is listed in column 3 of Table 20.7. For example, the net social benefit for alternative *B* is $455,000 (Table 20.3), which deviates by $30,000 from the goal of $485,000.

(c) The deviations of all four alternatives for each objective were summed (column 4) and averaged (column 5). The deviations for net social benefit

Table 20.7. An Illustration of Goal Programming Approach Applied to Alternative *B*

Objectives	Goal[a]	Deviation from Goal			Standardized Deviations for Alternative B	
		Alternative *B*	All Alternatives	Average[b]	Unweighted	Weighted
1	2	3	4	5	6	7
Net social benefit	485	30	538	134.5	0.22	0.15
Acquisition cost	0	90	709	177.3	0.51	0.36
Operating cost	0	100	300	75.0	1.33	0.93
Income distribution	8	8	23	5.8	1.39	1.25
Recreation	64.3	0	7.7	1.9	0	0
Research	2	1	3	0.8	1.33	1.33
Landscapes	1 (yes)	0	1	0.3	0	0
Kangaroo habitat	1 (yes)	0	2	0.5	0	0
Eucalypt habitat	1 (yes)	1	3	0.8	1.33	2.00
Total						6.02

[a] Units as in Table 20.3.
[b] Rounded to one decimal place.

are $0 for existing use, $23,000 for *A*, $30,000 for *B*, and $485,000 for *C*. These total $538,000 and average $134,500.

(**d**) The deviations were standardized with the weighted additive method. Other procedures are possible, as discussed in Chapter 9. We simply divided each deviation by the average for its objective. For net social benefit, the deviation of alternative *B* was standardized by dividing 30,000 by 134,500, which gave 0.22. The results for all objectives for alternative *B* are listed in column 6 of Table 20.7.

(**e**) The figures in column 6 were multiplied by their respective weights from Table 20.6 to give the weighted deviations of column 7.

(**f**) Column 7 was added to give the aggregate weighted deviations from all goals. This sum is the comparative value of alternative *B*. The comparative values for all alternatives are:

Existing use	Alternatives *A*	*B*	*C*
12.48	9.02	6.02	6.86

Because smaller deviations indicate that an alternative is nearer the goals, a lower number indicates a higher comparative value. Alternative *B* is the preferred choice, with alternative *C* as second.

Sensitivity Analysis. Except for net social benefit and acquisition cost, the outcomes of alternative *C* are closer to the park goals than those of alternative *B*. Would the comparative ranking of *B* and *C* change if the figures for some of these goals were different? A change in the largest goal from $485,000 to $285,000, with equal changes in the outcomes of existing use and alternatives *A* and *B*, would only raise the value of *B* to 6.26 and reduce that of *C* to 6.43. This sensitivity test indicates that the comparative values of *B* and *C* are, in fact, substantially different.

5.3. A Reflection on the Approach

We have illustrated three different ways of implementing a mixed approach to the analysis of complexity. There are other ways of applying the methods of Chapters 8 and 9, singly or in combination with other methods. In our example, the maximin and maximax methods both eliminated alternative *C*, even though their other results were contradictory. The goal-programming approach also eliminated alternative *C* from the first choice. This application seemed to combine monetary and nonmonetary values well. Because the goals and the standardization procedure are appropriate, alternative *B* can be recommended.

6. A COMPARISON OF THE APPROACHES

We have applied three different approaches to analyzing the complex valuation problem of the proposed Gorgelands national park.

The monetary approach gave the following comparative values for the alternatives:

Existing use	$1,009,000
Alternative *A*	997,000
Alternative *B*	984,000
Alternative *C*	653,000

This approach apparently eliminates alternative *C* from consideration and shows little difference in values between the other alternatives. However, a test showed that this comparative ranking is sensitive to differences in the figures used for ore quality and price. Different prices would not change the relationship of the first three alternatives, but a decrease in ore price that appears to be within the possible range would be sufficient to rank alternative *C* above the other three. The monetary approach, therefore, provides evidence that a national park of some kind would have a social value at least as large as that of the existing use of the area.

The utility approach eliminated alternatives *A* and *C*. It showed that two of the three kinds of people questioned preferred alternative *B*, and the other one preferred existing use. A sensitivity test showed that no reasonable changes in the figures would cause either of the first two to shift their preference to existing use. However, a reasonable valuation for preservation of the kangaroo and eucalypt by the miner would suffice to shift his preference from existing use to alternative *B*. The utility approach provides evidence that a national park of the kind proposed in alternative *B* would have greater social value than the alternative uses of the area that were tested.

Two versions of the mixed approach were used. The combined maximin and maximax approach eliminated alternative *C*, but failed to rank the other three alternatives. The goal-programming approach gave the following comparative figures for the alternatives:

Existing use	12.48
Alternative *A*	9.02
Alternative *B*	6.02
Alternative *C*	6.86

Because these measure deviations from desired goals, the smaller the figure, the greater the value. The mixed approach therefore provides evidence that a national park of the kind proposed in alternative *B* would have the greatest social value of the alternatives tested.

When the results of the three approaches are combined, there is strong evidence that a national park would be socially desirable, and that the most valuable form of park would be the one proposed in alternative *B*.

Choice between the Approaches. The choice depends on the nature of the decision and on how much access the analyst has to the decision makers. Both the utility approach and our version of goal programming accommodated descriptive and quantitative outcomes, as well as monetary and nonmonetary values. Both are restricted to comparisons within a sector and require access to decision makers. The monetary approach suits intrasector comparisons and is also suitable for such intersector analyses as comparing a park, a highway, and an educational investment. This approach often requires considerable time to value all unpriced things in money or to reduce the choice to a comparison of money and one unpriced thing, but it does not require access to the decision makers.

Cost of the Analysis. The costs of the monetary approach, in man-days, were:

Outcomes		Collection of Information	Calculations
Identification of significant outcomes	30 interviews	3	2
Net social benefit—cattle	32 farms	5	2
Net social benefit—mining	1 firm	10	2
Income compensation	8 families	3	3
Recreation	Interviews through season	12	3
Research		1	Nil
Preservation of: Natural landscapes, Kangaroo habitat, Eucalypt habitat	250 interviews	5	4

These costs are small compared with the usefulness of the information. The highest costs were in formulating the problem for Table 20.1 and in the search of the literature for concepts and methods. The costs of problem formulation must be incurred for every analysis. But we hope that this book will reduce the costs of literature search in future analyses.

Combination of Methods. In Part II we reviewed and illustrated each method separately. In this chapter we have combined methods to analyze a complex problem. The important benefits and costs were identified with the total utility estimation methods of Chapters 10 and 11. In the monetary approach we valued unpriced things with the opportunity-cost, direct-question, and net-social-value methods and aggregated the results.

Comparing New and Existing Uses. Choices between similar things are usually straightforward because the assumptions apply equally to everything. Valuation through characteristics of the environment assumes, for example, that characteristic level is a proxy for utility. This assumption is acceptable when the method is applied to choices between similar things but is probably unacceptable otherwise. The choice between a new alternative and an existing use is difficult when the new use is quite different from the existing one. In the gorgelands example, the full park alternative (*C*) was quite different from the existing exploitive use of mining and cattle grazing. But valuation can be simplified if the existing and new alternatives are examined and compared objective by objective.

7. AN OVERVIEW

Useful value information can usually be generated when decisions are clearly analyzed and when the comparative nature of the outcomes is clearly identified. Our analysis has illustrated the identification of outcomes by alternative and objective and the feasibility of valuation in complex situations.

The monetary, utility, and mixed approaches will not make choices for decision makers. They do not remove the need for judgment, but they do narrow the latitude for judgment and controversy. The approaches and methods we have presented model decisions and make explicit the basic nature of choices. The model of value in Equation 3.5 provides a basis for valuing unpriced benefits and costs of any kind and under any circumstances.

REFERENCES

Aaron vs. City of Los Angeles. 11 *CCH Aviation Cases* 17, 642 (1970).

Ackoff, R. L. "Does Quality of Life Have to be Quantified?" *Operational Research Quarterly*, **27**(2), 289–303 (1976).

Alchian, A. A. "The Meaning of Utility Measurement." *American Economic Review*, **43**(1), 26–50 (1953).

Alexander, I. "City Centre Redevelopment: An Evaluation of Alternative Approaches." *Progress in Planning*, **3**(1), 1–81 (1974).

Allison, R. C. and R. S. Leighton. *Evaluating Forest Campground Sites*. University of New Hampshire, Cooperative Extension Service, Extension Folder 64, Durham, undated.

Alston, R. M. and D. M. Freeman. "The Natural Resource Decision-Maker as Political and Economic Man: Toward a Synthesis." *Journal of Environmental Management*, **3**(3), 167–183 (1975).

Anderson, R. C. and C. Auster. "Costs and Benefits of Road Salting." *Environmental Affairs*, **3**(1), 128–144 (1974).

Anderson, R. J., Jr. and T. D. Crocker. "Air Pollution and Residential Property Values." *Urban Studies*, **8**(3), 171–180 (1971).

Anderson, R. J., Jr. and T. D. Crocker. "Air Pollution and Property Values: A Reply." *Review of Economics and Statistics*, **54**(4), 470–473 (1972).

Armstrong, F. H. "Valuation of Amenity Forests." *The Consultant*, **19**(1), 13–19 (1974).

Arthur, L. M., T. C. Daniel, and R. S. Boster. "Scenic Assessment: An Overview." *Landscape Planning*, **4**(2), 109–129 (1977).

Atkinson, W. A. "A Method for the Recreational Evaluation of Forest Land." Unpublished master's thesis. Berkeley: University of California, 1956.

Auburn University. *Environmental Quality: A Survey of Costs, Benefits, Citizens' Attitudes*. Department of Civil Engineering, Auburn, Alabama, 1971.

Babcock, L. R., Jr. and N. L. Nagda. "Indices of Air Quality." In W. A. Thomas, Ed., *Indicators of Environmental Quality*. New York: Plenum Press, 1972. Pp. 183–197.

Bach, W. *Atmospheric Pollution*. New York: McGraw-Hill, 1972.

Baier, K. "What is Value? An Analysis of the Concept." In K. Baier and N. Rescher, Eds., *Values and the Future*. New York: Free Press, 1969. Pp. 33–67.

Barrett, L. B. and T. E. Waddell. *Costs of Air Pollution Damage: A Status Report*. U.S. Environmental Protection Agency, Report No. AP-85, Research Triangle Park, North Carolina, 1973.

Beardsley, W. *Economic Value of Recreation Benefits Determined by Three Methods*. U.S. Department of Agriculture, Forest Service, Research Note RM-176, Fort Collins, 1970.

Becker, G. S. "A Theory of the Allocation of Time." *Economic Journal*, **75**(299), 493–517 (1965).

Bennett, A. E. and K. Ritchie. *Questionnaires in Medicine*. London: Oxford University Press, 1975.

Berry, D. *Landscape Aesthetics and Environmental Planning: A Critique of Underlying Premises*. Regional Science Research Institute, Discussion Paper No. 85, Philadelphia, 1975.

Bishop, J. and C. Cicchetti. "Some Institutional and Conceptual Thoughts on the Measurement of Indirect and Intangible Benefits and Costs." In H. M. Peskin and E. P. Seskin, Eds., *Cost-Benefit Analysis and Water Pollution Policy*. Washington: The Urban Institute, 1975. Pp. 105–125.

Bohm, P. "An Approach to the Problem of Estimating the Demand for Public Goods." *Swedish Journal of Economics*, **73**(1), 55–66 (1971).

Bohm, P. "Estimating Demand for Public Goods: An Experiment." *European Economic Review*, **3**(2), 111–130 (1972).

Boland, L. A. "Lexicographic Orderings, Multiple Criteria, and 'Ad Hocery'." *Australian Economic Papers*, **13**(22), 152–157 (1974).

Boster, R. S. and T. C. Daniel. "Measuring Public Response to Vegetative Management." In *Proceedings of the 16th Annual Arizona Watershed Symposium*, Arizona Water Commission, Phoenix, 1972. Pp. 38–43.

Boyet, W. E. and G. S. Tolley. "Recreation Projection Based on Demand Analysis." *Journal of Farm Economics*, **48**(4), 984–1001 (1966).

Brewer, D. and G. A. Gillespie. "Estimating Satisfaction Levels of Outdoor Recreationists." *Journal of Soil and Water Conservation*, **22**(6), 248–249 (1967).

Brookshire, D. S., B. C. Ives, and W. D. Schulze. "The Valuation of Aesthetic Preferences." *Journal of Environmental Economics and Management*, **3**(4), 325–346 (1976).

Brown, W. G. and A. Hussen. *A Production Economic Analysis of the Little White Salmon and Willard National Fish Hatcheries*. Oregon State University, Agricultural Experiment Station, Special Report 428, Corvallis, 1974.

Brown, W. G. and F. W. Nawas. "Impact of Aggregation on the Estimation of Outdoor Recreation Demand Functions." *American Journal of Agricultural Economics*, **55**(2), 246–249 (1973).

Brown, W. G., A. Singh, and E. N. Castle. *An Economic Evaluation of the Oregon Salmon and Steelhead Sport Fishery*. Oregon State University, Agricultural Experiment Station, Technical Bulletin 78, Corvallis, 1964.

Brush, R. O. Personal communication, 1976.

Buchanan, J. M. *The Public Finances: An Introductory Textbook*, 3rd ed. Homewood: Irwin, 1970.

Buchanan, J. M. and G. Tullock. *The Calculus of Consent: Logical Foundations of Constitutional Democracy*. Ann Arbor: University of Michigan Press, 1962.

Buehler, B. "Monetary Values of Life and Health." *Journal of the Hydraulics Division*, **101**, 29–47 (1975).

Burke, H. D., G. H. Lewis and H. R. Orr. "A Method for Classifying Scenery from a Roadway." In *Park Practice Guidelines*. Washington: National Park Service and National Conference on State Parks, 1968. Pp. 125–141.

Burt, O. R. and D. Brewer. "Estimation of Net Social Benefits of Outdoor Recreation." *Econometrica*, **39**(5), 813–827 (1971).

Burton, T. L. *Experiments in Recreation Research*. London: Allen and Unwin, 1971.

Burton, T. L. and G. P. Wibberley. *Outdoor Recreation in the British Countryside*. London University, Wye College, Studies in Rural Land Use No. 5, Ashford, 1965.

Buxton, B. M. and J. W. Hammond. "Social Cost of Alternative Dairy Price Support Levels." *American Journal of Agricultural Economics*, **56**(2), 286–291 (1974).

Candler, W. "Linear Programming in Capital Budgeting with Multiple Goals." In J. L. Cochrane and M. Zeleny, Eds., *Multiple Criteria Decision-Making*. Columbia: University of South Carolina Press, 1973. Pp. 416–428.

Candler, W. and D. Sargent. "Farm Standards and the Theory of Production Economics." *Journal of Agricultural Economics* **15**(2), 282–290 (1962).

Cerny, J. W. "Scenic Analysis and Assessment." *CRC Critical Reviews in Environmental Control*, **4**(2), 221–250 (1974).

Cesario, F. J. Jr. "Operations Research in Outdoor Recreation." *Journal of Leisure Research*, **1**(1), 33–52 (1969).

Cesario, F. J. "Value of Time in Recreation Benefit Studies." *Land Economics*, **52**(1), 32–41 (1976).

Cesario, F. J. and J. L. Knetsch. "The Time-Bias in Recreation Benefit Estimates." *Water Resources Research*, **6**(3), 700–704 (1970).

Christianson, J. B. "Evaluating Locations for Outpatient Medical Care Facilities." *Land Economics*, **52**(3), 299–313 (1976).

Churchman, C. W. and R. L. Ackoff. "An Approximate Measure of Value." *Operations Research*, **2**(2), 172–187 (1954).

Ciriacy-Wantrup, S. V. and W. E. Phillips. "Conservation of the California Tule Elk: A Socioeconomic Study of a Survival Problem." *Biological Conservation*, **3**(1), 23–32 (1970).

Clawson, M. *Methods of Measuring the Demand for and Value of Outdoor Recreation*. Resources for the Future, Reprint No. 10, Washington, 1959.

Clawson, M. and J. L. Knetsch. *Economics of Outdoor Recreation*. Baltimore: Johns Hopkins Press, 1966.

Cochrane, S. McL., A. Fitzgibbons, and H. P. Hendrikx. *Social and Economic Gains from Drilling in the Barrier Reef Area*. Paper presented to the 43rd Congress of the Australian and New Zealand Association for the Advancement of Science, Brisbane, 1971.

Cohon, J. L. and D. H. Marks. "A Review and Evaluation of Multiobjective Programming Techniques." *Water Resources Research*, **11**(2), 208–220 (1975).

Coomber, N. H. and A. K. Biswas. *Evaluation of Environmental Intangibles*. New York: Genera Press, 1973.

Cordell, M. L. and G. A. James. *Visitors' Preferences for Certain Physical Charac-*

teristics of Developed Campsites. U.S. Department of Agriculture, Forest Service, Research Paper SE-100, Asheville, 1972.

Cowling, K. and J. Cubbin. "Hedonic Price Index for United Kingdom Cars." *Economic Journal,* **82**(327), 963–978 (1972).

Craik, K. H. "Appraising the Objectivity of Landscape Dimensions." In J. V. Krutilla, Ed., *Natural Environments: Studies in Theoretical and Applied Analysis.* Baltimore: Johns Hopkins Press, 1972. Pp. 292–346.

Craine, L. E. "Comment." In R. Dorfman, Ed., *Measuring Benefits of Government Investments.* Washington: The Brookings Institution, 1965. Pp. 110–116.

Crawford, A. B. "Impact Analysis Using Differentially Weighted Evaluative Criteria." In J. L. Cochrane and M. Zeleny, Eds., *Multiple Criteria Decision Making.* Columbia: University of South Carolina Press, 1973. Pp. 732–735.

Crissey, W. F. "Prairie Potholes from a Continental Viewpoint." In *Saskatoon Wetlands Seminar,* Department of Indian Affairs and Northern Development, Canadian Wildlife Service Report Series, No. 6, Ottawa, 1969. Pp. 161–171.

Currie, J. M., J. A. Murphy, and A. Schmitz. "The Concept of Economic Surplus and Its Use in Economic Analysis." *Economic Journal,* **81**(324), 741–799 (1971).

Cuttance, P. *The Application of Some Recent Developments in Measuring Living Standards to the Study of Poverty.* Paper presented to the Fourth Conference of Economists, Canberra, 1974.

Dalkey, N. C. and O. Helmer. "An Experimental Application of the Delphi Method to the Use of Experts." *Management Science,* **9**(3), 458–467 (1963).

Daniel, T. C. and R. S. Boster. *Measuring Landscape Esthetics: The Scenic Beauty Estimation Method.* U.S. Department of Agriculture, Forest Service, Research Paper RM-167, Fort Collins, 1976.

Darling, A. H. "Measuring Benefits Generated by Urban Water Parks." *Land Economics,* **49**(1), 22–34 (1973).

David, L. and L. Duckstein. "Multi-Criterion Ranking of Alternative Long-Range Water Resource Systems." *Water Resources Bulletin,* **12**(4), 731–754 (1976).

Dawson, R. F. F. *Cost of Road Accidents in Great Britain.* Report of Road Research Laboratory, Ministry of Transport, London, 1967.

Day, J. C. and J. R. Gilpin. "The Impact of Man-Made Lakes on Residential Property Values: A Case Study and Methodological Exploration." *Water Resources Research,* **10**(1), 37–43 (1974).

Dee, N., J. Baker, N. Drobny, K. Duke, I. Whitman, and D. Fahringer. "An Environmental Evaluation System for Water Resource Planning." *Water Resources Research,* **9**(3), 523–535 (1973).

Denison, E. F. *The Sources of Economic Growth in the United States and the Alternatives Before Us.* Committee for Economic Development, Supplementary Paper No. 13, New York, 1962.

Dillon, J. L. "An Expository Review of Bernoullian Decision Theory in Agriculture: Is Utility Futility?" *Review of Marketing and Agricultural Economics,* **39**(1), 3–80 (1971).

Donnermeyer, J. F., P. F. Korsching, and R. J. Burdge. "An Interpretative Analysis of Family and Individual Economic Costs Due to Water Resource Development." *Water Resources Bulletin,* **10**(1), 91–100 (1974).

Doolittle, M. L., M. H. Kootsher, and C. V. Mercer. *Relationship of Personnel Characteristics to Fire Prevention Effectiveness*. U.S. Department of Agriculture, Forest Service, Research Note SO-191, New Orleans, 1975.

Downes, R. G. "Goals for Resource Management." In J. A. Sinden, Ed., *The Natural Resources of Australia: Prospects and Problems for Development*. Sydney: Angus and Robertson, 1972. Pp. 19–31.

Downing, P. B. "Factors Affecting Commercial Land Values: An Empirical Study of Milwaukee, Wisconsin." *Land Economics*, **49**(1), 45–56 (1973).

Duerr, W. A. *Fundamentals of Forestry Economics*. New York: McGraw-Hill, 1960.

Dupuit, J. "On the Measurement of the Utility of Public Works." Reprinted in A. T. Peacock, R. Turvey, F. A. Lutz, and E. Henderson, Eds., *International Economic Papers*, No. 2. London: Macmillan, 1952. Pp. 83–110.

Dutch Agricultural Investment Commission. *An Assessment of Investments in Land Reclamation: A Study from the Point of View of the National Economy*. International Institute for Land Reclamation and Improvement, Publication 7. Wageningen, Netherlands: H. Veenman and Zonen N. V., 1960.

Eckenrode, R. T. "Weighting Multiple Criteria." *Management Science*, **12**(3), 180–192 (1965).

Eckstein, O. *Public Finance*, 2nd ed. Englewood Cliffs: Prentice-Hall, 1967.

Edwards, A. L. *Techniques of Attitude Scale Construction*. New York: Appleton-Century-Crofts, 1957.

Edwards, W. "Social Utilities." *The Engineering Economist*, Summer Symposium Series IV, 119–129 (1972).

Epstein, L. I. "A Proposed Measure for Determining the Value of a Design." *Operations Research*, **5**(2), 297–299 (1957).

Erskine, H. "The Polls: Pollution and Its Costs." *Public Opinion Quarterly*, **36**(1), 120–135 (1972).

Field, D. B. "Goal Programming for Forest Management." *Forest Science*, **19**(2), 125–135 (1973).

Fines, K. D. "Landscape Evaluation: A Research Project in East Sussex." *Regional Studies*, **2**(1), 41–55 (1968).

Finn, R. M. "Effects of Some Variations in Rating Scale Characteristics on the Means and Reliabilities of Ratings." *Educational and Psychological Measurement*, **32**(2), 255–265 (1972).

Fischer, D. W. and G. S. Davies. "An Approach to Assessing Environmental Impacts." *Journal of Environmental Management*, **1**(3), 207–227 (1973).

Fischer, L. A. "Some Economic Aspects of Pest Control in Agriculture." *Canadian Journal of Agricultural Economics*, **16**(2), 90–99 (1968).

Fischer, L. A. "The Economics of Pest Control in Canadian Apple Production." *Canadian Journal of Agricultural Economics*, **18**(3), 89–96 (1970).

Fishburn, P. C. *Decision and Value Theory*. New York: Wiley, 1964.

Fishburn, P. C. "Methods of Estimating Additive Utilities." *Management Science*, **13**(7), 435–453 (1967).

Fisher, J., N. Simon, and J. Vincent. *Wildlife in Danger*. New York: Viking, 1969.

Fitzgibbons, A. J. and H. P. Hendrikx. "An Economic Evaluation of the Proposed

Cooloola Sand Mining Project." *Economic Analysis and Policy,* **1**(2), 58–73 (1970).

Foster, C. D. "Social Welfare Functions in Cost-Benefit Analysis." In J. R. Lawrence, Ed., *Operational Research and the Social Sciences.* London: Tavistock, 1966. Pp. 305–318.

Foster, C. D. and M. E. Beesley. "Estimating the Social Benefit of Constructing an Underground Railway in London." *Journal of the Royal Statistical Society,* Series A, **126**(1), 46–78 (1963).

Foster, J. H. Personal communication, 1977.

Frank, C. R., Jr. and K-P. Heiss. *Cost Benefit Study of the Earth Resources Observation Satellite System Grazing Land Management.* Princeton: Mathematica, 1968.

Freeman, A. M. III. "Air Pollution and Property Values: A Methodological Comment." *Review of Economics and Statistics,* **53**(4), 415–416 (1971).

Freeman, A. M. III. "On Estimating Air Pollution Control Benefits from Land Value Studies," *Journal of Environmental Economics and Management,* **1**(1), 74–83 (1974).

Galanter, E. "The Direct Measurement of Utility and Subjective Probability." *American Journal of Psychology.* **75**(2), 208–220 (1962).

Garrett, J. R., G. J. Pon, and D. J. Arosteguy. *Economics of Big Game Resource Use in Nevada.* University of Nevada, Agricultural Experiment Station, Paper B25, Reno, 1970.

Gauger, S. E. and J. B. Wyckoff. "Aesthetic Preference for Water Resource Projects: An Application of Q Methodology." *Water Resources Bulletin,* **9**(3), 522–528 (1973).

Geiger, P. H. and F. A. Firestone. "The Estimation of Fractional Loudness." *Journal of the Acoustic Society of America,* **5**(1), 25–30 (1933).

Gluck, R. *An Economic Evaluation of the Rakaia Fishery as a Recreation Resource.* Monash University, Australian Recreation Research Association, Monograph No. 6, Melbourne, 1975.

Goldstein, J. H. *Competition for Wetlands in the Midwest: An Economic Analysis.* Baltimore: Johns Hopkins Press, 1971.

Gray, E. C. "Alternative Strategies for Locating Transmission Lines." *Canadian Journal of Agricultural Economics, Workshop Proceedings,* 1975. Pp. 153–166.

Gray, J. R. and L. W. Anderson. *Use of Natural Resources in the Ruidoso Ranger District.* New Mexico State University, Agricultural Experiment Station, Bulletin 489, Las Cruces, 1964a.

Gray, J. R. and L. W. Anderson. *Recreation Economics in South-Central New Mexico.* New Mexico State University, Agricultural Experiment Station, Bulletin 488, Las Cruces, 1964b.

Gray, J. R., G. D. Fisk, and M. Mathews. "Environmental Costs of Recreation in the Sandia Mountains." *New Mexico Business,* **27**(10), 3–12 (1974).

Green, D. M. and J. A. Swets. *Signal Detection Theory and Psychophysics.* New York: Wiley, 1966.

Griliches, Z. "Research Costs and Social Returns: Hybrid Corn and Related Innovations." *Journal of Political Economy,* **46**(5), 419–431 (1958).

Gum, R. L., T. G. Roefs, and D. B. Kimball. "Quantifying Societal Goals: Development of a Weighting Methodology." *Water Resources Research,* **12**(4), 617–622 (1976).

Gupta, T. R. and J. H. Foster. "Economic Criteria for Freshwater Wetland Policy in Massachusetts." *American Journal of Agricultural Economics,* **57**(1), 40–45 (1975).

Haefele, E. T. *Representative Government and Environmental Management.* Baltimore: Johns Hopkins Press, 1973.

Haimes, Y. Y. and W. A. Hall. "Multiobjectives in Water Resource Systems Analyses: The Surrogate Worth Trade-Off Method." *Water Resources Research,* **10**(4), 615–624 (1974).

Halter, A. N. and G. W. Dean. *Decisions Under Uncertainty with Research Applications.* Cincinnati: South-Western, 1971.

Hamill, L. "Classification of Forest Land for Recreational Potential and Scenery." *Forestry Chronicle,* **47**(3), 149–153 (1971).

Hamill, L. "Statistical Tests of Leopold's System for Quantifying Aesthetic Factors Among Rivers." *Water Resources Research,* **10**(3), 395–401 (1974).

Hammack, J. and G. M. Brown, Jr. *Waterfowl and Wetlands: Towards Bio-Economic Analysis.* Baltimore: Johns Hopkins Press, 1974.

Hardie, I. W. Personal communication, 1977.

Hardie, I. W. and J. E. Kirkley. *An Alternative Method of Assessing Preferences for Potential Government Goods.* Paper presented to Annual Conference of American Agricultural Economics Association, Columbus, Ohio, 1975.

Harlow, H. F., J. G. Miller, and T. M. Newcomb. "Identifying Creative Talent in Psychology." *American Psychologist,* **17**(10), 679–683 (1962).

Harrison, A. J. and D. A. Quarmby. "The Value of Time." In R. Layard, Ed., *Cost-Benefit Analysis.* Harmondsworth, U.K.: Penguin, 1972. Pp. 173–208.

Harrison, H. A. *Coordination Problems—Dispersed Areas.* Paper presented to U.S. Forest Service Timber Management—Recreation Meeting, Bend, Oregon, 1962.

Harry, J., J. C. Hendee, and R. B. Stein. "A Sociological Criterion for Outdoor Recreation Resource Allocation." Unpublished review draft, undated.

Haveman, R. H. *Water Resource Investment and the Public Interest: An Analysis of Federal Expenditures in Ten Southern States.* Nashville: Vanderbilt University Press, 1965.

Haveman, R. H. "Comment." In S. B. Chase, Jr., Ed., *Problems in Public Expenditure Analysis.* Washington: The Brookings Institution, 1968. Pp. 209–213.

Haveman, R. H. and B. A. Weisbrod. "The Concept of Benefits in Cost-Benefit Analysis: With Emphasis on Water Pollution Control Activities." In H. M. Peskin and E. P. Seskin, Eds., *Cost-Benefit Analysis and Water Pollution Policy.* Washington: The Urban Institute, 1975. Pp. 37–65.

Havighurst, C. C. *A Survey of Air Pollution Litigation in the Philadelphia Area.* U.S. National Air Pollution Control Administration, Final Report, Contract Number CPA 22-68-112, Raleigh, 1969.

Heady, E. O. and J. L. Dillon. *Agricultural Production Functions.* Ames: Iowa State University Press, 1961.

Hedlin, R. "Economic Values of Small Wetlands." In *Saskatoon Wetlands*

Seminar, Department of Indian Affairs and Northern Development, Canadian Wildlife Service Report Series, No. 6, Ottawa, 1969. Pp. 25–28.

Helliwell, D. R. "The Amenity Value of Trees and Woodlands." *Scottish Forestry,* **21**(2), 109–112 (1967).

Helliwell, D. R. "Valuation of Wildlife Resources." *Regional Studies,* **3**(1), 41–47 (1969).

Helliwell, D. R. "Priorities and Values In Nature Conservation." *Journal of Environmental Management,* **1**(2), 85–127 (1973).

Helliwell, D. R. "The Value of Vegetation for Conservation I. Four Land Areas in Britain." *Journal of Environmental Management,* **2**(1), 51–74 (1974a).

Helliwell, D. R. "The Value of Vegetation for Conservation II. Ml Motorway Area." *Journal of Evironmental Management,* **2**(1), 75–78 (1974b).

Herfindahl, O. C. and A. V. Kneese. *Economic Theory of Natural Resources.* Columbus, Ohio: Merrill, 1974.

Hicks, J. R. "The Rehabilitation of Consumers' Surplus." *Review of Economic Studies,* **8**(2), 108–116 (1941).

Hicks, J. R. "The Four Consumer's Surpluses." *Review of Economic Studies,* **11**(1), 31–41 (1943).

Hicks, J. R. *A Revision of Demand Theory.* Oxford: Clarendon Press, 1956.

Hill, M. "A Goals-Achievement Matrix for Evaluating Alternative Plans." *Journal of the American Institute of Planners,* **34**(1), 19–29 (1968).

Hill, M. and R. Alterman. "Power Plant Site Evalutation: The Case of the Sharon Plant in Israel." *Journal of Environmental Management,* **2**(2), 179–196 (1974).

Hitch, C. J. and R. N. McKean. *The Economics of Defense in the Nuclear Age.* Cambridge: Harvard University Press, 1960.

Hoff, R. M. D. "The Case Against Cascadia Dam (a Slightly Biased Report)." *Wilderness River Drifting,* **1**(1), 17–18 (1972).

Hoinville, G. Personal communication, 1976.

Hoinville, G. and R. Berthoud. *Identifying and Evaluating Trade-Off Preferences: An Analysis of Environmental Accessibility Priorities.* Social and Community Planning Research, Publication P-117, London, 1970a.

Hoinville, G. and R. Berthoud. *Value of Time: Development Project Report on Stage 3.* Social and Community Planning Research, Publication P-119, London, 1970b.

Horner, G. L. "Internalizing Agricultural Nitrogen Pollution Externalities: A Case Study." *American Journal of Agricultural Economics,* **57**(1), 33–39 (1975).

Howe, C. W. *Benefit-Cost Analysis for Water System Planning.* American Geophysical Union, Water Resources Monograph 2, Washington, 1971.

Huber, G. P., V. K. Sahney, and D. L. Ford. "A Study of Subjective Evaluation Models." *Behavioral Science,* **14**(6), 483–489 (1969).

Hughes, J. M. *Wilderness Land Allocation in a Multiple Use Forest Management Framework in the Pacific Northwest.* U.S. Department of Agriculture, Forest Service, Research Note PNW-26, Portland, Oregon, 1965.

Iden, G. "Farmland Values Re-explored." *Agricultural Economics Research,* **16**(2), 41–50 (1964).

Jaksch, J. A. and H. H. Stoevener. *Effects of Air Pollution on Residential Property*

Values in Toledo, Oregon. Oregon State University, Agricultural Experiment Station, Special Report 304, Covallis, 1970.

Jaksch, J. A. and H. H. Stoevener. *Outpatient Medical Costs Related to Air Pollution in the Portland, Oregon Area*. U.S. Environmental Protection Agency, Report EPA-600/5-74-017, Washington, 1974.

Kalter, R. J. and L. E. Gosse, "Recreation Demand Functions and the Identification Problem." *Journal of Leisure Research*, **2**(1), 45–53 (1970).

Kasperson, R. E. "Political Behavior and the Decision-Making Process in the Allocation of Water Resources between Recreational and Municipal Use." *Natural Resources Journal*, **9**(2), 176–211 (1969).

Keeney, R. L. "A Decision Analysis with Multiple Objectives: The Mexico City Airport." *Bell Journal of Economics and Management Science*, **4**(1), 101–117 (1973).

Keeney, R. L. and E. F. Wood. "An Illustrative Example of the Use of Multiattribute Utility Theory for Water Resource Planning." *Water Resources Research*, **13**(4), 705–712 (1977).

Kelly, R. F. and R. Stephenson. "The Semantic Differential: An Information Score for Designing Retail Patronage Appeals." *Journal of Marketing*, **31**(4), 43–47 (1967).

Kielbaso, J. J. *Economic Value of Trees in the Urban Locale*. Paper presented to the Symposium on the Role of Trees in the Southern Urban Environment, Athens, Georgia, 1971.

Klingebiel, A. A. and P. H. Montgomery, *Land Capability Classification*. U.S. Department of Agriculture, Agriculture Handbook 210, Washington, 1961.

Kneese, A. V. *Economics and the Environment*. Harmondsworth, U.K.: Penguin, 1977.

Knetsch, J. L. and R. K. Davis. "Comparison of Methods for Recreation Evaluation." In A. V. Kneese and S. C. Smith, Eds., *Water Research*. Baltimore: Johns Hopkins Press, 1966. Pp. 125–142.

Krutilla, J. V. and C. J. Cicchetti. "Evaluating Benefits of Environmental Resources with Special Application to the Hells Canyon." *Natural Resources Journal*, **12**(1), 1–29 (1972).

Lancaster, K. J. "A New Approach to Consumer Theory." *Journal of Political Economy*, **74**(2), 132–157 (1966).

LaPage, W. F. *The Role of Customer Satisfaction in Managing Commercial Campgrounds*. U.S. Department of Agriculture, Forest Service, Research Paper NE-105, Upper Darby, Pennsylvania, 1968.

Lave, L. B. and E. P. Seskin. "Air Pollution and Human Health." *Science*, **169**(3947), 723–733 (1970).

Leopold, L. B. *Quantitative Comparison of Some Aesthetic Factors Among Rivers*. U.S. Department of the Interior, Geological Survey Circular 620, Washington, 1969.

Leopold, L. B. and M. O. Marchand. "On the Quantitative Inventory of the Riverscape." *Water Resources Research*, **4**(4), 709–717 (1968).

Lewis, J. N. "Public Policy for Pesticides." In *Proceedings of the Seminar on Wildlife Conservation in Eastern Australia*. Armidale: University of New England, 1965. Pp. 39–43.

Lichfield, N. "Evaluation Methodology of Urban and Regional Plans: A Review." *Regional Studies,* **4**(2), 151–165 (1970).

Liesch, P. W. and J. A. Sinden. *Market Failure or Utility Success in Land Use Analyses?* Paper presented to the 20th Annual Conference of the Australian Agricultural Economics Society, Armidale, 1976.

Likert, R. "A Technique for the Measurement of Attitudes." *Archives of Psychology,* No. 140 (1932).

Lime, D. W. *Factors Influencing Campground Use in the Superior National Forest of Minnesota.* U.S. Department of Agriculture, Forest Service, Research Paper NC-60, St. Paul, 1971.

Lin, W., G. W. Dean, and C. V. Moore, "An Empirical Test of Utility vs. Profit Maximization in Agricultural Production." *American Journal of Agricultural Economics,* **56**(3), 497–508 (1974).

Linton, D. L. "The Assessment of Scenery as a Natural Resource." *Scottish Geographical Magazine,* **84**(3), 219–238 (1968).

Lipscomb, D. M. "Indicators of Environmental Noise." In W. A. Thomas, Ed., *Indicators of Environmental Quality.* New York: Plenum, 1972. Pp. 211–242.

Little, I. M. D. *A Critique of Welfare Economics.* Oxford: Clarendon, 1950.

Litton, R. B., Jr. *Forest Landscape Description and Inventories: A Basis for Land Planning and Design.* U.S. Department of Agriculture, Forest Service, Research Paper PSW-49, Berkeley, 1968.

Litton, R. B., Jr. "Aesthetic Dimensions of the Landscape." In J. V. Krutilla, Ed., *Natural Environments: Studies in Theoretical and Applied Analysis.* Baltimore: Johns Hopkins Press, 1972. Pp. 262–291.

Luken, R. A. "Preservation of Wetlands: The Case of San Francisco Bay." *Natural Resources Journal,* **14**(1), 139–152 (1974).

Lynne, G. D. and E. N. Castle. *Trade-Off Ratio Calculations in Water Resource Planning.* Oregon State University, Agricultural Experiment Station, Special Report 429, Corvallis, 1975.

McCay, R. E. *Ohio Trail Users.* U.S. Department of Agriculture, Forest Service, Research Note NE-228, Upper Darby, Pennsylvania, 1976.

McCay, R. E. and W. B. White. *Economic Analysis of the Gypsy Moth Problem in the Northeast. I. Applied to Commercial Forest Stands.* U.S. Department of Agriculture, Forest Service, Research paper NE-275, Upper Darby, Pennsylvania, 1973.

MacCrimmon, K. R. "An Overview of Multiple Objective Decision Making." In J. L. Cochrane and M. Zeleny, Eds., *Multiple Criteria Decision Making.* Columbia: University of South Carolina Press, 1973. Pp. 18–44.

MacCrimmon, K. R. and M. Toda. "The Experimental Determination of Indifference Curves." *Review of Economic Studies,* **36**(10), 433–451 (1969).

McDermid, R. W. and J. R. McKnight. *Noise Hazards on Forestry Operations in the South.* Louisiana State University, Forestry Note 114, Baton Rouge, 1975.

McGaughey, E. E. and E. Thorbecke. "Project Selection and Macroeconomic Objectives: A Methodology Applied to Peruvian Irrigation Projects." *American Journal of Agricultural Economics,* **54**(1), 32–40 (1972).

McHarg, I. L. *The Least Social Cost Corridor for the Richmond Parkway.* Philadelphia: Wallace, McHarg, Roberts and Todd, 1968.

McKean, R. N. *Efficiency in Government through Systems Analysis, with Emphasis on Water Resources Development*. New York: Wiley, 1958.

McMillan, M. "Measuring Benefits Generated by Urban Water Parks: Comment." *Land Economics*, **51**(4), 379–381 (1975).

Mack, R. P. and S. Myers. "Outdoor Recreation." In R. Dorfman, Ed., *Measuring Benefits of Government Investments*. Washington: The Brookings Institution, 1965. Pp. 71–101.

Major, D. C. "Benefit-Cost Ratios for Projects in Multiple Objective Investment Programs." *Water Resources Research*, **5**(6), 1174–1178 (1969).

Mansfield, N. W. "The Estimation of Benefits from Recreation Sites and the Provision of a New Recreational Facility." *Regional Studies*, **5**(2), 55–69 (1971).

Markham, J. and P. N. O'Farrell. "Choice of Mode for the Journey-to-Work in Dublin: Some Multivariate Aspects." *Journal of Environmental Management*, **2**(1), 123–147 (1974).

Marsh, G. P. *Man and Nature*. New York: Scribner, 1864.

Marshall, A. *Principles of Economics*. London: Macmillan, 1890.

Marstrand, P. K. "Assessing the Intangibles in Water Pollution Control." *International Journal of Environmental Studies*, **5**(4), 289–298 (1973).

Matell, M. S. and J. Jacoby, "Is There an Optimal Number of Alternatives for Likert Scale Items? Study I: Reliability and Validity." *Educational and Psychological Measurement*, **31**(3), 657–674 (1971).

Mayntz, R., K. Holm, and R. Hoebner. *Introduction to Empirical Sociology*. Harmondsworth, U.K.: Penguin, 1976.

Merewitz, L. "Recreational Benefits of Water Resource Development." *Water Resources Research*, **2**(4), 625–640 (1966).

Michalson, E. L. *Development of Criteria for Evaluating Wild and Scenic Rivers*. University of Idaho, Water Resources Research Institute, unpublished paper, Moscow, 1972.

Michigan Department of Conservation. *Outdoor Recreation Planning in Michigan by a Systems Analysis Approach. Part III: The Practical Application of "Program RECYSYS and SYMAP."* Lansing, 1967.

Miller, S. F., L. L. Boersma, and E. N. Castle. *Irrigation Water Values in the Willamette Valley: A Study of Alternative Valuation Methods*. Oregon State University, Agricultural Experiment Station, Technical Bulletin 85, Corvallis, 1965.

Miller, W. L. and D. M. Byers. "Development and Display of Multi-Objective Project Impacts." *Water Resources Research*, **9**(1), 11–20 (1973).

Milliman, J. W. "Can People be Trusted with Natural Resources?" *Land Economics*, **38**(3), 199–218 (1962).

Milton, W. J., Jr. "National Forest Roadless and Undeveloped Areas: Develop or Preserve?" *Land Economics*, **51**(2), 139–143 (1975).

Mishan, E. J. "Realism and Relevance in Consumer's Surplus." *Review of Economic Studies*, **15**(1), 27–33 (1947–48).

Mishan, E. J. "A Survey of Welfare Economics, 1939–59." *Economic Journal*, **70**(278), 197–265 (1960).

Mishan, E. J. *Cost-Benefit Analysis: An Introduction*. New York: Praeger, 1971.

Moeller, G. H. and J. H. Engelken. "What Fishermen Look for in a Fishing Experience." *Journal of Wildlife Management*, **36**(4), 1253–1257 (1972).

Moeller, G. H., R. MacLachlan, and D. A. Morrison. *Measuring Perception of Elements in Outdoor Environments*. U.S. Department of Agriculture, Forest Service, Research paper NE-289, Upper Darby, Pennsylvania, 1974.

Mohring, H. "Urban Highway Investments." In R. Dorfman, Ed., *Measuring Benefits of Government Investments*. Washington: The Brookings Institution, 1965. Pp. 231–275.

Monarchi, D. E., C. C. Kisiel, and L. Duckstein. "Interactive Multiobjective Programming in Water Resources: A Case Study." *Water Resources Research*, **9**(4), 837–850 (1973).

Moore, J. R., Jr. and N. R. Baker. "Computational Analysis of Scoring Models for *R* and *D* Project Selection." *Management Science*, **16**(4), B212–B232 (1969).

Munro, D. A. "Introduction." *In Saskatoon Wetlands Seminar*, Department of Indian Affairs and Northern Development, Canadian Wildlife Service Report Series, No. 6, Ottawa, 1969. P. 2.

Murray, J. B. *Appalachian Trail Users in the Southern National Forests: Their Characteristics, Attitudes and Management Preferences*. U.S. Department of Agriculture, Forest Service, Research Paper SE-116, Asheville, North Carolina, 1974.

Nairn, R. J. *Community Involvement in the Noarlunga Freeway Review*. Paper presented to the Second Conference of Economists, Sydney, Australia, 1971.

Nash, C., D. Pearce, and J. Stanley, "An Evaluation of Cost-Benefit Analysis Criteria." *Scottish Journal of Political Economy*, **22**(2), 121–134 (1975).

Nordhaus, W. D. and J. Tobin. "Is Growth Obsolete?" *In Economic Research: Retrospect and Prospect*. Fiftieth Anniversary Colloquium, Vol. V. New York: National Bureau of Economic Research, 1972. Pp. 1–80.

O'Brien, W. T. and G. G. Roy. *The Multi-Objective Management of Natural Resources*. Paper presented to 43rd Congress of the Australian and New Zealand Association for the Advancement of Science, Brisbane, Australia, 1971.

Officer, R. R. and A. N. Halter. "Utility Analysis in a Practical Setting." *American Journal of Agricultural Economics*, **50**(2), 257–277 (1968).

O'Hanlon, P. W. and J. A. Sinden. "Scope for Valuation of Environmental Goods: Comment." *Land Economics*, **54**(3), 381–387 (1978).

Osgood, C. E. "The Nature and Measurement of Meaning." *Psychological Bulletin*, **49**(3), 197–237 (1952).

Owen, M. S. and W. R. Thirsk. "Land Taxes and Idle Land: A Case Study of Houston." *Land Economics*, **50**(3), 251–260 (1974).

Paul, M. E. "Can Aircraft Noise Nuisance be Measured in Money?" *Oxford Economic Papers*, New Series, **23**(3), 297–322 (1971).

Payne, B. R. Personal communication, 1976.

Payne, B. R. and R. M. DeGraaf. "Economic Values and Recreational Trends Associated with Human Enjoyment of Nongame Birds." In *Proceedings of the Symposium on Management of Forest and Range Habitats for Nongame Birds*. U.S. Department of Agriculture, Forest Service, General Technical Report WO-1, Washington, 1975. Pp. 6–10.

Payne, B. R., W. B. White, R. E. McCay, and R. R. McNichols. *Economic Analysis of the Gypsy Moth Problem in the Northeast. II. Applied to Residential Property*. U.S. Department of Agriculture, Forest Service, Research paper NE-285, Upper Darby, Pennsylvania, 1973.

Peacock, A. T., R. Turvey, F. A. Lutz, and E. Henderson. *International Economic Papers*, No. 2. London: Macmillan, 1952.

Pearse, P. H. "A New Approach to the Evaluation of Non-Priced Recreational Resources." *Land Economics*, **44**(1), 87–99 (1968).

Pendse, D. and J. B. Wyckoff. *Measurement of Environmental Goods: A Suggested Approach*. Paper presented to the annual meeting of the American Agricultural Economics Association, Gainesville, 1972.

Pendse, D. and J. B. Wyckoff. "Scope for Valuation of Environmental Goods." *Land Economics*, **50**(1), 89–92 (1974a).

Pendse, D. and J. B. Wyckoff. *A Systematic Evaluation of Environmental Perceptions, Optimum Preferences and Trade-Off Values in Water Resource Analysis*. Oregon State University, Water Resources Research Institute, Bulletin WRRI-25, Corvallis, 1974b.

Penning-Rowsell, E. C. and D. I. Hardy. "Landscape Evaluation and Planning Policy: A Comparative Survey in the Wye Valley Area of Outstanding Natural Beauty." *Regional Studies*, **7**(2), 153–160 (1973).

Perloff, H. S. *The Quality of the Urban Environment: Essays on New Resources in an Urban Age*. Baltimore: Johns Hopkins Press, 1969.

Peters, L. C. "Shade and Ornamental Tree Evaluation." *Journal of Forestry*, **69**(7), 411–413 (1971).

Peterson, G. L. and E. S. Neumann. "Modeling and Predicting Human Response to the Visual Recreation Environment." *Journal of Leisure Research*, **1**(3), 219–237 (1969).

Pickle, H. B., A. C. Rucks, and R. Sisson. *The Economic Benefits of Abating Water Pollution in the Steel, Textile and Paper Industries in Alabama*. Auburn University, Water Resources Research Institute, Alabama WRRI Bulletin 14, Auburn, 1973.

Pill, J. "The Delphi Method: Substance, Context, A Critique and an Annotated Bibliography." *Socio-Economic Planning Sciences*, **5**(1), 57–71 (1971).

Potter, D. R., J. C. Hendee, and R. N. Clark. "Hunting Satisfaction: Game, Guns, or Nature?" *In Transactions of the Thirty-eighth North American Wildlife and Natural Resources Conference*. Washington: Wildlife Management Institute, 1973. Pp. 220–229.

Prest, A. R. and R. Turvey. "Cost-Benefit Analysis: A Survey." *Economic Journal*, **75**(300), 683–735 (1965).

Prewitt, R. A. *The Economics of Public Recreation: An Economic Study of the Monetary Evaluation of Recreation in the National Parks*. Washington: National Park Service, 1949.

Prochaska, F. J. and R. A. Schrimper. "Opportunity Cost of Time and Other Socioeconomic Effects on Away-from-Home Food Consumption." *American Journal of Agricultural Economics*, **55**(4), 595–603 (1973).

Promkutkeo, J., R. Mook, and P. W. O'Hanlon. *The Relative Importance of Dif-*

ferent Environmental Benefits and Costs. University of New England, Recreation and Tourism Research Unit, Occasional Paper No. 3, Armidale, 1977.

Radtke, H. D. "Benefits and Costs of a Physician to a Community." *American Journal of Agricultural Economics*, **56**(3), 586–593 (1974).

Raiffa, H. *Decision Analysis: Introductory Lectures on Choices under Uncertainty*. Reading: Addison-Wesley, 1968.

Ramsey, F. P. "Truth and Probability." In R. B. Braithwaite, Ed., *The Foundations of Mathematics and Other Logical Essays*. London: Kegan Paul, Trench Trubner, 1931. Pp. 156–198.

Randall, A., B. Ives, and C. Eastman. "Bidding Games for Valuation of Aesthetic Environmental Improvements." *Journal of Environmental Economics and Management*, **1**(2), 132–149 (1974).

Reiquam, H. "Establishing Priorities Among Environmental Stresses." In W. A. Thomas, Ed., *Indicators of Environmental Quality*. New York: Plenum, 1972. Pp. 71–82.

Richardson, H. W., J. Vipond, and R. A. Furbey. "Land Prices in Edinburgh 1952–67: A Study of Edinburgh City Corporation Land Purchases." *Scottish Journal of Political Economy*, **21**(1), 67–75 (1974).

Rickard, W. M., J. M. Hughes, and C. A. Newport. *Economic Evaluation and Choice in Old-Growth Douglas-fir Landscape Management*. U.S. Department of Agriculture, Forest Service, Research Paper PNW-49, Portland, Oregon 1967.

Ridker, R. G. *Economic Costs of Air Pollution*. New York: Praeger, 1967.

Ridker, R. G. and J. A. Henning. "The Determinants of Residential Property Values with Special Reference to Air Pollution." *Review of Economics and Statistics*, **49**(2), 246–257 (1967).

Robinson, W. C. and V. Tanzi. "Economic Studies of Outdoor Recreation Benefits." In *Economic Studies of Outdoor Recreation*. Outdoor Recreation Resources Review Commission, Report No. 24, Washington, 1962. Pp. 45–69.

Romm, J. *The Value of Reservoir Recreation*. Cornell University, Water Resources and Marine Sciences Center, Technical Report 19/Agricultural Experiment Station, Report AE Res. 296, Ithaca, 1969.

Roskill Commission. *Report of the Commission on the Third London Airport*. London: Her Majesty's Stationery Office, 1971.

Rothenburg, J. *Economic Evaluation of Urban Renewal: Conceptual Foundation of Benefit-Cost Analysis*. Washington: The Brookings Institution, 1967.

Roy, B. "How Outranking Relation Helps Multiple Criteria Decision-Making." In J. L. Cochrane and M. Zeleny, Eds., *Multiple Criteria Decision Making*. Columbia: University of South Carolina Press, 1973. Pp. 179–201.

Ryan, J. G. "Using Input Demand and Production Function Models to Assess the Net Benefits of Dairy Herd Improvement." *Australian Journal of Agricultural Economics*, **19**(1), 23–38 (1975).

Samuelson, P. A. "Evaluation of Real National Income." *Oxford Economic Papers*, New Series, **2**(1), 1–29 (1950).

Sanderson, D. G. *A Utility Analysis of the Effects of Crowding on Recreational Experiences*. Unpublished B.Ag.Ec. thesis. Armidale: University of New England, 1974.

Schmid, A. A. "Nonmarket Values and Efficiency of Public Investments in Water Resources." *American Economic Review*, **57**(2), 158–168 (1967).

Schmitz, A. and D. Seckler. "Mechanized Agriculture and Social Welfare: The Case of the Tomato Harvester." *American Journal of Agricultural Economics*, **52**(4), 569–577 (1970).

Schuler, A. T., H. H. Webster, and J. C. Meadows. "Goal Programming in Forest Management." *Journal of Forestry*, **75**(6), 320–324 (1977).

Schwartz, A. "Interpreting the Effects of Distance on Migration." *Journal of Political Economy*, **81**(5), 1153–1169 (1973).

Seckler, D. W. "On the Uses and Abuses of Economic Science in Evaluating Public Outdoor Recreation." *Land Economics*, **42**(4), 485–494 (1966).

Seiler, K. "A Cost Effectiveness Comparison Involving a Tradeoff of Performance, Cost, and Obtainability." *Operations Research*, **14**(3), 528–531 (1966).

Shafer, E. L., Jr. *The Photo-Choice Method for Recreation Research*. U.S. Department of Agriculture, Forest Service, Research Paper NE-29, Upper Darby, Pennsylvania, 1964.

Shafer, E. L., Jr. and J. Mietz. *It Seems Possible to Quantify Scenic Beauty in Photographs*. U.S. Department of Agriculture, Forest Service, Research Paper NE-162, Upper Darby, Pennsylvania, 1970.

Shafer, E. L., Jr. and T. A. Richards. *A Comparison of Viewer Reactions to Outdoor Scenes and Photographs of Those Scenes*. U.S. Department of Agriculture, Forest Service, Research Paper NE-302, Upper Darby, Pennsylvania, 1974.

Shaw, M. E. and J. M. Wright. *Scales for the Measurement of Attitudes*. New York: McGraw-Hill, 1967.

Sinden, J. A. *Utility Analysis in the Valuation of Extra-Market Benefits with Particular Reference to Water-Based Recreation*. Oregon State University, Water Resources Research Institute, Bulletin WRRI-17, Corvallis, 1973.

Sinden, J. A. "A Utility Approach to the Valuation of Recreational and Aesthetic Experiences." *American Journal of Agricultural Economics*, **56**(1), 61–72 (1974).

Sinden, J. A. and R. K. Smith. "The Analysis and Management of Forest Landscapes: Exotics, Eucalypts or Solitude?" *Australian Forestry*, **38**(3), 183–200 (1975).

Sinden, J. A. and J. B. Wyckoff. "Indifference Mapping: An Empirical Methodology for Economic Evaluation of the Environment." *Regional Science and Urban Economics*, **6**(1), 81–103 (1976).

Smith, N. M., Jr. "Comments." *Operations Research*, **2**(2), 181–187 (1954).

Smith, R. J. and N. J. Kavanagh. "The Measurement of Benefits of Trout Fishing: Preliminary Results of a Study at Grafham Water, Great Ouse Water Authority, Huntingdonshire." *Journal of Leisure Research*, **1**(4), 316–332 (1969).

Snaith, R. "What Price Heritage? Estimating the Price Elasticity of Demand for National Trust Properties (and Some Related Issues)." In G. A. C. Searle, Ed., *Recreational Economics and Analysis*. Harlow, U.K.: Longman, 1975. Pp. 141–150.

Sokoloski, A. A. "Externalities and Empiricism in Water Resources." *Journal of Farm Economics*, **49**(5), 1521–1525 (1967).

Solow, R. "Technical Change and the Aggregate Production Function." *Review of Economics and Statistics,* **39**(3), 312–320 (1957).

Sonnenfeld, J. "Equivalence and Distortion of the Perceptual Environment." *Environment and Behavior,* **1**(1), 83–99 (1969).

Stankey, G. H. "The Use of Content Analysis in Resource Decision Making." *Journal of Forestry,* **70**(3), 148–151 (1972a).

Stankey, G. H. "A Strategy for the Definition and Management of Wilderness Quality." in J. V. Krutilla, Ed., *Natural Environments: Studies in Theoretical and Applied Analysis.* Baltimore: Johns Hopkins Press, 1972b. Pp. 88–114.

Steiner, P. O. "The Role of Alternative Cost in Project Design and Selection." In A. V. Kneese and S. C. Smith, Eds., *Water Research.* Baltimore: Johns Hopkins Press, 1966. Pp. 33–50.

Steinitz, C. "Landscape Resource Analysis: The State of the Art." *Landscape Architecture,* **60**(2), 101–105 (1970).

Stevens, S. S. "Measurement, Psychopsychics, and Utility." In C. W. Churchman and P. Ratoosh, Eds., *Measurement: Definitions and Theories.* New York: Wiley, 1959. Pp. 18–63.

Stilwell, F. J. *Australian Urban and Regional Development.* Sydney: Australia and New Zealand Book Co., 1974.

Stimson, D. H. "Utility Measurement in Public Health Decision Making." *Management Science,* **16**(2), B17–B30 (1969).

Stoevener, H. H. and W. G. Brown. "Analytical Issues in Demand Analysis for Outdoor Recreation." *Journal of Farm Economics,* **49**(5), 1295–1304 (1967).

Stoevener, H. H. and W. G. Brown. "Analytical Issues in Demand Analysis for Outdoor Recreation: Reply." *American Journal of Agricultural Economics,* **50**(1), 151–153 (1968).

Thampapillai, J. *An Analysis of Conflicts Between Income Maximization and Environmental Quality: A Linear Programming Approach to Multiple Objective Planning In Dumaresq Shire.* Unpublished M. Econ. dissertation. Armidale: University of New England, 1976.

Thedie, J. and C. Abraham, "Economic Aspects of Road Accidents." *Traffic Engineering and Control,* **2,** 289–595 (1961).

Thomas, H. A. "The Animal Farm: A Mathematical Model for the Discussion of Social Standards for Control of the Environment." In R. Dorfman and N. S. Dorfman, Eds., *Economics of the Environment: Selected Readings.* New York: Norton, 1972. Pp. 250–256.

Tideman, T. N. "The Efficient Provision of Public Goods." In S. J. Mushkin, Ed., *Public Prices for Public Products.* Washington: The Urban Institute, 1972. Pp. 111–123

Tintner, G. and M. Patel. "Evaluation of Indian Fertilizer Projects: An Application of Consumer's and Producer's Surplus." *Journal of Farm Economics,* **48**(3), 704–710 (1966).

Torgerson, W. S. *Theory and Methods of Scaling.* New York: Wiley, 1958.

Trice, A. H. and S. E. Wood. "Measurement of Recreation Benefits." *Land Economics,* **34**(3), 195–207 (1958).

Turban, E. and M. L. Metersky. "Utility Theory Applied to Multivariable System Effectiveness Evaluation." *Management Science*, **17**(12), B817–B828 (1971).

Tweeten, L. G. and F. H. Tyner. "The Utility Concept of Net Social Cost: A Criterion for Public Policy." *Agricultural Economics Research*, **18**(2), 33–42 (1966).

U.S. Department of Health, Education and Welfare. *Toward a Social Report*. Washington, 1969.

U.S. Department of the Interior. *The Third Wave*. Conservation Yearbook No. 3, Washington, 1967.

U.S. Water Resources Council, Special Task Force. "Proposed Principles and Standards for Planning Water and Related Land Resources." *Federal Register*, **36**(245), 24144–24194 (1971).

Viner, J. "The Utility Concept in Value Theory and Its Critics." *Journal of Political Economy*, **33**(4), 369–387 (1925).

Von Neumann, J. and O. Morgenstern. *Theory of Games and Economic Behavior*, 2nd ed. Princeton: Princeton University Press, 1947.

Waddel, T. E. *The Economic Damages of Air Pollution*. U.S. Environmental Protection Agency, Report EPA-600/5-74-012, Washington, 1974.

Wallace, R. F. *An Evaluation of Wildlife Resources in the State of Washington*. Washington State University, Bureau of Economic and Business Research, Bulletin No. 28, Pullman, 1956.

Walters, A. A. *Noise and Prices*. Oxford: Clarendon Press, 1975.

Warden, R. E. and W. T. Dagodag. *A Guide to the Preparation and Review of Environmental Impact Reports*. Los Angeles: Security World Publishing, 1976.

Watson, P. L. *The Value of Time: Behavioral Models of Modal Choice*. Lexington: Lexington Books, 1974.

Weintraub, S. "Price-Making in Forest Service Timber Sales." *American Economic Review*, **49**(4), 628–637 (1959).

Weisbrod, B. A. "Income Redistribution Effects and Benefit-Cost Analysis." In S. B. Chase, Jr., Ed., *Problems in Public Expenditure Analysis*. Washington: The Brookings Institution, 1968. Pp. 177–209.

Wennergren, E. B. "Valuing Non-Market Priced Recreational Resources." *Land Economics*, **40**(3), 303–314 (1964).

Wennergren, E. B. *A Probabilistic Approach to Estimating Demand for Outdoor Recreation*. Utah State University, Agricultural Experiment Station, Bulletin 478, Logan, 1968.

Wills, G., R. Wilson, N. Manning, and R. Hildebrandt. *Technological Forecasting*. Harmondsworth, U.K.: Penguin, 1972.

Wollman, N. B., R. L. Edgel, M. E. Farris, H. R. Stucky, and A. J. Thompson. *The Value of Water in Alternative Uses: With Special Application to Water Use in the San Juan and Rio Grande Basins of New Mexico*. Albuquerque: University of New Mexico Press, 1962.

Worrell, A. C. *Economics of American Forestry*. New York: Wiley, 1959.

Yntema, D. B. and W. S. Torgerson. "Man-Computer Cooperation in Decisions Requiring Common Sense." In W. Edwards and A. Tversky, Eds., *Decision*

Making: Selected Readings. Harmondsworth, U.K.: Penguin, 1967. Pp. 300–314.

Young, A. "Rural Land Evaluation." In J. A. Dawson and J. C. Doornkamp, Eds., *Evaluating the Human Environment: Essays in Applied Geography*. London: Arnold, 1973. Pp. 5–33.

Zionts, S. and J. Wallenius. "An Interactive Programming Method for Solving the Multiple Criteria Problem." *Management Science*, **22**(6), 652–663 (1976).

Index

Adjective, checklist method, 191
Administrative hierarchy, 88
Aggregation, 75, 164
Allocating a budget, 313
Allocation of percentage ratings, 226
Alternative choice situations, 84
Alternatives methods:
  analyze wide range, 134
  estimate data and design, 135
Annuity, 43
Assessment systems, 98
Attractivity models, 401

Baier, K., 7, 114
Benchmark method, 150
Budgeting method, 287
Budget line, 38

Checking for consistency, 230
Comparative descriptions, 192
Comparison method, 301
Compensation situations, 83
Conservation value, 177
Constraint procedure, 102
Consumers'-expenditure method, 258
Content analysis, 194
Converging direct questions, 312
Costing constraints method, 267
Costless-choice method, 322
Cost minimization, 256
Cost of replacement, 256
Costs, 41
Cost-saving method, 261
Costs, observation and interpretation of, 254
Cut-off method, 139

Decision situations, 82
Defensive expenditures, 256
Delphi method, 392
Demand, 18
  function, 29
  schedule, 18
Direct-midpoint method, 232
Display systems, 97
Disutility, 41
Double-judgement method, 234

Economic rent, 287
Either/or situations, 82
Elasticity, 31
Electre method, 152
Estimation of ratios method, 228
Exchange, 17

Fischer, L. A., 285

Goal-programming method, 154, 485
Gray, J. R. and L. W. Anderson, 251
Gross national product, 259

Half-judgement method, 232
Half-value sum method, 222
Hammack, J. and G. M. Brown Jr., 339

Imperfect competition, 51
Income capitalization method, 291
Index of recreation value, 268
Indifference curve, 36
Indifference map, 37
Indifference-mapping method, 149, 329, 471
Individual value, 53
  equation, 54, 57
Internal rate of return, 43

Judgement method, 300

Land-price method, 290
Lexicographic method, 138

Likert method, 202
Linear programming, 139, 253
  combined optimization, 157
  constrained optimization, 140

Marginal physical product, 23
Marginal revenue product, 270
Marginal value product:
  calculation of, 284
  definition of, 284
Market-comparison method, 299
Market failure, 47
Market-price method, 278
Market prices, 44
Market-value method, 300
Maximax criterion, 136, 484
Maximin criterion, 135, 484
Miller, S. F., L. L. Boersma and E. N. Castle, 284
Milliman's range method, 265

Net social benefit, 335
  Direct Methods, 347
  Structured methods, 364
Neumann-Morgenstern von, method, 236

Opportunity cost, 250
  definition, 41
Opportunity-cost methods, 250, 377
Order of merit technique, 198

Paired comparisons method, 219
Payne, B. R., W. B. White, R. E. Mc Cay and R. R. McNichols, 294
Performance budgets, 103
Present net worth, 43
Present worth, 43
Priority-evaluator technique, 324, 474
Production costs:
  as benefit indicators, 255
  for decision information, 255
Production function, 22
  definition, 25
  method, 283

Q-sort method, 199

Ramsey method, 240
Ranked comparisons method, 219
Ranking methods, 195
  complete, 197
  partial, 195
Rating methods, 200
Reference-contract method, 237
Residual method, 287

Satisfaction Index, 401
Semantic-differential method, 200
Scoring method, 206
Simple-betterness method, 102
Single direct question method, 307
Social value, 45, 63, 383
  equation, 64, 72
Standardization by ranked classes, 183
Standardization by utility ratings, 180
Standardized difference methods, 171
Standardized proportion methods, 176
Standard-gamble method, 237
Supply, 20
  curve method, 257
  function, 31
  long-run, 22
  schedule, 23
  short-run, 22
Surplus:
  consumer's, 33
  producer's, 33

Threshold comparison, 101, 310
Time:
  arithmetic of analysis, 43
  as cost, 42
  preference, 42, 48
Trade-off games, 315
  Single, 315
  Double, 319
  Comparative, 321
Travel-cost methods, 364
  for on-site experience, 368
  for whole experience, 366

Uncertainty, 48
Uniqueness ratio, 179
Utility, 34
  definition, 7
  diminishing marginal, 34
  estimation, 188, 213, 479

Valuation:
  definition, 119

processes, 78
Value-added method, 260
Value:
concept, 4
criterion, 7
definition, 57
determination, 12
equation, 111
function, 61

Weighting, 76
Weighting methods, 142
additive, 145, 479
multiplicative, 146
Weights, derivation of, 395

Z-score, 171

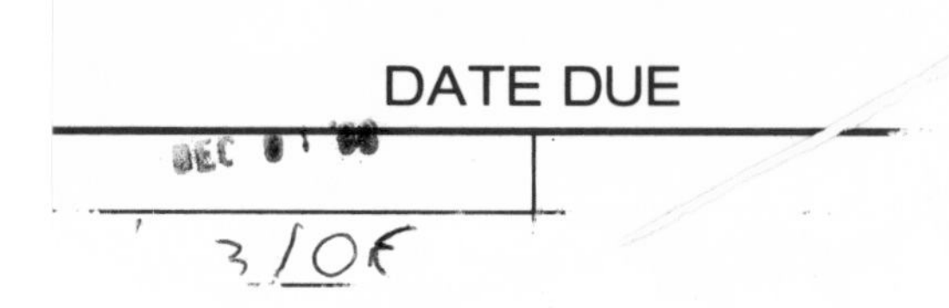
DATE DUE
DEC 01 '88
3/08

Lewis and Clark College - Watzek Library
HB201 .S599
wmain
Sinden, J. A./Unpriced values : decision
3 5209 00339 5478
OLLEGE LIBRARY
GON 97219